PLATE I

1. CHAMPOLLION IN 1822

2. THE ROSETTA STONE
Hieroglyphic, demotic, and Greek texts (British Museum)

The Nile
and Egyptian
Civilization

Alexandre Moret

DOVER PUBLICATIONS, INC.
Mineola, New York

Published in Canada by General Publishing Company, Ltd., 895 Don Mills Road, 400-2 Park Centre, Toronto, Ontario M3C 1W3.

Bibliographical Note

This Dover edition, first published in 2001, is an unabridged republication of the work originally published in 1927 by Kegan Paul, Trench, Trubner & Co., Ltd., London.

Library of Congress Cataloging-in-Publication Data

Moret, Alexander, 1868–1938.
    [Nil et la civilisation égyptienne. English]
    The Nile and Egyptian civilization / Alexander Moret.
        p. cm.
    Originally published: London : Kegan Paul, Trench, Trubner & Co., 1927.
    Includes bibliographical references.
    ISBN 0-486-42009-4 (pbk.)
      1. Egypt—Civilization—To 332 B.C. I. Title.

DT83 .M62 2001
932—dc21

2001047270

Manufactured in the United States of America
Dover Publications, Inc., 31 East 2nd Street, Mineola, N.Y. 11501

CONTENTS

CHAP.   PAGE

FOREWORD (by HENRI BERR) xix

INTRODUCTION. SOURCES AND CHRONOLOGY . 1
    I. Greek Sources and their Value, 1. II. The Decipherment of the Hieroglyphics, 7. III. Native Sources and Chronology, 16.

PART ONE

THE COUNTRY AND THE BEGINNINGS OF HISTORY

I. COUNTRY, NILE, AND SUN. THEIR INFLUENCE ON SOCIAL DEVELOPMENT 25

II. EARLY SOCIAL ORGANIZATION. CLANS AND NOMES 38
    I. The Clans, 38. II. The Nomes, 40. III. Ensigns and Gods of Nomes. Their Struggles for Political Influence, 44.

III. THE DIVINE DYNASTIES AND THEIR HISTORICAL SIGNIFICANCE 60
    I. Divine Dynasties and Gods of the Universe, 60. II. Horus the Elder, First King of Lower Egypt, and Seth, First King of Upper Egypt, 65.

IV. THE DIVINE KINGDOMS OF THE DELTA. WESTERN AND EASTERN NOMES. OSIRIS AND HORUS, SON OF ISIS 73
    I. The Delta and its Protohistoric Past. The Western Nomes of the Delta, 73. II. The Confederation of the Eastern Nomes of the Delta, 77. III. Osiris and Horus, Son of Isis, the Traditional Founders of the Kingship. The Historical Significance of the Legends, 80.

PART TWO

KINSHIP AND SOCIETY

I. The Protohistoric Monarchy. Servants of Horus and Thinite Kings. The Earliest Royal Institutions 101

    I. Simultaneous Reigns in Upper and Lower Egypt. The Moral Preponderance of the Delta, 103. II. The Servants of Horus in Upper Egypt. Their Wars with the Delta, 106. III. The Thinite Kings and their Synthesis of Royal Institutions, 116. IV. The Thinite Administration, 134. V. The Next Life, 141.

II. The Memphite Monarchy. The Autocratic King, Son of Ra 146

    I. Heliopolis and the Kingship by Right Divine, 146. II. The King as Son of Ra and Autocratic Sovereign, 157. III. The Dead King. Osiris and Ra, 168.

III. The Decline of the Memphite Monarchy. The Feudal Period and Social Revolution (VIth to XIth Dynasties) 188

    I. The Royal Family and the Government of Egypt, 188. II. The Privileged Imakhu, 196. III. From the VIth to the XIth Dynasty. Feudal Priesthood. Charters of Immunity, 202. IV. The Provincial Feudal Nobility, 208. V. The End of the Old Kingdom and the Social Revolution (VIIIth to XIth Dynasties), 216.

IV. The Rule of the Just Laws. The New Social State and the Administration of the Theban Kings 232

    I. The Reforms of the Theban Kings, 233. II. Funeral Rites for the People, 252. III. State Socialism. Peasants. Caftsmen. Local Administrators (XIIth to XXth Dynasties), 260. IV. The Central Administration, the Vizier, and the King, 276.

V. The Struggles of the Pharaohs with Mercenaries and Priests. Foreigners in Egypt 290

    I. Thebes as the Imperial Capital. Palaces, Temples, Necropoles, 291. II. The Military Class in the Theban State, 298. III. The Priestly Class in the Theban State, 302.

IV. Monarchy against Theocracy: 1. Dynastic Disputes in the Time of Hatshepsut, 306. 2. Reaction of the Kings. The Heresy of Akhenaten, 315. V. The Government of Egypt by the Gods, 327. VI. The Kingship in the hands of Priests and Mercenaries. Foreign Invasions of Egypt, 334.

PART THREE

INTELLECTUAL LIFE. RELIGION, ART, SCIENCE

INTRODUCTION 353

I. RELIGION 355

I. The God. Local Cults, 355. II. Material and Spiritual Forms of the Gods. Beasts. Statues. Names, 360. III. The Universal Gods and Theological Conceptions, 368. *A.* The Doctrine of Heliopolis, 369. *B.* The Doctrine of Osiris, 380. IV. The Rituals of Heliopolis and Osiris applied to Gods and Men, 385. V. Magic. Morality. Personal Piety, 403.

II. ART, SCIENCE, AND LITERATURE . . . 411

I. The Works of the King in Temples and Tombs, 412. *A.* Materials, 412. *B.* The Plan of Temples and Tombs, 415. *C.* The Decoration of Buildings : Draughtsmen, Sculptors, Painters, and Decorators, 425. Composition of Pictures, 433. Personal character of artists and periods, 436. II. Science, 444. Geometry and mathematics, 445. Medicine, 448. Chemistry, 452. Astronomy, 452. III. Literature, 455.

CONCLUSION 465

BIBLIOGRAPHY 477

INDEX 479

TABLES

						PAGE
Chronological Table of the Dynasties	.	.	.	.	.	23
Nomes of Upper Egypt	.	.	.	.	.	54
Nomes of Lower Egypt	.	.	.	.	.	57
First Dynasty of the Gods	.	.	.	.	.	61
Ist and IInd Dynasties .	.	.	.	.	.	117
IIIrd, IVth, and Vth Dynasties	.	.	.	.	.	148
VIth, VIIth, and VIIIth Dynasties	.	.	.	.	.	189
XIIth Dynasty .	.	.	.	.	.	232
XVIIIth to XXVIth Dynasties	.	.	.	.	.	336

EGYPTIAN TEXTS TRANSLATED OR ANALYSED

HISTORICAL TEXTS.

Decree granting immunities (Vth Dyn.), 206.

Occupations of the Vizier, 279. Instructions of the King to the Vizier, 285.

Biographies of Phtahshepses, 192; Uni, 193; Pepinefer, 211; Zau, 213; Ameni, 239.

SOCIAL WRITINGS.

Teachings for Merikara, 221, 237, 242, 256, 286.

Teachings of Sehetepibra, 288.

Sentences of Neferrehu, 221, 231.

Sayings of Ankhu, 222.

Dialogue of a Misanthrope with his Spirit, 223.

Song of the Harpist, 224.

Admonitions of an Old Sage, 225.

Tale of the Peasant, 283.

Condition of the peasant, 267; craftsman, 268; scribe, 270.

LITERARY WORKS.

Maxims of Ani, 459.

Complaint of a husband against his dead wife's Spirit, 459.

Love-songs, 461.

HYMNS.

To the Nile, 30, 82, 145.

To the Sun (Aten), 36, 325.

To Amon-Ra, 318.

To Thebes and Amon-Ra, 330.

To the Trinity, Amon, Ra, and Phtah, 331.

To Osiris, 97.

To Maat, 391.

To Min-Horus, 367.

To the King, 288.

To the Crown, 164.

THEOLOGICAL TEXTS.

Shabaka, 71, 94, 376, 386.

Legend of Ra, 371.

FUNERARY TEXTS.

Mysteries of Osiris, 249.

Funeral Ritual, 93–4, 143, 171–4, 178 ff., 198–200, 212–13.

Negative confession, 398.

Chapter of the Heart, 400.

ILLUSTRATIONS IN THE TEXT

FIG.   PAGE

1. The Egyptian Scripts   8
2. Demotic Spelling and Cartouche of Ptolemy   10
3. Ptolemaic Cartouches   12
4. Pharaonic Cartouches   13
5. Ensign of the XVth Nome, over the Sign *Spat*   41
6. Town (*Nut*)   41
7. Signs of the Memphite Period   42
8. House (*Per*) and Seat (*Ist*)   42
9. Totems and Ensigns of Clans   45
10. Ensigns of Nomes   47
11. The Falcon, Victor over the Oryx Seth   51
12. Nomes of Upper Egypt and six of Lower Egypt . . .   52
13. The Sign *Neter*, God   66
14. Horus Presiding over the Two Eyes   67
15. Seth   68
16. Booty from Libya   75
17. The Sign *Iment*   76
18. The Sign *Iabt*   77
19. The Black Bull (10th Nome)   78
20. Anzti on his Nome   79
21. Pillar of the Horus-Seth Khasekhemui   80
22. Zed Pillar and *Sez* Tree   81
23. The Vegetable Resurrection of Osiris   90
24. Isis suckling her Son Horus in the Papyrus-beds of Chemmis .   99
25. Life, Health, Strength 108
26. The Equipment of the Servants of Horus 110
27. *Per-ur*, the Palace of the Kings of Upper Egypt . . . 112
27a. *Per-neser*, the Palace of the Kings of Lower Egypt . . . 112
28. King Lion devouring his Enemies 114
29. King destroying Forts 115
30. Name of Horus Aha in Palace 118
31. The Titles *Nsut Biti* and *Nebti* 121
32. The Name of Horus Anzib, between the Arms of the Ka . . 121
33. The *Sma Taui* 124

FIG.		PAGE
34.	The White Wall of Memphis	125
35.	Episodes in the Coronation or the Sed	127
36.	Rising of the Kings of Upper and Lower Egypt in the Double Pavilion of the Sed-feast	128
37.	The Erection of the Zed on the Morning of the Sed-feast by the King	133
38.	Public Buildings	137
39.	Sign of the " Scribe "	138
40.	King Khasekhem in Sed Costume	139
41.	Sarcophagus of Mycerinus	142
42.	Horus-titles of Memphite Kings	149
43.	The Earliest Cartouche (Snefru)	151
44.	One of the First " Son of Ra " Titles	151
45.	Shu separating Nut and Geb	154
46.	Solar Temple of the Vth Dynasty	162
47.	Seti I before the Table of Offerings	166
48.	The Gesture of the Ka	175
49.	The Ba bringing the Veil and Sceptre	184
50.	Badge of the Imakhu	196
51.	" Offering given by the King "	200
52.	" What comes at the Voice "	200
53.	The Niles bringing Papyrus, Lotus, and Nourishment	201
54.	Civil War in Egypt	219
55.	The Ka of King Hor	230
56.	Royal Funeral Procession of a Plebeian	232
57.	The Zed of Osiris at Abydos	247
58.	The Casket of Abydos	247
59.	Pharaoh's Granaries	281
59a.	The Vizier's Antichamber	281
60.	The Royal Son of Kush receiving the Official Seal	287
61.	Egyptian Soldiers and Foreign Mercenaries	299
62.	Amenophis III accompanying the Barge of Amon-Ra	305
63.	Akhenaten addressing his Followers at el-Amarna	322
64.	Libyan Chief	351
65.	Worship of Sebek-Ra as a Crocodile	363
66.	Mummy being swathed in Wrappings	381
67.	Amenophis III sacrificing a Victim to Min	388
68.	Swaddled *Neter*	390
69.	Ushebti, or Answerer	395
70.	The Judgment of the Dead by Osiris	399

FIG.		PAGE
71.	Horus the Saviour	405
72.	Plan of a Palace at el-Amarna	417
73.	Temple of Khonsu at Karnak	418
74.	Ground and Roof-lines of the Temple	423
75.	A Visit to the Necropolis	424
76.	Harem at el-Amarna	427
77.	Cutting Vases in Hard Stone	437
78.	Talisman Bracelet	437
79.	Pectoral shaped like a Shrine	438
80.	A Property of the Theban Period	442
81.	Transport by River	445
82.	Gold Chains weighed in the Balance	446

PLATES

PLATE

I. 1. Champollion in 1882. 2. The Rosetta Stone   *Frontispiece*

FACING PAGE

II. 1. Cliff of the Libyan Desert at Der el-Bahari and Temple
of Hatshepsut. 2. Karnak. The Nile and the Great
Temple of Amon-Ra   26

III. 1. The God-king Chephren. 2. The Falcon Horus protecting Chephren. 3. Falcon Horus from the Temple at
Hieraconpolis   68

IV. 1. Great Pyramid of Cheops, Sphinx, and Granite Temple
at Gizeh. 2, 3. In a Mastaba : Statue-chamber and
Chapel   146

V. 1. The Dead Man coming out at the Voice. 2. Offering of
Incense by the Opening in the Serdab. Rites of the
Opening of the Mouth of the Mummy. 4. A Family of
the Old Kingdom   168

VI. 1. The Seated Scribe. 2. Offerings brought for the *Pert
Kheru*   198

VII. 1. The Sun born from the Lotus. 2. Maspero reading the
Pyramid Texts in the Chamber of Unas. 3. Osiris on
the Funeral Bed   202

VIII. Spearmen and Archers of the Princes of Siut .   .   .   218

IX. Peasants at Work : 1. Watering Gardens. 2. Fattening
Livestock. 3. Grape and Pomegranate Harvest. Corn
Granaries. Ploughing   268

X. 1. The Ka of King Hor. 2. Senusert I embracing Phtah.
3. Colossal Head of Senusert III   286

XI. 1. Diorite Sphinx from Tanis. 2. Woman bearing Offerings   290

XII. 1. Amenophis IV Akhenaten. 2. Nude Statuette from
el-Amarna. 3. Chair of Tutankhamen. 4. Statuette of
Queen Nefertiti   320

XIII. 1. Painted Pavement from a Palace at el-Amarna. 2. A
Family of the Theban Period   326

XIV. Theban Gods of the New Empire : 1. Worship of Osiris
with Isis and of Ra-Harakhti with Maat. 2. Sekhmet
in her Sanctuary. 3. Amon-Ra and Tutankhamen.   .   328

XV. 1. Rameses II. 2. Rameses II presenting an Offering.
3. Mummy of Rameses II   334

PLATE		FACING PAGE
XVI.	Osiris worshipped by the Goddesses	378
XVII.	Rameses II led before Osiris	388
XVIII.	1. Temple at Dakkeh. 2. Funerary Temple of Rameses II at Thebes	412
XIX.	1. Karnak. Great Hypostyle Hall. 2. Edfu. Court, Hypostyle, Sanctuary, Circuit Wall	416
XX.	1. Luxor. Central Colonnade of Tutankhamen. 2. Philae. Palm, Lotus, Papyrus, and Composite Capitals	422
XXI.	1. The Valley of the Kings. 2. Sarcophagi, Coffins, Boxes for Canopi	424
XXII.	The Golden Hall of the Tomb of Seti I	426
XXIII.	1. Amenardis on the Knees of Amon. 2. Amenardis, Divine Worshipper. 3. Panezem, First Prophet of Amon	430
XXIV.	1. Mentuemhet, Prince of Thebes	442

MAPS

I.	Lower Egypt and its Nomes	⎫
II.	Upper Egypt and its Nomes	⎬ AT END
III.	Nubia and Ethiopia	⎭

FOREWORD

EGYPTIAN CIVILIZATION AND RELIGION

I

*I*N From Tribe to Empire, *in this series, we saw that the
Mediterranean East offered a favoured region to the
development of mankind.*[1] *In that work, we followed political
organization from the humble germs of individualized power to
the formation of strongly centralized kingdoms and vast empires.
We observed that, as a consequence both of individual ambitions
and of collective needs, it was a kind of " internal impulse "
(p. xxix) which caused the institutions inherent in human
societies to develop ; and we were witnesses of struggles, for
ever breaking out anew through the advent of new racial elements
or the rivalry of growing groups, in which those institutions
were put to the test.*

*In the course of that complex history of which we have seen
the main lines, three civilizations attained a remarkable development and shed their influence over a large area—the Egyptian
civilization in Africa, the closely connected civilizations of
Babylonia and Assyria—the pool into which other Asiatic
civilizations flowed, which we may call the Mesopotamian
civilization—and the Ægean civilization in the heart of the
Mediterranean. All three contributed to the advance of logic in
the wide sense which I give this word,*[2] *but they present very
different characteristics, on which stress must be laid in the three
volumes which deal with them, including the present.*[3]

*Before historians knew of that Ægean civilization whose
brilliant light was so suddenly extinguished, Egypt was thought
to have played a chief part among the influences undergone by*

[1] *pp.* 116–17.
[2] *See my General Introduction and various Forewords, especially to* **Prehistoric**
Man, Language, *and* Greek Thought, *all in this series.*
[3] Mesopotamia *and* The Ægean Civilization, *in this series.*

Mediterranean Europe. In reducing that rôle to its true value, we must not depreciate its importance. Monsieur Moret, whose knowledge covers a wide field of Oriental study, here brings his masterly learning as an Egyptologist to the task of defining it exactly, without overestimating it.

II

The population of Egypt, even in the remote period in which we first encounter it, was composed of various elements, one of which, fair-skinned and brachycephalic, was probably of African origin. In the course of time inroads and immigration complicated the ethnic constitution of the country. Semites from Asia and Mediterraneans, not to mention Negroes, contributed greatly to the stock. We know that a mixture of races often has good results for a people; and in Egypt there was a mighty factor for unity, as M. Moret, following M. Pittard, has made clear—the Nile.[1]

Certainly there is nothing here which invalidates M. Febvre's reflections, in A Geographical Introduction to History, *on the capacity of man, of human societies, to break away from the dominion of the physical environment. For it is chiefly the harmful, inhibitive effects of his surroundings which drive man to react and free himself; and on the banks of the Nile it was not all blessings and kindliness. The Egyptian had to fight against the irregularities of the inundation, which might be devastating in their effects.[2] But in the valley of the Nile he found, together with singular advantages from material life, conditions which were especially favourable to the development of social life, and, at the same time, to racial fusion.*

The Nile made the men who dwelled on its banks into husbandmen, closely associated in the working of the soil, peaceable beings who, being protected on both sides by the desert and in the

---

[1] See Race and History, pp. 412 ff., and From Tribe to Empire, pp. 157–8, in this series.

[2] In Les Premières Civilisations, by J. de Morgan, there is a striking picture of Egypt in its primitive state. " Seven thousand years ago, the Nile, covering the bottom of its valley with gravel, left here and there long banks of shingle and sand. Constantly changing its course, everywhere leaving isolated backwaters, to-day overthrowing what it had built yesterday, it went through all Upper Egypt and part of Central Egypt without leaving deposit in any appreciable quantity." See the whole passage, pp. 217–20.

*North by the " Very Green ", only asked for the tranquil enjoy-
ment of a life maintained at little expense.*[1]

*Historians and travellers have striven to describe the very
special character of that long, narrow, fertile valley—as the
Egyptians made it, for one must distinguish between periods and
not imagine an absolutely unchanging country and population.
One of those who has succeeded best is Eugène Fromentin, who
was doubly an artist, for he painted, in words as well as in
colours.* His Notes d'un voyage en Égypte *are full of precise,
delicate, and wonderfully vivid observations.*[2] *He certainly saw that
land, " burning and fertile, warm and smiling."*[3] *But M. Moret
himself, being a historian who uses his eyes, depicts in happy,
picturesque terms, " that oasis created by the Nile, aired by the
north wind, green with meadows, golden with harvests, red with
the blood of vines, a paradise of water, fruit, and flowers, between
two torrid deserts."*[4]

*In this country one sees a creator more potent even than the
Nile. By shedding his " torrents of fire " on the Black Land,
it is the Sun who really gives well-being to the inhabitants. The
beneficent orb quite naturally takes on a moral character, and is
transfigured in men's imaginations into a divine being.
Fromentin, one evening as he watched the tremendous radiance
of the sunset on the Nile, lived with his eyes through " all the
myths, all the worships of Asia, all the fears inspired by night,
the love of the Sun,* King of the World, *the sorrow of seeing him
die, and the hope of seeing him reborn on the morrow ".*[5]

*So, in M. Moret's striking expression, " the Nile demands of
the Egyptians that they co-ordinate their efforts ; the Sun reveals
to them that a single power rules the world."*[6]

III

*In the eyes of the Greeks, the Egyptians were " the most religious
of men ". When we consider their tradition in the form in which
Herodotus, for example, learned it, we can say that they lived*

---

[1] See J. Baillet, Le Régime pharaonique dans ses rapports avec l'évolution
de la morale en Égypte, *pp.* 648–52, *for " the moral lessons of nature by the Nile ".*
" In Egypt, the Nile created justice and morality as it did geometry."
[2] Louis Gonse, Eugène Fromentin peintre et écrivain, *to which is added* Un
Voyage en Égypte (Oct.–Dec., 1869).
[3] Fromentin, p. 298.
[4] Below, p. 84.   [5] Op. cit., p. 272.   [6] Below, p. 37.

*and moved and had their being in the divine. M. Moret shows
the close bonds which united social life and political institutions
with religious life. He has devoted special pages to religion, in
order to summarize its characteristics, but his account of the
part which it played, by the very nature of things, runs from the
beginning of the book to the end. He has, however, made an
interesting, and often very original, attempt to distinguish the
work of properly social, political, and economic organization
which religious organization both supplemented and in great part
covered up. In the myths, he disentangles the historical realities
embodied in the traditions of thousands of years. His analyses
show immense erudition, and also exceptional acuteness and
ingenuity.*

*Starting from the moment when man becomes sedentary in
Egypt (and here we have a more detailed account of the stages
indicated in* From Tribe to Empire), *he traces the genesis, with
the nomes, of an organization which is agricultural and is also
religious. In the transition from clans to nomes, the totems play
a part on which M. Moret throws a vivid light.*

*Next we see, in the wars between different peoples, between
North and South, new gods appearing, not supplanting, but,
as a rule, uniting with the totems, which become gods of nomes,
so that divine society, like human, is composed of many elements.
Local, political causes create an order of rank among the divine
beings. In the course of its evolution, Egyptian religion, as has
been said, grows* more complex *and at the same time* simpler.[1]
*It is the object of a curious effort of collective elaboration, directed,
more and more consciously by the thought of the theologians.[2]
Finally the divine and the human are welded together by means
of a theogony which, on the one hand, reflects earthly events,
wars of different groups and the progress of centralization, and,
on the other, sets the great gods of nature at the beginnings of the
kingship.*

*Two of these gods take a supreme place in the Egyptian
Pantheon—Ra and Osiris. Ra is the Sun ; and he becomes the
Demiurge, the creator of the gods themselves, and the founder of
all order, divine and human. Osiris, the god of fertilizing water*

---

[1] *See G. Foucart, in Ad. Reinach,* Égyptologie et histoire des religions, *p.* 47.
(*Extract from* Revue de Synthèse historique, xxvii, 1913).
[2] *M. Moret makes a valuable contribution to the study of what one may call with
him " the logic of the first men civilized " (p. 169).*

and vegetation ; [1] *" fluid and varied, having many shapes and names,"* [2] *at war with his brother and enemy Seth, the desert, dryness, night, symbolizes not only a cosmic drama—the vital forces always reborn after apparent death—but also historical events, and a moral drama as well. Osiris undergoes a Passion ; he is the god of death and resurrection. All the gods end by being replicas of Ra and Osiris, and the god-king is an incarnation of them.*

Never was a kingship by right divine so absolute as that which ruled over this country, once the North and South were united. Pharaoh owns everything which belongs to his people, and owns his people itself. Through him alone the people communicates with the gods. It is just this apotheosis *of the King, in the literal sense of the word, which is the striking characteristic of Egypt. What happens (according to M. Davy's hypothesis in* From Tribe to Empire) *when clans are concentrated under a chief, and that chief gathers up the totemic* mana, *also happens as the result of a long process of concentration, more completely than in any other kingdom or empire, in respect of everything embraced by the Egyptian kingship. The King becomes the sole holder of the sacred force. And in this process of social organization we clearly see religion and power tightening their bonds as each supports the other.*

After judiciously reconstructing the origins, and explaining the " sacred despotism ", M. Moret describes the later stages in detail, and throws light upon the thorough-going transformations of the country which was so long supposed to have been incapable of change. There comes a day when an oligarchy of priests and nobles, a feudal vassalage, takes the power from the King ; later a popular revolution emancipates the masses ; and always in this country, where power is essentially religious, it is direct *participation in worship which, being extended, brings increased participation in the administration of the State and in the ownership of land.*

Too much stress cannot be laid—for this is one of the most novel ideas which Egyptology will owe to M. Moret, and a source of instructive comparison with Greece and Rome—on the

---

[1] *Isis, the sister and wife of Osiris, is the " fertilized soil" and " the prototype of woman in Egypt ". Through the myth of Isis, M. Moret reconstructs the formation of the family.*
[2] *p.* 85.

importance of the admission of the people to religious rights under the Middle Kingdom, and on the consequences to which it led. It is thanks to texts recently discovered that M. Moret has been able to follow, from the IIIrd Dynasty onwards and from the feudal lords to the proletariat, the advance of the spirit which claimed rights.

Ra continued to be the monopoly of the Pharaohs ; but the religion of Osiris gradually opened its doors, and the number of those who benefited by his passion and immortality constantly increased. Justice spread from heaven to earth. " Sacred despotism is succeeded by State socialism." [1] Pharaoh, growing more human, questions his conscience, in order to make law ; and the plebeian, fully awakened to religious and civic activity, questions his thoughts in touching accents, on the meaning of life.[2] If he has " set God in his heart ", if he is " pure ", he is confident of immortality ; the dead man justified becomes an Osiris, a Pharaoh. M. Moret demonstrates, with more force than anyone has done hitherto, this identification of the dead man with kings and gods.[3]

When Egypt comes out of her comparative isolation, when— after having borne the Hyksôs yoke and thrown it off—being taught by experience, she establishes protectorates outside her borders to prevent invasion, a new feudal vassalage of priests and warriors grows up, against which the king has to fight. One Pharaoh attempts a religious revolution which favours an " anticlerical " policy ; Akhenaten raises the worship of Ra to a monotheism ; and the new doctrine, which also moves one by its moral beauty, its feeling of human brotherhood, tends to restore to the King, as the incarnation of the god, the fullness of his power.[4] But in the end theocracy triumphs, with Amon, the god of the priests, and reigns until the ruin of Egyptian independence.

No historian has better brought out the especial character of this history, which is above all religious history. So, in the part of the book devoted to the life of the spirit and æsthetic production, M. Moret has only to summarize features which have struck the reader all through.

Over the development of Egyptian thought there presides (as

[1] *p.* 270.   [2] *p.* 223.   [3] *p.* 260.   [4] *p.* 325.

he has shown, and as he repeats with emphasis) the profound feeling that godhead is a vital force, a creative energy, a " potentiality ", divided among the gods—those gods of many forms, of which living beings are the visible images,[1] and innumerable names, which express and raise up energies. And, amid all this division of the force, the immanent unity tends to organize the divine in ranks, and to make the Word rule, the creator of physical and moral laws. In Egyptian thought there is a first outline of metaphysics, heralding Plato ; one day Egypt will be the home of Neo-Platonism.[2]

In a vigorous summary M. Moret explains Egyptian art, by the materials which the country supplies and by the religious symbolism which animates it entirely at its origin. We may say of the pyramid as of the Gothic cathedral, that it is an " act of faith".[3] The tombs and the temples, " abodes of eternity, the size of cities,"[4] in which the arts, not differentiated, all combine to convey the symbolic intention, are the supreme expression of the Egyptian genius, which loves greatness, but a calm, serene greatness, preserving " the sense of proportion even in the grandiose ".[5] Writing, which began as drawing, *literature, which began as the* decoration *of temples and tombs, and science, which has its seat in the temples, all the creations of the mind are seen under the sway of the pantheistic mysticism of the Egyptians.*

I should dwell still more upon the religion of Egypt, were it not that I hope to speak of religion in general, its origins, and its rôle in the evolution of mankind, in the Foreword to The Religious Thought of Greece, *which will be the first volume in this series to be devoted wholly to the study of a religion.*

---

[1] *The worship of animals, which was so deep-seated in Egypt, was not a mere survival of totemism.*

[2] *See* Greek Thought, *in this series ; Gomperz,* Greek Thinkers, *1901, vol. ii, pp. 255 ff.; J. Baillet,* Introduction a l'étude des idées morales dans l'Égypte antique, *p. 188.*

[3] *p. 174.*

[4] *See P. Montet, " Chronique égyptologique," in* Revue des Études anciennes, *Jan.–March, 1926, pp. 60–7. Renouvier, in* Introduction à la philosophie analytique de l'histoire, *speaks of " that kind of religion of death and its remains, unknown everywhere else. That religion was carried to the point where it became the biggest and costliest matter in public and family life, covered the land of the living with the monuments of the dead, absorbed a considerable part of the nation's labour, and set up, by the side of every city, a vast necropolis in which the complete and recognizable remains of the dead imposed themselves on the time and lay like a weight upon posterity " (p. 276).*

[5] *P. Lorquet,* L'Art et l'histoire, *p. 125.*

IV

Two important observations must, however, be made here.

First, the paradox of Egypt is that, while the divine surrounds all human activity, earthly life is carefully cultivated and tasted to the full in the advantages which it affords. Preoccupation with the " future " did not prevent the Egyptian from enjoying life ; on the contrary, it was because he valued it so much that he wanted to prolong it indefinitely—and in the same conditions.[1]

Jacques de Morgan's striking phrase, that Egypt " was not a kingdom of this world ", must not be taken too literally.[2] *What one can say is that the men who dwelt there were very different from the Semites, warlike, merciless, and " always thirsting for wealth and enjoyment ".*[3] *" A submissive, light-hearted race, content with little, singing at their toil, working with taste and patience,"* [4] *and essentially peaceful, they had managed to arrange their life judiciously and with ingenuity. On the reliefs of the Old Kingdom there are only " scenes of hunting and fishing, navigation and rural employments—always works of peace ".*[5]

Also, among these men, life became all the sweeter because in them the moral sentiment had gradually attained an " exquisite delicacy ", and the " law of doing good " had taken definite shape.[6] *Social necessity, here as elsewhere, and here more strongly than elsewhere, because of the conditions of environment of which I have spoken, imposed the principle of mutual helpfulness. Religion, in its growing domination, absorbed this principle, founding the worship of natural forces and morality ; and morality more and more assumed a religious character, until the time when the individual found the fine distinctions of his conduct in the privacy of his conscience.*

---

[1] " *It would be a mistake to imagine them as people who lived sadly, absorbed in meditation on death.*" See G. Foucart, *in Ad. Reinach, op. cit., p.* 47 ; cf. Söderblom, Manuel d'histoire des religions, *French ed., p.* 76.

[2] *Op. cit., p.* 251.

[3] *Ibid.* ; cf. Mesopotamia, *in this series.*

[4] *Below, p.* 216.

[5] *De Morgan, op. cit., p.* 220.

[6] *See Gomperz, op. cit., vol. i, p.* 135, *and Baillet,* Le Régime pharaonique, *p.* 652.

This takes me to my second observation. However centralized social life may appear, however socialized religious life may have been, we must not underestimate the part played by the individual. On the contrary, my law—or, more modestly, my hypothesis—of the three phases of social evolution [1] is, if anything, confirmed. In Egypt, as everywhere, technical and æsthetic inventions, which respond to practical interest and the need for play, come from the individual. It is the preoccupation of the individual with death which gives rise to the beliefs and rites connected with the next life which are most characteristic of Egypt. The knowledge, mixed with magic, which the priests acquire at an early date, is based on personal observation.[2] But the stage of socialization is here strongly marked. So it was that the arts, for example, as de Morgan has observed, while they developed rapidly, " at once encased themselves in rigid rules, and the artist's genius found itself restricted by religious canons." [3] So it was that " medicine had assumed a divine character, and the physician who departed from the sacred rules was liable to punishment by death as a murderer ".[4] Yet in the end the individual emancipated himself.

No doubt " old Egypt was but rarely a land of non-utilitarian culture, art for its own sake, pure scientific inquiry, abstract reasoning, or intimate literature " [5]—of all that bears the deepest impress of personality. Yet, after the popular revolution, art became realistic, psychological, and therein more personal, the spirit inquired more freely, and science " tended to become secularized ".[6]

The individual may not have expanded here as he did in Greece, but Egypt was none the less, like Greece, an exceptional success. In that happy valley, intelligence (notably in the scribe) [7] and morality (in great personages and humble people) played a

---

[1] *See Foreword to* From Tribe to Empire.
[2] *The tradition recorded by Plato made " Theuth " the inventor of writing, astronomy, land-measuring, and mathematics. See Gomperz, op. cit., vol. ii, pp. 257–8.*
[3] *Op. cit., p. 269.*
[4] *Op. cit., p. 250.*
[5] *Below, p. 463.*
[6] *S. Reinach,* Orpheus, *p. 46.*
[7] *On education and the part played by the scribe, see J. Baillet,* Idées morales, *p. 52, and Gomperz, op. cit., vol. ii, p. 256. The god Thoth is the scribe of heaven. On the writing of Egypt, see* Prehistoric Man, *pp. 256 ff., and* The Ægean Civilization, *p. 371, both in this series. For Egyptian mathematics, which represent a stage between pure empiricism and science, see an article by Abel Rey, in* Revue de Synthèse historique, *xli, June, 1926.*

part which explains the admiration of the Greeks for that venerable wisdom, that knowledge " old as the world ".[1]   For human unification, which could, at the same time as the mastering of nature, be the very work of civilization, Egypt did much.   And it was by moral law, rather than by violence and domination, that she brought men together.[2]   Her just administration, her pleasant adornment of this life, her serene conceptions of the after-life, all tempt the historian to ask himself whether, on the road which mankind is travelling in search of Paradise, the stage represented by ancient Egypt is not one of those in which it may sometimes have seemed that the goal was almost reached.

V

I do not think that I exaggerate when I say that in M. Moret's fine work the history of Egypt will be seen in an absolutely new light.

Since Maspero's time important evidence has made it possible to distinguish more between periods and to follow the development of the family and of institutions better.   No doubt works on Egypt in which new discoveries are utilized are not lacking ; but one does not find in them the historical sense and the spirit of synthesis in the same degree as here.   Elsewhere the matter is cut up into fragmentary studies ; here all is combined and blended in a powerful and living picture.

Not that M. Moret tries to create any illusions about the state of our knowledge.   For all the light thrown upon the past by the genius of Champollion, and for all the abundance of monuments and documents preserved in that land where it does not rain, there are matters about which " generalization is extremely hazardous ".[3]   But of these monuments and texts—often biassed, and often naively truthful—M. Moret makes use with marvellous judgment.   He is a complete historian, who can illustrate Egyptian history by happy comparisons.   He animates his broad canvas with picturesque details and curious quotations,

---

[1] *See Gomperz, op. cit., vol. i, p. 135; vol. ii, pp. 255–6.*
[2] *Cf. the part played by Persia ; see Ancient Persia, in this series.*
[3] *Below, p. 261.*

skilfully selected, which take one into the heart of a society thousands of years old. His exposition is completed and illustrated by the anthology no less than by the picture-book. And, if this work does not claim to be the last work in Egyptology, that science will only advance beyond it with its help.

HENRI BERR.

THE NILE AND EGYPTIAN CIVILIZATION

INTRODUCTION

SOURCES AND CHRONOLOGY

I

GREEK SOURCES AND THEIR VALUE

THE hieroglyphic writing invented by the Egyptians, which we find as a complete system on the earliest monuments of the Thinite period, about 3,500 years before Christ, gradually fell out of use, and was replaced by Coptic and Greek, when Egypt was occupied by the Ptolemies and the Cæsars. About the end of the fourth century of our era the Christians succeeded in having the Egyptian temples closed, by an edict of Theodosius of 391 ; the last schools of Egyptian priests which still studied the " sacred writing " disappeared at the same time. The written monuments of Egypt became unintelligible, and no direct interpretation was possible until the discovery of the bilingual Rosetta Stone and its decipherment by Champollion.

As far as we know, no scholar of the neighbouring peoples of antiquity was able to read the hieroglyphs. The historians who visited ancient Egypt and have left us their accounts of the country, obtained their information from intermediaries. They questioned learned and competent witnesses, but were not able to check the truth of their statements. Their conversations with their interpreters were full of pitfalls, facts often being distorted, misunderstood, and garbled, as still happens when the traveller relies on native dragomans in the East.

Lastly, the historical narratives left by the Greeks are not earlier than the fifth century B.C., by which time Egyptian civilization was between thirty-five and forty centuries old, and was so far from its origins and its most glorious days that it had lost much of its character.   In the eyes of the inhabitants themselves, already permeated by foreign influences, the monuments had become merely the relics of a past, of which they did not understand the true meaning.

So the classical historians,[1] obtaining their information second-hand, and living so long after the events, could only give us a very fragmentary and distorted history of Egypt. Yet, until the time of Champollion, they were the only sources available, and we cannot deny the great value of the evidence of eyewitnesses like Herodotus, Diodorus, and Strabo on the condition of Egypt at the time when they visited it. They could use their eyes, and their tourists' notes are often correct and picturesque, and well express the freshness of their impressions and the shrewdness of their judgment. In the traditions which they collected about earlier times, many facts have been recognized as true, through the ever-thickening veil of legend and the distortions due to the extreme remoteness of the events.

It was at the time of the Persian conquest in Egypt that the first Greek historians came in search of information. Hecatæos of Miletos, who lived about 520 B.C., visited the banks of the Nile and consulted the Egyptian priests at Thebes, in order to compile his *Genealogies* [2] and his history of " Libya ", forming part of his Περίοδος γῆς. Herodotus of Halicarnassos, inquiring into the causes of the wars between Greeks and Barbarians (that is Persians), devotes the whole second book of his *History* to Egypt, where he had spent some weeks shortly after the battle between Inaros [3] and the Persians of 454, that is somewhere about 450. He first visited the Delta, stayed at Memphis and Heliopolis, went up the

---

[1] I shall quote only the chief among them. Very detailed information about the classical sources for Egyptian history will be found in Alfred Wiedemann's *Aegyptische Geschichte*, i, pp. 102 ff.

[2] Hdt., ii. 143.   [3] Hdt., iii. 12.

Nile with stops at Panopolis, Thebes, and Elephantine, and on his way back made excursions into the oasis of the Fayum, completed his inquiries in the Delta, and left by Pelusium.[1] The questions which he asked of the priests of Heliopolis, Memphis, and Thebes refer chiefly to the origin and legends of the gods and to chronology. Priests told him that Menes had been the first king of Egypt, and after him they enumerated " 340 names of other kings. From the first king to the last there had been 341 generations of men ; allowing three generations to a hundred years, that gives 11,340 years, of human history ". Before these men, the gods had reigned over Egypt.[2] To these stories, which he repeats as he heard them, Herodotus adds " what he could observe for himself ".[3] This consists of entertaining pictures of popular life, and reflections on the monuments and on the legends attached to them, of which we can make use, for they are based on personal observation, and many of them bear the stamp of truth.

After the conquest by Alexander the Great, in 332, Egypt opened its doors wide to the Greeks, and history-writing was held in honour at the court of the Ptolemies. Hecatæos of Abdera, who lived at the court of Ptolemy I Soter, at the end of the fourth century B.C., wrote the Ægyptiaca, a work which only survives in fragments, but was much used by Diodorus Siculus, who quotes it from time to time (i, 45).

At the court of Ptolemy Soter and Ptolemy II Philadelphos there also lived Manetho of Sebennytos, the most important historian of Egypt. According to the Jewish historian Josephus, Manetho was an Egyptian by race, a high priest and temple scribe, equally conversant with his own language and Greek. At the request of King Ptolemy Philadelphos he compiled, from hieroglyphic sources, his Ægyptiaca, in which he set out to bring within reach of the Hellenes the historical events, the religious and political traditions, and the manners and customs of his country. The date of the work is later than 271 B.C.

These Ægyptiaca have come down to us as fragments by two different ways. Josephus, who was born A.D. 37, had written a pamphlet against the grammarian Apion of

---

[1] C. Sourdille, La Durée et l'étendue du voyage d'Hérodote en Égypte, 1910, p. 251.
[2] Hdt., ii, 142–3. But in ii, 100, he mentions only 330.
[3] ii, 99.

Alexandria, a violent anti-Semite, who ascribed the origin of the Jews to " lepers and other impure men ", driven with Moses from the valley of the Nile by the Egyptians. Josephus retorted that these impure men were the Hyksôs, descendants of Jacob and Joseph, who had indeed entered Egypt, but as conquerors, not as slaves. To support his argument, he quotes the text of Manetho's passages on the invasion of the Hyksôs [1] and their expulsion from Egypt by the Pharaohs of the XVIIIth Dynasty.[2] Then he gives a list of the kings of Egypt, from Thothmes I to Rameses IV—twenty-one names, with the years and months of each reign. It is probable that Josephus does not quote these from Manetho direct; he must have taken his account from a summary or *Epitome*, drawn up by the chronologists from the original Manetho.[3]

This *Epitome* at least proves that Manetho gave a complete list of the kings of Egypt, from Menes (who was preceded by the gods) down to the Ptolemies, with the exact dates of their reigns ; he had also made out synchronous tables of the kings of the other Eastern peoples. This very fact made him an invaluable source for the Christian apologists, when they tried to prove the extreme antiquity of the Jewish faith as compared with all the pagan religions.[4] For these polemics it was necessary to compare the annals of the various peoples of the East with the Old Testament, and to establish synchronous tables of Jewish and all the other histories, in order to prove the greater age of the Jews. So Manetho's *Epitome*, boiled down to an enumeration of Pharaohs arranged in dynasties, with a few brief notes, has been preserved for us by the Christian chronologists.

First of all, Sextus Julius Africanus (the African) gave the *Epitome* in his Chronology, composed about A.D. 220. Then Eusebius, Bishop of Cæsareia (270–340), in a Chronology which is partly preserved in Greek and more completely in

---

[1] See Moret and Davy, *From Tribe to Empire*, in this series, pp. 247–8. The first part of this work is by M. Davy.

[2] *Contra Apionem*, i, 14.

[3] Eduard Meyer, **XXIII**, pp. 100 ff.

[4] In addition to Meyer's *Chronologie*, which represents the latest results of modern criticism in respect of Manetho, the reader is referred to an old work by Brunet de Presles, *Examen critique de la succession des dynasties égyptiennes* (1850), where he will find the various lists given by the abbreviators of Manetho. The full text of all fragments of Manetho is in the *Fragmenta Historicorum Græcorum*, vol. ii (Didot's ed.).

Armenian, quotes the *Epitome* from the XVIth Dynasty onwards, but follows a different version from that of Africanus. Lastly, George, known as the Syncellus, a secretary of the Patriarch of Constantinople, compiled a Chronography, about A.D. 800, in which he quotes the *Epitome* (from Africanus and Eusebius), a *Book of Sothis*, attributed to Manetho, and an *Old Chronicle*.

From these abridgements, we know that Manetho's *Ægyptiaca* were in three books (*tomoi*), and that the kings were divided into thirty-one dynasties (royal families or lines), designated by a geographical epithet indicating their origin— the Thinite Dynasty, the Memphite, Elephantite, Heracleopolite, Theban, etc. The original text gave the years, months, and days of the reign of every king. The *Epitome* mentions only the most important kings, with the length of their separate reigns; for certain dynasties the names of the kings are not given, and we have only the sum total of all their reigns together. These figures, which would have been so valuable for establishing the true chronology of Egypt, have unfortunately been doctored by the Christian apologists, with a view to making them agree with the chronology of the Bible. The resulting arrangements are so arbitrary that when the years of individual reigns are added together they hardly ever correspond with the totals of the dynasties. Yet in spite of the suspicion attaching to this computation of years, the abridgment of Manetho is still a most precious document for the history of Egypt. The arrangement in *dynasties*, which no classical author had used, has been adopted by modern historians, as being authentic,[1] and indispensable for the chronological classification of the Pharaohs.

After Manetho we have to come down to Diodorus Siculus for a work on Egypt of any importance which has escaped the ravages of time. In his *Historical Library* Diodorus attempts a picture of the history of the world, and begins with the origin of the universe ; this takes him to Egypt, for there " tradition places the origin of the gods ", and " the Egyptians say that their country is the cradle of the human

---

[1] The hieroglyphic texts never mention dynasties, but sometimes designate royal families by the word " *house,* of such-and-such a city ".

race ".[1] Diodorus is inspired by Herodotus, and, above all, by Hecatæos of Abdera ; nevertheless, since he visited the Nile valley himself in the 180th Olympiad (between 60 and 57 B.C.), his evidence has a personal value. His natural bent inclines him to philosophical and religious digressions, in marked contrast to the realistic observations of Herodotus.

On several occasions Greek geographers came to study the country of the Nile. As early as the third century Eratosthenes of Cyrene, who lived in Alexandria, at the court of the Ptolemies (275–194 B.C.) travelled through Egypt, and was the first to estimate its extent by parallels of latitude. He is said to have obtained in the archives of the priests of Thebes, a list of thirty-eight Theban kings, " which he translated from Egyptian into Greek." This list, which has been preserved by George the Syncellus, really includes a variety of kings, from the Ist Dynasty to the XXth, but it is of especial interest in that it adds to each proper name a paraphrase of its signification, often based on true data.

Strabo, who visited Egypt up to the First Cataract, about A.D. 27, has devoted the seventeenth and last book of his *Geography* to the country. His descriptions are precise and interesting, but his historical information seldom goes back beyond the Ptolemaic period.

Plutarch of Chæroneia gives us the exegetical, moralizing point of view in his treatise *On Isis and Osiris* ($\Pi\epsilon\rho\grave{\iota}$ $"I\sigma\iota\delta\sigma$ $\kappa\alpha\grave{\iota}$ $'O\sigma\acute{\iota}\rho\iota\delta\sigma$), which he wrote about A.D. 120. It is the only systematic account which antiquity has left us of Egyptian religion, and in particular of the myth of Osiris and its profound significance. Plutarch was well-informed, and his testimony is very often confirmed by hieroglyphic texts, some of which are three thousand years earlier than his time. Apart from the tendency, which, indeed, he shares with Herodotus and Diodorus, to force the Egyptian gods into the scheme of Greek mythology, Plutarch displays a penetrating intuition into the Mysteries of Osiris and has made it possible for us to understand them.

In sum, the Greek historians, geographers, and philosophers studied Egypt with enthusiasm and often with discrimination ; the country exercised over them the fascination which classical antiquity has for us. Their curiosity has saved for us

[1] Diod., i, 9–10 ; cf. i, 42.

a certain number of historical facts, the names of the greatest kings, and a general idea of religion, institutions, and manners; but either from lack of capacity or from lack of information, they were not able to distinguish legend from fact, or to classify the periods methodically, or to establish an outline of the general history—they were on the whole retailers of anecdotes. Manetho, on the other hand, though he did not deny himself legendary stories, sometimes did real historical work; he has given us a practicable framework, namely the dynasties, with dates and totals for periods. Unfortunately, his abridgers have obtained from him contradictory or fabulous figures, and names which do not always agree with those of the other classical writers.

So, hidden behind the veil of ancient history, the past of Egypt, filled with wonders, threw an uncertain, wavering light. Yet, all the time, that infathomable Egypt was telling her own story on thousands of tombs, temples, stelæ, and statues, covered with hieroglyphics, mute witnesses, speaking a language to which the key had been lost. A man of genius was to find it.

II

THE DECIPHERMENT OF THE HIEROGLYPHICS

When, on the 14th September, 1822, Champollion deciphered the name of Rameses II, it was 1,400 years since any man had read the hieroglyphics correctly. Yet the actual language of the ancient Egyptians was not extinct; it survived in the form of *Coptic*.

Since Alexander's conquest, the Egyptian language had assumed a foreign mask; it was no longer written in hieroglyphs alone, but also in conventional, alphabetic signs, which the Greeks had borrowed from the Phœnicians. To render Egyptian sounds, unknown to spoken Greek, seven signs taken from the demotic script were added to the Greek alphabet (Fig. 1). In this guise, the Egyptian language, which had, moreover, developed in the course of classical times, was called Coptic,[1] and it continued to evolve as a popular

---

[1] In the name *Copt* we have the Greek word for " Egyptian "—*Ægyptios, Gyptios*—transmitted in the Arabic word *Qubt*.

tongue. Down to the end of the Roman Empire, three scripts
were in use in Egypt—the hieroglyphic of tradition, the Greek,
and the Coptic, which was intermediate between the two
others. The hieroglyphic writing disappeared with paganism,
at the end of the fourth century, and the Greek writing
succumbed after the Arab conquest. The Arabic language
and writing were then imposed upon the dwellers by the
Nile, but Coptic survived as the liturgical language of the
Christians, and continued in use in monasteries, churches,
and schools. A Coptic literature,[1] composed of translations
of the Old and New Testaments, apocryphal Gospels, lives
of Saints, familiar letters, etc., survived into our own time ;
in the nineteenth century there were still monks who not
only read Coptic but spoke it among themselves, but to-day
the language is known only by scholars.

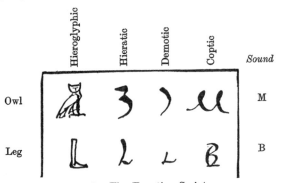

Fig. 1.—The Egyptian Scripts.

Thus Coptic was descended from the Egyptian dialects of
the late period, transcribed in Greek letters. Now, Coptic
grammars and Copto-Arabic and Copto-Greek lexicons exist,
through which one can get back to all the later vocabulary
and syntactical forms of ancient Egyptian, but on one
condition—that one can read the Pharaonic writing, that one
can decipher the hieroglyphics.

In the middle of the seventeenth century, the Jesuit priest
Kircher perceived that Coptic preserved, under its
alphabetical disguise, the old Egyptian language. His very

---

[1] On this subject, see Étienne Quatremère, *Recherches sur la langue et la littérature
de l'Égypte*, 1808. Written before the hieroglyphics were deciphered, this work
treats only of Coptic literature.

scientific researches restored to honour the study of Coptic, which he called the *Lingua Ægyptiaca Restituta* (1643); but when he tried to go beyond Coptic to Egyptian he failed utterly, for he came up against a strictly locked door. What were the hieroglyphs? Letters, sounds, ideas? And how could they be read?

About the hieroglyphs, antiquity had only left a few obscure definitions. Their very name was mysterious, γράμματα ἱερά, " sacred letters," Herodotus (ii, 36), and Diodorus (iii, 3) called them; γράμματα ἱερογλυφικά, " sacred carved letters," is the more specific description of Bishop Clement of Alexandria,[1] who, living in Egypt at the end of the second century of our era, knew Egyptians who spoke their language and read the hieroglyphics. These names implied that the hieroglyphic writing was perhaps reserved, among the Egyptians, for sacred or religious subjects. Yet Herodotus and Diodorus told us that there were two kinds of Egyptian " letters "—the " sacred," ἱερά, which the priests alone knew, and the " popular," δημοτικά, which were applied to common things. Clement of Alexandria was still more explicit. There are, he says, three distinct kinds of writing: (i) the type called epistolographic; (ii) the hieratic, used by the *hierogrammateis*; (iii) the hieroglyphic.[2] As for the signification of these various signs, the current tradition was that they expressed, not sounds (phonetically), but ideas (as symbols). Egyptian writing would perhaps be an unsolved problem at this day, had it not been for the chance find made in 1799 by a soldier of Napoleon.

The French expedition which Napoleon led to the land of the Nile had as its object, in addition to its military purposes, the elucidation of the problem of the writing, and consequently of the civilization, of the Pharaohs. The General was accompanied by an escort of scholars. Chance favoured them. In August, 1799, a captain of artillery named

---

[1] *Stromateis*, v, 4, Potter's ed., p. 657. Cf. Letronne, " Examen du texte de Clément," etc., in *Œuvres choisies*, i, 2, p. 237.

[2] Precise details on this ancient evidence will be found in H. Sottas and E. Drioton, *Introduction à l'étude des hiéroglyphes*, 1922.

Broussard unearthed, beneath the earthworks of the modern fort of Rosetta, a block of basalt engraved with a text in three writings. The lowest was in Greek epigraphic characters and recorded a decree issued in 196 B.C. by Ptolemy V Epiphanes. This Greek portion also said that the same text was given in the two writings above, one of which, being in hieroglyphs, was called " sacred letters " (γράμματα ἱερά), while the other, which was formed of linear signs, was described as ἐγχωρία γράμματα, "native letters," or " popular " (demotic) characters ; and, indeed these last were similar to those found on a number of known papyri (Plate I, 2).

So the Rosetta Stone was a bilingual document, and held the key to the mystery ; the meaning of the words was

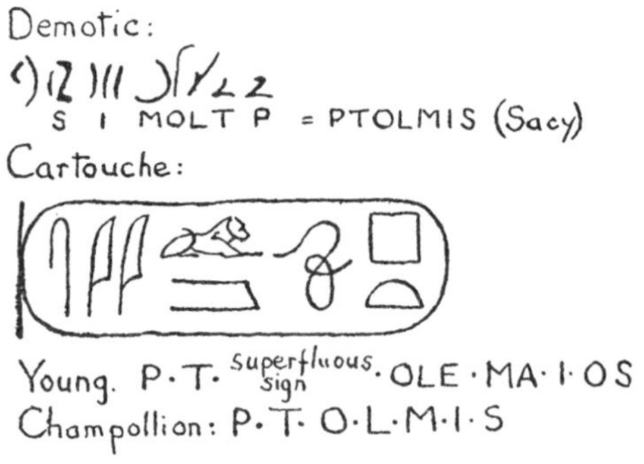

FIG. 2.—Demotic Spelling and Cartouche of Ptolemy, as read by Sacy, Young, and Champollion.

supplied by the Greek. A first inference to draw was that the hieroglyphic script was not, after all, strictly religious in character, since it could be used, like the demotic, for administrative documents. The next thing to do was to identify in the Egyptian versions the signs corresponding to the Greek words.

In 1802 the Arabic scholar Sylvestre de Sacy attacked the demotic portion, the cursive signs of which were not unlike Arabic and seemed to him likely to be alphabetical rather than figurative. With the help of the Greek he sought for the approximate position of the royal names Ptolemy and Arsinoë, which occurred several times. So, by mere measurement, he succeeded in identifying the demotic signs which wrote the name Ptlomis (= Ptolemy), from right to left. But neither he nor Akerblad, who took up the study of the demotic text in 1802, could obtain anything further from this purely empirical method. When the letters thus identified were applied to other passages, it was not possible to recognize, in the demotic text, a single Coptic word having an equivalent sound.

In 1814 Dr. Thomas Young, an eminent English physicist, grappled with the hieroglyphic text. Inspired by a shrewd observation of the Abbé Barthélemy, he saw that royal names, like Ptolemy, must be those which were surrounded by a loop or " cartouche " (Fig. 2); accordingly he classified the signs found in the cartouches as letters representing *P t o l e m a i o s.* He succeeded in identifying the total name Ptolemaios, but he was not able to define the exact phonetic value of every sign. When he applied the alphabet thus constituted to other words, he arrived at entirely incorrect readings, and could not find one Coptic word with a similar sound.

At the same time, a young man who was teaching history at the Faculty of Letters at Grenoble, Jean François Champollion (1790–1832), had devoted himself to the solution of the problem. From his early childhood he had had a passion for the history of Egypt, and had learned all that classical antiquity and the Coptic language had handed down to us about it. He pored greedily over the signs of the various hieroglyphic writings, on the Rosetta Stone and in the *Description de l'Égypte* published by the French scholars who had accompanied Napoleon. The work done by Sacy and Young proved to him that the Greek proper names must be written in alphabetical Egyptian characters. On this basis he built up his own discoveries, which, from 1821 onwards, followed with marvellous rapidity (Plate I, 1).

First of all, Champollion cleared up the question of the diversity of the scripts. He showed that the hieratic writing was an abbreviation of the hieroglyphic signs, and that the demotic in its turn was derived from the hieratic ; in these three forms Egyptian writing was one and the same. Therefore, in the hieroglyphic script as in the demotic, there must be signs having a phonetic, alphabetical value. Furthermore, he noted, on counting the hieroglyphic signs of the

Rosetta Stone, that they were more numerous than the words of the parallel Greek text; therefore each hieroglyphic sign did not represent a whole idea or a word.

Having established these points, Champollion returned to the study of the cartouches of Rosetta. In 1822 he received copies of two new cartouches, engraved on a small obelisk found at Philæ, the base of which bore a dedication in Greek to Ptolemy and Cleopatra. Champollion showed that one of these cartouches was like that of Rosetta, and gave *Ptolmis*; the second, which was new, must be read as *Kliopatra*.[1] Five letters are common to the two names: *p*, *t*, *l*, *o*, and *i*; and five similar signs are found in the right place in the two

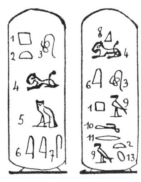

FIG. 3.—Ptolemaic Cartouches.

1 = P;   2 = T;   3 = O;   4 = L;
5 = M;   6 = I;   7 = S;   8 = K;
4 = L;   6 = I;   3 = O;   1 = P;
9 = A; 10 = D; 11 = R;   9 = A;
       2 = T; 13 is a determinative.

hieroglyphic names. On the other hand, the *s* of Ptolmis does not appear in the name of the queen, and new signs, corresponding to *k*, *a*, and *r* in the name of Kliopatra, do not appear, and ought not to appear, in the name of the king (Fig. 3). The conclusion is that, since similar signs in the two names express the same sounds in each cartouche, they are entirely *phonetic* in nature.

In a few weeks Champollion applied the rudiments of an alphabet thus obtained to all the names of Ptolemies and

---

1 The true reading is Kliopadra. Sign 10 is the dental *d* interchangeable with *t*. The final *t* is not pronounced.

Cæsars found in the plates of the *Description de l'Égypte.*
Seventy-nine cartouche-names were deciphered, one after
another, supplying new letters to the alphabet, and making
it possible to draw up a *Table of Phonetic Signs.* This appears
in a *letter to M. Dacier,* the Permanent Secretary of the
Académie des Inscriptions et Belles-lettres, dated 27th
September, 1822, in which Champollion announces that he is
reading the hieroglyphic cartouches !

So far he had read only the proper names of Greek and
Roman sovereigns, transcribed in hieroglyphics. How was he
to prove that the writing of the Pharaonic period contained
the same phonetic elements ? Yet the aforementioned letter
expressed Champollion's certainty that he would soon read

FIG. 4.—Pharaonic Cartouches. Ramesses, Thotmeses.

the cartouches of the Pharaohs, like those of the Ptolemies
and the Cæsars.

On the 14th September, 1822, Champollion had received
impressions of cartouches from a temple distinctly earlier
than the Greek period. On one of them (Fig. 4) he recognized
in the two hooked lines at the end of the name the last letter
of the name Ptolmis at Rosetta, and accordingly he read
s . . . s. At the beginning, the disk with a dot in the middle was
the symbol of the sun, the reading of which was supplied by
the Greek and Coptic texts—Ra. As for the middle sign,
Champollion had seen it at Rosetta, where it appeared, as
here, followed by *s,* in one single place, corresponding to the

Greek γενεθλία, " birthday," of the king. The conclusion was that this character was not alphabetic, and was equivalent to the Coptic word ⲙⲥ (*ms*) " be born ", or ⲙⲁⲥ (*mas*) " child ". Champollion put these elements together, and saw before him—the illustrious name of Ra-ms-ss,[1] *Ramesses*, mentioned by Manetho, Tacitus, and the Book of Exodus ! Not only could he read the name ; he could understand it, and translate it. According to Coptic, Ra-ms-s means " Ra begets him ", that is " Child of Ra ".

He at once checked his method by the other cartouche (Fig. 4). Here there is an ibis instead of the sun at the beginning of the name, the other elements being like those in the first cartouche. From the Greeks we know that the ibis was the symbol of the god Thoth. The name must read *Thot-ms-s* ; and Manetho gives the name of the Pharaoh Thutmosis. According to Coptic this means " Thoth begets him ", or " Child of Thoth ".

Then Champollion had a flash of genius. The writing on the Pharaonic monuments prior to the Græco-Roman epoch was not purely alphabetic, like that of the cartouches Ptolmis and Kliopatra ; and it was not exclusively symbolic, as had been too long supposed. At one and the same time it employed (i) symbolic or figurative signs, like those of Ra and Thoth, and (ii) phonetic signs, some syllabic like *ms*, and some alphabetic like *s*. The mistake of all his predecessors, under which he himself had laboured until now, had been to suppose that the hieroglyphic script was either entirely figurative or entirely phonetic. In reality " it is a complex system, a script at once figurative, symbolic, and phonetic, in the same document, in the same sentence, in the same word ".[2]

In his *Précis du système hiéroglyphique* (1824), an incomparable masterpeice of penetration and French clarity, Champollion declares that he can henceforward read the monuments of every period. What is more, he translates without hesitation. In the Coptic vocabulary and grammar, which he knows thoroughly, he finds words having the same sound as those which he has read in hieroglyphics, he understands their meaning, he defines their grammatical function.

---

[1] Champollion had guessed that in Pharaonic times Egyptian writing, like the scripts of the Semitic languages, gave only the consonants of words.

[2] *Précis du système hiéroglyphique*, p. 327.

In this way he interprets whole documents, with a surety of method and an ease which even at this day fill us with surprise and admiration.[1]

Champollion now undertook to review all the Egyptian monuments brought to Europe. He showed the learned world that many of the royal names cited by Manetho appeared authentically on the *Royal Tablet of Abydos* and in the *Turin Papyrus*; that the gods Amon-Ra, Osiris, Isis, Horus, and the rest lived again in their statues and the prescriptions for their ritual; that henceforth the monuments could be classified in periods; that a whole past, thousands of years long, was unveiling and would yield up its secrets, and might perhaps reveal the beginnings of civilization. From 1828 to 1829 he continued his researches in Egypt itself; for fifteen months he ranged the valley, as far as the Second Cataract, visiting every accessible monument, copying every important inscription, having reliefs drawn and plans of buildings made.

On his return a Chair of Egyptian Antiquities was created for him at the Collège de France, but, worn out by the fever of work, after ten years of prodigious activity, he died on the 4th March, 1832, leaving, he said sadly, " as a visiting-card on posterity," his *Grammaire égyptienne*, his *Dictionnaire hiéroglyphique*, and, in *Les Monuments de l'Égypte et de la Nubie*, those admirable copies taken at the sites, which trained to his own method the Egyptologists of coming generations.

A pioneer in an almost virgin territory, Champollion created, in addition to the method of decipherment, the method of scientific use of material by excavation, publication, and research, on a philological basis, in every domain— archæology, history, religion. He threw back the horizon of mankind more than three thousand years. To explore it, he stepped with a giant's stride over the threshhold at which the Greeks had halted, struck with awe and surprised at their ignorance, before the Veiled Isis, the symbol of the country which they called the Mother of Civilizations.

---

[1] For fuller details of the stages of the decipherment, see " L'Égyptologie ", by A. Moret, in *Livre du centenaire de la Société Asiatique*, 1922, and the same author's " L'Écriture hiéroglyphique en Égypte ", in *Scientia*, February, 1919. The specialist is referred to H. Sottas and E. Drioton, *Introduction à l'étude des hiéroglyphes*, 1922.

III

The Egyptian sources for history have a special character. No historical writing, in the modern sense of the word, has been found in Egypt. To reconstruct history we have to depend entirely on epigraphic monuments—biographical stelæ, accounts of victories, royal decrees—and on papyri, which have preserved literary compositions, Government correspondence, legal documents, and private papers (especially from the Ptolemaic period onward). Except these last-named documents, all sources have one feature in common : they were found in temples and in tombs. This fact of their origin would be almost enough to reveal their tendency ; the writer always had a preconceived intention and placed himself at a subjective point of view. Thus, a war or a peace treaty is not set forth objectively, but recorded as evidence of the power of a god, *ad majorem Dei gloriam.* The biography of an individual is conceived as an act of gratitude towards the king his benefactor. Above all, the bulk of the texts consists of funerary formulas, divine liturgies, rituals for the worship of the gods and the dead, and mythical narratives, on the walls of temples or of royal tombs. For the Old Kingdom we reconstruct the facts from the titles of kings, from lists of other titles, from decrees, and in a few rare cases from biographies inscribed in tombs. As for doctrines, we find them in the immense corpus of religious texts spread over the walls of the royal pyramids of the VIth Dynasty. Facts, therefore, are almost always presented from a religious angle, and events are related according to a well-established plan, or according to various theological systems—at any rate, in the way in which the Egyptians wanted posterity to regard them. It was history written with a purpose and embellished, rather than an account of what really happened. Human truthfulness may lose by the process, but the history of ideas and institutions gains, for the systematic, dogmatic twist given to the facts is itself a revelation of the spirit of a people ; it is a historical truth.

Among these Egyptian sources the chronological documents are of chief interest. As soon as Champollion could read the hieroglyphics, he sought for the historical, artistic, and religious monuments which were most likely to give him definite points on which to base a chronological system. At the beginning of this study of Egyptian civilization I must warn the reader of the very special features presented by the chronological problem in Egypt. As in *From Tribe to Empire*, I shall take as my foundation Eduard Meyer's *Ægyptische Chronologie*.[1]

The Egyptians had no era.[2] Their monuments are not dated from an official, accepted starting-point[3]; for example, we never see " In the year 1320 " this or that happened. We find " In the year 1, in the third month of the season of Shemu, on the third day, His Majesty made his first campaign against the Asiatics " ; facts are dated by the year of the Pharaoh's reign, and the computation recommences with every reign. To establish Egyptian chronology with these data, we should have to possess the names of all the kings, with all the years of their reigns, without omission or error, for a period covering almost 4,000 years. We could get this if we discovered monuments of all the kings of Egypt, mentioning the number of years each had held the throne, or if we found complete " king-lists ". The former condition is unattainable ; the second has not yet been attained.

Yet these king-lists did exist, and we have seen that Manetho endeavoured to establish a chronological table of his dynasties. The following are the chief hieroglyphic lists found up to the present, in order of antiquity, starting from the Old Kingdom :—

(i) A fragment of Annals, carved on a block of diorite, which is preserved in the Museum of Palermo, and is known as the *Palermo Stone*.[4] This document was probably drafted in the reign of Neuserra, a Vth Dynasty king, who died about

---

[1] French translation by A. Moret, revised by the author in 1912, **XXIII.**

[2] One solitary exception to this rule appears on a monument of Rameses II, which mentions the year 400 of a King Seth-Nubti, of the Hyksôs period. This isolated fact had no effect on official chronology. Cf. Meyer, **XXIII**, p. 95.

[3] Such as, for example, " From the foundation of the City," *Ab Urbe Condita*, among the Romans.

[4] This stele was first known by a fairly large fragment ; I shall quote it later, from H. Schaefer's edition. Four more fragments, now in the Cairo Museum, were found later. Three belong to the Palermo Stone, and one to another " tablet " (H. Gauthier, " Quatre Nouveaux Fragments de la Pierre de Palerme," in *Musée égyptien*, vol. iii ; G. Daressy, in **II**, *Bulletin*, vol. xii, p. 161).

2600. It recorded the reigns of kings since the beginning of time, even prior to the Ist Dynasty, giving a summary of the chief deeds of each early king, and, in the case of some later kings, their achievements in every year of their reign. If this stone were intact we should have the complete official tradition regarding the history of Egypt from the beginning to the reign of Neuserra ; unfortunately the fragments preserved are only an eighth of the whole.

(ii) A series of " royal tablets ", lists of dead kings, who are entitled to receive ancestor-worship in the temples where the lists were found. These date from the XVIIIth and XIXth Dynasties. They all merely give a *selection*, admittedly incomplete, of ancestral kings, named without dates (neither regnal years not totals) and without division into periods or dynasties. The choice of names varies according to the preferences of the royal donor, and the arrangement is not the same on one tablet and another ; it is clear that these tablets come from different sources. Of such lists we have :—

(*a*) A mutilated list, now in the Louvre, carved in the *Chamber of Ancestors* of Thothmes III (died about 1447) at Karnak ; it gives two names of the Old Kingdom and most of those of the Middle Kingdom, in a confused arrangement.

(*b*) A list in the temple of Seti I (XIXth Dynasty, after 1320) at Abydos ; this is the *First Tablet of Abydos* ; it gives seventy-six names, from Menes to Seti I.

(*c*) A *Second Tablet of Abydos*, carved under Rameses II (after 1300), which repeats the first, preserving names 40–52 and 61–76 ; it was transported to the British Museum in 1818, and was utilized by Champollion.

(*d*) A tablet found at *Saqqarah* in the tomb of a private person, which enumerates the kings from Miebis, of the Ist Dynasty, to Rameses II. A piece is missing from the middle ; forty-seven names have been preserved ; there should be fifty-eight. The Middle Kingdom names (XIth and XIIth Dynasties) are written backwards. It is not taken from the same original as the Tablets of Abydos.

(iii) The *Royal Papyrus* preserved in the *Turin* Museum, which is our most important document for chronology. This papyrus was complete when found, but was broken to pieces in transport. It is possible to make use of three hundred fragments. It was written under Rameses II (after 1300), and gave a list of all the kings of Egypt from the beginning. It begins with the gods who reigned on earth ; then come mortal kings. These are classified in groups which do not exactly correspond to Manetho's dynasties. The figures for reigns are given in detail, in years, months, and days ; at the end of each group, a total is written in red ink ; from time to time big historical divisions are indicated. For example, from Menes to the end of Manetho's VIIIth Dynasty, the total is 955 years ; for the XIIth Dynasty, it is 213 years. This papyrus is based on a tradition akin to that followed by the Saqqarah list ; the details given about the reigns are an anticipation of the procedure which Manetho adopted later.

If we compare these Egyptian lists with Manetho's *Epitome*, we are struck by the agreement which exists over many of the kings' names, and the disagreement presented by the number of kings enumerated. From the Ist Dynasty to the end of the VIIIth, Turin gives fifty-three kings and 955 years ; Manetho (according to Africanus), 145 kings and 1,643 years ; Saqqarah, 36 kings ; Abydos, 39. Moreover, the monuments discovered, which bear names of kings, confirm the existence of the kings given in these lists, but also mention other kings, who have been cut out of the official tablets.[1] These divergences are especially to be noted in the intervals separating the Old from the Middle Kingdom (IXth to XIth Dynasty) and the Middle Kingdom from the New Empire (XIVth to XVIIIth Dynasty). During these periods, which were disturbed, as we know, by internal revolutions and foreign invasions, the royal tablets completely suppress the names of kings. There are no monuments, or but few have been discovered. Manetho is content to give the names of dynasties with fabulous totals ; the Turin Papyrus alone supplies us with many names and dates. This example shows how insufficient and untrustworthy the chronological lists are for filling up the framework of the royal dynasties. The chronology of the kings of Egypt presents very serious lacunæ, which probably can never be filled.

---

[1] There is a catalogue of all the monuments giving the name of any king of Egypt, with the dates attached to each reign, in H. Gauthier's most excellent work, " Le Livre des rois d'Égypte ", terminated in 1917, in **II**, *Mém.*, vols. xvii–xxi.

We can, however, establish fixed points for the great periods of Egyptian civilization, by means of what are called *natural dates*, and by the establishment of *synchronisms* with the other peoples of the East.

Natural dates are notices of such phenomena as the rising of a star, and chiefly of Sothis, our Sirius. Some of the monuments mention its rising in a certain year of a certain reign. As I remarked in *From Tribe to Empire* (pp. 133–4), the Egyptian calendar distinguished between the vague year (the civil, or calendar year of 365 days) and the fixed solar year, that is, the time taken by the sun to return to the same point in the sky, $365\frac{1}{4}$ days. The Egyptians knew that Sothis completed its celestial revolution in $365\frac{1}{4}$ days, like the sun. They had taken, for the first day of the year, that on which Sothis rises at dawn, a little before sunrise. At the latitude of Memphis, this *heliacal rising* of Sothis occurred on the 15th June.[1]

The Egyptian astronomers had observed in very early times that the vague year of 365 days fell short of the Sothic and solar year by a quarter of a day for every year that passed; four years after a correct heliacal rising, it was a whole day out; after eight years it was two days out, and so on. It took 1,461 calendar years for the heliacal rising to come round to the first day of the calendar year again.[2] Consequently tables were drawn up, by which the difference between the calendar year and the Sothic or solar year could be followed from year to year. On certain monuments the Egyptians have noted that the heliacal rising of Sothis took place, not at the beginning of the civil year, but on such-and-such a day of such-and-such a year of King So-and-So. This is what we call a *double* date, that is a royal date synchronized with a natural date. Modern astronomers also have their tables, on which they have been able to trace the exact curve of Sothis throughout all past years. Therefore, whenever an Egyptian document states the difference between the

---

[1] " In the year 4241 (the supposed date of the inauguration of the calendar in Egypt), the *Julian* 19th July (the day of the heliacal rising of Sothis) corresponds to the *Gregorian* 15th June " (**XXIII**, p. 53).

[2] So the sun and Sothis come round and agree with the beginning of the civil calendar year after a revolution of 1,460 solar years, or 1,461 civil years. The Greek and Roman astronomers call this cycle of 1,460 solar or Sothic years a " Sothic cycle ".

heliacal rising of Sothis and a given day of the reign of some king, we can say that the difference occurred at such-and-such a point on the curve of Sothis, on such-and-such a day of such-and-such a year before our era.[1]

Now, for the period before Christ, the Egyptian monuments have so far disclosed three double dates :—

(i) A calendar of religious feasts, carved at Elephantine under Thothmes III (XVIIIth Dynasty) records that the feast of the heliacal rising of Sothis fell on the 28th day of the month of Epiphi, instead of on the 1st Thoth. According to our modern tables, this difference occurred in the course of the years 1474–1471 B.C. Therefore, these years fall within the reign of Thothmes III.

(ii) According to the Ebers Medical Papyrus, in the ninth year of Amenophis I (the second king of the XVIIIth Dynasty), the heliacal rising of Sothis fell on the 9th Epiphi. That takes us to the years 1550–1547. Therefore the first year of Amenophis I was between 1558 and 1555, and the beginning of the XVIIIth Dynasty may be placed about 1580.

(iii) A papyrus from Kahun states that under Senusert III (XIIth Dynasty), in the seventh year of his reign, the feast of the heliacal rising of Sothis took place on the 16th Pharmuthi, instead of on the 1st Thoth. This difference took place between 1882 and 1879 B.C. Therefore the first year of Senusert III was between 1888 and 1885, and the XIIth Dynasty began about 2000.[2]

So the essential results obtained from natural dates are that the XVIIIth Dynasty began about 1580, and the XIIth Dynasty about 2000.[3]

From these data we get another essential date—that of the adoption of the Egyptian calendar, which was based on the concordance of the 1st Thoth, the first day of the civil year of the Egyptian calendar, with the heliacal rising of Sothis. It seems evident that this calendar was inaugurated on a day when the 1st Thoth actually coincided with the

---

[1] The reckoning can only give the date within four years ; for, Sothis being a quarter of a day behind the civil year, the heliacal rising was visible on the same day for four years running.

[2] Senusert III was the fifth king of the XIIth Dynasty. The Turin Papyrus gives about 115 years to his four predecessors, so that the XIIth Dynasty must have begun about 2000 B.C.

[3] For details, see Meyer, **XXIII**, pp. 56–79 (pp. 52 ff. of the German).

apparition of Sothis at dawn. This phenomenon occurred, before the XIIth Dynasty, in the years 2781–2778, and 1460 years earlier, in the years 4214–4238.

The date 2781 must be rejected, for the interval between the XIIth Dynasty (2000) and the Ist Dynasty requires at least 1,300 years to accommodate the Thinite, Memphite, and Heracleopolite Dynasties.[1] There remains the earlier date, 4241, which would place the invention, or at least the adoption, of the calendar a thousand years before the Ist Dynasty. Indeed, this interval is necessary to allow time for the protohistoric kings who came after the clan chiefs, and I agree with Eduard Meyer in regarding it as acceptable, in the present state of our knowledge of the protohistoric period (see the Chronological Table below).

The *synchronisms* which can be established between historical events in the valley of the Nile and those among the neighbouring Eastern peoples support this chronological contention. In *From Tribe to Empire*, I have drawn the reader's attention to these matters on several occasions, and need not return to them in detail. The migrations of peoples which put an end to the empire of Sargon and Naram-Sin in Shinar, about 2500, made themselves felt in the Delta at the end of the VIth Dynasty, about 2400 [2]; the Kassite invasions which destroyed the empire of Hammurabi, about 2080,[3] coincided with the arrival of Asiatics in the Delta under the Heracleopolite Dynasties ; the invasion of the Hyksôs, who overwhelmed Hither Asia before Egypt, may conveniently be placed between 1700 and 1600, before the XVIIIth Dynasty.[4] For the same period, the relations between the Pharaohs of the Middle Kingdom and the Creto-Ægeans are best explained if we adopt this computation.[5] After 1600 the Tell el-Amarna Letters and the Assyrian sources make it certain that the XVIIIth and XIXth Dynasties must be placed between the XVIIth and XIIIth centuries (inclusive) before our era.

It is for these reasons that I have adopted, in these

---

[1] See *From Tribe to Empire*, p. 134.
[2] Ibid., pp. 212–15.
[3] Ibid., p. 218.
[4] Ibid., pp. 246–7.
[5] Glotz, *The Ægean Civilization*, in this series, pp. 23–6.

two works dealing with Egypt, the shorter chronological system, as being well established after 1600, and being the most probable before that date.[1]

CHRONOLOGICAL TABLE OF THE DYNASTIES

Prehistoric period.[2]

Protohistoric period.
    Divine Dynasties.
    Kings, Servants of Horus.

Introduction of the calendar	4241
Ist and IInd (Thinite) Dynasties	3315–2895

OLD KINGDOM.

IIIrd (Memphite) Dynasty	2895–2840
IVth ,, ,,	2840–2680
Vth ,, ,,	2680–2540
VIth (Elephantite) Dynasty	
VIIth Dynasty (imaginary)	2540–2360
VIIIth (Memphite) Dynasty	

Transitional period.

IXth and Xth (Heracleopolite) Dynasties	2360–2160

MIDDLE KINGDOM.

XIth (Theban) Dynasty	2160–2000
XIIth ,, ,,	2000–1785
XIIIth (Xoïte) Dynasty	1785–1660

Transitional period (parallel dynasties).

XIVth (Xoïte) Dynasty		
XVth (Shepherd) Dynasty (Avaris)	XVIIth	
XVIth ,, ,,	(Theban)	1660–1580
XVIIth ,, ,,	Dynasty.[3]	

NEW KINGDOM (EMPIRE).

XVIIIth (Theban) Dynasty	1580–1345
XIXth ,, ,,	1345–1200
XXth ,, ,,	1200–1100

---

[1] While *From Tribe to Empire* was in the press a new work on the chronology of the Old Kingdom appeared—L. Borchardt's *Die Annalen und die zeitliche Festlegung des Alten Reichs der aegyptischen Geschichte*, 1917. The author, arguing chiefly from the Palermo Stone, considers that the dates assigned by Meyer to the Ist–VIIIth Dynasties are too short, and places the beginning of these dynasties about 1,000 years earlier, while still making the XIIth Dynasty begin about 2000 B.C.

[2] See *From Tribe to Empire*, pp. 117–25.

[3] *Ibid.*, p. 252.

PERIOD OF DECLINE.

XXIst (Tanite and Theban) Dynasty	1100–945
XXIInd–XXIVth (Bubastite and Saïte) Dynasties . .	945–712
XXVth Dynasty. Ethiopian supremacy . . .	712–663
,, ,, Assyrian supremacy	670–663
XXVIth (Saïte) Dynasty	663–525
Conquest by Persians	525–332 [1]
Conquest by Alexander	332
Alexander and the Ptolemies	332–30
The Cæsars, from	30

N.B.—Except 525, 332, and 30, all these dates are approximate, especially before the XIIth Dynasty. From 2000 to 1785, and from 1580 to 1100, the approximation comes nearer and nearer to exact figures.

[1] The abridgers of Manetho ascribe the Persian kings, from Cambyses to Xerxes, to a XXVIIth Dynasty. After these, the native kings of the Delta, who rebelled against the Persians, form the XXVIIIth, XXIXth, and XXXth Dynasties. The last Persian kings, from Artaxerxes to Darius Codomannus, are placed in a XXXIst Dynasty.

PART ONE

THE COUNTRY AND THE BEGINNINGS OF HISTORY

CHAPTER I

Country, Nile, and Sun
Their Influence on Social Development

NO country in the East has its boundaries so definitely fixed by nature as Egypt. In the north is the Mediterranean ; east and west are the Arabian and Libyan deserts ; in the south are the cataracts of the Nile. These were hard barriers to pass, and behind them the oldest known civilization found, in the lower valley of the Nile, a very safe refuge. As Diodorus says (i, 30–1), " Egypt is fortified on all sides by nature."

Egypt, properly so called, extends from the First Cataract to the Mediterranean.[1] I have described its general physical characteristics in *From Tribe to Empire* (pp. 117–22) ; here I shall dwell only on the more special features of the country.

Nature has divided Egypt into two regions—the Valley and the Delta.

The Valley is a longitudinal rift in the rocky desert plateau of the Eastern Sahara, through which the Nile has forced a passage from Central Africa to the Mediterranean. Its waters have eroded the exposed edges of the plateau, forming cliffs (Pl. II, 1), which rise 600 feet above the plain, which is uniformly flat.[2] An interminable corridor, 500 miles in length,[3] and between 6 and 12 miles wide, at places narrowing down to the breadth of the stream, with steep, bare walls

---

[1] Herodotus says (ii, 17 ; cf. 18) : " The Oracle of Amon (in the Libyan Oasis) declares that all the country covered by the inundation of the Nile is Egypt, and that all those who, below Elephantine, drink the water of the Nile are Egyptians."

[2] These edges of the Sahara plateau are sometimes improperly called the Libyan and Arabian Mountains. Cf. Hdt., ii, 8.

[3] From Alexandria to Cairo it is 125 miles by railway ; from Cairo to Assuan, 554 miles.

on either side ; the two dry, burning rims of boundless desert, where the red and yellow sand drifts over the baked rocks, and between them a flood of blue water rolling across an unbroken carpet of pastures and cornfields, green and golden ; a draught of refreshing air under the blazing sun— these are the features of the land, *ta-shemâ*, which we call Upper Egypt. The epithet has only a relative value, for the ground is not at all high, falling imperceptibly from an altitude of 300 feet at the First Cataract to Memphis, at the apex of the Delta, barely 40 feet above sea-level.

North of Memphis, or of the present Cairo, the aspect of the country changes abruptly. The Libyan and Arabian cliffs, cut into a V by an old marine gulf, diverge more and more until they fall into the sea, and the Valley spreads out in a Delta [1] like a gigantic fan, 60 miles long and almost 400 miles in perimeter. The eyes of the traveller, hitherto accustomed to a narrow valley, marvel at the vast prospect of low-lying plain, stretching away to the distant sea, whose waters recede imperceptibly every year before the advancing silt. It is an *aequor*, in which land, canals, lagoons, and beaches merge in one absolutely level surface. There the dazzling light of the sun is veiled in transparent haze, and the heat is tempered by humidity. That is the " Northern Land ", *ta-meh*, Lower Egypt ; away from the heat and solitude of the African desert, it is in touch with the busy roads of the Mediterranean, it is attached to the Arabian isthmus, it reaches out towards Europe, and it is refreshed by " the delightful breezes of the North ".[2]

So nature has created a Mediterranean Egypt and an African Egypt. The differences between these " Two Lands ", as the Egyptians called them, are great enough to make a marked impression on the mythological and human history of the country, as we shall see. Nevertheless, the Two Lands are inseparable one from the other. They harmonize together ; the Valley is all length, the Delta all breadth, but their cultivable surface, their economic value, their population are equal, and the two equal forces balance one another. The

---

[1] The name appears in Hdt. (ii, 15), and Diod. (i, 33) explains it : the mouths of the Nile form a triangle, like the Greek letter *Δ*, *delta*, with its base on the sea.

[2] Hdt. (ii, 17) enumerates seven mouths of the Nile. The three chief are the Pelusiac on the east, the Sebennytic in the middle, and the Bolbitinic on the west.

PLATE II

1. CLIFF OF THE LIBYAN DESERT AT DER EL-BAHARI AND
TEMPLE OF HATSHEPSUT

2. KARNAK. THE NILE AND THE GREAT TEMPLE OF AMON-RA

two Egypts could never prosper apart; the Delta by itself lacks the resources of the country above, and the Valley, without the coast, is a blind alley, having no outlet on Europe or Asia. The Nile is what chiefly makes the indivisible unity of the Two Lands. Without the Delta, the Valley would be a stalk with no flower blooming at the end; cut off from the Valley, the Delta could no more live than a flower in full bloom, shorn from the slender stalk which feeds it.

The Nile [1] was the biggest river of the world which the ancients knew.[2] Where it enters Egypt, after the First Cataract, its deep bed is already over 500 yards wide, and lower down it spreads out to about half a mile. This huge volume of water flows between two immense barren deserts, which follow it all along its course towards the sea, not only in Egypt, but from as far up in the south as the Egyptians ever went. Now the sands do not absorb the river; on the contrary, the black mud carried by the water encroaches on the tawny ground and clothes itself in corn and greenery. There is no visible source, no persistent rain to feed its waters; no tributary comes in from the neighbouring countries, within the borders of Egypt, to swell the inexhaustible flood. What a wonder it must have been for the first inhabitants of the valley! We know that the Egyptians never solved the mystery of the origin of their river.[3] What is more, hardly less ignorant than they, we were still unaware less than a century ago of the great lakes in the centre of Africa. It was only recently that the sources of the Nile were discovered.[4] The Egyptians, admitting their ignorance,[5] declared that this sacred water came to the earth from heaven, or else rose by secret ways from the Lower World. For them, the majestic river which fed them was " the Great River ", *itr-âa*, or

---

[1] Cf. C. Palanque, *Le Nil à l'époque pharaonique*, 1903 (*Bibl. de l'École des Htes. Études, Sciences hist. et philol.*, No. cxliv).

[2] To-day the length of the Nile is estimated at 4,060 miles, which makes it the longest river in the world except the Mississippi-Missouri (4,155 miles).

[3] Cf. the allusions in the *Hymn to the Nile*, p. 30 below.

[4] To-day it is generally considered that the source of the Nile is the Nyava-rongo, an affluent of the Kagera, which feeds Lake Victoria Nyanza, in which the Nile rises.

[5] Cf. below, p. 326.

" the Sea ", *iumâ* ; they called it *Hapi* when they made it
into a god of human form. The name Nile, $N\epsilon\hat{\imath}\lambda os$, which
first appears in Hesiod, is of unknown origin. In Homer
$A\H\imath\gamma\upsilon\pi\tau os$ means first the Nile and then the country made by
the river ; for Egypt is a " gift of the river ", $\delta\hat{\omega}\rho o\nu\ \tau o\hat{\upsilon}$
$\pi o\tau\acute{a}\mu o\upsilon$, according to the very true description of the
Egyptian priests, recorded by Herodotus.[1]

The river has made the soil of Egypt of mud stolen from the
Abyssinian plateau by the Blue Nile and the Atbara. The
alluvium deposited on the rocky subsoil through centuries has
an average depth of 30–40 feet, and in certain parts of the
Delta, where the deposit is better preserved, it is as much as
80–100 feet [2] ; this soil is rich in potash, very fertile, and easy
to cultivate. Wherever the muddy water reaches it covers
the ground with a carpet of this humus, which forms the
" Black Land ", *kem-t*, and the ancient Egyptians gave this
name to their country [3] (Plate II, 2).

The Nile not only brings this black earth—it waters it.
First there are the infiltrations which take place through the
porous soil, all along the river. Generally these are invisible,
but in places they are sufficiently considerable to form a
natural channel alongside the Nile, such as the Bahr Yusuf
on the left bank, running from the Thebaïd to the Fayum.
The five oases of the Libyan desert, situated in a row, between
60 and 120 miles from the valley, are fed from a layer of river
water which has soaked through the sandstone of the plateau
to a depth of 500 to 650 feet ; this water comes out by natural
springs or artificial wells, and fertilizes the ground over
hundreds of miles.

But the annual inundation is the greatest of the miracles
of the Nile. By this the river keeps up the depth of cultivable
soil, compensates for evaporation, and gives it the humidity
needed in a rainless country. Did the Egyptians know the
real cause of the periodic flood ? Herodotus and Diodorus
are vexed that they could learn nothing, from the priests or
anyone else, about the nature of the Nile, the river which,

---

[1] ii, 10 and 5.
[2] Cf. *From Tribe to Empire*, pp. 118–19.
[3] Ibid., p. 167. In contrast the desert is called the " Red Land ", *ta-desher* ;
our Red Sea is the " Sea of the Red Land ". Hdt. lays stress on the difference
in colour between the black soil of Egypt and the red soil of Libya (ii, 12).

unlike all others, flooded in the height of summer. " The rising of the Nile is a phenomenon which astounds those who see it and appears quite incredible to those who hear of it. For, whereas other rivers shrink about the summer solstice, and grow smaller and smaller from that point onwards, the Nile alone begins to swell, and its waters rise, day by day, until in the end they overflow almost the whole of Egypt." [1]

The Greeks ventured upon hazardous explanations which Herodotus rejects with scorn. According to some the Etesian winds from the north caused the flood, by pushing back the water of the Nile and preventing it from falling into the sea. Others said that the flood was simply a movement of the ocean surrounding the earth, from which the Nile sprang. A third explanation ascribed it to the melting of the snows, followed by periodic summer rains, on the high plateau— but how could there be snow in a country where even rain was unknown, and the sun was so hot that it turned men black ? As far as one could ascend the Nile, in four months of sailing, the intense heat makes the country a desert.[2] Since no hypothesis was satisfactory, most of the Greeks were content simply to marvel at the phenomenon, as the Egyptians did.

To-day we know that the inundation comes chiefly from the regular winter rains in the region of the great lakes and from the melting of the snow on the lofty plateau of Abyssinia, the maximum effect of which is felt about the summer solstice. The White Nile sends down a mass of water which advances slowly down the 4,000-mile-long valley, passing Khartum at the beginning of April and reaching Elephantine towards the beginning of June. A wave of *green*, laden with vegetable detritus from the equatorial swamps heralds the inundation. One month later, the Blue Nile sends its *red* wave, coloured by the ferruginous mud brought down from the soil of Abyssinia. Descending from the plateau in spate, it imparts a rapid pace to the inundation and fills the water with humus. The two streams, combined, arrive in force in the lower valley about the 15th June, bringing to the Black Land, which has been burnt by the sun until it is dry, brittle, and as powdery as sand, " the

[1] Diod., i, 36.
[2] Hdt.. ii. 19–31 : cf. Diod.. i. 38–41.

water of renewal,[1] the water of life." [2] From June to September, during nearly a hundred days, the Nile rises 40 or 45 feet in the confined gorges of Upper Egypt and 20 or 25 feet in the wide plains of the Delta. It submerges the whole country, and, after remaining for some days at the same level, till the beginning of October, it falls. About the 10th November, it has lost half the height it had reached, and then it returns to its normal bed, shrinks in breadth, and loses by evaporation until the return of the flood in its season. So the Nile takes possession of the country during four months of the year, and leaves it deeply permeated with water and covered with damp, soft mud, ready to receive the plough-share and the seed.

The grand spectacle of the inundation and its effects, both terrible and beneficent, inspired the oldest religious literature of the Egyptians, engraved in the pyramids of the VIth Dynasty. " They tremble, they who see Hapi (the Nile) when he beats (his waves) ; but the meadows smile, the banks blossom, the offerings of the gods come down (from the heavens) ; men do homage, the hearts of the gods are lifted up . . ." [3] The hymns written later, in the Theban period, are still expressive, through the allegories and mythological elaborations. " Hail, Hapi, thou who dost rise on to this earth, and comest to give life to Egypt ; who hidest thy coming in the darkness [4] on this very day when we sing thy coming, a wave spreading over the orchards which Ra made, to give life to all who thirst, and refusing to water the desert with the overflowing of the waters of heaven ! When thou dost descend, Geb (the earth) is in love with bread, Nepri (the corn-god) presents his offering, Phtah makes every workshop to prosper. Do his fingers ail, are they idle ? Then all the millions of beings are wretched. Does he grow less in the sky ? Then the gods themselves perish, and men ; the beasts go mad ; and all on earth, great and small, are in torment. But

[1] *Pyr.*, § 589. I quote the texts of the Saqqarah pyramids (VIth Dynasty) from Sethe's ed.

[2] *Pyr.*, § 2063. The Gregorian 15th June (= Julian 19th July) is the official date of the first day of the inundation and of the first day of the Egyptian year (1st Thoth). This date fits the position of the seasons under the Old Kingdom. Cf. above, p. 20, n. 1.

[3] *Pyr.*, §§ 1553–4.

[4] Further on we find : " No man knows the place where he is ; his casket is not found by means of magic writings."

if the prayers of men are granted when he rises, and if he makes himself to be called Khnum (Creator) for them, when he goes up, then the earth shouts for joy, every belly makes glad, every back is shaken by laughter, every tooth munches." [1]

The flood of the Nile does not bring only blessings. It does damage. As it submerges the valley it destroys every-thing in its path, overturning the soil and shifting the boundaries of properties, and when it retires it carries away the mud which it brought in its advance. The earliest men had to learn to protect themselves against these dangers ; villages were built on artificial mounds, and fields were secured against too rapid currents by dikes, which at the same time served as raised causeways. [2] Another cause for anxiety was the volume of the inundation. The date of the floods may be constant, but the amount of water which they bring is not. In all ages the inhabitants have tried, by calculation, to foresee whether they would have the amount of water which their fields needed.

" The height required for thorough irrigation varied according to the province. It was known, and entered among

---

[1] *Hymn to the Nile*, from the Papyri Sallier II and Anastasi VII, translated by Maspero, **XX,** vol. i, pp. 40 ff.

[2] Diod. (i, 36) describes the flood and its consequences as follows : " Since the country is flat, and towns, villages, and even rural dwellings are built on earthworks, made by the hands of men, the appearance of the whole recalls the Cyclades Islands. Many land animals perish, victims of the flood ; others escape, taking refuge on high ground. At this time the cattle are kept in the villages and farms, where fodder is brought to them. The people, who are free from work all this time, remain idle, and give themselves up to pleasures, festivities, and merry-makings of every kind. The anxieties to which these inundations gave rise inspired the kings with the notion of constructing a Nilometer at Memphis, by means of which the rise of the water is measured exactly. The men who have this duty send messages to every town, announcing how many cubits or finger-lengths the river has risen and when it begins to fall. Thus warned of the rise and fall of the water, the people are relieved of all anxiety. Everyone can foretell the yield of the harvest, thanks to this arrangement, the results of which have been recorded by the Egyptians for a great number of years." We shall see later that the Palermo Stone gives the yearly figures of the rise of the Nile from very early times ; by these the rates of taxation were probably assessed.

The levels of the inundation given by the Palermo Stone prove the use, as early as the Thinite period, of Nilometers (Borchardt, " Nilmesser," in *Abh. Berlin Akad.*, 1906). Nilometer pits have been found in several temples. Strabo (xvi, 1, 48) describes that of Elephantine ; he says that the levels which it indicated told the peasants what water they could use and the Government what taxes it should levy. Every rise in the inundation meant a rise in taxes. This Nilometer has been restored, and is in use at the present day.

the information inscribed on the standard cubits of which specimens have been found in different localities. At Elephantine a good flood meant a rise of 28 cubits [1]; at Edfu, 24 cubits and $3\frac{1}{4}$ palms were required ; as one descended northwards, the rise needed was less, and at Mendes and Xoïs 6 cubits were deemed sufficient. At Memphis, about the Græco-Roman period, 16 cubits were held to be the desirable height. That is why the famous statue of the Nile, in the Vatican Museum in Rome, which represents the god reclining, holding ears of corn and a cornucopia, is surrounded by sixteen children, each a cubit high. If the inundation did not reach the sixteen cubits, it was as disastrous as if it exceeded 18 cubits." [2]

When the Nile was "small", that is to say, insufficient, the country was plunged in great distress. " I am very sorrowful," King Zeser, of the IIIrd Dynasty, is made to say, " because in my time the Nile did not overflow for a period of seven years. Corn is lacking ; the fields are dried up ; what serves for food perishes. Does a man beg help of his neighbours ?   All flee in order not to go to him. The child cries, the young man grows weak, and the heart of the old man fails ; their legs are without strength ; they huddle on the ground with folded arms." [3] If the Nile rises too much the distress is quite as great. In the reign of Osorkon III (XXIIIrd Dynasty), " the whole valley became like a sea ; the temples were invaded by the waves ; the people were like water-fowl, or swimmers in a torrent." [4]

To preserve Egypt from shortage and from excess of water the river had to be controlled. Mighty dikes, parallel to the bank, compelled it to keep to a regular bed. Menes, the founder of the Ist Dynasty, was said to have built those which protected the Nome of Memphis against an abnormal flood. " Even to-day," Herodotus wrote, about 450 B.C., " under Persian rule, special attention is paid to these dikes, and they

[1] The cubit is about 20 in.
[2] G. Daressy, " L'Eau dans l'Égypt antique," in *Mém. de l'Inst. Égyptien*, viii (1915), p. 205.
[3] The so-called Famine Stele, found on the island of Sehel. It was written by the priests of Khnum in the Ptolemaic period, and attributed by them to the very ancient King Zeser, who was supposed to have obtained from Khnum the cessation of the distress. See G. Roeder, *Urkunden zur Religion des alten Aegypten*, p. 177.
[4] G. Daressy, in *Bull. de l'Inst. Égypt.*, December, 1895.

are carefully strengthened every year." [1]   Other dikes ran perpendicularly from the river to the Libyan and Arabian cliffs, so as to divide the valley into a chessboard of basins, descending in terraces from south to north.   At a certain moment during the rising of the water, sluices were opened to let it in, and then they were closed to hold it when the river fell.   The basins were also connected together by small artificial canals, parallel to the Nile, by which the water flowed from south to north.   Within each main basin, the same methods of retention and distribution were repeated by a network of smaller dikes and subsidiary channels. The whole of Egypt was, as it were, squared out by this criss-cross of ditches and embankments ; so the hieroglyph designating the nome (province or district) reproduces the chequer pattern (Fig. 5), into which the ground appeared to be geometrically divided by the canals and ditches which irrigated it.

As I said in *From Tribe to Empire* (pp. 124–5), this reshaping of the valley had already been effected as early as the protohistoric period, by the first occupants of Egypt. It was improved and extended without interruption after that, but it was the prodigious labour of the generations before Menes which brought the phenomenon of the inundation into the service of agriculture. So the Nile, by its habits, compelled men to invent agricultural methods. Above all, the river made work in common, a collective, persevering effort, necessary ; it created a solidarity among the dwellers on its banks ; it imposed an organization upon them ; it united them into a society. From the top of the valley to the bottom, each great basin of irrigation formed the frame of an agricultural district, which became a nome, a province. So the Nile acted as a principle of division and organization in districts. Now every basin, every nome, commanded or depended on its neighbours, each in turn, as the water was passed on from one to the next through all the length of Egypt.[2] Therefore the inhabitants of all the nomes had to accept a reciprocal discipline, to make rules governing irrigation, which would be fair and satisfactory for the whole valley, and, lastly, to create an authority superior to all

---

[1] ii, 99.   [2] On this subject, see *From Tribe to Empire*, p. 148.

the nomes, to see that these rules were obeyed. So the Nile
acted as a principle of order and centralization ; it brought
about the subordination of all to one master, and absolute
monarchy. A good judge in the matter of authority, Napoleon,
after seeing Egypt with his own eyes, learned the lesson of
the Nile, and has passed it on to us in these words : " In
no other country has the administration so much influence
on public prosperity. If the administration is good, the canals
are well dug and well kept up, the regulations on irrigation
are carried out justly, and the inundation reaches far. If
the administration is bad, corrupt, or weak, the canals are
blocked with mud, the dikes are badly kept up, the regulations
on irrigation are disobeyed, and the principles of the system
of inundation are thwarted by the sedition and private
interests of individuals and localities. The Government has
no influence on the rain or snow which falls in Beauce or Brie,
but in Egypt the Government has direct influence on the extent
of the inundation which takes their place. That is what
makes the difference between the Egypt governed by the
Ptolemies and the Egypt already decaying under the Romans
and ruined by the Turks."

Since Champollion taught us to read the hieroglyphics we
have known that the Ptolemies introduced nothing new in the
matter of irrigation. Forty centuries before them the lesson
of the Nile had been understood by the earliest Egyptians.

A second and no less essential factor in the physical and
economic life of Egypt is the sun.

The valley of the Nile leads straight from the Mediterranean
to the Equator ; of the cultivated regions of the ancient
world Egypt comes closest to the tropics. There the sun
exercises a most important influence. The hours of sunlight
are almost constant, in winter as in summer, and dawn and
twilight are very short ; the sun lights and heats Egypt better
than any other civilized country. And the quality of its light
is no less remarkable than its duration and its calorific power ;
the dryness of the adjoining deserts of Africa rids the
atmosphere of all humidity and makes it wonderfully pure
and transparent. In Upper Egypt no mist veils the glory of

the sun; very rarely a passing cloud darkens the sky [1];
sun, moon, and stars shine in the firmament with marvellous
brilliance.

So the sun gives Egypt a more radiant and more clement
climate than is enjoyed by the other Mediterranean countries.
Even Herodotus noticed it [2]: "Perpetual summer reigns in
Egypt." Rain is almost unknown there, and only appears in
the form of short, violent storms, in March and April, the
season of the burning desert wind which the Arabs call
the Khamsin.[3] Yet, though the heat reaches a very high
degree, it is seldom overpowering, because it is dry. Moreover, the immense extent of the neighbouring deserts causes
a considerable cooling at night, so that abundant dew is
precipitated in the morning, taking the place of rain in Upper
Egypt. In summer the north winds blow regularly up the
valley, mitigating the heat of the sun deliciously.

The Delta also acts as a reservoir of coolness. On its
vast plains the evaporation of the widely spread water,
combined with the proximity of the sea, gives rise to the
temperate conditions of maritime climates. The sun's
radiation is still intense, but it is modified by mists. The
winter rains are frequent here, and the humidity is thrice as
high as in Upper Egypt.

To the sun the Egyptians owed the kindly climate which
favours man and plant, the clean, healthy light which kills
miasmas, prolongs life, and keeps the heart cheerful, and the
warmth which simplifies the conditions of existence,
stimulates germination, and when it is not overpowering,
excites activity everywhere.[4]

Need we, then, be surprised that the sun places his radiant
stamp on so many Egyptian monuments? The Nile makes
the Black Land; the sun lights it, heats it, fertilizes it, and
protects it by "dispelling storm, driving away rain,

---

[1] Diod., i, 38: "The Nile is the only river about which neither mists nor cold
vapours which thicken the air arise."
[2] ii, 16.
[3] Rain-storms are sometimes mentioned in the Egyptian texts. It should
be noted that the temples of all periods have channels, on the roofs (with
spouts) and underground, to carry off rain-water.
[4] Hence the legends of spontaneous generation, caused by the sun in the
land inundated by the Nile. "The sun, they say, which dries the surface of the
mud, produces animals, some of which are complete, while others are only half
made, and remain attached to the ground" (Diod. i, 10).

dispersing the clouds." [1] So the material sun, the star of day, always appears to the Egyptians as the king of the world, the dispenser of a light at once terrible and beneficent, in which every living thing, even the humblest, has his fair share. It is the visible splendid form of a power superior to the earth, which rules our material and moral life, and governs the universe with regularity, order, and justice. The gratitude which rises in the heart of every Egyptian when he beholds his benefactor is expressed with singular happiness in Egyptian literature, and especially in the hymns to the Solar Disk, the god Aten, composed by Amenophis IV, or Akhenaten. Here is one of these poems, which was composed and engraved at the end of the XVIIIth Dynasty, about 1370, but preserves for us the note, the imagery, and the poetry of popular hymns which were certainly more ancient.

" Thou dost rise beautifully, living Aten, Lord of Eternity ! Thou art shining, thou are beautiful, thou art strong ! Great and wide is thy love ; thy rays shine for the eyes of all thy creatures ; thy countenance [2] is lit up to make hearts to live.

" Thou hast filled the Two Lands with thy loves, O beautiful Lord, builder of thyself, creator of all earth, and begetter of all that is thereon, men and all beasts and all the trees which grow on the ground.

" They live when thou dost rise for them, for thou art a mother and a father to thy creatures. Their eyes, when thou dost rise, look towards thee. Thy rays light up the whole earth ; every heart is lifted up at the sight of thee, when thou appearest as their Lord. (But,) when thou liest down in the Western horizon of the sky, they lie like dead men ; their heads are covered, their noses are stopped, until thy splendour (renews) itself in the morning, in the Eastern horizon of the sky.

" Then their arms adore thy Ka, thou dost vivify their hearts by thy beauty, and they live ! When thou dost give thy rays, all the earth makes merry ; they sing, they make music, they shout for joy in the court of the Mansion of the Obelisk,[3] thy temple in Akhetaten, the great place where thou takest delight, where food-offerings are made to thee . . .

" Thou art Aten (the Solar Disk), thou livest for ever. . . . Thou hast created the distant heaven, to rise therein and to look down on all that thou hast made. Thou art (up there) all alone, and (yet) thousands (of beings) live by thee, and receive the breath of life for their nostrils (from thee). When they see thy rays, all the flowers live, they which grow on the ground and flourish by thy appearance ; they are drunk with the joy of thy countenance. All the beasts leap on their legs ; the birds, which were in their nests, fly joyfully ; their wings, which were folded, open to adore the living Aten." [4]

[1] *Pyr.*, § 500.
[2] Literally, " thy skin."
[3] *Het-Benben*, the name of the Temple of Ra, at Heliopolis and at Akhetaten (El-Amarna).
[4] *Little Hymn to Aten* (Davies, *El Amarna*, iv, pp. 32–3). For the *Great Hymn*, cf. below, p. 325.

Another hymn, by the same king, adds this :—

" Thou createst the Nile in the lower world, and thou bringest it (on to earth), where thou willest, to feed the men (of Egypt) . . . thou, the Lord of the Land." (Cf. below, p. 326.)

So the Nile himself, the creator of the Black Land, is the work of the Sun, the supreme author of the Universe, who gives life to every being and every thing. The Nile demands of the Egyptians that they co-ordinate their efforts ; the Sun reveals to them that a single power rules the world.

CHAPTER II

EARLY SOCIAL ORGANIZATION. CLANS AND NOMES

I

THE CLANS

AS I said in *From Tribe to Empire*, the first inhabitants of Egypt did not all belong to one race. The skeletons found up to the present and the types portrayed on the monuments permit us to distinguish three : a race of Semitic type, of medium height, with a dolichocephalous skull, one of Semito-Libyan type, brachycephalous and hook-nosed, and one of Mediterranean type, brachycephalous, with a short, straight nose.[1] These elements were fused together in the valley of the Nile as in a crucible, to form a people of tillers of the soil. Afterwards this people was to absorb the foreign elements which came in at intervals and the dweller by the Nile would retain a special Egyptian character.[2] Apparent diversity and fundamental unity are as true of the race as of the country.

The stages of progress among the earliest Egyptians have been described in *From Tribe to Empire*.

For the prehistoric period we find, first of all, on the edge of the still uninhabitable valley, on the terraces of the Libyan and Arabian plateaux, not the bodies of men, but their tools of knapped and shaped stone (*Palæolithic age*). These objects and the remains of food are characteristic of a people of nomads, living by hunting and fishing, not by agriculture or stock-breeding.

Later these nomads came down into the valley, which was in process of being transformed by the regular floods of the Nile, which continually heaped up the deposits of mud, and so raised the ground-level. The first permanent settlements, with tools of the *Mesolithic age*, have been found at a

[1] *From Tribe to Empire*, pp. 125, 157–8.
[2] Defined in op. cit., pp. 165, 167.

few points only. It is supposed that the villages of these earliest settlers in the valley are now covered by the silt of the Nile. How many centuries did it take for men, at last taught by repeated experience, and learning foresight, to discover how to forestall the effects of the inundation, to think of dikes, and to build artificial mounds to hold their dwellings above the ravaging floods? When settlements provided with *Neolithic* tools appear, we perceive immense progress. By the side of weapons of polished stone, pottery, and vases of hard stone, we find tools and ornaments of bone and ivory and weapons and other objects of gold and copper. The settled folk till the soil and raise cattle ; they have picked out the cultivable plants and the animal species suited to domestication. Wheat, barley, and millet furnish them with corn for bread, flax affords a textile material, sheep, goats, and oxen form, with game, reserves of foodstuffs, and they are aided by dogs in hunting, by oxen in ploughing, and by asses in transport. The Nile, gradually embanked, diverted, and disciplined, no longer lays their fields and villages waste, and already carries their boats.

This slow, patient, industrious adaptation of men to the soil of Egypt could not have been effected save by a strong social organization. From these centuries of toil and development no written monument has come down to us, by which we might see their origin and follow their stages. But they have left their witnesses, in pictures drawn on palettes of schist or vases, representing huts and boats beneath the ægis of various emblems, which stand out prominently, like banners set up for rallying marks. Among these we recognize a falcon, an elephant, a solar disk, arrows crossed on the hide of a beast, the outline of a tree, and that of a mountain. Now, many of these ensigns remained in use to the end of Egyptian civilization, as names of nomes, or provinces. It is therefore safe to assign to them an ethnic signification in the earliest times. They served to designate, to identify tribes [1] ; their presence indicated that of men and families belonging to the same group, agglomerations which were classified and distinguished from one another by these emblems, which were perhaps totems in the prehistoric period, and afterwards were to become gods.

[1] *From Tribe to Empire*, p. 123.

Prehistoric Egypt, therefore, seems to have had a division into clans, gathered round ensigns, and perhaps constituting totemic groups. As we have seen in *From Tribe to Empire*, authority in such a social system lies in the hands of the " Elders " of each clan. In Egypt, religious traditions, recorded in the pyramids of the VIth Dynasty,[1] call up a past, not far removed from the beginnings of history, in which men were ruled by " Saru ", who were probably the Elders of each clan. It seems that this gerontocracy, the usual form of authority among proto-civilized men at the clan stage, guided the earliest Egyptians in their century-long efforts to make the Nile valley healthy and cultivable.

About the year 4000 B.C. the historical period begins—that is, the epoch of which the Egyptians preserved an authentic tradition, attested not only by the later *Annals*, but also by *written monuments* of the time itself or of the period immediately following. Rudimentary organizations developed into institutions ; the clans became provinces (nomes), in which their primitive ensigns, whether fetishes or totems, were transformed into gods ; beside or over the Saru, there rose single chiefs and then kings ; the nomes were grouped into kingdoms, at first many, and then brought together and made one under a single king. At this point the dynastic period began, and wrote itself down in history. Writing set down in stone the names of kings, wars, great political events, traditions hitherto oral, and religious doctrines. The human community had become a state.

In *From Tribe to Empire* (pp. 128–58) I have endeavoured to follow the advance from clan organization to state organization, looking in the valley of the Nile for the features common to the history of all primitive peoples. Here we shall return to the subject only to discuss in more detail the especially Egyptian features of this development.

II

THE NOMES

The fixing of the clans in nomes is an important stage in the very remote history of Egypt. No account of it is supplied

[1] *Pyr.*, § 1041.

by the native sources. But the study of the nome and the examination of the oldest lists of nomes can give us useful information.

The original Egyptian word is *spat*, from the root *sp*, " divide " [1] (like its Greek equivalent νόμος from νέμω); it means then, " division." The division refers to the territory, for the word-sign *spat* represents a rectangular piece of ground, divided into squares by lines intersecting at right angles.

This fact reveals an essential difference between the nome and the clan. The clan is a group of individuals united by kinship and common veneration for an ancestor, a patron, a totem. These individuals may be nomadic or sedentary ; it is not by residence in a given district that a man becomes a clansman. The nome, on the contrary, defines a portion of territory, not a group of the population. When we find the organization by nomes, the clan system has been left behind. The population has attached itself to the soil to work it and it has been necessary to divide the valley into sectors of exploitation, the nomes, which supply the framework of an organization of

FIG. 5.—Ensign of the XVth Nome, over the Sign *Spat*.

FIG. 6.—Town (*Nut*).

sedentary folk in which the important thing is not man, but the ground, its ownership, and its cultivation.

Each nome comprises a territory and a capital. At this very early period we cannot conceive of the inhabitants of the towns as " townsmen ", as against the peasants of the territory. The city is merely the fortified place whither the peasants, herdsmen, and hunters, who live on the soil and spend their days in the fields, return every evening for shelter, and where they find the craftsmen, traders, and servants of the Government, who are tied by their occupation to their

[1] *Pyr.*, § 2069.

" seats ".[1] The town, *nut*, built at a road-crossing, as its
word-sign indicates (Fig. 6), is surrounded by a circular
defence. Within is the collection of wattle-and-daub huts,
in which ploughmen, herdsmen, and travellers, leaving the
unsafe country, take refuge at night from the attacks of
nomads. Huge barns, warehouses, stores for farm-gear,
cattle-byres, workshops of craftsmen, and booths of traders

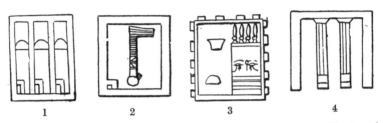

Fig. 7.—Signs of the Memphite Period. 1. Mansion, *het* (triple). 2. Mansion of
a god. 3. Building with a wide hall. 4. Hall with columns (proto-Doric).

are crowded round a public place, serving as a market, where
every man brings and barters the products of his industry
and foodstuffs. Above the houses rise the high walls of a
" Mansion of the God ", *het-neter*, the temple of the patron
deity of the nome, with the sacred stores and the dwellings
of the priests. The representative of the god on earth—the
King or the Nomarch, according to the period—also has his

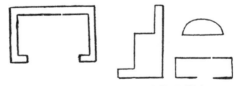

Fig. 8.—House (*Per*) and Seat (*Ist*).

" mansion ", *het*, a large building forming a closed rectangle,
differentiated by its great size from the ordinary house, *per*,
which is a small enclosure with a door (Fig. 8). The " seats "
of the royal or local administration, for the exercise of justice
and the regulation of taxes and agriculture, the storehouses,
the treasuries, the prisons, etc., stand out here and there,

---

[1] " Seat " (*is-t*) is one of the commonest Egyptian terms for the administrative
office, the place where authority sits.

with the columns of their wide " halls " of reception, or shelter their " sealed " hiding-places under the ground.

When the King founds a city he " separates each town from its neighbour, informs each town of its boundaries towards the other towns, sets up their boundary-stones, (lasting) as the sky, defines their waters, from what is in the books, and apportions water, fields, woods, and sands " [1] as far as the adjoining desert. On this territory, as the population grows, or agriculture extends, taking the workers further from the urban centre,[2] secondary towns or villages, also called *nut*, are founded, and mansions (*het*) ; the supervision of these is delegated to Regents of Towns (*heqa-nut*) and Regents of Mansions (*heqa-het*), subordinate to the Nomarch. The whole collection of land, villages, and capital forms the nome. Its dimensions are usually modest ; its length is between 15 and 25 miles, and its breadth depends on its position in the valley. Where the valley is narrow the nome covers the two banks, from one desert to the other ; where the valley widens the nome lies on one bank only, being bounded by an imaginary line down the middle of the river.

The lists of nomes carved on the walls of the Græco-Roman temples (to record the names of the gods and sanctuaries in the whole of Egypt) tell us that in the later period the nomes presented uniform divisions.[3] In these official lists we obtain information about the administrative organization and about the territory itself. From the administrative point of view, the lists mention (i) the official name of the nome, (ii) that of the capital, and (iii) that of the god who dwells in the temple ; then they give information about the chief sanctuary, the titles of the high priest, and high priestess, the name of the boat of the god, that of the sacred tree, a short catalogue of the local feasts, a mention of what is forbidden (*but*, food-taboo, or ritual prohibition), and the name of the protecting serpent, the *agathodæmon*, of the nome.[4]

---

[1] Great Beni-Hasan inscription, l. 40 (XIIth Dynasty).

[2] Maspero defined the nome (in its cultivated portion) as " an extent of land such that a peasant can go to market and return in one day " (**VII,** 4th November, 1909). The nomes of Lower Egypt are larger than those of Upper Egypt.

[3] Brugsch, *Dictionnaire géographique*, suppl., end.

[4] These lists also mention the part of the dismembered body of Osiris which the chief sanctuary of the nome preserved as a relic.

For the territory the lists mention (i) the chief channel or basin of irrigation (*mer*), (ii) the two divisions of the territory—first, the agricultural district (*u*), comprising the cornfields of the irrigated ground, high or low-lying,[1] according to their distance from the Nile, and the vineyards, and, secondly, the borders (*pehu*) of the nome [2] towards the deserts, a district of pasture, hunting, and also fishing, for it is often swampy.

These official lists show us what the Egyptians understood by a " nome ". On the one hand it was a division for agricultural exploitation ; on the other, it was an administrative division, in which traditional authority was in the hands of the god of the capital, who bore the title of Lord (*neb*) of the city. The rule of the god was exercised through the King or Nomarch, the latter being independent, or dependent on a king, according to the period. Power was in essence religious ; the man was the delegate of the god. Was this conception of administration peculiar to the late period, or did it go back to early Pharaonic times ? As early as the Memphite Dynasties, the inscriptions tell us, in scraps of information, that agriculture was already organized in the same divisions as in the Græco-Roman period ; and the gods are called " Lords of the Cities " on the most ancient monuments. We may conclude that the double organization of the nome, agricultural and religious, existed in Egypt ɟrom the beginning and always.

III

ENSIGNS AND GODS OF NOMES.   THEIR STRUGGLES FOR
POLITICAL INFLUENCE

These definitions being established, the transition from clans to nomes shows itself more clearly. One might think that one had only to make out a list of the nomes in the earliest times, to look among the gods, Lords of Nomes, for survivals of prehistoric totems or fetishes, and to note cases of the

---

[1] Sethe, *Urkunden*, iv, 31.
[2] On the products of the *pehu*, see the texts quoted by J. de Rougé, *Géographie de la Basse-Égypte*, pp. 68, 72, 90.

introduction of a new patron deity. So an approximate idea
might be obtained of the course of historical development.
But the task is not so simple.

A list of the nomes in early times is first given in a decree
attributed to a King of the VIIIth Dynasty (about 2400).
The King entrusts to the authority of a Vizier twenty-two
nomes in Upper Egypt, and their names follow, one after
another.[1] But in the pyramids of the VIth Dynasty, and on
the walls of the Memphite tombs, we find single nomes
mentioned. For Lower Egypt there is no official list, but the
same documents name a certain number of nomes in the
Delta. These sources go back to the end of the Thinite period.

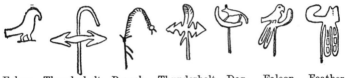

Falcon. Thunderbolt. Branch. Thunderbolt   Dog.   Falcon.   Feather.
                                and Feather.

Wolf.   Beast of Seth.   Ibis.   Falcon.   Arms of the Ka.

FIG. 9.—Totems and Ensigns of Clans.
From Loret.

We may take it that about 3000 B.C. the Two Lands were
already divided into provinces, with about an equal number
in each—from twenty to twenty-two in Upper Egypt and
twenty in the Delta.[2] In all these texts the nome is designated
and " written " by its ensign—an animal, tree, or other object,
on a stand, set on the word-sign of the squared ground. Each
of these figures gives its name to the territory which it rules ;
they are the eponymous patrons of the nomes, and they play
this part down to the end of Pharaonic civilization.

[1] A decree found at Coptos by R. Weill, and published and interpreted by
A. Moret, " Une Liste des nomes de la Hte.-Égypte," in **III**, 1914, p. 565.
[2] Certain nomes, in consequence of the growth of the population, were
doubled, making an " Upper " and a " Lower " (Terebinth, Palm-tree, Child),
or a " South " and a " North " (Two Arrows). On the variations in the number
of nomes, cf. G. Steindorff, *Die aegyptischen Gaue*.

Among these eponymous figures we find some of the ensigns which once stood over the prehistoric clans.[1] Not all survived ; the solar disk, the human face, the scorpion, the elephant, and certain plants did not come to preside over the destinies of nomes. On the other hand, in Upper Egypt, a falcon appears in the ensign of the IInd Nome ; the bucranium is the origin of the cow-headed sistrum of the VIIth ; the " thunderbolt " designates the IXth ; the flying falcon is in the XVIIIth ; and certain trees, which appear on Neolithic pottery as tribal ensigns, may perhaps be found in the terebinth of the XIIIth and the palm-tree of the XXth. In Lower Egypt,[2] we find the falcon in the 3rd Nome ; the two arrows crossed on an animal's hide designate the 4th ; the harpoon is preserved in the 7th ; and the three-peaked mountain in the 6th. What are we to infer, except that these ensigns of wandering clans became the ensigns of nomes when the clans attached themselves to the soil ? As we have seen in *From Tribe to Empire* (p. 136), the Thinite Kings of the Ist Dynasty introduced new clans marching under new ensigns—the greyhound (?) of Seth, the dog (or wolf), the ibis, the falcon of the West, an ingot (?), called the emblem of the East, and a piece of meat (Fig. 10). These became the eponyms of the XIth and XVIIth Nomes of Upper Egypt and the 15th, 3rd, 20th, and 2nd Nomes of Lower Egypt.

So a certain number of prehistoric ensigns and Thinite ensigns survived when the clans of kinsmen became sedentary and were confined within territorial, administrative limits. Although our evidence is still incomplete, we may assume that half of the forty or forty-two nomes of historical Egypt took their ensigns and patrons from the old clans. For other ensigns the same origin is possible, if not proved, in cases where there is no evidence of a historical derivation.

Moreover, there are *gods* in every nome-capital. These are the deities of the historical period, of whom some appear in

[1] *From Tribe to Empire*, p. 123.
[2] I shall use Roman numerals for the nomes of Upper Egypt and Arabic for those of Lower Egypt.

one capital only, while others—Horus, Hathor, Khnum, Osiris, Thoth—preside over several.   What relationship was there between the gods of the capitals and the ensigns of the nomes ?   We find two cases :—

(i) The god of the capital is blended with, or is indisputably connected with, the ensign of the nome.

In Upper Egypt, in the IInd Nome, the Falcon, as being the god Horus, rules over the territory, the ensign of which means " the Throne of Horus " ;   the cow-goddess Hathor governs the VIIth Nome, that of the Bucranium ; the god Min resides in the IXth, where the " Thunderbolt " designates both Min and the nome; in the XVIIth the Dog is at once the ensign and the god (Anubis) of the capital. In Lower Egypt the Crossed Arrows stand for the goddess Neith in Saïs, her city, and also

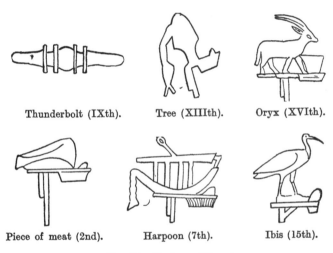

| Thunderbolt (IXth). | Tree (XIIIth). | Oryx (XVIth). |
| Piece of meat (2nd). | Harpoon (7th). | Ibis (15th). |

FIG. 10.—Ensigns of Nomes.

for the 5th and 6th Nomes, and the Ibis of the 15th is both the ensign and the god of the capital. In all these cases [1] the ensign of the nome is a survival, a legacy from proto-historic or Thinite times. The organization in nome-cities has preserved, in the places mentioned, the patron chosen by the earlier human group ; the totem of the clan remains that of the god of the town.

[1] And also, it appears, in the case of the XVIIIth and 3rd Nomes.

In this new capacity the totem becomes humanized; usually it takes on an anthropomorphic appearance.

This development is physically visible on some Thinite monuments. The beast of Seth appears endowed with the name *Ash* and transformed into a man with a greyhound's head; the viper Wazet becomes a serpent with a human head.[1] Here we perceive the origin of the hybrid figures which, by a synthetic process, represent the god with a human form, emerging from the old animal totem, but of a piece with it. Henceforward, until the end of the history of Egypt, these figures, which are true signs of writing, will " name " the various elements which " compose " the patron deity of the city.

The Falcon, in its capacity of the god Horus of the IInd Nome, is often a falcon-headed man; in the ensign it is simply a falcon. The Ibis, as god of the city of the 15th Nome, is an ibis-headed man; as ensign of the nome, it keeps the full shape of a bird. In the 5th Nome Neith has the features of a divine woman, but she holds in her hand the Two Crossed Arrows, the ensign of the territory. Certainly we must suppose that these animals and objects had lost their original meaning for the vulgar. The Falcon or Ibis of such-and-such a nome was no longer exactly an ancestor, a patron, or a totem; but it would never be an abstract symbol or a mere attribute, but the *living image on earth*, the " god-beast ", of this or that god. The Two Arrows would still be a fetish, a visible image, in which the goddess was incarnate, under another material form. Thus, the primitive idol was adapted to the advance of the new social system.

The historian should remember that, as early as the Thinite IInd Dynasty (between 3200 and 3000 B.C.), the hybrid figures of deities bear witness that the change from ensign to god, which seems to be the result of the transformation of the clan into a nome, was an accomplished fact.

(ii) The god of the capital is distinct from the ensign.

We have seen above that certain ensigns, whether prehistoric or Thinite, are not to be found in the nomes. Moreover, there are other significant divergences. In Upper Egypt the Two Falcons of the Vth Nome belong to the god Min, who is not a bird, but a man, whose fetish is the " Thunderbolt ".

---

[1] On this subject, see V. Loret, in **VIII,** vol. xi, p. 88.

The VIth Nome, that of the Crocodile, belongs to the goddess Hathor, a cow. The XVth Nome, Hare, belongs to the ibis Thoth, and the XIIIth and XIVth, Terebinth, are under the wolf Upuat and the cow Hathor. The XXth and XXIst, Palm-tree, belong to the ram Khnum and the cow Hathor-Isis. In all these cases there is no apparent connexion between the ensign and the god ; the former is not the visible shape of the latter, and ensign and god are represented differently in writing. Lower Egypt presents similar contradictions between the ensigns of the nomes and the patron deities of the towns ; these will be found in the table at the end of this chapter.[1]

So, in half the nomes, we find two patrons. The older one is probably the local totem, degraded from his rank, but still kept, out of reverence, as the ensign of the nome, and adored as a god-beast or fetish object ; his power has no longer any material foundation, and is only supported by tradition and superstitious affection. The new patron, the god and lord of the capital, is visible, either in the form of a god-beast or fetish (which are, however, distinct from the ensign), or in his humanized shape. These two classes of gods live harmoniously together, while remaining quite distinct. The texts of the pyramids expressly distinguish between " all the gods of the nomes and all the gods of the towns ".[2]

Really, the god of the nome, where he is different from the god of the capital, is usually an ancestor, or a conquered patron, who has yielded the effective lordship over the territory to a successor. After some social and political change, he has been supplanted, but not destroyed, by the god of the capital.

This supremacy of the god of the capital over the nome is asserted by the name of the capital. Every great town had a " vulgar " name, without definite meaning (at any rate, for us), of which many examples survive—Teni, Zebti, Shashetep, Saut, etc. (see the Table of Nomes). These place-names were replaced by a series of " sacred " names after the establishment in all the cities of the historical gods. The capital is called the House (*per*), Mansion (*het*), Town (*nut*), Shrine

---

[1] See the 2nd, 6th, 8th, 10th, 14th, 16th, 18th, and 19th Nomes.
[2] *Pyr.*, § 1522.

(*zebat*), Sanctuary (*sekhem*), Pillar (*iun*), or Sceptre (*uast, uâbu*) of such-and-such a deity. Above all, the great temple of the place imposes its name on the whole city ; all the capitals are described as " *House* of So-and-so " ; for example, Busiris means "House of Osiris ", Bubastis means "House of Bast ", etc. This sacred name gradually encroaches on the others, and on that of the nome. At various periods the whole nome is designated by the name of the capital, that is by that of the temple. The practice becomes general after the occupation of Egypt by the Greeks. These latter, adopting a procedure which must have already become customary in the administration, gave the provinces the names of the capitals, in their quality as the domains of Egyptian gods, and they looked for the equivalents of these gods in Hellenic mythology. The IInd Nome, that of Horus, was called " the Nome of the City of Apollo ", the Apollinopolite Nome. There were Diospolite, Aphroditopolite, Hermopolite Nomes, called after the cities of Zeus (Amon at Thebes), Aphrodite (Hathor at Denderah), and Hermes (Thoth at Khmunu).[1] This was the last stage of the age-long encroachment of the gods of the capitals on the eponyms of the nomes.

Sometimes a city was built on virgin territory,which had been reclaimed from the Nile, or had not been settled by any ancient clan or by the " Servants " of a god. At the apex of the Delta, on ground which had formerly been flooded, but had been won from the river by the construction of a gigantic dike,[2] Menes founded the city of the White Wall, which was to become Memphis. The adjoining territory took the same name as the city, and was inscribed as White Wall at the head of the nomes of Lower Egypt. The god Phtah, who reigned not far off, did not give his name to the city or to its province ; on the contrary, when he annexed Memphis from the religious point of view, he himself received a surname from the city,

[1] See Steindorff, loc. cit., and especially H. Gauthier, *Dictionnaire de noms géographiques*, vol. ii, pp. 50–144, in which all town-names composed of *Houses* of gods are classified.

[2] Hdt.. ii. 99.

and was called Phtah, South of his Wall, that is, Phtah whose sanctuary is outside the city. With the IVth Nome of Upper Egypt the same thing seems to have happened; the city of the Sceptre, *Uast* (later Thebes), imposed its name on its territory, then borrowed its god Mentu from a neighbouring city, Hermonthis (" House of Mentu "), and later adopted Amon as well.

In other cases the nome was an administrative creation in which respect had to be paid to the religious traditions of successive ages. The Ist Nome of Upper Egypt does not seem to have existed before the Memphite Dynasties. When this territorial division was created, for purely administrative purposes, it was called *ta-Setet*, " Land of the goddess Setet," whose true domain was the island of Sehel, to the south of the nome. The capital was placed at Abu, the city of the Elephant (the Elephantine of the Greeks), which may perhaps preserve the memory of a prehistoric clan whose animal ensign is known to us.[1] Lastly the god introduced into Abu was the ram Khnum, who took Setet from the island of Sehel as an associate goddess. So the organization of the Ist Nome, by its terminology, calls up three distinct elements— perhaps three stages of development.

FIG.11.—The Falcon,Victor over the Oryx Seth (XVIth Nome).

With our present evidence, still very scanty, it is hard to say definitely whether in other cases certain analogies may have led to assimilation or fusion, whether the god of the capital inherited certain features of the god of the nome; in fine, to what extent they may sometimes have affected each other, while remaining distinct. The nomenclature seems sometimes to reveal permanent assimilation, and sometimes persistent rivalry between the first occupants and the usurping gods imported by newcomers. Sometimes the figurative sign of the ensign has been modified in such a way that the conflict between successive occupants is evident.

[1] See *From Tribe to Empire*, p. 123.

In Upper Egypt the Crocodile of the IVth Nome is represented
in the historical period with a knife stuck in its eye—that
is, killed or mutilated after a battle. It is unlikely that a clan
would originally have chosen a patron who was seriously
wounded and in a state of physical inferiority ; therefore the
mutilation of the crocodile was introduced later. It
shows that a new god conquered the old patron ; the
invaders perpetuated the memory of their conquest by
allowing the ensign of the former occupants to survive in
humiliating conditions.   So, too, the White Oryx (a

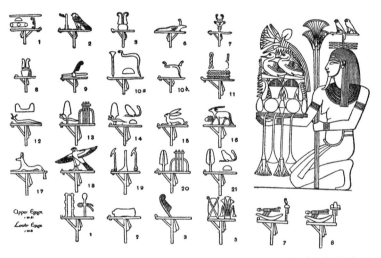

FIG. 12.—Nomes of Upper Egypt and six of Lower Egypt. (Caulfeild, *Abydos.*)

Typhonian beast) of the XVIth Nome bears on its back
the lordly outline of the Falcon Horus, its conqueror ;
here mythology comes to our aid, for tradition tells
of the triumph of Horus, setting his talons upon his
enemy Seth.   Thus, these allegorical figures preserve the
living memory of the wars waged by rival clans or
peoples for the possession of the nomes.[1]

When we read the table of the nomes we notice that many
of the cities of the Two Egypts took the same patron—Horus,

---

[1] Cf. *From Tribe to Empire*, p. 80, where M. Davy observes that, in Australian
communities, eagles, falcons, and crows have conflicts which are described in
the myths.

under his own name or in different forms, Hathor, who is made the wife of Horus by the traditions, but also governs other cities by herself, and Seth, their common enemy, who is still powerful and, in spite of his defeat, holds his own as the ensign of various places. Notwithstanding the splitting up of the soil and of the worships which this table of the nomes reveals, we perceive from almost immemorial time, a marked tendency towards religious and political concentration.

This development will take us from organization in nomes to organization in kingdoms.

TABLE OF THE NOMES [1]

UPPER EGYPT

Prehistoric Ensign (not localized).	No. and Emblem of Nome.	Gods of Capital.	Capital.	Greco-Roman and Modern Names.
ELEPHANT	I. *Ta-Setet*, Land of Setet	(Ram) { 1. KHNUM 2. Setet (Satis), *f.* 3. Anuqet, *f.*	*Abu*, City of Elephants	Elephantine
FALCON	II. *Utest-Hor*, Throne of Horus	(Falcon) { 1. HORUS (HARAKHTI, Hor-BEHEDETI) 2. Hathor, *f.* 3. Ihi, their son	*Zebat, Behedet, Mesent,* Sanctuary (of the Falcon) in Upper Egypt. Cf. 14th and 17th Nomes	Apollinopolis Magna (Edfu)
FALCON	III. *Nekhen* (?), Two Feathers	(Vulture of Upper Egypt) NEKHEBT, *f.* (Mummified Falcon) HORUS	*Nekheb*, R. bank *Nekhen*, L. bank, afterwards	Eileithyiapolis Hieraconpolis
			Iunit, Pillar	Latopolis (Esneh)
		(Falcon and Bakha Bull) MENTU	*Per-Mentu*, House of Mentu *Iunu-shemā*, Pillar of Upper Egypt, afterwards	Hermonthis
FALCON	IV. *Uast*, Sceptre	afterwards 1. AMON-RA (Ram, Goose) 2. Mut, *f.* (Vulture) 3. Khonsu, their son (Moon)	*Uast*, City of the Sceptre, *Nut-Amon*, City of Amon	Diospolis Magna (Thebes)

[1] *Col.* 1 : Ensigns of unlocalized clans, the shape or worship of which survived in the emblems of the nomes. *Col.* 2 : The numbers of the nomes, with their god-emblems. *Col.* 3 : Gods of capitals, conflicting or connected with the god-emblems of the nomes, with the primitive form (animal or other) of every deity who received, in addition, a human form, or characteristic object, as an attribute. (*Col.* 2) Names of the capitals. On the meaning of these names, some of which are "vulgar" and some "sacred", see above, p. 49. Every capital had some such name as "House of Ra" (at Heliopolis), "House of Hor-Nubti" (at Hieraconpolis, XIIth Nome) ; I have mentioned this sacred name expressly only where it was more commonly used than the vulgar name. *Col.* 5 : The corresponding Greco-Roman and modern names. For certain nomes, *Triads,* or divine families, are indicated. See the sources quoted above, pp. 44–63, and p. 74.

UPPER EGYPT—*continued*

Prehistoric Ensign (not localized).	No. and Emblem of Nome.	Gods of Capital.	Capital.	Græco-Roman and Modern Names.
FALCON AND BEAST OF SETH	V. *Neterui* (?), Two Falcons = Two Gods	(Thunderbolt, Ithyphallic Man) MIN	*Gebtiu*, City of Caravanmen	Coptos
	VI. *Zam* (?), Crocodile	(Cow) { 1. HATHOR, *f.* 2. Hor-Behedeti 3. Ihi, their son	*Ta iunt netert*, Pillar of the Goddess	Tentyris (Denderah)
BUCRANIUM	VII. *Seshesht*, Bucranium, afterwards Sistrum	(Cow) NEBT-HET (Nephthys), *f.* afterwards HATHOR, *f.*	*Het*, Mansion (of the Goddess)	Diospolis Parva
WOLF	VIII. *Ta-ur*, Great Land, afterwards *Ab*, Reliquary of Osiris-Anzti	(Wolf) KHENT-AMENTI, afterwards OSIRIS (in the necropolis)	*Teni* Necropolis : *Abdu*	This, Thinis Abydos
THUNDERBOLT	IX. *Khem* (?), Thunderbolt of Min	MIN (ithyphallic)	*Apu*	Panopolis
	X. *Wazet*, Serpent	(Cow) HATHOR, *f.*	*Zebti*, City of Two Sandals, and *Per-Wazet*, House of Wazet (in Upper Egypt)	Aphroditopolis
BEAST OF SETH	XI. *Seth*, Beast of Seth	(Ram) KHNUM	*Shashetep*	Hypselis
TWO-PEAKED MOUNTAIN	XII. *Zu-heft* (?), Mountain of the Serpent (?), or *Zu-f*, His Mountain	(Falcon on Nubti) HORUS-NUBTI (Horus Vanquisher of Seth)	*Per Hor-Nubti*, House of Horus Nubti	Hieraconpolis
TREE	XIII. *Atef-khentet*, Upper Terebinth (?)	(Wolf) UPUAT of Upper Egypt	*Saut*	Lycopolis (Siut)

[*page* 55

UPPER EGYPT—*continued*

Prehistoric Ensign (not localized).	No. and Emblem of Nome.	Gods of Capital.	Capital.	Græco-Roman and Modern Names.
TREE	XIV. *Atef-pehut*, Lower Terebinth (?)	(Cow) HATHOR, *f*.	*Gesa*	Cuse
	XV. *Un*, Hare	(Ibis) THOTH	*Unt*, City of the Hare, afterwards *Khmunu*, City of the Eight of Thoth	Hermopolis Magna
	XVI. *Ma-hez*, White Oryx (with the Falcon on its back)	(Falcon) HORUS, Vanquisher of Oryx	*Hebnu*	Hibis
	XVII. . . . (?), Dog	(Dog) ANUBIS, afterwards (Falcon) HORUS	*Kasa*, afterwards *Het-nsut*, Mansion of the King of Upper Egypt	Cynopolis
FLYING FALCON	XVIII. *Sepa*, Flying Falcon	(Falcon) HORUS	*Sepa* and *Het-benu*, Mansion of the Phœnix	Hipponon
	XIX. *Uabu*, Sceptre	(Sceptre) IRU-SHEPES, "August Form"	*Uab sep-meri*, or *Per-mezed*	Oxyrrhynchos
TREE	XX. *Nar-t khentet*, Upper Palm-tree (?)	(Ram) HERISHEF, "He who is on his domain"	*Khenen-nsut*, City of the King's Child	Heracleopolis Magna
TREE	XXI. *Nar-t pehut*, Lower Palm-tree (?)	(Falcon) HORUS	*Shedt*, *Per-Sebek*, House of the Crocodile Sebek	Crocodilopolis (Fayum) [1]
	XXII. . . . (?), knife	(Cow) HATHOR-ISIS, *f*.	*Mátenu* and *Per-hemt*, House of the Cow	Northern Aphrodito-polis

[1] The Lake of Upper Egypt (*Urk.*, i, p. 3), *Mer* (or *She*) *shemá* (= the Fayum, Lake Mœris), sometimes forms an autonomous district. See **I**, vol. v, p. 76.

LOWER EGYPT

Prehistoric Ensign (not localized).	No. and Emblem of Nome.	Gods of Capital.	Capital.	Greco-Roman and Modern Names.
	1. *Inb-hez*, White Wall	(Apis Bull) 1. PHTAH (Lioness) 2. Sekhmet, *f.* (Lotus) 3. Nefertum	*Inb-hez*, afterwards *Men-nefer*	Memphis
PIECE OF FLESH	2. *Duau*, Piece of Flesh, Thigh	God of the Necropolis: Sokar (Mummified HORUS KHENTI-IRTI, Falcon) Horus who presides over the Two Eyes	*Sekhem*, Sanctuary (of Horus)	Letopolis
OSTRICH-FEATHER FALCON AND FEATHER	3. *Imen* (West), Ostrich-feather	(Ostrich-feather IMENT (Amenti), on Goddess's Goddess of the West Head)	*Imu* and *Per neb Imu*, House of the Lord of the Imu	Apis (Libyan Nome)
TWO ARROWS CROSSED OVER A SKIN	{ 4. ....(?) *shemâ*, Two Arrows of Upper Egypt 5. ....(?) *meh*, Two Arrows of Lower Egypt	(Two Arrows) Neith, *f.*	*Zeka* *Sau*	Prosopis. Saïs
THREE-PEAKED MOUNTAIN (desert)	6. *Ka-khaset*, Bull of the Desert	(Bull) RA, afterwards AMON-RA	*Khaset*, (City of) the Desert	Xoïs
HARPOON.	7. ....(?) *Imenti*, Western Harpoon (Libyan side)	HA, a mountain god, afterwards 1. OSIRIS 2. Isis, *f.* 3. Horus the Child	*Per Ha neb Imenti*, House of Ha, Lord of the West	Metelis

[*page* 57

LOWER EGYPT—*continued*

Prehistoric Ensign (not localized).	No. and Emblem of Nome.	Gods of Capital.	Capital.	Graeco-Roman and Modern Names.
HARPOON	8. . . . (?) *Iabti*, Eastern Harpoon (Arabian side)	ATUM	*Teku* and *Per-Atum*, House of Atum	Patamos (Pithom), Heroönpolis
	9. *Anzti*, Protector	(God crowned with Two Feathers) ANZTI afterwards OSIRIS-ANZTI	*Per Osiris neb-Zed*, House of Osiris, Lord of the Zed	Busiris
	10. *Kem-ur*, Great Black (Bull)	(Falcon) HORUS KHENTI-KHET, Horus who presides over the (Divine) Body	*Het ta herj ib*, Mansion of the Middle Land	Athribis
	11. *Ka-heseb*, Heseb Bull	(Falcon) HOR-MERTI, Horus with the two Eyes	*Hesebt, Shednu*	Pharbæthos
BULL (?)	12. . . . (?) Bull-calf	(Falcon) ANHERT (Anhor, Onuris)	*Zebat-neter*, Sanctuary of the God	Sebennytos (Iseium)
SUN	13. *Heq-āz*	ATUM afterwards RA and the Ennead (Phœnix, Mnevis-Bull)	*Iunu (meh)*, Pillar (of Lower Egypt) *Per-Ra*, House of Ra	Heliopolis
INGOT (?) (EAST)	14. *Khent-iabti*, Point of the East	(Falcon) HORUS	*Zebat-meht, Mesent, Be-hedet-meht*, Sanctuary (of Horus) in Lower Egypt; cf. IInd Nome; *Per Hor neb-Mesent*, House of Horus, Lord of Mesent	Sele (Zalu)

[page 58

LOWER EGYPT—*continued*

Prehistoric Ensign (not localized).	No. and Emblem of Nome.	Gods of Capital.	Capital.	Græco-Roman and Modern Names.
IBIS	15. *Zehut*, Ibis	(Ibis) ZEHUTI (Thoth)	*Bâhet* and *Per-Zehuti*, House of Thoth	Hermopolis Parva
	16. . . . (?), Silurus Fish	(Ram, *ba*) KHNUM afterwards OSIRIS	*Per Ba neb Zedet*, House of the *Ba*, Lord of Zedet	Mendes
	17. *Behedet*, Sanctuary (of Horus)	(Falcon) HORUS afterwards AMON-RA	*Behedet, Per iu n Amon*, House of the Island of Amon	Diospolis Parva
	18. *Imu-khenti*, Upper Royal Child (of Upper Egypt)	(Cat) BAST, *f*.	*Per-Bast*, House of Bast	Bubastis
	19. *Imu-pehu*, Lower Royal Child (of Lower Egypt)	(Serpent) WAZET, *f*., and HORUS THE CHILD	*Immet* and *Per-Wazet*, House of Wazet	Buto
	20. *Ákhem* (?), Mummified Falcon	(Falcon) HORUS SEPED	*Per-Seped*, House of Seped	Arabia

CHAPTER III

The Divine Dynasties and their Historical Significance

I

DIVINE DYNASTIES AND GODS OF THE UNIVERSE

THE historical tradition preserved by the original Egyptian sources and by the Greek historians, and Manetho in particular, maintains that the first kings of Egypt were the gods. Are we to dismiss this tradition as a mere myth ? What we have learned about the part played by the ensigns and the gods compels us to inquire whether the legend does not conceal some facts. It is the historian's business to discern, behind divine heroes, the men or groups who did the work of which legend tells. When we examine the pious fictions about the divine dynasties, we shall see what was the mentality of the " Servants " (*Shemsu*) or " Followers " (*Imu-khet*) of the gods, who, in the name of their divine patrons, founded the kingdoms, after the nomes. The subjects which interest the historian of civilization are the rivalries and endeavours of men, inspired and led, as they believed, by their gods. What I shall try to bring out is the wholly religious character of the institution of kingship, as it appears at the beginning of Egyptian history, in this society of god-kings superimposed on the human community.

Official history, in Egypt as among many other peoples, claimed to go back to the creation of the world. Simply, and with conviction, it linked the first human kings up with the original Demiurge. Now, according to the theologians of Heliopolis, at the head of the gods of Egypt there were twenty-seven, divided into a Great Ennead, a Small Ennead, and a third Ennead without any special denomination.

Now let us turn to Manetho, in the summaries of Eusebius and the Syncellus. He gives the following plan of mythical history [1]:—

[1] E. Meyer, **XXIII**, p. 167.

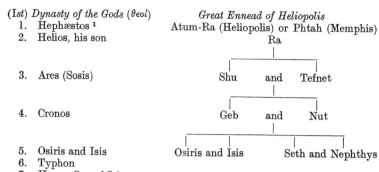

(1st) Dynasty of the Gods (θεοί)

1. Hephæstos [1]
2. Helios, his son

3. Ares (Sosis)

4. Cronos

5. Osiris and Isis
6. Typhon
7. Horus, Son of Isis

Great Ennead of Heliopolis

Atum-Ra (Heliopolis) or Phtah (Memphis)

Ra

Shu   and   Tefnet

Geb   and   Nut

Osiris and Isis   Seth and Nephthys

Replace these names by their hieroglyphic equivalents, complete the divine couples by the addition of the goddesses (as is authorized by the addition of Isis to Osiris in Manetho), set aside the Demiurge (we shall see that he is fused in Ra) and Horus, Son of Isis (who, in the summary of the Syncellus, belongs to the second divine dynasty); and we have,[2] in this first dynasty of Hellenized gods, the Great Ennead of Heliopolis, the traditional composition of which under the Old Kingdom is given by the Pyramid Texts.

Here is a second divine dynasty, from the Syncellus, with its approximate equivalents :—

Horus	. .	Horus
Ares .	. .	Anhor
Anubis	. .	Anubis
Heracles	. .	Khonsu
Apollo	. .	Horus Behedeti (of Edfu)
Ammon	. .	Amon
Tithoës	. .	Thoth
Sosos	. .	Shu
Zeus .	. .	Amon-Ra

This second dynasty, which I shall not discuss in detail. also contains nine members. Manetho must, therefore, have copied out names belonging to an Ennead, and it is probable that he was influenced by the second, or Small, Ennead of Heliopolis, the gods of which are given in the lists in the pyramids. Manetho's text is here corrupt, or he accepted a late tradition, for the names are quite different from those given by the Heliopolitans.

---

[1] Manetho, working from Memphite documents, substituted Phtah, god of Memphis, for Atum, god of Heliopolis, as Demiurge.

[2] G. Maspero, " Sur les dynasties divines de l'ancienne Égypte," in **XXXVIII**, ii, p. 279.

A third dynasty was composed of deified dead heroes called
" dead demigods ", νέκυες ἡμίθεοι. These were probably
beings intermediate between gods and human kings. No
names are given by the abbreviator of Manetho ; possibly
this third dynasty corresponded numerically to the third
Heliopolitan Ennead, which included " the children of
Horus, Son of Isis, God of Buto " and " the children of
Horus Khenti-Khet,[1] God of Athribis ".

Before we pursue this analysis of the traditions further, we
should note the presence in the first dynasty of Ra, Osiris,
Isis, Seth, and Nephthys ; in the second of two forms of
Horus, Thoth, Amon, Anhor, and Khonsu ; and in the third
of the children of the various Horuses. These gods, whom we
already know as the patrons of nomes or cities, reappear in
the historians, arranged in groups to suit a fanciful theological
system. In the Heliopolitan tradition of the Old Kingdom,
which Manetho sometimes respects, and sometimes distorts
or reshapes, Horus plays a variety of parts, but there is one
epithet which shows his parentage and origin—he is " Horus,
Son of Isis ". Later we shall see the historical importance of
this title.

The Turin Papyrus, too, though sadly mutilated, gives us
information about the divine dynasties in two fragments.[2]
One is complete, except for two names, and runs as follows :—

(King of Upper and Lower Egypt, Phtah) [3]
King of Upper and Lower Egypt, Ra
King of Upper and Lower Egypt, Shu
King of Upper and Lower Egypt, Geb, length (of life) . . .
King of Upper and Lower Egypt, Osiris
King of Upper and Lower Egypt, Seth, 200 years (reign)
King of Upper and Lower Egypt, Horus, L.H.S.,[4] 300 years (reign)
King of Upper and Lower Egypt, Thoth, L.H.S., 3,126 years (reign)
Queen of Upper and Lower Egypt, Maat (Justice), . . . years
King of Upper and Lower Egypt, Horus . . .

Total . . .

---

[1] E. Chassinat, " Les *Nékues* de Manéthon," in **IV,** vol. xix, pp. 23 ff.
[2] Meyer, **XXIII,** p. 160, and Table ii.
[3] I restore Phtah and Shu here from Manetho's tradition.
[4] L.H.S. = Life, Health, Strength.

The papyrus does not adopt the scheme of the Heliopolitan Ennead ; however, it gives, after the Demiurge, nine gods, and the end of the dynasty is indicated by the mention of a total. But it retains only the chief names, from the members of the Great and Small Enneads, and, moreover, introduces Horus, Thoth, and Queen Maat into the first divine family. It should be noted that here, again, Horus appears twice.

Another fragment of this papyrus,[1] to which we shall return, enumerates, immediately before Menes, the *Iakhu Shemsu-Hor*, the " Spirits, Servants of Horus ". The word *Iakhu*, Spirits, here corresponds to the *Manes*, Νέκυες, of Manetho. The Servants of Horus are human kings, placed under his protection, anterior to Menes. So the tradition which places successive dynasties of gods, demigods, and *Manes* at the beginning of the history of Egypt is recalled, though in a summary fashion, in the Turin Papyrus. Such a coincidence cannot be fortuitous, and it shows that, in spite of differences in detail, official history recorded the main phases of a development, bringing from heaven to earth, in three stages, the divine dynasties who were the ancestors and models of the human dynasties.

What is the historical significance of the first divine dynasty, corresponding to the Great Ennead of the theologians of Heliopolis ? The intention of the priests is obvious. Their aim was to expound the creation of the world briefly by the device, familiar to Orientals, of the story of the rise of a family of gods. The genealogical table represented by the Great Ennead shows us the main stages of the formation and government of the universe. The gods who make up the Nine are highly developed, compared with the gods of the nomes who succeeded the ensigns. They are not local patron deities, worshipped within the narrow confines of a district and tied down to a nome ; their power is not limited in space, or restricted to the few worshippers who can call on the Thunderbolt, the Sistrum, the Sceptre, or some other fetish. On the contrary, they are gods of the whole universe, cosmic deities,

[1] Frag. 1, **XXIII**, p. 163 and pl. iii.

whose sway covers all Egypt and goes beyond, taking in every
known land. Ra is the sun [1] ; Shu is the aerial " void ", the
air [2] ; Geb is the earth ; Nut is the sky. At first they have
no " personal " name, apart from the element or portion of
the universe which they represent. They have no definite
shape, until they come to be fused with other deities, whose
animal or human form they assume.[3]   Nor is their worship
peculiar to any one town or nome, doubtless because it is
common to the whole country. The four last-born are opposed
in pairs : Osiris represents the fertilizing Nile and vegetative
force and his wife Isis is the fertilized soil in which the seeds
grow, while Seth is the dry desert, with Nephthys as his
barren consort. The universe, then, has been made by the
successive work of a family of gods, the issue of the solitary
Demiurge, and their pedigree is as follows :—

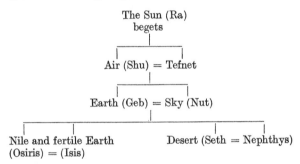

Over the patron deities of the nomes, the theologians set
the great nature-gods, as kings of the whole country ; these
were its first divine dynasty.

The supremacy of these great cosmic gods is only rarely
attested before the Thinite period [4] ; but as soon as royal
monuments with texts appear, we perceive, by unmistakable
signs, that their rule was imposed everywhere. By patient
research in the Corpus of the pyramids, which contains so
many memories of very early times, by cautious use of the

[1] Ra, the first god, has no divine wife at first.

[2] Shu's wife, Tefnet, seems to have been a creation of the mind, and had no
definite cosmic function.

[3] e.g. Ra, fused with Atum of Heliopolis ; Nut, with the cow Hathor ; Seth,
with the greyhound ; Osiris, with the god Anzti.

[4] But certain natural forces, represented by the ensigns of the sun, mountains,
trees, appear among the patrons of the clans, and later of the nomes. See
From Tribe to Empire, p. 123.

legends preserved in the classical period, and by the interpretation of the titles of the first human Pharaohs, it is
possible, if not to reconstruct the whole fabric of beliefs,
at least to see its general plan. In my opinion, the universal
gods gained the upper hand in certain towns, and then, thanks
to the speculations of the theologians, gradually extended
their influence. It is clear that the diffusion of their worship
helped to bring about the transformation from nomes to
kingdoms. The political centralization which little by little
superseded the numerous small units, was accompanied by
the retreat of the local gods and favoured the triumph of the
gods of universal character, who were thenceforward acknowledged all over Egypt.[1]

This does not mean that the moral and material conquest
of Egypt took place in the order presented by the Heliopolitan
genealogy, in which Ra, as Demiurge, is the first author of the
series of events. The theologians of Heliopolis would not have
any god but their own Ra at the head of the first divine
dynasty ; but we know that as things really happened, other
gods and other cities had already, before Ra, exercised a wide
influence and prepared the way for centralization.

II

HORUS THE ELDER, FIRST KING OF LOWER EGYPT, AND SETH, FIRST KING OF UPPER EGYPT

Of the gods of the universe, the oldest in authority seems
to have been a god of light and the sky. He is not the sun,
represented by a disk (Ra, Aten), but a being of still more
general significance, embodying the whole sky ; he is an
inhabitant of the celestial kingdom, a bird, the falcon.
This is a conception of entirely popular origin, appropriate
to the country of Egypt. A god of the universe, being supernatural, must live above the earth ; therefore, he is a winged
being ; and of all the birds of Egypt, is any more beautiful
and brave than the falcon ? From morning to evening he
sails in the light, a ravening, watchful lord of heaven and

---

[1] On the parallel development of the concentration of power in politics and
of the notion of a great God in mythology, see Davy in *From Tribe to Empire*,
p. 79.

earth. Even in prehistoric times we found the falcon as the patron of many clans ; later, when he became the god of several cities, his worshippers were so many that he was considered the divine being *par excellence*. In hieroglyphic writing, in the earliest period, the word-sign which determines the idea of " God " is the falcon on his perch (Fig. 13).

The god and the bird are named and written in the same way—*Hr*, *Hru*,[1] which the Greeks transcribe as *Ὧρος*,

FIG. 13.—The sign *Neter*, God.

and '*Aρ*- in composite names, whence comes the Latin transcription *Horus*. The earliest texts mention several gods named Horus, from different places of origin—Horus the Elder, and Horus the Younger, Son of Isis; Horus of the East, that is, Horus of the Eastern Horizon, *Harakhti* ; Horus of the Morning ; Horus of the Gods,[2] etc. At present let us ignore the two first, whose epithets are comparatively late, and do not correspond to the original idea. The four others, in the Pyramid Texts, are still entirely celestial beings, " those four Young Ones who sit on the Eastern side of the sky, those four Young Ones with the curly lock, who sit in the shadow of the tower of the Lofty One." [3]

The Egyptian language encouraged the localization of the Horuses in the sky by similarities of name. The word *hr*, with the adjectival inflexion *hrj*, means " upper ", " that which is above ". As a substantive, *hrt*, it is " the sky "— a further reason for mentally placing the Falcon God, *Hru*, in the sky. Another word, *hr*, means the upper part of a man, " the human face," " the head," and so " the chief " ; by association and pun, the god *Hr* becomes the heavenly face, the divine *head* whose Two Eyes, the sun and the moon, light the universe, and, as they open and shut, give day and night to living things. In classical times Amon-Ra is addressed as follows : " Thou art like Horus who lights the Two Lands with his Two Eyes. It is not the disk Aten which shows itself in the sky, but thy head, which touches the sky." [4]

[1] V. Loret, " Horus le Faucon," in **II**, *Bulletin*, iii (1903), p. 15.
[2] One of these four Horuses is sometimes called Horus Shesemti.
[3] *Pyr.*, § 1105. Kati (= the Lofty One) seems to be a name of the personified sky. A long curly lock, falling from the scalp to the shoulder, was a mark of noble children in Egypt.
[4] Maspero, " Études de mythologie et d'archéologie," in **XXXVIII**, ii, p. 12 ; Moret, **XLVIII**, pp. 129, 133 ; Sethe, *Zur Sage vom Sonnenauge*, p. 5.

The Horus who, of all the Horuses, should most particularly personify the divine face would be likely to obtain the supremacy among men. Now, in the Delta, at Letopolis, the capital of the 2nd Nome of Lower Egypt, there reigned a Falcon (Pl. III, 3), whom the oldest texts describe by an epithet of sovereignty—*Hor khenti-irti*, Horus who presides over the Two Eyes.[1] He was

FIG. 14.—Horus Presiding over the Two Eyes. Note the final sign of the mummified falcon.

made superior to the four celestial Horuses ; the theologians of Heliopolis tell us that they were his four sons.[2] Later, to emphasize his superiority and to distinguish him from the other Horuses, he came to be called Horus the Elder, *Hor-ur*, a tradition which was even known to Plutarch, who calls him ῏Ωρος πρεσβύτερος.[3] We have no direct, explicit evidence which casts light on the causes of this supremacy on earth, nor on the political circumstances which enabled the worshippers of Horus Khenti-irti to found the first kingdom in Egypt ; our texts give us rather allusions and reminiscences. We shall see that Horus the Elder was eclipsed in later history by another Horus, with whom he originally had no connexion. This was the Son of Isis, the god of Buto, who was called, to distinguish him, Horus the Younger, or Horus the Child.[4] He took advantage of the similarity of name to superimpose his cult and his kingship on those of the older Horus. So the history of Horus of Letopolis reads like a palimpsest manuscript, in which a later writing covers the still visible letters of a much older story.

Luckily for us the memory of Horus Khenti-irti survived, intimately mingled with that of another god, Seth. Seth was not obliterated by a successor ; his bad character and his rôle as the essential, inexorable, eternal opponent of the gods of heaven earned his preservation all through the history of ancient Egypt. Seth, as we shall see later, was the rival of

---

[1] *Pyr.*, § 1670, 2086.

[2] *Pyr.*, § 2078. An interpolation assimilates the four gods to the four children of Horus, Son of Isis.

[3] *De Iside*, 12, 54. In Greek *Hr ur* becomes Ἀρούηρις, Horus the Great, a name afterwards especially applied to Horus of Edfu, the Apollo of the Greeks.

[4] In the *Book of the Dead* (Budge's ed., p. 325) we find Horus the Great, Horus Khenti-irti, and Horus, Son of Isis, mentioned one after the other.

Horus the Elder before he became the opponent of Horus the Younger; with his aid, we shall go back to the beginning and obtain a better knowledge of the first divine monarchy.

On the ensigns of the Thinite period Seth is a quadruped, perhaps a greyhound or an ant-eater, which leads a clan. This animal survives as ensign of the XIth Nome of Upper Egypt. Seth is also the god and patron of the Vth Nome (Two Gods). He is worshipped near Negadah, in the town of Ombos. He is likewise a god at Shashetep, in the XIth Nome, where he is later replaced by Horus and Khnum, and in the XIXth Nome (Sceptre, Uabu), where he is represented by the sharp-nosed oxyrrhynchus fish.[1] In other Typhonian forms—Crocodile (VIth Nome), White Oryx (XVIth Nome)—Seth appears yet again, in various parts of the valley, as a personage whose hostile character compels respect and sometimes veneration. The most ancient centre of his worship, his place of origin, and the political headquarters of his adherents is Nubt

FIG. 15.—Seth.

(Ombos, near Ballas and Negadah, on the west bank, opposite Coptos). There Flinders Petrie's excavations in 1895 revealed an archaic necropolis and a temple, in which there are numerous prayers addressed to Seth Nubti (Seth of Nubt, Seth the Ombite), son of Nut (the Sky Goddess), " Lord of Upper Egypt " (*neb ta shemâ*).[2] These texts are not older than the XVIIIth Dynasty, but the tradition is ancient ; on the pyramids we read " Seth, he who dwells in Nubt, the Lord of Upper Egypt ".[3] As far as we know, Seth is the oldest god to bear this epithet of sovereignty ; therefore his worshippers and adherents must have imposed their god, at the beginning

---

[1] In the Osiris legend this fish appears as the ally of Seth. For the nomes of the worshippers of Seth, see the very complete account in H. Kees, *Horus und Seth als Götterpaar*, ii, pp. 40–50.

[2] Flinders Petrie, *Nagada and Ballas*, pls. 77–8.

[3] *Pyr.*, § 204. Here Seth is often called by the epithet *Nubti* alone—" He of Nubt ".

PLATE III

2. THE FALCON HORUS
PROTECTING CHEPHREN
(Cairo)

1. THE GOD-KING CHEPHREN
Diorite (Cairo)

3. FALCON HORUS FROM THE
TEMPLE AT HIERACONPOLIS
Wrought gold (Cairo)

[face p. 68

of historical times, on the other southern nomes which adopted Seth. They made Seth the first King of Upper Egypt.

It was also in his capacity of cosmic god that Seth conquered Southern Egypt. But he was not a light-god ; he lived in the sky, like the Sun,[1] but as the adversary of light. Seth is the angry, howling god, who personifies the storm,[2] the deadly wind,[3] the thunder.[4] Since his power is manifested against the light, his domain is darkness, the physical night, and, at a later, more highly developed epoch, moral night, Evil, becomes his work. How could these baneful qualities win Seth so many worshippers, so that his power extended through the whole valley ? The reason was that night, the antithesis of day, was as natural and necessary as the day. Moreover, Seth was a " great magician ",[5] whose " very redoubtable power " [6] thwarted the gods of light. Fear is a great force ; men and gods were afraid of Seth, and worshipped his brutal power.

Nature itself gave way before the attacks of Seth and gave him only too many opportunities of prevailing over the beneficent gods of light. First, there were the atmospheric disturbances which, though rare, are not unknown, and are all the more striking for their infrequency, in Egypt, where the spring equinox brings on the desert wind, now called the Khamsin, and disorders the serene harmony of the heavens. The sun might, indeed, " drive away the storm, repulse the clouds, and break the hailstones " [7] by which Seth showed his hostility, but how could he escape the recurring night, and eclipses, partial or total, and who could stop the regular waning and disappearance of the moon every month ? These were all attacks, ephemeral but successful, of Seth against the Right Eye (the sun) and the Left Eye (the moon) of Horus. They were what the Egyptians called " battles in the sky " (*khennu m pet*),[8] in which neither adversary ever succeeded in putting down the other. " Fear for the Eye of Horus " was one of the unavoidable conditions of human life. When the theologians tried to imagine a state anterior to the creation of the world, they described the time " when there were no

---

[1] *Pyr.*, § 370. [2] *Neshen*, §§ 298, 326. [3] *Qer*, §§ 261, 281.
[4] When the heavens roar, it is the roaring of Seth (*nhemhem*, § 1150).
[5] *Ur hekau*, § 204. [6] *Áa peht*, § 622. [7] *Pyr.*, § 500.
[8] *Pyr.*, § 304. Cf. " the Combatants " (§§ 289, 306), as a name for Horus and Seth.

sky, and no earth, and no battles (in the sky), and none of the
fear which there is (to-day) for the Eye of Horus ".[1] This
Horus was, as we have seen, in the earliest times, the god
of Letopolis in the Delta, " He who presides over the Two
Eyes." [2] For the opposition between Delta and Valley, which
nature had made different and complementary, there was a
corresponding rivalry between heaven and earth, day and
night, in the form of a pair of warring brothers,[3] " the two
lads," [4] whose *concordia discors* was necessary to the life and
equilibrium of the universe.

The details of these fratricidal wars for the mastery of the
universe were a favourite theme of the mythical literature
of the Egyptians.[5] Plutarch has preserved a faint echo of it
in his *De Iside et Osiride* (55).

> The Egyptians say that Typhon (Seth) sometimes *strikes* Horus on the
> eye, and sometimes *tears it out*, swallows it, and then gives it back to the
> sun. By the blow, they describe in allegory the monthly waning of the
> moon ; by the *total removal* of the eye, they mean the eclipse of that
> orb, which the sun remedies by illuminating it again when it escapes from
> the shadow of the earth.

Horus gave his enemy blow for blow ; " he takes away his
strength and his power. That is why, at Coptos, a statue of
Horus holds the private parts of Typhon in one hand." On
the pyramids, allusions to the removal of Horus's eye and the
castration of Seth are frequent. Before the creation, " the
eye of Horus was not torn out, the testicles of Seth were not
cut off." [7] We read of the agony of the rivals after the battle :
" Horus cries out for his eye ; Seth cries out for his testicles.
The eye of Horus is out, fallen on this side of the Basin of
the Lotus, (but) it protects its body against Seth. Thoth has
seen it on this side of the Basin of the Lotus," and the eye of
Horus " falls on the wing of Thoth the Ibis ".

In his capacity as Moon God (or guardian of the Moon),
Thoth intervened between the two " combatants ". According

---

[1] *Pyr.*, § 1040.
[2] In the Pyramid Texts, the God of the Two Eyes, *Khenti-irti*, often acts
in concert with Seth Nubti, in memory of the days of their parallel kingship
(§§ 17, 826, 852).
[3] *Pyr.*, §§ 712, 1963.
[4] *Rehui*, in *Book of the Dead*, chaps. xvii, xlii, cxxiii.
[5] See E. Lefébure, *Le Mythe osirien : les Yeux d'Horus*, pp. 19, 43.
[6] Sometimes Seth changes himself into a black pig which tries to eat the eye ;
this is the Great Woe (*nsheni ur*) of the Eye (*Book of the Dead*, ch. cxii).
[7] *Pyr.*, § 1463.

to the old traditions, he cured the wounds of both, by spitting on Horus's face, putting his eye back, and tying Seth's testicles on again.[1] The allusions to the god who " gives their portions to the two brothers ",[2] and tells each his rights,[3] refer to Thoth, for it was at Hermopolis (Magna ?), the capital where Thoth reigned, that the conflict had been settled judicially ; there Thoth had " pacified " the two adversaries.[4] If, as seems fairly likely, these legends preserve an echo of predynastic battles between two great parties, one consisting of the nomes which supported Horus and the other of the nomes which obeyed Seth, Hermopolis (Magna ?), lying between the Delta and the Valley, must have acted as arbiter in the dispute, as its god did in the legend.[5]

According to another tradition, equally ancient, but preserved for us on a monument which is relatively very late, the dispute was judged and settled by the god Geb, not Thoth. Having summoned the two opponents to his tribunal, Geb addressed them one after the other.

> Geb says to Seth : " Go there where thou wast born," and Geb says to Horus : " Go there where thy father was drowned." [6] Geb says to Horus and Seth : " I have given you your portions, Upper Egypt to Seth and Lower Egypt to Horus."

Details explaining this excessively terse judgment are supplied by an opportune gloss.

> Geb has given their portions to Horus and Seth. He has forbidden them to wrangle. He sets Seth as King of the South in Upper Egypt, in the place where he was born, at Su [7] ; then Geb sets Horus as King of the North in Lower Egypt, in the place where his father was drowned, apportioning the land. Then Horus and Seth stand (as kings) each on his territory (*iat*). They give peace to the two countries at Tura,[8] which is the frontier of the two countries. . . . (Henceforward) Horus and Seth (live) in peace ; the two brothers are united, and dispute no longer ; they are joined together at Het-Ka-Phtah (Memphis), the balance of the two countries, the place where the two countries are in equilibrium.[9]

[1] *Pyr.*, §§ 594, 947.
[2] *Pyr.*, § 141 ; *Book of the Dead*, ch. xvii.
[3] *Pyr.*, §§ 712, 1963, 1749.
[4] *Pyr.*, §§ 229, 311, 315.
[5] Cf. Patrick Boylan, *Thoth*, p. 40. The Pyramid Texts do not say whether it is Northern or Southern Hermopolis.
[6] This phrase is an interpolation, to make Horus the Elder the true son of Osiris.
[7] One would expect the town of Nubt here ; Su is in the Fayum (Brugsch, *Dictionnaire géographique*, p. 752).
[8] On the East bank of the Nile, at the level of Memphis ; celebrated for its quarries of fine limestone.
[9] A. Erman, " Ein Denkmal memphitischer Theologie," in *Sitz. der Akad. Berlin*, 1911, pp. 925 ff. The text is carved on a monument of Shabaka (XXVth Dynasty), but the tradition is mentioned on the Pyramids, § 480.

Let us leave aside the allusions to Memphis and Tura, which have been interpolated into a much earlier tradition (incidentally these allusions describe the historical rôle of Memphis by very happy metaphors) ; there remains, in this account, a memory of very ancient wars between the Delta and the Valley, followed by arbitration. The conflict is ended by a very fair division, which nature demands and geography has always imposed on the institutions of Egypt. Henceforward, whoever the god or human king may be, to whom Egypt is subject, the country will by tradition be divided into the " territory (*iat*) of Seth " (Upper Egypt) and the " territory of Horus " (Lower Egypt).[1] The simultaneous reigns of Seth and Horus in the Two Kingdoms at a very remote epoch—the earliest known—are an accepted fact, a constant tradition, for the Egyptians of all periods. In the Pyramids, Horus and Seth, " They who are in the Royal Palace," [2] one in the Palace of Upper Egypt, one in the Palace of Lower Egypt,[3] become the divine forerunners of the Pharaohs.

---

[1] *Pyr.*, §§ 487, 960, etc.   [2] *Pyr.*, § 141.
[3] *Pyr.*, § 370 (Seth in the Palace of Upper Egypt).

CHAPTER IV

I

THE DELTA AND ITS PROTOHISTORIC PAST. THE WESTERN NOMES OF THE DELTA

WHAT date and what duration can we assign to the kingdoms of the Delta and the Valley, founded by the adherents of Horus and Seth ? We have no historical datum save one—the reigns of Horus of the Two Eyes and Seth are earlier in history than the appearance of Horus, Son of Isis. As soon as the gods of the family of Osiris come on the scene as leaders of human groups, Horus and Seth are eclipsed and make way before them, like old chiefs who are respected for their past glory, but are given only secondary rôles ; and even these rôles are modified and varied at need. A new force rises in the Delta, and it is in the Delta that historical interest now concentrates, before it spreads to the Valley.

The Delta has preserved very few documents indeed, compared with the Valley, and that for physical reasons. The soil, often swampy and everywhere damper than in the Valley, does not keep the vestiges of the past so well or so long ; intensive cultivation demands the constant working of the rich, fertile ground, and ruins and waste land are barely tolerated ; and lastly, the Delta is not set among the rocky cliffs of the Libyan and Arabian deserts, where the inhabitants of the Valley found everlasting sites for their flint workshops, their first villages, and their later tombs and temples. In consequence, the history of the Delta, in all periods, is far less accessible than that of the Valley. Fortunately, this lack of archæological evidence is compensated by the Pyramid Texts, which were written by priests of Heliopolis at the end of the Vth Dynasty (about 2540), being based on a fund of legends and traditions which they had collected in the Delta. The intellectual activity of the inhabitants of the Delta is magnificently displayed in this Corpus of history with a purpose, fiction, and philosophical speculation. It was well up to the level of the material prosperity of the country, where the excellence of the soil and the vast extent of the cultivable land favoured the development of a dense, hard-working, progressive population.

It was in Lower Egypt that the Egyptians were first confronted with the great social problems, for it was here that collective labour first had to be organized on a very large scale. It is therefore probable that the first attempts to unify religious and political power were carried out by chiefs of the Delta.

The second stage in this half divine, half human history is marked by a transformation of the Delta. Through the veil of religious tradition, we have caught a glimpse of the unified kingdom of Lower Egypt, under the protection of Horus of the Two Eyes. The Delta is now divided into two groups of nomes, Western and Eastern. (Map I.)

In the West an influx of people of Libyan stock occurred.[1] What we to-day call the Libyan *desert* was known to the

---

[1] *Imen*, West, also means the right side; the Egyptians took their bearings facing south.

For our knowledge of the protohistoric Delta we have no sources but the politico-religious traditions preserved by the Pyramid Texts and by the reliefs on Vth Dynasty temples depicting the Sed-feast, the latter being supplemented by temples of the late period. The foundations of these researches were laid by the last editor of the Pyramid Texts, Prof. Kurt Sethe, in a series of publications : " Die Namen von Ober- und Unteraegypten," in **XII**, 44, pp. 1–29 (1907) ; " Zur altaegyptischen Sage vom Sonnenauge," in **XXXIX**, v, 3 (1912) ; " Ausdrücke für Rechts und Links," in *Nachrichten d. Göttinger Gesellschaft*, 1922.

The questions raised by the Vth Dynasty reliefs have been discussed by F. W. von Bissing and H. Kees in " Untersuchungen zu den Reliefs aus dem Re-Heiligtum des Rathures," pt. i, 1922 (*Abhandlungen d. Bayrischen Akad. d. Wiss., philos.-philolog. Klasse*, vol. xxxii), and by H. Kees, " Horus and Seth als Götterpaar," 1923–4 (*Mitt. d. Vorderasiatisch-Aegyptischen Ges.*, 28–9 Jahrg.). One may also mention H. Junker, *Die Onurislegende* (*K. Akad. Wien, philos.-philolog. Klasse, Denkschriften*, vol. lix), and Patrick Boylan, *Thoth, the Hermes of Egypt*, 1922, in which these questions are regarded from other points of view. I myself discussed these subjects at the Collège de France, in 1925, from the Pyramid Texts. Here I give only a very brief account of these highly complex and little investigated problems.

ancients (at least in the neighbourhood of the Delta) under a
very different aspect. The land was sandy, but covered here
and there by pastures, supporting huge herds of oxen, asses,
and sheep, and rich in trees.[1] There dwelled the Tehenu,
half nomadic, half sedentary, hunters, herdsmen, and
caravan-leaders, armed with arrows and boomerangs.

Their penetration into the western part of the Delta is
attested by the epithets borne by the gods of the nomes on
the Libyan side.[2] The 3rd Nome (West) worshipped a " Horus
Tehenu who lifts the arm up high " (the action of a hunter

Fig. 16.—Booty from Libya (*Tehen*).
Oxen, asses, sheep, trees. Protohistoric palette.

with his boomerang ?).[3] The goddess Neith, in the 4th and
5th Nomes, carries a hunter's arrows, crossed on the dappled
hide of an animal, and is also called " the Libyan " (Tehenut).
The epithet "Western", *Iment*, which was later given to
all the Libyan side of the Delta, is expressed in writing
by an ostrich feather, either alone, stuck in the ground, or
fixed in front of a falcon; now, this feather was an ornament
of the Libyans, who wore it in their hair.

---

[1] Probably not olives. See Charles Dubois, " L'Olivier dans l'ancienne
Égypte," in *Revue de Philologie*, 1925, p. 60.
[2] In *Pyr.*, § 908, there is an obscure allusion to " the boomerangs which
preside at Letopolis ". This 2nd Nome had undergone Libyan penetration.
[3] The 3rd Nome was called " Libyan " in the Greek period.

The temples of the Vth Dynasty preserved the memory of a time when these 3rd and 5th Nomes, together with the 7th (Harpoon), were grouped under the leadership of the goddess West (Iment), in the form of a woman wearing the characteristic feather on her head. Behind her, at the Sed-feast, march the Libyan Horus, the Libyan Neith, and Horus of Buto, and sometimes this last also holds the ensign of the West. In this case, the hieroglyphic for " West " is not a mere geographical name, but a banner, leading a group of nomes. This political and social character of the Western ensign *Iment* is very ancient. On a palette which bears the name of a Thinite King (now effaced),[1] we see warriors starting for the chase, guided by the Iment ; opposite them is another clan, preceded by the ensign of the East, the *Iabt*. These two signs, which later indicate merely the cardinal points, here have the concrete, living value of tribal emblems.[2] The religious texts always respected this classification of the gods by their districts of origin and ethnical features. The patron spirits of the West formed a group of " Souls of the West ", *Bau Imenti* and the Wolf Upuat, " He who opens the roads," born at Buto,[3] was named " He who presides over the West ", *Khenti-Iment*, an epithet which originally expressed Upuat's political ascendancy in the Western Delta.[4]

FIG. 17.—The Sign *Iment.*

The presidency of the Wolf Upuat, or the reign of this or that god, means that the royal power is in the hands of a clan or an individual, who exercises it in the name of that god. It was just in this western region that the monarchical institution got some of its significant features. The goddess Neith wears on her head the Red Crown [5] ; Wazet, the goddess of Buto, also has " the Mansions of the Red Crown " in her city ; and this crown, itself a goddess, was always to designate the Pharaoh of Lower Egypt.[6] The oil used for anointing the

---

[1] Reproduced in *From Tribe to Empire*, p. 127.
[2] V. Loret, in **VIII**, vol. xi, p. 78.
[3] *Pyr.*, § 1438.
[4] Only later did it have a funerary significance, when the West came to mean the necropolis.
[5] One of the names of the Red Crown, *Net*, is the same in sound as that of Neith (*Net*, from *Nert*).
[6] Cf. *From Tribe to Empire*, p. 132.

brows of gods and kings, mentioned as early as the Thinite monuments, was called *hatet*, perhaps in memory of the Libyan chiefs, the *Hatiu*,[1] but its epithet was " the Libyan ".[2] In the pyramids Pharaoh is likened to Upuat, who presides over the West, and is complimented in these terms : " You take the great White Crown from (the hands of) these very great foreigners who preside over the Libyans." [3]   These allusions refer to a past shared in common by the Western Delta and Libya.   It is an admissible hypothesis that in the protohistoric period there was an Egypto-Libyan kingdom of the West, with its axis on the great fluvial artery of the Western Delta, the Canopic Arm, and its centre—to judge from the importance of Neith in the Thinite period and in other historical epochs—probably at Saïs.

II

THE CONFEDERATION OF THE EASTERN NOMES OF THE DELTA

On the same Thinite palette which shows the Falcon of the West leading his men to the chase, there is another band of warriors, led by the ensign of the East, *Iabt*.[4]   While the West is marked by the ostrich-feather which the Libyans stuck in their hair, the East, a land of copper and other metals, is represented by a spear-head, probably of metal, or perhaps an ingot.   The temples of the Vth Dynasty perpetuate the tradition of the two forces opposed symmetrically—the gods of the East, led by the ingot Iabt, and those of the West, led by the Libyan feather Iment.[5]   In the Sed-feast the East leads

FIG. 18.—The Sign *Iabt*.

the procession, parallel to the West,[6] and in the religious texts we find, corresponding to the " Souls of the West ", the " Souls of the East ", *Bau Iabti*.

---

[1] Sethe, in Borchardt, *Das Grabdenkmal des Königs Sahure*, ii, Text, p. 73. The bringing of this oil to Pharaoh is attested by many royal palettes of the Thinite period.

[2] *Pyr.*, § 450 : *Tehent*.

[3] *Pyr.*, § 455.   The White Crown was later that of Upper Egypt.

[4] *From Tribe to Empire*, p. 127.

[5] *Sahure*, ii, pl. 11, 27.

[6] E. Naville, *Festival Hall*, pl. ix, 3.

For the existence in the Eastern Delta of a confederation of nomes under one leader we have definite evidence in the Pyramid Texts. There are several references to a personage of heroic aspect, " him who is in the Nome Anzti, chief commander of his nomes " (*herj zaza spaut-f*) [1] ; twice he is called Anzti, " he who presides over the Eastern Nomes " (*khenti spaut Iabti*). The context adds two significant features: when the dead King receives in heaven confirmation of all his royal office and all his domains, when he holds in his hands his sceptre and his club, to preside over men and gods (Spirits), then he is like

> Upuat, who presides over the West ;
> Anzti, who presides over the Nomes of the East. [2]

So there were two confederations of nomes, Western and Eastern, each under the command of a chief. Now let us see of what nomes the East was composed, and what was the character of their leader.

Among the Eastern nomes north of Heliopolis,[3] distributed right and left of the great fluvial artery of the Eastern Delta,

the Damietta Arm, there was, first, the 9th, that of Anzti himself. Of the others, two seem certainly to have existed in very ancient times—the 10th, the Great Black Bull, the 11th, the Heseb Bull, and the 12th, the Calf, which were founded by clans of herdsmen and husbandmen, and the 16th, in the swamps, with the ensign of the Silurus Fish. Along the Isthmus, near

Fig. 19.—The Black Bull (10th Nome).

the Bitter Lakes, the 8th Nome, Eastern Harpoon, lies symmetrically opposite the 7th, the Western Harpoon ; and the 14th Nome, Point of the East, *Khent-Iabt*, has the administrative name suitable to its geographical position. The town of Anzti occupies a central position with reference to " his nomes ", symmetrically with Saïs and in the same latitude.   Just as Saïs stands on the great western

---

[1] *Pyr.*, § 182.   Anzti is the name both of the hero and of the 9th Nome ; here the ensign and the god of the nome are fused.

[2] *Pyr.*, §§ 218–20 ; cf. 1833 : " Nut has made Osiris to rise as King of the South and of the North, in all his (royal) office . . . like Upuat Khenti-Iment (an interpolation follows) and like Anzti Khenti-Iabt."

[3] We do not know whether Heliopolis was at this time part of the " East ".

fluvial artery, the Rosetta Arm, so Busiris dominates the Damietta Arm.

The chief of this kingdom, Anzti, presents a very personal aspect. Alone of the ensigns of the nomes he has human form.[1]

In the classical period Anzti is represented as a man standing with his left foot forward, with two symmetrical feathers on his head, one hand raising the shepherd's crook in a gesture of authority and the other carrying the cowherd's whip horizontal. In the Pyramids he appears differently. In these texts figures of men and animals were mutilated on principle, for fear lest they should come to life and show themselves hostile to the dead man. Accordingly, Anzti is portrayed in only half his person, stuck on a pole—characteristic of the emblems of the earliest periods—without even the usual stand beneath him. He is an eerie figure, on his squared plot of ground, something like a scarecrow in a field. This is, perhaps, the most ancient image of a human ruler that the history of Egypt has left us.

Fig.20.—Anzti on his Nome.

From his appearance Anzti seems much earlier than the Thinite Kings ; his person, his attributes, his attitude of command, all indicate that he is a human hero deified. In his summary outline the very name which he bore is expressed—the " Protector ",[2] or the " Shepherd of Peoples ", who led the men of his kingdom, as he led his flocks and herds, with crook and whip.

Now this Anzti disappears from the historical and religious texts after the Pyramids ; his name no longer appears in the lists of the northern nomes, save as ensign of the 9th. Why ? Because he is supplanted, in his own province and everywhere else, by a god who takes his province and his name—Osiris.

In the Pyramids there is an invocation to Osiris which recounts the services done by Horus, Son of Isis, to his father :

---

[1] If we except the Children of the 18th and 19th Nomes, who may not have existed at this period.

[2] Anzti is derived from the root *ânz, âz*, " to be in good condition." As the name of an agent, with the inflexion *ti*, it would mean " he who keeps in good condition ", " protector ". The most ancient title of the Nomarch is *âz mer,* " protector of the water-channel, or irrigated land."

" He has set thee before the gods ; he has made thee to take possession of every crown . . . Horus has made thee to live in this thy name of *Anzti.*" [1] So we find that the capital of the 9th Nome, still keeping its old patron Anzti as its ensign, is called, in the very earliest texts known, " House of Osiris," the Busiris of the Greeks, who faithfully rendered the Osirian name in their transcription. The historical interest shifts, and from Anzti we pass on to Osiris.

III

OSIRIS AND HORUS, SON OF ISIS, THE TRADITIONAL FOUNDERS OF THE KINGSHIP. THE HISTORICAL SIGNIFICANCE OF THE LEGENDS

Who was this Osiris, who was to take such an important place in the religious, social, and political ideas of the Egyptians ? To answer this question, let us examine a fetish, the *Zed*, which is inseparably associated with Osiris and is probably the primitive form of the god.[2] The very name of the town of Busiris was Zedu, the City of the Zed, and in the 16th Nome, where the Silurus also surrendered his capital, Mendes, to Osiris, the new god was again represented by the Zed, the capital being called Zedet after it. What, then, was the Zed ?

The oldest form is found on granite pillars erected in the temple at Hieraconpolis by King Khasekhemui, of the IInd Thinite Dynasty (Fig. 21).

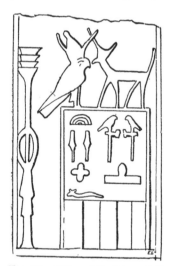

FIG. 21.—Pillar of the Horus-Seth Khasekhemui, adorned with the Zed of Osiris and the Knot of Isis. Cairo.

[1] § 614. Note that in § 648 a similar passage calls on Osiris by his name of Khent-Imenti, " He who presides over the West."

[2] There is no plausible reason for doubting that the Zed was associated with Osiris from the very beginning. At Hieraconpolis it is already connected with the Knot of Isis, another Osirian emblem. Quibell, *Hiérakonpolis*, pl. 2, 59. See Fig. 21 above.

For a long time two possible interpretations held the field.[1] Some regarded it as a pillar with four capitals, one above the other; that is, really, a drawing of four pillars seen one behind the other, according to Egyptian rules of perspective. Others took it for the lopped trunk of a tree with the stumps of branches, highly conventionalized, on the upper part. This latter seems to be the right interpretation; it is based on a passage in the Pyramid Texts, on which Mr. Newberry has made an ingenious commentary.[2] Osiris, mourned by his two consort-sisters, Isis and Nephthys, is far away from Egypt, beyond the " Very Green " (the Mediterranean); but he is restored to life and comes back to the Delta across the sea. " Thou takest the two oars, the one of *uân* wood, the other of *sez* wood, and thou goest over the basin of thy house, the Very Green." [3] Now the word *sez*, which is used for a tree whose wood has been taken to make an oar, is represented by a sign (Fig. 22) in which we see one of the forms given to the Zed on the monuments; this sign seems to depict the Zed, not yet completely conventionalized. Furthermore, the *uân* is the juniper, often mentioned by the Egyptian texts as a Syrian shrub,

Fig. 22.—Zed pillar and *Sez* Tree, from the Pyramids

while the *sez*, according to the sign representing it on the Pyramids, is a bigger tree, with horizontal, parallel branches— that is, a conifer. Lebanon, where the story is evidently laid, has three conifers [4]: the cedar (the Egyptian *sib*),[5] the fir (the Egyptian *âsh*), and the cypress, of which the variety with horizontal branches is probably the *sez*. The Zed, depicted as the *sez*, seems to be some kind of conifer. Such trees do not exist in Egypt, any more than the fir (*âsh*), of which the texts say that it comes from Osiris, or that its rustlings recall the plaints of

[1] Maspero, **XX**, i, p. 130; Moret, **XXIX**, p. 13.
[2] *Egypt as a Field for Anthropological Research*, 1923, p. 14.
[3] *Pyr.*, §1751. The Syrian origin of this episode is confirmed by the text: " Hathor, the Lady of Byblos, she makes the oars of thy boat." This text appears on the sarcophagi of the XIIth Dynasty (**XII**, xlv, 1908, p. 8), where the *âsh*, or Byblos fir, is also mentioned.
[4] Newberry, loc. cit., p. 14. According to Loret, the *âsh* is the fir.
[5] Loret, *La Flore pharaonique*, p. 41.

the dead god.[1]   Therefore the origin of the fetish Zed is probably to be sought on the coast of Syria, beyond that sea which Osiris crossed.

At this point we must make a clear distinction between certain features of the Osirian legend and the personality of Osiris as a whole.   The fetish Zed, resembling the lopped trunk of a Syrian tree, and certain other details or episodes may well have come from Syria ; but we need not conclude that Osiris himself was of foreign origin.   Was it not natural for the Egyptians, in their essentially agricultural country, to think of a vegetation-god for themselves, as all agricultural peoples do ?   The undoubted similarities which exist between Osiris and Adonis, the vegetation-god of Byblos, do not for a moment imply that he is a double of the Syrian god, transplanted to the banks of the Nile.   From the earliest historical times Syrian ships visited the ports of the Delta, and Egyptians settled with their gods, Osiris and Isis-Hathor, at Byblos.   There was mutual contamination between the myths of Osiris and of Adonis.   The episodes of the Osiris-legend which take place at Byblos may, therefore, be explained by the political and commercial relations which the Thinite and Memphite Egyptians maintained with the Syrians.[2]

The Zed, the fetish of a tree-god, recalls but one aspect of Osiris.   Many other features are of purely Egyptian origin. In the very earliest texts Osiris appears as a god of nature, personifying, not only vegetation, but various permanent forces of the life of the universe.   Son of Earth (Geb) and Sky (Nut), Osiris appears in several forms, which involve no contradiction.   For example, he personifies the water of sky and earth ; although the Nile is already represented by a special, anthropomorphic god, named Hapi, the fertilizing virtue of the river, which is manifested on earth after the inundation, is Osiris.   This is how his coming is hymned.

> The water of life which is in the sky, it comes. The water of life which is in the earth, it comes. The sky burns (with lightning) for thee, the earth trembles for thee, before the birth of the God. The two mountains [3] are

---

[1] **XII**, xlv, p. 41.
[2] Cf. *From Tribe to Empire*, pp. 163, 177.
[3] The two cliffs between which the Nile passes at the First Cataract.

opened, and the God manifests himself, the God takes possession of his body (the land of Egypt).[1]

The deceased King is compared to Osiris in these terms :—

He came, like the tide which comes before the fullness of the flood. . . . He came towards his well-watered lands, to the shore (bathed) by the inundation during the great rising, to the place of offerings, to the green fields.[2]

So, too, in the legend, when Horus seeks his father Osiris, he finds him at the moment when he is reborn, " is renewed, is rejuvenated, in his name of *Water of Renewal*." [3]

In the hymns of the New Kingdom, Osiris is clearly identified with Hapi, the special god of the Nile.

Thou art Hapi the Great, on the day of the flood-time, at the beginning of the year. Gods and men live by the moisture which is in thee.[4]

Osiris, as we have seen, also personifies trees, the force of vegetation. Now, there were in Egypt special gods for the trees, and for wheat (Nepri),[5] but Osiris was, in a way, their Spirit, their sap, the power by which they turned green.

Oh, he whose tree is green, the God who is on his field ! Oh, the God who opens the flower, who is on his sycamore ! Oh, the God, the shining shape of the banks, who is on his palm-tree ! O Lord of the green fields ! [6]

Trees and plants greet in Osiris the beneficent water which makes them live.

Thou art the flood among the fields growing green, the flood come to the children of Geb (the earth) . . . the *iam* tree is thy servant, the *nbs* tree bows its head towards thee.[7]

In his name of Water of Renewal, Renpu, Osiris presides over the *renput*, the first fruits and vegetables which appear, reborn, after the inundation every year.[8] Lastly, he is the " Lord of the flowering vine ".[9] In the later texts all these features are accentuated, made more definite, and treated didactically. In the *Book of the Dead*, Osiris declares : " I live as the Corn God (Nepri) ; I am the wheat (*bedet*)."

These traditions were afterwards greatly elaborated in Diodorus and Plutarch, and we shall return to them when we

---

[1] *Pyr.*, § 2063.   [2] *Pyr.*, § 507.   [3] *Pyr.*, § 589.
[4] XXth Dynasty hymn, in **XII**, 1884, p. 38.
[5] Represented in the temple of Sahura (Borchardt, ii, pl. 30) as an anthropomorphic god (like the Nile in every respect), but with his skin dotted with grains of corn.
[6] *Pyr.*, § 699.   [7] *Pyr.*, § 1018.
[8] *Pyr.*, §§ 874, 965.   [9] *Pyr.*, § 1524.

speak of religion. Here we are trying to bring together the various elements of which the primitive Osiris was formed, and we note that he ends by embodying the universal power of fecundation. All that oasis created by the Nile, aired by the north wind, thanks to the draught created by the current of the river, green with meadows, golden with harvests, red with the blood of vines, a paradise of water, fruit, and flowers between two torrid deserts, was the work of Osiris ; more, it was Osiris himself. In the Pyramid Texts these various characteristics all appear in this hymn, addressed to the Nile, which gives the whole personality of Osiris.

> This thy secret place [1] is the great hall of Osiris, which brings the wind. On to it the north wind bears, which raises thee, like Osiris. To thee the God of the Winepress comes, with the water of the grape . . . They tremble, who see Hapi when he thrashes (his waves), but the meadows smile, the banks flower, the offerings of the Gods come down, men do homage, and the heart of the Gods is lifted up.[2]

Now, in the fresh imagination of primitive men, the gods of vegetation or creative forces of nature become the heroes of a drama setting forth the inevitable vicissitudes through which they pass in their earthly course as the seasons come round. The Nile rises, overflows, and then shrinks until it looks as if it would dry up. The corn comes out of the ground, turns green, sends up a golden ear, and then dies, mown down by the sickle, broken in pieces by the flail, and ground by the stone which makes it into flour and by the teeth of hungry man. The vine, having brought forth its grapes, bleeds beneath the trampling feet of men and in the winepress. The tree gives its flowers and fruits, then withers and dies. Then comes the miracle. In the fertile earth the buried corn germinates and rises into the light ; the sap ferments in vine and tree ; the water rises ; and every year when the Nile has risen flowers, corn, and fruit are born again. From this abundance, dwindling to poverty, from this annual death followed by resurrection, the Sumerians took their myth of Dummuzi and the Syrians that of Adonis ; the Greeks conceived Dionysos ; the Egyptians had Osiris. The legend of Osiris, as told by Diodorus and Plutarch, is the beneficent *life* of a god, the inventor of agriculture, who *dies* murdered,

---

[1] *Tepehet*, the secret place from which the Nile was supposed to rise, at Elephantine.
[2] *Pyr.*, §§ 1551–4.

is *broken in pieces*, and manifests himself again in a *resurrection*—all characteristic stages in most agrarian myths. It is probable that, in his primitive form of an agricultural god, living, dead, and resurrected in turn, Osiris was of popular origin and worshipped everywhere.

New circumstances were to transform this universal nature-god into a political and local deity, with profound effects upon his character and his legend.

While his worshippers among the people made Osiris a victim who fell only to rise again, the hero of a Passion, one clan, or several clans, of warriors made his fetish tree, the Zed, a " banner ". They set it up in towns which would hence-forward be called the cities of the Zed—Busiris and Mendes. At the former city, Osiris supplanted the " Protector " Anzti, and established himself as " the Chief who presides over the Eastern Nomes " [1]; and so he became a political sovereign in the Eastern Delta. Far from abandoning the external signs of Anzti's power, he appropriated them to himself. One might say that Osiris stepped into his predecessor's skin ; the human form of a chieftain, the crest of feathers, the crook, the whip, and the very name of Anzti, Osiris assumed them all and so effectively that he would never lose them. The god of water and green things, fluid and varied, having many shapes and names, now concentrated his character and his power in the form of a shepherd of men, which he seems to have taken entirely from Anzti.

From Busiris, the followers of Osiris spread all over the Delta. No record tells us of their conquest ; but their advance and its stages are clearly marked by the annexation to the Osiris legend of gods and goddesses who were originally unconnected and worshipped in other places. In the 12th Nome, north of Busiris, there dwelt at Per-hebit [2] a goddess Isis. She had a famous Iseium there until late times, and its ruins still exist. It is suspected that this was the original habitation of the goddess who was placed at the side of

[1] See above, p. 78.
[2] The city was also called Neter, " the Divine " (*Pyr.*, §§ 2188, 1268).

Osiris as sister and wife, after her domain had been conquered by the men of Busiris.

Other eastern nomes then yielded up their falcon-Horuses, and later the ibis Thoth, to the Osirian family. From the east Osiris conquered the Western Delta. In the Harpoon, his power was established near Buto, at Chemmis, where Isis and Horus the Younger, her son, became so powerful that the goddess Wazet, ancient in sovereignty, shrank, as it were, into Buto, her own capital. Neith, the patroness of Saïs, the Libyan Horus of the Western Nome, and the warrior-wolf Upuat, entered, alive as they were, into the Osirian party; they must, therefore, have been conquered by the worshippers of Osiris. At Letopolis itself, the capital of the ancient sovereign of Lower Egypt, Horus of the Two Eyes, the spread of the power of Osiris is shown by the name of the *pehu* (territory), which was called the " Basin of Anzti " ; so the men of Busiris must have advanced that far.[1]

No doubt this sketch of the Osirian conquest is nothing more than a provisional hypothesis. There is no narrative document enabling us to date these stages, or to determine other points reached. But two things are certain ; there were in the Delta many religious centres where Isis, Horus, Thoth, Anubis, and Upuat reigned, and these cults were originally independent of Osiris.

How these gods and cities came into the orbit of the Osirian group, we do not know. Yet the Osiris legend, the essential elements of which are scattered about the Pyramid Texts, shows these gods as attached to Osiris. It was after the conquest of the Delta by the worshippers of Osiris that the legend took on the form in which we know it. Let us, then, examine it briefly, from a historical point of view, and try to arrange its successive elements.

The legend of Osiris contains four chief elements—the life, death, and resurrection of Osiris, and the transmission of his royal power to his son Horus.

---

[1] For the names of places and their ancient patrons, see J. de Rougé, *Géographie ancienne de la Basse-Égypte.*

The Life.[1]—Osiris was a great king, who had succeeded his father Geb (Earth) as lord of the terrestrial world. He taught men agriculture, making them acquainted with wheat, barley, the vine, and other useful plants, and thus abolished cannibalism. So he was the inventor of bread, beer, and wine, the staple foodstuffs of the Egyptian people. He also gave them laws and taught them to honour the gods. He conquered Upper Egypt, where he found mines of gold and copper, and he disclosed to the Egyptians the art of metal-working. Later, he extended his pacific conquest to the whole earth, everywhere teaching agriculture to men and introducing them to all the benefits of civilization.[2] In this labour of love, Osiris was not alone ; his wife Isis was his helpmate in various capacities. As a skilful sorceress she took an equal share in the agricultural inventions ascribed to Osiris [3] ; as an experienced queen she made codes of law, and ruled Egypt in person while her husband was conquering the world.[4] In addition, Thoth invented writing and the arts which beautify human life, and served Osiris with his gifts as an administrator ; he was the Vizier and sacred scribe of the kingdom.[5] Lastly, a dog-god, Anubis, and a wolf-god, Upuat,[6] the allies of Osiris, according to the Egyptian texts (his sons, according to Diodorus), accompanied him on his campaigns of conquest.

In the agricultural inventions of Osiris it is easy to see the boons which, in tradition, an agricultural god dispenses to his worshippers. The other characteristics must come from Anzti, for it is only after his fusion with the " Protector " of the Eastern Delta that we find Osiris as a king, with the insignia of command. In the nomes conquered by Osiris, in which Isis, Thoth, Upuat, and Anubis reigned as local gods, the latter were not evicted, but became the fellow-

---

[1] This résumé follows the accounts of Diodorus (i, 13 ff.) and Plutarch (*De Iside*, 12 ff.), whose details almost all go back to very early times, and are confirmed in the Pyramid Texts by allusions varying in extensiveness.

[2] The Egyptian text corresponding to this account is in the *Hymn to Osiris* engraved on a stele of the Bibliothèque Nationale, now in the Louvre, ll. 9–13. See below, p. 97.

[3] On the connexion of magic with agricultural skill, see Davy in *From Tribe to Empire*, p. 105. Women are sometimes accredited with the initiation of ocial customs (ibid., pp. 30–1).

[4] *Hymn*, l. 14.

[5] Cf. Boylan, *Thoth*, p. 53.

[6] Called Macedon by Diodorus (i, 18).

workers of Osiris. It will be noted that all have a personality and characteristics of their own. Isis is an heiress who, on her marriage with Osiris, brings as much as she receives ; in accordance with matriarchal custom, she reigns and administers by the side of her husband.[1] Thoth is already the scribe, the guardian of the arts and laws. Anubis and Upuat are still, as in the Pyramids, warrior-gods,[2] the allies, not the subjects, of Osiris. The legend admits implicitly that each continues to be the god of his nome, but Osiris " presides over " their federation.

The Death.—In the twenty-eighth year of his reign (or life), Osiris was slain by his brother Typhon (Seth), his violent and impious rival, and seventy-two fellow-conspirators. This happened on the 17th of the month Hathor (Greek Athyr, probably our November). The story was that Seth jestingly persuaded Osiris to get into a chest, which was at once closed and thrown into the Nile. Thus " drowned " in the river,[3] Osiris floated down through the Tanitic Mouth into the sea, and then to the coast of Byblos. Isis, seeking her husband in despair, found him at Byblos and brought the body in a coffin to Buto. Then Seth, hunting one night by the light of the moon, saw the coffin, and cut the body into fourteen (or more) pieces, which he distributed among his accomplices, that he might involve them all in his crime and be sure of their support.

The legend does not explain Seth's hatred for his brother. But the murder needed no explanation, for it was an unavoidable fate, repeated every year. Plutarch rightly describes Seth's deed as a phenomenon of nature. Seth was by destiny at war with Osiris ; he was the barren red desert, the stormy, drought-bearing wind, the born enemy of the fertilizing water and the vegetation which adorned the Black Land. All creative acts and good things came from Osiris, all destruction and badness belonged to Seth.[4] The rivalry of the divine brothers was that of two cosmic, universal gods. The traditional day of the death of Osiris fell at the fatal time when the Nile sank, and the desert wind began to

---

[1] Cf. *From Tribe to Empire*, pp. 29 ff.
[2] On this subject, see E. Meyer, **XII,** 1904, p. 104.
[3] Osiris is often called the Drowned One, he who is in the water, *mehi* (*Pyr.*, § 388, and text of Shabaka).
[4] *De Iside*, 45.

blow, and the trees shed their leaves, while the wheat-ear, already cut down by the sickle and beaten on the threshing-floor or trampled underfoot,[1] was broken up into grains to be buried in the earth. Here, again, all these features belong to the agricultural god and are part of the original core of the legend. It is the same with the story of the chest which went to Byblos. Landing in the country of Adonis, Osiris benefited by the worship there paid to tree-gods. A shrub of the Syrian coast, the erica, spread its leaves over the chest, and the stalk grew so big and strong that it surrounded it and hid it completely. " The king of the country, struck by the size of the bush, bade men cut the stalk which hid the chest in its bosom, and made it into a pillar to hold the roof of his palace." We may take it for probable that the Zed, the lopped trunk of a Syrian tree, which was the emblem of Osiris, was a memory of the adventure of Osiris at Byblos.[2]

The Resurrection.—After the death of Osiris, Isis takes first place in the story. It is she who transforms the god of water and vegetation, lying still in death, into a resurrected god. The body was mutilated. Isis, in her distress, set out upon a tragic *search* ; she *sought*, she *found*, and she *recognized*, one after another, every limb except the genital organs, which had been eaten by a fish, the oxyrrhynchus. Whenever Isis found a part of the body of Osiris, she set up a tomb on the spot, and that was why one found so many tombs of Osiris in Egypt.[3]

Even more was expected of the wisdom of Isis ; death must be vanquished. Isis, the great magician, " invented the remedy which gives immortality," and restored Osiris to life.[4] About this mystery the Greek texts maintain a religious silence, but the Pyramid Texts describe the means which she used. Isis and her allies, Thoth, Anubis, and Nephthys, collected the scattered limbs, protected the perishable flesh against corruption, and made of it an eternal body, *zet*,

[1] According to Diodurus (i, 14), in harvest-time, the first ears were given as an offering, and the Egyptian peasants called on Isis as they threshed the corn. The breaking-up of the corn caused the goddess to mourn over the dismembered body of her husband.

[2] In the Pyramids (§ 1485) there are invocations to the tree (called a sycamore) " which enfolds Osiris ", and other features of the erica story.

[3] According to the lists of nomes engraved in the Ptolemaic temples, each capital preserved a bit of the body of Osiris in its temple.

[4] Diod., i, 25. The *Hymn to Osiris* lays stress upon the magical knowledge of Isis ; see below, p. 98.

the first mummy, in which Osiris should live for ever. But
this new life was that of a king withdrawn from the world,
of a deified hero who, while still the protector of his race, left
the management of things to his successor.

These stories belong to the primitive foundation of the
legend. Osiris is reborn, like the grain which, buried in
November, rises from the ground in spring, like the tree
which sprouts new branches, like the Nile which the annual
flood reawakens from apparent death (Fig. 23). Every year
the " old god " of the husbandmen gives place to a scion full
of life, in whom his ancestor recommences, without, however,
being confused with him.   So, in the Osiris myth, the dead
god, called away to a superhuman life, is succeeded by his
son, full of new sap and vital force.[1]

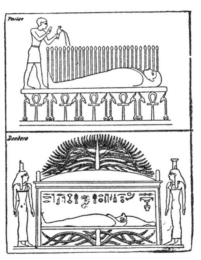

FIG. 23.—The Vegetable Resurrection of Osiris.

The Father Avenged by his Son.—We come to the last
episode in the legend. The son of Osiris, like the new wheat,
like the rising Nile, like the opening bud, is born after his
father's death ; he is a posthumous child.[2] Isis became a

---

[1] On this subject, see Frazer's fine work, *Adonis, Attis, Osiris.*

[2] *De Iside,* 19 : " Isis, with whom Osiris had had intercourse *after his death,*
bore him a son before her time . . . He is called Harpocrates."   This name
comes from *Hr pa kherd,* " Horus the Child," the epithet by which, in the Pyramid
Texts, one can distinguish Horus of Chemmis from Horus the Elder, the god of
Letopolis.

mother by supernatural means, which she took from magic. She contrived to reanimate the corpse of Osiris so that she was impregnated by the dead god ; so Horus is called the son of Isis, much more than of Osiris. He was born at Chemmis, in the swamps of Lake Burlus, not far from Buto, and was reared " in solitude ", in danger of the attacks of his uncle Seth. When he grew up he devoted himself solely to the duty of " avenger of his father ".[1] Many Egyptians went over to the side of Horus,[2] including even the concubine of Seth. In the end Horus and his following defeated Seth and his supporters after a battle lasting several days. Seth, however, took the dispute before a court of gods. " He brought a suit against Horus concerning his legitimacy ; but Horus, with the aid of Hermes (Thoth), obtained recognition from the gods,[3] and conquered Seth in two more battles. After that, Horus succeeded his father." Diodorus (i, 25) makes this remark : " Horus seems to have been the last god to reign in Egypt after the departure of his father for the sky."

We come back to earth with this episode of the " father avenged by his son ". The myth here takes on a historical aspect. The episode tells us how the kingdom of the Lord of the Eastern Nomes was transmitted to an heir, a falcon-god, consequently called Horus, or Horus the Young Child (*Hor pa kherd*), to distinguish him from the sky-god, Horus of Letopolis. In the Pyramid Texts, the rôle of Horus " the Avenger of his Father " (*Nez-itef*) is fully described, but it is made clear that he is not a normal son of Osiris.

We are told that Isis contrived to be impregnated by the slain god, to whom her magical arts had restored his virile force ; and the picture of Isis impregnated by the mummy of Osiris appears in the texts and the temple paintings,[4] as the highest evidence of the miracles which she performed.

---

[1] All this passage is in *De Iside*, 19. " When Osiris, returning from Hades, asked his son Horus what should be regarded as the noblest action, Horus replied, ' To avenge his father and mother on those who did them harm.' " In the Pyramid Texts, it is said that Horus avenges his father on him who has done him harm (§ 850).

[2] The supporters of Horus are mentioned : πολλῶν μετατιθεμένων ἀεὶ πρὸς τὸν Ὧρον, and τῶν περὶ τὸν Ὧρον. They are the equivalent of the *Shemsu-Hor* of the Egyptian texts.

[3] Compare the *Hymn to Osiris*, below, p. 99.

[4] *Pyr.*, §§ 632, 1635. See *Hymn to Osiris* below, p. 99. Cf. the relief at Abydos, Pl. VII, 3.

The connexion between Osiris and Horus the Child is, therefore, fairly loose. In the early form of the legend, Osiris was killed before he had a son. So it was not Horus who first paid the funeral duty to his " drowned " father, but Geb, the father of Osiris, and Anubis and Thoth, his allies. But Osiris had to have a son, to succeed to the kingdom and to avenge his father for the crime of Seth. Therefore the miraculous pregnancy of Isis, after the death of her husband, was invented. Why was this heir chosen among the falcon-gods ? It was probably in order to bring into the Osiris myth a Horus, who could, in view of the name, be passed off as the mighty King of Heaven, Horus of Letopolis.

Originally the god who was afterwards called Horus, Son of Isis, Horus the Child, was merely a local falcon, born at Chemmis, where his mother, Isis the Great, was sovereign. The Pyramid Texts tell briefly how the falcon of Chemmis became the heir of Osiris.

" When Osiris went down to the Very Green (brought back from Byblos by Isis), the Very Green bowed its head and lowered its arms before him. Then the Gods, the Children of the Sky, made the Red Crowns bloom [1] for Isis the Great, for her who put on the crown (girdle ?) in Chemmis, who made libation for her son, young Horus, when he crossed the land with his white sandals, and set forth to see his father Osiris." [2] The old capital of the Red Crown of Lower Egypt, Buto (*Pe*), acclaimed Horus when he left Chemmis and went away, purified, to " avenge his father." [3]

In this way Horus, after Osiris, became sacred chief of the Delta. He took possession of Letopolis, and henceforward Horus the Younger, son of Isis, was blended to his advantage with Horus the Elder, Horus of the Two Eyes, of Letopolis. The younger took up the feuds of the elder, and consequently the periodic " fight " between Horus the Elder, god of the sky, and Seth of Ombos became the personal affair of Horus the Younger. In the agricultural myth, Seth, as god of the desert, was the natural enemy of Osiris, the god of vegetation and the Nile. On to this endless conflict there was now grafted the political rivalry which formerly divided the sovereigns of Upper and Lower Egypt. Horus gathered together his

---

[1] At Buto the red crowns were kept in a mansion. Cf. above, p. 76.
[2] *Pyr.*, § 1213.   [3] *Pyr.*, § 2190.

supporters, who were already called "the Companions of Horus," *Shemsu-Hor*. There were among them warriors armed with the bow, and others with the boomerang (i.e. perhaps the Easterners of the Delta, bowmen like the Asiatics, and the Westerners of the Delta, who had boomerangs like the Libyans); they were led to battle by the warrior-god Upuat, whose ensign (Fig. 26) is crossed by a club.[1] There were bloody battles between the supporters of Horus and those of Seth. The stake was now the whole of Upper Egypt, and many places (see p.109) preserved the memory of terrible encounters. Seth had the upper hand for a long time, and among the gods as among men he had defenders who denied the crime of which he was accused, and were even more doubtful of the legitimacy of Horus, Son of Isis, as heir of Osiris. Finally, a lawsuit was brought before the supreme tribunal (transformed by tradition into a tribunal of the gods), to decide which was right (i) Seth or Osiris, and (ii) Seth or Horus.

(i) The case of Osiris is set forth briefly in the Pyramid Texts.

O Osiris, Horus is come, and embraces thee. He caused Thoth to turn back from thee those of the following of Seth, and he brought them to thee in bonds. He made the heart of Seth to fail, for thou art greater than he, thou wast born before him, thy virtue surpasses his. Geb saw thy merits,[2] and set thee in thy place. . . . Horus caused the Gods to join thee and to be brotherly with thee. . . . He caused the Gods to avenge thee. Then Geb set his sandal on the head of thy enemy, who retreats far from thee. Thy son Horus struck him, he saved his eye from his hand,[3] and gave it to thee; thy soul is within, thy power is within. . . . Horus has caused thee to grip thy enemies, so that they cannot escape from thee. . . . Horus has gripped Seth, and placed him beneath thee, that he may bear thee and tremble under thee. . . . O Osiris, Horus has avenged thee![4]

This brutal victory was not enough. For the pacification of the whole world, justice had to triumph in the person of Osiris. Besides, Seth had the outrageous effrontery to declare himself innocent. The memory of this famous trial is recalled in the following dramatic terms.

The sky growls, the earth trembles, Horus comes, Thoth comes. They lift Osiris on his side[5] and set him on his feet before the two divine Enneads.

[1] The bow, the boomerang, and the ensign of Anubis are determinative signs, attached to the name *Shemsu-Hor* (*Pyr.*, §§ 921, 1245). Cf. below, p. 110.

[2] See *Hymn to Osiris*, l. 10.

[3] This is an example of the way in which the texts combine the legend of Horus of Letopolis and that of Horus the Younger, in their rivalry with Seth.

[4] *Pyr.*, §§ 575 ff.

[5] Osiris is often portrayed lying on the ground, on his side, after the assault of Seth, in the place named Nedit (*Pyr.*, §§ 819, 1256).

Remember, O Seth, and lay up in thy heart this judgment which Geb gave out, and this threat with which the Gods threatened thee in the great city of the Sar, Heliopolis, because thou didst cast Osiris to the ground. Thou, Seth, didst say, " Truly, I did not do that to him ! " that thou mightest triumph here, and be saved, that thou mightest triumph over Horus. Thou, Seth, didst say, " It was he that attacked me (?) " . . . Arise, Osiris ! And Seth lifted him (Osiris) up, for he heard the threats of the Gods. " (Osiris) the heaven is given to thee ; to thee are given the earth, the fields of rushes, the territories of Horus, the territories of Seth ; to thee the cities are given ; for thee the nomes are gathered together . . . by order of Atum." This is the judgment of Geb in this matter.[1]

" Seth is guilty, Osiris is justified (*maâu*) "[2]; that, in brief, is the judgment of Thoth and the gods on Osiris.

Gods and men rejoice at the triumph of Justice. Osiris rises up (as King) ; the Powerful is purified ; the Lord of Justice is lifted up ; the Gods of the Ennead are satisfied, all the Gods of the earth are satisfied, and also those who are of (foreign ?) lands ; the Gods of the South and of the North, the Gods of the West and of the East are satisfied, all the Gods of the nomes, all the Gods of the cities are satisfied with this very great word, uttered by the mouth of Thoth for Osiris." [3]

(ii) In the case of Horus, the legitimacy of his birth and of his succession to the throne of Osiris was established before Geb, sitting in his court. In the same document which preserves the judgment by which Geb divided Egypt into the territory of Horus (Lower Egypt) and that of Seth (Upper Egypt), at the time of the conflict between Seth and Horus the Elder, of Letopolis, there is a significant addition. It tells us what happened when Horus, Son of Isis, took the place of Horus the Elder. The text makes no mention of the story of Osiris and the judgment by which Seth lost his power, and it attributes the revision of the apportionment to a regret on Geb's part.

There was grief in the heart of Geb, that the portion of Horus was equal to the portion of Seth. Then Geb gave (all) his inheritance to Horus, the son of his first-born son (Osiris). So Horus stood up over the country, and the country was united again. . . . The two great sorceresses, the White Crown and the Red Crown, prosper on his head, for it is indeed Horus who rises as King of the South and King of the North, and unites the Two Lands (*sma taui*) in the White Wall (Memphis), the place where the Two Lands are united.[4]

So the drama of Osiris ends. After Osiris, Horus in his turn sees his just cause prevail. He reigns over the Two Egypts. He is succeeded by the Servants of Horus, who, according

---

[1] *Pyr.*, §§ 955–61.   [2] *Pyr.*, § 1556.   [3] *Pyr.*, §§ 1522–3.
[4] Erman, continuation of the text quoted on p. 71.

to various traditions, are the first human kings. Thus it is from the gods that these last hold their inheritance, the legitimate possession of the country. It was on the right of Horus to the inheritance of his father Osiris that Menes, the first King of the Ist Dynasty, and the Pharaohs of thirty dynasties after him, based their right to ascend the throne. The line of descent was never interrupted, even by usurpers ; for three thousand five hundred years this fiction had the force and prestige of a historical reality.

The double kingship of Horus and Seth presents a character at once cosmic and mythical ; but the kingship of Osiris-Anzti, followed by the transmission of the power to Horus, has all the features of a human drama, and may have a historical foundation. Beneath the episodes of the "human" legend of Osiris one dimly perceives features taken from very ancient social customs.

Osiris-Anzti, King of Busiris, and later of the Delta, symbolizes one of those chiefs who concentrate in their own person the hitherto diffused authority of the clan (pp. 64, 68).[1] He settles the Nomads on territories, lays down the foundations of a methodical working of the soil, and creates institutions which make it effective (pp. 66–7).

At the same time as the clans become sedentary and the power is individualized in Osiris, the marriage custom changes. Being attached to the soil, man no longer goes out of the clan to look for a wife ; exogamy is succeeded by endogamy (pp. 20–1) ; Osiris marries his sister Isis. Hence a sacred prestige attaches to the consanguine marriage, which will continue to be a feature of Egyptian manners. The institution of marriage,[2] which the couple Osiris and Isis are supposed to have revealed to men, marks the evolution of a society from the uterine system, in which each woman of the clan believes herself impregnated by the totem, to the paternal system, in which the husband is the true father (pp. 20, 35–6, 87 ff.).

[1] The references are to Davy, in *From Tribe to Empire*.

[2] p. 67 : " When mythology echoes revolutions effected by certain ancestors in the ritual or in some institution, such as marriage or the system of kinship, it is only reflecting in the imaginary plot of the legend the history of advances " in social organization.

Henceforward the clan is divided into *families*, the members of which have obligations similar to those which were incumbent on the clansmen (pp. 13–14). Authority is now in the hands of the husband and father, just as, in the kingdom which the clan has become, the power passes to the King. Within the family, the authority will usually pass from the father to the eldest son, by paternal and masculine heredity (pp. 86 ff.). Horus ascends " the throne of his father " as his " heir ". From the time of Horus onwards, following his example, every Egyptian will claim as a right, not to be denied if justice reigns, the privilege of holding, from son to son, " the place of his father ". Thus the Osiris legend describes a society in which, in conformity with the theoretical development of primitive civilizations, endogamy and paternal power and inheritance appear as soon as the clans settle and individual chiefs arise.

Nevertheless, the Osirian family retains traces of the earlier social system, and these traces will survive indelibly in Egyptian society. They appear chiefly in the person of Isis, the prototype of woman in Egypt. Isis shares the authority with Osiris, she inspires his government, she invents magical rites, she creates mysteries which restore her husband to life ; in her are revealed the authority and intuitive knowledge with which primitive men invest woman, the depositary of the race, whom the totems visit (pp. 30–1). Uterine descent, which is characteristic of totemic societies, survives in the Osirian family and will always be recognized in social life in later times. Horus is the " Son of Isis " ; he owes his birth to his mother, who restored the virile force to the corpse of her husband. Like Horus, every Egyptian child will mention that he is " born of such-and-such a mother ", and will seldom give the name of his father. The uterine system of descent will survive, from this ancient past, even after paternal power and inheritance have been definitely adopted. The importance enjoyed by women in the family, and especially by Queens, the preservers of the royal race (p. 36), will be one consequence of the old respect for uterine descent.

The Osirian family also gives us some information about the obligations of the human family in very early times—the duty of taking part in worship, and that of avenging injuries done to a member of the community (p. 13). We shall see, in the course of this book, how the family worship paid to Osiris by his wife, his son, and his allies became the prototype of worship in all Egyptian families. Lastly, the essential title assumed by Horus, " Avenger of his Father," which all Pharaohs after him claimed, can only mean the survival of the *blood-vengeance*, that collective obligation of all the members of the clan, which had become the imperative duty of the members of the family. Horus, brought up by his mother, Isis, to carry on the blood-feud, supported by his " allies ", Anubis and Thoth, and by his " clients ", grimly perseveres until he obtains, by his own stength and by means of the divine tribunals, vengeance for the blood of Osiris.

In sum, beneath the anthropomorphic legend of the agricultural god, we see the development from clan to family, and the movement from the power of the community to that of the individual. That is why the kingship of Osiris served as a foundation for the later institution of monarchy ; that is why his reign is always recalled in the texts as the most ancient pattern of a lawful, civilizing government. That the reader may understand for himself what the Egyptians thought about it, I shall place before him the principal document, in a translation of the hymn which is the most complete account left by the Egyptians of the fortunes of Osiris as man and king.

THE HYMN TO OSIRIS [1]

Hail to thee, Osiris, Lord of Eternity, King of the Gods, whose names are manifold, whose destinies are sublime, whose forms are mysterious in the temples !

THE SANCTUARIES OF OSIRIS IN VARIOUS NOMES.—It is he whose Ka is noble in Busiris, it is he who is rich in domains at Letopolis, who is lord of acclamations in the Nome Anzti, who presides over the offerings in Heliopolis ; he is remembered in . . . ; he is the mysterious soul, which rules Kerrt ; illustrious in the White Wall, the soul of Ra and his very body [2] ; he takes delight in Heracleopolis, for ever acclaimed in the *Nart* tree which exists to bear his soul. He is Lord of Hermopolis Magna, greatly feared in Shashetep, Lord of Eternity, who presides at Abydos, and rests in his place in the Necropolis.

THE PRIMORDIAL GOD.—His name is very lasting (*zed*) in the mouth of men, as primordial god of the united Two Lands,[3] food and substance presented before the divine Ennead, perfect Spirit among the Spirits.

---

[1] On a stele of the XVIIIth Dynasty, prior to the Aten reformation, which was for a long time in the Bibliothèque Nationale, and is now in the Louvre. The text is published by Chabas, in **XXXVIII**, vol. ix, p. 95 ; here I have revised the text from the original. For the translation, cf. **XLIV**, p. 187.

[2] [3] Developments introduced into the Osiris legend at a relatively late date, when it was desired to make Osiris the equal of Ra and Atum.

OSIRIS AND NATURE.—Nun [1] has offered him his water, the North Wind goes up to the South for him, for the sky gives birth to the Air for his nose, to satisfy his heart. The plants grow at his wish, and the ground gives birth to its produce for him. The sky and the stars obey him, and the great doors (of the sky) open for him, the lord of acclamations in the sky of the South, and worshipped in the sky of the North. The imperishable stars [2] are under his authority, and his dwellings are the Unwearied Ones. [3]

OSIRIS, THE UNIVERSAL LORD.—The offering rises to him, by the order of Geb ; the divine Ennead worships him ; the dwellers in the Lower World nose the ground (before him) ; those (of the necropoles) of the desert bow down, all rejoicing when they see him, and they who are there (the dead) fear him. The Two Lands worship him at the approach of his majesty ; (for he is) the glorious noble who presides over the nobles, he whose (royal) office is established, whose government is firm. Good chief of the divine Ennead, gracious in countenance, loved by all who see him ! He puts his fear into all lands, that they may utter his name before (all) ; all make offering to him, the Lord who is remembered in the sky and on earth, for whom there are many joyful rites at the Feast of Uag, [4] for whom the Two Lands make rejoicing with one heart.

OSIRIS, THE HEIR OF GEB AND KING OF THE UNIVERSE, JUST AND FEARED.—He is the eldest of his brothers and the most ancient of the divine Ennead. [5] It is he who establishes Justice over the Two Lands ; he leaves the son in his father's place. [6] So he is praised by his father Geb, loved by his mother Nut, very strong when he overthrows the rebellious man, mighty in arm when he cuts his adversary's throat ; he puts his fear into his enemies, and takes the frontiers of them who plot evil, [7] and closes his heart when he tramples on the rebellious. He is the heir of Geb in the kingdom of the Two Lands, and (Geb) has seen his merit ; so he has given over to him the government of the lands for the good (of all), he has put in his hand this land, its waters, its winds, its plants, and all its cattle. All that flies, all that hovers, the reptiles, the beasts of the desert, have been given to the son of Nut ; and the Two Lands rejoice thereat. Rising up on the throne of his father, like Ra when he rises on the Eastern sky-line, he has brought light into the darkness. He has lighted up space with (the brightness) of his two feathers ; he has flooded the Two Lands with it, like the disk Aten in the morning ; his crown pierces the sky, and converses with the stars like a sister. He is the guide of every god, accomplished in command, the favourite of the Great Ennead, the beloved of the Small Ennead.

ISIS REIGNS WITH OSIRIS.—His sister has protected him, she who keeps the enemy far off, who wards off the acts of the Evil Ones by the charms (uttered by) her mouth, she whose tongue is subtle, whose words do not fail, accomplished in command.

---

[1] The primordial ocean, in which the germs of all things floated.

[2] Those which can be seen all the year round, and do not leave the visible sky.

[3] Those which are " wandering ", the planets.

[4] The feast of the dead and of rebirth.

[5] See p. 97, n. 2.

[6] A stock phrase, to describe the just king who deprives no one of his family possessions.

[7] The wars and conquests of Osiris are here presented as battles against evil.

Isis AVENGES OSIRIS.[1]—Isis, the inspired one, it is she who avenges her brother, who seeks him without wearying, going over the land in her grief; she does not stop till she has found him. It is she who then makes shade for him with her feathers, who gives him air with her wings, who utters acclamations and brings her brother to the shore.[2]

Isis PROCREATES HORUS.—It is she who lifts up what is faint in the God whose heart fails, and takes his seed, and procreates an heir,[3] and rears the Child in solitude, without any knowing where he is.

Isis CAUSES THE LEGITIMACY OF HORUS TO BE RECOGNIZED.—It was she who caused him (Horus) to go up, when his arm was strong, into the great hall of Geb. (Then) the divine Ennead, full of joy, (cried out) " Come, come, son of Osiris, Horus, stout in heart, justified, son of Isis, heir of Osiris ! "

Fig. 24.—Isis suckling her Son Horus in the Papyrus-beds of Chemmis.

The court of Justice was united for him —the divine Ennead, the Universal Lord himself,[4] the Lords of Justice, and her allies, who turn their heads at injustice.

They sit in the great hall of Geb, to give the (royal) Office to its lord, to give the kingship to him to whom it should be transmitted. They find that Horus and his word are truthful.

HORUS, KING OF THE UNIVERSE.—The Office of his father is given to him. He goes out crowned, by order of Geb. He has taken the government of the Two Lands, with the crown set firm upon his head. The earth is reckoned to him for his possession, the sky and the earth are under his authority. All mankind,[5] Egypt,[6] the Peoples of the North,[7] are given over to him. All that the disk Aten surrounds is under his law, the North Wind, the River, the inundation, the fruit-trees and all plants. The Corn God (Nepri) gives all his vegetation, the nourishment of the ground ; he brings repletion and gives it to all countries.

[1] It will be noted that the " Passion " of Osiris is passed over in " religious silence ", as Herodotus would say.

[2] Referring to the return of the chest, from Byblos to Buto.

[3] Cf. Louvre Papyrus No. 3079 (Pierret, *Études égyptologiques*, i, p. 22). It is a work on the " Spiritualization " of Osiris (of late date), in which Isis herself defines her part in the procreation of Horus. " I am thy sister Isis. There is no god, nor goddess, who has done what I have done. I acted as a man, though I am a woman, that thy name might live again on the earth. Thy divine seed was in my body, and I made it come into the world. He (Horus) will avenge thy virtues ; he will be safe, whereas thou dost suffer. He will deal a blow to him who has struck thee ; Seth will fall beneath his sword, and the allies of Seth will depart from Seth." A XIIth Dynasty sarcophagus has preserved an account of a similar episode (in **XLIX,** p. 204).

[4] The Universal Lord, one of the names of Osiris.

[5] Here come four names, *Nertu, Rekhetu, Pâtu, Hunemmtu,* corresponding to four categories of men, which cannot be identified.

[6] *Ta-meri,* one of the names of Egypt.

[7] *Hau-nebu.* The present edition of the hymn dates from the time when Egypt was dominant in Hither Asia and the Eastern Mediterranean.

THE GRATITUDE OF MEN.—All men are happy, their hearts are joyful, their thoughts are glad. All make merry, and all worship his goodness. "How sweet his love is to us! His grace surrounds our hearts, his love is great in every body."

SETH VANQUISHED.—The adversary of the Son of Isis is delivered to him. His violence is beaten down. Evil comes to the Evil One [1]; he who drives to violence (?), his (disastrous) destiny catches him. The Son of Isis has avenged his father; his name is made illustrious and perfect.

THE REIGN OF JUSTICE AND PEACE.—Strength has made a place for itself; abundance is established through his laws. The roads are free and the ways are open.

What peace there is in the Two Lands! Evil flees, crime goes far away, the earth is happy under its Lord. Justice is firmly established for its master, and all turn their back on injustice.

May thy heart rejoice, Unnefer! [2] The Son of Isis has taken the crown.

The Office of his father has been transmitted to him in the great hall of Geb. Ra has said it, Thoth has written it; the court of the Gods agrees. That is what thy father Geb has ordained for thee, and it has been done as he said.

Osiris, the god of the Nile and of corn, acknowledged king by all Egypt, transmitting the kingly office to Horus, to the Servants of Horus, and to the Pharaohs, what is he but the very land of Egypt, *justissima tellus*, imposing on its inhabitants the laws of its soil, with a social system based on submission to work and to authority, on distributive justice and necessary discipline?

[1] Literally, "the Howler."
[2] "The Good Being," a surname of Osiris, which often appears as a royal name inscribed in a cartouche.

PART TWO

KINGSHIP AND SOCIETY

CHAPTER I

THE PROTOHISTORIC MONARCHY. SERVANTS OF HORUS
AND THINITE KINGS. THE EARLIEST ROYAL INSTITUTIONS

THE institution of kingship was directly connected with
the reigns of Osiris and Horus. In these legendary figures
we distinguish the human chiefs, worshippers of these gods,
whose inheritance finally came to Menes about 3315 B.C.

The last god to reign over Egypt,[1] according to Egyptian
and Greek traditions, was Horus, Son of Isis. After him the
traditions place several more dynasties (seven in the Turin
Papyrus, four in Eusebius) of semi-divine and human kings.
Finally there come those whom the Turin Papyrus calls
" Spirits, Servants of Horus " (*Akhu, Shemsu-Hor*), whom
Manetho likewise calls " *Manes*, Demi-gods ". The Egyptian
accounts make these the immediate predecessors of the
historical dynasties.[2] Now, if the last of these protohistoric
kings call themselves the Servants of Horus, surely it proves
that they regard themselves as the heirs of that divine kingship, derived from Osiris and Horus, and transmitted to
themselves by the intermediate kings.

Between Osiris and Menes, tradition assigns enormous
totals to the reigns of the gods or demi-gods. The Turin
Papyrus gives 23,200 years to the predecessors of the
Shemsu-Hor, and 13,420 years to themselves, making a total
of 36,620 years ; and the gods are not included in these figures.
Eusebius assigns 13,900 years to the gods, and 11,000 to
the demi-gods, and Herodotus and Diodorus hold their own

---

[1] Turin Papyrus, in **XXIII**, p. 160 ; see above, p. 62 ; Hdt., ii, 44 ; Diod.,
i, 25, 44 ; Manetho (in Eusebius). Cf. **XXIII**, p. 167.
[2] **XXXIX**, Sethe, *Die Horusdiener*, p. 6.

against these almost astronomical figures. It is clear that the historian cannot take these fabulous computations into account. But we may note that all traditions agree on two points : (i) After Osiris and Horus, Egypt is governed by kings, and (ii) this period, during which the kingship is created, is extremely long.

Would it be unreasonable to suppose that this period, in which the way was prepared for the official dynasties, lasted at least as long as Pharaonic Egypt ? The Pyramid Texts are full of allusions, obscure to us, to facts which are real, but half-obliterated, like a damaged relief. One has the impression that they describe an enormously remote past, going back to the distant beginnings of the people of the Nile. For us, this is so much precious salvage from the protohistoric period ; it is like flotsam, borne in the texts on the current of later tradition. That is why I have thought it necessary to dwell so long on the divine dynasties which, under the veil of fable, disguise the age-long endeavours of the earliest pioneers and organizers of the Black Land, and that is why we must still dwell on the Servants of Horus and their immediate forerunners.

These kings come from the Delta. In the Turin Papyrus the lines preserved mention " nineteen (chiefs) of the (White) Wall,[1] and nineteen Venerables of the North ", before the *Shemsu-Hor* ; no mention is made of Kings of the South. Manetho, on the other hand, mentions thirty Memphite Kings, and then ten Thinite Kings, before the *Manes*. The fragment of the Palermo Stone has preserved nine names of a line of kings, wearing only the Red Crown of Lower Egypt. The general outline of this period must have been as follows :

I. Simultaneous, parallel reigns
{ Kings with the Red Crown (Lower Egypt).
Kings with the White Crown (Upper Egypt) = Manetho's Thinites.

II. *Shemsu-Hor* from the Delta conquer Upper Egypt and divide themselves into Kings of the North and Kings of the South.

III. Menes, King of the South, unites the Two Lands and founds the Ist historical Dynasty (Thinite).

[1] Of course these terms " White Wall " (Turin Pap.) and " Memphis " (Manetho) are taken from the language of a time later than the protohistoric period.

Since these three periods have been described, from the point of view of archæological material, in *From Tribe to Empire* (pp. 128 ff.), I shall here discuss only their main lines and essential character.

I

SIMULTANEOUS REIGNS IN UPPER AND LOWER EGYPT. THE MORAL PREPONDERANCE OF THE DELTA

We know nothing definite about these kings. Probably Buto in Lower Egypt and Nekheb in Upper Egypt were already their capitals, as they later became those of the *Shemsu-Hor*. The Kings of the North, who maintained the tradition, call themselves the heirs and successors of Horus, Son of Isis, the god of Buto ; we may therefore regard them as the earliest *Shemsu-Hor*. On the other hand, we may suppose that the Kings of Upper Egypt regarded themselves as the heirs of Seth of Ombos. For Seth continued to be a dynastic god, though secondary all through the history of Egyptian civilization ; the memory of his reign and the tradition of his inheritance were preserved by the " Followers of Seth " (*Imu-khet Seth*),[1] of whom the Kings of the South were probably the chiefs.

We know nothing of the names of these kings, with few exceptions,[2] or of the events of their time ; but, at least, we have a fairly clear notion of the political tendency and the fortunes of the two parallel kingdoms. There is no doubt that Lower Egypt dominated the Valley by the superiority of its civilization. It was in the Delta that royal institutions, which first appear in a primitive form in the group of the Western Nomes at Saïs and in the confederation of the Eastern Nomes at Busiris, developed until they became the " protectorship of Anzti " and then the " kingship " of Osiris, followed by that of Horus, Son of Isis, which embraced the whole of Lower Egypt. While the political monarchy was being organized, the myth of Osiris and Horus was elaborated. This myth retells, in one coherent scheme, the disconnected stories of the rivalries of the cosmic gods and their sufferings, the

---

[1] *Pyr.*, § 635.
[2] The nine names of Kings of Lower Egypt preserved on the Palermo Stone are archaic in form and are at present unintelligible.

" Passions " of the agricultural gods ; it reveals a first attempt at a synthesis giving an elementary explanation of the universe. This attempt at religious organization and concentration explains, and prepares for, the political concentration which we see going on, which found its expression in the kingship—first superhuman, then human—of Osiris.

Art, too, assumed a magnificent development. With the immediate predecessors of Menes, the first sculptured and written monuments appear. Before then we find, in Upper Egypt, only the products of the Neolithic workshops, perfect though they are—weapons, tools, jewels, etc., of polished stone and flint. The palettes are rudely carved and the statues are shapeless, but painted pottery and vases of hard stone are made. Suddenly, in the period just before Menes, copper and gold appear, and weapons, tools, and jewels have an excellence hitherto unknown ; the palettes are carved with " historical " reliefs ; the figures, formerly barely rough-hewn, have expressive features; the vases, cut in the hardest stone, are masterpieces of art and workmanship. Moreover, and this is an advance greater than all the rest, *writing* appears. It is very elementary, being still essentially pictorial, but it develops towards phoneticism. Above pictured scenes, there are short legends engraved, in which the pictorial signs begin to be used with a symbolic sense, and later with a phonetic. Half rebus and half alphabet, this writing is already formed, adult, capable of expressing abstractions, the result of groping efforts (lasting how many centuries ?) and a method which has at last triumphantly found its path.[1] To whom did Egypt owe this decisive transformation which took it, without perceptible transition, straight from Neolithic culture to a " historical " civilization of which it already possessed the religious, intellectual, and political elements and artistic materials ? By whom was Upper Egypt influenced, if not by Lower Egypt, which must have developed during the millenniums ascribed to the divine dynasties of the Delta ?

This theory is supported by a solid argument—the very early existence of the calendar,[2] which, as I explained in the Introduction, was adopted in 4241 at the latest. At this remote

---

[1] Palette of Narmer. Cf. *From Tribe to Empire*, pp. 138–9.
[2] Cf. op. cit., pp. 133 ff.

date the Egyptians effected a reform of the calendar, based on exact observations and experiments which had required thousands of years. But by whom were these made ? By the astronomers of Upper Egypt, or by those of Lower Egypt ? The date chosen for the starting-point of the calendar corresponds to our Gregorian 15th June ; now the heliacal rising of Sothis cannot, on this day, be observed below the 30th degree of latitude, that is, in the territory of Memphis and Heliopolis.[1] It is, therefore, to the astronomers of Lower Egypt that we owe the calendar, and the centre of their studies and observation of the heavens was certainly on the site of Heliopolis, for Memphis was founded much later. We know that " Seeing ", that is, the observation of the sun and stars, took an important place in the worship of the god of Heliopolis ; it is not a mere coincidence that the priests of Heliopolis call themselves " those who see " and the High Priest has the title of " Great Seer " (ur mau).[2]

The Pyramid Texts pass over the origin and the early political rôle of Heliopolis in silence. But the Nome of Heliopolis, Heq-âz, is contrasted with the West of the Delta [3] ; so it may perhaps have had a political organization apart from the rest of Lower Egypt. It is possible that Heliopolis was, during this period, a scientific and intellectual centre, and had no position as a political capital, such as Saïs and Bubastis enjoyed. One curious thing is that the ensign of the Heliopolitan Nome, Heq-âz, seems to be a recollection of the ensign Anzti of the 9th Busirite Nome. Was there contamination or influence ? Have we here a trace of the arrival at Heliopolis of men of Busiris, such as we have observed at Letopolis (above, p. 86) ?

This argument is supported by another fact. From the very earliest times, the intercalary days [4] were under the protection of " gods born in the five days placed at the beginning of the year ".[5] The Egyptian and Greek texts agree in calling these gods Osiris and Isis, Seth and Nephthys, and Horus.[6] The year began with the simultaneous rising of Sothis, Ra, and the Nile ; since Osiris, the god of the Nile

---

[1] **XXIII**, p. 27. As one goes up the valley, from one degree of latitude to another, the date of the rising of Sothis advances one day (**XXIII**, p. 191).
[2] Cf. **XII**, lv, p. 65.   [3] Pyr., § 222.   [4] From Tribe to Empire, p. 133.
[5] Pyr., § 1961.   [6] **XXIII**, p. 10 ; cf. Plut., De Iside, 12.

and vegetation, was placed at the head of it as its patron—
for he was supposed to have been born on the first of the five
intercalary days—we may conclude that the worshippers of
Osiris were powerful at Heliopolis itself at the time when the
astronomers of that city established the calendar.

So, with the calendar, Lower Egypt imposed on Upper
Egypt the authority of Osiris and Ra, the supremacy of the
Nile and the sun.

II

This conquest of Upper Egypt by the civilized men of the
Delta is probably the explanation of the radical changes
noted by ethnologists and archæologists.   These changes
appear in the population and in the monuments of Upper
Egypt immediately before the dynastic period.   The
inhabitants of Upper and Lower Egypt blend, and their
physical characteristics, as revealed by their bodies, tend
towards a unified type. The conquerors introduce innovations.
The tombs, hitherto mere graves dug in the sand, in which
the body was laid in the bare ground, or in a crude coffin
of clay (a cist), become small edifices of brick, in which the
body lies in a wooden coffin, surrounded by more artistic
funeral furniture.   In the place of terra-cotta ware and red
vases with black rims, or red-polished, with white ornament,
we find urns with wavy lugs, first egg-shaped and later
cylindrical, the development of which continues to the
Memphite period, in such regular fashion that Flinders
Petrie has established an approximate chronology of
" sequence dates " [1] from the successive shapes of this
pottery. This must have been imported from the Delta.
On other vases, and on the walls of a tomb at Hieraconpolis,
on which painting now appears, we see large boats, flying
the ensigns of nomes. Among these we often find the Harpoon,
the ensign of the 7th Nome, which bordered on that
inhabited by Horus of Buto.   The other ensigns belong
chiefly to nomes of the Delta.   We perhaps have another

---

[1] See the references quoted in J. Capart, *Les Origines de la civilisation
égyptienne*, Brussels, 1914, pp. 26 ff.

record of this conquest in the knife-handle from Gebel el-Araq (illustrated in *From Tribe to Empire*, p. 162), on which there is a scene containing ships flying the ensign of the 3rd Nome (Letopolis).[1] Lastly, certain archaic palettes adorned with battle-scenes, without names of kings, seem to represent combats between the northern conquerors and the settled folk of the Valley. These invaders seem, from all appearances, to have come from the Delta ; in any case, they were worshippers of Horus (and therefore of Osiris), for, in the Turin Papyrus, they bear the name of *Shemsu-Hor*, Servants of Horus.

The fact that the Servants of Horus conquered the Valley has long been admitted ; but the invasion has been supposed to have had a starting-point and a character quite other than those which I shall ascribe to it.[2]

In the great Temple of Horus at Edfu, as rebuilt by the Ptolemies, a long mythical narrative is inscribed—the history of the wars waged by Horus of Edfu (*Hor-Behedeti*) for the Sun King, Ra-Harakhti, in the 336th year of his reign, against his enemies, the Followers of Seth (*Imu-khet Seth*).[3] Horus defeats Seth in a series of battles, which are recorded in many sanctuaries of Horus, known as *mesent*, in various parts of the Valley and the Delta. Maspero incorrectly interpreted *mesent* as " smithy ", and its derivative, *mesentiu*, as " smiths ", and accordingly put forward the following hypothesis. A warlike tribe of " smiths " from the Upper Nile (where the negro smiths form a privileged caste), led by Horus, the Lord of the Smithy (*Neb-mesent*), conquer the Valley northwards, enter the Delta, and at intervals establish " smithies ", *mesent*, which are at once arsenals and centres of worship. The chief *mesent* was at Edfu (Zebat), which was the capital of the Horian smiths ; the other *mesent*, copied from it, are, according to this theory, witnesses to the conquest of Central Egypt

---

[1] These vessels, according to Flinders Petrie, are sea-going ships rather than Nile boats, and come from the Delta, thus illustrating the advance of the northern Egyptians up the river.

[2] Maspero holds that Horus comes from the south of Egypt, and his companions, the " Smiths of Horus ", are Africans from the Upper Nile. Loret thinks that Horus comes from Arabia, bringing Semitic Horians with him (cf. the Falcon Horus).

[3] E. Naville, *Textes relatifs au mythe d'Horus.* Cf. Roeder, **XLIX,** p. 121.

and the Delta by a people from the south, the Servants of Horus.[1]

This hypothesis must be abandoned. Horus of Edfu is not mentioned on the Pyramids, nor on any text before the XIIth Dynasty.[2] As the Falcon, he belongs, as we have seen, to the old foundation of the native religion ; but as god of the royal line, he is late ; he only becomes important after his fusion with the Sun, Ra. From this fusion a new divine type later develops, Ra-Harakhti,[3] in whom the local falcon becomes a god of the universe. Now, the legend inscribed on the Ptolemaic temple at Edfu refers less to Horus than to the Sun. It relates the battles of the Sun against his enemies, the " Followers " of the dark and stormy Seth. In this capacity Horus is rather the Horus who was god of Letopolis, the ancient sky-god, Seth's rival, who was never quite forgotten and was revived in the classical period in the Horus localized at Nekhen, and later at Edfu. As for the word *mesentiu*, its true ancient form is *mesenu*, which means " harpooners ", and more particularly those who hunt the hippopotamus with the harpoon ; the sanctuaries called *mesen* or *mesent* are the cities of the harpooners.[4] Now, the reliefs accompanying the texts at Edfu show the " Followers of Horus " with harpoons, hunting the hippopotamus (a Typhonian beast, personifying Seth). These " Followers " are sometimes called *Shemsu-Hor*, " Servants of Horus," but here the word, lacking the royal determinative, certainly does not mean the

---

[1] Maspero, *Les Forgerons d'Horus et la légende de l'Horus d'Edfou*, in **XXXVIII**, vol. ii, pp. 313 ff.

[2] Gardiner, in **XIII**, v, p. 223. I am speaking of the Horus locally established at Edfu (Zebat). The Horus Behedeti of Sahura's temple (Vth Dynasty) belongs to Behedet in the Delta.

[3] Harakhti, " Horus of the Eastern Horizon," appears, in the form of an anthropomorphic god with a falcon's head, on the cylinders of the superintendents of the vineyards of King Khasekhemui (end of IInd Dynasty) and King Neterkhet Zeser (beg. IIIrd Dynasty) (cf. Petrie, *Royal Tombs*, ii, pls. 22–3 ; Garstang, *Mahasna and Beitkhallaf*, pl. 9). A legend in front of the god states that he " gives life and strength ", or " gives all his life, strength, stability " to the King. This is the first mention of the formula L.H.S., " Life, Health, Strength," which accompanies the King's name as a blessing in the classical period. This Harakhti is not yet localized at Edfu.

FIG. 25.—Life, Health, Strength.

[4] Sethe, " Die angebliche Schmiede des Horus von Edfu," in **XII**, liv (1918), p. 50.

protohistoric kings ; in its proper sense, in its common acceptation, it simply means those who are in the service of the god. So Horus Behedeti, who wages war for Ra, is not originally a god of Upper Egypt. Nor does he lead a tribe of negro smiths into the Valley and the Delta. These are the exploits of Horus of the Delta, revived in a late period to the credit of Horus of Edfu.

For Horus of the harpoon takes us to the Delta sites. The country for harpooning is the swamps, which are especially frequent in the western and central part, in the 7th Nome of the Harpoon where Horus was born, among the reeds of Chemmis. This is not a mere wild assumption. From the earliest times to those of Herodotus and Pliny,[1] the swamps near Saïs were famous for the hippopotamus-hunting, which was done with the harpoon.[2] The harpooning-scenes which so often appear in Egyptian tombs, and in every period, call up the wars of Horus, Son of Isis, and Seth, in the guise of a hippopotamus.[3] An XVIIIth Dynasty tomb gives a fragment of text regarding this hunt. According to this, the goddess Neith of Saïs, the capital of the Western Delta, appears to Horus as he is about to cast his harpoon at the hippopotamus Seth. She prostrates herself before the Harpoon ; she shows her son Horus the place where the Hippopotamus is hiding in the river ; she promises the victory of his good cause— Horus will be " justified ".[4] Here we have another allusion to the ancient war of Horus of Buto against Seth.

For these reasons we may take it as probable that Horus and his Servants came not from Edfu, but from the Delta, when they conquered the Valley. With Maspero,[5] we may suppose that the *mesent* were sanctuaries of Horus marking the successive battlefields on which Horus met Seth, at Sele (14th Nome), at Heracleopolis Magna (XXth), at Edfu (IInd) ; but our founders of the *mesent* came from the North, not from the South. So, too, another term commonly used for the temples of Horus, *Behedet*, was applied to Edfu (IInd Nome) only in imitation of a Behedet in Lower Egypt (17th Nome) ;

---

[1] Hdt.,i i, 71 ; Pliny, *N.H.*, xxviii, 121.
[2] Diod., i, 35.   [3] Plut., *De Iside*, 50.
[4] Alan H. Gardiner, *The Tomb of Amenemhet*, pp. 28–30, pl. i.
[5] For these *mesent*, or harpoon-cities, see the details in Maspero, **XXXVIII**, vol. ii, p. 323, and the data supplied by Kees, *Horus und Seth*, pp. 40–50.

the epithet *Behedeti* designated Horus, Son of Isis, before it was used for Horus of Edfu.[1]

If we accept this explanation we understand how the whole Osirian family, with the Servants of Horus, took possession of the principal temples of the Valley (Map II).

Osiris established himself at Abydos, near Thinis,the centre of the future Thinite kingdom, and the VIIIth Nome took for its divine ensign the two feathers worn by Anzti of Busiris, and by Osiris after him. Anubis, the dog-god, who " dwelt in the West " of the Delta, settled on the left bank, from Abydos to Siut; becoming the god of the necropolis of Abydos, he there " presided over the Westerners " (*Khenti-Imentiu*), that is, the dead. In this name we see his old local title, " President of the West " (*Khenti-Iment*). We also find him in the XIIth Nome, on the Serpent Mountain, and in the XVIIth, at Cynopolis. His associate, the Wolf Upuat, installed himself in the Nome of the Sycamore (XIIIth), the capital of which was later called Lycopolis. The Ibis Thoth, who had a sanctuary (Hermopolis Parva, 3rd Nome) and a nome (the 15th) in the Delta, supplanted the Hare of the XVth Nome in Upper Egypt, and there founded his new city, Hermopolis Magna. Isis, in her form of Hathor, considered either as the Great Mother or as the wife of Horus the Elder, was worshipped in the nome of the ancient enemy, the Typhonian Crocodile Sebek (VIth), in the Sycamore (XIVth), and in the Knife (XXIInd).[2]

This active participation of the gods of the Delta in the Horus-worshippers' conquest explains many things—the presence of the Wolf Upuat as the determinative of the word " Servants of Horus " in the Pyramid Texts, and the representation of the Two Falcons, the Wolf, and the ensign of Letopolis on the war-ensigns of the Thinite Kings.[3] So, too, the existence of pairs of cities, in

FIG. 26.—The Equipment of the Servants of Horus. Ensign of Upuat, bow, boomerang (*Pyr.*, § 1245).

---

[1] Only from the XVIIIth Dynasty onward was the name Behedeti applied to Zebat, the capital of the IInd Nome of Upper Egypt, and used to designate Horus of Edfu (**XIII**, v, p. 223, n. 1, acc. to Gardiner).

[2] See the Table of Nomes, pp. 54 ff.

[3] Palette of Narmer (*From Tribe to Empire*, p. 139, fig. 7, and p. 153, fig. 11).

the Delta and in Upper Egypt, of Horus, Thoth, Anubis, etc., points to a veritable colonization of the Valley by kings, the Servants of Horus, who came from the Delta and marched to battle behind Osiris, Thoth, Anubis, Upuat, and Horus.

Having become masters of the South and the North, the *Shemsu-Hor* kings respected the natural division of the country, and Egypt was at first governed by two royal families, the Kings of the North (*Bitiu*) at Buto, and the Kings of the South (*Nsutu*) at Nekheb. Since I have given a résumé of this period in *From Tribe to Empire* (pp. 135–7), I shall here add only a few details obtained from recent research.

The Kings of the North did not establish their capital at Saïs, the ancient capital of the Western Delta, but at Buto, the city of a goddess who was worshipped in the north of the Delta, Wazet, whose name, turned into Uto by the Greeks, appears in Buto (*b* + *uto* = City of Wazet). Wazet was a serpent-goddess, who joined forces with Osiris and Horus, and so became, for ever, the royal goddess of the North ; in the form of the uræus, she was later attached to the crown, as the inseparable protectress of the King's head.[1] Her headgear, the Red Crown (*net*), which she had taken from Neith, also became the permanent emblem of the kingship of the Delta. Why did Wazet's city Buto supplant the ancient capital Saïs, the city of Neith ? It may have been because Neith did not go over to the Osirians, like Wazet. The worshippers of Neith were the warlike Egypto-Libyans, who always had a passion for liberty, and remembered their ancient independence.[2] The worshippers of Wazet, on the other hand, made common cause with the supporters of the Kings of the North. Besides, not far from Buto was Chemmis, where Horus was born ; and at Buto Isis had consecrated Horus, the posthumous son of Osiris, as heir to his father, and had equipped him for the war against Seth.[3] For all these reasons Buto became a dynastic and royal city. It contained two quarters—Dep, the sacred city of Wazet,

---

[1] Cf. *From Tribe to Empire*, p. 131, fig. 4.
[2] Cf. above, p. 75.   [3] Cf. above, p. 92.

where her temple stood, and Pe (meaning " the Place ", above all others), properly the royal city of Horus, where the King of Lower Egypt had two residences,[1] often mentioned on the Pyramids, the *Neser* palace and the *Nu* palace (Fig. 27a).

The second branch of these royal Followers of Horus, established in the South, created a faithful copy of the kingdom of Buto in the upper valley. The distinctive sign of the Kings of the South was the tall White Crown (*hezt*), which was worn by the goddess Neith ; in other respects they did as their brothers of the North. They, too, took for their capital the city of a goddess, the Vulture of Nekheb (IIIrd Nome) ; this goddess-mother, Nekhebt " with the long feathers, with the hanging paps ", was to suckle the children

FIG. 27.—*Per-ur*, the Great House, the Palace of the Kings of Upper Egypt.

FIG. 27a.—*Per-neser*, the House of Flame (?), the Palace of the Kings of Lower Egypt.

Wattle-and-daub constructions.

of the royal line. Having taken her " white headgear ",[2] of which they made the crown of the South, the Kings placed themselves under the protection of Nekhebt in order to inherit the influence which she had long exercised over the South. Just as there were two cities in Buto, Dep and Pe, so these Kings built opposite Nekheb, the city of the goddess Nekhebt on the right bank, a city of Horus on the left bank, named Nekhen, Horus of Buto's royal city in the South, Hieraconpolis. There the Falcon Horus was later worshipped in the same form of a mummified bird (Fig. 14 and Pl. III, 3) as was given at Letopolis to Horus of the Two Eyes.[3] To

---

[1] **XII,** liii, p. 57.

[2] *Pyr.*, § 729. Nekhebt, being a goddess-mother, was identified by the Greeks with Eileithyia, protectress of childbirth, and Nekheb was called by them Eileithyiapolis. In hieroglyphics, the vulture is also read as *mt* (= mother).

[3] *Pyr.*, §§ 729, 717.

complete the symmetry between North and South, in Nekheb the goddess Wazet was given a *Nu* palace, copied from the type of building so named in Buto. The Upper Egyptian palace is, however, often represented by a building of different appearance (Fig. 27).

The " artificial " character of these royal residences shows that a dynastic theory already existed, with its official terminology, which was imposed on cities as it was on royal individuals. What we chiefly perceive in this is the intention of establishing a monarchy under the protection of the gods.

It is not unimportant that these deities are *goddesses*, in the North and South of Egypt alike. When Horus installed himself at Buto, he presented himself as the son, and therefore the heir, of the local goddess Wazet. The right to the crown belonged to Wazet, as, in the South, it belonged to Nekhebt, both being " royal " goddesses. This fact explains a peculiarity in the royal title of the Pharaohs. Several very ancient royal ensigns bear names constructed with the feminine possessive suffix, which refers to the goddess Wazet, and perhaps also to Nekhebt. To designate the Uræus and adornment placed on Pharaoh's brow, the ancient language used the words " her frontlet " (*wpt-s*)—i.e. Wazet's. So, too, we find " her Crown of Lower Egypt " (*meh-s*), " her Crown of Upper Egypt " (*shemâ-s*), " her sceptre," " her stick," " her pectoral." [1] So the attributes of royal power originally belonged to goddesses. This may be a very curious remnant of an old matriarchal system,[2] turned to the profit of the Servants of Horus. These latter, who already owed a great part of their prestige to the queen-goddess Isis, seem also to have appropriated the inheritance of the royal goddesses at Buto and Nekheb.

The last stage achieved by these kings, the Servants of Horus, was the union of the two kingdoms, which was effected by the Southern family.[3]

---

[1] **XXXIX,** Sethe, *Zur Sage des Sonnenaugen*, p. 13.
[2] Cf. above, p. 96.
[3] For the details of the events, see *From Tribe to Empire*, pp. 136–7.

Two of the kings of Hieraconpolis-Nekhen, the Scorpion and Narmer, have left monuments on which they are represented as conquering the Delta. King Scorpion, with the ensigns of the Southern nomes borne before him,[1] celebrates his victory over the " Rekhetu " and the " Bows ", the former being Egyptian peoples and the latter Asiatics. Although he only wears the White Crown of the South on this palette, the Scorpion certainly conquered and held part of the Delta, without, perhaps, taking Buto.[2] Narmer, on the other hand, is represented with the two crowns. On the front of his famous palette,[3] where he is felling a man of the Harpoon Nome (7th) with his mace, he wears the White Crown of Nekhebt ; on the back, he marches, wearing the Red Crown of Wazet

Fig. 28.—King Lion devouring his Enemies.

and preceded by the ensigns which lead the *Shemsu-Hor*, towards a place where ten chieftains of the Harpoon have been beheaded.

What is the explanation of the bloody conflict which divided the two royal families of the Servants of Horus ? It seems to have followed upon new invasions of the Delta, by the Libyans in the West, and by the Semites in the East. On the palette of Narmer, there is no doubt about the Asiatic, and especially Semitic type of the overthrown enemy.[4] A

[1] Ibid., fig. 5, p. 136.
[2] Jars sealed with the name of the Scorpion have been found near Memphis.
[3] Op. cit., figs. 6–7.
[4] Cf. the man trampled by King Bull, op. cit., fig. 7 ; also fig. 9.

protohistoric palette, unfortunately incomplete and lacking a royal name, also shows us King Lion on the battlefield, devouring the dead and the living, and these present an equally distinct Semitic type. Above the scene there are the lower part of a person wearing a robe of embroidered wool of Semitic style, and the name of a people, unfortunately illegible, being incomplete, but having the elliptical determinative of foreign countries. This word probably designated the Asiatics. On another palette (Fig. 29) the front shows the king, represented by a scorpion, a lion, a falcon, or several falcons, dismantling a fort with picks, while the back shows the procession of booty—oxen, asses, and sheep among trees (Fig. 16). In the bottom compartment the

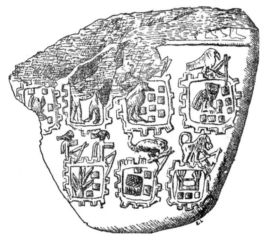

FIG. 29.—King destroying Forts.
Cf. Fig. 16.

boomerang of the Libyans is clearly drawn, set on the ellipse of foreign countries ; this sign, *Tehenu*, is the name of the Libyans.[1] What conclusion are we to draw ? That the Scorpion and Narmer, Kings of Upper Egypt, had to intervene in the Delta to save it from invaders, the Libyans in the West and the Semites in the East. Obviously the Delta was always in more danger from its close and hungry neighbours than the Valley, secure behind its protecting deserts.

[1] **XXIX**, p. 166 ; Sethe, " Zur Erklärung einiger Denkmäler aus der Frühzeit der aegyptischen Kultur," in **XII**, lii (1914), pp. 55–60.

The Kings of Buto may sometimes even have combined with those neighbours, for the Pyramid Texts preserve memories of a time when " the Kings of Lower Egypt in Buto " were regarded as enemies.[1] Was this why the Delta, the cradle of the royal dynasties, but sullied by foreigners, passed under the control of the Kings of Upper Egypt and even in the royal titles of later times yielded the precedence to the Valley ?   Certainly the conquest of the Delta by the Kings of Hieraconpolis left an indelible memory in dynastic tradition.   Royal titles and administrative formulas would always (except during a few periods which will be mentioned later) give the first place, the place of honour, to the king and the country of Upper Egypt.   In the united monarchy inaugurated by Menes,[2] the pre-eminence allowed to Upper Egypt shows the rather distrustful anxiety with which the Pharaohs thenceforward regarded the Delta.

III

THE THINITE KINGS AND THEIR SYNTHESIS OF ROYAL INSTITUTIONS

Egyptian and Greek sources agree in making Menes the first king of united Egypt, and the founder of the human lines of kings, after the gods and the Servants of Horus. In *From Tribe to Empire* (pp. 137–54) I have described the character of this earliest monarchy.   Here I would show : (i) how Menes and the Thinite Kings welded together and co-ordinated the various elements of the royal power which they had found existing before them and had concentrated in their own hands ; (ii) why they founded a new royal capital, on the site of Memphis ; (iii) how they laid the foundations of a royal administration.

For the results of this political concentration we must look to the titles assumed by the Thinite Kings, and taken on as a tradition by all their successors, including the Ptolemies and the Cæsars.

---

[1] *Pyr.*, § 1488.   [2] *From Tribe to Empire*, pp. 131, 137.

KINGS OF THE THINITE Iˢᵗ AND IIᴺᴰ DYNASTIES[1]

MONUMENTS.		KING-LISTS.	MANETHO.	APPROXI-MATE DATE.
			1st Dynasty. 8 Thinite Kings.	3315
Horus-name	King's Name.			
Aha	= Menes	Menes	1. Menes	
Khent	= Ka (?)	Atoti I	2. Athothis	
		Atoti II	Athotes (acc. to Eratosthenes)	
		Atoti III	3. Cencenes	
Zet			4. Uenephes	
Den	= Hesepti	Hesepti	5. Usaphaïs	
Anzib	= Merbapen	Merbapen	6. Miebis	
Smerkhet	= Samsu	Samsu	7. Semempses	
Qa	= Sen	Qebehu		
		Biuneter	8. Ubienthes	
			IInd Dynasty. 9 Thinite Kings.	3100
Hetepsekhemui		Bazau	1. Boëthus	
Nebra		Kakau	2. Sechous	
Neteren		Bineteren	3. Binothris	
Sekhemib	= Perenmaat	Uznas	4. Tlas	
Seth Peribsen				
?	Send	Senti	5. Sethenes	
			6. Chaïres	
Khasekhem		Neferkara	7. Nephercheres	
		Neferkasokar	8. Sesochris	
Horus ⎫		Huzefa	9. Cheneres	
⎬	Khasekhemui	Zazaï	(position	
Seth ⎭		Nebka	uncertain)	2895

[1] From E. Meyer, **XXII**, pp. 151, 156.

The official title used by the Thinite Kings comprises :
(i) a Horus-title ; (ii) a title as King wearing the Two Crowns ;
(iii) a title as King of Upper and Lower Egypt. Each of these
titles may be accompanied by a " name " assumed by the
King.

Horus-title.—This consists of some name such as Aha,
" Warrior," [1] inscribed in a conventional plan of a royal
palace, with a Falcon (Horus) perched on top. That means
that the King is the living incarnation on earth (i) of the
Falcon, (ii) of Horus (rendered in Greek by Ἀπόλλων).

This Falcon is clearly described by the texts of all periods
as a living bird, with which the King is identified.[2] For
example, the Thinite sculptors give the bird life, by making
it hold in its claws the shield and javelin [3] which are the
ideographic signs of the word *ahâ*, " Warrior." [4] He is,
without any doubt, the creature which leads so many clans
in protohistory. He lives again in the person of the King.
So the chain of tradition is maintained by this first title which
connects the clan-ensign with the Thinite King.

We have seen the Falcon become a god and assume various
aspects—first of all as sky-god of Letopolis, with the name
" Horus of the Two Eyes ", and King of Lower Egypt, the
rival of the god Seth-Nubti, the King of Upper Egypt. The
Thinite Kings are, in the human world, the living image of
this Horus, who still resides at Letopolis, but also, by right
of conquest, at Nekhen and Edfu ; and the Falcon which
stands before their royal name is also the name of the god
Horus. But the tradition of the royal power once enjoyed by

Seth in Upper Egypt survives in the Thinite
title; Seth is sometimes named in it by the
side of his " companion " Horus. On the
monuments of the first dynasties, " two
gods " (two falcons) frequently designate
the King as the incarnation of Horus-Seth.
Merbapen (Miebis), of the Ist Dynasty, often
puts two falcons before his name, that is

FIG. 30.—Name of
Horus Aha in
Palace.

---

[1] Cf. op. cit., fig. 8.   [2] *From Tribe to Empire*, p. 140.
[3] See also the fish Nar in the royal name Narmer (op. cit., fig. 9).   [4] Ibid., fig. 8.

" two gods " instead of one only [1]; and these two gods are Horus and Seth. Here Seth, still all-powerful despite his defeat, disguises himself as a falcon out of respect for the Osirian legend. Under the IInd Dynasty, on the other hand, there must have been some reaction on the part of the worshippers of Seth, the traditional King of Upper Egypt, for two kings take him as their eponymous patron, in the form of the Typhonian Beast (the greyhound?). King Peribsen never calls himself " Horus ", but " Seth Peribsen ".[2] Peribsen's two successors return to Horus, but at the end of the IInd Dynasty King Khasekhemui (whose spoken name means " the two Mighty Ones Rise ") places before his name a falcon and a greyhound, that is, Horus and Seth (cf. Fig. 21), and after his name he inserts a significant epithet—" the Two Gods unite in him ".[3] Nevertheless, the worshippers of Seth were afterwards obliged to consider the susceptibilities of the worshippers of Osiris. The name of Seth disappeared from the title, and was replaced by that of Nub(ti), the genesis of which will be explained in the next chapter. But the memory of Seth, King of Upper Egypt, the royal ancestor embodied and living again in the line of the Pharaohs, was never lost. In classical times the Queen was called " She who sees Horus and Seth "—that is, the King, in whom both gods were embodied. On temple-walls of all periods we find Seth Nubti, as the god of foreign lands, bringing captive foreigners to the King, and taking part, as an Egyptian god, in the ceremonies of the coronation. So, too, in the Vth Nome of Upper Egypt, the ensign of the Two Falcons recalled the heroic age of the Two Companions, while at Ombos, south of Edfu, Seth, in his crocodile form, was worshipped beside Horus.

Moreover, the Falcon Horus still represented the young god of Buto, the Son of Isis, the posthumous child of Osiris, who received the royal " office " from his father, after the sentence of the gods assembled to try the dispute between Osiris and Seth (above, p. 94). Pharaoh was an embodiment of Horus in this aspect, too; this is evident from numerous texts of

---

[1] Petrie, *Royal Tombs of the First Dynasty*, i, pls. 6, 26.
[2] An inscription on a seal of this king explains: " Nubti of Ombos (Seth) transmitted the Two Lands to his son, the King of the South and of the North, Peribsen." Cf. Petrie, op. cit., ii, pl. 22, No. 190.
[3] Petrie, op. cit., pl. 23.

the following periods and from the " Service of Horus " which the Thinite Kings celebrated as a dynastic ceremony.[1]

Lastly, from the Vth Dynasty onwards, the priests of Heliopolis, now become the inspirers of the Pharaohs, made up, out of the various aspects of the Falcon Horus, a composite dynastic god, in whom the predominant element was the " Sun of the Eastern Sky ", called Ra-Harakhti. The development was complete under the XIIth Dynasty ; thenceforward the Falcon of the royal title, crowned with the solar disk, signified " Horus-Ra ", or, rather, " Ra-Horus."

So, by this title of Horus, the King embodies the old king-gods who successively presided over the destinies of Egypt. Pharaoh is the incarnation at once of the Falcon, of Horus of Letopolis (and Seth Nubti), of Horus, Son of Isis and Osiris, and of Horus-Ra. He is not a spiritual heir, a symbolic representative of the divine race, but the real descendant and incarnation of these divine ancestors. The Thinite sculptor was so steeped in this " truth " that he expressed it in material form. The royal name of Horus, inscribed in the plan of a palace surmounted by the Falcon, is borne in the two arms of the Ka ; now, the Ka is the genius of the race, the divine substance (see Fig. 32). In later times the theologians would say " The King is the Ka ", or " He is Ra incarnate ".

The second title of the Thinite King is represented by a Vulture and a coiled Serpent on two baskets (these last symbolize the idea of totality, of universal overlordship). The two creatures are the totems of Nekheb and Buto, which afterwards personified Nekhebt [2] and Wazet, the goddesses of the capitals of Upper and Lower Egypt. In the royal title, they mean " the Two Mistresses " (*nebti*) of the White Crown and the Red Crown. So the King, with the qualification *nebti*, is the Double Crown incarnate ; he is White Crown and Red Crown, he is the Two Mistresses. The Greek translators, like ourselves, use an approximate expression, " Lord of the Two Royal Crowns," κύριος βασιλειῶν.

In *From Tribe to Empire* (p. 132) I have pointed out the essential importance of the crown among peoples in the earliest

---

[1] *From Tribe to Empire*, p. 145.   [2] *From Tribe to Empire*, fig. 10.

ages. What is for us modern folk merely an emblem of the royal office, is for them a living being, a deity who really reigns, the possession of whom constitutes a right. So it was in Egypt : the King, when crowned, became the goddesses themselves, and took their place in all their rights.

With his *third title*, a Reed (?) and a Bee, *nsut biti*, Pharaoh claims the personality of other gods who had royal rights in the South and the North, but we know little about them. In addition to the serpent Wazet, there was at Buto a bee (*bit*), who symbolized royalty, for the Pyramid Texts call the King of Buto " Him of the Bee ". The title *nsut* belonged to the lord of a district to the south of the Delta, or near Heracleopolis[1] ; when the Horians conquered the Valley, *nsut* must have extended its influence to Upper Egypt. Here we have gods localized on earth ; so the meaning of this third title is topographical—Βασιλεὺς τῶν τε ἄνω καὶ τῶν κάτω χωρῶν—" King of the Upper and Lower Countries."

Fig. 31.—The Titles *Nsut Biti* and *Nebti* of King Qa.

In addition to these three titles, the Kings bear the names of " Mighty Bull ", " Glaring Lion ", etc., which, like that of " Falcon ", may be followed by formal epithets. On the archaic palettes the King is represented as a bull overthrowing his enemies and knocking down fortress-walls with his horns or as a lion devouring the vanquished on the battlefield.[2] That means that these formidable animals were in early times held to be depositaries of part of the royal power, as totems or protectors of certain clans or nomes. The King absorbed these rival totems or protectors into himself, just as he absorbed

Fig. 32.—The Name of Horus Anzib, between the Arms of the Ka. Negadah

---

[1] *Nsut* means " he who belongs to the plant *sut* " ; see **XII**, xlix, p. 1 ; Newberry, op. cit., p. 8. Cf. **XXX**, p. 34.
[2] *From Tribe to Empire*, p. 139, and above, pp. 114–15.

the Falcon, Vulture, or Uræus. The less powerful figures did not take the same place in the royal title as the others,[1] but, at least, they were not altogether forgotten.

The variety of these formal titles proves that the elements of kingship, the experiments in government, the embryos, were many and various in protohistoric Egypt, at the time when the Thinite monarchy came to impose itself over the other powers. The tradition preserved in the legends of the divine dynasties in the Pyramids has already made a selection among historical facts, and concerned itself chiefly with the adventures of the Horians. We do not yet know what were the Kings of the Bee, the Reed, the Bull, etc. The political material which the Thinite Kings had to organize must have been rich in ingredients, complex in forms, and various in origins. So the kingship of Menes represents a bold synthesis and a deliberate choice ; for its divine protectors and fore-runners, it preserved the great cosmic gods, Horus and Seth, the pair inseparable in nature, the goddesses of the capitals, and a few emblems of Upper and Lower Egypt.

So, one may suppose, the Thinite Kings must have absorbed their political rivals and reduced them to complete impotence. The Pyramid Texts give us a striking picture of what a conquest was in protohistoric times. This is how, copying the methods practised on earth at the time, a deified King, arriving in Heaven, took possession of his domains and of their divine inhabitants :

The sky grows dark,[2] the stars weep, the dwellers in the skies are agitated, the bones of those who are on the horizon tremble . . . because they have seen King N. rise like a soul, as a god who lives upon his fathers, who feeds upon his mothers . . . King N. has his Gods upon him, he has his uræi on his brow . . . his sceptres defend him. King N. is the Bull of the Sky, with the aggressive heart, who lives upon the life of every God, who eats their entrails. . . . This King eats men and lives upon the Gods . . . this King eats their magic and swallows their spirits.[3] The great (Gods) are for his morning meal ; the middle ones, for his evening meal ; their young ones, for his night meal. Their old ones, male and female, are for his furnaces ; the great ones of the sky stir up the fire for their pots, filled for him with the legs of their elders. . . . N. renews his rising in the sky ; he holds the crown of the Lord of the Eastern Horizon. As he has counted the bones and the vertebræ, as he has taken out the hearts of the Gods, as

---

[1] *From Tribe to Empire*, p. 142.
[2] *Pyr.*, §§ 393–412. I omit several passages which would need long commentaries. Cf. Speleers, *Pyramides*, translation, 1923.
[3] Cf. *From Tribe to Empire*, p. 106 : " You eat your dead enemy in order to assimilate his substance. his *mana*. as food."

he has eaten the Red Crown and swallowed the Green (White ?) Crown, the King feeds himself on their lungs, he rejoices as he lives upon their hearts and their magic. . . . He grows green again, for their magic is in his belly. None can take the royal dignity from N., for he has swallowed the wisdom of every God. The length of the life of King N. is eternity ; his limit is everlastingness, in that dignity in which he does what pleases him and does not do what displeases him,[1] he who has no limit but the horizon, for ever and ever.

Obviously Menes did not eat his political opponents raw, whether chiefs of nomes or local kings; but let us remember the palettes on which King Bull tramples on dead and living and King Lion devours them. The texts and monuments are of an age which was already civilized. There were thinkers then, astronomers and theologians, and such barbarities no longer existed. But men still believed in magic, and they used these recollections of a long-vanished cannibalism as an incantation against the enemy. The brutal orgy of physical possession, ritual eating, was by that time only a nightmare, calling up a very distant past. The theorists who made up the Pharaonic title transmuted these practices into an " assimilation " of the Falcon, of Horus and Seth, of Nekhebt and Wazet, by the first King of united Egypt.

It was on the day of his coronation that the King became a Horus. The operation, which was magical in character as much as religious and political, was conducted with ceremonies which were already established in their essentials in the time of Menes and were observed with scrupulous respect by the Cæsars.

According to the Thinite monuments and the Palermo Stone, there were three principal ceremonies, three rites of coronation.

    i. { *Khâ nsut*, the Rising of the King of the South.
       { *Khâ biti*, the Rising of the King of the North.
    ii. *Sma taui*, the Union of the Two Lands.
    iii. *Pekhrer ha inb*, the Procession round the Wall.[2]

These took place in a palace or in " royal buildings ", which supplied the necessary setting. According to Manetho,

---

[1] This is the theory of the King's good pleasure. We shall find it again, expressed in the same terms, in the decrees of the Memphite Kings.
[2] Palermo Stone (Schaefer, p. 28). The Wall is that of Memphis.

it was Athothis, son of Menes, who built them at Memphis—
τὰ ἐν Μέμφει βασιλέα ; according to Herodotus,[1] Menes
himself founded Memphis (the White Wall). It is now
established that " Memphis ", as a city, really dates from
Pepi I (VIth Dyn.) ; but the White Wall is mentioned on
monuments as early as the reign of Khasekhemui (end of the
IInd Dyn.),[2] and we may allow that it and the royal buildings
were founded by Menes. Now let us describe these ceremonies.

(i) *Khâ nsut, Khâ biti*.—On a platform reached by a stair,
a chair of state, the throne, was set up. The King went up
the steps, sat on the throne, and " appeared " to men, holding
the crook and whip of Osiris in his hands. Then he " rose "

FIG. 33.—The *Sma Taui*.

The King, seated on his throne between the goddesses of Upper and Lower
Egypt, holding the Osirian crook and whip, tramples on papyrus and lotus,
which Horus and Thoth (replacing Seth) bind round *Sma* signs. Abydos.

(*khâ*), wearing the White Crown, as " King of the South ".
The sign *khâ* means that the King " rises like the sun "[3]
on the Eastern horizon. The same ceremony was performed on
another throne for the " Rising of the King of the North ",
wearing the Red Crown. The throne was that of Horus [4] ;
the King was called " the Horus of the living ". On his head

---

[1] Hdt., ii, 99 ; iii, 91 (cf. above, p. 32). Diodorus (i, 50) ascribes the building
of Memphis to Uchoreus, a mythical King, whose name recalls the " fore-
name " of the legendary Bocchoris (see below, pp. 347–8).

[2] Petrie, *Royal Tombs*, ii, 23, No. 193.

[3] Louvre, Stele C.213. " Behold, His Majesty Seti I rose like the Sun (*khâu
mi Râ*) in his palace of life and strength."

[4] **XXX**, pp. 92, 93, figs. 15, 16.

the two crowns were combined in the single diadem called the Pskhent.[1]

(ii) *Sma taui*.—The King was presented with a *Sma* pillar, with a cleft top,[2] round which were wound the papyri of the North and the lilies or lotuses of the South, symbolizing the Two Lands, *taui*. The composite sign thus obtained, *Sma taui*, signifies " the union of the Two Lands ". This pillar, garlanded with the two plants, was inserted in the base of the royal throne, so that the King was supported by the flora of the Two Egypts.[3]

On the monuments of the classical period the gods Horus and Seth, in their own persons (the parts being taken by priests wearing suitable masks), bind to the base of the throne, under the feet of their human successor, the lotus and papyrus [4] which grow in the " two portions " which Geb bestowed upon them in heroic times (Fig. 33).

(iii) *Pekhrer ha inb*.—With the divine ensigns going before him (Fig. 35), the King " went the round of the Wall ". The different versions of this scene on later monuments show that it always took place at Memphis, and was repeated regularly at the festivals of the local god, Phtah-Sokar. The " Wall " was the White Wall built by Menes.[5] The King went round the rampart which protected Upper Egypt against invasion from the Delta. As he went round the wall, on the south and on the north, he seemed to review the Two Egypts and to enclose the wall in a magic circle, under his protection. On the Pyramids, when the King dies and becomes a king in heaven, they say to him, " Seated on the throne of Osiris, with thy sceptre in thy hand, thou givest orders to the living . . . thou hast gone the round

Fig. 34.—The (White) Wall of Memphis.

---

[1] *Pa skhenti*, " That which embraces " the King's head. Cf. *From Tribe to Empire*, p. 132.

[2] Vase of Khasekhem, IInd Dynasty. The goddess Nekhebt presents the *Sma taui* to the King. Cf. op. cit., p. 146, fig. 10.

[3] Sometimes the King is represented (as a statue) borne on the *Sma taui* as on a stand. **XXX**, p. 106 (Pepi I).

[4] Gautier and Jéquier, *Fouilles de Licht*, p. 37. Sometimes Thoth takes the place of Seth (**XXX**, p. 95). The Niles of Upper and Lower Egypt also bring the heraldic plants, or bind them for the King (**XII**, liv, p. 138).

[5] Sethe, " Menes und die Gründung von Memphis," in **XXXIX**, iii, 2, p. 138.

(*pekhrer*) of the territories of Horus, thou hast gone the round of the territories of Seth." [1]

Since the wall was none other than the White Wall of Memphis, the coronation rites probably date from the foundation of the White Wall by Menes, after the recovery of the Delta by the *Shemsu-Hor* of the South.

For the united monarchy, a royal city was needed, distinct from Nekheb and Buto, and more central. Menes built it at the point which commands Delta and Valley, " there where the two countries are in equilibrium " (above, p. 71), at Memphis, " the balance of the Two Lands." In the Greek period Memphis was still the city where the Ptolemies took the Crowns and received " their great royal office ".[2]

What did these coronation rites mean ?   They chiefly recalled the double kingship of Horus and Seth, but the memory of Osiris was there. As soon as he " rose ", the King held in his hands the crook and the whip which had been wielded by Anzti, the shepherd of peoples, before he surrendered them to his supplanter Osiris. In another royal festival, the Sed, in which the ceremonies just described were repeated, Osiris was recalled as the prototype on whom the kings, his human successors, modelled themselves.

This Sed-feast played a very important part in the life of the Kings of Egypt. It was held several times in the course of a reign ; we find it observed in the Ist Dynasty, and it was kept up in Roman days. Unfortunately, though we know certain episodes of the Sed from monuments of all periods, no complete representation has been preserved. Moreover, the Sed was one of those " mysteries " performed inside the temples, which are depicted in the reliefs but are not explained by any precise text, and are the subject of a " religious silence " on the part of Herodotus. The interpretation of the Sed is, therefore, much disputed and quite hypothetical. The following are the general characteristics of the feast and the meaning which I see in them.

[1] *Pyr.*, §§ 134–5.
[2] Rosetta inscr., Greek text. l. 8.

Several ceremonies, at first distinct, and of different origins, seem to have been combined in a single liturgy. This includes at least three characteristic episodes :—

(i) A repetition of the coronation rites ;

(ii) A ceremony in which the wife and children of the King take part ;

(iii) A gathering in honour of Osiris, represented by his emblem, the lopped trunk, or Zed pillar.

(i) On the day of the Sed-feast the King renews his enthronement.[1] He performs his " risings " in two pavilions, each containing a throne, that of the South and that of the North; the word-sign *Sed* has as a determinative this double

FIG. 35.—Episodes in the Coronation or the Sed.

The King (Thothmes III) clad in the Osirian winding-sheet, and preceded by the ensigns of Upuat and Khonsu, goes a ritual round (*pekhrer*).
Seth-Nubti and Horus, the ancestral Kings, direct his shooting (see **XXX**, p. 105).

pavilion, with the two thrones together (Fig. 36).[2] There the King assumes the Two Crowns, the crook, and the whip. After the two risings, comes the " Union of the Two Lands ", and then the " Procession round the (White) Wall ". But there is a detail in the royal costume which is peculiar to the Sed ritual—the King wears a cope falling from the shoulders to the knees, with two slits through which his hands come to hold the crook and whip. When he is seated, this cope covers him like swaddling-clothes, or a winding-sheet. This costume is only worn by the King at the Sed-feast and at his

[1] Palermo Stone, p. 19, " Rising of the King of the South, rising of the King of the North, Sed-feast " (Ist Dynasty).
[2] On the Sed-feast, see Moret, **XXX**, pp. 235 ff.

coronation,[1] and by Osiris [2]—a fact of which we shall presently
see the importance.

With what object were the coronation rites repeated? It
was in order to renew in the King his consecration as Horus.
The latent force of the rites which had consecrated him the
first time tended to expire; it was therefore desirable to
repeat them at periods which may have been determined by
the King's age,[3] for, with his royal dignity, the very life of
the King was renewed—he received from the Sed a new youth.

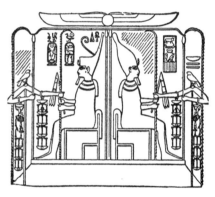

Fig. 36.—Rising of the King of Upper Egypt and Rising of the King of Lower
Egypt in the Double Pavilion of the Sed-feast.

The ensign of the Falcon with its two arms presents to the King the
whip of Osiris and the emblems of the Sed-feast and of longevity. Luxor,
Amenophis III.

This youth, this physical and royal "renewal", is one of
the incontestable effects of the Sed-feast recorded by the
inscriptions.   By the Sed the King receives "years in
millions".   The word-sign meaning "millions of years" (see

---

[1] Moret, **XXX**, pp. 240–4, 252, 263, 277, 281 (figs.). Coronation: Der el-
Bahari; cf. **XXX**, p. 80, fig. 12; p. 93, fig. 16.

[2] **XXX**, p. 271, from G. Moeller, in **XII**, xxxiv, pls. iv, v.

[3] The Rosetta decree translated the epithet of the King, "Lord of the Sed-
feast, like Phtah," as "Lord of the thirty-year gatherings"—κύριος τρια-
κονταετηρίδων. Accordingly, modern historians often call the Sed "Thirty-year
jubilee".   Under the New Empire the "Sed of the year 30" is mentioned
(cf. Moret, **XXX**, p. 259).   But where did they start—from the birth of the King,
or from his accession?   No certain reply is possible, with our present evidence.
It has been suggested that "thirty" is a vague term, like "generation" (op.
cit., p. 260).   All that can be said is, that "after this festival, the King commenced, as it were, a new reign.   The feast seems to prove that at the beginning
the kingship was given only for a determined period" (**XXII**, § 220).

Fig. 36) is a god of eternity holding in his hands young sprouts, the emblem of the years, and it is closely associated with the word " Sed-feast ". The temples built for the celebration of the King's Sed are called " buildings of millions of years ".[1] Then the gods say to the King : " I give thee years with the Sed-feast." [2] They address Seti I in these flattering terms : " For thee we have united the Two Lands beneath thy sandals ; for thee we have joined the lotus with the papyrus. Rising as King of the South and as King of the North . . . thou sittest on thy throne, when thou dost appear on thy stand of the Sed-feast . . . Thou art renewed and thou beginnest again, thou becomest young like the infant Moon God ; thou growest up again (like) him, from season to season,[3] like Nun at the beginning of his time ; (thou renewest) thy births by repeating the Sed-feast. All life is in thy nostrils, for thou art the King of the whole earth, for ever." [4] This explains an epithet frequently given to the King—" he who renews his births," *uhem mesut.*[5] But the " renewal " was not lasting. From the Ist Dynasty onwards, the King, after holding the Sed-feast, repeated it twice, thrice, or four times, according to the length of his life,[6] as if he needed to dip himself in a bath of youth more often as he grew older.

(ii) The episode which introduced the Queen and the royal children is an integral part of all representations of the Sed, but, for lack of explicit texts, it is hard to interpret. Mr. Newberry [7] regards it as a nuptial episode ; as a rule, accession to the throne was conditional upon the marriage of the royal candidate with a princess of the blood, who brought him her rights as heiress, and so this was recalled at the Sed feast. Moreover, at Soleb (XVIIIth Dyn.) and Bubastis (XXIIIrd Dyn.), there are texts in which the King declares that in holding the Sed-feast he assumes, in addition to the defence of Egypt, the special protection of the holy women of the Temple of Amon. Now, at this time the Queen was High Priestess of Amon, at once wife and worshipper of the god. In the festival in which the King was supposed to recover

---

[1] **XXX**, pp. 246, 265, 267 (figs.).   [2] Ibid., p. 257.   [3] Cf. *Pyr.*, § 1491.
[4] Mariette, *Abydos*, i, 51. Cf. **XXX**, p. 256.   [5] **XXIX**, p. 84.   [6] **XXX**, p. 258.
[7] *Egypt as a Field for Anthropological Research* (British Association,   Liverpool, 1923, pp. 11–13).

youth and longevity, it seems quite possible that the Queen and the royal children, representing the ancient and the future heirship of the crown respectively, should have taken a part ; but our evidence is so doubtful that we cannot say anything definite.

(iii) It has been positively denied that the Sed-feast had an Osirian character—that is, that it in any way showed the identification of the King with Osiris.[1] But the " Osirification " of the King by the rites of the festival seems to me to appear clearly in the third episode, which I shall describe briefly. This was the erection of the Zed pillar.

After the " Risings of the King " and the " Procession round the White Wall " came the " Erection of the Venerable Zed " of Osiris (sehâ zed shepes). In the classical period,[2] the festival of the Zed was connected with the feast of Sokar-Osiris, held on the first day of the first month of the germination of plants. This same day, the 1st Tybi, is, in the calendars, a fixed annual feast of the royal coronation, independent of the accession of the particular King. The erection of the Osirian fetish is, therefore, inseparable from the royal coronation, and from the Sed-feast by which that coronation is renewed.[3]

If the Osirian myth was one of the characteristic episodes of the Sed, was it not in order to establish the assimilation of the King to Osiris ?   Just as, in the Pyramids, the body of Osiris is set up, that he may resume his " great office " of royalty, so here the Zed was set up to bear witness that the Pharaoh's reign would be " stable and lasting ".[4]

There are many other Osirian features in the royal Sed. From Osiris the King takes, not only the whip and crook, but the special costume, like a winding-sheet, in which the god is ritually clad.[5] How could the King take on the whole outward aspect of Osiris, but by intimate assimilation with

---

[1] Newberry, op. cit., pp. 11–12 ; other scholars share this point of view.

[2] For good examples of the erection of the Zed, dressed up like a statue, see J. Capart, Le Temple de Séti Ier, pl. xxix (below, Fig. 56).

[3] Sethe has elucidated these problems in " Menes und die Gründung von Memphis ", in **XXXIX**, iii, 2, p. 138. In the classical period obelisks were set up (a rite with the same meaning) at each coronation. Cf. J. H. Breasted, "The Obelisks of Thutmose III," in **XII**, xxxix (1901), pp. 59–60.

[4] This is the meaning of the word zed in the language, apart from its use for the fetish of Osiris.

[5] See the costume donned by Rameses I for the Sed, and that which he wears as the dead god Osiris (**XXX**, pp. 277, 281).

Osiris ? That is why the King, in the course of the Sed-feast,
receives the rites which Isis, Anubis, Thoth, and Horus
performed over the body of the god when he was slain by
Seth, in order to reanimate it. Happily we have a text,
engraved under a picture of Pepi II (VIth Dyn.) enthroned
in the double pavilion, which expressly states that " the
mouth (of his statue) has been opened in the Golden Building,
the first time that he celebrates the Sed-feast ".[1] Anubis
and Horus opened the mouth of Osiris, to allow him to breathe,
to speak, to feed himself, to come back to life. So, in my
opinion, in the Sed-feast the King was supposed to " imitate "
the death and resurrection of Osiris. So surely as these rites
had reanimated Osiris, would they renew the failing life in
the old King. Since the King was not really dead, as Osiris
was, the Sed, with its Osirian rites, represented for him an
insurance against the chances of premature death.[2] A promise
of long life, of " millions of years by the Sed-feast "—that
was the meaning of the erection of the venerable Zed and the
obelisks, in the course of the festival.

We even hear of a Sed-feast which was held, not for a human
king, but for Osiris himself.[3] This is represented on sarcophagi
of the end of the Second Theban Empire. The " Royal
Rising " on the two thrones, in the double pavilion, the solemn
procession of the god, the special costume reserved for the
feast, the erection of obelisks, the presence of the Queen
and the royal children, the progress of the Apis Bull,[4] everything recalls the special rites of the royal Sed, as they are
represented at Abusir (Vth Dyn.), Soleb, and Bubastis.[5]
Nor can it be said that this attribution of the Sed to Osiris
is late. We have seen that the coronation rites, repeated in
the Sed, conferred on the King the sceptres of Anzti-Osiris.
The legendary kingship of Osiris inspired the coronation rites
of the Thinite Kings.

So the Sed presents sufficient Osirian elements for the

---

[1] Sethe, *Urk.*, i, p. 114.

[2] As I said in *From Tribe to Empire*, pp. 151–2, the Sed, from this point of
view, was the last vestige of a very ancient custom, common to many primitive
peoples, whereby the King when old was ritually put to death.

[3] G. Moeller, " Das *Heb-Sed* des Osiris," in **XII**, xxxix (1906), p. 71. The
figures are reproduced in my **XXX**, p. 271.

[4] Another episode which may be connected with the Sed, already mentioned
on the Palermo Stone.

[5] This is also the opinion of Moeller, op. cit.

definition proposed by Petrie and myself—that the Sed is an " Osirification " of the King—to contain an appreciable amount of truth.

It is none the less true that our present evidence does not allow of a complete explanation. The very name of the feast is of uncertain meaning. *Sed* means " tail ". Is it an allusion to the King's waist-cloth, girt with the tail of an animal ? But the " cope " worn by the King has no tail. Can we with Petrie understand " tail " in a figurative sense—" end," " last part," and so the " end " of a period in the King's life ? No definite answer is possible.

However that may be, the ceremonial of the coronation and of the Sed was a ritual which continually recalled the mythical reigns of Horus-Seth, Osiris, and Horus, Son of Isis. The mechanical repetition of obligatory rites, which overloads all royal festivals in ancient Egypt, in all periods, seems cumbrous and monotonous to us. For the Egyptians is was a peculiarly vivid evocation of the past, hailed by Court and people with the joy which attends any allusion to the " good old days ". The coronation and the Sed became festivals at which the great dignitaries of the State appeared, and the priests of the gods of cities and nomes, carrying the statues of deities and ancestral kings.[1] The people joined in with an enthusiasm which astonished Herodotus in the fifth century B.C. Certain episodes required that the crowd should take part in miming representations, like the Mysteries of the Middle Ages. By a stroke of fortune an XVIIIth Dynasty tomb has preserved a lively and picturesque representation of the erection of the Zed at the Sed feast by King Amenophis III.

" The King himself," aided by a few officers of his Court, pulls at the ropes " to set up the Zed ", which we must suppose previously lay on its side, like dead Osiris. The scene takes place in the presence of the Queen, the royal children, and the women of the Harem of Amon. Underneath the royal personages are gesticulating figures described as " the inhabitants of Pe " and " the inhabitants of Dep "—that is the people of Buto, the old capital of Horus. All these people are fighting and belabouring each other with fists and sticks ;

---

[1] The statues and ensigns carried at these feasts give information about the traditional groups of cities and nomes which has been used above (pp. 76 ff).

some fly routed ; others come to grips : some are shouting,
" I have taken Horus Kha-m-maat (Amenophis III)," and
others answer " Hold him fast ! " or " Don't resist ! "

What is the meaning of this little war, played by the actors
of a " royal mystery ", in connection with the setting up of
the Zed ?   It seems to have been a presentment of the
conquest of Buto by the *Shemsu-Hor* of Upper Egypt. The
people were divided into two parties, one of which " took "

Fig. 37.—The Erection of the Zed on the Morning of the Sed-feast by the King
himself.

From a sketch by A. Erman.

Horus who had come from Upper Egypt, to consecrate him
as King, while the others opposed it.[1] Thus Amenophis III,
on the anniversary of his coronation, at the moment when he
set up the Zed, the fetish of Osiris, caused a " mystery "
to be performed. Not only the legend of Horus, Son of Osiris,

[1] Sethe, " Menes und die Gründung von Memphis," pp. 136–7. Cf. Brugsch,
Thesaurus, p. 1190, and my *Mystères égyptiens*, p. 14.

at Buto, was represented ; the King himself, Kha-m-maat,
appeared. Amenophis III, and every other King at the time
of his coronation, regarded himself as still being Menes, or
Horus, King of Upper Egypt, striving against his enemies
for the union of the Two Lands, which was the necessary
condition of social progress and civilization.

To terminate, let me point out one essential feature. The
possession of the throne by Menes and his successors was
founded not only on divine inheritance, conquest, and
political tradition, but on principles which have as much
to do with magic as with dynastic right. Menes, and
every Pharaoh after him, certainly continued, in his own
person, his ancestors Horus and Osiris ; but he also *imitated*
the great facts of the " divine history ", with procedure
which was that of magicians. He claimed to identify himself
really, bodily, with Horus and Osiris, by *repeating* their
traditional deeds—rising, union of the Two Lands, erection
of the Zed. As a magician, conjuring a snake, threw a spell
on it, saying, " Fall !   Be overthrown ! I am Ra ! " [1] so,
with the same assurance, the King declared that he was
Horus, that he was Osiris, and forced human credulity to
accept his absolute identity with the gods. The rites of the
coronation and the Sed owed this imperative, ritual character
to their immense antiquity. They combined an act of
imitative magic with a religious and political ceremony.[2]

IV

THE THINITE ADMINISTRATION

In *From Tribe to Empire* (pp. 145–9) I have related what
the Thinite monuments tell us about the Thinite Kings of the
first two dynasties, who reigned some four hundred years
(about 3300–2900). Here the fragments of the Palermo Stone
supply the most precious evidence ; for every year of a reign

---

[1] *Pyr.*, § 442.
[2] In the Thinite tombs a certain number of wooden and ivory labels have been
found, which were once attached to oil-jars. These labels bear conventionalized
engravings of the feasts of the coronation and Sed, and of the Service of Horus,
in which the oil was used for anointing. Many of these labels are reproduced
in J. Capart, *Les Origines de la civilisation égyptienne*, pp. 16–17.

they give the event which was regarded as the most important and the most worthy to give its name to the year. We do not yet find " the year x of the reign of So-and-so ", but the year of such-and-such a feast, building, or (more rarely) victory. The great events of the reign of every King, which give their names to the year, are the royal feasts of the coronation and the Sed, the birthdays of the King and of the gods Anubis, Upuat, Sed, Min, Herishef, Mafedet,[1] the festival of Sokar, the procession of Apis, the shooting of the hippopotamus, the foundation of temples, palaces, and forts, the building of great divine barges, and occasionally deeds of war—a campaign in which the King " smote the Troglodytes " or the Easterners.[2] Certain events recur periodically, such as the feast held in honour of Horus every two years, which was known as the " Service of Horus ", *Shems-Hor*, clearly showing how it was desired to connect the reigning line with the *Shemsu-Hor*. From the IInd Dynasty onwards, a census of the revenues of the country was made every other year, alternately with the Service of Horus. Lastly, we have for every year a record of the height of the Nile flood (above low-water level)—" 4 cubits, 1 hand," and in the following years " 5 cubits, 5 hands, 1 finger," and so on. These annals of the Thinite Kings tell us about their duties towards the gods and towards their people.

For the gods they built temples. These were at first of wattle and daub, then of brick, and finally of good stone,[3] with timbers from Lebanon. In these temples, the foundation of which is recorded on the Palermo Stone, the Kings officiated as priests, following a ritual according to the calendar of festivals—the birthdays of gods, great religious gatherings at sanctuaries, etc. In order to ensure regular worship, the Kings created priests who were "servants of the god ", *hemu neter*. For the sacred furniture they set carpenters, joiners, metal-workers, potters, and goldsmiths to work. Statuaries carved figures of the gods in wood and stone, or hammered them in copper and gold, either in human form or with the head of a beast. Vases of hard stone and palettes

---

[1] Or perhaps the manufacture (*mest*) of statues for these gods (*Urk.*, i, 114).
[2] Palermo Stone, p. 18, and Tablet of King Den.
[3] Temple of Horus at Hieraconpolis (cf. Pl. III, 3, and *From Tribe to Empire*, p. 135).

of schist, deposited as votive offerings, were engraved with
scenes of battle—victories over Nubians, Libyans, and
Asiatics—or with the jubilee of the Sed, or with the feast of the
Service of Horus.

For the welfare of their subjects the Thinite Kings
developed irrigation and built dikes.[1] In order to increase
the supply of labour and of cattle they imported thousands of
prisoners of war and beasts taken in Libya and other foreign
countries. Holding, as they did, the copper mines of Sinai
and the gold mines of Nubia, they had the reserves of metal
needed for the arts of peace and for war.

We should be glad to know something of the situation of
persons and of land with reference to the Thinite Kings,
but we lack explicit evidence. The clay stoppers of provision-
jars deposited in tombs often bear impressions from the seals
of officials.[2] In the eyes of the King, the only people
who mattered, besides his wives, seem to have been the
officials of the Court or the royal administration.

Even in the Ist Dynasty we know of some queens—
Neit-hetep, the wife of Menes, and Mert-Neit, the wife of
Usaphaïs. Their names show that they were associated with
the worship of Neith, the goddess of Saïs. The Queens seem
to have brought to their consorts hereditary rights over the
Western Delta. Nemaat-hapi, the wife of Khasekhemui,
appears on the monuments ; other queens, whose names are
mutilated, are mentioned on the Palermo Stone. The King's
wives proudly bore the epithet " She who sees the Horus
and the Seth " (*maa Hor Seth*),[3] that is, the King, the living
image of the Two Gods, or else " She who follows Horus "
(*khet-Hor*). The " King's Mothers " and the " Mothers of the
Royal Children " hold these titles officially. In the Thinite
Court, therefore, the Queen, dowager or reigning, had an
important position, and she was given a " house " for her
maintenance.

---

[1] See above, p. 32, for the dike built by Menes to protect the region in which
Memphis was afterwards built. Methodical observation of the Nile and anxiety
to control the floods by irrigation-works are also attested by the annual records
of the inundation on the Palermo Stone.

[2] As in Shinar, engraved cylinders were rolled over the clay before it was
fired, so as to leave an impression. A great many of these cylinders have been
found.

[3] Petrie, *Royal Tombs*, ii, pl. 27, Nos. 96, 128, 129. This title survived in the
formal title of the Queens.

The King was surrounded by a Court personnel. There were " Princes " (*hati-â*)—etymologically, " First Ones "—who were not sons of the King. They were entrusted with offices, such as that of Director of the Soldiers (*imra meshâu*).[1] Therefore the King had an army. A " Chosen Guard " protected the King's palace, which was called the " House of the Chosen Guard " (*per setep-sa*). At the Court, too, lived Servants of the Royal Rising (*shems-khâ*), scribes (*sesh*), priests (*sem*), and officiants provided with rituals for the celebration of feasts (*kheri-heb*). Probably each king had a personal residence ; therefore the political capital changed with every reign, and there was as yet no fixed centre of government. The White Wall was the city of the coronation, where the King resided for his " Risings " and the Sed ; but the Thinite Kings must have had their individual palace,

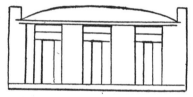

Sarcophagus reproducing the front of a palace.   Festival kiosk.

FIG. 38.—Public Buildings.

a great rectangular building with a double gate (of the North and the South), near Thinis, for their tombs have been found there. This palace was called simply the " House ", and later the " Great House " (*per-âa*), or the " Double Great House ". In the Memphite period this name came to designate the King himself, and is the origin of our word " Pharaoh ". In the palace there were at an early date central offices of administration, directed by the " First under the King of the South " (*tpi kher-nsut*) and by " Friends of the Palace " (*smer per-âa*), but we do not know what were the details of their duties with the King at that time.[2]

---

[1] *Imra* means that which is in the mouth, the tongue, i.e. him who speaks in the King's name to his subordinates, and passes their prayers to the King for them.

[2] For all aspects of Thinite administration, see the administrative seal-impressions collected by R. Weill in *La IIe et la IIIe Dynastie* (1908), and explained by Sethe, in J. Garstang, *Mahasna and Betkhallaf* (1902), and by E. Meyer, **XXII**, §§ 219 ff.

While the central administration of the palace is still obscure, the bipartite organization of the Two Lands, the inheritance of the *Shemsu-Hor*, is more apparent. In the two capitals the King posted trustworthy chiefs,[1] the Warden of Nekhen (*iri Nekhen*) and the Chancellor of Upper Egypt (*szati shemâ*) in the royal city of Nekhen (Hieraconpolis), opposite Nekheb, the capital of the South, and the Warden of Pe (*iri Pe*) and the Chancellor of the King of the North (*szati biti*) in the royal city of Pe, opposite Dep (Buto). The services directed by them were the House of the King of the South (*per-nsut*) and the White House (*per-hez*) in the Valley, and the Red House (*per-desher*) [2] in the Delta. For the desert country—Sinai, Libya—there were Protectors of Countries (*âz mer*), and then Directors (*imra*) and Scribes (*sesh*) of Foreign Countries (*Khaset*).

The royal officials devoted their whole attention to the

cultivation of the land, the breeding of cattle, and the agricultural and industrial crafts. What was the condition of the workers, and of the people of all classes ? We have no idea whatever, and the situation of the land is also hard to determine. From certain indications one may say that the King had a " personal domain " over the land in Egypt. It would be most interesting if we could follow the development which, in a few centuries, from the Thinite period to the Memphite, extended this limited royal domain to the whole of Egypt. With our present evidence we only see the starting-point and the end.

FIG. 39.—Sign of the " Scribe ". Showing the reed pen, pot of water, and palette with two cups, for red and black.

The Thinite cylinders speak of vineyards belonging to the King. One, which has the pious name of " Worship of Horus who presides in the Sky ", is known from the Thinite period to the XIIth Dynasty ; it had a special Protector (*âz mer*). Another vineyard is called the " Second " (*sen*) of the other. A third is the " Vineyard of the House of the King

---

[1] It is possible that the Vizier (*tati*) is already mentioned beside the King on the Palette of Narmer.

[2] These " Houses " have the colours of the South (white) and North (red). The White Wall of the new capital had the colour of the South.

of the South and of the Red House ". The King must also have had a great deal of arable land, woods, and livestock of all kinds ; certain officials are called Sealers or Wardens of all the Goods (*ikhut nebt*) of the King. Funerary foundations, of which I shall speak later, necessitated the " conveyance of provisions " (*uzeb*), for which there were " houses " managed by Inspectors (*za hr*).

There are numbers of other titles, designating " provision centres " (*ist zefa*), where the produce of the cornfields, vineyards, orchards, pastures, and workshops was collected. In primitive societies the chief is a " collector of property and provider of food ".[1] This service was entrusted to "Protectors", "Directors", " Great Ones ", "Recorders", whose employments are clear, though we do not know their relative ranks. The King's granaries were very important ; among those employed there, we may mention the " Criers " (literally, " Loud-voiced " *nekht-kheru*), who announced the quantities brought in by each tax-payer, or taken away as payment. As early as the Thinite period, we find a high official, the Royal Carpenter, directing the constructions in which wood played an essential part— tombs, palaces, boats, etc. Artistic workers and metal-founders were likewise under the orders and supervision of

Fig. 40.—King Khasekhem (IInd Dynasty) in Sed Costume. Hieraconpolis.

the King. We do not know if they were yet, as later, in the Memphite period, placed under the direction of the high-priest of Phtah (the " Great Chief of Works ").

Some significant facts indicate that property and the crafts were still partly free, but under some control from the King, which became increasingly strict and effective. From the IInd Dynasty onwards, the King held a census (*tenut*) of immovable property (fields) and movable goods (assessed in gold) every two years. He attached such importance to this

[1] Cf. Davy in *From Tribe to Empire*, p. 68.

that in the IInd Dynasty the years of reigns are given as
" the fourth time, fifth time, sixth time, etc., of the census ",[1]
while the intermediate year is still dated by the Service of
Horus. The two essential facts of a reign were, therefore, the
dynastic festival and the establishment of the budget for two
years. For this is the only character which we can ascribe
to the *tenut* ; it was an assessment of private fortunes, with
a view to establishing the total of taxes and impressed labour
due to the King. So, too, the recording of the Nile rising made
it possible every year to reckon the variable return of the land
and the movable scale of dues. From these facts it seems that
a large part of the land was still private property in the hands
of the inhabitants, and that gold (in bullion, dust, rings,
jewels) represented the movable fortune produced by trade
and industry freely conducted in the cities.[2]

So the existence of owners of landed and movable property
is proved by the very control exercised over them by the
King's administration. By the side of the royal domain,
there were private estates ; but these were destined to
disappear, as the kingship strengthened itself by its works
and established its doctrine of divine right. Already the
appropriation of all power by the King was on the highway to
realization. Most of the Thinite cylinders give the name of the
service without the personal name of the official; they are the
seals of offices, not of officials. This implies an administration
long established ; the man did not hold the office—the
office, delegated by the King, made the man. It indeed
seems, as Eduard Meyer says, that " the monarchy of Menes
was not an oligarchy of noble families, but a state composed
of officials ".[3] Nevertheless, the Saru of the primitive local
organizations managed to find a place in it. We do not yet
notice the predominance of the sons and relations of the King,
which strikes us in the Memphite period, in the high offices
of the State. In this respect the Court of Menes and the offices
of the royal city mark a transition between the system of
local authority which Egypt had known before the Thinites,
and the complete centralization achieved by the first
Memphite Pharaohs.

---

[1] Palermo Stone, pp. 22 ff.
[2] **XXII**, § 224.
[3] **XXII**, § 222.

V

THE NEXT LIFE

If Pharaoh's life was necessary to his people, his death interested them quite as much. A god on earth, the King, like all gods, possessed the secrets which triumph over physical death. Let his people help him to perform this last feat in his divine destiny, and he would remain the protector of his subjects for ever; after his decease, he would be the intermediary and intercessor between men and the gods of the other world. As I have said elsewhere,[1] "Even after death, the King's office towards his people is not over . . . Hence the people's eagerness and alacrity in building splendid tombs to protect the royal body from any hurt and to secure him fitting and eternal means of subsistence."

The royal tombs of the first two dynasties were discovered in the Thinite necropolis, near Abydos, by E. Amélineau, J. de Morgan, and Flinders Petrie between 1895 and 1900. The most ancient of these tombs are rectangular graves dug in the sand, about 23 feet long, 16 feet wide, and 10 feet deep. The sides are revetted with walls of brick, and a ceiling of wood, supported by wooden props, is covered with sand, so that the tomb is invisible from outside.[2] About the middle of the Ist Dynasty, these dimensions were tripled or quadrupled, floor, walls, and ceiling were faced with wood, and a funerary chamber was arranged in the centre with small cells at the side to hold provisions—jars, furniture, arms, ornaments, and woven stuffs. At the end of the IInd Dynasty, the tomb of Khasekhemui is nearly 280 feet long, and contains fifty-eight chambers. It is reached by a descending stair of brick; over the roof of sand a stone stele bears the name of the royal occupant; and inside are stelæ naming some of the familiar companions of the King, buried with him.[3]

When we see all this material heaped up in these great

---

[1] *From Tribe to Empire*, p. 152.

[2] The tomb of King Aha Menes is of a peculiar type. It is an edifice of unbaked brick, about 177 feet by 88, rising above the ground, without doors or windows. The body was placed in a central hall, while lateral cells served as store-rooms. The outside walls were adorned with projections.

[3] For the royal tombs, cf. J. de Morgan, *Recherches sur les origines de l'Égypte*, Paris, 1896–7, and Jéquier's résumé, *Histoire de la civilisation égyptienne*, pp. 92 ff. See also **XXVII**, " Avant les Pyramides."

buildings, intended for the future life of the occupants, we can obtain some idea of what the Thinite Kings expected after death. Only a belief in the survival of the body, defined by no written text as yet, can explain the piles of furniture and provisions. The theory of kingship set forth above allows us to infer that the King, being the successor of Horus and Osiris and their living image on earth, had to be treated after his death like those gods themselves. That the King might be sure of an eternal life, he had simply to be identified with Osiris in every possible way. The Sed-feast, by its Osirian rites, already restored youth to him in his lifetime ; the same rites, applied to his body, would reanimate him, as they had reanimated Osiris, for all eternity. In the other world, by the

Fig. 41.—Sarcophagus of Mycerinus (IVth Dynasty), reproducing the Front of an Archaic Palace.

side of Osiris, Pharaoh would act as the ancestor and protector of the reigning King, just as Osiris, according to tradition, had done for Horus, Son of Isis, when he succeeded his father on the throne.[1]

[1] In an inscription of Rameses II, the rôles of the dead King, Seti I, and of his living successor, Rameses himself, are contrasted in these terms. " Thou dost rest in the Underworld, like Osiris, while I have risen like Ra for mortals, and sit on the great throne of Atum, like Horus, Son of Isis, who avenged his father " (l. 77). Seti I replies to his son that he is asking Ra and Osiris to grant Rameses II " millions of years of eternity on the throne of Horus of the Living. I have said to Ra ' Grant him eternity on earth ' . . . I have said to Osiris ' Double for him the eternity of thy son Horus ' " (ll. 100, 103–4) (H. Gautier, " La Grande Inscription d'Abydos," in XII, xlviii, p. 65). Cf. the definition of the dead King's duties to men, given in the Pyramid Texts, below, pp. 172, 185.

The new life promised to the dead King will be described in the next chapter, for it is only in the texts of the Memphite pyramids that we find an account of it. But certain titles borne by the Thinite officials who were buried round their King are suggestive. They tell us that for the King rites were performed relating to his *Ka* and his *Akh*—that is, to the deified Substance and to the divine Spirit which the King rejoined in the next world. We have enough evidence to be sure that as early as the Thinite period men believed in a spiritual life, reserved to the King after his death. In the Memphite period we shall see the development of these doctrines which prolong the divine life of earthly Pharaohs after their decease.

As for the " people " ruled by the Thinite Kings, we have no text of the period telling us what became of them after death. But in the necropoles excavated by Junker and Reisner we find bodies laid on their left side, with the face to the West, and food, vases, tools, arms, and ornaments buried with them. The ritual attitude and the funerary furniture bear witness that, to ensure for the dead survival in another world, a cult was already paid to them.

We shall see that in the Memphite period the Osirian doctrine imposed itself on this cult with all its authority ; the funerary ritual became an adaptation to men of the magical methods invented by Isis and Horus to save Osiris from death. But some of the formulas in the VIth Dynasty Pyramids present a simplified version, in which the dead man is not called Osiris, and the officiant is not called Horus, Son of Osiris, but the rites are those which any son performs for the salvation of his father : " O Father, rise up on thy left side. Turn on thy right side towards this Water of Renewal which I have given thee . . . Take this bread which I have made for thee.[1] . . . It is I, thy son, thy heir . . . I have dug barley for thee, I have tilled wheat for thee." The dead man is told to " turn towards his house " ; there his heir occupies his (former) place.[2] " Thy son is in thy seat, furnished with thy forms. He does what thou wert wont to do among the living; he tills the corn, he tills the wheat, and he makes an offering of it to thee." [3] If the dead man has had an enemy, let him be easy, for his son protects and avenges him (*nez*). " Rise up,

---

[1] *Pyr.*, §§ 1802, 1046, 187 r. [2] § 1388. [3] § 760.

see, hear, what thy son has done for thee. He smites the man
who smote thee " . . . for " the son avenges his father ".[1]
I agree with Adolf Rusch, who drew attention to these texts,
in seeing here a pre-Osirian ritual. The Memphites later
remodelled it so as to adapt it to the Osirian revelation, by
means of very obvious interpolations.[2]

It is probable that such rites date back to the Thinite
period ; we discern here an individual family cult, not yet
brought under the sway of a funerary god and still free of
all priestly influence. But in my opinion the interest of these
passages goes beyond the strictly religious aspect ; they give
us a glimpse of Egyptian society in the days when the clan
was split up into families, grouped under the authority of the
father.[3]

We see here the social importance of the funerary cult,
its connexion with heredity in the paternal line ; if the son
has to feed his dead ancestors, it is because he is the heir,
and tills the family land. A very strong bond unites the dead
and living of the household ; the dead father lives again in
the person of the son, and remains, in theory, the master of
the family possessions. At the end of one of these formulas,
after the dead man has received the offering from the fields
tilled by his son, he is addressed thus : " O Master of the
House (neb per), your hand is over your goods ! " [4]

Another conclusion to be drawn from these texts is that in
the pre-Memphite period family property still existed for
a part of the population, and had not yet been absorbed by
the domain of Pharaoh ; this we had already deduced from
the examination of the administrative documents.[5]

So we come to the end of the Thinite period, about 2900.
At this remote date the Egyptian had already made an
enormous advance. Coming to a country which was full of
resources, but demanded unwearying effort, foresight, and
method, he controlled the forces of the Nile and disciplined

---

[1] § 1007. Cf. above, p. 100.
[2] " Osiris " was put in after " father ", " Horus " after " son ", and so on.
Cf. A. Rusch, " Der Tote im Grabe," in **XII**, liii (1919), p. 75.
[3] Above, p. 96, and *From Tribe to Empire*, pp. 35–6, 71.
[4] *Pyr.*, §§ 1881, 2641.   [5] Above, p. 140.

Nature, submitting himself to their laws. In the Nile which he transformed into Osiris, the Egyptian worshipped a master, an educator, and the creator of his food and his life ; he knew that the Nile had exercised a salutary constraint over him, which he translated into the beneficent kingships of Osiris, Horus, and the human Pharaohs. The interdependence which the Nile had created between the dwellers on its banks, limiting every man's rights by the needs of others, had for its consequence collective labour, organized with a view to the welfare of all. So, at the sight of Egypt, peaceful and prosperous, the Egyptian of very early times lavished his feelings of gratitude, in many forms, on the divine Nile which had inspired his institutions. This is how a hymn, preserved in the Pyramid Texts, celebrates the inundation, which was the cause every year of the renewal of the health and wealth of the King (living and dead) and the gods, of the administration, of agriculture, of the calendar—in a word, of the material and social life of Egypt.

The Rising of the Nile.—It comes, the water of life which is in the sky. It comes, the water of life which is in the earth. The sky burns for thee, the earth trembles for thee, before the birth of the God. The two mountains are opened,[1] the God manifests himself, the God takes possession of his body.[2]

Kings and Gods purify themselves in it.—See this King N. ! His feet are nosed [3] by the pure waters. . . . (The Gods) are come, they bring thee the pure water (issued) from their Father. They purify thee, they incense thee, O King N. ! Thou bearest the sky with thy hand, thou dost spread the earth beneath thy foot. The fresh libation is served at the Door [4] of this King N. Every God washes his face (with it), and thou dost wash thy two arms, Osiris ! Thou dost wash thy two hands, O thou King N. !

Effects of the Inundation. (i) *Food ensured for the King and the Gods.*—Thou renewest thyself as a god, O thou Third Orderer of the Offerings.[5] So the perfume of the Goddess Khetutet is for this King N. ; the bread is in the mansion of Sokar, the meat in the house of Anubis.

(ii) *Social organization.*—King N. is prosperous.[6] The palace stands. The month is born. The nome lives. The lands are measured. The barley is grown, the wheat is grown,[7] with which this King N. is gratified here, for ever. (*Pyr.*, §§ 2063–70.)

[1] The two rocks of Elephantine, from which the Nile was supposed to issue.
[2] The land of Egypt.
[3] We should say " kissed ". In ancient times the Egyptian "nosed"; he did not know about kissing. In this paragraph the rebirth of the King after death is compared to that of the Nile after the drought.
[4] The palace or tomb.
[5] The King is called " the Third at Heliopolis " in § 363 (after Atum and Ra ?).
[6] *Uza*, to be healthy, in good condition, later became the formula used by the royal officials to say that " all was well " with the King and the administration.
[7] Literally, " thou dost cultivate."

CHAPTER II

The Memphite Monarchy. The Autocratic King, Son of Ra

THE IIIrd and IVth Dynasties are called Memphite by Manetho. The political centre shifts from Thinis to Memphis and Heliopolis, and a new period begins—the Memphite Old Kingdom. It comprises the IIIrd and VIIIth Dynasties and covers rather more than five hundred years, roughly from 2895 to 2360. In respect of the kingship, two processes appear : first, a steady development ending in the full maturity of an autocratic monarchy by right divine, from the IIIrd to the Vth Dynasty (2895–2540), described in the present chapter, and then the decline of the royal authority, under the assaults of the priests and nobles, who set themselves up on the ruins of the autocratic monarchy (VIth to VIIIth Dynasty, 2540–2360). A period of confusion follows ; the country is at the mercy of factions and foreigners, a revolution jeopardizes the very existence of Egypt, and, after two centuries (about 2360–2160), a new political and social order is established (Chap. III).

I

HELIOPOLIS AND THE KINGSHIP BY RIGHT DIVINE

The northward movement of the Thinite Court and administration began early, and was progressive. The White Wall (Memphis), the coronation city, had an attraction for the Horus Kings, from Menes onwards, which is apparent in the IInd Dynasty, and explains the reaction of the followers of Seth under Peribsen, mentioned above (p. 119).

Most of the Kings of the IInd Dynasty were not buried at Abydos. The ruins of their tombs are found between the Fayum and the White Wall. Now, we know that the residence of each King was built near his last dwelling-place. Even Seth Peribsen, who returned to Abydos to build himself a

146

PLATE IV

1. GREAT PYRAMID OF CHEOPS, SPHINX, AND GRANITE TEMPLE
AT GIZEH

INTERIOR OF A MASTABA

2 STATUE-CHAMBER (SERDAB)
(Reisner's excavations)

3 CHAPEL AND STELE-FAÇADE
(Tomb of Phtahhetep)

tomb there, had a funerary cult in the necropolis of the White Wall, and so had his successor Send.

The movement towards Memphis and Heliopolis reached its height with the IIIrd Dynasty. The founder of the dynasty, Zeser, adopted new architectural forms for his tomb. At Bet-Khallaf, near Abydos, he built a great edifice of brick, with sloping walls like a truncated pyramid, a kind of gigantic pedestal to raise the king above the ground.[1] This first effort led him to make another experiment : south of the White Wall he raised a rectangular tower, surrounded by buttresses of limestone blocks, built one over the other in five stories, and diminishing upwards, so as to look like a colossal staircase facing in four directions. This is the famous Step Pyramid of Saqqarah,[2] a tomb conceived on a new plan, inspired by a fresh ideal of the next life. Zeser's successors vied with him in daring. Still further north, at Zawyet el-'Aryan, Neferka hewed the lower portion of a pyramid in the rock [3] ; it was never finished, but at Medum and Dahshur Snefru successfully accomplished his gigantic undertaking. After him come the other Pharaohs of the IVth Dynasty, Cheops, Chephren, and Mycerinus, who built the great pyramids of Gizeh. So the residence of the King came, reign by reign, nearer to the White Wall ; it was finally established there when Pepi I (VIth Dyn., about 2500) built for the Court a new quarter of the White Wall—the Good Harbour, Mennefer, Μέμφις, Memphis.

So the royal city henceforward merges into the religious city, Heliopolis, just as, formerly, the royal palace of Pe was near Dep, the city of Wazet, and Nekhen was opposite Nekheb.

Certainly it was the prestige of Heliopolis that drew the Pharaohs northwards ; we see it in the change which appears in their names, the mirrors of their moral personality. On the King-lists (Turin, Saqqarah), we find Kings of the IInd Dynasty with names like " Fair is the Ka of Ra " (Neferkara), or " Fair is the Ka of Sokar " (Neferkasokar) ; so the gods of Heliopolis and Memphis had already won the allegiance of the Thinite Kings. Soon Ra the Sun would become the rival of Horus as patron of the dynasty.

---

[1] Photograph in **XLVII,** p. 8.
[2] Photographs, ibid., p. 42 ; **XXVII,** p. 158.
[3] Photographs in **XLVII,** p. 47 ; **XXVII,** p. 154.

KINGS OF THE IIIrd, IVth, AND Vth DYNASTIES [1]

MONUMENTS.		KING-LISTS.	MANETHO.	APPROXIMATE DATE.
Horus-name	King's Name		*IIIrd Dynasty.* 9 Memphite Kings (214 years)	
Neterkhet	Zeser	Zeser I	2. Tosorthrus	2895
Khaba		Zeser II	The other names	
		Sezes	differ from those	
Sanekht	Nebka	Nebkara	in the lists	
	Neferka Huni	Neferkara		
		Huni		
			IVth Dynasty. 8 Memphite Kings (277 years)	2840
Nebmaat		Snefru	1. Soris	
Mazedu		Khufu	2. Suphis	
		(Cheops)		
Kheper		Zedefra		
Userib		Khafra	3. Suphis	
		(Chephren)		
Ka		Menkaura	4. Mencheres	
		(Mycerinus)		
			5. Ratœses	
			6. Bicheris	
		Shepseskaf	7. Sebercheres	
			8. Thamphthis	
			Vth Dynasty. 8 Kings (*sic*) from Elephantine (248 years)	
Irmaat		Userkaf	1. Usercheres	2680
Nebkau		Sahura	2. Sephres	
Neferirkara		Kakaï	3. Nephercheres	
		Shepseskara	4. Siophes (Sisires)	
Neferkhau		Khaneferra	5. Cheres	
Isitibtaui		Neuserra	6. Rhathures	
Menkhau		Menkauhor	7. Mencheres	
Zedkhau		Zedkara Issi	8. Tancheres	
Uzataui		Unas	9. Onnus (Unus)	2540

[1] Cf. E. Meyer, **XXII**, pp. 189, 199, 225.

In the Step Pyramid of Saqqarah, the door of the funeral chamber is faced with enamelled bricks, on which is engraved the title of the King who built it, the Horus Zeser.[1] After the phrase " King of Upper and Lower Egypt, Lord of the Two Crowns, Neterkhet " comes the Sun Ra over the sign of Seth of Ombos, *Nubti*. What does this new title mean ? That the Sun Ra has mastered Seth.[2] As a signal act of grace, the god of Heliopolis has taken up the cause of Horus against Seth,[3] and even takes the place of Horus to defeat his enemy. However, out of respect for ancient tradition, Ra did not maintain his claim ; Horus would resume his traditional

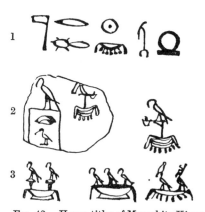

FIG. 42.—Horus-titles of Memphite Kings.

1. Neterkhet, called *Râ-Nubti*. Cartouche-seal at the end of the line.
2. Khaba, called *Hor-Nubti*. 3. Other forms of the title *Hor-Nubti*, with the Two Gods (Horus and Seth), sometimes expressed by the plural (three falcons).

rôle as conqueror of Seth. The next King, Khaba, replaces the sun by the Falcon Horus standing over *Nubti* ; henceforth *Hor-Nubti*, with or without an accompanying epithet (cf. Fig. 42), appears in the titles of all Pharaohs. All the same, the Ra of the priests of Heliopolis did not willingly give up what he had once captured. The new title *Hor-Nubti* retained

[1] Photographs in **XX**, vol. i, p. 243, and **XLVII**, p. 95 ; cf. **XXX**, p. 22, n. 3.

[2] A text composed in the Ptolemaic period and ascribed, by a pious fiction, to Zeser, replaces the Sun Ra by the Falcon Horus, over the sign *Nubti*. This shows that the two titles were equivalent in the eyes of the Egyptians.

[3] The Greeks translated *Hor-Nubti* by ἀντιπάλων ὑπέρτερος, " He who is over his enemies ", meaning that Horus is over Seth, like the falcon on the back of the gazelle (above, p. 51).

a certain " solar " character. As time went on, the original meaning was distorted ; *Nubti* (He of Ombos) suggested, by the sound, *nub*, " gold " ; but gold is the " liquid of Ra ", since the sun is all of gold, so *Hor-Nubti* becomes *Hor-nub*, *Hor n nub*, " Golden Horus." This confusion was further encouraged by the assimilation of the Falcon Horus, the sky-god, with the Sun Ra, which was expressed in a new divine type, " Horus-Ra, the great god, lord of heaven." The Pharaohs, from the Middle Kingdom onwards, called themselves, not " Horus ", but " Horus-Ra ", or, better, " Ra-Horus ".[1]

About the same time, at the beginning of the IIIrd Dynasty, the practice arose of inscribing the King's name, or sometimes the whole of his ceremonial titles, in an oval set on a flat base, *shenen* (Fig. 43), which we call a cartouche. For the Egyptians this oval represented the elliptical course of the sun round the world, and defined the limits of the kingdom which it lighted—" all that the disk (*shenen*) of Aten illuminates." It is Zeser, again, who, on the same bricks of his pyramid, placed after his name this *shenen*, which here appears as a royal seal (Fig. 42). With Snefru (beginning of the IVth Dyn.), the cartouche comes into use, at first optionally, and then as a matter of course.[2] Chephren adds to the royal name inscribed in the cartouche [3] two epithets which had a great future : " The Great God " (*neter âa*), that is, Ra, and " Son of Ra " (*sa Râ*) (Fig. 44). The decisive step was taken ; Pharaoh, while still Horus Son of Isis, now became, in addition, Son of Ra, and, at the same time, Ra Incarnate.

In the Vth Dynasty, Kakaï, the third King, accepted a second name on the day of his coronation, Neferirkara,[4] which should express his especial devotion towards Ra. The custom was maintained after him. From the VIth Dynasty onwards, Pharaoh would have two names—that given him at his birth, and the coronation name, which he held direct from Ra, the god who dispensed crowns. This new name

---

[1] For references, see **XXX**, pp. 21–4. For the meaning of the title " Golden Horus ", see Moret, " Le Titre d'Horus d'Or," in **IV**, xxiv, p. 23, and **X**, xi, p. 35.

[2] Relief from the Wady Maghara (Sinai) : Lepsius, *Denkmäler*, ii, 2*a*.

[3] Statues of the King in Borchardt, *Statuen A.R.* (Cairo), Nos. 15, 17.

[4] H. Gauthier, " Le Livre des rois d'Égypte," in **II**, *Mémoires*, vol. xvii, pp. 114, 358 ; cf. **XXII**, § 250.

became the specially royal name. It had a truly *Solar* character, for the sign of the Sun was written at the beginning of the word composing it—" Ra is strong," " Ra whose Ka is venerable," " Beloved of Ra," and the like. Thus, with few exceptions, the disk of the sun would henceforward shine before the name given to the King at his coronation.

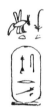

Fig. 43.—The Earliest Cartouche, that of Snefru.

Fig. 44.—One of the First " Son of Ra " Titles.

(From Petrie, *History of Egypt*, 1923, pp. 46, 87.)

A King of the IXth Dynasty, Kheti (Achthoës), established the whole title of Pharaoh in a form which was afterwards generally followed. The royal coronation-name was inscribed in a first cartouche, then came the epithet " Son of the Sun ", and then a second cartouche containing the Pharaoh's birth-name. Then the full normal title comprised five names ; that of Rameses II will serve as an example.

(i) *Horus-Ra*	(ii) *Lord of the Two Crowns* (*Nebti*)	(iii) *Golden Horus* (*Hor-Nubti*)
Mighty Bull, Beloved of Justice	Defender of Egypt, Binder of Foreign Lands	Rich in Years, Great in Victories

(iv) *King of Upper and Lower Egypt* (*Nsut Biti*)	(v) *Son of Ra*
Rich in the Justice of Ra, Chosen of Ra	Beloved of Amon, Rameses
(1st cartouche, royal coronation-name)	(2nd cartouche, birth-name)

The influence of Ra on the moral personality of the King is here despotic. Ra takes half of the Horus-title, he modifies the sense of the title *Hor-Nubti*, he imposes a new coronation-name, asserts himself as the father of Pharaoh, and encloses the two names in the seal of his heavenly kingdom. Thus, from the Vth Dynasty, the Sun of Heliopolis, just as he rules over the physical world, in Egypt more than in any other country, becomes the head of the spiritual world and the patron of the Pharaohs.

How did Ra obtain this spiritual ascendancy, which at the same time brought him political power, first as the rival and then as the supplanter of the prestige of Horus and Osiris ? It was by the increasing influence of the clergy of Heliopolis. We do not know how this priesthood began. In the time of the *Shemsu-Hor*, Heliopolis was already the intellectual centre of the Valley, where the calendar was established and imposed on the rest of Egypt, with all the consequences entailed by such an innovation. But in this pre-Thinite period Heliopolis had no political authority, or the Kings of Thinis would have called themselves Ra, and not Horus, from the accession of Menes onwards. Indeed, Ra himself was not dominant at Heliopolis before the IInd Dynasty.

The local god of Heliopolis was Atum, who was represented in human form. With him were associated, in a triad, a lion and lioness, Shu and Tefnet, who belonged to the neighbouring town of Leontopolis.[1] This Heliopolitan triad already had solar elements, for the lions represented the sun in the sky, but without any extensive radiation or influence beyond the boundaries of the Central Delta. However, the theologians of Heliopolis, who were metaphysically inclined, wished to explain the origin of the universe, so they taught that Atum had created the world, and had produced from his own substance Shu and Tefnet, his first children, who gave birth to other gods.

As creator and lord of the world, Atum of Heliopolis found himself, by the force of circumstances, in rivalry with a god who represented the mightiest of natural forces—the Sun.[2] We know little of the earliest forms of the worship paid to the universal Sun ; but we may take it that, like the Nile, the material sun was adored everywhere, without being the local

---

[1] On the right bank of the Damietta Arm, north of Athribis.

[2] For the origins and development of Heliopolitan conceptions, see Maspero's " Études de mythologie et d'archéologie " (**XXXVIII**, vol. ii) and the clear and suggestive account published in 1924 in the series *Das Alte Orient* by Adolf Rusch : *Die Stellung des Osiris im theologischen System von Heliopolis*.

god of any particular city. Among the prehistoric ensigns we find the sun, in the form of a disk, set on a pole [1]; we do not know whether this disk was already called Aten, or Ra, as it was later. Nor can we trace the transition from the solar ensign to the Sun God. The Pyramid Texts, however, which were written by the priests of Heliopolis, give legends about the Sun which conflict with the teachings of their city and must come from outside sources.

According to these stories, which were inspired by the observation of nature, the material sun was the son of the sky-goddess Nut, who gave birth to him every day on the Eastern horizon.[2] At once, without losing his universal character, the Sun became a being with a definite form, born at daybreak, growing towards noon, and then declining and dying every evening. Popular imagination gave him various shapes, sometimes like those of local gods. He was represented as a falcon hovering in the sky, as a scarab beetle rolling his ball before him, or else as a child of human form or a " milk-calf with pure mouth ", according as his mother Nut was imagined as a divine woman or as a cow.[3] He was given a history full of mythical episodes, battles against clouds and storms, personified by the serpent Apophis,[4] victories, and conquests, in which the parallel adventures of the legend of Horus and Seth were mingled.

The object of these wars was the lordship of the world, of which the Sun remained undisputed sovereign. The lord of the world needed a *name*. The word *Râ* defines the association of the material solar disk, in its manifold aspects, with the conception of glorious and beneficent power, which henceforward made up the personality of the universal Sun.

It was a stroke of genius on the part of the Heliopolitan theologians to adopt as the patron of their city this Sun, Ra, universally adored and so easy to understand. They rejected none of the various forms with which popular superstition had invested him ; as calf, falcon, beetle, or human child, Ra lent himself to all kinds of poetical or speculative developments. He was first blended with Atum, the god of Heliopolis, to form a composite deity, Atum-Ra. He appropriated the work of Atum, the creation of the world, as it had been

---

[1] *From Tribe to Empire*, p. 123.   [2] *Pyr.*, §§ 1688, 1835.
[3] *Pyr.*, § 27.   [4] From the XIIth Dynasty onwards.

elaborated by the metaphysicians of Heliopolis, and he brought to Atum the popularity, prestige, and splendour of the golden orb and his authority as universal lord. The lowest date which can be assigned to this fusion of Ra and Atum is the middle of the IInd Dynasty, when the Thinite King Neferkara (Fair is the Ka of Ra) for the first time introduced Ra into a royal name.

Ra could not establish himself at Heliopolis without his

FIG. 45.—Shu (the Air) separating Nut (the Sky) and Geb (the Earth).

family. Now, according to the popular conception, his mother Nut was the wife of Geb, the Earth God. As we have seen, Earth and Sky were the parents of Osiris and Isis, Seth and Nephthys. The daily opponent of Seth, the celestial Horus, was attached to the same group in the popular mind. So the gods of the earth and the sky formed a natural society which could not be arbitrarily broken up. Accordingly, when Ra was promoted to patron of Heliopolis and associate of Atum, the priests thought it wise to accept all the great Nature-gods in a body, and to make Heliopolitans of them. Thus was constituted " that great body of the gods born in the beginning, who are at Heliopolis ",[1] in which the Heliopolitan triad and the Osirian group are so strangely associated, the former ranking first to preserve the honour of the gods of the city.

1.   Atum-Ra.
2–3.   Shu and Tefnet.
4–5.   Geb and Nut.
6–9.   Osiris and Isis ; Seth and Nephthys.[2]

In this group of nine deities, the politico-religious system of Heliopolitan Ennead, what became of the great gods of the Thinite Kings, Osiris and Horus ?

Osiris holds a good position, in the third generation from Ra, but below the Sun, who is the central moving power of the universe. As god of the Nile and vegetation, he has by nature a rôle which never brings him into conflict with the god of Heliopolis ; but he is a god of the earth, and therefore

---

[1] *Pyr.*, §§ 1041, 1250, 1689.   [2] § 1655.

inferior in situation and sometimes hostile to the great shining god of the sky—one of the Lower Beings (*khert*),[1] below the Upper Gods (*heru*).[2] Moreover, Osiris had been the dynastic god of earthly kings, and even after yielding his place to Horus he was still the god who renewed the life of the King and saved him from death. The theologians of Heliopolis therefore welcomed Osiris and all his prerogatives gladly. With his legend, his special rites, and his character as a dead and resurrected King, Osiris came into the Ennead. His rôle was reconciled with that of Ra as well as possible ; it was by Ra's order that the murdered Osiris had been resuscitated by Anubis,[3] Thoth, and Isis, and it had been the tribunal of Heliopolis which declared the rights of Osiris, justified (*maâu*) against the accusations of Seth.[4] Thereupon, Osiris, "taken up from among the gods of the earth, was counted among the gods of the sky." [5] We shall see later that Osiris, after his promotion to the sky, continued to be the protector of the dead Kings, thanks to ingenious devices by which the rites proper to the gods of the earth were combined with those reserved for the gods of the sky.

Horus presented a more delicate problem. As celestial Horus, he was the natural rival of the Sun, and exercised, like the Sun, supreme sway in the sky and in Nature. In places the Heliopolitan texts retain the memory of an equality of power between Ra and Horus of the Eastern Horizon, Harakhti,[6] who are both given the exceptional title of " Great God ".[7] Now, at the head of the Ennead there could only be one master, and that was Ra. Horus, although a very powerful sky-god, was not originally admitted into the " Great " Body of the gods of Heliopolis. This exclusion of Horus is a very remarkable thing ; may we not see in it the counterpart, in the society of the gods, of Ra's gradual usurpation of the place held by Horus in the royal title—that is, in human society ? Only the second Ennead, the " Small Ennead ", would receive Horus, and he was an inferior Horus, the Child, the Son of Isis, whose kingdom was chiefly terrestrial, having only his name in common with the old lord of the sky. It

[1] *Pyr.*, § 1203.   [2] *Pyr.*, § 2038.
[3] Sarcophagus of Sbeek-aa (XIIth Dynasty) in Roeder, **XLIX**, p. 222.
[4] *Pyr.*, §§ 957, 1689.   [5] *Pyr.*, § 1523.
[6] *Pyr.*, §§ 337, 560, 621. The Eastern horizon where Ra rises.
[7] *Pyr.*, § 1690.

was as posthumous son of Osiris that he was admitted into the company of Ra.[1]

So in the religious sphere the theologians of Heliopolis effected, to the advantage of Ra, a synthesis parallel to that which the Thinite Kings had brought about in the political sphere, to the advantage of Horus and of themselves. Now, in Egypt, where society was essentially religious, the gods governed kings as they did men; the victory of the theologians therefore meant a political triumph.[2] History shows that similar situations generally lead to the same results. The gods of Heliopolis, that is their priests, would end by controlling the monarchy. This they seem to have achieved at the beginning of the Vth Dynasty.

According to Manetho, the Vth Dynasty came from Elephantine.[3] A much older legend makes it come from Sakhebu, a city in the 2nd Nome, near Memphis. In any case, there is a breach between the Pharaohs of the IVth Dynasty and those of the Vth. According to the Turin Papyrus, the split comes in the reign of Kakaï. Now, this is the Pharaoh who first assumed a solar coronation-name, inscribed in a second cartouche. Here we are helped by popular tradition, which we have in a version of the XIIIth Dynasty. According to the story, the first Kings of the Vth Dynasty, Userkaf, Sahura, and Neferirkara-Kakaï, were usurpers, the sons of the wife of a priest of Ra, Lord of Sakhebu, their true father being no less than Ra himself.[4] The god had announced that these three children " would fill this beneficent office (the kingship) in this Whole Land ". Ra himself watched over the child-bed of the mother and the birth of the three; and each was born with the appearance of " a lusty boy, with limbs of gold ", already marked with

---

[1] *Pyr.*, § 176. Cf. above, p. 91.

[2] As I said above (p. 118), in the royal title and official documents the titles relating to Upper Egypt always have the place of honour, i.e. come first, in memory of the victory of the South over the North in the time of Narmer and Menes. There are not many exceptions to this rule, save on monuments of the IIIrd, IVth, and Vth Dynasties, and more rarely of the VIth, and sometimes in the Pyramid Texts. This was the period when Heliopolis imposed its teaching on the royal family; at these times, the North has the ascendancy over the South (**XII**, xliv, p. 15).

[3] In *Pyr.*, § 812, Setet, goddess of Elephantine, is mentioned, " who takes the Two Lands, the flame who captures her two regions." Does this refer to a temporary conquest by a family from Elephantine ?

[4] G. Maspero, **XLVI**, p. 23, 38–44.

the colour of the Sun. Such legends are often a remnant of historical tradition, true but distorted. It is possible that in this case the popular imagination embroidered on authentic facts,[1] that it made a story out of a striking event, for which the way had long been prepared by the Heliopolitan synthesis of the Ennead and the influence of the priests on the title of the King—the conquest of the monarchy by the son of a high priest of Ra.

II

THE KING AS SON OF RA AND AUTOCRATIC SOVEREIGN

The Memphite Kings of the Vth and VIth Dynasties did not become priests of the Sun ; the monarchy did not develop into a theocracy. But the sons of Ra were autocrats who took as their example their father, the Demiurge, King of Heaven and creator of the universe. The Heliopolitan texts describe the occupations of Ra, and this picture is applicable in every detail to the earthly King, for, in Egypt as elsewhere, the gods were made in the likeness of men.[2]

The King lived in a castle or mansion (*het*),[3] which had a different shape and name according as it was the Palace of Upper Egypt (*per-ur*) or the Palace of Lower Egypt (*per-neser*)[4]; together the two palaces were the two regions (*iterti*)[5] of the sky or of the earth ; they symbolized the Two Egypts over which the King ruled. Before the palace stood tall masts (*senut*),[6] sometimes obelisks.[7] An avenue led to the doors, lined with ram-headed or lion-headed sphinxes, which mounted guard and " kept men away ".[8] Stout doors with massive bolts defended the entrance to the palace, and likewise " kept away " the vulgar[9] ; sometimes they were adorned with protomæ of bulls, the images of the god

---

[1] Cf. **XXII**, § 250.
[2] In the following quotations from the Pyramids the reference is either to Ra, King of Heaven, or to the deified Pharaoh after his death, now a king in the sky like Ra. The texts found in the Memphite tombs which describe the occupations of the Pharaohs confirm the evidence of the Pyramids.
[3] § 14. The mansion of the *Sar* in Heliopolis, i.e. of Ra.
[4] § 852. Each palace had a special architecture. Cf. fig. 27.
[5] §§ 731, 757, 1182.   [6] § 645.   [7] 1178.
[8] § 1726 ; cf. 1178*b*.   [9] § 655.

Khonsu.[1] A large staff of guards, door-keepers, and watch-men mounted guard (*sa*) round the palace, [2] which was, moreover, called " the house where the guarding of the King is done " (*step-sa*) (cf. p. 192).

The King was supposed to rise (*khâ*) at dawn, like the Sun. As soon as he opened his eyes, the women of the harem greeted him with a song of good omen, accompanied by instrumental music : " Wake in peace, as the Goddesses of the Crowns wake in peace ! Thy waking is peaceful." [3] In the temples, the gods were waked in the same manner ; in fact, the word for " morning ", *dua*, took on the sense of the morning greeting, or worship, and came, with a suitable determinative, to mean " worship ". When he had woken up the King performed his ablutions in a bathroom (*qebehut*), where his servants bathed, massaged, and dried him. He is compared to the god Ra who, when he awakes, finds the goddess Coolness (*Qebehut*), the daughter of Anubis, waiting to serve him with her four pots of water, with which she " refreshes the heart of the God on his waking " [4]; after the bath, " Horus rubs the flesh of Ra, and Thoth rubs his legs." Then, washed and clean, the King put on his divine garments [5] and took his morning meal.[6]

When the moment was come to perform his " great office " as King, he went into his palace, where he found his special scribe (the scribe of Ra was the god Uneg),[7] and the other scribes. Each of them sat before his writing-palette, with its two cups for red and black ink, and his rolls of papyrus.[8] The King took note of reports and letters, opened the sealed papyri, dictated or himself wrote replies and " royal orders ", sealed them with his great seal,[9] and sent out his messengers (in heaven these are the " Unwearied " planets).[10] The King went into accounts of receipts and expenditure ; a scribe in charge of the Book of the God (the King) supervised food-supplies (*kau*) [11] and communicated the returns of goods

---

[1] § 416.   [2] *Urk.*, i, pp. 41, 52.
[3] A. Erman, *Hymnen an das Diadem der Pharaonen*, p. 18, from a papyrus of the New Empire ; but this hymn was in use as early as the Old Kingdom (*Pyr.*, §§ 56, 383, 1478, 1518).
[4] § 1180.   Cf. 519, 525, 542.   [5] § 533.   [6] §404.
[7] § 952.   [8] § 954.
[9] Sethe, *Urkunden*, i, 60, for the King writing himself ; i, 128, for his sealing himself.
[10] *Pyr.*, § 491.   [11] § 267.

and livestock.[1] In the intimate circle of the King lived his counsellors—that is, his sons, brothers, and grandsons, the King's Acquaintances (*rekh*), his Friends (*smeru*),[2] and the " learned men " of the House of Life, whom he placed at his right hand.[3] Among these were chosen the Chiefs of Secrets [4] of the different services (later they became *secretaries*, in the ordinary sense), in whom the King placed his trust ; he spoke to them with condescension,[5] and could be friendly and confiding with them, for most of them were of the royal family and had been brought up at the Court with himself (see below, p. 192).

When the King held an audience, he sat on his throne before the palace door. It was there that he publicly performed his royal office. The essentials of power were " commanding" and " judging ".

Commanding consisted in " uttering words " (*uzu medu*),[6] which were made into " royal orders " (*uzu nsut*), that is decrees, written on tablets or papyrus and afterwards engraved on stelæ, which themselves were given this name *uzu*.[7] In these words the King " spoke justice " (*maât*). Just as the Demiurge had created the world and living things by his Word, so the King emitted words which became realities ; his command, once issued, engendered acts, being immediately executed and blindly obeyed by his subjects. It was a compliment to say to a royalty, " All that you say is realized." [8] The King, consequently, " says what is, and causes what is not yet to come into being." [9] If, at the moment of speaking, he wishes to maintain the *status quo* of the world, " he says what is, and does not say what is not." [10]

In accordance with Egyptian custom, this power of command which marked the King was personified as a deity, Hu, the God of Command. " What Hu commands " and

---

[1] *Urk.*, i, 55, 106. Cf. Palermo Stone.

[2] See below, p. 190. In heaven, Ra has his own " Friends " and " Acquaintances " (*Pyr.*, § 856).

[3] § 267. The " House of Life " was the school of the scribes, soothsayers, magicians, astrologers. Cf. **XLVI**, p. 130, n. 1.

[4] [5] Below, p. 192.   [6] § 272.   [7] *Urk.*, i, 62.

[8] *Urk.*, i, 39. " All that issues from His Majesty's mouth becomes reality at once." See the theory of the " Issuing Voice " (*pert kheru*) below, p. 396. In primitive societies it is believed that, by magic, " the sign creates the thing . . . the word (creates) the event " (*From Tribe to Empire*, p. 48).

[9] *Pyr.*, § 1146.   [10] §§ 1159–60.

" the divine command given by His Majesty " [1] are expressions employed by the King himself, and signify the King's command.

Judging was " dividing words " (*uza medu*), making a decision between one thing and another. " Behold all ! The King utters words for men, and he divides words for the living (Gods) " [2] is said of the dead King when he reaches heaven. To give judgment the King held audience at the door of the palace or " before the palace ". He donned his royal head-dress, took the sceptre and whip in his hands, and gave his decisions. Even in heaven, the King continued to perform his great office of judge, and " transmitted his decisions to men ".[3]

These sentences, these orders of the King, constituted Justice, Truth (*maât*), that is, public Law. There were as yet no codes of law ; law was made up impromptu by the King's dooms, as circumstances demanded. Law was " what the King loves " ; the opposite was " what the King hates " [4] ; and what he hated above all was that " his word should be transgressed ".[5] Pharaoh's subjects did not discuss the law given by the King : " I have spoken the law that the God loves, every day." [6] " I am the King's true liegeman, I am the Great God's true liegeman ; I love good, I hate evil ; what the God loves, is acting justly." [7]

The King " spoke " to his subjects in person, uttering his august revelations to them ; but he also employed spokesmen, heralds, who both spoke in the name of the King and answered in that of the people. Hence arose the expressive titles borne by the most ancient officials of the Court—the Mouth (*ra*), the Tongue (*imra*), the Repeater (i.e. he who repeats the words of the King, the herald, *uhemu*), the King's Eyes and Ears, etc. So, too, Geb has, under the Demiurge Atum-Ra, the same rôle of herald to mankind and to the commonalty of heaven, and is called Mouth of the Earth [8] and Wise Mouth (*ra pânt*).[9]

---

[1] *Urk.*, i, 49, 108–9.   [2] *Pyr.*, § 272.   [3] §§ 1124, 1160, 1166.
[4] Decrees of Coptos, and above, p. 123 (*Pyr.*, § 412).
[5] *Pyr.*, § 1161.   [6] *Urk.*, i, 57.   [7] *Urk.*, i, 71.
[8] *Pyr.*, § 2169.   [9] § 1618.

The greater part of Pharaoh's time was not given up to military matters. It is true that he founded arsenals, recruited men, and saw to their instruction ; but he was a warrior in wartime only, on the battlefield. In *From Tribe to Empire* I have described the warlike activity of certain conquerors in Nubia and Asia. In time of peace, the monuments do not show us the Memphite King inspecting his troops or training them for fighting. In the temples, apart from the battle-scenes, we see the King employed in peaceful occupations. He draws his bow against the beasts of the desert. Hunting was a favourite pastime, but also a ritual duty. The tawny hides of the beasts of the desert sometimes concealed the supporters of Seth, the traditional enemies of the *Shemsu-Hor* ; and to kill the gazelle, the lion, or the hippopotamus was to act like Horus and to " defend men against all the ill that Seth might do them ".[1]

Though one of the King's rôles was that of leader of the warriors, his subordination to Ra, since he had become the son of the god, involved a certain *diminutio capitis*. Certainly he still fought in the front rank and bore the brunt of the battle, but he acknowledged that he was helped and protected by Ra and the other gods ; credit for victory was given to his prowess, but also to divine assistance. In the Vth Dynasty, in the time of Sahura, we see Horus Sepdu, a winged griffin, rending the Eastern Barbarians with his claws for the King.[2] In the same way, Horus of the Delta and Seth of Upper Egypt bring him files of Asiatic and Libyan captives in chains.[3] We should remember, too, the very characteristic dialogue between Rameses II and Amon-Ra in the middle of the Battle of Kadesh.[4] This opportune invocation, this appeal for divine assistance, takes us a long way from the Ist Dynasty, when the King all by himself beats down his enemies, rends them or tramples them under-foot, in his form of falcon, lion, or bull. By Memphite times the son of Ra was more concerned with justice than with war and with religious duties than with military glory.

For religion held the predominant place in his daily pursuits. In Egypt, as in many ancient societies, the King

[1] § 1594. Cf. *From Tribe to Empire*, p. 186, and above, p. 108.
[2] Borchardt, *Grabdenkmal des Königs Sahure*, pl. viii.
[3] Ibid., pl. v.　　　[4] *From Tribe to Empire*, p. 323.

was, by definition, the chief priest, above all others, in every temple and to every god. Later we shall see the daily ritual duties which fell to him in this capacity. Now, since Pharaoh had called himself the son of Ra (and of other gods), he had, in addition to the duties of a king, those of a son [1]; for him the worship of the gods became the family cult of his own ancestors. No doubt, even in Thinite times the building of sanctuaries and the celebration of worship fell to the King. The Palermo Stone mentions buildings, statues, and feasts as the chief events of each reign. But after the triumph of Heliopolis this active piety, the construction of temples for the gods, and especially for Ra, became the principal duty of

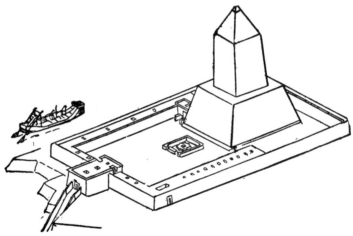

Fig. 46.—Solar Temple of the Vth Dynasty.
A table of offerings in front of the obelisk ; the Evening Boat of the Sun on the right side of the temple.

Pharaoh. The popular legend quoted above states quite definitely what the priests thought themselves entitled to expect from the King whom they maintained on the throne. In announcing to the gods the coming birth of his sons, the future Kings, Ra says : " They will fill this beneficent office in this Whole Land, building you your temples, furnishing your altars with offerings, supplying your tables with libations, and increasing your divine foundations." [2]

The kings of the Vth Dynasty showed their filial piety to Ra by building on the west bank of the White Wall the first great temples which we find in Egypt. They were huge edifices, open to the sky and very simple in arrangement.

[1] Moret, **XXX**, chaps. iv–v.   [2] Maspero, **XLVI**, p. 38.

In a central court stood a " mastaba ", surmounted by a high massive obelisk of white stone, in front of which was a wide table for offerings. The obelisk was a petrified ray of the sun, the symbol of Ra himself. The names of six such temples and of the six kings who built them are found on the monuments and on the Palermo Stone—" Time of Ra " (Userkaf), " Country of Ra " (Sahura), " Place of the Heart of Ra " (Kakaï), " Repose of Ra " (Neferfra),[1] " Glory of the Heart of Ra " (Neuserra),[2] and " Horizon of Ra " (Menkauhor)[3]; they are like a litany of stone in honour of the Sun. In each of these temples the royal bounty maintained clergy, lands, and offerings. The King was supposed to officiate as high priest every day, either in person or by a priest delegated for the service. The reliefs preserved in the temple of Neuserra describe the foundation of the temple by the King and the celebration of the Sed, over which the Sun Ra now presided, since the royal jubilee took place in his sanctuary. Materials, sculptures, everything in this building bears witness to a pious choice, a refined art, and the constant anxiety of the King to show his filial gratitude to Ra his father.

As priest, warrior, and judge the King was inspired by the example of Ra. By living among the gods and modelling his conduct on theirs, he acquired the authority and prestige of the gods themselves, and his subjects expressed their veneration in many forms.

If the King went a journey in a palankeen or on the royal barge, he was preceded by running messengers[4]; the courtiers lined the way, the soldiers of the escort bowed before him, and all raised their hands in sign of worship, crying " Adoration to thee, God of the living who see thy beauty ! "[5] When he came to the palace or temple, for some " coronation feast ",[6] he took his seat " on his ebony throne, like Ra

---

[1] The position of this King in the dynasty is uncertain ; he probably reigned after Kakaï.

[2] In this temple, the porticoes of the court, with their reliefs, and the base of the obelisk are partially preserved, and the table of offerings and court of sacrifice are intact. Cf. Borchardt, *Reheiligtum des Newoserre*, and **XXIX**, " Sanctuaires de l'Ancien Empire," pl. xvi and p. 309.

[3] Cf. Sethe, " Die Heiligthümer des Re im alten Reich," in **XII**, xxvii (1889), p. 111.

[4] *Pyr.*, § 1539.   [5] Borchardt, *Grabdenkmal des Königs Sahure*, ii, pl. xii.

[6] *Urk.*. i. 53.

presiding over the Ennead ",[1] or " on an iron throne, with the heads of glaring lions and the legs of the Great Victim Bull ".[2] He stood up, holding his sceptres, and lifted his hand towards men, and the gods came to him, with bowed heads . . . "for this Sar is the Sar of all the world," as they said of him.[3] " Nosing the ground " before the King—that was the posture demanded of all who presented themselves to him.   Sometimes, in his graciousness, he allowed someone to kiss (nose) his feet instead of the ground ;   this was a sign of especial favour.[4]   Dressed in his golden ornaments, shining like Ra's own, with the artificial beard on his chin [5] and the two living Crowns, the goddesses Nekhebt and Wazet, on his head, and protected by the Uræus-viper flashing above his eyes, the King inspired his humble subjects with an awe which is expressed in certain hymns, such as this, addressed to the Crown of the North :—

O Red Crown Net ! Great one ! Great magician ! O Flame (Uræus) ! Grant that the fear of King N. may be like the fear of thee. Grant that the respect of King N. may be like the respect of thee. Grant that men may pray to King N. as they pray to thee. Grant that King N. may be loved as thou art loved. Grant that his Soul may preside over the living. Grant that his Power may preside over the Akhu (the Spirits). Grant that his knife may be strong against his enemies ! [6]

This god on earth, raised to superhuman stature, was, nevertheless, subject to needs, like the humblest of his subjects. He required moments of relaxation from his august office, and his pleasures had to be provided. So he " gladdened his heart ", listening to singers accompanied by flutes and harps, and watching dances performed to the clash of castanets by slim girls, or by the pygmies brought by his emissaries from the Sudan, who were the talk of every house and every street.[7] Sometimes a sorcerer would present himself before His Majesty and do marvellous tricks, such as "making a lion follow without a leash ", or " restoring a

[1] *Pyr.*, § 1906.
[2] *Pyr.*, § 1124. Iron is the metal of which the heavenly vault is made. The seats of royal statues have lions' heads and animals' legs (Pl. III, 1 ; XII, 3).
[3] *Pyr.*, § 1127.   [4] *Urk.*, i, 53.   [5] *Pyr.*, § 573.   [6] § 196.
[7] § 1189 ; cf. *Urk.*, i, 135, and *From Tribe to Empire*, p. 180.

cut-off head to its place ". When His Majesty was bored, or required distraction from his cares, he summoned his magicians, and bade them do something to lighten his heart. Then one or another would suggest : " 'Let Your Majesty deign to have a barge manned by all the fair girls of the royal harem. The heart of Your Majesty will be lightened when you see the lovely reed-beds of your lake, when you look upon the fair country which surrounds it and its beautiful shores. Let them bring me twenty oars of ebony, fitted with gold ; let them also bring twenty women, of them who have a fair body, fair breasts, and beautiful hair, and have not yet had a child ; and then let them bring twenty hair-nets, and give them to the women as clothing.' It was done as His Majesty had ordered. The women came and went, and the heart of His Majesty rejoiced to see them rowing the barge." [1]

Another most important moment in Pharaoh's life was his meal-time, when the abundance and the choiceness of the dishes marked him out for the admiration and envy of his subjects.

On ceremonial occasions, at least, the royal repast was preceded by purifications—mouth-rinsing, hand-washing, fumigations, anointings, rougings, and donning of clean linen—which were not merely acts of personal cleanliness, but ritual observations.[2] To take food into oneself was, in a sense, a ceremonial action, a sacrifice, for which the agricultural gods gave their flesh and blood.

Purified in body and soul, the King sat down at a table. Originally this was a plain mat, on which a conical loaf or a pot of beer was placed, bread and beer being the staple diet, the typical ration, of the Egyptian.[3] So, in hieroglyphic writing, the word sign " offering " (*hetep*) is a loaf, or a pot, on a mat, and the determinative for a meal is composed of a conical loaf, a pot of beer, and a round cake.[4] The " King's Offering " (*hetep nsut*) shows how much agriculture and stock-breeding had increased the supply of foodstuffs. The fare was extremely rich and varied. Loaves of bread or cakes were

[1] **XLVI**, pp. 29 ff.
[2] Cf. G. Maspero, *La Table d'offrandes des tombeaux égyptiens*, reprinted from *Revue de l'Histoire des religions*, 1897, pp. 4–27.
[3] See the information of the popular legends on this subject, **XLVI**, pp. 32, 37, 57, 97, etc.
[4] Maspero, *La Table d'offrandes*, pp. 30, 36.

arranged in fourteen compartments, then came onions, then ten pieces of meat (beef, goat, antelope), and five kinds of poultry (geese, ducks), with scones between the courses. The drinks included two kinds of milk, four of beer, a brew of fermented figs, and four brands of white and red wine. Then came cakes, with all the vegetables of the year, and fresh or preserved fruit.

FIG. 47.—Seti I before the Table of Offerings.
Behind the King, his Ka guards him (*sa*) and carries his Horus-Ra name. Abydos.

Variety and abundance without stint—that was what marked the King's table. Like the god Ra, the King had at his disposal " thousands of loaves, thousands of beers, thousands of beasts, thousands of poultry, and of all the things on which a god lives ".[1] Like the divine beings, he was the " lord of five meals " a day [2] ; for him, too, " his water was wine ", that is, his ordinary drink was a luxury.[3] Like the gods, he " never knows thirst or hunger ".[4] To keep

---

[1] *Pyr.*, § 2006.
[2] § 717. Does not Rudyard Kipling use the same expression to describe the well-fed British soldier of to-day ?
[3] *Pyr.*, §§ 128–30.   [4] *Pyr.*, § 382.

him alive he has " all the good and pure things which the sky gives, the earth creates, or the Nile brings from his hiding-place " [1] (Fig. 47).

The list of dishes gives us not only the King's bill of fare, but, at the same time, a kind of catalogue of the foodstuffs and supplies (*zefau*) of Egypt which the King stored in his " seats of supplies " which were so numerous even in the Thinite period (above, p. 139).

Victualling and supplies were personified by deities named Zefau, Spedu, detached from the deified Substance, the Ka, whose name in the plural, *kau*, properly means foodstuffs. Now, the King bore a title which was of capital importance to the maintenance of his subjects—he " presided over the food of all living " (*khenti kau ânkhu neb*),[2] and *he made a gift of it* to the gods whom he worshipped and the men, living or dead, whom he wished to take into his service.

From this point of view the " Offering given by the King " (*hetep rdu nsut*) was a social institution, and greatly furthered the policy of centralization. Gods and men became *nourris*, " fed ones," as retainers were called in the Middle Ages ; their physical life and their feeding depended on the bounty of the chief. The King's meal, with its amazing plenty, the menu of which was posted up in temples and tombs, asserted the unmatchable superiority of Pharaoh and increased his prestige and authority. We should remember the competitions in generosity, the solemn distributions of food and gifts, by which candidates for power in primitive societies display their wealth. In *From Tribe to Empire* (pp. 90–1), M. Davy has defined the essential importance of these in the stages by which the clan-chieftain advances to kingship. The acceptance by gods and men of this " Offering given by the King " is, moreover, a recognition of authority, a promise of obedience ; it binds gods and men, as by a contract, to him who feeds them.[3]

---

[1] The formula used of the funeral repasts in the Middle Kingdom, the elements of which are found in the Pyramid Texts.

[2] Borchardt, *Grabdenkmal des Königs Sahure*, ii, pls. v, viii.

[3] M. Davy shows, in *From Tribe to Empire* (p. 92), how this reveals wholly new points of view in the conception of power. Authority is acquired not only by heredity, but by individual contract.

III

King and god in his lifetime, Pharaoh commenced a new existence after his death, in which he was still king and god. In the Thinite period, we were reduced to hypotheses in trying to imagine this prolongation of the royal activity, but in the Memphite period, thanks to the texts engraved in the Pyramids, we know the future promised to the King in the next world. Here we meet a conception characteristic of Egyptian thought, and one which had the most far-reaching consequences.

In the very earliest texts we note that the royal funeral cult is at the same stage of development as that reached at the same time by political institutions ; funeral rites, at the beginning of the IIIrd Dynasty, are crystallized round the person of the King. Just as there is now but a single chief, so it seems that there is but one dead man who matters in Egypt, and that is Pharaoh. That royal corpse must be protected, reanimated, and made to last for ever, for with its fate the destiny of the whole race is bound up, in the struggle against death.

The first stage described by the texts is the assimilation of the King with Osiris, the royal god, slain and resuscitated. Then the theologians of Heliopolis intervene, during the IIIrd and IVth Dynasties. The living King, Horus, they had already made into a son of Ra ; of the dead King, Osiris, they will make a god, Ra himself.[1] The two destinies reserved for the King in the next world, Osirian destiny and Solar destiny, are blended together, without the second annihilating the former. Finally, under the VIth Dynasty (the time at which the Heliopolitan texts were engraved at Saqqarah, in the chambers of the Pyramids), there is a compromise ; the dead King becomes Ra, without ceasing to be Osiris ; in the person of the King, Osiris ascends to heaven and shares the dominion with Ra.[2]

[1] §§ 135, 698, 703.
[2] For what follows, consult J. H. Breasted's fine work, *Development of Religion and Thought in Ancient Egypt* (1912), pp. 99 ff.

PLATE V

1 THE DEAD MAN
COMING OUT AT
THE VOICE
(Tomb of Mera, Saqqarah)

2 OFFERING OF INCENSE BY THE OPENING
IN THE SERDAB
(Tomb of Tı, Saqqarah)

3 RITES OF THE OPENING OF THE MOUTH OF
THE MUMMY
(New Empire)

4 A FAMILY OF THE OLD KINGDOM
Limestone (Musée Guimet)

The Osirian destiny of the dead King is frequently described in the Pyramid Texts, which have preserved traditions of different dates and origins side by side without always combining them in a coherent corpus. An analysis of these documents leads us to observe that in the earliest period the Egyptians distinguished two elements in the person of the King—(i) the human, earthly body (*khet*), and (ii) the spirit, of which the principal forms are the Ka, the Ba, and the Akh.

What became of the body after death, we know from the corpses found in Thinite cemeteries. They were laid in the sand or in a cist, either contracted in the crouching attitude of the fœtus in the womb, or cut up, limb from limb, with the bones in a pile and the head on top. The flesh has disappeared, either through putrefaction or through ritual laceration and removal intended to mitigate the process of decay.[1]

The Osirian myth was invented in order to explain these rites and to perfect them. The dismemberment of the body became the starting-point of a resurrection. The dead King, cut in pieces, was Osiris, dismembered by Seth ; and, since Isis had found the " remedy against death" (above, p. 89), it was enough to apply the Osirian rites to the royal corpse for its reanimation to ensue, as had happened with Osiris.

This reasoning is applied with the imperturbable logic of the first men civilized. " The King's body is for the earth " [2] ; it is condemned to " pass " ; it is made of perishable flesh, " subject to putrefaction " in the sand where it has been laid [3]; but, since the King is the successor of Osiris, his death is explained like that of Osiris—he has been drowned in the river and cut in pieces by Seth. Once that is assumed, the dismembered King becomes dismembered Osiris. In the Pyramid Texts the King is called " Osiris N." Then the sacred drama is reconstructed ; the episodes of the " mystery " played by the Osirian family are now played by the royal family. The Queens take the parts of Isis and Nephthys, the eldest son acts Horus, the " darling son " (*sa mer-f*), and the grandsons, brothers, relations, and friends play the children of Horus, Anubis, and Thoth. At the beginning there is no doubt that the royal family personally

---

[1] **XXVII,** p 175.
[2] *Pyr.,* § 474. " The spirit (*akh*) is for heaven, the body (*khet*) is for the earth."
[3] *Pyr.,* §§ 145, 617, 1878.

took part in the Osirian rites ; but after the very early date
when the ritual was established in writing, in all its minute,
complicated details, the assistance of specialists, professional
priests of the funeral cult, became indispensable. Then there
appeared the officiant (*kheri-heb*), the priest (" pure one ",
uâb), the sacrificer (?) (*sem*), the embalmer (*uti*), the sculptor
(*mesenti*), the associate, or wife (*smat*), the two weeping-
women (*zerti*), the servant of the Ka (*hem-ka*), etc., all experts
in the ritual, who performed the episodes of the mystery before
the assembled family. However, it is probable that the Queen
and the Heir Apparent often took part personally. In any
case, the priests and priestesses announced themselves
with the words : " I am Isis," " I am Horus, thy darling son,"
" I am Anubis," etc., the actors thus assuming the character
of the different members of the royal family, transformed into
the Osirian family.[1]

The funeral rites of the King comprised the following
episodes, which I shall describe very briefly (cf. above, p. 89).

(i) The " search " for the body, which, being drowned or
scattered like that of Osiris, must, in theory, be *sought,
found*, and *recognized*[2] by Geb, the father of Osiris, by Isis,
his wife, and by Horus, his son.

(ii) The putting together of the dismembered flesh, and
its transformation into a *mummy*, a new body (*zet*),
undecaying[3] and imperishable, and also into a *statue*,[4] a
" living image " of the former body, with the appearance of
physical strength and youth which the mummy cannot
reproduce.

(iii) The restoration of physical life to the mummy and
statue by rites of imitative magic. With the same instruments
which were supposed to have been used for Osiris, " the
Opening of the Mouth and of the Eyes " was imitated.[5] To
imitate the movements of life was to create that life in inert
bodies, the mummy and statue, to restore to them the
physical faculties, breath, sight, hearing, taste, touch, speech,
thought, movement, and the capacity of taking nourishment

---

[1] On this subject, see G. Maspero, " Le Rituel du sacrifice funéraire," in
XXXVIII, vol. i, p. 289.

[2] *Pyr.*, §§ 2144, 1255, 1799, 1335.

[3] § 1257.

[4] § 1329, and *Ritual of the Opening of the Mouth*.

[5] *Pyr.*, §§ 11 ff., 1329.

and resisting decay. In the statue and the mummy the heart, likewise reanimated, was put in its place.[1] Henceforth the mummy and the statue would live again, like Osiris.

(iv) It was in the domain of the god who " presides over the West " (*Khent-Amenti*),[2] in the " divine Lower Region " (*Khert neter*),[3] that is, underground, far from men and the celestial gods, that the King would find a new kingdom. There his nourishment was ensured—he would never know hunger or thirst. We do not know the details of the life in the *Khert neter*, but Pharaoh found his ancestors there and protected the fortunes of his successors in the presence of Osiris.

Nor do we know anything of the *spiritual* side of this new life. The dead King was certainly in possession of his Ka, his Akh (spirit), and his Ba (soul), for we find these words even in the Thinite period. We have seen that the Ka bore in its arms the *name* of the falcon-king (Figs. 32, 47), and therefore protected Pharaoh's intellectual personality. The word *Ba* appears in such royal names as Biuneter, " Souls of the God," and on Thinite stelæ the servants of the Kings are called *skhenu akh*, " Embracing the Spirit," a title which describes a funeral rite performed by Horus, Isis, and Nephthys for Osiris and for the Osirian King.[4] So the Ka, the Akh, and the Ba are elements of a spiritual character, which dwell with the resuscitated body, the Zet. Of their nature and their rôle in the Thinite period, in the case of the dead Kings admitted to the paradise of Osiris, we as yet know nothing. Everything that I shall say of them below belongs to the Heliopolitan system, and refers to the paradise of Ra.

After this explanation, a few texts, chosen out of hundreds, will be the easier to understand.

O Osiris Teti ! Horus comes. . . . He recognizes thee, for Horus loves thee. . . . Horus has sought thee. . . . Horus has made thee to live in thy name of Anzti. . . . Nephthys has made an armful of all thy limbs . . . Thou art given to thy mother Nut, in her name of Sarcophagus ; she takes thee in her arms, in her name of Sarcophagus. . . . Horus has joined thy limbs to thee, and does not allow thee to fall asunder ; he has put thee together, whole, and there is no disorder in thee. . . . Ah,

[1] § 835.
[2] Khent-Amenti was at first Upuat, Anubis, and afterwards Osiris.
[3] The Lower Region (*iat khert*) is mentioned in the Pyramids, in opposition to heaven, the sky (§ 1201).
[4] *Pyr.*, §§ 11, 1797, 1799, 1280.

> Osiris Teti ! thy heart is set up, thy heart is strong, thy mouth is open, for Horus has avenged thee . . . Horus has set thee up,[1] in thy name of Sokar.[2] Thou livest, thou movest every day. Thou art Spirit (*Akh*), in thy name of Horizon (*Akhet*), from which Ra rises ; thou art strong, thou art fortified, thou art Soul (Ba), thou art Mighty, for ever.[3]

Other passages give more detail. Here we have the reconstruction of the dismembered body.

> Thy mother is come to thee, that thou mayest not perish away ; the great modeller, she is come, that thou mayst not perish away ; she sets thy head in place for thee, she puts together thy limbs for thee ; what she brings to thee, is thy heart, in thy body. So thou dost become he who presides over his forerunners, thou givest commands (*uzu˙medu*) to thy ancestors, and also thou makest thy house to prosper after thee, thou dost defend thy children from affliction. Thou art pure, as the Gods are pure, the lords of their possessions, who go to their funeral provisions (*kau*).[4]

The twofold position of the dead King, reigning in the necropolis among his ancestors, and from there protecting the royal house and his children on earth, is here perfectly clear. In the lower world, his chief care is to be well fed.

> Hunger, come not near Teti . . . Teti is filled ! . . . Teti is not hungry, thanks to the bread of Horus, which he has eaten, which his sister, the Great One (Isis), made for him ; he is filled, and (by this bread) he takes possession of this country. Teti is not thirsty, like the God Shu ; Teti is not hungry, like the Goddess Tefnet.[5] Hapi, Duamutef, Qebehsenuf, and Imset (the four children of Horus) drive away the hunger in the belly of Teti, the thirst on the lips of Teti.[6]

That the King may not be like those neglected dead, who are reduced to eating their excrement and drinking their urine, horrible as it is to them,[7] it is necessary that he should, in his lifetime, have taken precautions by signing *foundations*, that his royal meals may be served to him in the next world, under the name of " King's Offerings " (*hetep nsut*). Hence the very decided reflections ascribed to the deceased King.

---

[1] Setting up = resurrection.

[2] Sokar or Sokaris, god of the Memphite necropolis.

[3] *Pyr.*, §§ 609–21. The end of the passage, implying admission to heaven, to the side of Ra, is an addition. For the expressions " thou art Soul ", " thou art Spirit ", see *From Tribe to Empire*, p. 47. " *Mana* is not merely a force, a being . . . The word is simultaneously a substantive, an adjective, and a verb. People say . . . of an object that it is *mana*, meaning that it possesses that quality." In Egypt they say of a being that *he is Soul*, *Spirit*, meaning that he has soul or spirit.

[4] *Pyr.*, §§ 834 ff. Cf. above, p. 142, and below, p. 185.

[5] Shu, the deified Air or Void, and Tefnet, his consort, can engender inanition.

[6] *Pyr.*, §§ 551–2.		[7] §§ 127, 718.

The Spirit (*Akh*) is for heaven, but the body (*khet*) is for the earth. When men take their tombs, and their thousands of loaves and their thousands of beers on the offering-table of Khent-Amenti, the heir (who has to perform the funeral cult) is empty (of provisions for his ancestors) if he has not before him a writing (a deed of foundation). Now, Unas has written, of a truth, with his big finger, and he has not written, of a truth, with his little finger.[1]

Such is the life of the King in the next world according to the Osirian conception. It explains for us the enormous size of the royal tombs. Conversely, the huge dimensions of the pyramids bear witness to the capital importance attached by the Egyptian people to the protection of the bodies and souls of its dead Pharaohs, who continued to be the patrons of their children and their kingdom (cf. *From Tribe to Empire*, p. 152). In Part III I shall describe the royal pyramids. Let us here merely note that the Pyramid of Cheops is a mountain, 475 feet high and 760 feet wide, containing over 3,000,000 cubic yards of stone. Inside are the chambers for the mummies of the King and Queen. On the eastern front stood a massive temple, 330 feet long and 98 feet wide, in which the statues of the King were housed in perfect strongholds built of enormous stones. A covered way, about 500 yards long, led from the temple to the valley ; its entrance took the form of another temple, smaller than the first, but quite as solidly built. The Temple of the Sphinx, built by Chephren at the end of the road leading to his pyramid, is a magnificent example of the kind. The " Great Pyramids " are, by themselves, the largest monuments ever constructed by man. What must the whole site have been like,[2] with the pyramid, the temple and its statues, the covered road, and the entrance in the valley ? (Pl. IV, 1.)

Imagine the transportation of this pile of materials, limestone and granite blocks, sometimes weighing 350 or 400 tons—the long convoys trailing overland and by water, the constant tramping of men and beasts in the dust, donkeys braying, workmen shouting, boatmen fighting, the hauling at the quay, the hum of the building-yards, the gangs grunting

---

[1] § 474. Perhaps the finger was used, as among the Sumerians, to make an impression on deeds of foundation, as a personal seal.

[2] On this subject cf. **XXIX**, " Sanctuaires de l'Ancien Empire." It is only within the last few years that the whole architectural scheme, of which the pyramid was but one element, has been reconstructed. In the Pyramid Texts there is mention of the pyramid (*mer*) and its temple (*het-neter*), §§ 1277–8.

in unison, or heaving in time to a chanty. Reckon up all the toiling men and beasts of burden, masons, stone-cutters, polishers, outside and indoor workers, camping on the fringe of the desert as far as eye could see, with their wives and children, to say nothing of the offices of Government officials, supervisors, surveyors, accountants, auditors, and caterers.[1] Estimate the years devoted to the interminable task, where almost the only machinery was human hands, and the workers were in part foreign slaves and prisoners of war, and estimate the expense of maintaining offices and feeding and equipping all these beasts and men.[2] It is almost impossible to conceive such a gigantic effort. And this effort was demanded by every King in his turn. It gives one some idea of the material power and moral authority of Pharaoh ; it enables one to see the better into the mentality of the people which worked for the salvation of a single man, the master whose protection was perhaps despotic, but pretended to the justice, foresight, and benevolence of a god ; it helps one to understand the religious reverence with which a whole people bowed down before the dead body of the King, who conquered death by the grace of Osiris, and protected his kingdom after his decease. We see that the royal pyramid was an act of faith.

Although the pyramid was a fortress protecting a body whose paradise was down below, on earth, with Osiris, the Heliopolitan texts place it under the protection of the gods of the sky and the Ennead of Heliopolis.

O Tum, Scarab, who hast gone up to the top of the Stair,[3] who hast risen like the Phœnix of the Obelisk, in the Great Dwelling, in Heliopolis . . . thou who hast put thy arms behind the Gods in the form of a Ka [4] . . . that thy Ka may be in them ! O Tum, put thy two arms behind King N., behind this building, behind this pyramid, in the form of a Ka, that the Ka of King N. may be in it, for ever. Ah, Tum ! place thy protection on this King N., on this his pyramid, on this building of N.

---

[1] This summary is based on many reliefs in Memphite tombs, in which men are shown doing all kinds of work. On this subject, see P. Montet, La Vie privée dans les tombeaux égyptiens de l'ancien empire, which I have not been able to use, since it appeared while this work was in the press.
[2] See Hdt., ii, 124–6.   [3] See below, p. 370.
[4] A gesture of protection (Fig. 48).

Let no evil come here to the body (*zet*) for ever. Ah, Great Ennead of Heliopolis, Tum, Shu, and Tefnet, Geb and Nut, Osiris and Isis, Seth and Nephthys, children of Tum ! . . . (let each of you) protect this pyramid of N., protect this building against every God, against every death ; let him prevent that any evil come here, for ever. O Horus ! This King N. is Osiris ; this building is Osiris ; this pyramid is Osiris. So come to him ; do not stay far from him, in his name of Pyramid. . . . Horus, here is thy father Osiris, in his name of Fortress of the Prince.[1] O Great Nine of Heliopolis ! make King N. to prosper ; make this pyramid prosper for King N. ; as the name of Tum, who presides over the Great Ennead, prospers, so may this pyramid prosper, for ever.

FIG. 48. — The Gesture of the Ka.

So each of the gods of the Ennead is taken as a guarantor ; prosperous is his name, and prosperous the pyramid will be, for all eternity.[2] In the wording of these formulas we discern two streams of influence. First of all, the pyramid belongs to Osiris, it is Osiris himself ; here we have an old portion of the text. Later, this passage was incorporated in a Heliopolitan version ; the pyramid is placed under the protection of Atum and of the Ennead, to which Osiris belongs, but in a subordinate position, being placed in the third generation born of the Demiurge. We may conclude that in the course of the VIth Dynasty the Osirian pyramid became a " Solar " edifice, in which the dead King was no longer under the sole influence of Osiris, but was also dependent on Ra.

Moreover, the theologians influenced the architects, and gave a mystical meaning to the arrangement of sepulchral buildings. The great triangles formed by the sides of the pyramids seemed to fall from heaven, like the rays of the sun when his face shines through clouds, sending a ladder of light to the earth.[3] Now, the Egyptians worshipped this triangle of light in many aspects. They had made it the symbol of the goddess Sothis (Sirius) and of the zodiacal light.[4] The point of the obelisk, too, cut in a pyramidion, suggested the same triangle to them, and was dedicated to the Sun.

---

[1] The name of the temple at Heliopolis. The dead King is not only compared to the Osirian pyramid, but to the Solar temple.

[2] *Pyr.*, §§ 1659–71.

[3] There are many representations of the sun emitting rays, which are sometimes formed of small triangles, one over the other. Cf. Maspero, **XX**, vol. i, pp. 109, 192, 194.

[4] H. Brugsch, " *Δ* ou la lumière zodiacale," in **XIV**, xv, p. 233.

According to a tradition recorded by Pliny the Elder, the name of the obelisks meant that they were dedicated to the Sun, and they were an image of his rays.[1] We have, indeed, seen that in the Sun-temples of the Vth Dynasty the sun was represented by the obelisk, a petrified ray ; we should remember, too, that in the Sed-feast setting up an obelisk meant " causing Ra to rise ".[2] When we turn from the pyramidions of obelisks to the pyramids themselves, we find the same intention. The Egyptians adorned small votive pyramids [3] and the extreme apex of the large pyramids with the emblem of the sun's disk rising on the horizon, or that of the winged disk aloft in the sky. By luck a pyramidion has been found which formed the apex of the pyramid of a King of the XIIth Dynasty, Amenemhat III, at Dahshur. It is a fine block of granite, polished like a mirror, bearing on its eastward face a winged disk, flanked by uræi, and, underneath this, the two eyes of the heavenly face, from which fall the rays of the sun. There are inscriptions, saying : " The face of King N. has been opened, that he may see the Lord of the Eastern Horizon (Ra-Harakhti) when he crosses the sky in his barge," and " The Soul of King N. rises higher than the heights of Orion (Sahu), and he is brotherly with the Region of the Morning. Ra-Horus has established the son of his body, King N., above the stars ".[4]

All this shows that the dead King lay, in the pyramid, under the protection of a solar symbol, and that the pyramid raised him to the sky. Indeed, the sloping sides of the pyramid recalled the stair (uârt) by which Atum rose above Chaos [5] and the gods go up to heaven. We shall see later that the King, in his turn, reached the firmament by the same way. " Thou dost climb up," they say ; " thou dost ascend the rays (iakhu) ; thou art the Ray on the Stair of Heaven." [6] Anyone who has seen the pyramids rising in the sunlight and reflecting the glory of the rays to the four sides of the horizon will understand what the Heliopolitans meant.

---

[1] N.H., xxxvi, 14, 1 . . . obeliscos vocantes, Solis numini sacratos. Radiorum eius argumentum in effigie est, et ita significatur nomine Ægyptio.
[2] IV, xxiv, p. 167.
[3] e.g., in Maspero, LI, 1915, p. 193.
[4] G. Maspero, in I, iii, p. 206 ; H. Schaefer, XII, xli, p. 84. The block is 4 ft. 7 in. high and 6 ft. wide.
[5] See p. 374 and Pyr., § 1659.   [6] Pyr., § 751.

The names given to the Great Pyramids correspond to this interpretation—" Horizon (*akhet*) of Cheops," " Great is Chephren," and " Divine is Mycerinus " or " The One on High ". These names are of the sky ; they take us away from the earth and from Osiris enthroned in the lower world ; they show how the priests of Heliopolis encroached upon the dead King and finally took possession of him.

The Great Pyramids of the IVth Dynasty, colossal though they be as architectural feats, do not mark the height to which piety to the Sun rose. With the Vth and VIth Dynasties, this devotion grows finer and deeper, and no longer needs to display itself with so much ruinous prodigality. The Kings of the Vth Dynasty devoted the greater part of their resources to the Sun-temples, and their tombs were accordingly of smaller dimensions. The pyramid of Sahura at Abusir is only 164 feet high and 255 feet wide.[1] The pyramids of the VIth Dynasty Kings at Saqqarah are still smaller. That of Unas is 69 feet high and 131 feet wide, and the latest, built by Pepi II, who lived ninety years and worked at his tomb for a long time, is 102 feet high and 262 feet wide. But, though the fever of building had abated, the faith in the next life was none the weaker. The material rampart protecting the royal body was less thick, the stair rising to heaven was not so ambitious, but a far mightier spiritual rampart and a far swifter way of approach were offered to the Pharaohs Unas, Teti, Pepi I, Mehtimsaf, and Pepi II ; these were the texts [2] inscribed inside the chambers of granite. The Great Pyramids of Gizeh contain no inscriptions ; the chambers of the small pyramids of Saqqarah are covered with them (Pl. VII, 2). Under the influence of the priests of Heliopolis, prayer took the place of stone, as an efficacious defence against death. The royal tombs of Saqqarah, though meagre in comparison with the massive piles of Gizeh, outshine them by their spiritual radiance. For us, they mark the most decisive victory of spirit over matter in ancient Egypt.

---

[1] See **XLVII**, p. 44, for the plan of a pyramid of the Vth Dynasty.

[2] Discovered (1881), published, and translated by Maspero, *Les Inscriptions des Pyramides de Saqqarah*, 1894, and **IV**, iii–xiv. Critical edition, K. Sethe, *Die altaegyptischen Pyramidentexte*, 1908, which I quote. Index and a new translation by L. Speleers, *Les Textes des Pyramides égyptiens*, 1924.

The Solar destiny of the dead King, which the Pyramid Texts of Saqqarah describe in every detail, may be summed up in one sentence—the King is assured of life in heaven, by the side of Ra.

The Osirian rites gave the dead King an " eternal body " (*zet*), which he kept for ever,[1] but this body was the prisoner of the earth and of Osiris. Now, according to the priests of Heliopolis, the dead King, " dreads the earth [2] and eternal sleep."   So we find the cry uttered before the pyramids, " Rise up, you who are in your graves !   Cast off your wrappings ! Shake the sand from off your heads ! " The god Ra comes in person ; " he delivers King N. from the God below, and does not give him to Osiris, that N. may not die in death." [3]

For the Demiurge in the primordial Ocean, Nun, has " by decree assigned King N. to Tum of Heliopolis ; he causes the gates of heaven to be opened for King N. He has recognized King N., among men who have, of a truth, no longer a name. He has taken the King on his arm, he has lifted him to the sky, that the King may not die on earth, among men ".[4] The King, then, had left the paradise of Osiris, with which he had been content for hundreds of years, perhaps for thousands, having learnt from the Heliopolitans to disdain it. The West (Amenti), the country of Osiris and the dead, was a gloomy abode. " Do not go upon the waterways of the West ! Those who go there do not come back. But go upon the waterways of the East, among the Servants of Ra ! " [5]

Between earth and heaven, the King finds before him, as in his kingdom of the Nile, a country watered by a broad river, lakes, and marshes. It is a miraculous country, where everything has a magical life—the ground, the waters, the plants, and even the means of conveyance such as the boat by which the gods reach heaven.   This boat, the prototype of Charon's, is a goddess. She is guided by a silent, crabbed ferryman, whose name means " he who turns his head away ".[6] He waits for others to address him, like his classical descendant.

> *Le rameur qui m'a pris l'obole du passage*
> *Et qui jamais ne parle aux ombres qu'il conduit.*

[1] *Pyr.*, §§ 616, 1299, *Skhem k n zet k.* For all the following, cf. **XLI.**
[2] § 312.   [3] § 349.   [4] § 604.
[5] § 2175.   [6] § 1201.

The King tries to cheer him up, by telling him that he is the celebrated Danga, the dancing dwarf,[1] who gave King Pepi and his Court many a laugh, and that without a doubt Ra will welcome him with delight. Or else the King deigns to reveal who he is, namely, he of whom it is said on earth that Ra calls him and is keeping a place of well-fed " Privileged One " for him.[2] After a long wait, the ferryman replies with a definite request ; he demands a certificate of origin. " Whence comest thou to this place ? " So the King proceeds to prove his relationship to Ra. That is not enough. Then the King beseeches Ra, " Bid this Turn-head take his boat where the gods pass, to bear me to the East of heaven." If the ferryman still refuses, the King conjures the oar, that it may propel the boat, even against the ferryman's will. The magical spell will defeat the obstinate fellow. But if the boat resists, there remains a craft of a more primitive kind—two floats of reeds, which you hold under your arms, so that they support you in the water (*skhenui*). This ancient mode of transport, which is used in Nubia to this day, was used by all, even by Ra, at the beginning of time. There are many passages in which the dead King uses the two floats of heaven, the two floats of Ra.[3]

There are many other ways of going to heaven ; the texts offer them to the King without preference. Sometimes the ibis of Thoth, or the falcon of Horus, or the scarab of Ra, or the grasshopper, lends its wings.[4] A pinch of incense is thrown on the fire as the spells are recited ; the smoke of the incense spreads, rises skyward, and carries the King with it.[5] " The King flaps wings like a bird. He flies, he flies, O Men ! King Unas flies away from you ! "[6] Lastly, the rays of the sun which fall on the earth offer the King a convenient slope by which to go up to heaven. " O Ra, King N. has trodden thy rays, as a stair for his feet," [7] and this radiant stairway was built by the Souls of Heliopolis.[8] The rays stretch out their arms and King Unas goes up " like a flame in the air ".[9] Less splendid, but perhaps more practical is the wooden stair, bound with leather, which the gods make with their own

---

[1] §1189.   [2] §§ 1190–1.   [3] §§ 1091, 599, 1743, 337–63, 464.
[4] §§ 387, 913, 366, 1772.   [5] § 365.   [6] § 463.
[7] § 1108 : cf. § 751.   [8] § 1090.   [9] § 324.

hands [1] and set up on the horizon to enable the King to " go
far from (death) the dread of men ".[2]   By the virtue of
numerous spells, the King succeeds in setting up the ladder.
The whole universe looks on at the spectacle, and encourages
the King. " Men and Gods say ' Your hands under King N. !
Lift him up, bear him to the sky ! To the sky, to the sky !
To the great place, among the gods ! ' " [3]   From afar, men
implore Ra to help their King. " ' Here is the son of Ra.
He comes, the beloved of Ra, he comes . . . O Ra,' men say,
' thou who risest in the East of the sky, give thy hand to
this King N. ! Make him rise with thee, to the Eastern side
of the sky ! ' " [4]

The gates of heaven open, the bolts slide of themselves,
the door-keepers make no opposition,[5] for the origin of the
King is declared. " O Ra! Heliopolis is Unas. Thy Heliopolis
is Unas. The mother of Unas is Heliopolis. The father of
Unas is Heliopolis. Unas himself is a Heliopolitan, born in
Heliopolis." If any god were to thrust him back with his hand,
or to show ill will, " he would no longer find his bread among
the Gods ; the doors of the Barge of the Evening would no
more be opened to him, nor of the Barge of the Morning ;
he would no longer govern as a dweller in his city." [6] Pharaoh
arrives, at last, in the regions of Horus and Seth.[7] Men and
gods have followed all the incidents of his ascension with
emotion, and, indeed, it symbolizes a fact of immense
importance—the access of man to heaven.

> " How fair it is to see," say the Gods, " how satisfying it is to con-
> template, this God rising to heaven, this Unas rising to heaven, his Souls
> with him, his book of spells at his girdle, his magics attached to his feet ! "
> There are come to him the Gods, Souls of Buto, and the Gods, Souls of
> Nekhen, the Gods of the sky and the Gods of the earth. They have caused
> Unas to be borne on their arms. So, then, thou risest to heaven, O Unas ! [8]

We hear the joyful clamour of a whole people supporting
the effort of its King. How many millenniums did it take for
man's stupefaction in the presence of death to be replaced
by this prodigious hope of rising to heaven ?

---

[1] § 1474 ; cf. §§ 971, 2080 ff.   [2] § 2082.   [3] § 1101.
[4] §§ 1495–6.   [5] §§ 194, 502, 520, 525–30.   [6] § 482 ff.
[7] § 487.   [8] § 476–9.

So the dead king has joined the gods. He will undergo rites which will make him an inhabitant of heaven, a Spirit (*Akh*). The texts of the Old Kingdom call these rites " making Akhu " (*sakh*), that is *spiritualizing* the deceased.

The chief text which describes this spiritualization, once certain adventitious phrases have been cleared away, clearly sets forth the transformation of the King, the earthly god, into a King, god of heaven.[1]

> (i) *Purification of the Body (Zet).*—This Unas washes himself. O Ra, arise ! Shine, Gods of the Great Ennead ! Stand up, Nubti,[2] before the Palace of the South ! This Unas puts off the humanity of the flesh which is in him. This Unas takes the Great Crown from the hand of the Nine Gods. Isis suckles him, Nephthys feeds him, Horus takes him on his fingers. He purifies this Unas in the Basin of the Jackal.[3]
>
> (ii) *Purification of the Ka.*—Horus strips the Ka of this Unas in the Basin of the Morning.[4] He brushes the flesh of the Ka of this Unas clean for his Zet body . . .
>
> (iii) *Reunion of the Zet body and the Ka.*—He guides the Ka of this Unas to his Zet, to the great Mansion (of Ra) . . .
>
> (iv) *The King becomes a complete god.*—Then, this Unas guides the imperishable stars, he sails towards the Fields of Rushes.[5] This Unas perfects perfection, he is not corrupted ; this Unas excels excellence, for his Ka has come to him.

This text deserves a brief commentary, for it is the most precise explanation which the Egyptians of the Old Kingdom have left us of their ideas about the soul and the body and their relations one to another.

First we should note that we are dealing with the King, and not with mankind as a whole. At this moment in history there was no question of men, other than kings, having any right to eternal life with the gods of heaven. The Pyramid Texts describe the physical and spiritual condition of the god-king alone. We shall see later that this royal monopoly of immortality was the starting-point of a social revolution.

The complete being, the god which the King has become, is composed of a body and a Ka. The Zet, the " eternal "

---

[1] §§ 370–5, the interest of which has been pointed out by F. Lexa, *Geist, Seele, und Leib bei den Aegyptern*, reprinted from *Vestnikceské Akademie*, xxvi, 1918.

[2] Here Seth Nubti, as a sky-god (above, p. 69), aids in the establishment of Osiris in heaven. In this rôle he is not the enemy of Horus, but one of the primordial gods of the universe.

[3] Anubis, the inventor of funeral rites.

[4] The Morning, *Duat*, is the place where Ra and the dead King, who is compared to him, are born.

[5] The Fields of Ialu, the Eastern region of the sky, where the imperishable food-supplies of the sky-gods are.

body, given to him by the Osirian rites, is as imperishable as iron, incorruptible ; it is the body of the gods.[1] Yet it is made of flesh, and like a human body, although it is sometimes furnished with wings,[2] by means of which the King flies far away from men. The Osirian Zet still had an earthly character and a mouldy scent of humanity. When the King comes to heaven, by the East, " that side of the sky where the gods are born," appearing at the moment when the sun rises, daybreak, the hour when Ra and the gods are reborn every day, he is himself born to a new existence. These facts are given definitely in many texts.   We need lay stress on one point alone : Isis and Nephthys suckle the King like a new-born god. The King's arrival in heaven is compared to the child-bed of the goddess-mothers. " Unas comes out from the loins of Isis, and clambers on the lap of Nephthys. The father of Unas has taken the arm of Unas and presents him to the perfect, well-fed, and imperishable Gods. O mother of Unas, Goddess Ipy, give thy breast to this Unas ; let this Unas put it to his mouth ; let Unas suck thy milk, white, shining, and sweet." [3] So the King becomes Horus the Child, suckled by his mother, Isis.[4] And Isis speaks to him as a mother to her babe. " My son, Pepi, my Prince ! Take my breast ; suck it, my Prince, that thou mayest live, my Prince, thou who art small, my Prince." [5]

The Ka which comes and unites itself with the Zet body is a divine being, which lives in heaven and only appears after death. I was in error when, with Maspero, I defined it as a " double " of the human body, born with every man on earth, living with him, leaving the body at the moment of death, and brought back to the mummy by the Osirian rites. The formula for the spiritualization of the King makes this plain : while Horus purifies the Zet, dematerializing it in the Basin of the Jackal, he purifies the Ka in another basin, that of the Morning. Therefore the Ka and the Zet were previously separate, and have never lived side by side on earth. Another proof is, that the texts of the Old Kingdom have an euphemism for " die "—they say " to go to one's Ka " (*seb n ka-f*).[6] Other texts state definitely that there is

---

[1] §§ 530, 193. All the members of the Zet are gods (§§ 148–9).
[2] §§ 137, 1484.   [3] §§ 379–81.   [4] § 734.
[5] § 912.   [6] *Urk.*, i, 50, 71, 73.

in heaven an " essential " Ka ; " Thou art the Ka (i.e. *the* Ka, *par excellence*)," [1] is sometimes said to the deified King. This Ka is the father (*it*) and the being which causes men to live [2] ; it is the protector which defends the King from all fear of death [3] ; it presides over nourishment, for foodstuffs (*kau*) are simply the Ka converted [4] ; it also presides over the intellectual and moral forces ; it at once makes the flesh healthy, embellishes the name, and gives physical and spiritual life.[5] It therefore seems that what happens at the moment of spiritualization is this : from the essential and collective Ka, a primordial substance living in heaven, the gods detach an individual Ka for the King, and after purification this Ka is united with the Zet in the Mansion of Ra.

Once Ka and Zet are united, they form the complete being who achieves perfection. From then onwards this being has new properties which make him one of the inhabitants of heaven which are called Ba (Soul) and Akh (Spirit).

The Soul, Ba, represented as a *ba* bird, with a human head, lives in heaven among the gods. It does not live on earth with the human King, and it has nothing in common with our idea of a soul which animates the body during its earthly life.[6] To be Ba is the condition of the gods in their celestial life. As soon as the King is joined to his Ka, he automatically becomes Ba. " Ah, King N., thou hast been given all life and eternal strength, from Ra, what thou dost call thy body ; thou hast taken the shape of a god. Thou art great here, among the Gods who hold their place (from Ra). Ah, King N., thy Ba stands up among the Gods, among the Akhu " [7]— that is " he is Soul, he is God ".

The Ba which results from the divine life is sometimes simply a magical force, assimilated like food, which clings to some material object, and is kept in oneself and on oneself like a talisman. When Unas eats his bread and drinks his beer, they say to him : " Take them, thou art Soul through them." [8] When Unas devours the gods, he eats their souls (Bau) [9] ; when he appears in glory, " his Ba is on him, his

---

[1] *Pyr.*, § 149. [2] §§ 136, 1623. [3] § 63.
[4] F. von Bissing, " Versuch einer neuen Erklärung des Kai," in *Sitzungsber. Akad. München*, 1911 ; H. Sottas, in **X**, xvii, p. 33.
[5] *Pyr.*, § 908. [6] Breasted, *Religion and Thought*, pp. 59–62.
[7] *Pyr.*, §§ 762–3. [8] § 139. [9] § 413.

magic is at his girdle." [1] Altogether, the Ba is a divine force external to the human King, and added to the Zet, like the Ka, giving it divine life. " Thy Soul is with thee, thou livest, thou dost not die," [2] or " Thou livest by thy Soul ".[3] We cannot say that the Ba is a human soul, surviving in the King on his deification ; on the contrary, it enters into the King on his arrival in heaven, to cause him to live as a god.

In the classical period, the Ba brings the " breaths of life " to the Zet body (Fig. 49) ; therefore it is convenient to translate it as " soul " (*animus* = breath).

At the same time as the King becomes a Ba, he also becomes a Spirit, Akh. This likewise results from the union of the Zet and the Ka. The Akh is not a new form of soul ; it is the characteristic state of the perfect being. The King is reborn in the glory of the Eastern horizon (*akhet*) ; and he who is

Fig. 49.—The Ba bringing the Veil and Sceptre, symbolizing the " Breaths of Life " and Power.

born in the East becomes an *akh* (glorious, shining one). " You rise on the Eastern horizon (*akhet*), in the place where you are *akh* [4] . . . Thou dost become an Akh, which is in the Morning." [5] How do the gods confer this state of glory on the King ?   By the rites of spiritualization which I have described.

The perfect being takes his place in the boat of Ra, and sails above the universe, with the Stars. Henceforth he will lead in heaven " the delectable life which is that of the Lord of the Eastern Horizon (Ra) ".[6] The solid element in this felicity is, first of all, the food which is ensured to the divine beings. Near the Field of Rushes (*Sekhet ialu*), where the gods reside, is a Field of Offerings (*Sekhet hetepu*), which is kept

<hr>

[1] § 992.   [2] § 2201.   [3] § 1943.   [4] § 152.
[5] §§ 1172, 1986.   [6] §§ 1171–2.

constantly supplied with food and drink. In an undetermined spot in the celestial world there is a divine storehouse (*uhit*), placed under the protection of the Akhu. There, divine officials, called Regents of Offerings (*hequ heteput*), " bring down the provisions to Those who Preside over the *Kau* in heaven ".[1] The King who has been admitted among these Privileged Ones (*imakhu*) of Ra has his house (*per*) in heaven and takes his share of the food supplies (*kau*) proceeding from the primordial substance, the Ka.[2] All the gods go regularly to obtain supplies in the Field of Offerings ; it is said that they " go to their Kau ",[3] and the King does like them. " Thou goest down to the field of thy Ka, to the Field of Offerings." [4] There the fare is so choice that " the water of N. is wine, like Ra's ".[5] " O King, thou livest even more than the year (which renews all things) ; thy abundance of offerings is greater than the Nile. O Ka of King N., come ! King N. eats with thee." [6] (Cf. Fig. 47.)

The deified King still has his royal power, but it is infinitely increased, for he now rules with Ra. This is how his position is summed up :—

> Thou hast been washed in the Basin of the Jackal ; thou hast been purified by incense in the Basin of the Morning. . . . Thou hast established thyself in the Field of Offerings, among the Gods who go to their Kau. Thou sittest on this thy throne of iron ; thou hast taken thy mace, and thy sceptre ; thou givest orders to the Gods. Thou dost become an Akh, by the grace of thy Akh.[7]

In this character, the King is identified with Ra (as he had once been with Osiris) and with Ra he rules the universe.

> The heavens are joyful, the earth is glad, when they hear that the King has set justice in the place of iniquity. (They rejoice) that the King sits in the tribunal of Ra, because of the just sentence which issues from his mouth.[8]

Here a question arises of great moral importance. Is the King admitted to heaven simply by the more or less mechanical force of the formulas which have allowed him to

---

[1] § 1220. For this formula, see above, p. 167. [2] § 1219.
[3] § 1145. [4] § 563. [5] § 128.
[6] § 564. The King is called "the Lord of Offerings ". Like the god Ra, he is " he who unites, who subjugates the Kau " (*Neheb-Kau*).
[7] § 1164. [8] 1175.

imitate Osiris and Ra, or must he *deserve* to ascend to Ra's side ?

There is no doubt that *imitative* magic alone was not enough to save the King ; as early as the beginning of the VIth Dynasty the King's access to heaven was subject to a judgment of his actions before the tribunal of Ra.

Among all Eastern peoples, the Sun is the just god, above all others, who distributes his light impartially to all, drives away monsters, and condemns injustice and evil. Now, the Pyramid Texts say : " No evil has been found in what King N. has done. Broad is the sense of this saying before thy face, O Ra ! " [1] The King is just, and justified (*maâu*), but it is not merely because he has presented himself as an Osiris that he is described as justified. No doubt, all that was efficacious for Osiris is equally so for the King, and the sentence given by the tribunal of Heliopolis against Seth and for Osiris benefits the King, being himself an Osiris. But the King is not content with this " imitated " justification, obtained by the magical identification of his person with that of Osiris ; he must obtain a personal justification, based on good reasons.

A very important chapter shows us Unas on his way to heaven. When he arrives among the gods he appears before a tribunal.

> He wishes to be just in voice by his deeds.
> Inasmuch as Tefen and Tefnet have judged Unas ;
> Inasmuch as the Two Justices have heard him ;
> Inasmuch as Shu has been witness ;
> Inasmuch as the Two Justices have given the verdict ;
> He has taken possession of the thrones of Geb, and he has raised himself there where he wished. Gathering together his flesh which was in the tomb, he joins himself to those who are in the Nun, he brings the sayings of Heliopolis to fulfilment.
> So Unas goes out this day, in the just form of a living Akh.[2]

The scene of the trial begins with a declaration of principle. Unas " wishes " (lit. loves, desires) " to be *maâ-kheru* by what he has done ", by his deeds. The expression *maâ-kheru*, which has given rise to so many commentaries, and is, indeed, full of successive meanings, clearly means in this case " who has the voice of rightness (correctness) and justice " (Lefébure), him who speaks the truth, and speaks

----

[1] § 1238.   [2] §§ 316 ff.

it in the right way, following the prescribed ritual and legal formulas, which alone are valid. So the dead King who is *maâ-kheru* is a " just one " who becomes a " justified one ". This result he obtains by a magical process, and at the same time by an action of religious merit. In uttering his ritual formulas, " the words of Heliopolis," the King employs a *magical* procedure, which must work more or less mechanically. But the *moral excellence of the actions* of the dead King is also invoked, as a means to becoming *maâ-kheru.*

Truth-and-Justice (*Maât*) will plead his cause before the judges and save him from the fury of the monsters which devour guilty kings.

> O Gods of the South, of the North, of the West, of the East, protect Unas, for he was afraid, when he took his place with the Hyena of the Double Hall. (Otherwise) this Uræus Dennut will devour you, she will grind your hearts ! . . . But here is Unas, coming out on this day. With him he brings Justice (Maât) of a truth. Unas is not given to your flames, O Gods ! " [1]

In Part III I shall return to the importance of this long-misunderstood text, in which we have the earliest version of the famous Judgment of the Dead, followed by the punishment of the guilty. Let us especially note that at this time it was only the King who had to justify his actions before the gods ; for he alone of all men rose to heaven after death. Already, in the third millennium before Christ, the Egyptians made divine Justice the stern guardian of immortality.

From the King, the Servant of Horus, to the King identified with Ra on earth and in heaven, the distance covered is immense. Pharaoh, while still remaining Horus, slowly detaches himself from the Falcon and merges in the Sun, the King of the World. The processions of the Service of Horus are no longer held. The worship of Ra absorbs all the King's devotion ; and with Ra justice triumphs, to ensure order in the universe. Moral excellences begin to be regarded, in men's minds, with the same consideration as physical strength, or material riches. The King is responsible before Ra for his conduct on earth. A few more centuries and men will consider Pharaoh's responsibility to his people ; after the autocratic monarchy, will come the age of the claims of society.

[1] A. Moret, " Le Jugement du roi mort dans les textes des Pyramides," in *Annuaire de l'École des Hautes Études (Section des Sciences religieuses)*, 1922–3.

CHAPTER III

The Decline of the Memphite Monarchy. The Feudal Period and Social Revolution (VIth to XIth Dynasties)

I

THE ROYAL FAMILY AND THE GOVERNMENT OF EGYPT

AS far as we have been able to tell from the Pyramid Texts, Egypt was governed, about 2500 B.C., by an absolute monarchy by right divine. The King based his *de facto* power on the theory that he was the god Horus among men,[1] the heir of Osiris, and, at the same time, the son of Ra. Pharaoh concentrated in his person the whole authority, which was religious in essence. Alive, he was worshipped like Horus and Ra ; dead, he became Osiris in Amenti and Ra in the sky. Between gods and men he alone was the Intermediary, the Intercessor, he who knew and performed rites (*ir ikhet*), he who knew how to pray (*dua*) to the gods, he who held " all the secrets of magic ".[2]

The result, in practice, was that the King held all the highest offices ; he was priest, judge, and army commander. Moreover, he had become the owner of all the land in Egypt. This is proved by the transformation of the " census ", which was still held every two years. Under the Thinite Kings, the census included fields and gold, landed and movable property ; under the Kings of the IVth, Vth, and VIth Dynasties it only applied to livestock, large and small. " Landed property was, therefore, no longer a taxable thing, either because it belonged to Pharaoh himself, or because the soil had become free property in the hands of landed proprietors, or of the gods." [3]

---

[1] Under the Old Kingdom, Pharaoh is called " the God " (*Urk.*, i, 10, 57, 70, 80, 83, 86, 112), or " the Great God " (ibid., 9, 48, 88).
[2] " Secret magic " and the " secrets of the Court ". Cf. *Urk.*, i, 84, 89.
[3] **XXII**, § 244.

KINGS OF THE VITH TO VIIITH DYNASTIES

KING-LISTS.			MANETHO.	APPROXIMATE DATE.
Horus-name.	Coronation-name.	Birth-name.	*VIth Dynasty.*	
			6 Memphite Kings.	
Seheteptaui		Teti	1. Othoes	2540
Meritaui	Merira	Pepi I	2. Phius	
Neterkhau	Merenra I	Mehtimsaf	3. Methesuphis	
	Neferkara	Pepi II (reigned 94 years, acc. to Turin)	4. Phiops (lived 100 years)	2485–2390
	Merenra II	Zesamsaf	5. Menthesuphis	
		Neteraqert (Turin)	6. Nitocris (Queen)	
After Merenra II, the Tablet of Abydos names 17 Kings (= VIIIth Dyn.), and goes on to the XIth Dyn.			*VIIth Dynasty.* (imaginary)	
The Tablet of Saqqarah goes from Pepi II to the XIth Dyn.			70 Memphite Kings in 70 days	
The Turin Papyrus has preserved only a total, of 181 years for the Kings of the VIth–VIIIth Dyns. It gives the total years from Menes to the end of the VIIIth Dyn. as 955, and makes a big historical division at this point.			*VIIIth Dynasty.*	
			27, or 14, or 15 Memphite Kings, whose names are not given	2360

When a portion of land was given to a god as an estate, to an official as pay, or to a favourite as a present, if the recipient wished to dispose of it by a donation [1] or as funeral property, he could only do so if a "royal letter" [2] authorized the detachment of the land from the domain. Thus Pharaoh maintained eminent ownership of the land. That being so, it seems that we may accept the first hypothesis suggested above—that the limitation of the census to livestock meant that the land all belonged to Pharaoh. This eminent ownership of the soil, all over Egypt, fits in very well with the theory of divine and absolute monarchy revealed by the Pyramid Texts.

But to manage this land the King needed helpers. It is noted that, down to the VIth Dynasty, the King entrusts most of the great offices of State to his sons, grandsons, brothers, or relations. The royal family, which, though not divine, enjoys something of the superhuman condition of its head, supplies : (i) the priests, of the King or of the gods (*hem neter*), readers or officiants (*sem, kheri-heb*) ; (ii) the judges, the highest of whom is the Vizier (*tati*), the first official of the State ; (iii) the high officials of the Palace and of the Treasury, the Chancellor of the God (the King), the directors of the provision-stores, domains, and troops, and the very numerous " Chiefs of Secrets " of the various services ; (iv) the Nomarchs, who govern the nomes of Upper and Lower Egypt.

Under the IVth Dynasty, all the Viziers are sons of the King ; under the Vth, most of them are his grandsons. At Pharaoh's Court, which is a large family, in the strict sense of the word, the high employments are given by the King to his " darling sons ", the sons of his own body (*sa mer-f, sa n khet-f*), to the " King's Acquaintances " (*rekh nsut*), that is to his very numerous grandsons, then to his " Friends " (*smer*, including several categories), who mount guard in the palace, and, lastly, to men who are not always of royal blood, but are favoured by the King, the " Privileged Ones " (*imakhu*), a kind of " clients " of the Palace, whose duties and advantages we shall see later on.

To hold a royal office is to have some part in divine things. So when the King chooses a high official he " consecrates "

---

[1] *Urk.*. i. 4.　　　　[2] *Urk.*. i. 2.

him by an " anointing " (ureh),[1] and actually does homage (nez) [2] to the man thus consecrated, as he does to the gods. To be a high dignitary of the Court, is to be admitted to the religious and magical secrets of the King [3] ; for an outsider it is almost tantamount to entrance into the royal family. To reward his agents the King feeds them from his kitchen, if they are at Court, and gives them, especially if their duties are in the provinces, lands detached from his domain, in some cases almost as personal property, in others as the stipend attached to an office, obtained and resigned with the office itself.

Let us look at some of the careers of these royal officials, which are known to us from the biographical accounts inscribed in their tombs. We shall see how their situation evolves, from the IIIrd Dynasty to the VIth. Here is what Mten, who lived under Snefru, at the beginning of the IVth Dynasty, tells us about himself in his tomb at Saqqarah.

" The son of a judge-scribe, who gave him (to establish himself) neither corn nor household goods, but only servants and small livestock," he started in the royal administration as " the scribe of a provision-centre, the director of the goods of that centre ", and then became " Crier [4] and collector of the peasants' taxes ". He was attached to the Protector (âz mer) of the Xoïte Nome, and promoted to " Scribe-Crier and Director of all the King's Flax ". Then he became " Regent " of a royal domain, then Protector of the city of Dep (Buto), then Protector of the Xoïte Nome ; he received an estate as his own property, by the bounty of the King. Later on, he became a Nomarch with the official title of the period, " Guide of the Country, Regent of a Nome, Director of Messages for the Cynopolite Nome and of Tax-collectors (?) for the Mendesian Nome." Still later he " subdued and placed beneath his feet the Saïte and Western Nomes, as Superintendent of Declarations of Domains ",[5] and was

---

[1] **IV,** xxviii, p. 184.
[2] " I was saluted (nez) as First under the King " ; " I was saluted as Friend " ; " I was saluted as Sole Friend " ; " I was saluted as Priest of Min," in texts of the Old Kingdom published by me ; **III,** 1915, p. 554 ; 1916, p. 108.
[3] " I found my way into every secret of the Court " (Urk., i, 84) ; " I have known all secret magic," a Nomarch says (ibid., i, 89).
[4] See above, p. 139.
[5] The declaration (upet) was an act necessary to the foundation of a domain attached to any particular Government service.

given, for himself, twelve estates in the Saïte, Xoïte, and Letopolite Nomes.[1] We should note that Mten bears the title King's Acquaintance (*rekh nsut*), which was reserved for the grandsons of Pharaoh. Yet Mten's career was not at Court ; he started in small employments, and worked his way up to higher posts and from nome to nome, until he became a Nomarch.

We get quite a different impression from the career of Phtahshepses, who lived at the end of the IVth Dynasty or in the first third of the Vth.

> Born in the time of Mycerinus, he was brought up among the Royal Children,[2] in the Great Palace of the King, inside the harem, and was esteemed by the King more than any (other) lad. . . . Since His Majesty favoured him, he gave him the Great Royal Daughter Maatkha as wife ; for His Majesty would sooner that she was with him than with any other man. In the time of Userkaf, as Great Chief of Works,[3] esteemed by the King more than any other servant, he had access into every royal barge, and kept guard (over the King) ; he went on all the ways of the Palace of the South at all coronation feasts. In the time of Sahura, being esteemed by the King more than any other servant, as Chief of the Secrets of all the works which it pleased His Majesty to do, he embellished the Court of his Lord, every day. In the time of Neferirkara, being esteemed by the King more than any other servant, he was praised by His Majesty for (every)thing, and His Majesty permitted him to nose his feet, for His Majesty did not wish that he should nose the ground. In the time of Neferfra, being appreciated by the King more than any other servant, he went on board the barge *She who Carries the Gods* at all coronation feasts, being loved by his Lord. So, too, in the time of Neuserra, he kept guard for him, by the desire of his Lord, for his Lord loved him.[4]

Another official, Sabu, who was High Priest of Phtah at Memphis under Unas and Teti (beginning of the VIth Dynasty), describes his career at Court in the same terms, and adds :—

> "His Majesty made me enter the Court ; he gave me victuals in all places, of which I found the road there. Never was such a thing done to any servant, by any prince, because His Majesty loved me better than any other servant of his, because he favoured me every day, because I was a Privileged One (*imakhu*) in his heart. I was accomplished in all that I did under His Majesty, finding my way into every secret of the Court, esteemed by His Majesty." Sabu also calls himself "Chief of the King's Secrets in all his places " and " Privileged under every Prince ".[5]

[1] The text is in Sethe, *Urk.*, i, pp. 1–7 ; translation and commentary in A. Moret and L. Boulard, " Donations et fondations," in **IV**, **xxix**, pp. 57–75.

[2] On the Royal Children brought up at Court, see below, p. 197.

[3] High-priest of Phtah at Memphis.

[4] Mariette, *Mastabas*, p. 112 ; Sethe, *Urk.*, i, 51–3.

[5] *Urk.*, i, 81–4.

Phtahshepses and Sabu were favourites, who chiefly distinguished themselves in Court service, whereas Mten spent his life in the provinces in active official work.

Now let us see the career of Uni,[1] an administrator who, at the beginning of the VIth Dynasty, started in humble employments and rose to the highest positions. He himself tells us his story :—

First posts at Court.—" I was a child, the wearer of a girdle, under the Majesty of Teti. My office was that of Director of the House of Agriculture. Pharaoh made me Inspector of (his) Tenants. . . . (I was promoted to) Majordomo of the (King's) Chamber under the Majesty of Pepi (the First). His Majesty placed me in the office of Friend, Supervisor of the Prophets of his Pyramid. Although my office was (that of Inspector of Tenants) yet His Majesty appointed me Judge, Warden of Nekhen, because his heart was full of me, more than of any other of his servants. For the hearing of business, I was alone with the Judge of the Door, Vizier, in all secret business, (dealing) in the King's name with the royal harem and the six great courts of justice, because I filled the heart of His Majesty more than any other of his Saru, more than any other of his dignitaries, more than any other of his servants."

Uni receives a tomb.—" I asked the Majesty of my divine Lord to bring me a sarcophagus of white stone from Tura. His Majesty made the Chancellor of the God set off by boat, with crews of sailors and gangs of men under his hand, to bring me this sarcophagus from Tura. He came back in a great transport of the Court, with the sarcophagus and its lid, the stele-door, the jambs, the opening (of the door), and the foundation. Never was the like done to any servant, so much was I esteemed by the heart of his Majesty, so much did I please the heart of His Majesty, so much did I fill the heart of His Majesty."

Uni Judge of the Court.—" When I was Judge and Warden of Nekhen, His Majesty made me his Sole Friend, and Director of Pharaoh's Tenants. . . . I supplanted (?) the four Directors of Pharaoh's Tenants who were there. I acted in such fashion that His Majesty praised me, in my conduct of the guarding of the Palace, making the King's path or ensuring respect for etiquette. In all things I acted so that His Majesty praised me on this matter, more than everything.

" When an inquiry was made in the royal harem, regarding the Great Royal Wife, Amtsi, in secret, His Majesty made me come in, to hear. I was all alone, and there was no Judge of the Door there, nor Vizier, nor any Sar, but only I, all alone, because of my experience, because of my favour in the heart of His Majesty, because His Majesty filled his heart with me. It was I who did the writing, all alone, with only one judge, the Warden of Nekhen. And yet my office was that of Director of Pharaoh's Tenants. Never had such an opportunity to hear the secrets of the royal harem (been offered to anyone) before, except when His Majesty made me hear them, because I was esteemed by the heart of His Majesty more than any other of the Saru, more than any of his nobles, more than any of his servants."

Then came the war of Pepi I against the Asiatics, which

---

[1] The latest edition of the text of Uni is that of P. Tresson, *L'Inscription d'Ouni*, in **II**, *Bibliothèque d'étude*, vol. viii, 1919 ; cf. *Urk.*, i, 98–110.

I have narrated in *From Tribe to Empire*, pp. 213–14. The King made up an army of contingents from the South and from the North, of Negroes and Nubians.

> *Uni Director of the Army.*—" His Majesty sent me at the head of this army. Now, there were there Princes (army-leaders), and Chancellors of the King of the North, and Sole Friends of the Great Mansion, and Commanders-in-Chief (Nomarchs), Regents of Mansions of Upper and Lower Egypt, and Friends, Directors of the Interpreters, Directors of the Prophets of Upper and Lower Egypt, who directed the people of each half of Egypt (?), at the head of the troops of Upper and of Lower Egypt, of the mansions and the cities of which they were regents, and of the Negroes of those foreign countries. But it was I who organized them (although my office was that of Director of Pharaoh's Tenants) and established the balance of all things, so well that not a man was put in his neighbour's place, so well that not a man took loaves or sandals from those who were on the way, so well that not a man took clothing in any town, so well that not a man stole goats from anyone."

Uni was victorious, but he had to return to the enemy's country five times to put down rebellions (*From Tribe to Empire*, pp. 213–14).

> *Uni Director of all Upper Egypt.*—On the accession of Merenra, Uni was " in the Great Mansion as Bearer of the (Kings') Sandals ". Merenra made him " a Prince, Director of Upper Egypt, from Elephantine (Ist Nome) to the north of the Nome of the Knife (XXIInd) ", because of his excellent service. " When I was Bearer of the Sandals, His Majesty praised me for my vigilance and for the careful watch I kept in the service of etiquette, better than any of his Saru, better than any of his nobles, better than any of his servants. Never had this office been held by any servant before. I acted for him as Director of Upper Egypt, in the interests of (public) peace, so well, that no one there took his neighbour's place. I executed all works, and I kept accounts [1] of all material paid in for the Court, in this Upper Egypt, twice, and of every hour of impressed labour done for the account of the Court in this Upper Egypt, twice ; acting like an administrator in all that should be done in this Upper Egypt. Never was such a thing done in this Upper Egypt before. I acted, in all things, so that I was praised for it by His Majesty."
>
> *Uni's missions for the building of the pyramid of Merenra.*—" Then His Majesty sent me to Ibhat,[2] to fetch a sarcophagus (" chest of the living ") with its lid, and the august and venerable pyramidion [3] of the pyramid Khanefer-Henut of Merenra ; and His Majesty sent me to Elephantine, to fetch a door-stele of granite, with its substructure, the leaves of the doors of granite, and the doorways of granite, and basements for the upper chamber of the pyramid Khanefer-Henut of Merenra. I sailed north, from there, to the pyramid of Merenra, with six lighters, three rafts, and three boats of eight fathoms,[4] in one single expedition. Never was Ibhat or

---

[1] On the materials (supplies in kind) and hours of impressed labour of which accounts were kept, see below pp. 204–5.

[2] Granite quarries near Assuan.

[3] The pyramidion is called *benbent*, like an obelisk. See above, pp. 175–6.

[4] As we should say a boat of so many feet or tons.

Elephantine done in a single expedition, in the time of any King. Everything which His Majesty ordered of me was done in full, according to all that His Majesty ordered of me in this place.

"His Majesty sent me to Hetnub [1] to fetch a great offering-table, of Hetnub alabaster. I brought that offering-table down to him in seventeen days (after it had been) hewn at Hetnub, causing it to sail down the river to the North, in the lighter—for I had made for it a lighter of acacia-wood, 60 cubits long and 30 cubits wide, which I built in seventeen days, in the third month of Shemu. Although there was no water in the Rapids,[2] I landed successfully by the pyramid Khanefer of Merenra, and all was effected for me, in accordance with the divine Command given out by His Majesty my Lord.

"Then His Majesty sent me to dig five canals in Upper Egypt and to make three lighters and four rafts of acacia-wood of the country of Uauat. Since the Regents of the foreign countries of Iertet, of Uauat, of Imam, of Mazoï,[3] collected wood for this, I did everything in one year, placing on the water and loading very large blocks of granite for the pyramid Khanefer of Merenra. Of a truth, I made this economy (of time) for the Palace, by means of the five canals completed, by my merit, my zeal, my favour with the Souls of King Merenra, more than for all the Gods, and because everything was realized for me in accordance with the divine Command given out by his Ka (?) " [4]

Conclusion.—" I, then, I was the beloved of his father, the object of the great praise of his mother, the charm of his brothers, (I,) the Prince, active [5] Director of Upper Egypt, the Privileged One (*imakhu*) of Osiris, Uni."

No commentary could say more than the plain text of this biography of Uni—the most complete preserved from ancient Egypt—to show the despotic and meticulous authority of the King. He exerted it through a trustworthy servant, a factotum who had learned to cope with every difficulty and could show initiative in every sphere, even at a time when the administration was carried on by a corps of officials, very complete and elaborately graded, and was no longer wholly in the hands of the royal family. If the King's authority was so complete about the middle of the VIth Dynasty, what must it have been like under the IVth and Vth, when his family held all the important posts ?

---

[1] Alabastronpolis, celebrated alabaster quarries near el-Amarna.
[2] The rocks of the First Cataract, which can only be passed by channels kept in good condition.
[3] See *From Tribe to Empire*, p. 179.   [4] See above, p. 159.
[5] Lit., " true," applied to offices actively exercised, and not merely honorary.

II

THE PRIVILEGED IMAKHU

The King's relations, the courtiers, and the officials of high rank enjoyed, as we have seen, privileges which they described by saying " I am the King's Imakhu ". I do not think that this word has the vague sense of " dignitary " which is ascribed to it. It is true that the term was stretched by the inevitable wear-and-tear of time and social evolution, and from the XIIth Dynasty we may safely translate it as " liegeman " or " devotee " of the King or of a god. But in the Old Kingdom it has a strict sense. It definitely signifies a *privileged* status of the individual in respect of the King and the gods ; it designates the man who serves the King, whether he be his son, his grandson, his friend, or his client. In recompense for his services, the Imakhu receives " the favours of the King's presence " (*hesut net kher n nsut*). These consist in daily rations of food, the beneficiary being admitted direct to the King's meals, or allowed to draw income in foodstuffs from the royal stores [1] or a given royal domain, or presented with an estate which produces these supplies.[2]

FIG. 50.—Badge of the Imakhu.
The Imakhu are designated by this sign. It is not certain what object it represents.

The Imakhu are, therefore, *nourris*,[3] retainers fed by the King. One should remember the primitive societies in which the right to a share in distributions of food determines the whole scale of the ranks of the vassals (*From Tribe to Empire,* p. 105).

It is probable that the members of the royal family and the high officials were Imakhu, *ipso facto* and by definition. Others only attained this enviable position at the end of their career ; for them to become an Imakhu was to be an old man, grown white in the royal harness, one whose days of service were over and who thus reached the summit of rewards and

---

[1] See A. Moret, " Conditions des Féaux," in **IV**, xix, pp. 128–31.

[2] On this subject, see Moret and Boulard, " Donations et fondations," in **IV**, xxix, pp. 79, 89.

[3] Similar retainers are also found under the kings of Shinar, and in the feudal society of the Middle Ages.

honours. Such importance was attached to the Imakhu that the priests transported the institution to heaven, into the ideal society of the gods. When the King arrived in the presence of Ra, he assumed the rights and obligations of an Imakhu in respect of his lord, " like Horus, who takes the house of his father." [1]

So, too, the King's relations, friends, clients, and high officials enjoy the privilege of Imakhu in the next world. The biography of Uni gives us an example of these funeral favours. Almost at the outset of his career, he received from Pepi I the gift of a tomb, with a sarcophagus and funerary chapel (above, p. 193). Here, too, is what Sahura's chief physician asks of the King.

" May thy Ka command, O (King) beloved of Ra, that I may be given a stone door-stele for this tomb of the divine Lower Region." His Majesty caused two door-stelæ of Tura stone to be brought for him ; they were placed in the hypostyle hall of the Khaurret Palace of Sahura ; the two Great (Chiefs) of Works and the artisans of the sacristy (?) were charged with the execution of the work, in the presence of the King himself. The stone came in every day ; they were watched as they worked in the Palace ; His Majesty caused engravers (?) of inscriptions to be put among them, and they wrote (the texts) in blue. Then, His Majesty said to the chief physician, " As sure as this nose (breathes) health, (the nose of me) whom the gods love, thou shalt make thy way to the Khert-Neter, very old, as an Imakhu." Then I worshipped the King greatly, and I sang the Morning Hymn to every God for Sahura, for he knows all those who are among his servants. Now, everything which issues from the King's mouth becomes reality at once, for the God gave him knowledge of what is in men's hearts, because he is more august than any God. Therefore, if you love Ra, sing the Morning Hymn to every God for Sahura, who has made me what I am. I am his Imakhu, and I have never done ill to any man. [2]

We may complete the picture with the account which Sinuhet (XIIth Dynasty) gives of his reception by the King, who conferred the rank of Imakhu upon him.

The King said to him, " Since to-day old age comes to you . . . you think of the day of burial, and you will advance (to the dignity of) Imakhu. . . . There will be a procession for you on the day of your burial. . . . The invocations of the offering-tables will be recited for you, victims will be slain for you, beside your tomb-stones, and your pyramid·will be built of white stone, in the circle of the Royal Children." And, indeed, Sinuhet tells us : " The house of a Royal Son was assigned to me, with its riches and its bath-room, its heavenly decorations and furniture from the Double White House, stuffs from the royal wardrobe and choice perfumes. . . . And they brought me delicacies from the Palace thrice and four times a day, in addition to what the Children gave me without ceasing. A pyramid

---

[1] *Pyr.*, § 1219. [2] *Urk*, i, 38–40. For these tombs, see Pls. IV, V.

of stone was founded for me in the midst of the funeral pyramids. The chief quarryman of his Majesty chose the site ; the chief sculptor carved it ; the chiefs of the works which are done in the necropolis ranged all Egypt with this object. Every kind of furniture was placed in the stores. . . . A body of ' Ka-servants ' was formed for me . . . then I gave land, and formed a funerary domain thereon, with lands, in front of the city, as is done for Friends of the first rank. My statue was plated with gold, with a waist-cloth of silver-gilt, and it was His Majesty who caused it to be done. Not for a man of the common herd (*sho au*) would so much have been done ; but I was in the King's favour (*hesut net nsut*) until the day came for me to land (on the other shore)." [1]

What conclusion are we to draw from these texts ? The society which moved in the immediate circle of the King—his family, friends, and officials—constituted a class of privileged persons. First, they had a share in the political power, and took part in the government. Secondly, they had a tomb, generally in the circle of the pyramid of their Pharaoh, and built at the expense of the King, who supplied the site. Thirdly, just as the King fed his Imakhu while they were alive, he provided their funeral offerings when they were dead. As a rule, these were provided by villages in the Royal Domain, which supplied " the Offering given by the King ". At fixed dates, men and women bearing offerings came to the tomb to pay their due ; we see them in long files, each with the name of its village, engraved on the walls of chapels (Pl. VI, 2).

The texts state quite definitely that it was because of their personal tie with the King as Imakhu that his relations, friends, and officials were thus honoured. " The funeral offerings—and the villages—which the King has given me as an Imakhu," says a contemporary of Chephren, " whose tomb is in the necropolis attached to the pyramid of Chephren." [2] A noble of the XIIth Dynasty sums up this privileged status in these terms : " The King's Friend rests (in peace) as an Imakhu, but there is no tomb for him who rebels against His Majesty ; his body is thrown in the water." [3]

This gift of a tomb involved one consequence—the King allowed his Privileged Ones to imitate the magical rites of which he himself made use in order to survive after death. But the Pyramid Texts formally distinguish between " the

---

[1] From Maspero, **XLVI**, pp. 91–2, 101–3.

[2] *Urk.*, i, 12, 14.

[3] Cairo, Stele 20538. ii. ll. 18–19.

PLATE VI

1 THE SEATED SCRIBE
Limestone
Vth Dynasty (Louvre)

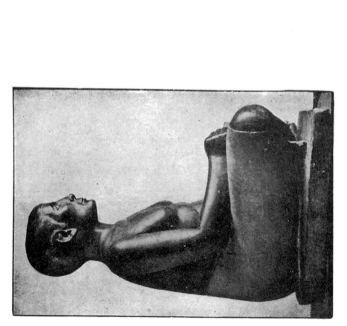

2 OFFERINGS BROUGHT FOR THE PERT KHERU
Vth Dynasty (Tomb of Sabu, Saqqarah)

[face p. 198

death of the King " and " the death of every dead man ",[1]
and even the Imakhu were only admitted, very properly, to
an inferior kind of after-life, in order that the distance might
be kept between the King and his subjects in the next world
as in this. The King had many supremely efficacious means of
survival, but he kept them to himself, and communicated
only a very small part of them to his family and friends.
On the other hand, as we have seen, he made gifts for the
preservation of their bodies—tombs, sarcophagi, coffins,
mummies.[2] But without the rites of consecration all this
material apparatus would be useless. He therefore revealed
to those about him the rites of the " Opening of the Mouth "
and of the " spiritualization " (*sakh*), which would cause the
mummy and the statue to live again as an eternal body, Zet,
henceforward imbued with the Ka, the Spirit (Akh), and the
Soul (Ba).[3]

For the nourishment of the dead, the King added to his
material gifts the right to use formulas, by which food
(imaginary, but endowed with a magical existence) would
appear perpetually on the offering-tables in the tombs.
Pharaoh's voice, as we have seen (p. 197), created things by
merely uttering their names. A similar power belonged to
every man who knew and uttered the master-words, being
initiated into the secrets of magic. This power was at the
service of the Imakhu ; their " voice issued " (*pert kheru*,
Figs. 51–2) and created, at will, the heaps of offerings which
the King's " menu " enumerates by name on the walls of the
tombs.

When the dead man, the relation or friend of the King,
was animated by these divine elements, he was thereby
assured of a new life, but where ? Until the beginning of the
VIth Dynasty his abode was underground, in the " divine
Lower Region ", whereas the King had already escaped and
inhabited a celestial dwelling-place. The formulas in the
tombs (which we wrongly call *proscynemata*, from the Greek
word meaning " prayers spoken kneeling "), at the beginning
of the Memphite Dynasties, show us that the Imakhu received

---

[1] *Pyr.*, § 1468.   [2] **IV,** xix, p. 123.
[3] These rites are already mentioned in the tomb of Mten, the official whose
career at the beginning of the IVth Dynasty we have seen (Lepsius, *Denkmaler*,
ii, pls. iv–v).

two favours from the King, which are arranged in the *bipartite* formula [1]:—

1. *Offering given by the King.*   That the Imakhu may be buried in the Khert-Neter.
2. *Offering given by Anubis.*   That the voice may issue for him (offerings) in all the feasts of the necropolis.

Formulas for feeding in the tomb.

Fig. 51.—" Offering given by the King." Fig. 52.—" What comes at the voice,
The King's meal in kind.   bread, beer, oxen, geese," etc.
Magical appearance of perpetual
offerings.

In the Vth Dynasty the King granted a third favour to his Imakhu—the power of leaving the tomb to go to Osiris, the god of the earthly dead. Here is an example of the *tripartite* formula [2] :—

1. *Offering given by the King and Anubis.*   That he may be buried in the Khert Neter, in the Mountain of the West, after a long old age, beside the Great God, as an Imakhu of the King.
    To the Sole Friend N.
2. *Offering given by Osiris, who presides at Busiris, Lord of the Thinite Nome.*   That the voice may issue for him (offerings) in the feasts of the year and those of the necropolis.
3. *Offering given by Khent-Amenti, Lord of the Mountain of the West.*   That he may travel in peace on the fair roads on which the Imakhu of the Gods travel.

There was no question of heaven being accessible to the Court before a date which we may fix, roughly, at the VIth Dynasty. The King alone would go to live with Ra. Moreover, the religious rights of the King's friends were still very limited.[3] Even the members of the royal family had no direct relations with the gods during their life on earth. Except in the titles of priestly offices, and in the formulas in which the King founds certain services of offerings, for some

[1] Mariette, *Mastabas*, p. 108.   [2] Ibid., p. 149.
[3] M. Davy has told us that in primitive societies the " Fed ones " are initiated into magical rites, by which good hunting and fishing are ensured, and also benefit by the magical prestige attached to eating (*From Tribe to Empire*, pp. 105–7).

deceased person, with Anubis, Osiris, or Geb (all gods of the earth), the gods are never mentioned or portrayed in the tombs of this period. " When one enters a tomb of the Old Kingdom," writes Mariette, who first discovered the mastabas, " what at once attracts attention and gives a date to the monument is the absence of any figure of a god, of any religious emblem or symbol." [1] Individual piety did not exist, and could not exist, at the time. The King alone was qualified to speak to the gods. When he wishes to show great favour to a relation or friend, or to thank him for some special service, " the King prays to the God for him." Men can, it is true, go so far as to supplicate the gods for Pharaoh, but

Fig. 53.—The Niles bringing Papyrus, Lotus, and Solid and Liquid Nourishment. Abydos.

for their own benefit they must avail themselves of the intermediacy of the King, who alone offers sacrifice to the gods.

In sum, down to about 2500 B.C., religious and political rights, even in this limited form, still existed only for the royal *gens*. This *gens* was entrusted with the administration of the country ; it lived in the royal residence, with the King ; officials whose duties took them away from the capital returned to the Court in their old age ; and all met in the end in the necropolis, round the royal body, and continued their service after death. We may reckon the number of these Privileged Ones as about five hundred in each reign.

What was the lot of the mass of the population ? Millions

[1] *Mastabas*, p. 50.

of townsfolk and peasants, craftsmen and serfs of the soil made their livelihood by working for the King and the Court, without being able to claim a legal status or any political or religious right. Thousands of plebeians were attached to the great cemeteries—architects, sculptors, joiners, painters, stone-cutters, and masons for building the tombs and making the funeral furniture, priests and officiants for the cult of the dead, embalmers for the preparation of the mummies, and, still more numerous, the craftsmen and peasants of the Domains, who toiled and reaped for the regular service of the offerings. The scenes in the mastabas show us the people at their tasks, tilling the soil or plying a craft with the boisterous gaiety of the care-free poor. In the bare sand we find their bodies, naked, not mummified, not enclosed in coffins, and supplied with but scanty provisions. In the burials of the poor, " the funeral statuettes, canopi, amulets and boxes which form the furniture of later tombs are absolutely unknown at this time." [1] For these plebeians there was no Paradise, unless the King should have chosen out one of them to admit him among his friends and servants. In Egypt, as in other ancient societies where religion was the foundation of institutions, religious, political, and civil rights were inseparably connected ; and before the VIth Dynasty none of them belonged to any but the " Privileged " relations, friends, and officials of the King (Plates V, VI).

III

FROM THE VITH TO THE XITH DYNASTY.   FEUDAL PRIESTHOOD.

CHARTERS OF IMMUNITY

Let us come down five hundred years, towards the year 2000, at the beginning of the XIIth Dynasty, and visit one of the great necropoles of the Middle Kingdom, such as that of Abydos. There, no longer round a royal pyramid, but near a tomb of Osiris, no longer round Pharaoh, but beside the Gods of the Dead, tombs and funerary stelæ stand in crowds. On them we read, all mixed together, the names of Kings,

[1] Mariette, *Mastabas*, p. 18.

PLATE VII

1. THE SUN BORN FROM THE
LOTUS
(Cleveland, U.S.A.)

2. MASPERO READING THE PYRAMID
TEXTS IN THE CHAMBER OF UNAS
(Saqqarah)

3. OSIRIS ON THE FUNERAL BED, WATCHED BY HORUS
ISIS (BIRD), AND NEPHTHYS
New Empire (Abydos)

sons and daughters of Kings, Viziers, and officials, and also of burghers, craftsmen, peasants, and other private individuals holding no administrative post. All claim, in their own name and in that of their relations, friends, and servants, " the Royal Offering," admission to heaven ; they declare that in the next world they are gods, justified Osirises (*Osiris maâ-kheru*) ; they engrave their stelæ with formulas identifying them with Ra, the King of Heaven ; and every one of them claims to be in the next world a Privileged One (*neb imakhu*).[1] So all Egyptians, without distinction of class, about the year 2000, had obtained the privilege of " royal death " ; presently we shall see that it was not a mere empty word. Let us consider the consequences of this in social life. The development took several centuries before it was complete, although at certain times it was so rapid and violent as to be of the nature of a revolution.

The VIth Dynasty, Memphite in origin, according to Manetho, comprised six principal sovereigns, who reigned, roughly, from 2540 to 2390. One of the last Kings, Pepi II, lived a hundred years ; according to the Turin Papyrus and Manetho, he reigned, from the age of six (Manetho), for ninety-four years. If so, it is the longest reign in the history of the world (from about 2485 to about 2390). Such a reign, during the years of childhood and of senility, gives ambitious men the opportunity of encroaching on the royal prerogatives ; and it is in the time of Pepi II that we see the decline of the royal authority and the advance of an oligarchy of priests and nobles becoming marked.

In Egypt, as later in Greece and Rome, the transition was from absolute monarchy to oligarchy. First of all, the ascendancy of the clergy of Heliopolis led to an extension of the privileges of the priestly class. The Kings of the Vth Dynasty who built the Sun-temples were already clearly under the control of the priests of Ra, and under the VIth Dynasty the Solar doctrines enjoyed a brilliant prestige. We have seen how Teti, the Merenras, the Pepis, and the rest of

---

[1] Lit., " Master of (the status of) Imakhu."

them gave up building enormous piles of stone, on which
there was no text speaking of the gods, and replaced them by
smaller pyramids, covered with long formulas, in which
Osiris and Ra were, turn and turn about, prayed or ordered
to make Pharaoh their equal after death. The display of
material power gave way to creations of the intelligence,
but this advance did not prove favourable to the doctrine
of royalty by right divine. The priests, followed later by
educated men in general, took an interest in religious, political,
and social problems,[1] and reflected on the sacred egoism
revealed in the Pharaonic institution. They caused more
moral and human conceptions to prevail, in which justice
and right had a larger place in the society of this world and
the next. Already we have seen King Unas appearing before
the tribunal of Ra after his death, and obliged to prove that
he deserved eternal life by his deeds.

The advance of the mind, therefore, meant the diminution
of Pharaoh's power, and the transformation of the Superman,
which the god-king had been, into a Man, the first of all,
sacred in character and divine in birth, but having something
in common with ordinary humanity. The stages of these
intellectual aspirations, which were to bring about a political
and social upheaval, can be seen in material facts, such as
the rapidly increasing break-up of the Royal Domain in
favour of privileged persons and the emancipation of the royal
officials. The first to benefit were the priests.

Of the priests, those who performed the cult of the dead
King in the *temples of the royal pyramids* were, as far as we
know, the first to be liberated. At the beginning of the
IVth Dynasty, Snefru decreed that " the two cities of his
two Pyramids shall be eternally exempted from doing any
impressed labour due to the King and from paying any tax
to the Court " ; at the same time, the tenants (lit. those
presiding over the domains, *khentiu she*) of these two cities
were exempted from the maintenance of the royal messengers
who went into their cities or into the lands dependent on

[1] This is proved by the output of literary works on these social questions,
which I shall quote later.

them. The King forbade that these tenants should be compelled to do impressed labour of ploughing, harvesting,
hunting, or quarrying, or that their lands, beasts, and trees
should be included in the census for taxation. The two cities
had a charter (âr), " declared " (upet) in the royal offices,
which defined their rights and obligations. In return for their
privileges, the tenants had to celebrate the divine rites for
Snefru. The charter was renewed by Pepi I in the year
21 of his reign, and the Director of Tenants, Uni, whose
brilliant career we know, was ordered, with the Vizier and
other officials, to cause the decree to be applied.[1] Thus,
immunities, defined by a " charter ", were what the priest-
tenants obtained from the King's benevolence.[2]

There is a series of similar documents of the reign of
Pepi II, which show us how Pharaoh made foundations in
order to ensure the regular service of offerings to himself
in the temples. At Coptos, in the Temple of Min, the god of
the Vth Nome, Pepi II had placed a statue of himself, of
bronze gilt. In order to serve this statue with daily offerings,
a domain was formed, with three arourai of fields and vineyards, under the House of Agriculture of the Vth Nome.
The peasants received a charter, which laid down their
obligations. The cult and the offerings supplied by the domain
were entrusted to the Director of Prophets of the Temple of
Min. Some years later, we find this foundation classed among
the " cities with immunities (nut n khut) which are in Upper
Egypt ". The King abstained from raising any tax there,
or sending any royal messenger there. It was a protected
domain (khut), reserved to the Temple of Min. Any official,
even the Director of the South, who should infringe this
decree would be expelled from the category of Priests of the
Royal Pyramid. Henceforward the foundation constituted
a " new city " (nut ma), in which a mast of Syrian wood was
set up and the decree of immunity was posted up in stone,
to bear witness to its rights and privileges. In a third decree,
of uncertain date, Pepi II renewed the immunities of this

---

[1] All the charters of immunity of the Old Kingdom, many of which, discovered
by R. Weill at Coptos, were published by him in his Les Décrets royaux de l'Ancien
Empire, are collected and commented on in Moret, " Chartes d'immunité dans
l'Ancien Empire égyptien," in Journal Asiatique, 1912–17. All useful references
will be found there.

[2] Moret, " Chartes," Journ. Asiat., 1917, pp. 387 ff.

same domain, which he had perhaps granted unwillingly. He relinquished the taxes and forced labour due to the Court, which are carefully enumerated in the list, which we shall examine in the chapter on administration. On the other hand, he demanded of the peasants and craftsmen on the domain the contributions in the form of hours of service and offerings, which were required for the cult of the King.[1]

At Abydos a fragment of a decree tells us that the Temple of Khent-Amenti had received statues of Pepi II, his wife, his aunt, and the Vizier Zau, and at every feast of the year these statues were to be given a portion of beef and pots of milk, supplied by a foundation which enjoyed the customary immunities.[2] If we multiply these instances by the number (unknown) of all the funerary temples and all the statues of the Memphite Kings, we can imagine the loss of territory and revenues suffered by the Royal Domain. Certainly the very renewal of the charters proves that the King, as eminent owner, tried, whenever he could, to recover property, of which he really only ceded the enjoyment, but, as the monarchy went on impoverishing itself, the clergy, growing rich on these properties in mortmain, ended by claiming the permanent ownership of them.

The *temples of the gods* obtained the same exemptions. Unfortunately, we have no text regarding the immunities of the Sun-temples of the Vth Dynasty, nor those of the priests of Heliopolis. But we can get an idea of them from the privileges granted to temples of far inferior standing, for which the excavations have yielded more evidence. I shall take the documents found in order of date.

In the Vth Dynasty, Neferirkara-Kakai (the first King who took a Solar coronation-name) addressed the following decree to the Director of Prophets of the Temple of Khent-Amenti at Abydos.

> The Horus Userkau. Royal Decree for the Director of Prophets, Hemur. I have not permitted that any man should have power to take any of the prophets in the Nome where you are, for the condition of craftsmen or for any impressed labour in the Nome, apart from the service to be done for

---

[1] Ibid., 1916, pp. 296–331. [2] Ibid., 1917, pp. 441–7.

the God, personally, in the temple where he is, and the good maintenance of the temples by the prophets in them

(I have not permitted) that the burden of any impressed labour should be laid on . . . Nor that any peasants should be taken who are on . . . } any field of the God, of which all the prophets have the charge.

For they are exempted (*khut*) for the length of eternity, in accordance with the decree of the King of the South and of the North, Neferirkara, and no (contrary) charter exists on this matter, in any service.[1]

Any man of the Nome who should take any prophets who are on the field of the God (*ahet neter*), of which they have charge in this Nome—or any peasants, who are on the field of the God—for the condition of craftsman, or for any impressed labour in the Nome—you must send him to the House of Agriculture of the Temple, that he may be posted . . . in the service of agricultural labour of that temple.

Any Director of Upper Egypt, any Sar known to the King, or Chief of Police (?) who should act contrary to this decree taken in the Hall of Horus (in the Palace)—all persons and goods belonging to him shall be used for the field of the God. . . .

Sealed in the presence of myself, the King, in the second month of the season Shemu, the 10th day.[2]

Now that we have seen this typical decree, I can speak more briefly of the others. At the beginning of the VIth Dynasty King Teti was advised that royal officials had dared to enter the domains of this very Temple of Khent-Amenti at Abydos, " to take the census of the fields, of the large cattle, and of the impressed labour due to the King." The King at once sent off a decree in which he proclaimed that the fields and prophets were " reserved " for Khent-Amenti and released from all contributions to the King, and that the King's men could not quote any contrary charter.[3] It was the same at Coptos, where M. Raymond Weill dug up, in 1912, a very long decree of Pepi I, renewed in the same terms by Pepi II, which established the immunities of the Prophets of Min at Coptos, and of their people of all conditions, in respect of the taxes, labour, and services levied by the King, for " they are reserved for Min of Coptos for the length of eternity ". The King denies false reports according to which other royal decrees had imposed royal contributions on the priests of Coptos. These stories are lies. " What the most just King loves, is that men should act in

---

[1] The King sometimes indicates that a decree is applicable " in every mansion, in every temple, and there is no immunity which can be opposed to it " (*Urk.*, i, 131).

[2] " Chartes," *Journ. Asiat.*, 1917, pp. 422–36.

[3] Ibid., 1917, pp. 436–41.

accordance with the present decree " ; " what the King hates," [1] is that they should act contrary to his real intention. No royal messenger can go into the domain of the temple. Any official violating this decree will no longer be admitted among the Priests of the Royal Pyramids. [2]

These texts are most instructive for the history of institutions, and lay the whole situation before our eyes— the Kings vainly resisting while the priests nibble away the Royal Domain, bit by bit. We see them alternately making concessions and taking them back. A charter of immunity, granted in a moment of generosity or weakness, is later contested, and annulled by the King's officials. Usually the King is reduced to disowning his agents and consenting to further surrenders, which end with the draining of the Treasury, the exhaustion of resources, and the disappearance of the Royal Domain, while the Fields of the Gods (the $\iota\epsilon\rho\grave{\alpha}$ $\gamma\hat{\eta}$ of the Ptolemaic texts) spread wide at the cost of the King. [3] If we should one day find the charters of immunities and privileges granted to the priests of Ra at Heliopolis, there is no knowing what they would tell us.

So, at the end of the VIth Dynasty, Pharaoh, the sole priest in theory, found himself confronted by an oligarchy of priests, initiated by their calling into the religious rites, who managed, and finally owned the Fields of the God, and were exempt from burdens and control, yet claimed a position and an authority at Court which the King himself had rashly relinquished to them. At the expense of the monarchy the priesthood came to form what we may call a feudal clergy.

IV

THE PROVINCIAL FEUDAL NOBILITY

In the same way the great civil officials, the Nomarchs, broke loose from the Court during the VIth Dynasty. Egypt had become a populous and wealthy state, as advanced in

---

[1] On these expressions, see above, p. 123, n. 1.
[2] " Chartes," in *Journ. Asiat.*, 1916, pp. 274–95.
[3] At Tehneh, near Minyeh, in the IVth Dynasty, Mycerinus " created fields " for the Prophets of Hathor (*Urk.*, i, 25).

intellectual culture as in material. That the royal *gens* was sufficient to form the framework of a State administration, was a political conception adapted to the small Egypt of the earliest Pharaohs. In the Egypt of the Vth and VIth Dynasties, it was inadequate, and was overwhelmed by its own achievements. At the end of a few generations, the sons, grandsons, and friends of the King had fortified themselves in their positions ; they were emancipated from his paternal control, and grew up, like the priests, on the ruins of the Royal Domain and the royal authority. Furthermore, princely families which had long broken their ties with the Court, or had raised themselves on their own resources, appeared here and there at the head of nomes, and laid the foundations of a provincial aristocracy, in natural opposition to the King's officials.

It is in Upper Egypt [1] that the decentralization of power, wealth, and political influence meets the eye. Powerful families appear in most of the nomes. Their tombs are preserved almost everywhere, and tell us their names, their achievements, and their ambitions. As one goes up the Nile, from Memphis to Elephantine, one finds their hypogea dug in the cliffs which dominate the valley. Deshasheh (XIXth Nome), Zawyet el-Meitin (opposite Beni-Hasan, XVIth Nome) Shekh-Said (near el-Amarna, XVth), Meir (XIVth), Der el-Gebraui (XIIth), Panopolis (IXth), Abydos (VIIth), Chenoboscion (VIIth), Denderah (VIth), Hermonthis (near Thebes, IVth), Edfu (IInd), and Assuan (Ist)—these are the sites of the princely necropoles, which mark the line of capitals of the provincial nobility, from the VIth Dynasty onwards.[2]

The heads of these princely families often begin by being great officials of the King. They bear the title of Regent of a Mansion (*heq het*), designating the governor of the capital of a nome, and also such appellations as Guide of the Country (*seshem ta*) and Superior Chief of a Nome (*herj zaza hesept*),[3] which belong to the Nomarch (in his civil capacity). In addition, every Nomarch is the Director of the Prophets of

---

[1] So far, the Delta has yielded no monument by which one can follow the gradual decline of the royal authority, as in Upper Egypt.

[2] For further details, cf. **XXII**, § 263, note. Most of these tombs are described in local monographs, published by the Egypt Exploration Fund.

[3] With or without the epithet " Great " (*âa*). To designate the nome, the spelling *hesept* is substituted for *spat*.

the principal god of the province. He also commands the soldiers (*meshâu*) of the local militia. Administrator, priest, and army commander, he represents the King in all his essential capacities. The Nomarch prides himself on being an official of Pharaoh, but this is not so much from real obedience as to give a legal basis to his authority. He adorns himself with the title of Chancellor of the King, that he may have the right to be holder of the royal seal in his nome. He sues for Court offices, as Sole Friend, Prince (*r-pât*), or Chief (of an army) (*hati-â*), and the King gives them to him, sometimes, as a posthumous reward (see p. 213).

Nevertheless, the Nomarch is no longer a " man of the Court ". He lives and dies " in his nome which he loves ", which he cultivates and develops, and he seldom goes near the King. In the Nomes, by the side of the " properties of the Court " (*ikhet n khenu*) [1]—that is, the Royal Domain, of which the Nomarch takes charge—there are, for him and his family, " properties of the house of the Prince," [2] " properties of his father," [3] that is, a princely estate which he has inherited, and increases when he can at the expense of the properties of the Court. As Director of Prophets, the Nomarch enjoys the immunities extorted by the priests from the piety or weakness of Kings [4] ; and he is given lands and exemption from taxation on his own account. Like the King and the clergy, the Nomarch founds new cities (*nut ma*),[5] which are so many " free towns " to which settlers are attracted by the liberties which they enjoy. In the XIIth Nome, the Nomarch Hanku (Vth Dynasty) ingeniously explains his method of competing with the King. " I refounded decayed (?) cities in this nome, with men of sense (summoned) from other nomes. Those of them who came as peasants hold office as Saru here, and I have never taken the goods from any man, who would have accused me of it before the god of the city." [6]

It is now the god of his own city, and not Ra, that the Nomarch calls as witness to his virtue ; it is to his own personal, provincial god that he confides his hopes and declares

---

[1] See the inscription of Pepinefer quoted on p. 212.
[2] *Siut*, pl. vii, l. 268 (XIIth Dynasty).
[3] *Urk.*, i, 144 (inscription of the Nomarch Ibi). Cf. *Siut*, pl. vii, l. 268.
[4] e.g. at Tehneh (XVth Nome) (*Urk.*, i, 24).
[5] *Urk.*, i, 24, 87.   [6] *Urk.*, i, 78–9.

his attachment as an Imakhu.[1] Finally, the local character of these families becomes more and more marked as the Nomarchs obtain from the King—when they do not confer it themselves—investiture with the same office for their eldest son, either in their own lifetime or after their death. At Tehneh, in the Vth and VIth Dynasties, Nekankh, Director of Prophets and Director of New Cities, " spoke " (*uzu medu*) to his children (as the King to his subjects), creating them priests of Hathor, from father to son, to perpetuity.[2] At Abydos the Vizier Zau, brother-in-law of Pepi I, dug a tomb in the necropolis of Thinis, " out of love of the nome where he was born," for himself and his father.[3] At Edfu the Nomarch Pepinefer, under Pepi I and Merenra, succeeded his father in high offices ; at Assuan, a line of princes of one same family established themselves ; at Meir, a powerful dynasty of local princes has been found—one Black Pepi had three sons, Pepi-Ankh the eldest, Pepi-Ankh the second, and Pepi-Ankh, the youngest, who shared his offices and his tomb.[4] From all these facts we may conclude that, with the great offices becoming hereditary in the provinces, the old State of officials, organized by the first Dynasties, broke up into small feudal States, which found their framework in the primitive division by nomes.

One striking thing is the tone assumed by these provincial magnates when they brag of their own power, or of their care for those under them. Take the Nomarch of Edfu, Pepinefer, who lived, like Uni, under the first three Kings of the VIth Dynasty. His father was already Superior Chief of the Land of the Nome of Utest-Hor (IInd) under King Teti, and Pepinefer was sent to Court for his education. Let him speak for himself.

> Being a child, wearing a crown, in the time of King Teti, I was brought to King Pepi (Ist) to be brought up among the children of the Nomarchs, and to be appointed as Sole Friend, Director of Pharaoh's Tenants, under King Pepi. (Later) King Merenra's Majesty made me go up the Nile to the Nome of Utest-Hor, in the capacity of Sole Friend, Nomarch, Director of the Corn of Upper Egypt, and Director of the Prophets of Edfu, because of the excellence of the consideration which I enjoyed in the heart of His Majesty. My consecration (*nez*) [5] came to me on the occasion of a feast, and set me above every Nomarch in Upper Egypt.

[1] *Urk.*, i, 32, 76, 80. [2] *Urk.*, i, 25. [3] *Urk.*, i, 118–19.
[4] See my report in Blackman's account of the tombs at Meir, in *Revue critique*, 1917, Nos. 38–9.
[5] i.e. as Nomarch. Cf. above, p. 191.

Management of the properties of the Court.—I acted so that the livestock of this nome was superior to the beasts (previously delivered) in the King's stalls, and at the top of the whole South (not at all what I found in the case of the Nomarch who was in the Nome before), by my vigilance and the perfection of my administration of the property of the Court (*ikhet n khenu*). I was the Chief of the Secrets of every word which came from the Gate of Elephantine and from the foreign countries of the South.

Having done such good work for the King, Pepinefer did no less for those under him. He made himself popular by a judicious use of the resources of the funerary properties (*per zet*, perpetual foundation).

I gave bread to the hungry,[1] and clothes to the naked, by means of what I found in the Nome. I gave pots of milk and measured out bushels of Southern corn, from the perpetual foundation, to the hungry whom I found in the Nome. All that I found in this Nome, who had no corn for themselves but the corn of others, I changed their condition, by means of the perpetual foundation. I buried every man in this Nome who had no son, with stuffs from the property of the perpetual foundation (*ikhet n per zet*). I established peace in every foreign country dependent on the Court, by the perfection of my vigilance in this respect, and I was praised for this by my Lord. I delivered the poor man from the hand of him who was richer than he, and I decided the portions of brothers, so that they were at peace.[2]

Other inscriptions show the processes by which the Nomarchs obtained from the King funeral rites for themselves, a necessary complement to their political and social prestige. The Nomarch Ibi, at Der el-Gebraui, tells us that he founded his tomb with the revenue of his own cities, thanks to his stipend as a priest, and thanks, too, to the King's Offering conceded by His Majesty.[3] At Elephantine, Sebni relates that his father Mekhu was killed on an expedition in the Sudan ; Sebni found his body, placed it in a coffin, and informed Pharaoh. The King at once sent an embalmer, an officiant, sacristy-priests, mourners, and a service of magical offerings (*pert kheru*) to honour (*nez*) Mekhu. " They brought him the oils of the White House, the secrets of the

---

[1] These self-laudatory declarations at this time became mere conventional commonplaces, which are found repeatedly in the biographies (*Urk.*, i, 77, 122, 133, 143).

[2] Text published by G. Daressy, " Inscription du Mastaba de Pepinefer à Edfou," in **I**, xvii (1917), p. 130 ; interpreted by Moret, " Un Nomarque d'Edfou au début de la VIᵉ dynastie," in **III**, 1918, p. 105.

[3] *Urk.*. i. 144 : cf. the case of the Vizier Zau, i, 119.

Double Sacristy, weapons (of state) from the arsenal, garments from the Double White House, and all the funeral gear which came from the Court." The consignment was accompanied by a letter from the King, congratulating Sebni on having brought back his father. Sebni himself received his funeral gear in advance, and thirty *arourai* of land, in Lower and Upper Egypt, with the rank and privileges of Tenant of the Pyramid of Pepi II.[1]

The case of Zau, the Nomarch of the Serpent Mountain, is equally typical. He says :—

> I buried my father, Prince Zau, in more honourable state than any of his contemporaries of Upper Egypt. I claimed from King Pepi II the honour of obtaining a sarcophagus, funerary garments, and oils for that Zau. When His Majesty sent to me, as for a Tenant, a sarcophagus of wood, ritual oils, perfumes, and two hundred pieces of Southern linen, of first quality, taken from the Double White House of the Court, for Zau, such a thing had never been done for any other of his time. Then I made for myself a sepulchre in one tomb with Zau, that I might be with him in one place. Not, in truth, that I have not a charter [2] to make another tomb. But I did this for the pleasure of seeing Zau every day, for the pleasure of being with him in one place. . . . And when I asked His Majesty to consecrate (*nez*) Zau with the dignity of Prince (*hati-â*), then His Majesty made a decree, that he should be made a Prince, with the Offering given by the King.[3]

Heredity in office and heredity in royal favours, even granted after death, as to Zau—such are the ways of all oligarchies. Just as Horus had succeeded Osiris, and just as Pharaoh, the son of the gods, held his " great office " by heredity right, so the Nomarchs considered themselves entitled to found local hereditary dynasties. In their own districts, they refrained from " despoiling any son of the goods of his father ",[4] thus making the principle of heredity respected everywhere (cf. pp. 96, 144).

On the other hand, we see the Kings of the VIth Dynasty trying to check the movement. They tried to inculcate docility and Court habits into the provincial Nomarchs by " bringing up the Nomarchs' children at Court ",[5] thus holding them as hostages for their parents' loyalty.[6] In addition, the King created a Director of Upper Egypt to inspect the twenty-two Southern nomes, and this post, which was entrusted to

---

[1] *Urk.*, i, 135–40.   [2] Or the position, means.   [3] *Urk.*, i, 145–7.
[4] *Urk.*, i, 123 (Herkhuf).
[5] Inscription of Pepinefer. See above, p. 211.
[6] The same tactics were practised at the Court of the Ptolemies (Bouché-Leclercq, *Hist. des Lagides*, iii, p. 107).

a single official, proves that the Court was making a real effort to correct the independence of the Nomarchs. Subsequently this very office came into the hands of several Nomarchs, such as Zauti of the VIIth Nome and Ibi of the XIIth ; the title became chiefly honorary and the post sometimes dwindled to being nothing more than a sinecure with a Court title. So even the measures of repression weakened the royal authority.[1]

Once the provincial nobles had obtained the right to be buried in their nomes at the King's expense, the Osirian destiny no longer satisfied them. The melancholy after-life under the ground, which Pharaoh had left with scorn to enter heaven, did not respond to their princely ambitions or their intellectual aspirations. Having been admitted to some kind of share in their master's immortality, they now wanted to follow him to heaven. This supreme favour, the application to themselves of the Heliopolitan theory which had been conceived for the King, they obtained from the Pharaohs of the VIth Dynasty. The Nomarchs of Assuan, of Der el-Gebraui, of Shekh-Said, boast in their funeral inscriptions [2] that they can " travel in peace on the sublime ways of the West, where the Akhu travel, and go up to the God, the Lord of Heaven, as Imakhu in the sight of (Ra) ". They are secure of reaching heaven " thanks to the two outstretched hands of the Goddess Amenti ", and of " there traversing the firmament " in the boats of Ra. The detailed royal ritual is not yet engraved on their tombs, but at least they have won the principle ; heaven is open to them after death, as to the King.

So, towards the end of the Memphite monarchy, the fact of belonging to the priestly class and that of holding the royal offices brought the priests and princes social and religious advantages of a kind which constituted a *jus civitatis* in an Oriental form—not, as in Greece and Rome, access to elective magistracies, but the right, which was on the way to becoming

---

[1] **XXII**, § 264.   On the distinction between active and honorary Directors of Upper Egypt, see above, p. 195, n. 5.   The list of the Directors of Upper Egypt has been established by H. Gauthier, in *Bibl. Hautes Études*, sec. iv, No. 234, pp. 225 ff.

[2] Herkhuf, in *Urk.*, i, 121 ; cf. *Der el-Gebraui*, ii, 8 ; *Shekh-Said*, 19 ; Mariette, *Mastabas*, pp. 369, 433 ; J. Capart, *Rue de Tombeaux*, pl. xi.

hereditary, to administrative offices, with a privileged position beside the King, in this life and the next.

The penalty decreed by the Pharaohs of the Vth and VIth Dynasties against those who should infringe the decrees of immunity is characteristic. It forbids the offenders to continue to be priests among the royal pyramids,[1] thus cutting them off from the prospect of "ever being counted among the Spirits (Akhu), or among the Living of the kingdom of Osiris and Ra".[2] Does this not prove that religious and civic rights were inseparable ? Both had been snatched from the Pharaohs by priests and nobles.

At the end of the VIth Dynasty, then, absolute monarchy had undergone an evolution, and society lived under a system which had analogies to the feudalism of Mediaeval Europe.

Of the mass of the people, our documents only show us the husbandmen and herdsmen who belonged to the *mertu* (= peasants) and the craftsmen who belonged to the *hemutiu* (= workers). These were dependent on the royal services (funerary and royal temples, *per zet*, new cities), working for the priests of the divine temples and for the Nomarchs. They were enumerated in the foundation-charters and shared in the legal status of the domains which enjoyed immunities. Had they a share in civil and religious privileges ? We do not know. Outside the exempted domains, the peasants and workmen perhaps had no status.[3] But the intensive cultivation of the land required a big peasant population. The building of royal pyramids, Solar and royal temples, and tombs granted to Imakhu, the sculptured adornment of edifices, and the manufacture of luxurious furniture, stuffs, jewels, etc., for the palaces of the living and the dead, all the needs of a very refined civilization, had increased the class of craftsmen, labourers, and peasants to a very considerable size. The trade in articles of luxury, at home and

---

[1] Moret, "Chartes," in *Journ. Asiatique*, 1916, p. 280, decrees of Pepi I and Pepi II.

[2] Ibid., 1917, p. 369, addition to the decree of Demzibtaui.

[3] In the inscriptions of Mten (beginning of IVth Dynasty) the people are attached to the soil (*Urk.*, i, 3–4); they are distinguished from the "royal" (tenants).

abroad, had grown greatly, to supply the Egyptian market with all the things needed by the Court, the temples, the tombs, and daily life—choice furniture, statues, metals, incense, precious woods, etc.[1] Therefore, a large working population certainly lived in the towns, apart from the workshops of the King and the priests, being especially congregated in the Delta (see below, p. 225). Down to the end of the Memphite Dynasties, these plebeians do not seem to have benefited by the slow evolution which was of such advantage to the oligarchy of priests and Nomarchs. We only see them in the reliefs on mastabas and hypogea, disciplined and skilful, a submissive, light-hearted race, content with little, singing at their toil, working with taste and patience as they polish and repolish the article intended for Pharaoh, or for the priests, or for the princes, in exchange for their meagre food. Of their aspirations, of their thoughts when they saw the emancipation of the priests and nobles, no text has yet told us anything. But this appearance of tranquillity is deceptive. The time is near, when we shall see the masses driven by the same ambitions as the officials, and they in their turn will find an opportunity to obtain a share in religious and civic rights.

V

THE END OF THE OLD KINGDOM AND THE SOCIAL REVOLUTION
(VIIIth TO XIth DYNASTIES)

Between the end of the VIIIth Dynasty (about 2360) and the beginning of the XIIth (about 2000), conditions favourable to a political and social revolution affecting the mass of the people presented themselves more than once.

The royal power, already greatly weakened at the end of the long reign of Pepi II, foundered in anarchy. The VIIth Dynasty, to which Manetho assigns seventy Kings in seventy days (!), never really existed. The VIIIth Dynasty contained eight Kings, according to the Turin Papyrus, seventeen, according to the Tablet of Abydos, and twenty-seven, fourteen, or five, according to the abbreviators of Manetho. The monuments tell us of only one of the Kings enumerated

[1] Below, p. 228, last quotation.

at Abydos, Neferkauhor, and of two others not named there. Such chaos as this means the hopeless decay of the Memphite kingship, and the texts of the period strengthen the impression that Egypt was drifting towards revolution with increasing rapidity.

Several decrees of King Neferkauhor have been found at Coptos. By one of them, a foundation is made for the service of a statue of the King in the Temple of Min at Coptos. The order is sent to the Chief of the Scribes of the Fields of the Vth, VIth, VIIth, VIIIth, and IXth Nomes of Upper Egypt. The appointment of a single chief scribe over the royal land of five nomes shows how the Royal Domain had been reduced by all the donations extorted from Kings.[1] Another decree, one of the most important administrative documents of the Old Kingdom, appoints the Vizier Shemaj Director of Upper Egypt, and places all the twenty-two nomes under his authority, enumerating them from the first to the last.[2] Some time later, the King appoints to the post of " Director of the South ", as " deputy (or herald ?) of his father, the Vizier . . . j ", who seems to be the son of the same Shemaj. Thus the Vizier gets his own son attached to him in his post of Director of the South, though it is true that the latter's jurisdiction extends only to seven nomes (Ist to VIIth) of Upper Egypt.[3] Here we have a noble acquiring the Director-ship of the South, which had been created as a check to the authority of the Nomarchs, as a hereditary office. At Coptos, M. Weill has discovered a decree of King Demzibtaui (who is not found on the king-lists, but belongs to the same period, from the names of the Vizier mentioned in it), which is no less significant. The King pronounces the most severe penalties on " any of this Whole Land who should violate or damage the foundations, inscriptions, chapels, offering-tables, or statues of the Vizier Idi, which are in all sanctuaries and all temples ". Surely it is abnormal for the Vizier Idi to have so much power that he can obtain a grant of statues and offerings in so many temples of the South, with so many

[1] " Chartes," in *Journ. Asiat.*, 1916, pp. 108–18.
[2] Moret, " Une Liste des Nomes de la Haute-Égypte sous la VIIIe dynastie," in **III**, 1914, p. 565.
[3] A stele which I found at Luxor in 1914, and published after the " Liste des Nomes " in op. cit., p. 570. The original is now in the Metropolitan Museum, New York.

guarantees that they shall be respected. There is something still more curious : in addition to earthly punishments (the destruction of the offender's property), the King attaches great importance to the penalties of the next world, saying emphatically, " the guilty shall never join the Spirits (Akhu), but shall be held and bound prisoners of King Osiris and of the gods of their cities." [1] Here Osiris and the local gods appear as judges, in the place hitherto reserved for Ra ; that shows well enough how strong was the reaction against Heliopolis and the Memphite monarchy. Finally, Demzibtaui threatens to visit with his wrath all officials, and indeed every one, including the King, the Vizier, and the Saru, who should oppose the execution of his decree. A similar threat against the King himself is found in a decree dating from the end of the Middle Kingdom, another period of disorders and invasions. It must be indeed a time of anarchy if Pharaoh does not separate the King from the Vizier and Saru by an impassable gulf ! [2]

It is at this point that the Turin Papyrus makes up the Total of Dynasties from Menes to the end of the VIIIth, regarding the Old Kingdom (3315–2360) as ended and a new age as beginning about 2360.

The IXth and Xth Dynasties (about 2360–2160) form a transition from the Memphite Old Kingdom to the Theban Middle Kingdom. Probably a Nomarch of Central Egypt usurped the power ; in any case, the capital of the country was now Heracleopolis. Few names of Kings have survived ; Achthoës (Kheti) seems to have been the usurper, and one of the last Kings, Merikara (who appears in a pseudo-historical work which I shall quote) is known from the inscriptions of the princes of Siut (XIIIth Nome), who were his stoutest supporters. From the sea to the First Cataract, Egypt was in the hands of the Nomarchs, who had become hereditary feudal princes. Central Egypt supported the King of Heracleopolis, but Upper Egypt, from Elephantine to

[1] " Charters," *Journ. Asiat.*, 1917, pp. 367–86.

[2] *Ibid.*, p. 137. " If any superior chief . . . does not oppose the offenders . . . even to the point of taking action against the King, the Vizier, and the Saru, his charter ceases to exist for his office and for his seal, his charter ceases to exist for all his goods, the charter of his children, ceases to exist in this respect, whereas he who opposes these offences remains established a Sar." Cf. Petrie, *Koptos*, pl. viii, decree of King Antef.

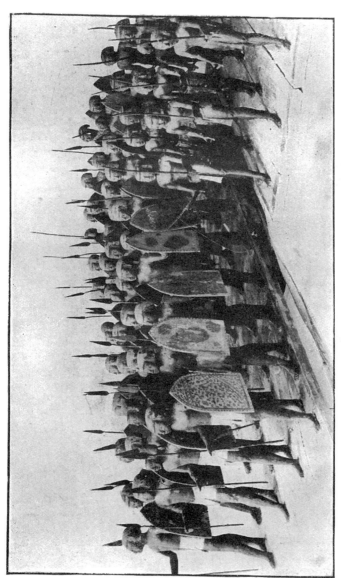

SPEARMEN AND ARCHERS OF THE PRINCES OF SIUT
Middle Kingdom.   Wood (Cairo)

[face p. 218

Abydos (VIIIth Nome), rallied round the Princes of Thebes, Antefs and Mentuheteps. The Delta had in part fallen once more into the hands of the Libyans and Asiatics who invaded the North in every period, as soon as the country weakened. For two centuries Thebes and Siut contested the crown.[1] In the tombs of this period of internal strife there is abundance of warlike scenes ; and we find soldiers training, battalions on the march, archers, spearmen, and Libyan and Nubian mercenaries, represented in sets of statuettes, which the princes took with them to the next world (Pl. VIII).

Among all these rival princes, warriors with conflicting ambitions and unstable parties, the government of Egypt was an uncomfortable task. The *Teachings for Merikara,*

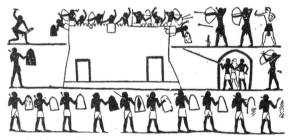

FIG. 54.—Civil War in Egypt.
From a XIIth Dynasty tomb. Newberry, *Beni-Hasan,* ii, pl. 15.

which have been preserved on a papyrus, bring an echo of those days, when the King, surrounded by intrigues, gave his sons the counsels of craft and patience which his difficult position inspired. He mentions revolts of Nomarchs, attacks of Asiatics,[2] and the defeat of the royal troops by the Thebans near Abydos. About 2160, the Heracleopolites and the princes of Siut were finally beaten by the Antefs of Thebes. The Tablet of Saqqarah, which omits all Pharaohs after Pepi II, recommences the official enumeration of the Kings with one of the Antefs. These Thebans of the XIth Dynasty consolidated the power so successfully that with the XIIth Dynasty (about 2000) peace and prosperity were

---

[1] Cf. **XX,** vol. i, pp. 455 ff., and **XXII,** § 274.
[2] It is in this connexion that Merikara's father is supposed to describe the Asiatics in the expressive terms quoted in *From Tribe to Empire,* pp. 218–19.

re-established.   But   for   two   centuries   (2360–2160)   the
institutions of absolute kingship had undergone a destructive
assault.   Authority   had   been   whittled   away,   the   Royal
Domain had vanished, civil and religious rights had gone to
whoever was strong enough to take them, and the individual
had given rein to his appetites and kicked over every kind
of discipline.   This   long   period   of   anarchy   had   brought
with it insecurity, scarcity, and moral disintegration.   Many
literary   works   inspired   by   this   crisis   show   the   common
people   of   Egypt   flinging   itself   on   the   prey.   Sometimes
oppressed and always forgotten, it took its revenge on the
recognized authorities and overwhelmed them in a wave of
violence and rapine.

It is not customary in Pharaonic documents to mention,
save by the most discreet allusion, anything disagreeable
which might have happened to the King, the Court, or the
Government.   We lack, not only " historical " texts for this
troublous epoch, but the monuments, private and   royal
buildings and other evidences of civilization, which are so
plentiful in the preceding Memphite period and the subsequent
Theban   period.   This   absence   of   monuments,   which   is
characteristic of all times of dynastic strife or invasion (for
example,   in   the   Hyksôs   period   and   between   the   Middle
Kingdom and New Empire), is eloquent by itself.   But, if
we   have   no   official   documents,   popular   literature   speaks.
The crisis so impressed the minds of men, that for centuries
it served as a theme for the meditations of the sage and the
fancies of the story-teller. Every revolution has tragic aspects,
but it also has its curious, and even   comic, side, which lends
itself to picturesque description and imagery.   In the usual
Eastern way, abstract ideas and expositions of doctrine are
given in a setting of everyday life, in the form of dialogues
and parables.   If we remember the Bible stories and the
Arabian tables we shall understand the meaning and scope
of the writings which we are about to consider.
     First we may mention certain literary documents of an
intimate kind, reflecting personal thought and observation,
in which the writer, without bias and without blinking the

facts, estimates the spectacle of the world in all sincerity. Some of these are veritable examinings of conscience, such as the papyri which we call *The Meditations of a Priest of Heliopolis*, *The Dialogue of an Egyptian with his Spirit*, *The Admonitions of a Sage*, the *Teachings* addressed by a King or Vizier to his children, and the *Songs of the Harpist*.[1] The royal personages who appear in these works belong to the IXth Dynasty (Merikara, Neferhetep), the XIth (Antef), and the XIIth (Amenemhat I), although the anarchy which they describe belongs rather to the IXth and Xth Dynasties. They were originally handed down by word of mouth, and put into elegant style by the literary men of the Middle Kingdom, as is shown by certain peculiarities of language and grammar, but most of them have come to us in late copies of the XVIIIth Dynasty.[2]

In the *Teachings* (*sebaiut*) which are supposed to have been addressed by a King to his son Merikara,[3] we see the preliminaries of the revolution and the splitting up of the country by usurpers.

> The turbulent man throws the city into disorder. He creates two parties in the younger generations. The country (of the N.E. Delta) destroyed by the Asiatics, is divided into districts. What was the principality of one (Nomarch ?) is now in the hands of ten. The priest is yoked to the land, he works like a gang (of farm-labourers). Elsewhere, troops of soldiers attack other troops, as it is said in the prophecies of the Ancestors. Egypt fights in the Necropolis.

The *Sentences* of the priest Neferrehu paint a still gloomier picture.

> The country is utterly lost ; no one any longer cares for it, no one speaks of it, no one weeps over it. And yet, what has become of the country ? The Sun is covered and no longer shines. . . . The river of Egypt is empty, it can be crossed dry-shod. . . . The (Typhonian) South Wind annihilates the North Wind. . . . All that was well is lost, the land is brought down to misery. . . . Enemies have arisen in the East, Asiatics have entered Egypt. . . . Wild beasts of the desert drink in the river of Egypt. . . . This land is taken (by plunderers), and no man knows what will come of it . . . I see this land in mourning and woe. That which had never happened is happening now. Men take up arms for battle, because the land lives on disorder. They make spears of copper, to beg their bread with blood. They laugh with an unwholesome laugh. There is no more weeping at funerals. . . . Every man slays the next. I show you sons becoming enemies,

---

[1] Besides the excellent publications of Gardiner, which will be quoted, cf. Erman's translations in **XLIV**.

[2] For the date of the papyri, cf. **XLIV**, pp. 3, 106, 131, 149, 158.

[3] Petersburg Papyrus 1116 A, translated by Alan H. Gardiner in **XIII**, i, p. 22.

brothers becoming adversaries; and a man kills his father. . . . Hate reigns among the people of the towns. The mouth which speaks is silenced, and is answered by words which bring the stick into the hand. . . . The speech (of others) is like fire to the heart, and men cannot endure what the mouth utters. . . . The land is diminished, and (yet) its chiefs become more numerous. . . . The Sun turns away from men. . . . I show you this country in distress and misery. The Nome of Heliopolis is no longer a country—Heliopolis, the city where every god is born ! [1]

The man who speaks thus, the *kheri-heb* (officiant) Neferrehu, was born at Heliopolis ; one can imagine the grief of the Heliopolitan in the presence of the unprecedented happenings in which the prestige and the doctrines of the city of the Sun collapsed tragically.

A tablet of the XVIIIth Dynasty has preserved the *Collection of Sayings* [2] issuing from the " ingenious heart " of another priest of Heliopolis, surnamed Ankhu.   The situation so astounds him that he " seeks unknown words, expressed in new language, free of all repetition of the usual formulas, and removed from the traditions left by our Ancestors ". For the first time, to our knowledge, *tradition* no longer avails an Egyptian thinker, who had been accustomed to invoke it as a rule and to follow it as an example.   The support thus lost he seeks in personal meditation ; he tries to define events which baffle him, giving up the attempt to understand them.

I squeeze my heart to extract what is in it, casting off all that was said to me formerly. . . . I shall tell of these things as I have seen them. . . . Oh, if I could understand what others do not yet understand ! . . . If I could tell of these things, and my heart would answer ! So I should explain my grief to it, and unload on to it the burden which weighs on my back. . . . So, then, I meditate on what is happening, on the events which arise all over the land. Changes are going on ; (to-day) it is not at all like last year ; every year weighs heavier than the last. The land is in confusion. . . . Right is driven out. Evil is in the council-chamber. Men fight against the plans of the Gods, and transgress their ordinances. The land is rushing towards misery ; mourning is in every place ; cities and provinces weep. All men are criminals ; on all which was respected they turn their back.

In the despair inspired by this spectacle, the only comfort left is to " speak with one's heart ", for " a courageous heart in time of distress, is the companion of its master ".   Then

---

[1] Petersburg Papyrus 1116 B, **XIII,** i, p. 100. The narrator makes Neferrehu live in the time of King Snefru, thus giving his description, the end of which foretells the coming of King Amenemhat (XIIth Dynasty), the kudos of a prophecy.

[2] Published by A. H. Gardiner as an appendix to *The Admonitions of an Egyptian Sage*, pp. 96 ff.

Ankhu meditates thus : " Come, my heart, that I may talk with thee, and thou mayest answer my words. Mayest thou explain to me what (is happening) all over the land."

In such melancholy examination of causes and responsibilities, and poignant questioning of destiny and conscience, many others indulged in those days. There is the *Dialogue of an Egyptian with his Spirit* in which, a thousand years before Job and the Preacher, a man uttered a cry of despair at the vanity of all things.

At the point where the text begins, the dialogue is already in progress. The Man is telling his spirit (*Akh*) that life on earth is so grievous that it is better to die.

> Lead me to death, and make the West pleasant for me. Is it then a misfortune to die ? Life is an evolution. See the trees ; they fall. So pass over my sins and give peace to the unhappy man. Thoth will judge me, Khonsu will defend me, and Ra will hear my words.

But the Spirit is less confident of eternal life than the Body, and replies :—

> If thou dost think of burial, it is a grief for the heart, it is what brings tears, troubling a man. It is taking a man from his house, to lead him to the Hill (of the desert). Nevermore wilt thou rise towards heaven, to see Ra, the Sun of the Gods. . . . They who have been carved in pink granite, for whom chambers have been made in the pyramid, who have achieved works of beauty, the builders who have become gods—their offering-tables are empty, like those of the neglected dead, who died on the shore (of the river), without survivors (to maintain their cult). The wave robs them of their might, and the sun likewise ; (only) the fish of the shore speak to them. Hear me, then, for it is good for man to harken. Give thyself up to following the happy day, and forget care.

In reply, the Man protests that " on earth, his name is slandered ", and that he no longer knows in whom to trust.

> To whom shall I speak to-day ? The hearts of men are violent, and every one takes his brother's goods. To whom shall I speak to-day ? Gentleness disappears, and violence rises over all the world. To whom shall I speak to-day ? The man who enrages (the good) by his wickedness makes all the world laugh by his sins. To whom shall I speak to-day ? There are no longer any just men ; the earth is delivered over to sinners. To whom shall I speak to-day ? The evil which beats the land is without end.

Hence the conclusion :—

> Death is before me to-day, as when a sick man is cured, as when one comes out of a sickness. . . . Death is before me to-day, as when a man desires to see his house again, after many years of captivity.

At these eloquent words, the Spirit decides to accept

death, which will reunite it with its body, in eternal rest, far away from the wicked.[1]

There is the same note of bitterness and scepticism in the voice of the people. On the tomb of one of the King Antefs of the Theban Middle Kingdom, in front of the harpists playing to the King, this melancholy song is engraved.

> Bodies have gone, and others have remained (in their place), since the time of our Ancestors. The Gods (deceased Kings) who once lived sleep in their pyramids, and the nobles also, the glorious ones, are buried in their tombs. They built houses, of which the place no longer exists. What, then, has become of them. I have heard the words of Imhetep and Hardedef,[2] whose sayings are repeated everywhere. Where are their places now? Their walls are destroyed, their places no longer exist, as if they had never been. No one comes back from down there, to tell us how it is with them, to tell us what they need, to calm our hearts until the day when we too shall go where they have gone. So, be joyful, follow thy desire, so long as thou livest. . . . Do all that thou dost wish on earth, and trouble not thy heart, until the day of (funeral) mourning comes for thee. The God of the Tranquil Heart (Osiris) does not hear mourning, and lamentations can save no man in the tomb. See, make a happy day! Have no care! See, no one takes his goods away with him; see, no one comes back, who has gone.[3]

The disenchantment, the scepticism, the materialism expressed in literature speak of a time of revolution. An age of general demoralization had set in, of impiety in the people, of hatred which questioned everything, authority and men alike. This collapse of Egypt under the Heracleopolite Dynasties is described in the *Exhortations of a Prophet*, or *Admonitions of an Old Sage*, to adopt the title chosen by Gardiner, the editor of the papyrus (which has come down in an XVIIIth Dynasty copy, preserved at Leyden).[4]

The treatise shows an old King, at a time when the country is plunged in anarchy. Tranquil in his palace, the aged man (who makes one think of the centenarian Pepi II) suspects nothing; but a sage, named Ipour, who has grown old in the harness of the royal administration, enters the palace and reveals the truth, calling out for arms against the revolution and prophesying the reforms and restorations of the future. The document gives a strong impression that the writer has

---

[1] Erman, *Gespräch eines Lebesmüden mit seiner Seele*, 1896. Cf. **XLIV**, p. 122.
[2] Personages of the Court of the Kings who built the Great Pyramids.
[3] W. Max Müller, *Die Liebespoesie der alten Ægypter*, p. 29, pls. 16–17. Cf. **XLIV**, p. 177.
[4] Gardiner, *The Admonitions of an Egyptian Sage*, 1909. Cf. **XLIV**, p. 131, and **XLI**, pp. 204 ff.

seen what he describes. At the beginning, every sentence begins with " So it is ". It is a statement of things as they were in a time prior to the moment when the narrator describes them—foreign invasions, intestine strife, insecurity, unemployment, famines, epidemics, a declining birth-rate, and shifting of social values ; in one word, revolution.[1]

The people of the desert take the place of the Egyptians everywhere (i, 9). The Foreigners come ; there are no more Egyptians anywhere The land becomes a desert ; the Nomes are laid waste ; the foreign Archers come into Egypt from outside (from Asia) (iii, 1–2). The ship of Upper Egypt is adrift ; the cities are destroyed, and Upper Egypt is a desert (ii, 11). The Delta is no longer protected ; the defences of the country are a much-trodden road (iv, 5). The hearts of men are violent ; the Plague (*iadt*) [2] overruns the land ; there is blood everywhere ; death is never idle (iii, 5–6).

The nobles are in mourning ; the common people exult ; every city says, " Come, let us put down the mighty among us " . . . The country is in revolution (turning) like the potter's wheel. Thieves become owners of goods, and the old (rich) are robbed (ii, 7–9). The townspeople are put to the corn-mills, and those who are clad in fine linen are beaten. Those (ladies) who had never seen the light go out of doors (iv, 8–10). The land is full of the factious ; the man who goes to till the soil carries a shield. The Nile rises in vain ; no one tills the ground, (for) all say, " We do not know what is happening in the land " (ii, 2–3). A man kills his brother, born of his own mother. The roads are ambushed. Men lie in wait in the bushes, until (the peasant) shall come, returning home in the evening, that they may take his load from him ; he is thrashed with sticks, and slain shamefully (v, 10–12). The beasts wander uncontrolled. There is no longer anyone to gather them together. Every man takes the beasts which he has marked for himself (iii, 2–3). All that one saw yesterday has vanished. The country is deserted, like a reaped field. The harvests perish on every side ; men lack clothes, spices, and oil. Filth overruns the land ; there are no more white clothes to-day (ii, 8). Every one says, " There is nothing left." The stores are destroyed, and their keepers thrown to the ground. Men eat grass and drink water ; they steal the food from the mouth of the pigs, without saying (as they used to do), " That is better for you than for me," so hungry are they (v, 12–vi, 3). All the materials necessary for the crafts are lacking (iii, 10). Men penetrate into every secret place. The Asiatics work in the workshops of the Delta (iv, 5). No (Egyptian) worker works any more ; the enemies of the country have despoiled the workshops (ix, 6).

Men are growing fewer. On every hand one sees a man burying his brother (ii, 13). The dead are thrown into the river ; the Nile is a sepulchre (ii, 6). The women are barren. No more children are born. The God Khnum no longer fashions mankind, because of the condition of the country (ii, 4). Great and small say, " Would I might die ! " Little children say, " (My father) should never have made me live." The

---

[1] The text of the *Admonitions* is prolix and confused, with lacunæ. I have had to put it in some order and to bring out the most striking features ; but I have endeavoured to keep the main divisions of the original.

[2] Cf. *From Tribe to Empire*, p. 249.

children of princes are dashed against the walls (iii, 2–3). Men flee the
cities. Tents—that is what men build (x, 2). Doors, walls, pillars are set
on fire. But the Palace of the King, L.H.S., still stands and remains solid
(ii, 10–11). But what is the use of a Treasury which has no more revenues ?
(iii, 12.)

The evil grows worse.   Here is the account of the looting
of the royal offices :—

> In the sublime Hall of Justice, the writings are taken away, and the
> secret places are thrown open. The magical formulas are disclosed and
> become inefficacious (?), because men have them in their memory. The
> public offices are open ; their declarations (title-deeds of ownership) are
> taken away ; so the serfs become masters of serfs. The (officials) are slain ;
> their writings are taken away. Woe is me for the sadness of this age !
> The scribes of the land-survey, their writings are taken away. The food of
> Egypt is for him who says, " I come, I take." The laws (hapu) of the
> Hall of Justice are thrown in the vestibule. Men walk on them in the
> public place ; the poor tear them in the streets. The poor man attains to
> the condition of the divine Ennead. This rule of the Hall of the Thirty
> Judges is disclosed. The Great Hall of Justice is to him who enters and
> goes out. The poor come and go in the Great Houses (of Justice). The
> children of the Great are thrown into the street. The wise men says, " Yes
> (it is true)," and the fool says, " No (it is not true)." But he who knows
> nothing (the King ?) thinks that all goes well. . . . (vi, 5–14).

This apathetic ignorance on the King's part becomes fatal
to him. We come to a new series of sentences, which now
begin with " But see ! " These may perhaps refer to events
which are still going on when the Sage is supposed to be
speaking. The revolutionaries attack the Palace and destroy
all government.

> But see ! Things happen which never happened before. The King is
> carried off by the plebeians (huru = poor). Those who were buried as divine
> Falcons are in coffins. That which the pyramid hid is now empty. Some
> men without faith or law [1] have despoiled the land of the Kingship. They
> have dared to revolt against the Uræus which defends Ra and pacifies
> the Two Lands. The secrets of the land, whose bounds are unknown, are
> disclosed (that is) the Court, which was overthrown in an hour. . . . The
> Serpent (the protector of the Palace) is taken from his hiding-place. The
> secrets of the Kings of Upper and Lower Egypt are disclosed (vii, 1–5).

Even if one admits that the attacks on the King and his
family are no more than a local, accidental riot, the situation
of the Court is desperate and beyond repair.

> Lower Egypt weeps. The King's granary is to every man who says, " I
> come. Bring me (this)." All the House of the King, L.H.S., has no more
> revenues. Yet it is to him (the King) that the wheat, the barley, the birds,
> and the fish belong ; his are the white linen, the fine stuffs, the bronze, the

---

[1] Lit., " without plan," i.e., without legal status (?), or without intelligence (?)

oils ; his are the mats and the carpets . . . the palankeens and all the beautiful gifts ! (x, 3–6.)

The people of the Court are in an equally bad plight.

When the Director of the City (the Vizier) goes on a journey, he has no longer an escort (x, 7). Those who are still strong in the country are told nothing of the condition of the people. They are marching to ruin (ix, 5). No official is at his post any longer. They are like a frightened flock without a shepherd (ix, 2).

Now the " revolution ", that is the reversal of social conditions, turns everything upside-down. With a pity not lacking in humour, the narrator depicts the distress of the nobles and the former rich, many of whom have emigrated, and the brutality, greed, and stupidity of the new rich.

The Great are hungry and in distress. The servants are now served (v, 2). Noble ladies flee . . . (their children) prostrate themselves, for fear of death. The chiefs of the country flee, because they have no more employment, for lack of . . . (viii, 13–14).

So the proletariat comes to the top.[1]

The poor of the land have become rich, while the owners no longer have anything. He who had nothing becomes the master of treasures, and the Great flatter him (viii, 1–2). See what happens among men ! He who could not build himself a chamber now owns (domains surrounded by) walls. The Great are (employed) in the stores. He who had not a wall (to protect) his sleep, owns a bed. He who could not sit in the shade now owns the shade [2] ; those who had the shade are exposed to the winds of the storm. He who had never made himself a boat now owns ships ; their (former) owner looks at them, but they are no longer his. He who had not a yoke of oxen owns herds ; he who had not a loaf for himself becomes the owner of a barn ; but his granary is filled with the goods of another. He who had no corn of his own now exports it (vii–viii, *passim*).

The luxury of the new rich becomes insolent.

The poor own the wealth ; he who never made himself shoes now has precious things (ii, 4). Those who had clothes are in rags ; but he who never wove for himself now has fine stuffs. He who knew nothing of the lyre now owns a harp ; he who never had people singing to him now calls upon the Goddess of Song. The bald man who never used pomade owns jars of scented oil. The woman who had not even a box now has a wardrobe. She who used to look at her face in the water owns a mirror of bronze (vii–viii).

Servants are out of the question, at least for the former masters.

---

[1] The same theme appears on an ostracon published by Sottas, in *Recueil Champollion*, 1922, p. 484.
[2] In Eastern countries, to own shade is a form of wealth.

He who had no servant is a master of serfs. He who was a distinguished person does his own commissions (ix, 5). He who went messages for others now has messengers in his service (vii, 11).

For the " noble ladies " the reversal of positions is especially tragic.

Let those who were in their husbands' beds sleep on skins (on the ground ?) . . . They suffer like servant-girls. . . . The slave-women are mistresses of their mouths,[1] and when their mistresses speak it is hard for the servants to bear it (iv, 9–13). Gold, lapis lazuli, silver, malachite, cornelian, bronze, and marble . . . now adorn the necks of slaves. Luxury runs all over the country, but the mistresses of houses say, " Oh, if we had something to eat ! " (iii, 2). The ladies . . . their bodies are sore from their old dresses [2] . . . their hearts are confused when they are greeted (iii, 4).

Worse is in store for the noblewomen.

The noble ladies are reduced to hunger, while butchers glut themselves on the meat which they used to prepare for the ladies (ix, 1). The noble-women, the great rich ladies, give their children on beds (prostituting them?) (viii, 7) ; he who used to sleep without a woman, from poverty, now finds noble ladies . . . (vii, 14).

The children of the rich can no longer be told from others.

The son of a man (of quality) [3] can no longer be told among the rest ; the son of the mistress becomes the son of the servant woman (ii, 14). The hair falls from the heads of all men ; one can no longer tell the son of a man (of quality) [4] from him who has no father (iv, 1).

What becomes of the gods and the dead in this complete upheaval ? The people, eager to enjoy life, has become sceptical about the next world. Through impiety, indifference, or lack of funeral gear, the dead are neglected. Moreover, the secret of the pyramids has been violated and the tombs have been plundered.

Those who used to build tombs have become ploughmen ; those who rowed in the barge of the God are under the yoke.[5] There is no more sailing to Byblos to-day. How should we have for our mummies the pines, with the products of which the Pure are buried, with the oils of which the Great are embalmed, as far as the land of the Keftiu (Crete) ? They no longer come. Gold is lacking, the (raw materials) for all (funerary) works are exhausted. . . . How important that seems, now that the people of the Oases come with their produce ! (iii, 6–10.) So the dead are thrown into the Nile (ii, 6). Those who used to have pure places (tombs) lie exposed on the sand (of the desert) (vii, 8).

[1] They speak as they please.
[2] They are ashamed of being seen in rags.
[3] i.e. well-born.
[4] Young princes wore a curly lock falling over the shoulder.
[5] The priests or servants of the gods.

As for the gods, we have already seen how emphatic the writer is in his indignation at the disclosure of the magical and religious secrets which were the monopoly of the King and a few intimates. What is more, *the poor man attains to the condition of the divine Ennead* .(vi, 11). What does this mean, if not that after this rush of all society towards equality on earth, believers have even forced the gates of Paradise ? Divine immortality is no longer the privilege of Pharaoh or of the select few ; the latter, in refusing to confine their future life to the Lower Region, and demanding a future in heaven like the King's, have set a contagious example. Henceforward, every human life will be prolonged up above, every man will be summoned before the tribunal of Ra,[1] and every one " justified " (by his virtue or by magic) will become a god.

Meanwhile demoralization is rampant ; unfaith is appalling ; no one any longer honours the gods. The sacrifices of oxen are given up for more mundane and urgent needs.

He who never killed (cattle) for himself, now kills oxen. The butchers cheat (the gods) with geese, giving them to the gods instead of oxen (viii, 11–12).

Men even make a parade of impiety.

Ah ! . . . If I knew where God was, I should certainly make offering to him ! (iv, 3.)

From this distracted Egypt there goes up an unceasing, heartrending complaint, in striking contrast with the carefree, exuberant, patriarchal life of the old times. There is no gaiety in the joy of bullies and destroyers. From the very beginning of the troubles,

the slaves were sad, and the Great no longer joined with the people in a brotherly way in their rejoicings (ii, 5).

Now the new rich " spend the night in drinking " (vii, 10), but, in spite of the artificial stimulation,

laughter has died, and is no more heard ; grief runs through the land, mingled with lamentations (iii, 13).

We come upon outbursts of tragic despair :—

These things, which one saw yesterday, have perished. The country is beaten down with exhaustion, like flax when it is torn up. Oh, if there

[1] See the dialogue with the Spirit, p. 223.

were an end of mankind ! No more begettings ! No more births ! Oh, let the country silence its cries ! Let there be no more tumult ! (v, 12 ; vi, 1.)

What remedy does the old Sage see for this universal frenzy ? To take refuge with the gods, to " remind them of the offerings, the sacrifices, which the men of the old days piously paid to them " (x, 12–xi, 6), and to trust in the goodness of Ra, the creator of mankind, who " will throw cold water on the fire " (xi, 11).

It is of Ra that he says :—

He is the Shepherd of all men ; nothing evil is in his heart. His flock dies, but he spends all the day guiding it, with fire in his heart. Oh, if he had known their nature (that of mankind) since the first generation, he would of a truth have chastised their sins [1] ; he would have lifted his

Fig. 55.—The Ka of King Hor, protecting the King and Egypt. Dahshur, XIIIth Dyn. Cf. Plate X, 1.

arm against them, he would have destroyed their seed and their inheritance. But (men) desire to beget offspring . . . the seed will still come out of women. . . .

Since the vital instinct is too strong, and man prefers his misery to the horror of nothingness, the sinners must receive their chastisement and return to the right way, the way of goodness, of the tried traditions. For that, a leader is awaited ; but whence will salvation come ?

There is no pilot in their time. Where, then, is he to-day ? Is he asleep ? We do not see his might (xii, 1–6).

[1] An allusion to the legend of the revolt of men against Ra. See Pt. III, Chap. I.

The end of the text of the *Admonitions* is missing. The conclusion may be imagined from the end of the *Sentences of Neferrehu*, where the *kheri-heb*, Heliopolis-born, starts to prophesy :—

A King will come from the South called Ameni . . . He will take the White Crown and he will wear the Red Crown, and the Two Lords (Horus and Seth), who love him, will take delight in him. . . . Rejoice, you who will live in his time ! The son of a man (of quality) will once more find (in his reign) esteem for his name, for ever. Those who wish to do evil and meditate enmity lower their mouths, for fear of him. . . . Right will resume its place, and injustice will be driven out. Happy he who will see these things and serve this King !

CHAPTER IV

The Rule of the Just Laws. The New Social State and the Administration of the Theban Kings

A MENI, the Saviour foretold by the prophecy, was King Amenemhat I, who founded the XIIth Dynasty about 2000 B.C. During the period which we call the Middle Kingdom (the Theban XIth to XIIIth Dynasties, 2160–1660), the Theban Kings restored order and prosperity in Egypt. In *From Tribe to Empire* (pp. 222–34, 243–6), I have

FIG. 56.—Royal Funeral Procession of a Plebeian.
Theban New Empire.

explained how these Pharaohs developed a Greater Egypt, extending their empire up the Nile Valley and in Palestine. This achievement, which was one of defence rather than of conquest, did not save Egypt from the invasion of the Shepherds, who interrupted the work of the Pharaohs for a century (1660–1580). The national reaction drove out the

	XIIth Dynasty MONUMENTS AND TURIN PAPYRUS		MANETHO 7 Diospolite (Theban) Kings.	
	1. Amenemhat I [1]		2000–1971	1.
	2. Senusert I		1980–1936	
	3. Amenemhat II		1938–1904	2.
213 years	4. Senusert II		1906–1888	
	5. Senusert III		1887–1850	3.
	6. Amenemhat III (Nemaatra)		1849–1801	4. 5.
	7. Amenemhat IV		1800–1792	6.
	8. Sebekneferura (Queen)		1791–1788	7.

[1] **XXII,** § 282. Some Kings called in their sons as associates, so that the date of the son's accession is earlier than his father's death.

invaders and strengthened the sovereigns of the Theban New Kingdom, or Empire, as it is called (XVIIIth–XXth Dynasties, 1580–1100). The various Kings named Thothmes, Amenophis, and Rameses, anxious to protect their frontiers, sought for advanced bastions. They were led on to conquer Hither Asia and to commit themselves to the gamble of a world-policy.[1] Thebes was not only the capital of the New Egypt ; it became the metropolis of the civilized East.

This splendid development of the Greatest Egypt was only possible through the reforms of the Kings, who had learned a hard lesson of experience in the revolution. We see the Pharaohs of the Middle Kingdom widening their conception of government, making the administrative framework less rigid, elaborating a new order of society, making laws, and in general, basing royal institutions on principles which remained those of the New Empire—the reduction of class-privileges, the admission of all to civil and religious rights, and the extension of justice to the whole of society, now levelled under the ægis of Pharaoh. The old rule of the god-king, at once patriarchal and despotic, the rule of the King's good pleasure, was replaced, for King and people alike, by the rule of the " just laws ".

I

THE REFORMS OF THE THEBAN KINGS

The revolution described in the preceding pages has left its trace in the material ravages undergone by the monuments of the Memphite age—the violation of chambers in the pyramids, the destruction of the attached royal temples, the mutilation of the statues of Kings, and the abandonment of the sanctuaries of Ra and the royal funerary temples of the Vth Dynasty.[2] It is also seen in the dismemberment of Egypt between the IXth and XIth Dynasties. While the " house of Achthoës " was ruling at Heracleopolis, the Delta relapsed, for a time, into its primitive historical divisions, namely a Western, where the Libyans were predominant,

[1] *From Tribe to Empire*, pt. iii.
[2] Cf. the defamatory stories preserved by Herodotus (ii, 128–36).

and an Eastern, under the Asiatics, while the South, from Elephantine to Thinis, formed a principality under the monarchs of Thebes, Antefs and Mentuheteps. In spite of the support which the Prince-Nomarchs of Siut gave to the Heracleopolites Achthoës and Merikara, we see the Thebans assuming first the princely title of *r-pât* (" Mouth of Men ") and then the royal title of *Horus*, with a single cartouche, in which the name Antef or Mentuhetep is followed by the epithet " Son of Ra ". Gradually the Thebans gained ground in the direction of Heracleopolis ; the fourth Antef made Aphroditopolis (Xth Nome) the northern gate of his realm.[1] The true restorer of united Egypt seems to have been Mentuhetep IV, who built himself a great funerary temple with a pyramid at Der el-Bahari, and took as his Horus-name " He who unites the Two Lands ".[2] A relief in the temple at Gebelein (south of Thebes) shows us this Mentuhetep or his predecessor casting an Egyptian (of the North), a Nubian, an Asiatic, and a Libyan to the ground.[3]

The Theban Kings revived the celebration of the Sed-jubilee,[4] and took the precaution of associating their sons with them on the throne before they died, in order to forestall competition and usurpation by rivals. The director of the capital, which was at Thebes, became the Vizier. Under the last Mentuheteps, one Amenemhat held this post of first official in the State and " directed the administration of the Lord of the Two Lands ".[5] It was perhaps he who, about the year 2000, succeeded the Mentuheteps and became the first Pharaoh of the XIIth Dynasty.

The history of the XIIth Dynasty seems to be better known than that of any other family of Egyptian Kings. We have the number of the Kings, the years of their reigns, and their place in general chronology, while epigraphic monuments, royal pyramids, tombs of nobles, stelæ of private individuals, and documents of every kind abound, giving us concordant information and constituting a mass of homogeneous historical material such as we do not find again except for the XVIIIth Dynasty. All this evidence is a proof that Egypt

---

[1] *Teachings for Merikara*, in **XIII**, i, pp. 29–30.
[2] **XXII**, §§ 276–7.
[3] Bissing and Bruckmann, *Denkmäler Aegypt. Skulpturen*, pl. 33a.
[4] **XVII**, vol. i, § 435.
[5] Ibid., § 445.

had returned to order, and that the individual was prosperous in a firmly established State. This is also a period in which clearly-marked personalities emerge, reflected in literature and art. The Theban Middle Kingdom produced a perfect efflorescence of popular tales, and also of written dialogues and treatises, which, as we have seen, were examinations of conscience and expositions of politico-social morality or popular philosophy, in the form of parables. Everywhere we see the memory of the revolution and the dread which it left behind it, an inexhaustible theme for meditation and criticism. The intellectual impulse came from the Court, which produced *Teachings* galore, expounded theories and methods of government, and discussed social problems. The statues of the Kings of this period bear the mark of this intellectual effort. The faces are intelligent, sometimes careworn, and furrowed deep by anxiety over public affairs, in striking contrast with the calm, majestic countenances of the Pharaohs of the Old Kingdom, who knew no bounds to their divine authority (compare Pl. X, 3, with Pl. III, 1). In the Middle Kingdom the social question came to the fore ; Egyptian society turned its course towards new goals. It was no longer the King alone who constituted the State ; the State was the whole population, and all members of it, nobles, priests, and plebeians of the towns and countryside, were called to take a share in the benefits and also in the burdens in the exploitation of the magnificent domain created by the Nile and the sun.

The revolution had opened the way to this new order of things by sweeping away the social classes under a deluge of proletarians. When the wave had passed, the Kings could start rebuilding on a levelled ground ; there remained but few traces of the social strongholds in which the nobles and priests held out behind antique privileges.

However, the whirlwind of the revolution had spared certain points in the country. In Central Egypt, especially, noble families managed to retain their power. At Cusæ, the capital of the XIVth Nome, the Pepi-Ankhs of the VIth Dynasty, whom I mentioned above (p. 211), show an uninterrupted line. Their descendants, Senbis and Ukheteps, Nomarchs and Directors of Prophets, have superbly decorated tombs. In one of these, there is an engraved list of the princes (*hatiu*) of Cusæ, with their wives—fifty-nine couples in all, before Ukhetep III, who lived under Amenemhat II (1938–1904).[1] A little to the north, in the Nome of the White Oryx (XVIth), and a little to the south, at Siut (XIIIth Nome), other Nomarchs held princely state. The inscriptions found in the tombs of Siut describe the power of the Nomarch Kheti, a stout supporter of King Merikara. Kheti is " the heir of a Regent (of a Nome), Regent of Regents, son of a Regent, son of the daughter of a Regent ". At a time when the Court and all Central Egypt are trembling with fear, he keeps his city and his province in complete prosperity.

> Here every official is in his place, and no one fights with spear and shield or draws the bow. Children are not killed beside their mothers, nor small folk (*nezes*, men of the people) beside their wives.[2] So the god of the city (Upuat) is content ; Kheti builds him a temple there, in which King Merikara will be able to hold his Sed jubilee [3] and win millions of years thereby.

These are the duties of a King, which the prince thus takes on himself in his province. Another Kheti boasts of having procured for his city all the hydraulic material required for good irrigation ; he leads water from the Nile right on to the Tells of ancient cities and fulfils the wants of the farmers. Having a great supply of corn, he was able, when the country suffered from scarcity, to feed his city with bushels of wheat, allowing every " small man " to take loads of corn for himself and his wife, for the widow and the orphan. Levying (?) for himself all the taxes which he had found " reckoned " in the country, by the care of his fathers, he stocked the fields with cattle, and so successfully that the cows calved twice a year and the pastures were full of calves. The militia of the nome formed regiments, and his ships satisfied His Majesty.

> I was the friend of the King, because his supporters knew me, those who maintained him at the head of the South. He made me govern when I was still but a child, a cubit high ; he gave me advancement among the young generations. He made me learn to swim with the Royal Children. I was correct in manners, and free of any opposition to my master, who brought me up when I was a child. Siut was quiet under my administration and Heracleopolis prayed to the God for me. Upper and Lower Egypt said (of me), " These are the Teachings (*sebaiut*) of the Prince ! " [4]

[1] Aylward M. Blackman, *The Rock Tombs of Meir*, iii, pp. 16–20.
[2] Griffith, *Siut* ; cf. **XVII**, vol. i, § 404.
[3] **XVII**, vol. i, § 403.
[4] *Siut*, pl. xv, 1–24, *passim*.

In short, it was the King's doctrine which the Nomarch of Siut applied ; and the monarchy would have had still more prestige if it had itself set an example of authority.

That is what the Thebans understood. The *Teachings* (*sebaiut*) ascribed to Merikara's father [1] and to Amenemhat I expound their wise *policy towards the nobles*. They will no longer tolerate revolt.

> If you find (the lord) of a city . . . who has broken the law . . . a dangerous man who talks too much, a fomenter of disorder, then put him down, kill him, wipe out his name, destroy his race and his memory and his supporters who love him. [2]

The Great who think and act rightly should be called by the King to be his helpers.

> Honour the Great Ones and protect your people. . . . Magnify the Great Ones that they may act on your orders, for he who is rich in his house acts impartially ; having (everything), he desires nothing. The poor man does not speak according to Right. A man who says, " I should like to have . . ." is not just ; he is partial to him whom he loves, he inclines towards him who pays him. Great is a great (King) who has great counsellors. Strong is the King who has a Court. Exalt him who is rich in nobles. [3]

These *Teachings*, addressed by the King to his heir, we see put into practice in the relations of Pharaoh with a powerful family who owned the tombs of Beni-Hasan. The inscriptions tell us of the relations of these princes with the first Amenemhats and Senuserts. At the beginning of the XIIth Dynasty, Amenemhat I made an inspection of his kingdom, to restore it to order.

> He came in his own person, and he drove away sin (the rebels), rising up (on the throne) like Atum himself. He restored that which he found in ruins, separating every city from its neighbour ; he caused every (city) to know its frontier towards its (neighbouring) city ; he set up again the boundary-stones, (lasting) as heaven ; he reviewed their waters from what is in the books, and assessed the tax from the old writings, by reason of his great love for justice. [4]

What does this tour of inspection mean, if not that Pharaoh

[1] Written in the Theban period, the *Teachings* ascribed to the father of Merikara, King of Heracleopolis, reflect, as if in anticipation, the Theban doctrine and the *Teachings* of Amenemhat.

[2] *Merikara*, § 5.   [3] Ibid., §§ 10–11.

[4] Great Beni-Hasan inscription, in Newberry and Griffith, *Beni-Hasan*, i, pls. xxv–xxvi ; cf. **XVII**, §§ 619–39.

resumed possession of the land of the nomes as State Domain, which he might entrust to the great local families for administration, but meant to hold henceforward as his own property ?   It is true that at the beginning of the XIIth Dynasty the Nomarchs retained some honorary privileges out of their past sovereignty—the right of reckoning in years of their office, as the King reckoned in years of his reign, and that of attaching L.H.S. to their names [1] ; but they were once more obedient to the King, and this is illustrated by what happened in the XVIth Nome of the White Oryx.

There Amenemhat I conferred distinctions on a noble named Khnumhetep I, who held the city of Menat-Khufu. He made him Nomarch, and set up stones marking the boundaries between this nome and its neighbours, the Hare (XVth) and the Dog (XVIIth).   Later, on the pretext of honouring the Nomarch's children, Pharaoh interfered with his inheritance.   The eldest son, Ameni, " Son of a Prince," became Chancellor of the King of the North, Great Director of the Soldiers of the Nome, leading hundreds of nomesmen in the King's armies, and, finally, Nomarch of the White Oryx.   A younger son, Nekht, was appointed Governor (*heq*) of the city of Menat-Khufu, which was thereby detached from the XVIth Nome.   The daughter, Beqet, Princess and Nomarch's daughter, married a Regent of New Cities, a favourite of the King, named Neheri, who governed the city of the royal necropolis.[2] Khnumhetep II, the son of Neheri and Beqet, was subsequently chosen by Pharaoh to receive Menat-Khufu (which did not go to the heirs of Nekht), with the title of Prince. He lived at Court, in great favour with the King, and married the daughter of the Nomarch of Cynopolis (XVIIth Nome). Of the two sons born of this union, King Senusert II made one, Nekht, Nomarch of the XVIIth Nome, as heir of his mother's father, and Director " at the head of Upper Egypt ". The second son, Khnumhetep III, was consecrated as Director of Menat-Khufu, and received many favours from the Court.

Here we have an example of the King's policy, taken from the life.   Rich and powerful as the Princes of Beni-Hasan

[1] Cf. above, p. 108, n. 3.
[2] Cf. xvii, § 628. Neheri is perhaps the Nomarch of the Hare (XVth Nome), who will be mentioned later on.

are, their "inheritance" is not in their sole control, but
depends on the King, who reshapes their domains and breaks
them up with every new generation. Khnumhetep I alone is
both Regent of Menat-Khufu and Nomarch of the Oryx.
His sons have one of these governments or the other, but
not both. In the third generation the XVIth Nome is out of
their hands, and they govern the XVIIth (Dog); after
that, the family disappears. At each succession the King
steps in, consecrates (*nez*) the Nomarch, divides the territory,
and never allows the union of two nomes in the same hands
to establish a dangerous power. On the other hand, he heaps
personal favours and honorary distinctions on the family,
and lavishes his friendship on those who go to Court.[1]

In general the princes who held nomes became, in the
administration of their provinces, mere royal officials. Ameni,
the eldest son of Khnumhetep I, who governed the Oryx
for twenty-five years (1963–1938), tells us of his duties.
First, as " Great Director of the Soldiers (*meshâu*) of the
XVIth Nome, in the place of his superannuated father ",
he commanded the contingents of 400 or 600 picked men,
supplied by the nome for the Nubian expeditions. He
describes his activity, on his return to his province, as
" beloved Regent of his city ".

> I passed my years as Regent of the White Oryx. All the impressed
> labour (*baku*) due to the King's House existed by my hand. The Directors

---

[1] The genealogical tree of this Beni-Hasan family is as follows (**XVII**, § 620):

Khnumhetep I,
Regent of Menat-Khufu
and Nomarch of the White
Oryx (XVIth).

Ameni,	*Nekht,*	*Beqet*
Nomarch of the Oryx.	Regent of Menat-Khufu.	= Neheri, Regent of the
(XVIth)		Royal City.
		Khnumhetep II, Regent
		of Menat-Khufu
		= Kheti, d. of the
		Nomarch of Cynopolis
		(XVIIth).

Nekht,	*Khnumhetep III,*
Nomarch of Cynopolis	Regent of Menat-Khufu.
(XVIIth).	

of Classes (of cultivators) of the Domains and of Herdsmen, in the Oryx, gave me 3,000 yokes of their oxen ; so I was praised for this in the Royal House, every year (of the census ?) of the cattle. I caused all their taxes to be taken to the King's House, and there was no surcharge (?) against me in any of his offices. While the whole Nome of the Oryx worked for me, and with full returns (?), there was no daughter of a plebeian (*nezes*) whom I abused, no widow whom I oppressed, no husbandman whom I turned back, no herdsman whom I threw in prison. There was no manager of (a gang of) five men whose men I took to work (for me). There was no one unhappy in my time, nor hungry in my day. When years of scarcity came, I tilled all the fields of the Oryx, to its southern and northern borders, causing the inhabitants to live, creating their sustenance, so that no one was hungry here. I gave to the widow as to the married woman. I did not favour the great man more than the small, in all that I gave. When the great Niles (high inundations) came, bringing harvests (?) and riches, I did not levy the arrears of taxes on the land.

So the pride of this Nomarch is no longer that he is an independent noble on his feudal land. The whole country has to make account to him, but he in his turn makes account scrupulously to the King, and his only ambition is to be considered an able administrator.

It was the same in the adjoining nome, the Hare (XVth). The princes of the capital, Hermopolis, were the heirs of feudal lords emancipated under the VIth Dynasty, whose tombs are at Shekh-Said. They honoured their ancestors and gloried in their origin, but they had no more real independence than their neighbours of the XVIth Nome. The inscriptions in their magnificent hypogea at el-Bersheh give us dates by the computation of the Nome, not by that of the King, a glorious past of liberty asserting itself in a less brilliant present, stamped by total submission to Pharaoh. The Nomarch Thothetep, who lived under Amenemhat II and Senusert II, still held his post as the successor of his maternal grandfather, Neheri.[1] On the walls of his tomb he has left a picture of a colossal statue being hauled from the quarry at Hetnub, about 12 miles away, to his city, by 172 men in four files. These are the " classes " (*sau*) of the priests, the recruits (*zamu*) of the troops of the nome, and the young men of the two banks of the province, eastern and western.

> The Princes (*hatiu*) who used to rule and the Judge Protectors, created inside this city, whom I established in their offices over the valley, their hearts had no idea of what I have been able to do (here, for myself).

[1] Perhaps the same as the Neheri mentioned at Beni-Hasan.

What was the source of this remarkable power ? Thothetep obtained it " by the King's favour ", and because he was " Sole Friend, Favourite of the Horus, Lord of the Palace ".[1]

After the reign of Senusert III (about 1880) the great necropoles of the princes were no longer used. No more monuments of Nomarchs appear in the valley of the Nile. The titles *heq spat* and *herj zaza âa*, borne by the Regents of Nomes and Great Superior Chiefs of the feudal period, cease to occur. One can only conclude that with the title the office disappeared. The princely families surviving from the old régime effaced themselves ; the provincial nobility became a Court nobility once more. The nomes were now under royal officials. So the Court recovered its position as hub of the administration. But it was no longer the royal family which governed, but agents, whatsoever their origin, chosen by the King. Such is the impression which one gets from the biographical stelæ of the Viziers of the XIIth Dynasty, who are once more the supreme officials in the Two Lands. Amenemhat, who was Vizier [2] to one of the last Mentuheteps, perhaps himself taking the Crowns as Amenemhat I, Mentuhetep, the Vizier of Senusert I,[3] and Sehetepibra, the confidant of Amenemhat III,[4] have left long-winded inscriptions, in which they have the titles of the great royal officials of the Old Kingdom. Thus the direct authority of the King was re-established in the nomes ; the princes had returned into the framework of the royal administration.

Towards the priesthood, the King's policy was simplified by circumstances. In the course of the Heracleopolite Dynasties the princes seem to have absorbed the feudal clergy, in that they appropriated to themselves the management of the property of the temples. Having become independent, the Nomarchs called themselves Directors of Prophets and watched over the temporal goods of the " classes " of priests, leaving the daily performance of the sacred rites to the *uâbu*, the Pure Ones, who were officiants by profession and instructed in divine matters. Pharaoh's

---

[1] Newberry, *El-Bersheh*, i, pls. xii–xvi.   [2] **XVII**, i, § 145.
[3] Ibid., § 531.   [4] Ibid., § 745.

resumption of his sovereign rights, therefore, meant also
the possession of the goods of the temples, so that the clerical
vassalage—or what remained of them, merged in the lay
vassalage—disappeared with the latter before the royal
authority. By resuming their guardianship of the priestly
class, the Theban Pharaohs once more became benefactors
of the gods and builders of temples. Different priesthoods
intrigued for the King's favour and the influence which
it gave.

In the matter of doctrine, *the priests of Ra* had not lost
ground. On the contrary, it is in the Theban works of this
time that we find the most eloquent panegyrics of Ra, Master
of the World and protector of the King, alive and dead. It
is he who is called simply " the God ". He had gone out of the
sight of men during the disorders of the anarchy, but his
invisible presence still dominated the government of the
universe.

> A generation of men goes by, and God, who sees through appearances,
> has hidden himself. . . . But honour God on his path, in his shape of a
> precious stone, or under his face of bronze. (He is like the river ?) ; no
> river lets itself be bound, but it breaks the dam which hides it.   (He is
> like the soul) ; the soul goes towards the place which is known to it, and
> does not turn aside from its path of yesterday. So, establish your house
> (tomb) in the West ; beautify your place in the necropolis, like a just man
> who has practised justice. It is in that that the heart of man finds rest.
> The virtue of one just in heart is more pleasing (to God) than the ox of
> one who practises injustice.[1] Work, then, act for God, that he may like-
> wise work for you, with an offering which will fill your table and with an
> inscription which will perpetuate your Name. God knows him who works
> for him. Men are well guided, that flock of God. It is he who made
> heaven and earth at their desire. He slakes their thirst with water, and
> creates the air to give life to their nostrils. They are his own images, pro-
> ceeding from his flesh. Ra rises in the sky at their desire.[2] It is he who
> made the plants for them, and the beasts, the birds, and the fish to feed them.
> But he also slays his enemies, and chastises his own children, because they
> have plotted to rebel against him. . . . (Yet), when they weep, he hears
> them. Ra has made leaders for them in the egg,[3] supports to support the
> backs of the weak. Ra has created magic for them, as an arm to defend
> them against evil fortunes, and he sends them dreams, night and day.[4]

Although the Kings of the XIIth Dynasty chose for their
residence the city of Itet-taui, " She who conquers the Two
Lands," near Dahshur and the point where the Fayum opens

---

[1] Cf. 1 Sam. xv, 22.
[2] Every morning.
[3] Ra shaped the kings as soon as they were conceived in their mother's womb.
This theme was developed and represented in the temples of the XVIIIth Dynasty.
[4] *Merikara*, §§ 27–8.

into the valley—a more central site than Memphis, and less exposed to invaders from the Delta—they did not abandon Heliopolis, the religious capital of the Old Kingdom. In the year 3 of his reign, Senusert I held a solemn audience, in which he conveyed to his counsellors and courtiers his desire to set up a stele to Harakhti—that is, to Ra, in his form of the Falcon Horus rising on the Eastern horizon.

"Harakhti," says the King, " brought me into the world to do as he did, to bring about what he decreed should be done. He has given it to me to lead this land. He has known it and he has united it, and he has favoured me with his support. I have caused the eye which is in him to shine, acting in all things as pleased him. . . . I am a King by birth, an overlord, who has not made himself. I have ruled since my childhood, I have been prayed to in the egg. I have dominated on the ways of Anubis, and he has raised me up to be Lord of the two halves of the world, since the time when I was a babe ; I was not yet out of my swaddling-clothes, when he had already enthroned me as master of men. . . . (Therefore) I have instituted divine offerings ; I accomplish works in the mansion of my father Atum ; I give provisions for his altar on earth ; I found my mansion near him, that the memory of my good deeds may endure in his dwelling ; for this mansion is my name, the lake is my monument, and the glorious and useful things which I have done for the God are my eternity." [1]

To this speech the King's Friends reply as follows :—

"The God Hu (speaks) through your mouth, and the God Sia [2] is behind you, O Prince, L.H.S." Then the King himself says to the Chancellor of the North, Sole Friend, Director of the Double White House, and Chief of Secrets, "Take counsel, that the work may be done according to My Majesty's desire."

On a chosen day the King " arose ", crowned with the royal diadem and the two feathers, followed by all men, and the officiant-in-chief, the bearer of the Sacred Book, ran a line round stakes planted in the ground according to the ritual of the foundation of temples. To this day, in the plains of Matariyyeh, where Heliopolis once stood, an obelisk of Senusert I, the sole surviving vestige of the temple, proclaims the glory of the King and of the god Ra.[3]

Amon-Ra at Thebes.—The Amenemhats and Senuserts also lavished their bounty on other sanctuaries still existing in Lower and Upper Egypt, which they restored, and built new ones as well.[4] Among these latter there appears, for the

[1] On a parchment preserved in the Berlin Museum. **XII**, xii (1874), p. 85 ; Maspero's translation in **XX**, vol. i, p. 504.
[2] Hu and Sia, the gods of Command and Knowledge.
[3] Illustrated in **XX**, vol. i, p. 507.
[4] See the list of foundations made in the XIIth Dynasty, in a fragmentary text translated by Breasted, **XVII**, vol. i, § 500.

first time, a monument dedicated to *Amon-Ra, Lord of Nesut-taui* (" Thrones of the Two Lands ", a name of Thebes). This was a shrine of pink granite, presented by Amenemhat I to his father, Amon-Ra, in the Temple of Phtah at Karnak.[1] The beginnings of Thebes and of Amon are obscure. In the vast plain in which, in the IInd millennium, the greatest city of the Eastern world was to rise, we hardly find the name of Amon before 2000, nor that of his abode, Uast, the " City of the Sceptre ". The Pyramid Texts do not mention Amon. The few monuments earlier than the XIth Dynasty found on the site name, as the religious centre, the Heliopolis of Upper Egypt, the city of Iunu-shemâ (Hermonthis), with its falcon-headed warrior-god Mentu.

On the stele of a " Nomarch of the Nome " found in the Theban necropolis of Asasif, and probably dating from the end of the VIth Dynasty, the names of Amon and Uast do not appear, but the Nomarch calls himself the Imakhu of Mentu, Lord of Iunu, of Hathor of Denderah, of Phtah-Sokar, who had a temple on the site of the future Karnak (Pl. X, 2),[2] and, finally, of Osiris, Lord of Busiris. Yet the plain north-east of Hermonthis formed the territory of the IVth Nome (Uast, Sceptre). With the XIth Dynasty, officials appear, residing in the capital of the nome, which is named, like the nome itself, Uast, and is the future Thebes. The god whom they worship is still Mentu, not Amon.[3] But then comes the founder of the XIIth Dynasty, Amenemhat I. He had taken for his patron [4] a local god of Uast, the curly-horned ram Amon. The new King dedicated chapels to the new dynastic god, in the temples of the gods previously worshipped on the site of Uast, and he must also have built him a temple of his own. Lastly, Amenemhat gave the god of Uast supreme authority over the gods of the other cities, making him a form of the patron deity of Heliopolis, under the name of *Amon-Ra*.

[1] **XVII**, vol. i, § 484 ; cf. **XX**, vol. i, p. 507.
[2] Newberry, " A Sixth-Dynasty Tomb at Thebes," in **I**, iv, p. 97. This monument seems to me to belong rather to the beginning of the Middle Kingdom. Cf. the stele of Senusert I, in the Louvre, on which the King does homage for his Nubian conquests to " Mentu, Lord of Uast ". Illustration in Maspero, **XX**, vol. i, 485.
[3] Cairo *Catalogue*, Nos. 20001, 20005, 20009. Under Senusert I, the general Nessumentu, commanding the recruits of Thebes, does not yet invoke the protection of Amon (Louvre, C.1).
[4] His name means " Amon is before ".

From then onwards, most of the gods of cities and nomes are associated with Ra—Solarized, one might say—with a view to a religious centralization, reinforcing the monarchical centralization effected by the Theban kings. Thus, Khnum of Elephantine, Horus of Edfu, Min of Coptos, Amon of Thebes, Mentu of Hermonthis, Thoth of Hermopolis, the Ram of Heracleopolis, Sebek of Crocodilopolis, etc., all become *kheperu*, forms or manifestations of Ra,[1] and members of the great body of the Ennead. The process by which Ra had superseded the old god of the royal family, Horus, son of Osiris, began again for similar reasons, but it took a less drastic form.

In this fusion of Ra with the local gods, did Heliopolis gain ? Ra the Demiurge, who in old times had had to reckon with the ineffaceable prestige of the ancient sky-god Horus, now had to come to terms with the newcomer from the capital, Amon, whose material power was growing with that of his city. In reality, it was Amon-Ra, not Ra, who reigned over all the gods of Egypt after 1600. We shall see that, while the doctrine of Heliopolis maintained its moral ascendancy, the Theban god imposed himself by a formidable earthly power, and that in Amon-Ra the predominant member was often Amon. The celestial Ra of Heliopolis remained more especially the god of the royal family, in the rôle in which he had once supplanted Osiris and Horus.

But it had not been possible to confine *Osiris* to his position as god of the earth and the dead. When the Heliopolitan clergy had secured the authority of Ra, they had been obliged to admit Osiris into heaven and to incorporate him in the Great Ennead. The devotion of the Theban Kings restored the doctrine of Osiris to favour. Compared with the doctrine of Ra, it was more within reach of the popular intelligence. Osiris had lived on earth, ruling over men ; Ra guided the destinies of the universe from the heights of heaven. Metaphysical theories of the creation of the world by the generations of the gods did not interest the masses so much as the practical recipes invented by Isis, Anubis, and Thoth to make an " eternal body ". What the Egyptian asked, was to be initiated into the Osirian mysteries which

[1] **XXII**, § 272 ; **XX**, vol. i, pp. 137 ff. Originally Khnum was a ram, Horus a falcon, Thoth an ibis, and Sebek a crocodile.

conferred immortality. This meant admission to the privilege hitherto reserved for Pharaoh and a select few, and, indeed, the growing popularity of Osiris came to signify, to some extent, the diffusion of democratic ideas in Egyptian society. Whereas the worship of Ra and the celestial gods was shut away in temples and done by the priests, the King's devotion to Osiris, reaching the public, extended both to the living and to the dead, in temples and in cemeteries alike, and created an immense wave of faith among the people. In Part III, Chapter I, we shall see how small temples of Osiris were attached to most of the great temples of various local deities, and how all sanctuaries were invaded by the Osirian ritual, which gradually forced them to adopt its fundamental practices and the details of worship.

Under the XIIth Dynasty there grew up in Upper Egypt a holy city of Osiris, which became the pendant of Busiris in the Delta. This was Abdu, Abydos, where the head of Osiris, the most precious relic of the dismembered body of the god, was kept in a vase, *ab*. Under the Old Kingdom, the local god of Abydos was the wolf Upuat from the Western Delta, now surnamed Khent-Amenti, " Presider over the West." [1]   By the confusion of the Wolf Khent-Amenti and the Jackal Anubis, who were brother-gods, the former became, like the latter, a god of the dead and of funeral rites (above, p. 87).   In his temple, discovered by Petrie at Thinis, the buildings and votive offerings of successive dynasties have been found—ivory statues of an unnamed Thinite King, a statuette of Khufu (Cheops), charters of immunity of Neferirkara and Teti (above, pp. 206–7), statues of Pepi II (above, p. 206), etc. With the Thebans, evidences of devotion to Upuat reappear in the temple ; here are admirable statues and reliefs dedicated to him by Mentuhetep III and Senusert I. At the end of the XIIth Dynasty, in this same sanctuary, the dedications mention Osiris, with the epithet Khent-Amenti, as lord of the temple and the capital.[2]

This assimilation with Khent-Amenti was late, only coming into effect after the year 2000, but Osiris had long ago con-

[1] Cf. above, p. 78.
[2] Petrie, *Abydos*, ii. Moreover, Khnum is mentioned at Abydos with Heqet, in funerary formulas on stelæ of the XIIth Dynasty (e.g. C.3 in the Louvre).

quered the necropoles of the nome and the tombs of the Thinite Kings. As our Table of the Nomes shows, the ancient name of the Nome of Abydos, Ta-ur, "the Great Land," refers to Osiris wearing the characteristic feathers which he took from Anzti of Busiris, and the ensign of the nome was already the vase, surmounted by feathers, which held the revered head of the god (Fig. 58). Furthermore, one of the Thinite tombs, that of King Khent, was transformed into a

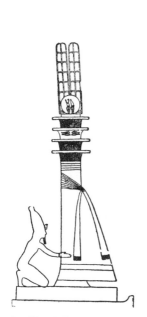

FIG. 57.—The Zed of Osiris at Abydos. Temple of Seti I.

FIG. 58.—The Casket of Abydos, with the Head of Osiris.

cenotaph of Osiris, perhaps on account of the similarity of Khent and Khent-Amenti, which had already become a surname of Osiris. Transplanted to Abydos, the god of Busiris there became the great god of the dead, this being expressed by the simple addition of the plural to his surname ; *Khent-Amenti* is frequently changed to *Khent-Amentiu*, "Presiding over the Westerners," that is, the dead buried in the West. In the tomb of King Khent, Amélineau discovered a funeral bed of sandstone, adorned with heads and feet of lions, on which lies the mummy of Osiris, wearing the White Crown of the South. At the four corners, four falcons, who are the four sons of Horus, keep vigil ; but on the mummy, on the end of the erect phallus, is a bird (*zert*), which is the goddess Isis, represented at the moment of impregnation by the resuscitated god (above, p. 99).[1] This monument dates from the New Empire, but it is probably simply a replica of a more ancient cenotaph, which perhaps existed under the Old Kingdom and even in Thinite times, and certainly under the XIIth Dynasty. The tombstones in the necropolis of Abydos very often express the wish to be laid near " the stair of the Great God, at Abydos, on the much-feared, much-acclaimed mound (*uart*), to which living and dead come, on which the Great God lies ".[2] The necropolis was called Peqer or Ra-peqer ; we shall see the rites of which it was the scene.

The Mysteries of Osiris at Abydos.—The Kings of the XIIIth Dynasty did for Osiris what those of the Vth had done for Ra of Heliopolis ; they created a cult. Instead of expressing itself in gigantic monuments, like the obelisk-temples, the worship of Osiris, being of a more intimate, personal character, manifested itself in feasts in which the entire people, sharing the same sentiments as the King and Court, took a direct and passionate interest. This age saw the appearance of the first ritual of the Osirian Mysteries, which were celebrated, not for the sole benefit of the King, but for the eternal resurrection of all worshippers of Osiris, from the King, his relations, and the high officials to the humblest craftsman, herdsman, or husbandman. Religion had become more democratic, like other institutions, and here we come to a capital fact in the history of kingship and society : under the Middle Kingdom the admission of the masses to religious rights changed the social system of Egypt for good. The result achieved by the revolutionaries of the Heracleopolite period was the admission of the common people to everlasting life in the next world and to civic life in this.

Breaking away from venerable traditions, the Kings of the XIIth Dynasty caused the highest officials of the Court

---

[1] Amélineau, *Le Tombeau d'Osiris.* There is a cast of the same subject in the Musée Guimet. Cf. Plate VII, 3.

[2] Louvre, Stelæ C.3 and 170 ; Musée Guimet, C.5 ; Cairo, 20024, 20153 ; Leyden, ed. Boeser, pl. iv, etc.

to enact, in public ceremonies, at the expense of the State, the episodes, hitherto kept secret (*seshtau*) of a sacred drama—the death, resurrection, and triumph of Osiris. The scene of these representations was the Nome of Abydos ; the principal episodes were performed on the banks of the river, at the cenotaph in the Peqer necropolis, and in the Temple of Osiris Khent-Amenti.

Under Senusert I, the Vizier Mentuhetep set up at Abydos a stele, on which he describes, in pompous terms, the supreme charges entrusted to him. Which gives him most cause for pride ? His conduct, as Chief of the Secrets, of the ceremonies of the Osirian drama in the temple and the necropolis of the Lord of Abydos, and his own performance of the part of " Horus, darling son " of Osiris.[1] This is indeed a privilege, which will ensure the glory of his name for ever ! Under Senusert III, Prince Sehetepibra, the intimate counsellor of the King, manages the same ceremonies, plays the part of the " darling son " also, and expects the same reward.[2] Lastly, another stele from Abydos, in the name of Prince Igernefert, Director of the Treasury and Buildings of Senusert III, and Chief of the Secrets of the Divine Sayings, describes the chief " acts " of the holy mystery, with a prudent reticence as to their true meaning, which is partly veiled from the vulgar. This important text runs as follows [3] :—

1. " *Royal Command* for the Prince, Chancellor of the King of the North, Sole Friend, Director of the Two Houses of Gold and of the Two Houses of Silver, and Director of the Seal, Igernefert.

" My Majesty has ordered that you should be taken up to Abydos, in the Nome of Ta-ur, to make a monument to my father Osiris Khent-Amenti, to adorn every secret (sanctuary) with electrum, which he has permitted My Majesty to bring from Nubia, as a conqueror and a Justified One. You, then, will do this, as well as it can be done, to satisfy my father Osiris. . . ."

Therefore I did according to all that His Majesty had commanded, in order to accomplish what my Lord had commanded for his father Osiris Khent-Amenti, Lord of Abydos, in the Nome of Ta-ur.

2. *Manufacture of accessories—statue, barge, scenery. Actors.*—I played the part of the Darling Son (*sa mer-f*) [4] for Osiris Khent-Amenti. Also,

---

[1] Cairo, Stele 20539, ii, ll. 6 ff.

[2] Cairo, 20538, ii, ll. 3 ff.

[3] Stele preserved at Berlin, and published by H. Schaefer, *Die Mysterien von Osiris in Abydos*, 1904, in **XXXIX**.

[4] *Sa mer-f*, " his darling son," the name given to the son who performs the funeral cult for his father in every family, and then to Horus celebrating for Osiris the rites invented by Anubis, Thoth, and Isis (cf. p. 143).

I completed (his statue), to be an eternal work, and I built him a shrine to hold the beauties of Khent-Amenti, in gold, silver, lapis lazuli, bronze, and wood, and I carved (*mes*) the gods of his following, making new shrines for them.[1]

I caused hour-priests [2] of the Temple to be appointed, to perform their services, teaching them the rule (of the worship) of every day and that of the feasts (held) at the beginning of the seasons.

I directed the work connected with the barge *Neshemt* [3]; I carved the cabin, I adorned the body of the Lord of Abydos with lapis lazuli, malachite, electrum, and all kinds of precious stones, fit to adorn the flesh of a God. (Then) I furnished the god with his gear, in my office of chief of the mystery. My office was that of Sem [4] (master of ritual ceremonies), for I have pure hands to adorn the God, I am a Sem with purified fingers.

I. *Beginning of the Mystery. Arrival of Upuat. Battle for the possession of the dead Osiris.*—After having led the procession of Upuat, [5] coming to save (*nez*) his father, I drove back those who attacked the barge *Neshemt*, and I overthrew the adversaries of Osiris. [6]

II. *Anubis and Thoth lead Osiris to his tomb in Peqer.*—When I led the great procession (of Osiris), [7] I followed the God in his footsteps; I caused the divine barge to sail, Thoth guiding the sailing. [8] I furnished the barge *Khammaat* of the Lord of Abydos with a shrine, providing all its gear when it sailed to Peqer. [9]

---

[1] The *sa mer-f* either made or caused to be made the statues and all the necessary setting. " I acted the *sa mer-f* in the direction of the Mansion of Gold (*het-nub*) for the Mystery (*seshta*) of the Lord of Abydos " (Mentuhetep). Hetnub is the name of the sacred workshop where ritual statues, of gold hammered on wood or cast, were made ; there, too, the statues were consecrated by the Opening of the Mouth.

[2] Priests who do hours of duty.

[3] The barge of Osiris.

[4] The Sem directed the rites of the Opening of the Mouth and the accompanying sacrifices. So Igernefert " officiated " on the statues of Osiris which he caused to be carved.

[5] *Per-t*, lit. " outgoing ". Upuat, the Opener of Roads, a wolf-god, on his stand, preceded and guided the procession of the feast of Osiris (Inscr. of Neferhetep, 1. 18). This is what is called the " chief procession " (*per-t tep-t*) of Upuat.

[6] Schaefer sees in this episode a representation of the departure of Osiris, as a living king, for the conquest of the universe (op. cit., p. 2), before his assassination by Seth. But our text says that Upuat comes to protect, or avenge (*nez*), Osiris. This can only apply to an already dead Osiris, the murder being regarded as having been done, and as the starting-point of the Mystery.

[7] The " Great Outgoing " of Osiris was the principal festival of the Osirian cult. The worshippers of Osiris often express the wish that they could " prostrate themselves before Khent-Amenti at the Great Outgoing " ; it was a funerary feast. In the Decree of Canopus (1. 7), these words are used to translate the Greek μέγα πένθος, the great annual funeral ceremony held in commemoration of the death of Berenice, the daughter of the divine Euergetæ. It is probable that at the Great Outgoing the mummification, entombment, and resurrection of Osiris were enacted in mime. See, on this subject, my **XXIX**, pp. 18 ff.

[8] Thoth helped Anubis to save Osiris, purified the limbs of the god (*Pyr.*, § 830), spiritualized him (*sakhut*) (§ 796), seized and slew his adversary (§ 635), sails in the sky as a pilot (§ 130), and helped Osiris (and helps the dead King) to cross the infernal river on his ibis-wings (§ 976).

[9] From many texts, cited by Schaefer (p. 27), it is clear that Osiris used to be crowned in the locality of Peqer. The two feathers and the royal circlet were placed on the god's head, which, set on a pole, represented the relic of Osiris

III. *Horus avenges his father. The battle at Nedit.*—When I directed the God's way to his tomb before Peqer, and I avenged Unnefer, on that day of great battle, I overthrew all his adversaries in the basin of Nedit, and I caused him to be borne in the great barge which bears his beauties.[1]

IV. *The triumph of Unnefer, whose statue is taken back to the temple at Abydos.*—I caused the heart of the hillmen of the West to swell, when they saw the beauties of *Neshemt.* She touched the shore at Abydos, at his palace.[2] I accompanied the God to his dwelling, doing his purifications and amplifying his sanctuary. I ended the feast inside (the temple), (leaving the statue of Osiris with his associate gods) and his courtiers.

The Service of Osiris at Abydos, performed by the highest officials, seems, therefore, to be the equivalent of the Service of Horus under the Thinites, or of the cult of Ra under the Memphites. The Middle Kingdom saw the triumph of Osiris. It was from this time onwards that the King was called the successor, not of Horus the Great, the master of heaven and sun-god, but of Horus the Child, born at Buto, the posthumous son of Osiris. Thus, Mentuhetep IV (XIth Dynasty) calls himself " heir of Horus, in his Two Lands, whom divine Isis [3] . . . has reared for the sovereignty of the two portions of Horus ".[4]

The priesthood of Heliopolis did not combat the Osirian doctrine, and claimed, on the contrary, to know it better than anyone else. In the XIIIth Dynasty, King Neferhetep, before holding the Service of Osiris at Abydos, took pains to find out how the books of Atum at Heliopolis described the ritual statue of Osiris, with its costume and equipment. In the year 2 of his reign he gathered together the nobles, the friends of his retinue, the royal scribes of the divine scriptures, and the chiefs of secrets, and said to them :—

" My heart desires to see the ancient writings of Atum. . . . Let me know the God in his (true) shape, that I may fashion him as he was in old

which was preserved in the Nome of Abydos and the actual ensign of this VIIIth Nome. Peqer seems to be the present Umm el-Gaab, where Amélineau discovered, in the tomb of the Thinite King Khent, the cenotaph representing Osiris dead and impregnating Isis, described above (pp. 247–8).

[1] Igernefert is here speaking in the rôle of Horus, the Darling Son, who avenged his father, hewing the followers of Seth in pieces (cf. above, p. 93). Nedit was the place where Osiris was killed by Seth and left dead on the shore (above, p. 93, n. 5). The return of Osiris to his temple was accompanied by acclamations and shouts of joy from the people of Abydos, as is often mentioned on stelæ of the Middle Kingdom (Louvre, Stele C.3). Unnefer, the " Good Being ", is a surname of Osiris.

[2] The Temple of Osiris at Abydos.

[3] After Isis, the inscription in the Wady Hammamat, a region under the influence of Min, adds " Min and Mut ".

[4] **XVII,** vol. i, 441 ; Lepsius, *Denkmäler,* ii, 149*d.*

time." The Friends reply, " Let Your Majesty go into the libraries, and see all the secret words." The King searches in the books, and finds the Book of the House of Osiris Khent-Amentiu, Lord of Abydos. Then he says to his Friends, " I shall represent (Osiris) according to what My Majesty has seen in the books, in the form of a King of Upper and Lower Egypt, as he came out of the womb of Nut " . . . And, indeed, King Neferhetep caused them to make before him, in the Building of Gold, the statue of Osiris. He himself put his hand to it ; he could do this, for His Majesty was pure with the purity of a god, and he was now better informed on the shape to give to the God than any scribe who had not found what the King had found. The text ends with the payment of filial homage by the King to his father Osiris, who has given him his inheritance, the possession of the land, and with threats against anyone who should not respect the decree. Not to honour Osiris is to attack the King ; the name of the rebel will not be inscribed among the Living (the deified dead) ; his Ka will not appear before the tribunal of Osiris in the next world.[1]

The Service of Osiris at Abydos went on all through the New Empire, and many foundations were made for his temple. In the XVIIIth Dynasty, Thothmes I passed a decree for the renewal of the statue, barge, and setting of the feast of Peqer, and, as we have seen in the case of Igernefert, the director of the works himself performed the secret rites, " without anyone seeing or contemplating or knowing the body of the God." [2] Seti I, of the XIXth Dynasty, built a splendid temple at Abydos, in which Osiris was worshipped with the King, and Merneptah added a building wholly consecrated to the litanies, prayers, and rites performed by Horus for his father Osiris. Rameses IV increased the foundations in honour of Osiris and set up a great stele to him, in which he magnified the glory of the patron of his line.[3]

II

FUNERAL RITES FOR THE PEOPLE

The Admission of the Masses to the Osirian Mysteries.—The Osirian doctrine extended until it became a general religion, truly binding all classes of Egyptian society. The Service of Horus of the Thinite Kings, and the celebration of the Sed-feast and the erection of Sun-temples to Ra by the

---

[1] **XVII**, vol. i, §§ 755–65. [2] **XVII**, vol. ii, §§ 96–8.

[3] See especially the dedicatory inscription of Seti I at Abydos (**XVII**, vol. iii, §§ 259, 266, 270), and the stele of Rameses IV, in **XII**, xxiii (1885), p. 15. Cf. Murray, *The Osireion at Abydos*, 1904, p. 3.

Memphites were official ceremonies, performed in honour of the gods by the King and Court. The people took no interest in them, and only benefited by them in so far as the health of the living King and the survival of the dead King made for the prosperity of Egypt ; they did good to the community, not to the individual.

In the service of Osiris, on the other hand, the adventures, death, and triumph of the god interested every Egyptian. Since the revolution, the King's salvation had not been the sole concern of the State and of religion ; every individual thought that his own life, in this world and the next, should be considered. Osiris, who had been the benefactor of men during his reign, had undergone his Passion and " deserved " salvation after death. It was an example on which every man should meditate. All were eligible for immortality ; but they must first be " justified " before the tribunal of Osiris.

How was this extraordinary change brought about, whereby all men became equal in the next world, and the relative positions of the King and his people were greatly modified ? We must remember that, during the revolution, " the secrets of the Court were disclosed," the magical incantations were given up to the eager curiosity of the public. The plebeian had invaded the great Court of Justice ; he had learned the formulas which give admission to the divine tribunal and the heavenly life among the gods ; in short, he " attained to the condition of the divine Ennead " (p. 226).

Let us summarize the main facts which prove that the people were admitted to religious rights.

First, the Osirian Mysteries which the King solemnly performed every year took on the character of a *social* manifestation. It was now the whole people of Egypt, in every city, that took part in the Great Outgoing of Osiris, and aided him to triumph, with fists, sticks, weapons, and also prayers and acclamations. By thus taking active part in the mysteries, witnessing the Passion of the god, and understanding the meaning, the people acquired the certainty of resurrection after death, by the grace of Osiris.

Herodotus, visiting the towns of Egypt long afterwards, was much struck by the spectacle of these feasts and processions, which, he says, the Egyptians were the first to have.[1] He estimates the number of pilgrims who poured into Bubastis for the local festival at 700,000 persons. He says only a few words about the Feast of Isis at Busiris, in which he must certainly refer to the Passion of Osiris.

> After the sacrifices they all beat themselves, men and women, in tens of thousands ; but in honour of what god they beat themselves, it would be impious for me to say.[2]

At Saïs he saw the feast of lamps, at which (not only in Saïs, but all over Egypt) " lamps burn all night long ", in every house. What was the object of these illuminations ? That the flames might ward off the evil spirits, the companions of Seth ; for, in the description which follows, we can recognize certain incidents in the Great Outgoing of Osiris.

> At night, thousands of people, armed with sticks, watch round the temple. The priests take a statue of the god, in a small shrine of gilded wood, back to its temple ; some try to prevent them, while others help them. The actors in the entrance bar the way into the temple ; the crowd, rushing to the help of the god, beats them, and there is a great battle with sticks, in which many a head is broken.[3]

Since the Middle Kingdom, it was at Abydos, the city where dead Osiris reigned, that the mysteries were held with the greatest splendour, and were therefore deemed the most efficacious. Abydos became the holy city ; just as the Mediaeval pilgrim went to Rome to seek salvation, and the Mussulman returns from Mecca with the ritual sanctity of a *hadji*, so the Egyptian who " knew the rites of Abydos " [4] through taking part in the mysteries there believed himself henceforward in a state of grace with Osiris. Thousands of Egyptians made the journey to " nose the earth before Khent-Amenti and to see the beauties of Upuat in the Great Outgoing ". They rowed in the processional barges, thrashed the companions of Seth, and watched over the body of Osiris on its bed, " in the night when the God is in his bed ".[5] They walked on the fair ways leading to Peqer, and found, " on the greatly acclaimed mound, full of offerings and provisions, and on the altar of Osiris, incense to revive their

---

[1] ii, 58. [2] ii, 61. [3] ii, 63.
[4] *Rekh ikhet Abdu* (Tomb of Neheri, at Beni-Hasan, XIIth Dynasty).
[5] On this subject, see **XXIX**, p. 50.

nostrils and thousands of loaves and offerings, which they could take after the Ka of the God was satisfied." [1] In memory of their pilgrimage, the visitors left a stele near the sacred mound, beside the stair of the temple. This stele was like a cenotaph (*mâhât*) for them, an imaginary burial beside Osiris. When they returned to their towns, they built their real tombs in the local necropolis ; but on the day of the funeral the priests performed mimic rites of a journey by the river to Busiris, the city of Osiris, King of the Living, and to Abydos, the city of the dead Osiris,[2] in order that the deceased might boast in the next world " that he had accompanied Osiris in every feast of the necropolis ".[3] Those who had never been to Abydos obtained the grace of the god and made sure of life with him by engraving the Osirian formulas on their tombs or coffins. But the highest aspiration was to write :—

> This tomb I made in the mountain of Abydos, that island girt by walls, predestined by the Universal Master,[4] a place illustrious since the time of Osiris, which Horus founded for his fathers, for which the stars work in the sky, the queen of (the first) men, to which the Great come from as far as Mendes, the second of Heliopolis, the glory of Horus, on which the Universal Master rested.[5]

The People before the Tribunal of Osiris.—So Abydos had become a rival and second to Heliopolis, since Osiris had won a place in religion and politics symmetrical with that held by Ra, the King of the Gods (Plate XIV, 1). The god of Heliopolis allowed none into paradise but the King, the royal family, and some of the Friends ; Osiris welcomed to his bosom every individual who took him as a guide and example. Now, since Osiris had himself become a god of the sky, equal to Ra, men would in the end live in the heavenly kingdom of Ra, which was that of Osiris. But they could only enter after being justified by their deeds. Just as Osiris had been received into the Ennead only after the judgment which declared

---

[1] These expressions are taken from stelæ of the XIIth Dynasty, the most complete specimen of which is Stele C.3 in the Louvre. Cf Maspero, in **XXXVIII,** i, p. 10.

[2] Moret, " Monuments égyptiens du Musée Calvet à Avignon," in **IV,** xxxii, p. 145. These boat-journeys are already mentioned, being for the sole use of the King, in *Pyr.*, §§ 1260–1.

[3] Sharpe, *Egyptian Inscriptions*, i, 18.

[4] An epithet of Osiris. Cf. above, p. 99, n. 4.

[5] *Egyptian Stelæ of the British Museum*, ii, 23. Cf. Moret, *La Profession de foi d'un magistrat, sous la XIIe dynastie* (*Bibl. de l'École des Hautes Études*, Historical and Philol. Sec.. No. 230).

him " justified ", so every initiate into the Osirian rites must appear before the sacred tribunal. This high ideal was already in the mind of the people in the Middle Kingdom, and it is clearly expressed in the literary texts of the period, describing the past revolution. The good man, who flees the disordered world and âspires to death, consoles himself with the thought that, if he is misunderstood on earth, in the next world, at least, " Thoth will judge him, Khonsu, the Scribe of Truth, will justify him, and Ra, in his sun-barge, will hear his words." [1] And this is the tone, at once inspired and menacing, in which a plain peasant dares to speak to the King, demanding his rights :—

> Put down the theft, protect the wretched. . . . Take heed that Eternity is coming . . . (Remember) that it is said, " It is the breath (of life) for the nostrils to do justice." [2]

King Merikara received teaching which he passes on in these terms : no one on earth should slay or act contrary to justice, for he will render account for his actions. For, after death,

> . . . the soul goes to the place of those who know it, and does not turn aside from its ways of yesterday. No magic stops it. It comes to Them who give the water (of welcome). The divine magistrates who judge the oppressed, you know that they are not gentle, on the day when the unhappy are judged, in the hour when the law is applied. Woe if the accuser is well-informed ! Do not trust to length of years, for they see the span (of a life) in an instant. Man survives after his landing (on the other shore) ; his deeds are heaped beside him. It is of a truth Eternity (that awaits) him who is there ; he is a madman, who despises that. But he who comes there without having committed sins, he will live down there, like a god, walking freely like the Lords of Eternity. [3] . . . Life on earth flows by (quickly), it is not long. . . . It avails not the Lord of the Two Lands to own thousands of men. (The virtuous man) will live for ever. He who passes with Osiris goes (to the next life), but he who has been indulgent to himself is annihilated. [4]

The application of this morality in the Middle Kingdom led to a religious equality which was truly democratic. Every man, of every condition, took the name of " Osiris justified " (*maâ-kheru*) on his funeral monument. Now, on the one hand, Osiris was King, and, on the other, the reigning Pharaoh was Osiris on earth and after death ; therefore " Osiris " meant

---

[1] **XLIV**, p. 123.
[2] *Peasant*, B., l. 145 ; cf. **XLVI**, p. 58.
[3] *Merikara*, §§ 12–13. Cf. E. Drioton, " Les Confessions négatives," in *Receuil de mémoires publiés pour le centenaire de Champollion*, 1922, p. 535.
[4] *Merikara*, § 10.

" Pharaoh ". Every one who died an Osirian thus became a Pharaoh in the next world, for the Egyptians drew the last logical consequences from the extension of the funeral rites to all.

Extension to the People of the Funeral Rites of the King.— From the XIIth Dynasty, the dead of every class of society were mummified like the King, on the model of Osiris ; and all received, as equipment for the next world, the clothing, crowns, headgear, and weapons of gods and kings.[1] The robes were, we are told, of " royal " material ; the crowns were those of Upper and Lower Egypt ; their heads were girt with the royal Uræus ; the necklaces, bangles, and anklets with which their bodies were adorned are called the ornaments of gods and Pharaohs ; their sticks were sceptres ; their weapons were those of the King ; and the vessels in which their hands and feet were washed were, we are assured, the very vases used for the toilet of the Lord of the Two Lands.

Previously, the ritual texts engraved in the Pyramids were confined to the Pharaohs alone. With the XIth Dynasty, they came into general use, and private persons, like Kings, princes, and great officials, had them painted on the sides of their coffins. By the side of a selection from the Pyramid Texts, we now have other formulas, composing a new theological Corpus.[2] In these, not only is the deceased treated as an Osiris, as a Pharaoh of the next world, but he is identified with the supreme gods, Atum and Ra [3] ; he dwells in the stars, with the gods. On the funerary stelæ, which are found in thousands in the cemeteries, the old formulas regarding offerings still appear, but those about the journey to the necropolis are replaced by others, promising the deceased that they shall enter into heaven, and sail in the barges of the Sun, by the side of Ra, and be enthroned in paradise, on the right hand of Osiris. From the XVIIIth Dynasty onwards, we find papyri deposited on every body, containing chapters of what we call the *Book of the Dead.*[4] These prepare the dead

---

[1] For the funeral equipment, see Jéquier, " Les Frises d'objets des sarcophages du Moyen Empire," in **II**, *Mémoires*, xlvii (1921). This gives a complete picture of all the material used by the living, as by the dead.

[2] A résumé of the texts published by Lacau, *Textes religieux*, will be found in Breasted, **XLI**, pp. 273–84.

[3] See also chap. xvii of the *Book of the Dead*, in **XXVII**, p. 222.

[4] **XXVII**, chap. v, pp. 199–244.

man to go before the tribunal of Ra (which later becomes the tribunal of Osiris), where his conscience and deeds will be weighed in the Balance of the god.[1] So every one has books of the rites needed in order to enter into the divine life.

These rites were the very same as had served for the Kings. The officiants for the dead were professional priests, or else the children and kinsfolk of the deceased. Whichever they were, they assumed, to celebrate the funeral cult, the names of the members of the royal family and of the Court officials. Those who were supposed to officiate, for the plebeian who had become King and Osiris by his death, were Horus, Son of Isis and Darling Son, the Father, beloved by the God (= the King),[2] the Royal Children, the King's Acquaintances (his grandsons), the Friends, the Princes, the Chief, the Man of the Court, the Chancellor of the God (i.e. of the King), the Chief of Secrets, the Prophets, the Officiant, the Reader, etc.[3] So it was, so long as the Pharaonic civilization lasted. Every dead man received royal honours ; he became, in theory, the head of the royal family ; his children and kinsmen represented the Court, and did worship to him as was done to the real Pharaoh. At the end of the funeral rites, the Friends carried the dead man on a stand, like a King, and cried, " The God comes !   Keep good watch on earth ! " [4] for it was thus that the coming of Pharaoh was announced on earth.

For his tomb every individual was entitled to a " place of burial " (ist qers), for, after death, he caused his name to be followed by the epithet of the initiates and favoured ones of former times, neb imakhu, " Privileged Lord." The offering might be modest, but for all that it became, by the virtue of the ritual formulas, the equivalent of the royal meal. Every one proclaimed that he was entitled to " the Offering given by the King " (hetep rdu nsut), and made the offerings which " come out at the voice " of the officiant (pert kheru) appear magically on his table. Every man's Ka, reunited to

---

[1] Lacau, Textes religieux, p. 87.
[2] Atef meri neter, originally the King's father-in-law.
[3] For the XIIth Dynasty, see especially Newberry, Beni-Hasan, i, pls. 18, 51 ; El-Bersheh, ii, pl. 9 ; Blackman, Meir, pl. 23, p. 5 ; Gardiner, Tomb of Antef-Ager, pl. xxi. For the XVIIIth, see Davies, Theban Tombs, pls. ii, vii, ix–x, and Virey, Rekhmara, pls. xx–xxiv.
[4] Antef-Ager, pl. xxiii ; Rekhmara, pl. xxxv.

his eternal body (*Zet*), feasted on these offerings, and also took its fill " from the table of the Gods, when they were sated ". Moreover, the funeral formulas were addressed to the Ka. In the past, the Ka had only manifested itself in the case of the King ; now every one joined his Ka after death.

With these rites and offerings which ensured material well-being in the future life, the deceased also associated his relations, friends and colleagues. The formulas on the stelæ are valid " for the Ka of his father, the Ka of his mother, the Ka of all whose names are written on this stele ".[1] There may be fifty names, and more, of kinsfolk, friends, clients, and servants, who benefit collectively by the deifying rites and the offerings. The rituals provide for the reunion in the next world of every dead man with his ancestors and descendants, his wife, sons, daughters, brothers, sisters, friends, and servants ; all the kin (*abt*) will live together once more, as they lived on earth.[2]

So, after the year 2000, religious equality was triumphant. No doubt there were inevitable differences in practice. For the King and the great, the funeral rites were celebrated with a care for detail and a display of luxury which the common man could not afford. A poor man would not be buried with the magnificence which a Sinuhet (see above, p. 197) obtained from the royal favour. What did it matter ? His obscure name, traced on a wooden tablet, or an ostracon, would be followed by the qualification, " Osiris N., Justified (*maâ-kheru*), Privileged Lord (*neb imakhu*) " ; he would have the right to a formula of offerings for his Ka (*n ka-f*) ; in the next world he would have the divine offerings ; and he would go to heaven like a Pharaoh. For his equipment, tiny clay amulets, costing little, would represent the ritual furniture and the necklaces, crowns, sceptres, and talismans of the King. From the Middle Kingdom on, we find in the tombs " Answerers " (*ushebtiu*)[3] humble statuettes of wood, enamelled clay, or hard stone, which took on a magical life when called, to relieve the poor man, like the rich, of the

---

[1] Boeser, Leyden, *Stelæ of the Middle Kingdom*, pl. xiii; Cairo, Stele 20161, with sixty-eight names, etc.

[2] P. Lacau, " Textes religieux," in **IV**, chaps. ii and lxxii, translated by J. Baillet, in *Journal Asiatique*, 1904, p. 307, and in Roeder, **XLIX**, p. 201.

[3] On the appearances of these statuettes in the Middle Kingdom, cf. **IX**, iv, p. 92.

labours of the next world. The manufacture of *Books of the Dead* in series [1] allowed every one to possess the rituals at small cost, so that the luxury of a tomb adorned with figures and prayers became superfluous. Every simplification was permitted, to bring the funeral rites within the reach of all. The name Osiris was enough to turn a dead man into a god and a king ; the epithet Justified ensured the favour of the divine tribunal ; the title *neb imakhu* made him the friend of Pharaoh ; and the very humblest plebeians took these three qualifications, claimed to be the equals of the noblest and wealthiest, and entered, after death, into the bosom of the royal and divine family, by the virtue of the Osirian rites.

This fact (the historical and social importance of which has hitherto been overlooked), that, from the Middle Kingdom onwards, every Egyptian who died was identified with the King and the gods, points to a social transformation, the greatest which the history of Egypt has revealed to us.[2] The concession which the Pharaohs made to their people is an extraordinary fact. It can only be explained if we admit the complete triumph of the masses in the revolutions described in the preceding chapter. Moreover, once the secrets of religion, of magic, of the administration, of the person of Pharaoh himself had been violated, it became impossible to restore the ancient kingship in its august and superhuman form, or to base its authority on mysteries which were no longer mysterious.   The Pharaohs resigned themselves to giving up their monopoly ; they accepted the extension of the rites to the whole population, *with the political and social consequences which this entailed.*

III

STATE SOCIALISM.   PEASANTS.   CRAFTSMEN.   LOCAL
ADMINISTRATORS (XIIth TO XXth DYNASTIES)

All the religious rights thus conferred brought with them what we may call political rights, that is, a share in govern-

---

[1] They were to be had ready-made, in the temples or from dealers, with a space left empty in each formula, so that the name of the person who was to benefit by the rites on his death might be inserted.

[2] I have tried to demonstrate this in my memoir, " L'Accession de la plèbe égyptienne aux droits religieux et politiques sous le Moyen Empire," in *Rec. Champollion*, 1922.

ment, admission to the offices, employments, and secrets of the royal administration.

The feudal princes and priesthood having been mastered and replaced by royal officials, the whole of society, nobles, priests, and plebeians, became the helpers of the royal line. Every one, without distinction of birth or wealth, was called to play a part in the State, according to his capacity, as priest, judge, militiaman, ploughman, or craftsman, just as he was deemed worthy to share in the religious ceremonies which were the foundation of royal institutions. King Merikara's father admits this equality.

> Do not distinguish between the son of a noble and the man of humble birth. Take men into your service according to their capacity.[1]

The extension of funeral ceremonies to all classes was, therefore, certainly accompanied by a democratic policy. By obtaining religious rights, the plebeians, in Egypt as in Greece and Rome, obtained a share in public offices, that is, in the administration of the State, and, in a certain form, in ownership.[2] Here the agrarian question arises in quite definite form.

What was the condition of the peasants and craftsmen under the Middle Kingdom ? How did they come to be admitted to a part in the administration, and even to the ownership of land and industry ? The sources are scarce, fragmentary, and localized in a few places. We are obliged to infer the general organization from a few local facts, and I would warn readers that in a work like the present such a generalization is extremely hazardous.

Let us first survey briefly *the social condition of the people under the Old Kingdom*. We find the peasants (*mertu*) still attached to the soil ; they remained bound to it if it changed its owner. When the King, the owner of all the land in Egypt, gave away an estate to his relations, favourites, or officials, the " men and beasts " went with it. This was the position of the *colonus* of the later Roman Empire and of the mediaeval serf, attached to the soil. So, too, the craftsmen in the royal

---

[1] *Merikara*, § 15.
[2] " To have a part in mysteries, religious ceremonies, and public offices " —so Demosthenes (*Neaera*, 113) defines the conquest of religious and political rights by the people. For a comparison with social crises in Greece, cf. my " Accession de la plèbe ", quoted above, p. 347.

workshops continued to work for the temples or nobles to whom the King ceded them. In agriculture, industry, and even commerce, the labourers were not separated from the fields, workshops, or stores.

The workers were divided into " hands ", that is, into gangs of five men under a *kherp* (holder of the rod of discipline).[1] The *kherpu* brought together the products of the soil or workshops for the Regents of cities or villages, who delivered them to the Nomarchs or to the royal storehouses. The gangs of five were grouped in gangs of ten and of a hundred, under the orders of " decurions " and " centurions ".

It is possible that from the beginning the men of a gang of five or ten all belonged to one family; this, at least, is what we find under the XIIth Dynasty. In this case the *kherp* must have been the father, or, failing him, the eldest brother ; things were arranged thus among the nobles, when a service like that of the priests of family or divine worship was organized.[2] But was it possible for the lower orders to remain in families for long on the same land or in the same workshop ? Since they were bound to the soil and to their trades, the caprice of administrative officials or the sale of landed property, which the King allowed privileged persons to effect, might scatter a family, distributing its members among different masters and domains.

The peasants, naturally, did all the work of corn-growing, stock-raising, and the engineering needed in a country like Egypt—dikes, canals, and causeways. In addition, they were liable (i) to " impressed labour " (*kat*), other than agricultural, such as transporting stones and building pyramids, temples, palaces, etc. ; (ii) to " taxes " (*mezed*), comprising the delivery of corn in the form of sheaves or loaves, and of manufactured goods (gold, silver, bronze, hides, textiles, ropes) ; (iii) the maintenance of royal messengers, the Court, and the King, when these passed through the district. Sometimes relations of the King, officials, or Negro allies (mercenary troops) might requisition the services of the craftsmen and peasants. All

---

[1] A Russian proverb says, " He who takes the bâton becomes a corporal." In Egyptian, authority in a certain matter is frequently described by saying that the matter is " at the rod " (*r khet*) of someone.

[2] See Moret and Boulard, " Donations et fondations," in **IV**, xxix, pp. 77, 92 ; G. Lefebvre and Moret, " Nouvel Acte de fondation," in **VIII**, N.S., i, p. 34 ; *Urk.*, i, 25–8.

these duties were performed under the supervision of the House of Agriculture (*per-shenâ*, literally, House of the Granary), which made the *mertu* and prisoners of war work; the serf was in almost the same position as the prisoner. Of the craftsmen (*hemutiu*) and office employees, each was confined to his own special work in the workshop or bureau of the King, priests, or nobles to whom he was subject.[1]

We do not get these facts from documents specifying the obligations of every man, but we can infer them from the charters of immunity of the Old Kingdom, by contrasting the lot of the " common people " with that of those exempted. So far, these common people do not seem to have had a legal status of any kind ; in practice they were liable to taxation and impressed labour without restriction. We do not know the limits of their obligations nor the wages of their labour.

As we have seen, there were, even under the Old Kingdom, a certain number of peasants and craftsmen who gradually escaped from the arbitrary power of the King; namely, those who worked on land given to relations of the King, Privileged Ones, priests, and lords. The royal decrees tell us that privileged estates had a " charter " defining the status of the peasants and craftsmen. The foundation of these domains was the occasion of a declaration (*upet*) in the King's offices. In the registers of the local administrators (*Saru*), meeting in a court, were entered (i) the " list of names " (*im ren-f*) of lands, buildings, etc. ; (ii) a "declaration of the persons " (*upet remtu*) belonging to them ; these people, in the texts of the Middle Kingdom, are grouped in families (*zam*) or in associations of kinsmen (*smait*), working together. The inventory and declaration were made the subject of a deed certified by witnesses and sealed in the offices of the Vizier. We do not know what was the purport of this deed, but it must have defined the taxes and impressed labour due to the King on the one hand and to the beneficiary on the other. It " governed the condition of persons and lands " [2] ; it was the first step towards a legal status for the common man (above, p. 205).

---

[1] *Journal Asiatique*, 1912, ii, p. 100 ; 1916, i, p. 330.
[2] *Journ. Asiat.*, 1916, p. 312.

Usually, after the VIth Dynasty, domains of this kind became " immunity cities " with a " charter " which abolished the work due to the King and restricted the obligations of the peasants and craftsmen to the work due to their owner. It was just the same with the common people in the " new cities " founded by the feudal lords. Thereby the lot of the plebeian was greatly improved ; the *mertu* in these cities were deemed to be equal to the Saru on the Royal Domain.[1] The charters of the freed cities were inscribed in the Vizier's archives, and enumerated all the forms of forced labour and taxes which were abolished for those exempted. Now, we have seen that in the feudal society of the Heracleopolite period these charters of immunity marked a first stage in the emancipation of the peasants and craftsmen. By conferring a privileged status on a certain number, they furnished a model on which the others based their demands.

The revolution enabled the masses, in certain places and for a certain time (both undetermined), to overthrow the social and political fabric of the Old Kingdom. We have seen the " poor " invading halls of justice and administrative offices, throwing regulations, records, and accounts into the street, stealing for their own use title-deeds and " declarations " of goods and persons, and taking by force what belonged to the King and to the rich.

When Society was reorganized it could not, as in Greece and Rome, culminate in pure democracy. We can hardly see the Pharaohs, the god-kings, the potentates by right divine, creating elective magistracies and organizing Councils of Elders and Assemblies of the People. Nevertheless, within the framework of a patriarchal system, they managed to improve the social and political position of the plebeians, by giving them a legal status and opening the doors of the administration to them.

Papyri found by Flinders Petrie at Kahun and Gurob, small towns of Central Egypt, give us a glimpse at the records of plebeian families, who lived from the XIIth to the XVIIIth Dynasty. There we see such a change in society as can hardly be explained except by the revolution which I have described. There is no more mention of privileges and

[1] Above, p. 210.

charters of immunity. There is no word of the Royal Domain, for all the Black Land belongs to the King. The plebeians of the agricultural villages and the cities (*nut*) are now called " peasants " (*sekhetiu*) and " town-dwellers " (*ânkh n nut*). They are classified by professions, their rights and duties are defined, and every man plays a part in the State. From the texts found, employments seem to have been divided as follows :—

The Kahun papyri have preserved " declarations of persons " (*upet remtu*) made by a soldier and by an officiant (*kheri-heb*), which " declare " the number of persons— mother, wife, daughter, sisters, servants—who are dependent on them and must live with them,[1] on the revenues of their employment. Other documents mention " house-inventories " (*imt-per*).[2] A checker of a " class " of priests makes an inventory of his goods for his son, to whom he gives his office, on condition that the son serves him as a " staff of old age ". The sealer of a director of works bequeaths his goods in town and country to his brother, a priest, who, in his turn, leaves them to his wife, with four servants. A priest, the head of a sacerdotal " class ", sells his office to a scribe in the bureau of the seal. Attached to one of these *imt-per* is a receipt for the sum paid to the Vizier's office as duty on the transfer. Other texts give lists of the men liable to impressed labour in the funeral cities of the Kings, and of the taxes in kind to be paid by the holders of various offices.

There are still many obscurities to be cleared up in the interpretation of these records of a small Egyptian town, but we are struck by one fact—we find here the same adminis- trative formalities which, in the VIth Dynasty, the King imposed on those who were granted royal charters. Every- thing is done as if the system of charter-holders had been extended to the whole population. Every individual was entered as the holder of a definite employment, as priest, soldier, peasant, or craftsman, with the family dependent on him or the servants employed by him. Moreover, just as the Privileged Ones of the Old Kingdom could sell and

---

[1] This family group (*abt*), comprising relations, friends, clients, and servants, will be united again, by a formal decree of the gods, in the next world, together with its ancestors (above, p. 259).

[2] " What is in the house," and therefore, *originally*, a list of movable goods, the only personal property formerly allowed to Pharaoh's subjects.

bequeath the land which they had from the King, provided that they obtained the King's permission and entered the fact in the revenue office, so those who hold land and public offices under the Middle Kingdom can bequeath to their children, or sell to their relations (?) their official post, civil, military, or priestly, on condition that they have the transfer properly confirmed in the Vizier's office and pay a transfer-fee ; and the same people can make over their houses and land in the same way.

The documents of the Theban New Empire give us a clearer notion of the position of the *peasant* in the new order of things. The land of Egypt, which is now called " the fields of Pharaoh ", is divided by the Vizier and his representatives into portions (*shedu, peseshut*), which are distributed among the families of peasants who cultivate it.[1] These households are under the head of the family or a member, man or woman, who takes the title or office of " inspector " (*rudu*), and is responsible for the tilling of the soil. From time to time, as the distribution of work within the family is affected by age or sickness, a house-inventory (*imt-per*) and " declaration of persons " are taken, in accordance with which the portions are again distributed among new members under a new *rudu*. The names of the fields and of the persons who till them are entered in duplicate survey-registers, in the Double House of the Treasury and in Pharaoh's Granary. In case of dispute, it is possible to refer to these records, even hundreds of years later, to establish a man's right to cultivate some particular field.[2] This organization corresponds fairly exactly with the account which Herodotus gives (ii, 109), from the information of the priests, of the condition of the land and the peasants in the reign of Sesostris—that is, under the Theban New Empire. Sesostris, according to this account, divided the land among the Egyptians, giving to each an equal square portion for which they drew lots (κλῆρον ἴσον

---

[1] The story of the *Peasant*, which dates from the beginning of the Middle Kingdom, already shows the " peasant " (*sekheti*) living on his portion of land (*shedu*), in his house, with his wife and children (**XLVI**, pp. 48, 54, 66).

[2] This is clear from an inscription found in a tomb of the time of Rameses II, which describes a family lawsuit regarding a royal donation made at the beginning of the XVIIIth Dynasty, nearly 400 years before. Cf. V. Loret, *La Grande Inscription de Mes* ; Moret, " Un Procès de famille sous la XIXᵉ dynastie," in **XII**, xxxix, pp. 1 ff. ; A. H. Gardiner, *The Inscription of Mes*, 1905.

τετράγωνον).[1] Thus the King formed the revenues of the State by fixing the taxes to be paid by each man yearly (ἀποφορὴν ἐπιτελέειν κατ' ἐνιαυτόν). If the Nile floods carried away part of an allotment, the King sent inspectors to assess the loss of ground and to reduce the tax accordingly.

In sum, the peasant paid taxes and did forced labour in accordance with legal tariffs which are unknown to us.[2] No doubt they were very heavy, but they were not arbitrary, and when he had discharged his dues he had the enjoyment of his portion. The head of the family disposed of the portion by donations to his wife and children (a primitive form of the will) and for distributions and exchanges among the members of his family.[3] But every transfer of property had to be inscribed and taxed in the offices of the Government. So the fiscal authorities raised considerable revenues and always knew who was responsible for the cultivation of the allotments. So much did the peasant profit by the revolution : from a serf, he rose to a free, hereditary tenant with a legal status.

The situation of the peasant was improved, but can we say that it was secure from danger and want ? The free man, subject to impressed labour and menaced by the exactions of the tax-office, which were always the same, whatever the harvest might be like, may sometimes have had more cares and responsibilities than the serf. Can we trust the very dark picture painted by a certain scribe, who is delighted with his official post and contrasts his security with the hard lot of the peasant ?

> I hear that you are giving up writing . . . that you are turning to the work of the fields. . . . Do you not remember how it is with the farmer, when the harvest is taxed ? The worms have destroyed half the corn, and the hippopotamus has eaten the rest. The rats are numerous in the country, and the locust comes down, and the cattle devour, and the little birds pillage. . . . What a disaster for the farmer ! Anything that may be left (after that) on the threshing-floor is finished by robbers. And the straps . . . are worn out, and the team kills itself, dragging the plough . . . and the scribe (of taxes) arrives at the port, and taxes the harvest. . . .

---

[1] The unit of area was, indeed, a square surface, the "*aroura*" (*stat*), with a side of 100 cubits, the cubit being about 20 inches. In distributions or donations, the beneficiary receives so many *arourai* of land. We have no evidence of drawing lots, at any rate under the Pharaohs.

[2] One-fifth of the harvest, according to Genesis. Below, p. 303.

[3] Transfers do not seem to have been allowed at this time, outside the members of the families inscribed.

The porters are there with their cudgels, and the negroes with their palm-sticks. " Give up the corn ! " they say. There is none. . . .   Then they beat (the farmer), stretched out on the ground ; he is loaded with bonds, and thrown into the ditch ; he plunges into the water, and wallows, head downwards. His wife is loaded with bonds in front of him, his children are put in chains, his neighbours abandon him and fly, carrying off their corn.[1]

The *crafts* of the cities were offices (*iaut*), just like the employments of the peasant and official.   From the stelæ dedicated to Osiris, on which the townsfolk give their names and professions, we see that industries and trades were growing numerous.

The revolutionaries had stolen the secrets of the crafts (above, pp. 225–6). The craftsmen, hitherto attached to the workshops of the King, the temples, or the nobles, were now freed, and, as it were, secularized. The career of the artist or craftsman, who used to be recruited from apprentices trained to " secret " processes, now gave scope for every kind of curiosity and initiative.

No doubt the craftsman, like the peasant, had to make a " declaration " and to pay registration-duties ; but once he had settled with the fiscal authorities he was free—at least, we have no ground for presuming that he was subject to restrictions. We have the proof in a literary treatise of the XIIth Dynasty, another collection of *Teachings*, which continued to be in vogue under the New Empire. A man takes his son to the school attended by lads of good family, and tries to dissuade him from adopting a manual trade, dwelling on the need in which craftsmen often live, and on the inevitable risk of all these professions, in which success depends on personal initiative—and into which, therefore, there is free access. Here are some extracts from this *Satire of the Trades*. The picturesque descriptions give a lively portrayal of the mass of the people, which might be illustrated by the many scenes of arts and crafts painted in the tombs of the period (Pl. IX).

I have seen the metal-worker at his task, at the mouth of his furnace, with fingers like a crocodile's (skin) ; he stank worse than fish-spawn. Every workman who holds a chisel suffers more than the men who hacks the ground ; wood is his field, and the chisel is his mattock. At night, when he is free (from his day's work), he toils [2] more than his arms can do ; even

---

[1] *Pap. Anastasi V*, 15, 6 ff.   [2] Overtime work.

PLATE IX

1. WATERING GARDENS,
SHADOOF

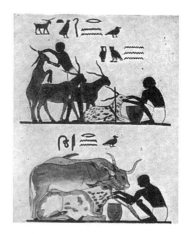

2. FATTENING LIVESTOCK

3. GRAPE AND POMEGRANATE HARVEST. CORN GRANARIES,
PLOUGHING
PEASANTS AT WORK
Tomb-paintings of the XIIth and XVIIIth Dynasties

at night he lights (his lamp, in order to work). The stone-cutter seeks work in every hard stone. When he has done the great part of his labour, his arms are exhausted, he is tired out. . . . The barber shaves till late in the evening . . . he goes from street to street seeking for men to shave ; he wears his arms out to fill his belly, like a bee which eats at its work (?). The boatman who carries his goods down to the Delta, to get their price, works more than his arms can do ; the mosquitoes kill him [1] . . . The farmer has accounts to settle which last to all eternity ; he cries louder than the *abu* bird. . . . The weaver in the workshop is worse off than a woman ; (he squats) with his knees to his belly, and does not taste (clean) air. . . . He must give loaves of bread to the porters, to see the light. . . . The courier starting for foreign lands leaves his goods to his children,[2] fearing lions and Asiatics. The cobbler is very wretched ; he is for ever begging . . . he eats leather.[3] The bleacher bleaches (linen) on the quay ; he is the neighbour of the crocodiles. For the fisherman it is worse than for all the other trades. Why, is his work not on the river, where he mingles with the crocodiles ? [4]

In contrast to this highly-coloured picture, we have the felicity of the scribe—that is, of the Government employee. The author of the *Satire of the Trades* is supposed to be the father of a minor employee, taking his son to Court to place him in " the place of the teaching of the books " (i.e. school), " with the children of the Great who have a post at Court." The young candidate learned reading, writing, and arithmetic, and was also initiated in the sacred characters, the " divine words " of Thoth, that is, in the handling of hieroglyphics in all their aspects. Next, he studied the laws, the administrative regulations, and the language of Government correspondence, with all the different forms of address required when writing to the King, the Vizier, a Court official, or a subordinate employee.[5] After many years of study, the scribe took his place among the Saru, or notables,[6] from whom were chosen the officials and members of the administrative councils and tribunals (the Thirty and the *Zazat*).

[1] See Herodotus (ii, 95) for the mosquitoes, the scourge of the Delta, and the use of mosquito nets to keep them off.
[2] Makes his will.
[3] The cobbler tears strips of leather with his teeth.
[4] *Pap. Sallier II* and *Anastasi VII*. The text is full of technical terms, the sense of which is not yet clear. Cf. Maspero, *Du Style épistolaire*, pp. 48–73 ; **XLIV**, pp. 100–5.
[5] Many collections of administrative letters, with the forms to be employed in the most usual cases, have been preserved from the Ramessid period. See Maspero, *Du Style épistolaire*, and **XLIV**, pp. 252–67.
[6] Maspero, *Du Style épistolaire*, pp. 25, 28 ; **XLIV**, p. 247.

" Write with your hand, read aloud with your mouth, question men wiser than you ; so you will fill the office of a Sar, and you will get this employment when you are old. Happy is a scribe who is fit for his office." [1]
" There is no office in which one has not a superior, except that of a scribe ; it is he who commands (*kherp*) " [2]; or else, " The scribe is released from manual tasks ; it is he who commands. . . . Do you not hold the (scribe's) palette ? That is what makes the difference between you and the man who handles an oar. . . . The scribe comes to sit among the members of the Assemblies (*qenbet*). . . . No scribe fails to eat the victuals of the King's House. The goddess Meskhent [3] makes the scribe prosper ; he comes to the head of the *Qenbetiu* ; his father and mother thank God for it." [4]

From this example, we see how the plebeian could become an official.

Who were the *Qenbetiu* among whom the scribe was to take his place ?   Under this name, from the Middle Kingdom onwards, we must recognize the Saru found in the texts of the Old Kingdom, whom I have tried to define [5] as the successors of the Councils of Elders, which are so important in primitive societies. [6] Under the Old Kingdom, the Saru met in assemblies (*seh*) ; they also formed councils of administration, or tribunals (*zazat*). [7] Contracts regarding property, movable and landed, were submitted to them (sales by exchange, funerary foundations), distributions, inventories, and declarations of persons and cattle were made before them, they defined the status of peasants and craftsmen and the charters of exempted persons, they kept the accounts for the levy of taxes, they made the administrative regulations (*seru*) required for the local application of the royal decrees (*uzu*), and they tried offenders.

Under the Middle Kingdom, the assembly of the Saru was no longer called *seh*, but *qenbet*, or council, and it seems always to have been blended with the *zazat*, or tribunal. There were Qenbets of districts (*uu*) ; there were some for peasants, for craftsmen, for soldiers, for sailors, for priests, in the towns

---

[1] *Pap. Anastasi III*, 3, 10 ff.
[2] End of the *Satire of the Trades*.
[3] Who presided over birth, like a fairy.
[4] **XLIV**, p. 105.
[5] On this subject, see the texts quoted by Moret, " L'Administration locale sous l'Ancien Empire égyptien," in **III**, 1916, pp. 378 ff.
[6] *From Tribe to Empire*, p. 124
[7] To the documents quoted in the study which I here summarize, one should add the deed of sale of a house, dating from the IVth Dynasty, which was sealed in the presence of the Zazat of the funeral city attached to the Great Pyramid of Cheops (H. Sottas, *Étude critique sur un acte de vente immobilière*, 1913).

and in the villages. These councils were competent for all administrative jurisdiction and for civil and criminal suits. As under the Old Kingdom, we find Qenbetiu everywhere opposite the royal officials of the central administration, as auxiliaries rather than as opponents. We may therefore suppose that the Saru or Qenbetiu constituted a local administration, perhaps more ancient than the royal administration, and preserved by the Kings even when political centralization was at its height. A text of the Vth Dynasty suggests that they represented the élite of the rural or urban population; when peasants (*mertu*) grew rich, they rose to the estate of Saru (above, p. 210). A person who founds a " city " or property, instals there *mertu* and " Saru to keep the accounts ". Their position is vague and ill-defined, but Maspero seems to estimate it rightly :—

" Among the tenants of land (*mertu*), some, by their birth, connexions, wealth, wisdom, or age, had acquired an authority over the people among whom they lived; it was these who were called the Saru, the Meshekhs of modern Egypt. These Saru were the old men and notables who collected at the gates of the village on market-days, and dealt with the private affairs of the community. They were, by their position, intermediaries between their humblest fellows and the established authorities." [1]

Were they appointed by a vote of the population or by a kind of co-optation ? We do not know. Certain conditions, however, had to be fulfilled before one could become a Sar. Were they of a social nature (e.g. the condition of a free tenant), or pecuniary (the payment of a certain amount as tax) ? Was only their personal wisdom considered ? None of these questions has been answered ; nevertheless, from the Middle Kingdom onwards, education was a necessary, and perhaps sufficient, condition for becoming a Sar and a member of a Qenbet. The scribes belonged either to the royal offices or to these Qenbets.

Peasants, craftsmen, and scribes—the best of whom rose to administrative posts and the assemblies of the Saru—

[1] **VIII.** 1912, No. 38.

all were written down for the service of the State. The King guided and controlled them by his hordes of local representatives—directors, chiefs, commanders, inspectors, themselves under the supervision of the Vizier and the central administration (below, p. 276). From time to time the King " made a census of the whole country and wished to know the names of the soldiers, priests, royal servants, and all officials (*iautiu*) of the whole country, with large and small livestock ".[1] A papyrus of the Ramessid period shows us how a royal scribe made out a statement of the division (*denit*) of a town by trades. Families of farmers, manual craftsmen, shoemakers, wicker-workers, stonemasons, quarrymen, storehouse-keepers, bakers, butchers, cooks, wine-tasters, artists, sculptors, draughtsmen, literary men, scribes, barbers—all are put down, with their inspectors and their chiefs.[2] The State took part of the harvest from the farmers and of the receipts from the craftsmen ; the remainder represented the wages which the State gave its employees for their labour, and became their property.

Conditions such as these were favourable to the growth of a middle class making its wealth by work and dependent on no master but Pharaoh. The story of the *Peasant* shows us the humble beginnings of the social class of " lordless men " liberated since the revolution. For a long time these " solitary " or " isolated ones " (*uâj*) [3] had to fight against the vexations of the rich and the exactions of the officials. They were contemptuously dubbed the " small folk ", or the " poor " (*nemhu*).[4] But they had the right of direct appeal against violence to the King and the gods.[5] The pride and wholesome joy of having a house built with their own hands on their own fields sustained and uplifted them. Listen to a director of the sculptors of the time of Thothmes I. " I made my tomb myself. I have my own house, my own boat. I possess fields which I myself made, and till them with my own oxen." [6] In this way the *nemhu* rose in society. The

---

[1] *Urk.*, iv, p. 1006 (Thothmes III).
[2] *Leyden Papyrus*, studied by Chabas, *Mélanges égyptologiques*, iii, vol. ii, p. 730, and Revillout, *Précis de Droit égyptien*, p. 86.
[3] *Tale of the Peasant*, B., l. 93.
[4] *Peasant*, B., l. 62 ; cf. Moret, *L'Accession de la plèbe*, p. 355, n. 1.
[5] Moret, *L'Appel au roi*, p. 147.
[6] *Urk.*, iv, p. 132. For the Middle Kingdom, cf. **III**, 1915, p. 368, and *Urk.*, i. 151.

Kings who stood for Law protected them against the exactions of the revenue office, forbidding (in terms which are very obscure to us) that all means of existence and work should be taken from them, in case of delay in paying their taxes, and ordering that they should be left a home and receive a distribution of food.[1] At the end of the Theban period there were in the valley many *fields of nemhu*.[2] Then their despised name changed its meaning; preserved in the Coptic *remhe*, the word *nemhu* took the meaning of " free men ",[3] showing how they had gone up in the social scale.

The rôle assigned to the family after the revolution only hastened the advance of the *nemhu*. Under the Old Kingdom the family only appears in the performance of the funeral worship rendered by children to their parents (above, p. 143). In the Middle Kingdom the texts show the enrolment for the service of the State of the family group (*abt*), which was maintained (as we saw, p. 259) in the next life. It was in families that peasants, craftsmen, and officials worked for the King.[4] Children succeeded their fathers in fields, workshops, and offices. But we should note that this heredity was always uncertain, not giving complete ownership and in no way impairing the principle of the King's eminent ownership of lands and employments. In consequence, there were no social *castes* in ancient Egypt, and a man could always change his calling, at his wish or by desire of the King.

Things being so, the father, as the trainer of his children for a social calling which he would bequeath to them, acquired chief importance in the family. This is quite clear from the *Teachings* of Phtahhetep, as well as from the administrative papyri. The wife, brothers, and sisters, allies, friends, and clients, also came into the gang and obeyed the chief. The State recognized the authority of the *eldest* (who was sometimes a woman), whom it regarded as the *rudu* (inspector) of the gang, entrusted with the distribution of lands or

---

[1] *Peasant*, B., l. 62; Edict of Horemheb; cf. Revillout, *Précis de Droit égyptien*, pp. 48–55.

[2] Moret, *L'Accession de la plèbe*, p. 355, n. 1.

[3] Spiegelberg has shown that in the demotic contracts of the Saïte period the condition contrasted with that of the *bak*, the servant engaged for perpetuity, is that of the *nemhu*, which therefore corresponds to "free man" (**XII**, liii, 1917, p. 116).

[4] Cf. Hdt., ii, 174, who classifies employments and trades in γένεα, but only mentions seven.

employments among the people of the family, and compelled to keep the accounts of work and taxes.[1]

Yet the mother, or wife, had not lost her ancient prestige and privileges (cf. above, p. 96). Children base their claims on uterine descent far more often than on paternal, and in certain cases the maternal uncle remains the natural protector of children, as in matriarchal societies.[2] In the service of the State, the woman sometimes commands the gang, when the husband is dead and the children are too young.[3] Above all, the married woman enjoyed a privileged position in respect of the family property.

When a man married, he " founded a house " (*gerg per*),[4] for the State allowed him to build a home on one of the allotments which he cultivated, or in a town. The married pair " entered the house " (*âq r per*). The real value of this expression does not appear before the IVth century, when it is applied in the demotic papyri to those who are married with a contract. Now, the expression was in use under the XIXth Dynasty.[5] From this it is inferred that the marriage contract may have existed in the time of the Ramessids. Perhaps one should go back even further. As early as the XIIth Dynasty the married woman is very often given the epithet (not found under the Old Kingdom) of *nebt per*, " mistress of the house." Is this an allusion to the " entrance into the house ", defining union with a contract ? Since no contracts have been preserved, we cannot say so with certainty. Yet we know that *nebt per* is not a mere polite formula ; it is an epithet with a real meaning. In the Theban love-songs, the " sister " ardently longs to consolidate her union and to receive " the goods (*ikhet*) of her beloved as the mistress of his house ".[6] We can hardly imagine that she would enjoy his goods in this way, without a contract defining the terms. Hence it is concluded that, in the Theban texts as in the demotic papyri, *nebt per* refers to the legal wife of the highest grade.[7] It is possible that the title already

---

[1] *Mes* (**XII**, xxxix, p. 34).   [2] **LI**, p. 183.   [3] *Inscription of Mes.*
[4] *Prisse Papyrus*, x, 9 ; *Urk.*, iv, p. 3.   [5] Spiegelberg, **XII**, lv (1918), p. 94.
[6] *Harris Papyrus*, 500 ; Maspero, " Études égyptiennes," in *Journal Asiatique*, Jan., 1883.
[7] Cf. **LI**, p. 180 ; and A. Wiedemann, *Das alte Aegypten*, 1920, p. 94, who summarizes the matter as follows. The married woman (in the demotic texts)

had this meaning under the XIIth Dynasty. In any case, it appears that this " house ", the home which sheltered the Egyptian's individual (no longer social) life, became the property of the wife who gave birth to the heirs. The practice of polygamy, at least among the rich, made it the more necessary to have a precise definition of the rights of the legal wife.

So, about the time when the people were getting religious rights and being admitted to public offices, the plebeian family was empowered to make contracts (endorsed by the State) for sales, purchases, the cession of offices, trades, the use of land, and perhaps, too, for marriages, a thing which, under the Old Kingdom, had only been possible for the favourites of the King. It obtained a partial ownership of the " house of the living " ; in addition, it got another partial ownership of real property—the house of the dead, " the place of burial " (*ist qers*), " the goods of burial " (*ikhet qers*), which were indispensable for the funeral cult which the revolution had made open to plebeians. In the tomb, ancestors and descendants would be united after death ; it, too, was a family house, the ownership of which (ground and offerings) was granted by the King. The Theban papyri mention the tomb among the goods of which the family claims the use and apportionment.[1]

What is the meaning of these successive gains—the management of royal lands to be farmed, the free exercise of trades and administrative offices (open to the scribes), the partial ownership of houses and tombs ? In them we see the

---

is designated by three epithets, which seem to mark three successive grades in her position as wife. (i) " Sister " (*sent*) ; this shows the frequency in all periods of consanguine marriage, which was especially the rule in the royal family. This title was probably that of the woman during the first year of marriage, in which her fertility and character were tested. After this trial marriage, either partner could repudiate the other on payment, by the one who left the house, of an indemnity laid down by contract. (ii) The " Wife " (*hemt*), who shared in the ownership and management of the family property. (iii) The " Mistress of the house " (*nebt per*), who received and maintained the husband in the house which he had given her. How far these various grades in the wife's position were really distinguished before the IVth century, we do not know. The wife could also bring a legal action and acquire or inherit property personally. For marriage in the Græco-Roman period, see Bouché-Leclerq, *Histoire des Lagides*, vol. iv, p. 76. For a contract of trial marriage, valid for five months, at the beginning of our era, see Spiegelberg, **XII**, xlv (1909), p. 112.

[1] *Westcar Papyrus*, pl. vii, l. 17 ; Spiegelberg, *Studien . . . zum Rechtswesen*, 1892, pp. 15, 19, 31 ; Revillout, *Précis de Droit égyptien*, p. 58.

tangible results of the revolution, the consequences of the admission of the mass of the people to the " secrets " of the State and of religion. Beneath the religious question, we should see the agrarian question and the political demands of the people. The whole people seems to have become, even in this earthly life, what it aspired to be after death, through the Osirian rites—members of the great royal family which, in the Old Kingdom, had ruled Egypt by itself, and since the revolution had become open to all men. In the service of the State every one was given a place, and worked according to a definite legal status. After the rule of the King's good pleasure comes, as the Pharaohs themselves admitted, the rule of Law. Sacred despotism is succeeded by State socialism.

IV

THE CENTRAL ADMINISTRATION, THE VIZIER, AND THE KING

The central administration employed a whole army of scribes. There were numbers of offices to deal with the land, industry, justice, the police, the army, the temples. We cannot study these offices or their chiefs in detail. We may be content to define certain prerogatives of two great officials who, from the XIIth Dynasty, really guided the State, with the King. These were the Director of the Seal (*imra szat*) [1] and the Vizier (*tati*).

The Director of the Seal was the chief treasurer, the finance minister (the *dioiketes* of the Ptolemaic period). That is, he controlled the raw materials and manufactured goods which came into the royal stores as revenue and went out as payments. He supervised the expenses of the King's House, checking the accounts for the feeding and maintenance of the Court and the royal palaces. [2] The guardianship of the royal storehouses—the Treasury, as we should say—was a complicated business. From the lists of payments preserved in the papyri from Kahun and elsewhere, we see that the most

---

[1] The meaning is certain, but the reading *szat* is doubtful.

[2] A list of payments in kind, for the maintenance of the Court, at the end of the Middle Kingdom, is preserved in the Cairo papyri; see A. Scharf, " Ein Rechnungsbuch des königlichen Hofes," in **XII**, lvii (1922).

disparate things went into the royal storehouses and were kept there. " On the same page, we find enumerated corn, dates, flour, fish, cakes, worked wood of various species, dressed hides, frankincense in balls, dry ink, mallets, boxes of gold, bronze, and copper, black for the eyes, wigs, a woman's seal ... In order to form a notion of what the tax-collector's offices looked like, one should imagine something like a pawn-shop, where the most unlikely objects are accepted, provided that they are of commercial value. The difference was that the Egyptian State paid its servants in kind, and had to dispose of all sorts of goods which could not be kept more than a day or two,[1] and which modern loan-offices would refuse to accept." [2]

Every day the Director of the Seal reported on the economic situation to his immediate superior, the Vizier. The latter's activities were unbounded, for he controlled all services, and placed his Vizierial seal on all documents required for the distribution of land, trades, and administrative offices of all kinds, including the army and the temples. He received the reports of the Nomarchs, now styled " Princes and Regents of Mansions " (*hatiu hequ het*), and of all other officials. He issued his orders by means of " messengers " (*uputu*), who went everywhere, instituting inquiries and " reporting " (*smi*) direct to the Vizier. Not only the royal officials were under the Vizier's authority ; he made use also of the Saru and Qenbetiu, described above, for the work of administration. When a difficulty arose, the local Qenbet caused one of its members to be appointed by the Vizier to make an inquiry ; this commissioner was called " the (man delegated) as administrator " (*nti m sar*). The Vizier alone could take a decision. Under the Ramessids, one or more councils, called the Great Qenbet, sat at Heliopolis, Memphis, and other places, and the Vizier presided over this supreme court.[3] Lawsuits and other business already submitted to the local Qenbets could be then referred to the Great Qenbet, whose decision, backed by the authority of the Vizier, was final.

---

[1] Animals, alive or slaughtered, fruit, beverages, etc.
[2] Maspero, in **XXXVIII**, vol. viii, pp. 431, 452.
[3] We know this from the inscription of Mes, already quoted. See Gardiner's edition, pp. 32–8.

It is interesting to note that, for all the progress made in the centralization of power in the King, the local Qenbets culminated in a Great Qenbet, governing under the presidency of the Vizier. In autocratic monarchies, such as Tsarist Russia, local institutions, relatively independent, sometimes correct the abuses of an excessive centralization. Such appears to have been the rôle which fell to the assemblies of the Saru, in respect of the Vizier and the other officials of the King.[1] They enabled the people to take part in the central government, in what was perhaps the most absolute monarchy known in the ancient world.

With the XVIIIth Dynasty, the duties of the Vizier became so complex that the office had to be divided. There were, in certain periods, a Vizier for Lower Egypt, at Memphis, a Vizier for Upper Egypt, at Thebes, and a Viceroy of Nubia, called " the Royal Son of Kush ".[2]

These powerful personages were not, as in the Old Kingdom, chosen by the King from his own family. There were officials by career, like the Nomarchs. On the other hand, according to the constant rule for officials, the Vizierate could be hereditary. We know of a Theban family under the New Empire which supplied several Viziers (User, Rekhmara), and of a similar Memphite family, that of the Phtahmes. As under the Old Kingdom, the Vizier administered the " City ", that is, the royal residence, Thebes in the South and Memphis and Pa-Rameses in the North. In the tombs of the Theban family of Viziers several copies have been found of a most instructive inscription, regarding the occupations of the Vizier. Many passages of this text are obscure or incomprehensible, through the frequency of technical terms of which we do not know the exact meaning. What follows is a résumé rather than a translation.[3]

---

[1] In the New Empire the Saru did not escape the interference of the King. The Vizier nominated the commissioners of inquiry (nti m saru) and presided over the Great Qenbet. Royal and local officials even came to have the same title of Sar.

[2] Cf. From Tribe to Empire, p. 261.

[3] The text is in Sethe, Urkunden, iv, p. 1103. Translation in XVII, vol. iii, §§ 663 ff. Cf. G. Farina, Le Funzioni del Vizir (Reale Accad. dei Lincei, xxvi, Nos. vii–x, 1916). There is a commentary by Maspero in Journal des Savants, Sept., 1900, pp. 534–47.

No (local) Sar has power to judge. If such a usurpation of power occurs, the Sar is taken before the Vizier, who causes him to be punished. The messengers whom the Vizier sends to every Sar, from the first to the last, must come into the nomes unexpectedly. The messenger takes the Nomarchs and Regents of Mansions to the tribunal,[1] and communicates the regulations to them. If a Sar has committed an offence, the Vizier judges and punishes him, according to the various circumstances and according to the case. All administrative documents must be sealed by the Vizier. If they are not secret documents, the auditors and scribes of the Vizier take them, and send them to the Vizier, who reads and seals them. If they are secret documents, they are conveyed by special messengers of the Vizier.

For all complaints regarding cultivated land, the Vizier convokes the complainant, after the Director of Fields and the Zazats have been heard. The case is examined within two months if the land in question is in Upper or Lower Egypt; if it is in the district of the capital, Thebes, it must be examined within three days. When the complainant has been heard, the Qenbetiu of his district are summoned, and make their report. Every relevant "inventory" is produced; the Vizier seals them and effects a grouping (by families) of the portions of land (distributed to each member). If a man says, "The boundary-stones of our fields have been moved," the contents of the documents previously sealed are verified, and the Vizier redistributes the portions, and passes the matter on to the Zazat, which will set up the boundary-stones in their lawful places.[2]

The Vizier is informed of all complaints received by the King, provided that these are presented in writing.[3] He sends the King's Messengers to the Nomarchs and Regents of Mansions, for all necessary inquiries.

The Vizier appoints all Commissioners (*nti m saru*) for Upper Egypt, Lower Egypt, and Central Egypt. They report to him on all that comes into their hands, every four months, and also pass to him all documents coming from the Zazat of their district.

The Vizier collects the army to escort the King when he goes up or down the Nile. He causes the Zazats of the soldiers to be brought to him, gives them his instructions for the troops, and receives all the leaders in audience, from the first to the last.

The Vizier causes the trees to be cut as demanded by the King's House; he sends the Qenbetiu of the districts to make dikes all over the country; he sends to the Nomarchs and Regents of Mansions (orders) to plough and reap; he appoints the heads of gangs of a hundred; he gives audience (to receive the reports) of the Nomarchs and Regents of Mansions.

Report is made to the Vizier of all that concerns the forts of Upper Egypt and of all arrests for robbery; he does the policing of every nome; he sends soldiers and scribes for the escort of the King. The documents regarding every nome are opened in his tribunal, at the Audience on all the Fields; he creates the offices of every nome, of every territory (?), creates all the property of the temples, and establishes every contract.

The Vizier makes every mouth speak, and hears every declaration, when a man comes to speak with an adversary. He invests every (official) invested for the Palace.

---

[1] Lit., "the gate" (*ârit*). Justice was originally given at the gate of the King's palace.

[2] On the loss of arable land which sometimes followed a disastrous flood and made a rectification of the allotments necessary, see Herodotus, ii, 109.

[3] On this written procedure, cf. Diod., i, 75–6.

The Vizier holds audience on the profits and losses (?) of all property of the temples ; he imposes every tax on the income (of the temples). . . . He makes the receipts (?) of the taxes due to the royal storehouses. The Great Assembly (*zazat urt*) reports to him on the taxes. He inspects [1] all (tribute) brought to the tribunal, all provisions brought to the tribunal. He opens the door of the Golden House with the Director of the Seal ; he sees what is brought from the (Whole) Land. . . . He makes the declarations (*upet*) of all the large cattle which are declared ; he inspects the reservoirs of drinking-water, every ten days, and the supplies of solid foodstuffs likewise.

The Vizier holds audience [2] on all that is said at the tribunal. Nomarchs, Regents of Mansions, and all private persons (?) report to him on all their taxes ; all Directors of Territories, all Heads of Hundreds refer all complaints to him. The . . . report to him on business every month, to justify the taxes. Report is made to him on the rising of Sothis and on the inundation of the Nile [3] ; report is made to him on the rain from heaven, and he issues all regulations to Directors of Territories and Heads of Hundreds to build forts. He taxes (?) every cargo-boat . . .

The Vizier sends every messenger from the King's palace ; he administers the Two Lands when the King is at war, with the army ; he reports on the Two Lands to His Majesty ; to him all the Qenbetiu report, from the first to the last ; he seals every decree of the King.

The Vizier's audience is described at the beginning of this document, and in the tomb of Rekhmara a picture (Fig. 59*a*) accompanies the text :

Regulations for the Sitting of the Director of the City, Vizier of the City (capital) of the South and of the country, in the Pillar Hall of the Vizier.

For every audience in the Hall of the Vizier, the Vizier sits on an armchair, with a footstool on the ground, a canopy over him, a skin under his stern, a skin under his feet, a white garment on him, a sceptre in his hand, and forty rolls of parchment open before him. [4]

The ten Great Ones of the South are in two sections [5] before him. The Director of the Cabinet is on his right ; the Keeper of the Things which Come In is on his left ; the Vizier's scribes are near him. Each of all (these) persons speaks in turn ; audience is not given to the man at the back before the man in front. When the man in front says, " No one else has audience before me," then he is introduced by the Vizier's messengers.

Report has been made to him (on) the closing [6] of every building to be closed at the moment (desired), and (on) their opening at the moment desired. Report has been made to him on what concerns the forts of the South and of the North ; the incoming of all that comes into [7] the King's House is reported to him ; the outgoing of all that goes out [8] of the King's House is reported to him. As for all that comes in and all that goes out

---

[1] Lit., " sees." [2] Lit., " listens."
[3] Above, p. 20. The flood of the Nile coincides with the heliacal rising of Sothis. On the inundation the harvest depends, and so does the rate of taxation.
[4] These were four collections of ten laws, four decalogues. Cf. Diod., i, 75.
[5] Lit., " in two territories " (*iterti*), alluding to the two halves of Egypt.
[6] Lit., " closing with a seal."
[7] Tax, revenue. [8] Payment.

FIG. 59.—Pharaoh's Granaries.

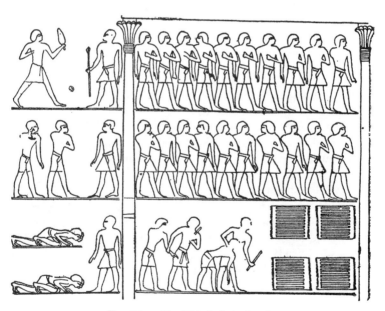

FIG. 59a.—The Vizier's Antechamber.
Tomb of Rekhmara.

on the soil of the Court, when it comes in and goes out, it is his messenger who makes it come in and go out, for the Directors of the Heads of Hundreds, the Heads of Hundreds, and the Directors of *Kherpu* of Lands report to him on their business.

Every morning the Vizier is received by Pharaoh.

Then he goes in, to inquire about the health of the Lord (King), L.H.S., and reports to him on what concerns the Two Lands, in his palace, every day.

He goes into the Double Great House [1] at the same time as the Director of the Seal, and keeps by the North Colonnade. Then the Vizier walks forward, going up to the door of the Two Great Palaces. Then the Director of the Seal comes to meet him, and reports to him as follows : " All the affairs of my Lord are safe and sound.[2] All the heads of services have reported to me as follows : ' All the affairs of my Lord are safe and sound.' The King's House is safe and sound."

In his turn, the Vizier reports to the Director of the Seal as follows : " All the affairs of my Lord are safe and sound. Every office of the Court is safe and sound. All the heads of services have reported to me the closing of buildings to be closed at the moment desired and their opening at the moment desired."

Then, after each of these two officials has made report to the other, the Vizier sends persons to open every door of the King's House, to let all come in, which comes in, and to let all go out, likewise. And his messengers cause all incoming (and outgoing) to be put down in writing.

What part did the King take personally in the administration ? There is no doubt that the Pharaohs were great workers, and that they took their business of kingship, their " great office ", as they called it, to heart. The Vizier was their confidential servant, but in principle authority lay with the King alone. Pharaoh saw everything and heard everything himself, or through his high officials who were called " the King's Eyes and Ears ".[3] Every Egyptian, rich or poor, had the right to appeal to the King, in a written petition, against any abuse of power. Such petitions have been found, dating from the XVIIIth Dynasty, but as early as the XIIth Dynasty we see royal investigators going about the country to collect complaints and petitions.[4] A popular tale, often copied out

[1] The King's palace.
[2] An administrative formula of the scribes, to say that all is well and there is nothing to report.
[3] An epithet of the Vizier User and several others.
[4] See the texts collected by Moret, " L'Appel au roi en Égypte au temps des Pharaons et des Ptolémées," in *Actes du Xe Congrès des Orientalistes* (Geneva, 1894), sec. iv, pp. 141–65.

by the Egyptians, has preserved for us the picturesque lamentations of a peasant to his King in the days of the Middle Kingdom.

A peasant was going to market, driving before him his donkeys, laden with salt, wood, and various victuals. He came to a road running past fields where another peasant was working for the King's Majordomo. Confident that his position under a powerful patron would protect him from the laws, this other peasant made plans to steal the donkeys of the first, who was soundly beaten into the bargain. The appeal of the victim forms the " Complaints of the Peasant " which are the subject of the story. First of all the ill-used hero complained to the Majordomo, calling upon sacred Law and divine Justice. The Majordomo consulted the Saru, and reported to the King.[1] The monarch, while meaning to do justice, hoped to have some fun at the expense of the robbed man, who had " the gift of the gab ". He ordered that the matter should be submitted in writing, but that they should wait, in order to draw forth the complainant's eloquence. (This is necessary to bring the story into line with the law.) He took care that in the meantime the peasant and his family should be fed and treated well. The peasant jumped at the splendid opportunity for relating his woes. Nine times he addressed the Majordomo in a speech, which for rhetoric and loftiness of sentiment is comparable to the language of the great Christian orators. Then he challenged the King's confidant, as if he were Pharaoh himself, and preached morals at him in the following terms :—

" O my Master ! You are Ra, the Master of the Sky ; you are also like the tide of the inundation ; you are the Nile, who fattens the fields. . . . (So be just like the Sun and the Nile.) Put down robbery, protect distress. Do not be a ravaging torrent against him who complains to you, but take heed that Eternity approaches, (and remember the saying) ' to do justice is life '." [2] Elsewhere he says, " Do the Justice of the Master of Justice, which is the Justice of Justice . . . for Justice is for Eternity ; it goes down into Khert-Neter with him who practises it. . . . Act according to this excellent saying, from the mouth of Ra himself : ' Speak Justice, do Justice, because Justice is mighty, because it is great, because it is lasting, and because it leads to Bliss '." [3] At the end of his ninth speech, the peasant's energy begins to fail, and his last words of protest are :

[1] The King in the story is Nebkaura, of a Heracleopolite Dynasty, at the time of the social revolutions.

[2] Lit., " is air to the nose."

[3] i.e., the condition of the Imakhu with the gods.

"Alas! I have complained to you, and you have not listened to my complaint; so I shall go and complain of you to Anubis." [1] The King and his Majordomo made an end of the unkind game. To compensate the complainant, the King caused his donkeys and their load to be restored to him, and, in addition, he gave six slaves, male and female, to the eloquent wind-bag who had amused His Majesty. [2]

This peasant was perfectly well acquainted with the doctrine of kingship of the Middle Kingdom. The author of the story sets forth in this humorous form, which is a feature of the Egyptian character, the very high principles of justice which the Kings of the XIIth Dynasty (and of the XVIIIth) really taught to their officials. If the peasant dares to lecture the royal judges, with a certain emphasis, it is because the King has been at pains to acquaint all his subjects with the duties which he expects of his officials.

Among the most curious writings of the time are certain *Teachings*, supposed to have been written by the Vizier Phtahhetep, of the Vth Dynasty, to inculcate in the young nobles and all budding officials good manners for the young and for decent men in general (behaviour in company, at table, in the drawing-room), the duties of a good King's Messenger, the respect due to the Great and the Qenbetiu, and the art of conducting oneself with dignity and skill in encounters with bullies, chatterers, or ill-disposed persons. Respect for justice and tradition, politeness, prudence, cleverness, and goodwill—such are the qualities of the good son, who " knows how to listen", that is, to obey, and of the loyal servant of the King. He who puts these qualities into practice becomes a " Servant of Horus "; he follows the road laid down by the founders of the Pharaonic government. [3]

This literary document is of historical value. It shows that the Pharaohs were careful to establish a doctrine, a " Teaching " (*sebait*) of justice and goodness, which should cause the government of the " *just laws* " [4] to reign everywhere. We have proof of it in the high morality which royal officials are careful to proclaim on their tombstones, as a guarantee that their deeds have been in accordance with the

---

[1] In the next world.
[2] From Maspero, **XLVI**, pp. 48–70.
[3] French edition by Virey, in *Bibliothèque de l'École des Hautes Études*, sec. iv, No. 70. Cf. Erman's translation, in **XLIV**, pp. 87–100.
[4] The expression occurs on the Stele of Antef (Louvre, C.26, l. 11).

doctrines of the Palace.[1] Moreover, we can tap the royal doctrine at its fountain-head, thanks to an official document, engraved in the tombs of Viziers (Rekhmara and his family), the inspiration of which probably goes back to the XIIth Dynasty. This is the speech which Pharaoh used to make to the Vizier on the day that he " consecrated " him in his august office.

Instructions given to the Vizier Rekhmara.—The Qenbetiu are introduced into the Hall of Audience of Pharaoh, L.H.S. The Vizier N. is brought in, when he is saluted (as Vizier). His Majesty says to him :

" Have your eyes on the Vizier's Hall of Audience. Supervise all that is done there. The constitution of the whole country (has its foundation) there.

" Look you ! to be Vizier is not to be mild ; it is to be firm, as the name shows.[2] He is a wall of bronze, around gold, for the house of his Lord. Look you ! You must not take sides with the Saru and with the Zazat, nor make a slave of any man. Look you ! a man in the house of his Lord must act for his Lord's good, and owes nothing of the kind to another man.

" Look you ! when a complainant comes from Upper or Lower Egypt . . . it is for you to see that all is done according to the law (*hap*), and that all is done according to the regulations concerning the case, doing so that every man has his rights. Look you ! a Sar[3] must (live) with his face uncovered. The water and the wind report all that he does. Nothing is unknown of his doings. . . . Look you ! it is safety[4] for a Sar to act according to the regulations, in answering the complainant. He who is judged must not say, ' I have not been given my rights.'

" Look you ! the sentence which was found, at the investiture (?) of the Vizier, at Memphis, in the mouth of the King . . . Take heed of what was said of the Vizier Kheti : ' He took sides against men of his own kin, in favour of other men who were not near to him.'[5] Now, that is more than justice. What God loves, is that justice should be done ; what God hates, is the favouring of one side (more than the other).[6] That is the Doctrine (*sebait*). So act likewise. Regard him whom you know as him whom you do not know, and him who is near to you in person as him who is far from your house. Look you ! a Sar who acts thus will prosper long on this seat.

" Do not send away any complainant before hearing his words. When a complainant is there, who comes to complain to you, do not reject what he says with one word ; but, if you must refuse him, you should let him

---

[1] The best examples are given in British Museum Stele 197, published by me under the title *La Profession de foi d'un magistrat sous la XIIᵉ dynastie* (*Bibl. de l'École des Htes. Études*, sec. iv, No. 230, 1921, pp. 7 ff.), and in Louvre Stele C.26 (XVIIIth Dynasty), a translation of which will be found in **XVII**, vol ii, §§ 763–71.

[2] The Vizier (*tati*) is *the* man, *vir*, *par excellence*. Cf. above, p. 256.

[3] In the general sense of " official."

[4] Lit., " an asylum."

[5] For fear of being suspected of partiality.

[6] These expressions, defining law in the time of the rule of the " just laws ", should be compared with those defining law in the time of the King's good pleasure (above, p. 160).

know why you refuse him. Look you! they say, 'The complainant likes his tale of grievances to be heard kindly even more than to see them put right.'[1]

"Do not fly into a rage with a man wrongfully. Only be in a rage when rage is (necessary).

"Set fear before you, that you may be feared. He is a Sar, the Sar who is feared. Therein lies the dignity of a Sar, when he renders justice. But if a Sar is too much feared, he is accused of violence, in the opinion of men. They do not say of him, 'There is a man!' . . . You will attain respect in filling (your) offices if you act according to justice.

"Look you! men expect the exercise of justice in a Vizier's very nature. Look you! that is the just law, from the time of the God (Ra). See what is said of the Vizier's scribe; he is (called) 'Scribe of Maat (Justice)'. The hall where you hold audience is the Hall of the Two Justices, where judgment is given; and he who distributes justice before men is the Vizier.

"Look you! when a man is an official, he should act as is prescribed for him. Happy the man who does as he is told! Never depart from Justice, whose laws you know. Look you! this is what happens to the arrogant (Sar); the King sets the timid one above the arrogant. Act, then, according to what has been prescribed for you."[2]

We may be sure that these noble words found an echo, and inspired a sincere, generous endeavour to put them into practice. We cannot criticize the laws (*hapu*) of Egypt in the actual text, for no code, like that of Hammurabi for Babylonia, has come down to us. But the King and his officials constantly invoke the law. It is the King who defines it to men, in teaching them his doctrine.

Another feature is characteristic of the manners of the new Egypt—the esteem in which intelligence and the art of speaking are held, as a means of government.

"Be an artist in words," a King says to his heir Merikara, "that you may be strong, for the tongue is a sword for (a King) and talking does more than fighting. Nothing takes an intelligent man by surprise. . . . A wise (King) is a (school ?) for the Great . . . no misfortune befalls him. 'Truth comes to him ready-brewed,'[3] as our Ancestors said." When the King sets the example, the courtiers vie in zeal and initiative. It is said of great officials, "Kind when listening, clever when speaking, skilful in disentangling all knots (of business),"[4] "Expert scribes who handle words well," "Teaching of the Whole Land," "More accurate than the weight, like the scales of Thoth, or Thoth in all things," "Psychologists, penetrating the secret thoughts and all the winding ways of the heart."[5]

What the King demands of his officials is not mere passive

---

[1] Like the peasant in the story, who was heard with so much ironical indulgence.

[2] From Sethe's edition and translation, "Die Einsetzung des Vizirs," in **XXXIX**, vol. v, 2, 1909.

[3] Like beer ready for drinking.

[4] *Merikara*, § 8.

[5] From the stelæ of Sehetepibra, Antef (C.26), British Museum 197, etc.

PLATE X

2 SENUSERT I EMBRACING PHTAH
XIIth Dynasty (Karnak)

1. THE KA OF KING HOR
Wood
XIIIth Dynasty (Cairo)

3 COLOSSAL HEAD OF
SENUSERT III

obedience, nor simply zeal and devotion, but mental agility, intelligence, and initiative—in short, character, personality. The King himself tries to set an example of a noble will applied to generous objects. We have already noticed how the images of the sovereigns of the Old Kingdom reflected an imperturbable consciousness of their superhuman authority and majesty. After the revolution, the god-king was assailed by doubts. He reflected, calculated; he had to come to terms with men, to learn how to govern. So the face of an Amenemhat or a Senusert seems to us a long way from the lofty serenity of his predecessors; it is harassed with care, and haggard with anxiety, questioning, or meditation. One

FIG. 60.—The Royal Son of Kush receiving the Official Seal. Tomb of Hui.

feels that they made an effort of will, struggling against themselves and others in their conscientious determination to do their duty and maintain their rights (Pl. X, 3).

Men listened with rapture to the royal promises; courtiers addressed the reforming Pharaohs in hymns full of wonder. A high official named Sehetepibra, who lived under Amenemhat III, hands down to his children the " Teachings " which he has received from his sovereign in these words :—

I say aloud, I make you hear, I make you know the eternal rule, the rule of new (or just) life, the means of passing to a life of bliss. Worship King Menmaat-Ra in your breast! Be brotherly with His Majesty in your heart! (The King) is the God Sa,[1] who dwells in hearts, whose eyes see into every breast. He is the God Ra whose rays make us see, who gives light to the Two Lands, more than the sun's disk (Aten), who makes (the earth) grow green more than the Nile in flood. He has filled the Two Lands with strength and life, and he refreshes the nostrils, when he goes forth against Evil. . . . He gives provisions (*kau*) to those who serve him, and his sustenance to those who tread his roads. The King is the Ka; his mouth is abundance [2]; his being is creation. He is the God Khnum (who fashions) all flesh, the begetter who begets all men. He is the Goddess Bast who defends the Two Lands. Whoever worships him is protected by his hand. (But) he is also the Goddess Sekhmet [3] to him who transgresses his commands. . . . Fight for his name, defend his life. . . . Abstain from any hostile act. The King's friend reaches the state of Imakhu, but there is no tomb for him who rebels against His Majesty; his body is thrown in the water. Therefore do (as I have told you); your flesh will be healthy, and it will profit you for ever.[4]

Lastly, here is a hymn in honour of Senusert III. Under the poetry of the Oriental images there is the throbbing gratitude of a whole people towards the good masters who had brought back to the country order, peace, wealth, and full enjoyment of earthly life, and had restored confidence in the future life. It consists of a series of strophes, in which each line begins with the same words.

I

How great is the rejoicing of

the gods : thou hast increased their offerings.
thy (children) : thou hast made their boundaries.
(thy fathers) of old time : thou hast increased their portions (of offerings ?).
the Egyptians at thy strength : thou hast protected their ancient rights.
men at thy designs : thy power wins their food.
the two banks at thy strength : thou hast enlarged their possessions.
thy young men (*zamu*) of the army : thou hast made them grow up.
thy (old) Imakhu : thou hast made them grow young.
the Two Lands at thy power : thou hast defended their ramparts.

---

[1] Knowledge, taste, satiety.

[2] The King's mouth creates by its words. For the creative power of the word, cf. above, p. 197. For the Ka, as a protective genius, cf. pp. 357–8.

[3] The lion-goddess who devours the enemies of Ra.

[4] Cairo Stele 20538. Cf. Maspero, **XXXVIII**, vol. viii, p. 142 ; and Erman, **XLIV**, p. 120.

II

How
great
is the
Lord
for his
City !

Alone, he is millions ; other men, they are small.
He is the dam dividing the river for his water-pipes.
He is the cool hall where man can sleep (sheltered) from the day.
He is the rampart which fortifies Goshen.[1]
He is that sanctuary where none can be pursued.
He is the refuge which saves the fearful man from his enemies.
He is shade in spring, a cold bath in summer.
He is a warm, dry corner in winter-time.
He is a rampart against the wind, when there is storm in the sky.
He is Sekhmet to the enemies who attack his frontier.

III

He has
come
to us :

he has seized Upper Egypt and set the Pskhent on his head.
he has united the Two Lands and wedded the reed to the bee.[2]
he has conquered the Black Land and subdued the Red Land.[3]
he has protected the Two Lands and given peace to the two banks.
he has given life to Egypt and done away with her sufferings.
he has given life to men and made the throats of the dead to breathe.
he has trampled on the Foreigners, and smitten the Troglodytes who did not fear him.
he has fought for his frontier and driven back pillagers.
he has allowed us to rear up our children and to bury our old men ! [4]

[1] Goshen, the Regent's Wall, mentioned in *From Tribe to Empire*, p. 228.
[2] Above, p. 121. [3] Above, p. 28.
[4] Griffith, *Hieratic Papyri from Kahun*, 1898, pls. i ff. For translation, see also Maspero, in **XXXVIII**, vol. viii, pp. 406–9 ; and Erman, **XLIV**, pp. 179–82.

CHAPTER V

THE STRUGGLES OF THE PHARAOHS WITH MERCENARIES
AND PRIESTS. FOREIGNERS IN EGYPT

BY calling their people to take a share in the administration, by giving every one, according to his social
position and his capacity, a certain access to political and
religious rights, and by making laws which were inspired by
justice and applied by trained and conscientious officials, the
Theban Pharaohs of the XIIth and XVIIIth Dynasties
prevented any return of the social revolutions which had
upset Egypt at the end of the Old Kingdom. In the good
years of the Kings of the XVIIIth Dynasty, one has the
impression that Egypt has reached a decree of prosperity
which she will never surpass, that the King is the " good
shepherd " who knows how to lead his flock, and that the
Government has managed to adapt itself, with a rare success,
to the natural conditions of the country.

This wise administration, which made the strength of the
Theban Pharaohs and was a pattern to the sovereigns of the
Oriental world, developed, like the society which it sustained,
under the pressure of historical events, most of which occurred
outside the valley of the Nile.

One event fraught with consequences was the invasion of
the Hyksôs. They ruled Egypt for about a century (1660 to
1580),[1] without, it seems, altering what we might call the
constitution of the kingdom. In return, the King and people
found themselves drawn, in the interests of their own
security, into a world policy, and the Pharaohs became the
conquerors and organizers of an Empire reaching from the
Upper Nile to the Euphrates. In *From Tribe to Empire* [2]
I have described the alternations of greatness and decline
through which this Empire passed, and noted the capacity
of the Pharaohs for governing their Syrian provinces with a

[1] See *From Tribe to Empire*, pp. 221–61.   [2] pp. 261–349.

PLATE XI

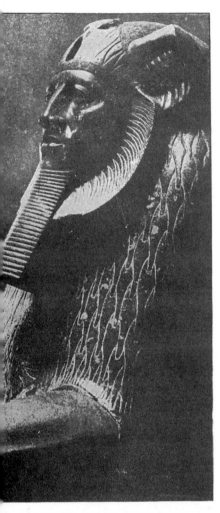

1. DIORITE SPHINX FROM TANIS
Old Kingdom (?)

2. WOMAN BEARING OFFERINGS
Stuccoed and painted wood
XIIth Dynasty (Louvre)

[face p. 290

prudence, adaptability, and intelligence which recall the methods of administration which they had tested at home in Egypt. What repercussion had this imperial policy on Egyptian society and civilization ? That is what I shall try to define in this last chapter, which will bring us to the disappearance of Egypt, at last overflowed and submerged by the foreign peoples whom she had tried, all in vain, to master.

I

THEBES AS THE IMPERIAL CAPITAL.   PALACES, TEMPLES,
NECROPOLES

Take it for all in all, the royal authority only gained by the state of war with the Hyksôs. The recovery of the country, city by city, from the Asiatics, the patient conquest effected by the Theban Kings of the XVIIth Dynasty and completed by Ahmes I, the founder of the XVIIIth (1580), strengthened the prestige of the kingship. The princely families disappeared [1] ; the whole of Egypt formed " Pharaoh's Fields " ; never was the country more effectively in the hands of the King than at the beginning of the New Empire. Did this practical ownership of the land lead to modifications of the more liberal status which the Pharaohs of the Middle Kingdom had given to the land-workers and trades ? We have no reason to think so. The texts of Rekhmara (middle of the XVIIIth Dynasty) prove, as we have seen, that the Vizier closely supervised, but also maintained, the administrative regulations which had to some extent emancipated peasants and craftsmen. Moreover, victory not only gave the land back to the Kings; it also brought them slaves. Hyksôs and Asiatics, Nubians, Peoples of the Sea, and others, vanquished on the field of battle, were captured in masses—those " smitten down alive ", as the texts say ; that is, defeated, perhaps wounded, but not dead. In addition, there were the prisoners taken in towns and in the country. All these men and their families arrived in Egypt to serve their conquerors.

[1] The monuments mention, in the XVIIIth Dynasty, only one princely family, and it was devoted to the monarchy—the Princes of el-Kab, who received from the King the duty of governing the districts from the south of Thebes to el-Kab (**XVII**, vol. iii, §§ 1 ff.).

Throughout the whole of the Egyptian domination in the Eastern world, from Ahmes I to Rameses III, we find at Pharaoh's disposal *slave labour*,[1] plentiful and easily assimilated, working on the land, plying trades, and holding humble posts in the administration. The introduction of these increasing masses of slaves among a relatively free population was an economic and social danger which we shall see growing more serious. Moreover, certain slaves succeeded in gaining the confidence of their masters ; at the Court of the Pharaohs, as at that of the Cæsars, we can observe the influence of foreign favourites,[2] whose servile condition guaranteed their devotion and explains the favour which they enjoyed.

The first to benefit by the spoils of the conquered, raw materials or slaves, was naturally Pharaoh. From the XVIIIth Dynasty onwards, the royal treasury grew continually richer. Into it flowed gold, silver, and bronze, raw or worked, furniture, vases, precious tissues, and rare woods ; all the wealth captured in Asia or paid as tribute by the subjects of Canaan and Syria and the allied Kings of Mitanni, Babylon, Assur, Khatti, Cyprus, and Crete. At the same time the storehouses and depots (*per-shenâ*) received captives in whole families, followed by cattle, goats, sheep, and horses, and housed outlandish creatures such as bears, elephants, and giraffes, which had come over Syria or by the Upper Nile.

It was to Thebes that Pharaoh took his captures and made them pass in procession before Amon-Ra, the protector of the dynasty. The City of the Sceptre, which came to be called the " City " (*nut*) above all others, contained the usual residence of the King and centre of the administration, especially during the XVIIIth Dynasty, and it was in the Theban necropoles that the tombs of the Kings were dug, from the XVIIIth Dynasty to the XXth. As the capital of the Kings, living and dead, Thebes became a city of marvels, where buildings were piled up as far as eye could see—

---

[1] J. Baillet has pointed out the indefiniteness of the terms used for the slave class in Egypt (**IV**, xxvii, pp. 30 ff. ; cf. *Le Régime pharaonique* (1913), p. 553, chap. xiv). When applied to foreign captives, taken in war and distributed to the soldiers, the word *hemu* certainly seems to mean slaves. Among the Egyptians of that time, it is doubtful if true slavery existed.

[2] On the rôle of foreign cup-bearers (*udpu*) at Court, cf. **XL**, p. 117.

Government offices, palaces, and temples ; the dwellings of the Court (the King's House), of officials of all ranks, of priests of all classes, and of the scribes of the bureaux ; shops, workshops, and factories. Workers in every branch of architectural construction and decoration, embalmers and funeral specialists, peasants who fed the townsfolk by tilling the rich land of the Thebaïd, baggage-porters and runners, royal guards and policemen, boatmen from the river-fleets, negroes and slaves of every hue, swarmed in a motley throng, in their hundreds of thousands, about the streets of the majestic, picturesque city, extending over an immense area, which the amazed Greeks, following Homer, would call " Hundred-gated Thebes ".[1]

Of the private city and that seething activity of which the Eastern towns of to-day give us a faint idea, nothing has survived. The religious and political city still speaks to us. Temples stand, by the side of a few substructures of palaces, and in the necropoles visitors can enter the yawning mouths of the hypogea. All that was not built in light, perishable materials—that is, the " eternal monuments " dedicated to gods and deceased Kings—bears witness to the splendour of the City of Amon.

The site was well suited to the construction of a capital. The valley spreads out to a width of 7 to 10 miles between the Libyan and Arabian plateaux. The Nile, the main stream of which is here about 1,000 yards broad, divides the city of the living (Luxor and Karnak) on the east bank from that of the dead on the west bank.

Karnak (Ipet-Isut) and Luxor (Southern Ipet) were two groups of colossal temples at the side of the city, forming an architectural scheme unique in the world. They were consecrated to the glory of Amon-Ra, and were called " the Throne of the Two Lands " (*Nesut-taui*). At the present day, the site of Karnak is still bounded by a ruined wall, the monumental gates of which survive in places ; it forms a quadrangle of 1,750 by 660 yards, running north and south along the river-bank. The principal group of temples occupies the whole breadth of this space on the north. In the middle,

---

[1] See the text and beautiful illustrations of J. Capart's *Thèbes : la gloire d'un grand passé*, 1925, translated as *Thebes : the glory of a great past*, London, 1926.

a few piers survive of the older sanctuary, erected to Amon-Ra by Amenemhat I and Senusert I ; the uninterrupted building of the XVIIIth Dynasty has caused this first temple to disappear. On the expulsion of the Hyksôs, Ahmes I, in the year 21 of his reign, set architects and labourers to work, and thenceforward every victorious campaign against the Asiatics was the occasion of new foundations (Pl. II, 2).

At first the temple was of modest dimensions—a little sanctuary of granite, halls with small columns, a court with a pylon in front. But every King, from Thothmes I to the Ramessids, contributed to the development of the plan, adding a court, a chapel, or a hall to the original nucleus. In consequence, in front of the sanctuary, there are no less than five pylons, separated by courts or pillared halls (hypostyles). The gigantic consummation of these constructions was the Hypostyle Hall of Seti I and Rameses II, between the pylons of Amenophis III and Rameses I. On a space 340 feet wide and 170 feet deep, a forest of columns in sixteen rows rises to a terrific height. The central nave has pillars 78 feet high, those of the lateral aisles rise 45 feet, and the whole of Notre-Dame would go inside it. These evidences of the strength and power of the Pharaohs must indeed have made a deep impression on contemporaries, since we, in the presence of what remains, can only repeat Champollion's admiring words : " No people, ancient or modern, has conceived the art of architecture on so lofty, broad, and grand a scale as the old Egyptians. They had the conceptions of men a hundred feet high ; the imagination, which soars far above our European porticoes, stops and falls powerless at the feet of the hundred and forty columns of the Hypostyle Hall " [1] (Pl. XIX, 1).

Colossal though it was (and I have not spoken of the extensions made by the Bubastite Dynasties), this central edifice was only a small part of Karnak. Inside the great temple itself, chapels, colonnades, and temples sprang up like toadstools on the trunk of a giant oak. Behind the sanctuary, an immense pillared hall, known as the Promenade of Thothmes III, closes the circuit of the great temple, forming a pendant to the Hypostyle Hall of Seti I. On the

---

[1] *Lettres écrites d'Égypte et de Nubie*, p. 98.

right side of what was afterwards the Bubastite Court, Rameses III built a complete temple.

On the side towards Luxor, two monumental avenues are laid out. One, which is lined with rams and contains four successive pylons (from Thothmes III to Horemheb), leads to the great temple raised by Amenophis III to Mut, the Goddess Mother, wife of Amon-Ra. The other, starting from a temple built by Rameses III to Khonsu, the son of Amon and Mut, is likewise lined with rams and runs 2,000 yards to Luxor, where Amenophis III, Tutankhamen, Horemheb, and Rameses II erected a mass of buildings, 720 feet long, to the glory of the Theban Triad. Here, again, obelisks, pylons, pillared courts, and splendid colonnades rise, one after the other, to express the love and gratitude of the Pharaohs of the XVIIIth Dynasty to their father Amon-Ra. The statue of the god was conveyed by water from Karnak to Luxor in ceremonial procession on the great feast-days, and the episodes of the journey are engraved on the walls. So, for two miles, Amon proceeded along a triumphal way, lined with temples, statues, and rams, in his city of Thebes.

The west bank, where the royal and private necropoles were, was equally covered with buildings, and was like an immense hive, its cells loud with the din of busy tools and wailing mourners. In the gorges called the Valley of the Kings and the Valley of the Queens, dried-up wadys of the Libyan plateau, the Pharaohs from Amenophis I onwards, from the XVIIIth Dynasty to the XXth (Pl. XX, 1), had their subterranean palaces dug, with rock-hewn passages leading to hypostyle halls and burial chambers, 300 feet deep and more. There lay the royal mummies, " eternal bodies ". Some have been found in their place,[1] but most were in hiding-places in which, to protect them from pillagers,[2] the bodies of Kings—Amenophis, Thothmes, Rameses—were heaped. Among all the other wonders of ancient Egypt, it is an extraordinary thing that the bodies of her Kings should have been kept for us, as lasting as their statues of bronze and granite. To no other people has fate granted the signal privilege of

[1] Amenophis II, Amenophis IV, and, lately, Tutankhamen.
[2] Such hiding-places were found by Maspero in 1881 (the pit of Der el-Bahari) and by V. Loret in 1898 (the tomb of Amenophis II). Cf. Moret, " Maspero et les fouilles dans la Vallée des Rois," in **VIII**, N.S., ii (1924), p. 38.

surviving in the features of its chiefs. The condition of these bodies to-day is pitiful enough, as they lie exhibited in the cases of our museums, but they are the symbols of an energy and a power such as the world had not known before.

On the edge of the Libyan plateau, at the foot of the beetling crag of rock the colour of blood, the funeral temples of the Theban sovereigns stand in a row, from north to south. In these temples worship was paid to the statues of the Kings, which were more accessible than the mummies buried in the depths of the hypogea. Mentuhetep III and IV, of the XIth Dynasty, had already erected a pyramid, surrounded by porticoes and chapels, on the site of Der el-Bahari, but their successors of the XIIth Dynasty placed their pyramids in the neighbourhood of the Fayum, and there, too, was their residence, at Itet-taui. The Theban Pharaohs, from the XVIIIth to the XXth Dynasty, on the other hand, chose Thebes for their earthly and funeral city. Each of them built himself a temple or a chapel on the west bank, and also a palace in the neighbourhood, on the fringe of the cultivated land.   The palaces have disappeared,[1] but the funerary temples survive. Those best preserved are the temple of Queen Hatshepsut at Der el-Bahari, which is built on terraces (Pl. II, 1), with porticoes borne by " proto-Doric " columns and rock-hewn sanctuaries ; those of Seti I at Gurnah, with marvellous sculptures ; the " Ramesseum " of Rameses II (described by Diodorus as the tomb of Osymandyas), which still has a pylon, a hypostyle, and a sanctuary, of splendid materials and very pure in style (Pl. XVIII, 2) ; and that of Rameses III at Medinet-Habu, the enclosure of which contains both a palace in the form of a stronghold and a huge sanctuary. Of the edifice of Amenophis III nothing remains except the monolithic colossi, facing east, which represent the King seated, guarding the entrance-gate. Sixty feet high and visible from all sides, they dominate the plain with a majesty which has in all ages won them the superstitious reverence of the fellah. For the Greeks, the northern colossus was the famous Memnon, who greeted his mother Eos in the morning with a harmonious murmur exhaled by the stone, trembling under the caress of the sun.

[1] Vestiges of the palaces of Hatshepsut and Amenophis III have been unearthed in the last twenty years.

Among the many *graffiti* left on the pedestal by admiring visitors who had heard the stone speak, we read these lines of an Imperial Procurator of Rome, named Asclepiodotus :—

" Know, Thetis, who dwellest in the sea, that Memnon lives still, and, at the warmth of his mother's torch, raises a sonorous voice at the foot of the Libyan mountains of Egypt, where the Nile, in his course, divides Thebes of the Hundred Gates. But thy Achilles, once insatiable for battle, now lies dumb in the fields of Troy, as in Thessaly."

Memnon is silent to-day ; but the texts, recalled to life by Champollion, are as eloquent as ever. On the walls of temples and palaces, crowded side by side along the ruddy cliff, lit by the rising sun, they bear witness to a magnificent past, and the statues still sing the glory of Thebes, living and immortal.

Above the line of temples, the Libyan cliff rises sharply, riddled with holes which mark the tombs of Theban officials. They can be reckoned in thousands. Some are marvellously decorated and covered with texts, such as those of the Viziers and high officials of the Crown. The Pharaohs, who lay not far off, in the Valley of the Kings, contributed to the cost of the burial of their best servants.

It must not be supposed that the thousands of temples, chapels, palaces, and tombs built in the Thebes of the living and the dead absorbed all the resources which the Nubian and Syrian campaigns procured for the conquering Pharaohs. All the cities of Egypt strove to set up monuments worthy of their gods. Abydos, the holy land, was lavishly adorned by Kings who wished to have a cenotaph there; those of Seti I and Rameses II assumed the dimensions of funerary temples, in which their worship was associated with that of Osiris, and they are among the most perfect monuments. At Memphis, especially under the XIXth Dynasty, many palaces and temples were built. The residence of Rameses II and his successors at Pa-Rameses, on the eastern edge of the Delta, the political capital of the Syrian provinces, vied in beauty with Thebes and Memphis. Great builders, Thothmes III, Amenophis III, Seti I, Rameses II, Rameses III, restored monuments all over Egypt, or built new ones, even beyond Elephantine, and as far away as Napata. The great dynastic gods, Amon, Ra-Harakhti, and Phtah, the royal donors, and the Nubian god Dudun had splendid palaces built by various Kings named Amenophis and Rameses at Kalabshi, Bet el-Wali, Dendur, Gerf Hussen, Sebua, Amada, Derr, Abu-Simbel, Soleb, and Napata (Gebel Barkal). Of these buildings, the temples at Abu-Simbel, entirely hewn in the Libyan cliff by Rameses II, the building of the Sed-feasts set up by Amenophis III at Soleb, and the sanctuary of Amon-Ra at Gebel Barkal bear comparison with the finest monuments of the lower valley.

The Pharaohs at all times had a passion for survival in everlasting monuments, but this thirst for glory and immortality, this eagerness to exalt their power, never possessed them with such force and could never be gratified so fully as in the days of the conquests and the riches of empire. When one sees what still remains, after the ravages and looting of so many centuries, when one counts the thousands of buildings, and thinks what they must have been like when intact, in all their splendour, one stands astounded before the incredible prodigality of expenditure and the immensity of the effort achieved. In vain one tries to calculate the amount of work furnished by the multitudes of foreign captives and Egyptian labourers who transported the materials and set up the walls, of decorators who painted, carved, and inscribed them, of craftsmen who made the furniture, of peasants who provided the daily offerings and victims, of priests who sacrificed in the sanctuaries, of stewards who managed the property of the gods—the imagination cannot rise to the reality and surrenders to stupefaction.

II

THE MILITARY CLASS IN THE THEBAN STATE

A military empire depends almost entirely on its soldiers ; so one of the essential facts of the Theban New Empire is the development of the military class in society.

The brothers-in-arms of Pharaoh were granted especial favours in return for their services. These were not only the gold necklaces, " the gold of valour," [1] decorations, and

---

[1] Cf. *From Tribe to Empire*, pp. 260, 265, n. 1.

weapons of honour with which honest officers liked to deck themselves out for reviews and solemn processions ; more substantial rewards awaited them. The chief of the sailors, Ahmes, received a share of spoil (*haqt*) in the form of slaves, male and female (*hemu*), ten *arourai* of land in his city of Nekheb, sixty *arourai* in another place, and a number of *arourai* elsewhere, the whole composing a property which was vested in him.[1] Another warrior of the same family, Ahmes Pen-Nekhebt, obtained from the King rings, bangles, sceptres, armlets, six flies and three lions of gold (decorations), two golden axes, two silver axes, etc. In the same period, a servant of Queens Aahhetep and Sebekmsaf was rewarded with " fields on high level and low ",[2] and became *kherp* of the Queen's property at Edfu, for the service of funeral offerings. A sailor, one Nesha, who had served under King Ahmes,

FIG. 61.—Egyptian Soldiers and Foreign Mercenaries.
El-Amarna.

received a donation of thirteen *arourai* of plough-land. This estate was described as " the property of one single person, (transmissible) to one single person " ; it was, therefore, distinguished from ordinary tenures, which were " divisible " among all the members of a family. Donations (*feqau*) of this kind constituted indivisible property, which could only be bequeathed to one single heir, from eldest son to eldest son. The inscription of Mes describes the rivalries which sprang up in families in order to bring these indivisible properties, so precious to their possessors, into the distributions which took place at intervals. Violence, forgery, every means was employed to cheat the lawful heir out of his indivisible estate, which fell into the family pool. Not till four

[1] Sethe, *Urkunden*, iv, 2 ; cf. iv, 6, 11.   [2] *Urk.*, iv, 31.

hundred years later did one Mesmen, a descendant of Nesha, succeed in establishing his right, with the aid of the records of the survey and treasury. The Vizier and the Great Qenbet of Heliopolis recognized the fraud of which he was the victim, and restored the distant heir of Nesha in his indivisible fief.[1]

We may conclude that a certain number of war-leaders thus received indivisible estates, detached from " Pharaoh's Fields ". To judge from rather later documents, the constitution of these fiefs required the following deeds : an inventory (imt-per) ; an order, detaching the estate from the royal lands ; and a receipt for the transfer duty[2] ; all verified and sealed in the office of the Vizier, who could thus follow up the fate of the domain, of which the King still kept the eminent ownership. These fiefs do not seem at first to have been exempt from control ; there is no mention of immunities here, and the King was careful not to repeat the mistake of the Old Kingdom. His administration maintained all his rights, and supervised the succession on the death of the holder, when the ownership passed to the eldest son.

So the war had created a " military nobility ", holding land which enjoyed certain privileges. Did the common soldier have any share in these rewards and was he allowed to own land ? The Kahun papyri tell us of the existence of " combatant " soldiers (âhâtiu = μάχιμοι), entered on the records of the nomes as officials. On many monuments of the time we find mention of people who " live as soldiers ", ânkhu n mshau,[3] as opposed to the ânkhu n nut, the " town-dwellers ". This expression seems to indicate that the Egyptians received, in return for military service, their subsistence by means of royal land, which the administration gave them in holdings divided by families, as was done for the peasants. The soldier's career does not seem to have conveyed privileges. During the XVIIIth Dynasty his social position was raised. The active army was divided into two main classes (sa), one for Upper Egypt and one for Lower. In the field we hear of the divisions of Amon, Ra, Phtah, and Sutekh,[4] in addition

---

[1] Moret, " Un Procès de famille," in **XII**, xxxii, pp. 19–23.
[2] Ibid., p. 21.
[3] Cf. *From Tribe to Empire*, p. 266, n. 1.
[4] These " divisions " appear with the conquests of the Thothmes. On this subject, cf. Moret, " La Campagne de Séti Ier en Palestine," in *Revue de l'Égypte ancienne*, i (1925).

to the special " guard " of Pharaoh, the Nubian mercenaries (*Mazoï*), and the Asiatic contingents (*Merinau*). This army was recruited on a new, territorial basis. The soldiers' families, settled on royal lands, seem to have been favoured, as compared with the peasants. In a celebrated passage in the poem of Pentaur,[1] Rameses II reminds his men, who have allowed themselves to be surprised in the camp of Kadesh,[2] of the exceptional position which he has granted them on his lands, in return for their military service.

" See, His Majesty calls his soldiers and his chariot-men, and also his great (leaders) who had not known how to fight. He says to them, ' How cowardly you have been in heart, my chariotmen ! . . . (And yet) there is not one man among you to whom I have not given a good portion on my land. Have I not acted there as (your) Lord, and are you not *nemhu* there ? I have made you become Great Ones by the provisions (*kau*) (which I have given you) every day. I have set the son on the property of his father. All that can be burdensome in the country is spared (you). I have relieved you of your taxes (*bkau*), and I have given you other things which had been taken from you. When any man came to me with a prayer, I said, " Yes, I shall do it," every day. Never did a Lord do for his soldiers what I have done for you, according to your desire. For I let you dwell in your houses and your cities, even when you made no declaration (did no service ?) as under-officers ; and, indeed, for the chariot-men, I showed them the way to many cities. And I said to myself : " I shall find them likewise, on the day and at the hour for marching to battle." But see, all together you do a deed of baseness ; not one of you stands up to give me his hand ! ' " [3]

As one often finds in the Egyptian texts, the phraseology, though redundant and sometimes obscure, proves, on closer inspection, to contain precise expressions which deserve attention. Rameses II gives his soldiers on his " land ", a favoured position (*sep nefer*), which no previous Lord had granted to his soldiers. He provides them with food, makes their employment hereditary, gives them houses and cities,

---

[1] Erman, **XLIV**, p. 331.
[2] *From Tribe to Empire*, p. 323.
[3] Cf. Revillout, in **VIII**, iii, pp. 101–4 ; and *Précis de Droit égyptien*, p. 75.

and relieves them of taxes (*baku*), even if they have not had themselves entered as under-officers. He himself receives all complaints of his soldiers and protects them in person. In sum, he is the lord of free men, *nemhu*.

So the soldiers constituted a hereditary privileged class from the Theban period onwards. In general, the hieroglyphic texts confirm what Herodotus could still see for himself in the IVth century. " The soldiers alone of the Egyptians, save the priests, have the privilege of twelve *arourai* of good land, free of taxation, for each man.[1] In the nomes of the Central and Western Delta, the people call these soldiers Hermotybies; they number 160,000. In the Eastern Delta and Valley, they are called Calasiries, and number 250,000. None of them has learned any trade but that of arms, and they hand it down from father to son.[2] Every year 1,000 Calasiries and 1,000 Hermotybies form the King's guard. These receive, in addition to their land, a daily ration of 5 minas of baked bread, 2 minas of beef, and 4 pots of wine." [3] Diodorus confirms that the land of Egypt was divided between the King, the priests, and the soldiers.[4]

The King maintained the eminent ownership of the military fiefs and the lands ceded to the soldiers of the nation : none the less, the concession was a first weakening of the royal authority, resulting from the warlike policy which had been forced upon the Pharaohs by circumstances.

III

THE PRIESTLY CLASS IN THE THEBAN STATE

No less exacting in their claims were the priests of Amon, the god of the Theban family, who gave the King victories and conquests.[5] Diodorus tells us :—

---

[1] ii, 168. [2] ii, 164–6.

[3] ii, 168. Spiegelberg (**XII**, xliii, 1906, p. 87) has shown that the name Calasiries comes from an Egyptian word, which originally meant the Nubian mercenary infantry, and that Hermotybies at first designated the chariot-men, the cavalry. In Herodotus's time these μάχιμοι were foot-soldiers. For their organization in the late period, see Maspero, " Études égyptiennes, ii," in *Journal Asiatique*, 1888, reprint, entitled *Un Manuel de hiérarchie égyptienne*, p. 35 ; and J. Lesquier, *L'Armée romaine d'Égypte*, 1918. G. Möller (**XII**, lvi, p. 78) regards the Hermotybies as spearmen.

[4] Diod., i, 73. [5] Cf. *From Tribe to Empire*, pp. 278–9.

The whole soil of Egypt is divided into three portions. The first and largest belongs to the college of the priests, who are held in the highest esteem among the natives, both on account of their religious office and because they have received the most complete education. Their revenues are used for the costs of sacrifices, for the keep of their subordinates, and for their own needs. . . . Among the Egyptians, those whose business is sacrifices and the worship of the gods are numerous. They are exempt from taxation, and they come next to the King in dignity and privileges. The second part of the land belongs to the Kings. From it they raise the taxes required for the expenses of war and the upkeep of the Court. The third part belongs to the soldiers.[1]

This evidence from a late period should be compared with the story of Joseph in the Book of Genesis. The Biblical writer is greatly impressed by the land system in Egypt ; all the soil belongs to the King, except the estates of the priests. Only he attributes this fact, with simple pride, to Joseph's influence over Pharaoh. In a year of dearth Joseph, who has become Vizier, fills the Treasury by selling the corn of the royal granaries to the starving people ; and when all the money of the country has gone into the King's purse, the people sells its livestock as well, and says to Pharaoh :—

"There is nought left . . . but our bodies and our lands. . . . Buy us and our land, against bread and seed." . . . So Joseph bought all the land of Egypt for Pharaoh ; and the land became Pharaoh's. And as for the people, he removed them to the cities from one end of the border of Egypt even to the other end thereof.[2] Only the land of the priests bought he not : for there was a law of Pharaoh in favour of the priests, who lived on the revenue which Pharaoh ensured to them ; wherefore they sold not their land.

Lastly, Joseph fixes the rate of the tax to be paid by Pharaoh's serfs :—

Then Joseph said unto the people, "Behold, I have bought you this day and your land for Pharaoh : lo, here is seed for you, and ye shall sow the land. And it shall come to pass at the ingatherings, that ye shall give a fifth unto Pharaoh, and four parts shall be your own, for seed of the field, and for your food, and for them of your households, and for food for your little ones." . . . And Joseph made it a statute concerning the land of Egypt (which has lasted) unto this day, that Pharaoh should have the fifth ; only the land of the priests alone became not Pharaoh's.[3]

The Bible story, which aims at a general impression rather than accuracy, is silent about the soldiers. The division of Egypt into three in respect of the revenue and land seems to be confirmed, in the reign of Thothmes III, by a scribe who mentions among his duties " the taking of the census of the

---

[1] i, 73.
[2] Cf. above, p. 301, for what is said about the soldiers in the poem of Pentaur.
[3] Gen., xlvii, 18 ff.

Whole Land, namely soldiers (*menfitiu*), priests (*uâbu*), and King's servants (*hemu-nsut*)—all the officials (*iautiu nebt*) of the Whole Land ".[1] If we accept this as a starting-point, we may conclude, from texts of various dates from the XVIIIth to the XXth Dynasty, that the temples, and consequently the priests, also held the land on special conditions, which placed them at least on a level with the soldiers.

These gifts and foundations of the Pharaohs in favour of the temples may be illustrated by a few examples.

Ahmes I gave Queen Teta-shera a revenue of bread and offerings supplied by persons (*remtu*) having fields and live-stock, each of whom knew his status.[2] Thothmes I created for Osiris of Abydos a staff of hour-priests and officials known as *semdet*,[3] divided into categories corresponding to priestly functions—divine fathers, priests, officiants, officials, and hour-servants of the god.[4] To the sacred domain (*hetep neter*) of Amon at Karnak Thothmes assigned 1,800 *arourai* of fields and many territories (*u*) in Upper and Lower Egypt. " The house of the God is full of peasants (*mertu*) ; His Majesty has chosen them from among his captures in the foreign countries of the South and the North—children of the Princes of Lotanu, children of the Princes of Nubia—obeying the order of his father Amon, the Lord of the Throne of the Two Lands." [5] To the temple of Abydos, Thothmes gave 500 *arourai* of gardens and 500 *arourai* of high land, with *mertu*. Amenophis III founded for his favourite, the wise royal scribe Amenhetep, son of Hapu, a funerary chapel, in which he " established (*smen*), for the duration of eternity, servants (*hemu*) of both sexes " ; he fulminates against all who should dare to alter their status, " against any chief of soldiers or scribe of soldiers who should take them away, to place them under Pharaoh or themselves." These *hemu* must remain on the funerary estate, from father to son, from one heir to another, " till eternity." [6] This is very like the constitution of the indivisible estates of the soldiers.

---

[1] *Urk.*, iv, 1006 ; small and large livestock are added to the population. The " King's servants " are the rest of the population, excluding the priests and soldiers.

[2] *Urk.*, iv, 28.

[3] Originally, perhaps, taking up their duty every half-month (*semdt* ?).

[4] *Urk.*, iv, 95.   [5] *Urk.*, iv, 171.

[6] H. Sottas, *Protection de la propriété funéraire*, p. 147 ; Möller, " Das Dekret des Amenophis," in *Sitz. der Berl. Akad.*, xlvii, 1910, p. 952.

Rameses II, being compelled to allow and increase the privileges of the soldiers, also confirmed those of the priests. When he founded the magnificent temple at Abydos for the funerary cult of his father Seti I, the scribes made inventories of the fields, from oral declarations ; the King furnished them with families of cultivators with their *rudu* and provided all the officials for the temple—hour-priests, craftsmen, and land-workers (*semdet*), all contributing to the service of the temple ; and territories in Upper and Lower Egypt were also to supply revenues. But all these real properties, men, and beasts, wherever they were, formed, in the State registers, one single body, entered in the name of the temple and its priests.

FIG. 62.—Amenophis III accompanying the Barge of Amon-Ra. Luxor.

" I have brought together (*sehu*)," says the King, " all those under thy administration, collected in one place, set beneath the rod of the prophet of thy temple, that thy possessions may remain in one single body, to be transferred to thy temple, to perpetuity." [1] This is the system of the indivisible property, detached from Pharaoh's Fields, like the military fiefs. It was a dangerous concession. Although the King's administration continued to control these properties, they came to be concentrated more and more in one man's hands—in this case in the grasping hands of the First Prophet, who was the administrator of the temple. Priests and soldiers who held fiefs ceased to regard themselves

[1] H. Gauthier, *Grande Inscription d'Abydos*, ll. 82 ff.

as mere tenants, and tended to become true owners, under the supervision, watchful or otherwise, of the Viziers.

So, in this highly centralized state, two classes constantly enriched themselves at the King's expense, for they held the religious authority and the military power.

IV

MONARCHY AGAINST THEOCRACY

The priests, securely established on territorial property and a wealth which increased with every reign, assumed a remarkable influence in Egypt from the XVIIIth Dynasty onwards. The priests of Amon, who were the most powerful of all, tried to keep the royal family under their thumb, but their intrigues led to reactions on the part of the Kings. The latter were supported by the rival priesthood of Heliopolis, which had inherited the monarchic traditions of the Old Kingdom, and perhaps by a military party as well. These struggles make the interest of two characteristic episodes in internal history, the reigns of Queen Hatshepsut and King Amenophis IV. There we see, in the full limelight, the political ambition of the priests, and the efforts of the sovereigns to escape from their dominion.

1. *Dynastic Disputes in the Time of Hatshepsut* [1]

The royal family allowed the priesthood an opportunity when questions of dynastic right arose. Egypt had kept very ancient traditions of the eminent right of women to inheritance. Traces of the primitive system of matriarchy (cf. p. 96) survived in certain instances in the manners of the people, where the wife, though subordinate in fact, was independent by right. The wife of a private individual was the " mistress of (his) house " (*nebt per*) [2] and could dispose of it, so far as the social laws allowed this at all, more freely than anyone else. The wife of a prince gave her sons the right to rule. The wife of royal race was the keeper of the royal heritage and transmitted the right of kingship to her children alone.

---

[1] For the whole episode, cf. **XXVIII**, p. 1.   [2] Cf. above, p. 274.

At the beginning of the XVIIIth Dynasty this custom was observed more strictly than at any other time. It seems to be established that the Thebans who fought the Hyksôs and founded the XVIIIth Dynasty sat on the throne of the Two Egypts because one of them, Seqeninra Tiuaqena, married a princess, Aahhetep I, who inherited the royal rights. We know of her influence at the Court,[1] and her mummy, once covered with splendid jewels and gold ornaments,[2] bears witness to the veneration in which she was held. Aahhetep is the first whom we know of a line of princesses who, from Ahmes I to Thothmes III, played a singularly important part. Maspero wondered whether there was not a moment during the Hyksôs wars, when all the men of the royal family had fallen in battle, and only women remained to perpetuate the race of the blood of the Sun. " We see," he says, " at least as many queens as kings among those who then presided over the destinies of Egypt." [3]

Princes had a right to the crown only if they were born of a father and mother who themselves had equal rights, as was the case when they were brother and sister, born of a " royal wife ". If the prince was the son of a concubine, his right to the throne fell before that of a sister whose mother was a Queen by birth. In this case, the sister married her own brother, who shared the throne with her. " The prince then ruled for her and relieved her of those of the duties of kingship which only a man could legally perform, the worship of the supreme gods, the command of the troops, and the administration of justice ; but she never ceased to be the sovereign. When she died the succession passed to her children. The father had to invest the eldest of them formally, in the place of the deceased Queen, and shared the outward show of power with him, if not the reality." [4]

This being so, it can be understood that the priests, the preservers of the royal doctrine and licensed witnesses of the Solar descent of the Pharaohs, seized the opportunity to intervene and exercise their control, whenever a prince or princess had to be selected, according to the purity of his

---

[1] The Inscription of Kares, the manager of the Queen's property, **XVII**, vol. ii, §§ 51–3.
[2] In the Cairo Museum, cf. **XX**, vol. ii, p. 97.
[3] **XX**, vol. ii, p. 77. [4] **XX**, vol. ii, p. 77.

or her pedigree. Now, this opportunity came to them several times. At the beginning of the XVIIIth Dynasty, Ahmes I married his sister Nefertari. In this " perfect " pair, husband and wife had equal rights, and Nefertari yielded to the King. When he died, their son, Amenophis I, still a minor, was inferior to his mother, Nefertari, who kept the rank of Queen after her son had attained his majority. Amenophis I carried on the tradition, and married his mother's daughter, Aahetep II. Their sons died young, and their daughter, Ahmasi, had to marry a prince, Thothmes I, whose mother was not of royal stock. Ahmasi allowed her husband to rule, but he had to share the power with his sons, who, through their mother, had more right to the throne than himself. The two sons of Thothmes I died young ; there remained a daughter, Hatshepsut, and Thothmes declared her Queen when his wife Ahmasi died.

Hatshepsut, who is one of the most interesting figures of the XVIIIth Dynasty, has left splendid monuments, such as the obelisks at Karnak and her funerary temple at Der el-Bahari.[1] Now, although she reigned over twenty years, it would be useless to look for her name in the king-lists. The Pharaohs kept this woman out of their Annals. The records say nothing of her, and tell us, on the contrary, that her father Thothmes I was succeeded by two sons, Thothmes II and Thothmes III. On the monuments erected by the Queen, her royal names are obliterated, the outline of her figure is effaced on the bas-reliefs, and the names or figures of Thothmes I, II, or III are engraved over the place. Why did her father and brothers combine against her ?

Thothmes II and III were sons of Thothmes I by a non-royal woman, and therefore had none of the rights to the succession which Hatshepsut had through her mother. Yet Thothmes I had just led his armies beyond the Euphrates on one side [2] and to the Upper Nile, beyond the Third Cataract, on the other. Could he entrust the destinies of Egypt to a woman, who· could not command the army ? It may have been that an anti-feminine party, probably composed of soldiers, was disturbed by the danger, and

---

[1] Cf. Plates XIX, I, and II, 1.
[2] See *From Tribe to Empire*, pp. 266–8.

resolved to prevent Egypt being ruled by a petticoat (about 1501).

The monuments declare that Hatshepsut and her husband, Thothmes III, were crowned together after the death of Queen Ahmasi, during the life of Thothmes I, and that they reigned conjointly before Thothmes II. Little is known of the first two years of their joint reign. The Queen only appears in the subordinate position of a woman, her name is not preceded by the royal titles, and sometimes Thothmes III is mentioned alone on the monuments. This was the result of an intrigue which we can infer from an inscription found at Karnak.

The inscription relates how Thothmes III came to the throne. The young royal bastard held a modest post as prophet in the Temple of Amon, when the anti-feminine party cast their eyes on him. Things were arranged so that on the day of a procession the statue of Amon was carried about in all directions, as if the god were seeking the young man. He was placed before the statue, in a reserved position known as the " King's station ", where the King alone had the right to stand. Amon indicated his satisfaction, and the secrets " which were in the heart of the God and known to no man " were revealed before the people. The god gave audience to the prince.

> He opened the gates of the Sky to me; he opened the gates of the Horizon of Ra to me.[1] I took flight into the sky like a divine falcon, contemplating his form in the sky. I worshipped his majesty. I saw the glorious forms of the God of the Horizon on the mysterious ways of the sky. Ra himself established me (as King). I was consecrated with the Crowns which were on his head, and his Uræus was set on my brow. . . . I received the dignities of a god . . . and he established my great royal names for me.[2]

Then follows the full title of Thothmes III; there is no mention of Hatshepsut in the narrative. Yet Thothmes III, in order to establish his right, had had to marry Hatshepsut. Her supporters countered the militarist plot with a legitimist plot.[3] Between the years 2 and 5 of the reign, the

---

[1] The Sky, the Horizon of Ra, are names of the Holy of Holies, the sanctuary in which the god resides.

[2] Cf. Breasted, " A New Chapter in the Life of Thutmose III," in **XXXIX**, vol. ii, 1900.

[3] For an account of the party-struggles of Hatshepsut's time, see Sethe, " Die Thronwirren unter den Nachfolgern Königs Thutmosis I," 1906, in **XXXIX**, vol. i.

Queen began to build the temple of Der el-Bahari, the
" Sublime of Sublimes ", for her own glory.   Whereas she
had formerly been called only the Great Royal Wife, she now
caused herself to be called " Horus " (in the feminine,
Hor-t) and " Ra " (in the feminine, *Ra-t*) ; she assumed the
royal titles (*nsut biti*), the two cartouches ; she was also
represented in art as a man, with short waist-cloth, false
beard, and bare chest, flat like a man's [1] ; then her name,
which means " First of the Nobles ", was made masculine—
Hatshepsu, instead of Hatshepsut.   Lastly, she caused two
series of splendid reliefs representing her birth and coronation
to be carved in her temple.

To prove that she alone was the lawful heiress, Hatshepsut
revealed to her subjects the mysteries of the royal nativity.[2]
The theory of descent from the Sun was very ancient, as we
have seen (p. 156), but Hatshepsut for the first time caused
it to be depicted on the walls of a temple.   Being inspired by
the priests of Amon, she proclaimed to the world in general
that her true father was Amon-Ra ; accordingly, the
sculptures on the walls represent the carnal union of Amon-Ra
with Ahmasi, the heiress-wife of Thothmes I and the earthly
mother of Hatshepsut.

On a bed of state, adorned with lion's head and feet, the
god and the Queen sit facing one another, with their legs
crossing, under the protection of the goddesses Neith and
Serqet.   There is a text giving a lyrical commentary on the
scene, and it leaves no doubt of the carnal nature of
the union.

This is what Amon-Ra, King of the Gods, said, when he had taken the
shape of that man, King of the South and of the North, Thothmes I.   He
found the Queen lying in the splendour of her palace.   She awoke at the
scent of the God, and marvelled when His Majesty at once went to her,
and possessed her, and laid his heart upon her, and made her see him in his
shape of a god.   And, on his coming, she was at once exalted at the sight
of his beauties ; the love of the God ran through her members, and the
scent of the God and his breath were full of the perfume of Punt.

And this is what the King's wife, Queen Ahmasi, said in the presence of
Amon.   " How great are thy souls !   It is a *noble* thing to see thy *face* [3]

---

[1] In the scene of her birth described below, she is born in the form of a little boy.
[2] The scenes are carved on the walls of the second terrace, at a place to which
the public had access.
[3] Lit., " thy front " (*hat*, which also means first, prince).

when *thou dost join thyself* [1] to My Majesty in all grace ! Thy dew impregnates all my members." Then, when the God's Majesty had accomplished all his desire with her, Amon said to her, " *She who Joins herself to Amon, she the First of the Nobles*, such of a surety, will be the name of the daughter who will open thy womb, for these are the words which came from thy mouth. She will rule with a beneficent kingship over this Whole Land, for my soul belongs to her, and my heart, and my will, and my crown belong to her, that she may govern the Two Lands, that she may guide all the Kau of the living."

Other reliefs show the god Khnum (who fashioned the living on his potter's wheel) making the visible form of the royal child (a little boy) and her Ka.[2] When her time comes, the Queen gives birth, and the Ka and the child are seen issuing from her body. Amon, to whom the twins are presented, embraces them, dandles them, causes the " purifications of birth " to be given to them, and promises them the kingship on the throne of Horus, in the presence of all the gods.[3]

The bastard Thothmes was left far behind. Moreover, there is no sign of him in this scene, nor in those which follow, which relate what happened to Hatshepsut, the " virgin in flower ". Her earthly father, Thothmes I, crowned her Queen during a visit to Heliopolis, by the traditional royal rites (above, p. 123). The ageing King summoned the royal nobles, the Friends, the high officials, into his Throne Room, and presented his daughter to the assembly, holding her in his arms with the ritual gesture of protection.

" This daughter, Khnumt-Amon Hatshepsut, living, I make to take my place. It is she who sits on my throne, and gives orders to the Rekhetu in every place in the Palace. It is she, of a surety, who will guide you. You hear her words, you unite to (carry out) her commands. He who worships her, of a surety, will live ; he who says anything evil, in hatred of Her Majesty, of a surety will die. Now, whoever of you shall hear the name of Her Majesty proclaimed, of a surety will come at once to bear witness to it before the King, as has been done for my own name. For this Goddess is the daughter of a God ; of a surety, the Gods fight for her, and form a guard behind her, every day, by order of her father, the King of the Gods."
The royal nobles heard . . . and they prostrated themselves. The word of the King went into them, and they worshipped all the Gods for King Thothmes I. They went out rejoicing, they danced and made merry. The official statement (*nekheb*) of the royal names of Hatshepsut was drawn up ;

---

[1] With the words of good omen uttered by the Queen when the god visited her, the latter composes the names of the child who is to come—Khnumt-Amon Hatshepsut.
[2] The King, being a god on earth, had the privilege of living with his Ka from his birth, whereas ordinary mortals only joined their Ka on death.
[3] I have described all these scenes in **XXX**, pp. 53–9, and, in summary, in **XXVIII**, pp. 19–24.

the god Amon-Ra suggested to the drafters of the title that they should " compose these names as he himself had already made them ".[1]

Then the Queen is led by the officiant Inmutef into the Great House (*per-ur*), where the pavilions of the two thrones are set up, that she may perform the Rising of the King of Upper Egypt, the Rising of the King of Lower Egypt, the Union of the Two Lands, and the Procession round the Wall, all the rites of the Feast of the Crown, handed down from the time of Menes.[2] Priests, wearing masks of the animal heads of Horus and Seth, falcon and greyhound, set the White Crown and then the Red Crown on the royal brow, and the procession is led by the totemic ensigns which once led Narmer and Menes.[3] Finally, Thothmes I presents Queen Hatshepsut to the Theban Triad, Amon, Mut, and Khonsu, and each deity welcomes her and compliments her at length. Thoth, pen in hand, writes down many Sed-feasts for the Queen in advance, and communicates the glorious accession of Hatshepsut to the Great Ennead. The Queen receives the embraces of the gods, and henceforward enters the position, more divine than human, of Pharaoh.

We should note that in this official description of the coronation nothing is said of the Queen's husband, Thothmes III. This is an answer to the systematic silence which he had maintained regarding his wife in the first years of their reign. Things had gone against the husband, and the wife was paying off the score. This is what makes one suppose that the Queen had these scenes carved after a *coup d'état* by the legitimist party. The title of King was left to Thothmes, but he was relegated to the background, and the Queen came to the fore.

Her apotheosis lasted only a few months. About the end of the year 6 of their reign, the texts of her birth and coronation were hammered out, and the figures of the Queen were completely obliterated. The names of Thothmes I and Thothmes II (his other bastard son) were substituted for those of Hatshepsut and Thothmes III, who were dispossessed of the throne. Did this restoration of masculine power coincide with military expeditions, for which a woman seemed

---

[1] From the words uttered by Queen Ahmasi on seeing Amon.
[2] Above, pp. 123.
[3] For all these scenes, cf. **XXX**, pp. 79–113 ; **XXVIII**, pp. 24–8.

unfitted ?   It is possible. for hardly had Thothmes I and II ascended the throne, when they led the armies into Nubia and Mitanni. Then Thothmes I died. Thothmes II called in as collaborator, not Hatshepsut, but her despised husband, Thothmes III. This dual government lasted until the death of Thothmes II, about the year 9 of Thothmes III. Then Hatshepsut came back and joined her husband on the throne, which she held until her death. This is how a contemporary describes the situation on the death of Thothmes II :—

> The King rose to heaven and joined the Gods. His son (that is, his successor,[1] Thothmes III) kept his place as King of the Two Lands ; he reigned on the throne of him who had begotten him. His sister, the Wife of the God,[2] Hatshepsut, did the business of the country of the Two Lands, according to her own plans. Egypt, bowing its head for her, tilled the excellent corn come from the God. She was the cable by which Lower Egypt is hauled, the post to which Upper Egypt is moored ; she was the perfect tackle of the helm of the Delta, the Mistress who gives commands, whose excellent plans give peace to the Two Lands, when she speaks.[3]

The Queen's position was once more what it had been before the coalition of her father Thothmes I with Thothmes II. This is confirmed by the sculptures of the temple at Der el-Bahari, the building of which was resumed by the Queen in the year 9. All the honours go to her ; her husband Thothmes III is seldom depicted, and always in a subordinate rôle. That being so, how is one to explain why Thothmes III recalled Hatshepsut, if not by the triumph of the legitimist party, which must have forced his hand a second time ? Now, this party, of which we have hitherto only been able to guess the presence, actually comes on the scene. We know its leaders, from the reliefs on the temple at Der el-Bahari and the statues at Karnak. They were Senmut, the architect of the admirable works at Der el-Bahari, Karnak, and Luxor, and steward of the domains of Amon-Ra, Nehsi, the Director of the Seal and chief treasurer, Thuti, the chief of the House of Gold and Silver, and Hapusenb, the First Prophet (high-priest) of Amon, the Director of all the Prophets of Upper and Lower Egypt, a kind of Pope of the official church, and, at the same time, Vizier, holding all civil and religious powers in his hands.[4]

[1] This is also the interpretation of Sethe and Breasted.
[2] On this title of the Queens, see below.
[3] The biography of Ineni, in **XVII**, ii, § 341.
[4] **XVII**, vol. ii, §§ 290, 363, 369, 389.

The Queen's party was, therefore, the Amon party, and shows the influence of the priests of Amon in the Theban State. Accordingly, the Queen displayed her devotion to the god. It was for him that she sent to the land of Punt the famous expedition,[1] commanded by Senmut and Nehsi, which brought back frankincense-trees which were planted on the terraces at Der el-Bahari.

> The first time that one had the fortune to measure out spices for Amon and to offer the marvels which Punt produces. . . . Her Majesty herself, with her own hands, made of them a scented essence for all her limbs; she exhaled the odour of the divine dew; her perfume reached to Punt; her skin was as if modelled in gold, and her face shone like the stars.[2]

The Queen died after the year 20 of her reign, and was buried by her faithful Vizier and First Prophet, Hapusenb, in a hypogeum hidden behind the cliff against which her great temple is built. Two empty sarcophagi have been found there, those of Thothmes I and of Hatshepsut.[3] The mummy of Thothmes I, taken from its sarcophagus, was among those which were crammed by the priests of the XXth Dynasty into the pit found at Der el-Bahari. That of Hatshepsut has not been identified among them. Egypt has not given us the remains of its greatest Queen; perhaps the body fell victim to the violence of the anti-feminine party.

These dynastic disputes are still far from being cleared up, and Egyptologists have different opinions about the part played by Thothmes II and Thothmes III by the side of Hatshepsut,[4] but all agree on one point—that the high-priests of Amon fomented these intrigues, giving their support to one competitor or the other and withdrawing it in turns. However this may have been, after Hatshepsut's death, her temple was abandoned to the fury of iconoclasts, the tombs of her supporters, Senmut, Nehsi, Thuti, and Hapusenb, were ravaged, and her husband Thothmes III, alone at last, set out in the year 22 for the famous Syrian expeditions (1479), which gave Egypt the empire of the Near East.[5]

---

[1] **XXVIII**, pp. 36–9, pl. ii and figs. 5–6.

[2] **XX**, vol. ii, p. 245.

[3] Davis and E. Naville, *The Tomb of Hatshopsitou*, 1906.

[4] E. Naville, who cleared and published the temple of Der el-Bahari, is far from accepting the order of events which Sethe and myself obtain from the texts quoted. Maspero regards Thothmes III as a nephew of Hatshepsut, younger than herself. With Breasted, I think that Sethe's reconstruction of the facts is, in its general lines, acceptable.

[5] See *From Tribe to Empire*, pp. 269 ff.

The priests of Amon gained all round ; the booty collected in these twenty years of warfare increased the wealth and influence of the god and his clergy tenfold.

2. *Reaction of the Kings. The Heresy of Akhenaten* [1]

Soaring fortunes sometimes have to halt. The triumph of Amon-Ra had one such check, lasting about twenty years, from 1370 to 1350, a century after the brilliant intervention of his priests at the court of Hatshepsut. For a short time Egypt witnessed such things as it had never seen before— Amon-Ra denied by his son Pharaoh, his priests driven from their temples, and Thebes abandoned by the Court, in favour of a new god, Aten, and a new capital, Akhetaten or Ikhutaten (Tell el-Amarna).

This episode lasted for a period, often called that of the Heretic Kings, covering the reigns of Amenophis IV Akhenaten and his successors, Saakara, Tutankhamen, and Aï. The names of these four have been struck off the official lists, although their monuments are many, and include some of the most beautiful and interesting in Egypt. There was, therefore, a political and religious crisis, brought about by the high-handed, desperate, but finally fruitless attempt of certain Pharaohs to free themselves from the growing domination of the priests of Thebes.

Thothmes III and his immediate successors, Amenophis II, Thothmes IV, and Amenophis III, were conquerors, who can really be called Emperors of the East. Their Empire stretched from the Upper Nile to the Euphrates. Having learned from the Hyksôs invasion, and being compelled, in order to preserve their frontiers, to pursue the invader into his distant retreats, they conquered peoples and made treaties of alliance, ruling Nubians in the South and Semites and Mitannians in Hither Asia, and treating Babylonians, Assyrians, Hittites, and Cretans as friends or allies. By contact with such diverse races, the ideas of the Pharaohs were widened ; an administration made for the narrow limits of Egypt, with its seat at Thebes, at the foot of the throne of Amon-Ra, seemed small, and unfit for the government of the world. A new spirit took hold of the Pharaohs, inspiring a broader policy and a

[1] For the whole episode, cf. **XXVIII**, p. 47.

religion which was less exclusively national, less formal, and more universally human.[1] But how were they to break with the august traditions of centuries, without coming into conflict with the sentiments and interests of the faithful guardians of religious institutions, and especially of the priests of Amon-Ra ? To conciliate the priests, the Kings heaped treasures, lands, and slaves on the temples of Thebes, but by this very action they were working for the ruin of Amon.

The breach with tradition was already marked by a first innovation—the Mitannian marriages. Scruples regarding purity of Solar blood, complicated calculations of dynastic rights, according to the decree of heirship on the mother's side, all the centuries-old jurisprudence of the royal family, yielded to political necessities when the Pharaohs decided to take Mitannian princesses as their Great Royal Wives.[2] Thothmes IV married the daughter of Artatama, King of Mitanni, and she was treated as the true Queen of Egypt, where she bore the name of Mutemuia. Amenophis III, at the height of the glory of the Egyptian Empire, took into his harem first the sister and then the daughter of Dushratta, King of Mitanni, but his Great Royal Wife was Tii, who was not " born " at the Court, a foreign lady, whose father, Iuya, was probably a Syrian.[3] Their son, Amenophis IV, took as his Great Wife Nefertiti, as the Egyptians called Tadukhipa, Dushratta's daughter ; she, having been sent to Egypt to marry Amenophis III a few days before his death, married his son instead.[4] It is therefore clear that the Solar blood was very much diluted in the veins of the Pharaohs of the end of the XVIIIth Dynasty. They were the sons of Aryan or Semitic women, from whom they also inherited certain religious tendencies. It was a great shock for the priests of Amen. They tried to gloss over the brutal facts by obtaining from King Amenophis III that, on the walls of the Temple of Amon-Ra at Luxor, the dynastic miracle of the divine birth should be repeated, figure for figure and word for word—

---

[1] Cf. *From Tribe to Empire*, pp. 295 ff.

[2] Cf. *From Tribe to Empire*, pp. 290–2.

[3] This is the conclusion drawn by Elliot Smith from the examina on of Iuya's mummy.

[4] See the articles of Erman, Evetts, and P. Jensen, in **XII**, xxxv (1890), pp. 112–14.

Amon visiting Queen Mutemuia, as he had visited the daughter of the Sun, Queen Ahmasi. Of this carnal union Amenophis III was born, as Hatshepsut had been born.

The desire of the Kings of the new race to be emancipated from Amon and his priests threw them into the arms of the priests of Heliopolis, and took them back to the cults of the Old Kingdom. This change was facilitated by the frequent and lengthy stays of the Court at Memphis and in the cities of the Delta, in order to prepare for military expeditions and to govern the Syrian provinces. A return to a special devotion to the Sun, Ra, appears as early as Thothmes IV. Besides, the Sun was the chief god of the royal families of Hither Asia to which the Pharaohs now went for their wives. The son of Amenophis II was not born of a royal wife. Like his illustrious grandfather, Thothmes III, he led the obscure and idle life of a royal bastard, being mainly given up to hunting lion and other game in the Libyan desert, west of Memphis, and making high speeds in his chariot, " with horses swifter than the wind, accompanied by one or another of his servants, unknown to everybody."

At the hour of the siesta, the prince and his companions used to rest by the side of Harmachis (the Great Sphinx),[1]

in that sublime place of ancient days, near the (Gods) Lords of Babylon and the road of the Gods, west of Heliopolis. There lies the very great statue of Khepri (the Sphinx), in that place, rich in souls and greatly feared, over which hovers the soul of Ra. . . . Now, one day this befell : the royal Prince Thothmes arrived at the hour of noon. He sat down in the shadow of the great God, and sleep and dreams took hold of him, at the moment when the sun is at its height. His Majesty perceived that the august God was speaking to him with his own mouth, as a father speaks to his son.

" See me, behold me, O my son Thothmes ! It is I, thy father Harmachis-Khepri-Ra-Atum. I give thee my kingship over my land, at the head of the living. Thou shalt wear the White Crown and the Red Crown over the land of Geb. Thine is the land in its length and its breadth, (all) that the eye of the Lord of All [2] illuminates ; (thine) are the provisions of the Two Lands and the great wealth which comes from every foreign country."

After these ravishing promises, the god uttered his desire ; he complained that he was sunk in the sand of the desert, which was overwhelming him.

" Come to my help, since thou art my son and my protector ! "

The Prince woke up ; he understood the promises of the God, and kept silence in his heart.

Later, when he became King, Thothmes IV cleared the

[1] The Great Sphinx of Gizeh, the image of Ra in his form of the rising sun, Harmachis. The Babylon in question was a place near Heliopolis.

[2] An epithet usually reserved for Osiris, but also applied, under the New Empire, to Ra, Amon, etc.

Great Sphinx of the sand which was stifling it, and built between its paws a chapel, the back of which is a block of granite on which the story of the prophetic dream is engraved. In this way he revealed to his people the miracle by which Ra-Harmachis had made him King.

Under Amenophis III, the great temple-builder, the special cult of the Sun, Ra-Harakhti, as distinct from Amon-Ra, regained importance.   The glorious star which caused the universe to live was now designated by a name which was not new, but was given a singular importance—*Aten* of the Day, that is, the Solar Disk, from which the light of day proceeds, a name which in its form recalls Adonai, the " Lord " of the Syrian cities, the Adonis of Byblos.   In the Hymn to Osiris quoted above (p. 98), Aten is invoked ; and this is how two directors of works of Amenophis III sing the praises of Ra, under the name of Amon, greeting the star of day in accordance with the new worship of the royal family.

Adoration to Amon, when he rises as Harakhti, from Seth and Horus,[1] Directors of the Works of Amon.   They say :

" Hail to thee, fair Ra of every day, who dost rise in the morning without ceasing, Khepri, who never tirest of thy labours !   Thy rays are on (our) heads, one knows not how.   Gold does not shine like thy rays.   Thou art Phtah, (for) thou dost model thy own flesh [2] ; thou art thy own creator, not having been created.   Unique in kind, he ranges over Eternity, on the ways, with the millions (of men) whom he leads.   Thy brightness is as the brightness of the sky ; thy colour shines more than its colour.   When thou sailest in the sky, all faces watch thee ; when thou walkest in the mysterious region (*iment*), the faces pray to thee. . . .   When thou givest thyself (to men) in the morning, they prosper ; when thou sailest in all thy majesty, the day passes quickly ; (and yet) thou dost go thy road, millions, hundreds of thousands of *itru* [3] long.   The measure of thy day depends on thee. . . . Thou dost accomplish the hours of the night in the same way ; they hasten for thee, and thou dost not halt in thy labours.   All eyes look at thee ; but thy labours do not cease when thou dost rest (at night).   Thou wakest to rise, in the morning, and thy brightness opens the eyes of the beasts.   When thou dost rest in Manu (the Mountain of the West), then they sleep as if they were dead.   Hail to thee, Disk (Aten) of the Day, who dost create mortals and make them live, great Falcon with the feathers of many colours . . . who creates himself, and is not begotten, Horus the Elder (dwelling) in the heart of Nut (the Sky), to whom acclamations are made alike when he rises and when he sets ; who models the creatures of the soil, Khnum and Amon of men ; who conquers the Two Lands, from the great to the small, august mother of gods and men, craftsman great-souled and unwearying in endless creation ; valiant shepherd who pastures his

---

[1] They were two brothers, equally favoured by Amenophis III.
[2] Phtah is the modelling god, the patron of artists and craftsmen.
[3] A measure of length. Cf. p. 445.

flock, who is their fold and makes them live. . . . He is heat when he wills and coolness when he wills ; he wearies bodies, and he embraces them (to revive them). Every land prays when he rises every day, to adore him." [1]

Do we not hear in this hymn the echo of the Solar teaching of Merikara's father (above, p. 242) ? Echoes from the past and hymn of the new age were only the prelude to a mighty voice, which would proclaim the worship of the Sun, but dissociated from Amon—the voice of Amenophis IV Ikhunaten, or Akhenaten.

When he ascended the throne, the man who was to be the Heretic King and break with the official church was barely fifteen years old. The statues and reliefs portray him as a stripling of medium height, with slender bones and delicate modelling, which afterwards became rounded and effeminate—a hermaphrodite figure, with prominent breasts, wide hips, and thighs too much curved, which makes one suspect a morbid nature, with some pathological flaw. This character is accentuated by the curious look of the head. In contrast with the very gentle oval of the face, the dreamy, rather oblique eyes, the slight curve of the long, fine nose, and the soft, sensual mouth with its prominent underlip, the skull is huge, being at once round and receding, with a hydrocephalic development towards the back of the neck (see Pl. XII, 1).

So the mixture of the Aryan blood of the princes of Mitanni with that of the Theban Pharaohs, further complicated by the Syrian descent of Tii, resulted in this refined, but degenerate individual, who had no physical resemblance to the vigorous scions of the ancient stock, but seemed much rather the last of a race. [2]

When this youth ascended the throne, he lived for some years under the patronage, if not under the guardianship, of his mother, Queen Tii. [3] The few monuments dating from the

---

[1] British Museum Stele 826 ; Pierret, **IV,** i, p. 70 ; Birch, **XIV,** *Transactions,* viii (1885), pp. 144 ff. ; cf. **XLVIII,** p. 9.

[2] The body found in the secret burying-place of Queen Tii, which was in a sarcophagus bearing the name of Amenophis IV Akhenaten, quite fits the physical characteristics and probable age of that King. The head in its fleshless state presents the prognathism and occipital development of the portraits. Dr. Elliot Smith therefore identifies it with Akhenaten (*The Royal Mummies,* 1912, p. 51).

[3] All the important texts about Akhenaten will be found in H. Schaefer's small treatise, *Die Religion und die Kunst von El-Amarna,* 1923 ; cf. A. Weigall, *The Life and Times of Akhnaton,* 1910.

first four years of his reign already announce the vocation which called him to the service of Ra. Crowned at Hermonthis, the Heliopolis of the South, he began, on the occasion of the Sed, by building an obelisk, not for Amon, but for Ra, in Karnak itself, the sacred domain of Amon. Many fragments still remain, including two blocks of pink granite, adorned with reliefs, in which the King presents an offering to Amon-Ra, the King of the Gods. So far, there is nothing in the scenes and figures which is not customary and traditional ; but the text introduces us to surprising projects. There the King takes the title of " First Prophet of Ra-Harakhti ", a thing without precedent. It was fairly bold to set himself up as the opponent of the First Prophet of Amon, that very powerful dignitary of the royal administration, who had, in the case of Phtahmes, under Amenophis III, been at the same time " Director of all the Prophets of the South and of the North, Director of the City of Thebes, and Vizier of all Egypt ".[1] As prophet of the Sun, the King made arrangements to erect an obelisk at Karnak to " Harakhti, in his name of Shu, who is Aten ". This title given to Harakhti was new. It, too, indicated that a new doctrine was being developed ; it gave the Solar theory a metaphysical meaning (the fusion of Ra, Harakhti, and Shu as gods of heaven ?) and a material meaning (the solar disk Aten being the true name and visible form of Ra).

In a monument of the beginning of the reign we see Aten of the Day. He has a falcon's head on a man's body, and above is a great red disk, adorned with an Uræus in profile. This is the traditional image of Harakhti under his new name, " Shu who is Aten." [2] But we also have a new representation of Aten—falcon's head and human body are gone, and there is nothing but a great red disk, seen from in front, with the Uræus in the centre of the lower edge ; from the disk long rays spread out fanwise, terminating in hands, which hold the signs of life and strength, or rest on the face and embrace the body of the King and Queen. Already, in the time of Amenophis III, it had been said of Amon-Ra, " Thou art the unique one, thou hast many arms, thou dost direct thy arms towards him whom thou lovest " ; but none had ever presented the metaphor in material form, or depicted a god

[1] **XXVIII**, p. 50.   [2] **XII**, lv (1919), p. 11.

PLATE XII

1. AMENOPHIS IV AKHENATEN
Alabaster (Louvre)

2. NUDE STATUETTE FROM
EL-AMARNA
(University College, London)

3. CHAIR OF TUTANKHAMEN
Wood, plated with gold, enamel, and
coloured glass (Cairo)

4. STATUETTE OF QUEEN
NEFERTITI
Painted limestone (Berlin)

[face p. 320

emitting rays and arms of light. Henceforward, on all monuments of the Aten period, the disk with arms would supplant the winged disk of Harakhti ; it became the official seal of the monuments of the new faith (Fig. 63).

As early as the year 4 of his reign, the King manifested his emancipation from Amon and his priests by radical measures. Amon was no longer the dynastic god ; Thebes, his city, was supplanted as the capital by a new city. Half-way between Thebes and Memphis, nor far from the present Beni-Hasan, on the right bank of the Nile, a fertile plain, which no King or god had yet colonized, offered a favourable site. At this spot, which the Arabs call Tell el-Amarna, the King founded the "Horizon of Aten", Ikhutaten or Akhetaten. The territory, 6 miles long and 3 wide, was marked off by boundary-stones, fourteen of which have been found on the two banks of the river, and consecrated to Aten. The inscriptions of the stelæ, which run from the fourth to the sixth year of the reign, announce the construction of temples for Aten, palaces for the King and Queen, a tomb for Mnevis, the sacred bull of Heliopolis, and hypogea to be dug for the royal family and the Court in the rocky cliffs of the Arabian plateau, which were reached by deep wadys.[1]

That Thebes and the Valley of the Kings were thus abandoned for the city and hypogea of Akhetaten is an indication that a revolution had taken place. The King had broken away from Amon and his priests, whose hostility is evident, although we only know their attitude from a few utterances.[2] To leave no doubt of the breach, the King took a new name, which should define his new moral personality. Instead of "Amon is satisfied" (Amen-hetep = Amenophis), he henceforth called himself *Ikhu-n-Aten*, or *Akhenaten*, "Glory (or, Pleasure), of Aten." The King naturally

[1] There is a good description of the new capital, Akhetaten, in C. Lagier, *L'Égypte pittoresque et monumentale*, 1914, pp. 96 ff.
[2] In the tomb of Rames, Vizier (but not high-priest of Aten) in the Aten period, is a mutilated inscription, in which the King complains of the hostility of the priests of Amon. "By the life of my father Ra . . . (the words) of the priests are more perverse than the things which I heard in the year 4 . . . more perverse than the things my father and grandfather ever heard." This brings us back to the ancient opposition between Amon and Ra, before their forced fusion, and at the same time shows us that the breach with Thebes probably began about the year 4 of the reign.

appointed himself the prophet or spokesman of Aten, and a doctrine (*sebait*) was built up, of which very remarkable expositions are preserved in the tombs of el-Amarna (see the

Fig. 63.—Akhenaten addressing his Followers at el-Amarna.

Hymn, below, p. 325). The King gave his wife a new name ; *Nefert-iti* (" the Fair One comes ") was now called *Nefer-neferu-Aten,* " Aten is the Fairest of the Fair." His daughters were named " Slave of Aten " (*Baket-Aten*), " Beloved of Aten " (*Merit-Aten*), and the like. His sons-in-law changed their names, and the future King *Tut-ankh-Amen* (" Living Image of Amon ") was for a time called *Tut-ankh-Aten* (" Living Image of Aten "). Akhenaten preached the good tidings himself :—

" He spends the day in instructing me, so great is the zeal with which I practise his teaching," says one of his courtiers, named Tut,[1] and another, May, repeats : " My Lord gave me advancement, because I practised his teaching. I heard his voice without ceasing. My eyes saw his beauties every day, my Lord, wise as Aten, making Justice his pleasure ! How the man prospers, who hears your teaching of life ! " [2]

Indeed, May declares, " I was only a *nemhu* (man of free estate) by my family, but my Master raised me up (made my fortune). I was a man without fortune ; he gave me men, a city, provisions ; he made me a proprietor." [3]

[1] Davies, *Rock Tombs of El-Amarna,* vol. vi, 15.
[2] Ibid.. vol. v. 2.   [3] Ibid., vol. v, 4.

And in the tombs of Tell el-Amarna we find only scenes of festivities, gifts of necklaces, jewels, and red gloves of honour to right-thinking courtiers, whose rejoicings make the roofs of the palace ring, while the people, loaded with like gifts, join in the enthusiasm of the great and in the general gaiety.[1]

At Thebes, and wherever the supporters of Amon dared to resist, life was less cheerful. The city of Amon had lost its god and its very name, for it was now called the " City of Shining Aten, the Great (God) ". Amon and his divine wife Mut were outlaws. The persecutors of the memory of Hatshepsut had shown an effective method of destroying the physical and divine life of a god or a king, namely, to destroy his sculptured image, to efface his name on monuments, to forbid the god to manifest his form or his spirit to men, to suppress his services of offerings, and, in brief, to annihilate his existence on earth and in heaven. Georges Legrain, who cleared the chaos of the ruins of Karnak with such admirable skill, and knew all its secrets, tells us that the movement against Amon assumed the dimensions of a veritable religious persecution.

" At that time, the images of Amon were everywhere forbidden or destroyed by the King's command. Few monuments, tombs, statues, statuettes, or even small objects escaped mutilation. At Thebes, wherever the fanatics found the name of Amon they destroyed it. Gradually, as success increased their ardour, not only the name of the great Theban god went, but also those of Phtah and Hathor ; and all the gods would have had the same fate if Amenophis had stayed at Thebes. They climbed to the tops of obelisks, they went down into the depths of tombs, to destroy the names and images of the gods. There were in the temples groups in which the Ancestral Kings were represented by the side of Amon, their arms entwined in his with filial respect. The iconoclasts vented their rage on the divine figure and obliterated every trace of it, while they respected that of the sovereign." [2]

When Tutankhamen restored the persecuted cult, this is how he describes the effect of the persecutions :—

---

[1] See Lagier, op. cit., pp. 104–5, on the festival in honour of the divine-father Aï.

[2] Legrain, " Thèbes et le schisme de Khouniatonou," in *Bessarione*, xi (1906), p. 17.

The supplies (of the temples) were forbidden. The land was as in the time of Chaos. . . . The temples of the Gods, (abandoned) from Elephantine (to the Delta), fell on an evil hour. Their sanctuaries were ruined, and became (deserted) heaps of earth; the storehouses were as if they no longer existed; the buildings became thoroughfares. The country was in decline. The Gods turned their heads away from this land. . . . If one called upon a God, to obtain his advice, he no longer came (to the call); if one besought a Goddess, she, likewise, no longer came at all. Their hearts were disgusted with their bodies [1]; they allowed creation to die away.

Of the fate of the priests the text says nothing, but it is very probable that they were expelled, outlawed, or reduced to slavery. The lower employees, " male and female slaves, singers, dancing-girls, were transferred to the King's House and inscribed for service in the Palace." The eternal properties (*hetep-neter*) of Amon-Ra thus returned to the Treasury; the fields of the god were once more the Fields of Pharaoh. The priesthood of Aten did not succeed to the inheritance of the priests of Amon. The King, as we have seen, was the First Prophet of Aten; therefore the administration of the goods of Aten was under his direct authority, and this appropriation of the property of the temples shows us what lay beneath the religious revolution, the economic and political objects of the rupture. The power and wealth of Amon had become so great that the control of the throne went to the bolder—the King or the First Prophet of Amon. This time, it was the King, reformer and revolutionary, who won the day; but two hundred and fifty years later the priests' turn would come, and they would take possession of the kingship.

Religious reform and anticlerical policy (in the true sense of the word) would not by themselves explain such an upheaval, which challenged the most august traditions in the country most attached to tradition. In reality, as I have explained in *From Tribe to Empire*,[2] this experiment in a more or less strict monotheism [3] was imposed by the needs of the time; it served the interests of Pharaonic imperialism. Egyptian expansion on the Upper Nile and towards the Euphrates necessitated certain measures applying to all the nations of the Empire alike. A sun-god could be the bond between the Egyptians and other peoples, standing above all

---

[1] That is, their mutilated statues.   [2] p. 300.
[3] They avoid mentioning any god but Aten.

other deities. His symbol was easy to understand, his natural supremacy would be accepted by all, and Pharaoh should be his sole prophet and interpreter—such was the new doctrine, which pressed the Pharaonic theory to its last logical conclusion, and had already been set forth in the *Teachings for Merikara* and in those of Sehetepibra. Religion and kingship were merged, as in ancient times, but the King alone knew and understood the god, and represented him among men. Now, this divine kingship was that of Ra, the god of heavenly justice. It soared far above the democratic religion of Osiris, who was still tolerated by the doctrinaires of Akhetaten, but no longer mentioned by name. The Osirian privileges to which the people attached such importance, the paradise of Osiris which made up for the social inequalities and miseries of earthly life, were held of no great account in the circle of the King. Akhenaten's attempt was, first and foremost, an act of political unification, but it was also, in Egypt itself, an effort to restore the King to his privileged position in the religious domain of dogma and ritual, while reducing the temporal power of the priests. Once more it was from the King, and by his favour, that man would win immortality, and not by the universal grace of the Osirian revelation.

And yet there is a generousness in the doctrine of Akhenaten, with a nobility of intentions, a sincere love of nature, an enthusiasm for moral truth, and a respect for material truth, which give his reign and monuments a unique character (Pls. XII–XIII). We shall see later that the art of el-Amarna expressed these tendencies, carrying realism to a photographic degree, as if the necessary and sufficient condition of beauty were truth and lifelikeness. The religious literature of the time bears the same stamp. A feeling of filial tenderness and human brotherliness inspires the famous hymn composed in honour of Aten.[1]

Hymn to Aten

Thou risest beautifully on heaven's horizon, O Aten, initiator of life ! When thou dost form thy circle on the horizon, thou fillest the earth with thy beauties. Thou art delightful, sublime, radiant high above the earth. Thy rays envelope the lands and all that thou hast created. Since thou

---

[1] The most complete text was found at el-Amarna, in the tomb of King Aï, the third successor of Akhenaten. See *From Tribe to Empire*, pp. 298–9. A shorter hymn has been given above, p. 36.

art Ra (creator ?), thou winnest what they give and thou bindest with bonds of thy love. Thou art far, but thy rays are on the earth.

When thou dost rest in the Western horizon, the earth is in darkness, as if dead. Men sleep in their rooms, with their heads wrapped up, and not an eye sees another. All their goods, which they have put beneath their heads, could be stolen without their feeling it. Then, every lion comes out of his cave, every snake bites. It is dark as in an oven. The earth is silent; for he who created it all rests in his horizon.

But the dawn comes, thou risest on the horizon, thou shinest as Aten of the Day; the darkness is banished when thou sendest forth thy shafts. The Two Lands make merry. (Men) awake, and leap to their feet; it is thou who makest them rise. They wash their limbs, they take up their clothing. Their hands worship thy rising; the Whole Land sets to work.

All the beasts are content with their provender. The trees and plants grow. The birds fly from their nests, their wings worshipping thy Ka. All the wild beasts leap; all things that fly and all that flutter live again when thou risest for them (cf. Plate XIII, 1).

The boats go up and down the river, for every road is open when thou risest. The fish of the river leap towards thee; thy rays go down to the very depths of the sea.

It is thou who raisest up children in women, and createst the seed in men; it is thou who feedest the child in the mother's belly, who soothest him that he may not weep, who feedest him by the breast, who givest air to animate all that thou makest. When the child comes forth from the womb (of his mother), on to the earth, on the day of his birth, thou openest his mouth that he may speak, and thou dost satisfy his needs.

When the fledgling is in the egg, a chirping in the shell, thou givest him breath to make him live. Thou givest him strength in the egg, to break it; he comes out of the egg to chirp . . . and he runs on his feet as soon as he comes out.

How numerous are thy works, all that thou hast created and all that is hidden, O thou, the unique God, to whom none is equal! Thou hast created the earth according to thy heart, thou all alone, with men, cattle, and every wild beast, all that exists on earth and walks on its feet, all that is in the air and flies upon wings, and the foreign countries (*Khast*), Syria (*Kharu*) and Nubia (*Kush*), and the land of Egypt (*Kemt*).[1] Thou settest each man in his place, creating what is needful for him, all with their inheritance and their property, with their languages, differing in words, their forms different too, and their skins different (in colour), for thou hast divided the foreign peoples.

Thou makest the Nile in the Lower World, and bringest him (to earth) where thou wilt, to feed the men (of Egypt). Thou art the Lord of them all, thou hast cared for them, the Lord of this Land, who risest for it, the very powerful Disk of the Day. And for distant peoples (too), thou dost make that whereby they live. Thou hast set the Nile in the heavens also, that it may come down to them, and beat the mountains with its waves like a sea, to water their fields in their lands. How excellent are thy designs! There is a Nile in the heavens for the foreign peoples, and for all the beasts of the desert that go upon feet, and there is also the Nile which comes from the Lower World for the land of Egypt.

Thy rays give milk to every territory, and when thou risest they live and grow for thee. Thou makest the seasons of the year, to hold all that

[1] For the importance of this passage from the point of view of Egyptian imperialism, see *From Tribe to Empire*, pp. 299–301.

PLATE XIII

1. PAINTED PAVEMENT FROM A PALACE AT
EL-AMARNA

2. A FAMILY OF THE THEBAN PERIOD
Painting on stuccoed stone
(Unpublished ; Musée Calvet, Avignon)

thou hast created, winter to cool them and summer (to warm them). Thou hast created the distant sky, to rise in it, and to look down from there on what thou hast created, thou all alone. Thou comest in thy form of living Aten, thou risest radiant, thou goest away and returnest. Thou drawest millions of forms from thyself alone—the nomes, the cities, the country-sides, the ways, the waters. Every eye beholds thee above it, Disk of the Day above the earth. Thou art in my heart; there is no other that under-stands thee, except me, thy son . . . issued from thy flesh, Akhenaten.

V

THE GOVERNMENT OF EGYPT BY THE GODS

Akhenaten's revolution left a profound impression on Egyptian art, but religious and political institutions retained no trace of it. After about fifteen years of a reign which went by, in the eyes of his subjects, like a glittering incomprehensible pantomime, the King vanished, struck down by a strange malady which hollowed the features of his face but bloated his misshapen body. He did not have the mere time to accomplish a work which needed many years. Then came still shorter reigns. He left only daughters, and his two sons-in-law, Saakara and Tutankhaten, reigned, the first for two years and the second for six or seven. Under the latter the inevitable reaction occurred. At the very beginning of his reign he returned—willingly or otherwise ?—to the worship of Amon. Going backwards along the road taken by Amenophis IV Akhenaten, he forswore the name of Aten, and instead of *Tut-ankh-Aten,* " Living Image of Aten," he called himself henceforward *Tut-ankh-Amen,* " Living Image of Amon," while his wife, the Heretic King's own daughter, had to follow the example of her husband who had returned to the fold of Amon (Pl. XIV, 3).

About the year 4,[1] a solemn decree restored Amon and the other gods to all their privileges. In a preamble, Tutankhamen announces that " he re-establishes all that was ruined among the eternal monuments ; he drives the lie far from the Two Lands, and everywhere re-establishes the truth ". There follows the account of the persecution under-gone by Amon, of which we have seen the text (above, p. 324).

---

[1] An approximate date. The last known year of the reign is the year 6, and the figure 6 is too long to go into the place at the beginning of the decree, where there is a lacuna.

" But, after days had gone by over these things, His Majesty rose on the throne of his fathers, and governed the lands of Horus. The Black Land and the Red Land were under the supervision of his countenance, and the whole country bowed before his Spirits."

Then the King, returning to Thebes, and taking up his residence in one of the palaces of the Thothmes, considered means of restoring the honours and fortune of his father Amon. Only one way occurred, or was suggested, to him—to do for Amon much more than all that had been done for him before. The statues and state barges which had been destroyed were, by the King's order, recast and rebuilt, and so embellished that Amon now needed thirteen bearers instead of eleven, and Phtah needed eleven instead of six. So both gods and priests benefited by the change.

His Majesty caused monuments to be made for all the Gods, and made their images in real mountain gold. He rebuilt their sanctuaries, as eternal monuments. He established their divine offerings in daily services, to supply their services of loaves on earth. He gave more than had existed before, since the time of Ra and the Ancestors. He consecrated the priests and prophets (choosing them) from the children of the Great of their cities and from the sons of people of known name. He filled their workshops with slaves and prisoners of war. . . . He doubled, tripled, and quadrupled the goods of the temples, in electrum, gold, lapis lazuli, turquoises, precious stones, cloths of royal linen, byssus, oils, face-paints, frankincense, resin, beyond numbering. . . . His Majesty purified the male and female slaves, the singing-girls, the dancing-girls, who had been transferred to the King's House and whose services had been inscribed for Pharaoh's palace. They were henceforth set apart and consecrated [1] to the Father of all the Gods. . . . So, all the Gods and Goddesses of this land, their hearts are joyful. They give eternity, long years, life, wealth, all things, for the nostrils of Tutankhamen. [2]

This decree is deceptive, like so many other historical inscriptions, when it speaks of the gratitude of the gods and priests to Tutankhamen. For all the munificence of the King who had returned to the official religion, the rage of the priests of Amon, recalled from exile in person or inheriting the rancour of their predecessors, was not content with material compensation. Their prestige demanded that they should once more have the King under their control. We must not forget that the First Prophet of Amon directed the other priesthoods, which had also suffered at Akhenaten's hands.

---

[1] A formula of the ancient charters of immunity.
[2] G. Legrain, " La Grande Stèle de Toutankhamanou," in **IV**, xxix, pp. 162 ff.

PLATE XIV

1 WORSHIP OF OSIRIS WITH ISIS AND OF RA-HARAKHTI WITH MAAT
Door-top, Tomb of Neferhetep
Painted limestone (Brussels)

2 SEKHMET IN HER SANCTUARY   3 AMON-RA AND TUTANKHAMEN
Granite (Karnak)   Granite (Louvre)

THEBAN GODS OF THE NEW EMPIRE (XVIIIth DYNASTY)

[face p 328

They joined forces; the people favoured the reaction, glad to return to the private worship of Osiris and to enjoy the Osirian privileges once more; lastly, the military class, ashamed of serving Pharaohs who had lost the Syrian provinces,[1] supported the restoration of Amon by force. A general named Horemheb,[2] whom we find in Akhenaten's reign growing up at Memphis, far from the Court, remained in the background behind Tutankhamen and his successor Aï, but finally, about 1345, he had himself raised to power, and received the crown at Thebes, from the hands of Amon.[3]

Horemheb brought to the restoration of Amon the weight of his authority and military force. He proceeded to make a general inspection of Egypt, to bring back order and justice—that is, he re-established the old order of things, in favour of the priests and soldiers, while putting down abuses of justice and protecting the people against the exactions of undisciplined soldiers and dishonest tribunals.[4] That done, he took up the broken dynastic tradition. The king-lists make him the immediate successor of Amenophis III, as if nothing had happened in Egypt since the reign of that King. There is no word of the passing supremacy of Akhenaten; the years of the reigns of the Aten-worshipping Kings are put down to Horemheb.[5] The memory of the heretic and his successors, who were tainted with heresy although they abjured it officially, was banned, and persecuted even in the next world. The dreadful days of el-Amarna were nevermore mentioned, save in periphrases in which the King who called himself the " Darling Son of Aten " became the " Vanquished One of Akhetaten ".[6]   The tombs prepared at Akhetaten for King Akhenaten and his family were emptied. By the piety of his son-in-law Tutankhamen, the body of the reforming King was saved from profanation, conveyed to the Valley of the Kings at Thebes, and buried in a secret place with his

---

[1] See *From Tribe to Empire*, pp. 302 ff.
[2] Horemheb first built himself a tomb in the necropolis of Saqqarah, while the school of art of Akhetaten flourished ; cf. **XVII**, vol. iii, §§ 1 ff.
[3] **XVII**, vol. iii, §§ 22 ff. ; cf. **XII**, xliv, p. 35.
[4] Stele in the temple of Karnak, the most important legislative document left by the Pharaohs, but deplorably damaged. **XVII**, vol. iii, §§ 45–57.
[5] This appears from the great inscription of Mes. In the same way, Louis XVIII reckoned the years of his reign from the death of Louis XVII, appropriating the interval of the Revolution and Napoleonic Empire to himself.
[6] Inscription of Mes. See also the hymn to Thebes, below, p. 330.

mother Tii.[1] Tutankhamen himself, despite the guarantees which he gave of his conversion, was consigned to a secret place, which was found in 1922 by Mr. Howard Carter, excavating for Lord Carnarvon.[2] The place was heaped with the furniture of the palaces of el-Amarna, marvellous specimens of a new art with a fresh inspiration. The capital Akhetaten, suddenly deserted, fell to ruins. To-day it is rising, under the excavator's spade, in the actual state in which it was left by the great nobles and artists who lived at the Court of the heretic royal family.

Horemheb wanted to take all the glory of the restoration to himself. He seems to have devoted a special hatred to Tutankhamen, robbing him of all his monuments, inscriptions, and statues. Even on the decree restoring the authority of Amon, the name of Tutankhamen has been hammered out and replaced by that of Horemheb.

The Kings of the XIXth Dynasty adopted as their political residence Pa-Rameses in the Delta. But Thebes was still the religious capital. The papyri of the XIXth Dynasty extol the revived glories of Thebes and the supremacy of Amon, more dazzling than ever.

PRAISE OF THEBES AND ITS GOD AMON [3]

Thebes is holier than any city. Water and land began to exist there. . . . (All cities) are founded after her true name [4]; they are called " cities " after (her) name, and they are placed under the watch of Thebes, the Eye of Ra.

The Wicked [5] broke loose from Thebes. She is the mistress of cities, mightier than any city. She gives the country to one single Master by her victory, she who wields the bow and holds the spear. Near her there is no fighting, for her might is too great. Every city takes pride in her name ; she is their mistress, being more powerful than they.[6]

This is (the order) which issued from the mouth of Ra. The enemy of Ra is reduced to ashes, and all belongs to Thebes—Upper and Lower Egypt, heaven and earth, the Lower World with its shores, its waters, and its mountains, and all that is brought by the Ocean and the Nile. All that existed for Geb grows for her, and all belongs to her in peace, wherever the Sun goes round. Every land pays tribute to her as a vassal, for she is the Eye of Ra, which none resists.[7]

---

[1] Davis, *The Tomb of Queen Tiyi*, 1910, pl. xxx.
[2] Carter and Mace, *The Tomb of Tut-Ankh-Amen*, vol. i, 1923.
[3] A. Erman, **XLIV**, p. 365, from a papyrus of the time of Rameses II, published by Gardiner in **XII**, xlii, pp. 12 ff.
[4] One name of Thebes was *Nut*, The City, *par excellence*.
[5] Probably the heretics of Aten.   [6] **XLIV**, p. 364.   [7] Ibid., p. 373.

Amon, thy name is great, and thy will is heavy; mountains of bronze cannot withstand thy will. . . . The earth shakes when he makes his voice heard, and all men fear his power. . . . He is the Master of fields and domains; his is the fore-arm (cubit) by which the stones are measured; it is he who stretches the line (for foundations), who founds the Two Lands, the temples, and the sanctuaries. Every city lies in his shade. . . . He is hymned in every sanctuary, and every place keeps his love always.[1]

The Nile rolls beneath his feet; he is Harakhti in the sky; his right eye is the day, his left eye the night. It is he who leads men on every road. . . . The field is his wife whom he makes fertile; his seed is the fruit-tree; his emanation is the corn.[2]

Happy is he who comes to die at Thebes, the abode of Justice, the place of Silence. . . . Evil-doers come not here, into the places of Justice. . . . Happiness to him who comes to die here ! He will be a divine soul ![3]

Not only security for the living and salvation for the soul are found at Thebes, but also, the priests say, the very government of Egypt and the world. Let us see this theory of the *Theban theocracy* which brings all the gods of Egypt into a divine " triumvirate ", composed of the gods of the three historical capitals, with Theban Amon at their head :—

All the Gods are three—Amon, Ra, and Phtah, who have no equals. (Of this triumvirate) the name [4] is hidden, being Amon [5]; Ra is the head; Phtah is the body. Their cities on earth, established for ever, are Thebes, Heliopolis, and Memphis, for eternity. When a message comes from heaven, it is heard at Heliopolis, it is repeated at Memphis, for the God with the Fair Face (Phtah), and it is made into a letter, written in Thoth's characters, [6] for the city of Amon. The answer is given at Thebes, and an order goes out from there. . . . (It is Thebes) which must slay or let live. Life and death depend on Thebes, for all beings. (Nothing exists) save Amon, Ra, and Phtah, together three.[7]

Who, then, governs Egypt, and even the world ? It is no longer the King alone, with the aid of his Vizier ; his decisions are submitted to the council of the gods. Every " message " from heaven to earth is considered at Heliopolis, for Ra is the thinking head of the trinity ; it is repeated and put into writing at Memphis by Phtah, conceived as the concrete image of the God among men, with the help of Thoth, the scribe of the gods ; but the decision lies with Amon, the hidden soul which rules the universe. Amon alone causes the divine thought to be put into execution as a decree of life or death.

The government of the gods, exercised by the priests, began

---

[1] Ibid., p. 367.   [2] Ibid., p. 372.   [3] Ibid., p. 373.
[4] i.e., the Soul, the Spirit.   [5] *Imen* (= Amon) means " hidden ".
[6] The hieroglyphics, which Thoth invented.
[7] " Unity-Trinity " ? Ibid., p. 371. Cf. **XXIX**, pp. 127–9.

to play an important part in the temporal administration. It was no longer a matter of solemn intervention of the gods in certain difficult situations, at critical moments in the history of the people—the enthronement of Hatshepsut and Thothmes III, the oracular prediction of the accession of Thothmes IV, or the support of the usurpation of Horemheb. These were purely political acts, *coups d'état* which profoundly affected the dynasty, and had their repercussion on society, but did not tamper with the mechanism of the royal administration. From the XIXth Dynasty onwards, on the other hand, we find the gods intervening more and more in private affairs, and giving advice to individuals. The usual procedure was for the statues of the gods, carried in their barges, on the shoulders of the priests, in the course of a solemn procession, to indicate their wishes by signs. If a person favoured by the gods (or priests) supplicated or questioned the statue as it went by, it would stop before him, and incline its head in assent.

This is what happened, under Rameses II, to an officer of the Mazoï ; by the favour of Isis, he obtained advancement in his career.[1] In the year 14 of the same reign, a priest named Pasar, who had made a complaint regarding a field, obtained a sign of assent from the statue of the deified King Ahmes I as it passed him, and it was confirmed by the priests who carried the barge ; this won him his case.[2] Here, then, we see the beginnings of a kind of appeal to priestly justice. The popularity of the gods and the influence of the priests gained by it, but at the expense of the royal authority and lay justice. The gods of the temples interfered in worldly matters by expressing *particular wishes*, not, as before, in the public interest and by general measures of government. So things were making ready for a transition from human monarchy to priestly theocracy. Soon the Kings, who had allowed such encroachment on their rights, would be supplanted by the priests.

This development was precipitated by the disasters which came falling upon Egypt at the end of the XIXth Dynasty and in the course of the XXth—the invasion of the Peoples of the Sea (through Phœnicia and through Libya), and the

---

[1] Petrie, *Koptos*, pl. xx. Cf. Erman, **XLV**, p. 234.
[2] Moret, " Un Jugement de Dieu sous Ramsès II," in **III**, 1917, p. 157.

final loss of the Syrian provinces.[1] On the one hand, the last
Ramessids could only hold their own with the aid of Nubian
and Libyan mercenaries (Mazoï and Meshau), or Shardana,
who had come with the Peoples of the Sea. Rameses III
(1200–1169), for example, settled them in " tens of
thousands " in the cities of the Delta, where they soon made
themselves at home.[2] On the other hand, the same papyrus
which tells us of this military colonization of Lower Egypt
by foreigners gives us an inventory of the property owned by
the temples of the three great cities, Thebes, Heliopolis, and
Memphis, where a member of the divine Triumvirate had his
seat, and a list of the taxes paid by their subjects. Here, as
it is summarized by its latest editor, Herr A. Erman, is
this " inventory " of priestly Egypt, at the end of the reign
of Rameses III.

PROPERTY OF THE TEMPLES

	Thebes.	Heliopolis.	Memphis.
Men	81,322	12,963	3,079
Livestock . . .	421,362	45,544	10,047
Gardens . . .	433	64	5
Fields	591,071 acres	108,927 acres	6,916 acres
Boats	83	3	2
Building-yards (?) . .	46	5½ (sic)	—
Villages . . .	65	103	1

CONTRIBUTIONS PAID BY SUBJECTS OF TEMPLES

Gold	114 lb. 5 oz.	—	—
Silver	2,200 lb. 3 oz.	117 lb. 10 oz.	19 lb. 10 oz.
Copper	5,281 lb. 3 oz.	252 lb. 13 oz.	—
Clothing . . .	3,722 pieces	1,019 pieces	133½ pieces
Thread	761 lb. 8 oz.	—	—
Frankincense, honey, oil .	1,047 pots	482 pots	—
Wine and must . .	25,405 pots	2,383 pots	390 pots
Amount in silver of con-signments sold . .	723 lb. 9 oz.	391 lb.	28 lb. 6 oz.
Grain	309,950 sacks	77,100 sacks	37,400 sacks
Vegetables . . .	24,650 bundles	4,800 bundles	600 bundles
Flax	64,000 bundles	4,000 bundles	—
Birds taken with the net	289,530	37,465	—
Oxen	866	98	15½
Geese for the fisc . .	744	540½	135
Wooden boats . .	82	8	—

In this table[3] we have evidence that the priesthood of Amon

---

[1] From Tribe to Empire, pp. 336–49.   [2] Ibid., pp. 347–8.
[3] **XL,** pp. 340–1.

far outdid both the others in wealth, greed, and ambition.
The policy of the priests of Amon, after a momentary check
from the Heretic Kings, was now triumphant.

VI

THE KINGSHIP IN THE HANDS OF PRIESTS AND MERCENARIES.
FOREIGN INVASIONS OF EGYPT

From the time of Rameses II onwards, the First Prophet
of Amon was the highest personage in the royal
administration.[1]

We happen to know how Rameses II chose the First
Prophet Nebunnef, in the year 1 of his reign. The King had
already marked out this man, who was at the time First
Prophet of Onuris, at Thinis, and of Hathor, at Denderah,
and Director of all the Prophets of all the gods, from Thebes
to Thinis ; but Nebunnef was only nominated after Amon
had uttered an oracle. The King " presented to the God the
names of all the officials of the Court, all the prophets, and
all the great ones gathered in his presence, at Karnak. The
God was not satisfied with any, save Nebunnef, when the King
had spoken his name ". After Amon had thus made his
selection, Rameses II went to Thinis, and told the story to
Nebunnef, ending with the words : " You are now the First
Prophet of Amon. His two treasuries and his double granary
are under your seal. The Temple of Hathor will be under the
rod (of your son, who will there hold) the office of your
fathers, in the post where you were yourself." The whole
Court and the Thirty (Judges) acclaimed the King and the
Prophet. Then " His Majesty gave his two signet-rings of
gold and his sceptre of gold to Nebunnef, hailed as First
Prophet of Amon, Director of the Double Treasury and the
Double Granary, and Director of the Soldiers and all the
Craftsmen of Thebes." [2]

We see the extent of the powers which fell to the First
Prophet. Soon they would be like the hereditary property of
one family, favoured by Amon and by the Kings.

[1] A list of the Prophets has been made out by W. Wreszcinski, in *Die Hohen-
priester des Amon*, 1904.
[2] Sethe, " Die Berufung eines Hohenpriesters des Amon unter Ramses II,"
in **XII,** xliv (1907), p. 30.

1. RAMESES II
Granite (Turin)

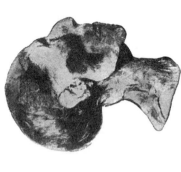

2. RAMESES II PRESENTING AN OFFERING
Schist (Cairo)

3. MUMMY OF RAMESES II
(Cairo)

[*face p. 334*

The " Prince " Bakenkhonsu tells us how he climbed up the degrees of the hierarchy. At the age of sixteen, he was a priest (*uâb*) of Amon for four years ; at twenty, he was a " divine father " of Amon for twelve years ; at thirty-two, Third Prophet of Amon, for fifteen years ; at forty-seven, Second Prophet of Amon, for twelve years ; at fifty-nine, being distinguished by his unusual merit, he was made First Prophet, and held the office for twenty-seven years. Among his attributions he mentions especially the " directorship of all the works of Amon ", in the course of which he built a chapel for Rameses II at Karnak.[1] Bakenkhonsu was perhaps the ancestor of a family of First Prophets, Rome, Roy, and Bakenkhonsu.[2] Roy, who lived from the reign of Merneptah to that of Seti II, tells us :—

" The King granted that my children should be gathered together in a tribe of my blood, establishing them among the prophets who are under my direction. I am the First Prophet of Amon, and my son is established at my side as Second Prophet . . . The son of my son will get the titles of the Fourth Prophet of Amon, Divine Father, Officiant, and Priest." [3] From now onwards the priestly family erected buildings at Karnak on its own account. Near the eighth pylon rose the palace of the high-priests, which was incessantly embellished and enlarged.[4] The district of Thebes was formed into a religious principality, which became a kind of repository of the royal tradition.[5] In twenty-five years, from Rameses III to Rameses IX, six Kings held the throne in turn, but the same First Prophet, Ramesesnekht (afterwards succeeded by his son Nesamon and his grandson Amenhetep) held Thebes. In the temple-pictures, the First Prophet was now represented as of the same height and in the same plane as Pharaoh.[6] His wife shared in his power, presiding over the harem of Amon with the title " First Concubine of the God " ; soon she was to supplant the Queen in one of her essential prerogatives.

---

[1] Statue at Munich, published by Devéria, in **XXXVIII**, vol. iv, p. 276.
[2] Statues of these First Prophets were found by Legrain at Karnak during the systematic clearing of the ruins.
[3] G. Legrain, in **IV**, xxvii, pp. 27, 72.
[4] **XVII**, vol. iii, § 619.
[5] Cf. Maspero, " Les Momies royales de Deir el-Bahari," in **II**, *Mémoires*, vol. i.
[6] **XVII**, vol. iv, § 492.

THEBAN NEW EMPIRE[1]
XVIIIth Dynasty

1580–1557.	Ahmes I
1557–1501.	{ Amenophis I / Thothmes I
1501–1447.	{ Thothmes II / Thothmes III } Queen Hatshepsut, omitted in the king-lists
1447–1415.	{ Amenophis II / Thothmes IV
1415–1380.	Amenophis III
1380–1362.	Amenophis IV Akhenaten
1362–1350.	{ Saakara / Tutankhamen } Four Kings omitted by the king-lists
1350–1345.	Aï
1345–1321.	Horemheb

XIXth Dynasty

1321–1300.	{ Rameses I / Seti I
1300–1234.	Rameses II
1234–1224.	Merneptah / Amenmeses / Seti II / Siphtah } Period of disorders[2]

Period of anarchy. Usurpation by a Syrian.

XXth Dynasty

1200.	Sanekht
1200–1169.	Rameses III
1169–1100.	Rameses IV to Rameses XII

XXIst Dynasty, 1100–945

{ First Prophets of Amon at Thebes (from Herihor) / Smendes and his successors at Tanis and Thebes

XXIInd Dynasty: Northern Libyans[2] at Bubastis		Southern Libyans at Napata
945.	The Sheshonqs / Osorkons / Takelots	5 generations
		Kashṭa

XXIIIrd Dynasty[2]	XXIVth Dynasty[2] at Saïs (Tefnekht)	
745. Petubastis		Piankhi
Osorkon III	718–712. Bocchoris	XXVth Dynasty, 712–661 / Shabaka / Shabataqa / Taharqa. (Esarhaddon, 671) / Tanutamon (Ashurbanipal, 668)

Saïte XXVIth Dynasty, 663–525

663–609.	Psammetichus I
609–593.	Necho II
593–588.	Psammetichus II
588–569.	Apries
569–525.	Amasis
525.	Psammetichus III
525.	Conquest of Egypt by Cambyses
332.	Conquest of Egypt by Alexander
30.	Conquest of Egypt by Cæsar.

[1] Cf. **XXIII**, p. 98.
[2] Periods of great confusion, with parallel, contemporary dynasties. The general classification of the Northern Libyans is still uncertain. Cf. Daressy, **IV**, xxxv, and Gauthier, *Livre des Rois*, vol. iii, pp. 230, 377, 407.

We have seen that, by the dynastic doctrine of the divine birth, Amon-Ra was at Thebes the carnal husband of the Queens, and the true father of the young kings, and the Queen was accordingly called " the Wife of the God " (*hemt neter*).[1] When, under the Ramessids, the Court resided for choice in the Delta, at Pa-Rameses, the absence of the Queen deprived Amon of his spouse. It seems that the wife of the First Prophet was called to play this theoretic rôle, and we shall see the political consequences which ensued under the XXIInd Dynasty. By the end of the XXth Dynasty, the royal heredity, which had lain in the Queen, first by ancient tradition and later through her marriage with Amon, was numbered among the privileges of the family of the First Prophets.

On the death of Rameses XII, the kingship was assumed by the real masters of Egypt. In the Delta, a princely family of Tanis, who were descended from Rameses II and governed Tanis and Mendes (that is, the ancient Eastern Delta), made themselves Kings and were regarded as having lawfully founded the XXIst Dynasty. Smendes, the first Tanite King, and his successors are barely mentioned on the monuments, and are only known through their relations with the First Prophets of Thebes.

At Thebes the First Prophet Herihor took the crown for life. He quite frankly wrote in his first cartouche " First Prophet of Amon ".[2] We can follow him and his children who succeeded to his priestly office all through the hundred and fifty years which the XXIst Dynasty lasted (Pl. XXIII, 3).

For the first time since Menes, Egypt, in a period when she was free from foreign invasion, was divided into two kingdoms—that of the South, comprising Kush, rich in gold-mines and inhabited by negroes, who furnished an excellent militia, and the central valley down to Siut ; and that of the North, which was in the hands of Libyan mercenaries commanded by the Egyptian royal family of Tanis. In theory,

---

[1] A title of Hatshepsut, for example.
[2] **XVII**, vol. iv, § 621.

the moral authority still resided at Tanis, with the descendants of Rameses II. So true is this, that the first son and successor of Herihor was not King, but his grandson Panezem I married the daughter of the King of Tanis and reigned more than forty years over the two Egypts,[1] at first keeping his post of First Prophet of Amon, and afterwards handing it over to his sons. After him the family of Herihor kept the Theban priesthood, and three other insignificant Kings reigned at Tanis. The true power, even without the royal title, was at Thebes.

It was at this time that the power of Amon was made plain to the people, being expressed in a childish form. Every important act of public life was submitted to his statue, which replied by moving its head or making gestures of approval or dissent. The statue was jointed, a priest being especially appointed to work it, and in the sanctuaries hiding-places were arranged in the thickness of the wall, from which an officiant skilfully caused the oracular voice of the god to be heard.[2] The royal decrees were now decrees of Amon. Theocracy had effectively taken the place of human kingship.

Moreover, the First Prophets, whether Kings or not, were genuinely anxious to act as true successors of the great Theban Kings. Whereas the last Ramessids had been power-less to prevent the open and unashamed pillaging of the royal hypogea, Herihor and his successors visited the necropoles of the Valleys of the Kings and Queens, restored the tombs, and, to save at least the royal bodies from destruction, took them from their sarcophagi and laid them in successive hiding-places, and finally in the pit behind the temple of Der el-Bahari, where Maspero found them in 1881, three thousand years later.[3]

Between the two kingdoms of Thebes and Tanis, and within each of them, other princely houses succeeded in making themselves independent. The days of feudalism had returned,

[1] Ibid., § 607.
[2] Ibid., §§ 615, 654, 671, 675, 726, 769 ; cf. the Stele of Bakhtan, and I, xv, p. 140 ; Erman, XLV, pp. 234–6.
[3] Cf. Moret, "Maspero et les fouilles dans la Vallée des Rois," in VIII, N.S., ii (1924), p. 38.

but under the XXIst and XXIInd Dynasties the King hardly intervened to grant immunities ; the leaders of mercenaries took them by force, or in virtue of their authority. The following is the best-known example. At Heracleopolis in Central Egypt, Buyuwawa, a leader of the Tehenu (Libyan mercenaries), seized the power about the time when Panezem I was King. Six of his descendants in succession held the titles " Divine Father of Herishef " (the local god) and " Great Chief of the Mashauasha ".[1] The seventh, Sheshonq I, conquered the Delta and founded the XXIInd Dynasty at Bubastis. The eighth, ninth, and tenth descendants were Kings Osorkon I, Takelot I, and Osorkon II. But Heracleopolis again became an independent principality, ruled as an apanage by royal sons, descended from Osorkon II, bearing the title of " Director of the South, High Priest of Heracleopolis, General of the Army ". We know the names of the princes, from the eleventh to the sixteenth, who continued the line of Heracleopolis, till the year 39 of Sheshonq II.[2]

Here we should note the persistence of local traditions. After the fall of the Ramessids, Egypt fell back, as if naturally, into the divisions which it had presented at the end of the Old Kingdom—Delta, region of Heracleopolis, and region of Thebes, the three great centres of provincial life when the central power was weak.

The Libyan Kings of the XXIInd and XXIIIrd Dynasties of Bubastis were soldiers, whose strength lay in the warlike tribes of the Mashauasha whom they commanded. To make sure of the loyalty of their comrades, now become their subjects, they settled them by the side of the first Libyan mercenaries whom Rameses III had already taken into the Delta.[3] Just as Rameses II had given land to his Egyptian militiamen, so Sheshonq I distributed the best of Pharaoh's

---

[1] The name of the Libyan tribe which furnished the mercenaries, *Máshau, Meshau.*

[2] **XVII**, vol. iv, §§ 745, 789–91.

[3] *From Tribe to Empire*, p. 347.

Fields among his Libyans. He is the King of whom Diodorus relates : [1]

> He chose out the strongest men and formed an army worthy of his great undertakings. In this way he raised 600,000 foot, 24,000 horse, and 27,000 war-chariots. He shared the command with the comrades of his youth, all experienced in fighting and full of daring, to the number of over 1,700. Sesostris had given them the best land, that they might have a decent income and, being secure from want, might give themselves up entirely to war. [2]

Diodorus, who no doubt gives the totals of the old and new militias, returns to the subject elsewhere :

> The third and last portion of the land [3] is allotted to the soldiers and all who are under the command of the leaders of the militia. Being devoted to their country on account of the property they hold there, they will face any danger in war to defend it. . . . The sons, encouraged by their father's example, eagerly train in military duties, and make themselves invincible by their daring and experience.

It is very probable that Sheshonq based the legal status of his Libyans on the model of the militiamen and mercenaries of Rameses II. With this newly organized military force, Sheshonq tried to reconquer Palestine,[4] but he did not long hold Jerusalem, which he had taken by storm in 925. He wished at least to restore the unity of the kingdom, and married his son, Osorkon I, to the daughter and legal heiress of the last of the Tanite Ramessids. The son born of this marriage called Sheshonq II, also became First Prophet of Amon.[5] Thenceforward, Thebes and Upper Egypt, with the dynastic god, joined forces with the Northern Libyans.

This unity was only nominal ; in reality, the whole valley broke up into nomes ruled by local houses, which were in fact independent, although vassals of Bubastis. The First Prophet Shesonq put his name in a royal cartouche [6] ; Thebes became a principality which vied with Heracleopolis. It was at this time that the porticoes of the great court at Karnak were built, in front of the Hypostyle Hall. King Osorkon II, who appears to have been powerful, to judge from his splendid buildings at Karnak and Bubastis,[7] addresses a prayer to the gods that they may give his descendants authority over the

---

[1] Eduard Meyer, " König Sesonchosis als Begründer der Kriegerkaste bei Diodor," in **XII**, li (1913), p. 136. In the place of " Sesostris ", an unidentified king, one MS. gives " Sesonchosis ", Sheshonq.
[2] i, 54. [3] i, 73 ; cf. 94. [4] *From Tribe to Empire*, p. 352.
[5] **XVII**, vol. iv, § 739. [6] Ibid.
[7] The great hall of the Sed-feasts, a precious monument for the study of that festival, published by E. Naville, *The Festival Hall of Osorkon*.

First Prophets of Amon, the leaders of the Mashauasha, and the Prophets of Heracleopolis.[1] Herein he admits the real independence of the three great principalities and the local military leaders. He could only maintain his authority by acts of generosity. The system of immunities recommenced ; Thebes was relieved (*khut*) of burdens, protected, and set apart for its god Amon, no inspector of the King's House could enter its territory, and the people of Amon were exempted and their service reserved for the god.[2]

Under the Bubastite XXIIIrd Dynasty, authority was still more split up. Several military leaders took the title of King ; there were many local wars ; Thebes and Heracleopolis vied for supremacy. At Saïs, the ancient capital of the Western, Libyan Delta, a chief named Tefnekht usurped the kingship and tried to conquer the rest of the Delta.

In the folk-tales, those faithful echoes of historical facts, we have stories of the days of King Petubastis which sound like romances of chivalry. They are all about civil wars and rival princes, Egyptians and Nubians and Negroes. Fine weapons, armour of gold and bronze, tournaments, and challenges were now the chief interest of the governing class, which was feudal once more and, for the first time in Egyptian history, in love with a soldier's life [3]—sure sign that they were foreigners, whose home had been but a few centuries in the Valley.

National unity was, however, partially restored, from about 722 to 670, but for the benefit of newcomers, who descended from a region whence they were hardly expected, Kush, the Ethiopia of the Greeks.

Under its Theban governors, the " Royal Sons " (above, p. 278), Kush had become a second Thebaïd. At Napata, Amon reigned in his sanctuary at the foot of the Pure Mountain (*du uâb* = Gebel Barkal).[4] There the authority of the governors and priests still made itself felt, when the

---

[1] **XVII**, vol. iv, § 745. [2] Ibid., § 751.
[3] **XLVI**, pp. 230–80. These romances are written in demotic, and are translated by Maspero under such titles as *The Fight for the Armour*, *The Fight for the Throne*.
[4] A small isolated crystalline massif, shaped like a table, which rises from the plain on the right bank. Upstream are the pyramids of el-Kuruw.

Valley below the First Cataract was a mere battlefield, contested by Thebes, Heracleopolis, Bubastis, Saïs, and a score of lesser cities. The Egypt of the Upper Nile was rich in its gold-mines and its trade with the Sudan, and strong in its armies of Negroes. These economic and military resources were to make the chiefs of Kush the arbiters of the situation in the Valley.

Who were these chiefs ?   About 800 there appears at Napata a royal family whose monuments for centuries form a solid, consistent mass, compared with the fragmentary evidences of the same period littered about Lower Egypt. These Kings—Kashta, Piankhi, Shabaka, Shabataqa, Taharqa—conquered the Thebaïd and Delta, imposed their authority (from 722 to 670) on Bubastis and Saïs, fought the Assyrians as far as Syria, and played such a big part that Manetho makes them into his " Ethiopian XXVth Dynasty ". They distinguished themselves by their piety to Amon and the other gods.   On all these grounds they were regarded as descendants of the old Prophets of Amon, of the family of Herihor, who were supposed to have left Thebes, being dispossessed by the Bubastites, and taken refuge at Napata.

This hypothesis is now overthrown by recent excavations, made on the site of Napata by Mr. Reisner.[1]   Whereas no royal tomb is known in Egypt after the XXIInd Dynasty, Napata has yielded the sepulchres of all the Ethiopian Kings.[2] The mummies have disappeared, but weapons, jewels, statues, and stelæ with long inscriptions have come in great numbers from the Temple of Amon, the pyramids, and other more ancient tombs.

At el-Kuruw, these tombs cover five generations before Kashta, the first King—that is, from about the year 800. In the oldest tumulus, flint arrow-heads, heavy gold beads, and fragments of pottery were found. This material indicates a race far less civilized than the Thebans of the time, and is just what one would expect of the Libyans.   Moreover, a daughter of Kashta had the title of Great Mistress of the *Temhu*, the Southern Libyans.   We may conclude, with

[1] *Bulletin of the Museum of Fine Arts* (Boston), Nos. 80 (1915), 89 (1917), 97 (1918), and esp. 112–13 (1921).

[2] At el-Kuruw, the tombs of Kashta, Piankhi, Shabaka, Shabataqa, and five previous generations; at Nuri, the pyramids of Taharqa, Tanutamon, Aspalut, and the other Kings of Ethiopia.

Reisner, that these chiefs, the ancestors of the "Ethiopian" Kings, were Libyans, who effected in the land of Kush a conquest parallel to that of the Northern Libyans in the Delta.

Their funerary gear shows them as hunters, warriors, and great horse-lovers. On the stele on which he relates his conquest of Egypt, Piankhi expresses his disgust at finding "Pharaoh's great horses" in the stables of the Delta badly fed, and has the chargers which were brought to him as tribute engraved in outline.[1] In the royal necropolis four horses of Piankhi, eight of Shabaka, and eight of Shabataqa lay beside their masters; their frontlets and trappings of silver-gilt and bronze have been found. The spirits of the war-horses accompanied those of their riders into the next world.[2]

During the first five generations, the Libyan chiefs of Kush remained vassals of their cousins of Bubastis.[3] Kashta, who was the first to take the royal cartouches, probably owed his crown to the Theban priests of Napata, who were interested in maintaining the traditions of the authority of Amon and of Pharaoh, his image on earth. Nowhere did the oracle of Amon take part in the acts of the Government more regularly than at Napata, with these Ethiopian Kings. The choice of the King was determined, not by heredity, but by the intervention of the jointed statue of Amon, who "apprehended", among the "Royal Brothers" marching past him, the candidate preferred by the priests.[4] The King asked Amon's advice for every decision, the interpretation of a dream, a campaign against the Delta, or the excommunication of an impious priest.[5] When, later, Piankhi took Egypt, he visited every temple, celebrating in person, as befitted the priest-born King, daily worship or special feasts. It is probably to these Ethiopian kings that we should refer the half-mythical picture which Diodorus draws (i, 70)

[1] Cf. **XX**, vol. iii, p. 174; there are also horses on the reliefs of the temple at Napata.
[2] Reisner, *Bulletin*, Nos. 112–13, p. 37. There is no trace of chariots; besides, the Ethiopian Kings, unlike the Pharaohs, rode on horseback.
[3] At Nuri the name has been found of a son of Sheshonq II (or III), named Pashedenbast, who was still Commander-in-Chief there (**XIII**, vi, p. 53).
[4] Stele of the Enthronement of King Aspalut, in **XXXVIII**, vol. vii, p. 143. Diodorus (iii, 5) records the custom.
[5] Cf. Maspero, "Annales éthiopiennes," in **XXXVIII**, vol. iii, p. 217, and H. Schaefer, *Die aethiopische Königsinschrift des Berliner Museums*, 1907.

of the strictly regulated life of the Pharaohs, with their food-taboos and their ritual obligations. So the Libyans complied with the exacting demands of the priests, to prove themselves the authentic heirs of the real Pharaohs.

As soon as Kashta had assumed the royal titles, he aspired to restoring sole kingship in the Valley. The Ethiopians took Thebes at the end of the XXIIIrd Dynasty. They respected the power of the lady known as the Divine Worshipper of Amon (below, p. 349), who was at the time Seshepenupet, the daughter of Osorkon III, but Piankhi made her adopt as her heiress [1] Kashta's daughter, Amenardis.[2] From Thebes, the Ethiopians descended northwards.

A stele of Piankhi,[3] in excellent preservation, gives in forty-two lines a picturesque and very instructive account of the campaign which took him to the Mediterranean. The Libyan kinglets had sent, begging him to come and deal with Tefnekht, the King of Saïs, who had conquered the Central and Eastern Delta, and the lower valley as far as Hermopolis, and was forcing the King of Bubastis and the other princes to serve under him. King Piankhi, already master of Upper Egypt down to Heracleopolis, conquered the valley with his army and fleet, recovered the kingdom of Amon city by city, and, like the pious king he was, everywhere celebrated worship in the temples. Thanks to this we have a most precious description of the cities, temples, and worship about 722. Finally, three kings (including Osorkon III of Bubastis) and five princes, not to mention Tefnekht, accepted the overlordship of Piankhi. But the peace was short-lived. In 720 Osorkon III retook Thebes, and Tefnekht's son, Bocchoris, King of Saïs, became so powerful that Manetho gives him the XXIVth Dynasty all to himself (718). The Ethiopians came down the valley again under Shabaka; Bocchoris was defeated, and, according to the Greek tradition, burned alive as the enemy of Amon[4]; and the Ethiopian Kings founded the XXVth Dynasty of Egypt.

Unfortunately, they came to the Delta just when the Kings of Assyria were making their greatest effort to conquer

---

[1] See below, p. 350.
[2] **XII**, xxxv (1897), p. 29.
[3] **XVII**, vol. iv, §§ 796 ff.
[4] Manetho, *F.H.G.*, ii, p. 593; cf. Moret, *De Bocchori Rege*, 1903, p. 17.

Palestine and Syria, and became involved in the intricate game of alliances and rivalries. Taharqa could not prevent Esarhaddon from invading Egypt. In July, 671, Memphis fell, and the Assyrians reinstated the local ruling families under the supervision of governors.[1] Soon Taharqa retaliated ; Ashurbanipal went up the Nile, sacked Thebes in 668, and returned in 661. For some years Egypt was an Assyrian province. The last Ethiopian King and overlord of Egypt, Tanutamon, was driven back above the Second Cataract, and the history of the kingdom of Kush ceased to be merged in that of Egypt.[2]

Deliverance came for Egypt from the Kings of Saïs. It is remarkable that in the last centuries of its existence the Delta recovered the balance of power which we have noted in the pre-Thinite period (above, p. 78). The Tanites and Bubastites had first restored the ancient supremacy of the Eastern Delta ; now it was the turn of the Western Delta. Saïs, fallen from its high estate for thousands of years, became the capital again.

Psammetichus I, the successor of the opponents of the Ethiopian Kings,[3] started as a vassal of the Assyrians, but took advantage of their difficulties with Babylon and Elam to drive them step by step from the Black Land. Herodotus, who is a mine of information for this last period of the Saïte restoration, relates that Psammetichus was one of twelve Kings who had divided Egypt among themselves at the time ; an oracle indicated him as the future master of the country, and, having been banished by his eleven rivals, he found supporters in Ionian and Carian mercenaries [4] whom Gyges,

---

[1] Cf. Delaporte, *Mesopotamia*, in this series, p. 262.

[2] After the loss of Egypt, the kingdom of Kush at first kept its prosperity, its theocratic government, and its Egyptian civilization, under Kings Aspalut, Horsiatef, and Nastesen, known from the fine stelæ of Gebel Barkal, and five or six others. A few centuries later, the capital of Kush was transferred to Meroë, above Atbara. The Meroïtic kingdom lasted till the end of the Roman period, but was rapidly Africanized, by the mingling of Egyptians and Negroes. Civilization declined ; hieroglyphic writing gave place to the Meroïtic script, which Mr. Griffith has interpreted.

[3] His father Necho I, King of Saïs, had been killed by the Ethiopians (Hdt., ii, 152).

[4] Hdt., ii, 152–4.

King of Lydia, had sent to Egypt to fight the Assyrians, the common enemies of Lydia and Egypt.

The great characteristic of the Saïte Dynasty was that they fought the Ethiopians and Libyans *with Greek mercenaries*.[1] After the soldiers came the traders. The Saïtes opened the Delta to them. Hitherto the Greeks had lived in separate quarters, something like the Concessions which Europeans obtained in China until the last century ; but after 660 they had permission to go anywhere. Necho II constituted a navy for the Mediterranean trade, and placed a fleet at the disposal of some Phœnician mariners for the circumnavigation of Africa. This latter feat really seems to have been accomplished, although no practical benefit ensued from it, since nobody would believe in it.[2] Under the last Kings, Apries and Amasis, relations with the Greeks developed. Ionians and Carians got permission to settle as far south as Memphis, where they numbered 200,000 souls. Others established themselves along the Canopic Arm and founded the port of Naucratis. There, for the first time, the Greeks were authorized to have a city, with its national gods, elected magistrates, and special laws.[3] Soon the Greeks were able to

---

[1] **XX**, vol. iii, p. 494.

[2] Hdt., iv, 42. In ii, 158 (cf. iv, 39), Herodotus says that Necho made the first attempt to connect the Nile with the Red Sea by canal; his work was interrupted, but Darius I finished it. The canal started north of Bubastis, passed Pithom, and, by the Bitter Lakes, reached the Gulf of Suez (see Map of Lower Egypt). Its length was equal to four days' sailing, and it was wide enough for two triremes to pass. Necho stopped in the middle of the work, being warned by an oracle that " he was working for a Barbarian ". Strabo (xvii, 25) describes the line of the canal across the Bitter Lakes and its sea-mouth near the town of Arsinoë. The traditions which he uses ascribed the first attempt at a canal to Sesostris (Senusert I, XIIth Dynasty), or to Necho. According to his story, Darius I did not complete the canal, having been told that Egypt might be submerged by the Red Sea, which was at a higher level than the country (this argument was brought up in modern times when the project of the Suez Canal was under discussion). The Ptolemies, Strabo says, took the risk, and completed the cutting, building a lock at the sea-mouth.

The line of the canal is still visible. It is marked by five monuments, or stelæ, with inscriptions in hieroglyphics and Persian (cuneiform). That best preserved is the stele of Shaluf, the Persian text of which runs : " I Darius, I am a Persian and I rule Egypt. I ordered this canal to be dug from the Nile (that is the name of the river which flows in Egypt) to the sea which comes from Persia . . . Then this canal (was dug) here . . . I, I ordered this canal, and I said, ' Go, from . . . this canal, to the shore of the sea ' " (J. Menant, " La Stèle de Chalouf," in **IV,** ix, p. 150). Therefore Darius did not abandon the undertaking. Herodotus and Strabo saw the canal working. Maspero places its opening under Rameses II (**XX**, ii, p. 408) ; others, under Senusert I (XIIth Dynasty), on the strength of Strabo's mention of Sesostris (**XL**, p. 31 ; **XXXIX**, vol. ii, p. 22).

[3] Cf. D. Mallet, " Les Premiers Établissements des Grecs en Égypte," in **III.** xii.

live anywhere on Egyptian soil. A colony of Milesians at Abydos, and one of Samians in the Great Oasis, show the extent of Greek penetration in old Egypt. After Libyans and Ethiopians, the Greeks, a new foreign element, from the Mediterranean, entered that melting-pot of nations.

During the last eighty years of the Saïte period, internal peace revived economic prosperity and the love of the arts.

In the course of the three previous centuries, the central government had been split up, but local administration had gone on as before, restoring order and prosperity as soon as there was a respite from the wars of princes. The favoured classes, the priests in the Thebaïd and Kush and the soldiers in the lower valley, had greatly extended their advantages ; but the free peasants and craftsmen (*nemhu*) also benefited by the weakening of the Kings. The popular classes were given, or took, the right of disposing—not only within " families ", among kinsfolk (see above, p. 267), but to third parties—of the fields which they tilled or the trades which they plied for the King, as the eminent owner, or for the priests and soldiers, as privileged tenants.[1] In the Bubastite period, deeds of sale, lease, and mortgage, marriage-contracts, and wills begin to appear, domestic records which bear witness to a comparative emancipation of goods and persons. Private individuals give portions of their land to the local temple, even without the intervention of the King.[2] Real and movable property is transferred, provided that the deeds are properly submitted to the scribes of temples or royal bureaux, the duty is paid, and every transfer of real estate and change of tenant is entered in the State registers. So it became necessary to adapt the hieroglyphic script to practical purposes ; the cursive form (hieratic) was shortened into a rapid, conventional script, which the Greeks called the " writing of the country ", or " of the people ", demotic (cf. p. 9).

Diodorus credits Bocchoris with the codification of the laws regarding these contracts (τοὺς δὲ περὶ συμβολαίων νόμους). Moreover, the emancipation of landed property allowed free men who were in debt to give their creditors a mortgage on their land and earnings as security. Bocchoris is also said to have abolished arrest and enslavement for

---

[1] Revillout, *Précis de Droit égytpien*, p. 206.

[2] **XII**, lvi (1920), p. 57.

debt, made regulations regarding usury, and decreed that in the case of loans, where there was no written contract, the oath of the borrower that he owed nothing released him from all obligations. All these laws brought such relief to the mass of the people that Diodorus not only compares them to the famous *seisachtheia* of Solon, but says that Solon copied that beneficial law from Egypt.[1] Herodotus (ii, 177) declares that Solon was indebted to the laws of Amasis for the regulation that every citizen should make a yearly declaration of his means of livelihood to the authorities, with a view to taxation. Revillout believes that codes of Bocchoris and Amasis really existed; nothing of them has come down, but the demotic contracts survive, the earliest of which actually date from the time of Bocchoris. In any case, the economic liberation of lands and persons would explain the immense popularity of Bocchoris and his reputation as a great lawgiver and a kindly judge, to which the strange legends of his life and his tragic death bear witness.[2]

At the end of the Saïte period, says Herodotus (ii, 177), the prosperity of Egypt was very great indeed. With the wealth which resulted from order and justice, the taste for costly works of art revived. The Ethiopians had already taken up the tradition of great " works of the King ", and built splendid monuments at Karnak and Napata. The royal sculptors had not lost the admirable craftsmanship of the Theban period : the jewels and small objects found by Reisner are very pure in taste, and as orthodox as can be in religious type. For the Ethiopian and Saïte Kings, artists cut stones chosen among the hardest, and loaded bronze with gold and silver overlay. Tomb-decoration and sculpture were inspired by the Memphite masterpieces, two thousand years old.[3] The Pyramid Texts were copied out ; Shabaka reproduced the text of a venerable manuscript, the treasure of the theologians of Memphis, on stone [4] ; the inscriptions aped the archaic language. The creative spirit being absent, erudition made a style for refined tastes. Industrial art also

---

[1] Diod., i, 79. Cf. Revillout, *Précis de Droit égyptien*, p. 206 ; Moret, *De Bocchori Rege*, p. 74.

[2] On the legendary literature of the Bocchoris-cycle, see *De Bocchori Rege*, pp. 34 ff.

[3] G. Bénédite was in favour of the term "Neo-Memphite" to describe Saïte art.

[4] Cf. pp. 79, n. 9, 94.

throve. Amulets and statuettes of bronze and enamelled clay were turned out of moulds by the million, and the works of the great masters were popularized by cheap reproductions which were brought by townsmen and peasants who had made money.

Such are the characteristics of this last period, which should be called the Ethiopian and Saïte Renaissance. As soon as power was concentrated in the hands of energetic or able Kings, the old administration recovered its efficacity, and brought back order, justice, and prosperity, while adapting itself to the necessary development of manners and laws.

The Saïte Kings, who were upstart adventurers of obscure origin, made themselves popular by their democratic laws and their simple, unceremonious ways.[1] None the less, they meant religion to continue to be the pillar of the State. Neither Psammetichus nor his successors abandoned the priestly traditions ; when they recovered Thebes, they made use of the hereditary prestige which lay in the Temple of Amon. Since the Bubastites had taken possession of the priesthood, the real authority had not been in the hands of the usurpers. Popular feeling placed it at Thebes, in what remained of the ancient Court of Amon. There the god's harem of priestesses was directed by a woman who was not, as before, the wife of the First Prophet, but was still called the Wife of the God (Pl. XXIII, 1), and, like the Queens, the " Worshipper (feminine) of the God " (*duat neter*). Was this woman chosen among the survivors of the Ramessid family ? At all events, she ruled Thebes, and had great estates. Since she did not marry a mortal, she had no children, but she adopted a young girl who succeeded her in her political and sacerdotal office. There is no doubt that this was a remnant of the old matriarchal tradition, a survival of the female royal heredity, which had been so powerful as late as the XVIIIth Dynasty. The apparently unreasonable choice of a woman as head of the priests of Amon and governor of Thebes was a confirmation of the most ancient and venerable tradition of the nation and its kings. Psammetichus I did

[1] See the anecdotes quoted by Herodotus, ii, 151 ; 162 ; 172–4.

not hesitate to make use of it to strengthen his authority, as Bubastites and Ethiopians had done before him.

The earliest Worshipper of Amon at present known is Seshepenupet I, the daughter of Osorkon III, of the XXIIIrd Dynasty. The Ethiopians found her at her post when they took Thebes, and forced her to adopt a daughter of Kashta, Princess Amenardis I (Pl. XXIII, 2). Amenardis I chose as her heiress Seshepenupet II, the daughter of Taharqa. When Psammetichus I took Thebes, he found this Ethiopian lady there. He compelled her to accept his own daughter, Nitocris, as her heiress ; a large stele unearthed at Karnak by Legrain gives us a full account of this adoption and of the transmission of property which was the consequence.[1]

On the Stele of Nitocris we find the fine language, imbued with royal and religious tradition, of the great Theban Pharaohs. Psammetichus first speaks, to define his position with regard to Amon :—

" I am his son, the first in the favour of the Father of the Gods, I am he who makes offering to the Gods, whom he has begotten for himself, to satisfy his heart. I have given him my daughter, to be the Wife of the God, that she may (call upon the divine protection for the King) more than those who were here before me, that he may be satisfied with prayers, and that he may protect the land. . . . Now, I have heard say that a daughter of King Taharqa (Seshepenupet II) is here, whom he has given to his sister (Amenardis I) to be the Worshipper of the God. But I am not one who drives an heir from his place, for I am a King who loves justice ; I am a son who avenges his father (Horus), who takes his inheritance from Geb, who unites the Two Portions (of Seth and Horus). So I have given this maiden (Nitocris) to her (Seshepenupet) to be her Great Daughter."

In sixteen days Nitocris went up from Saïs to Thebes, where she was received by Amon in magnificent state. Then Seshepenupet II had an inventory (*imt-per*) made of her real and movable property, which included 33,000 *arourai* of land in various nomes and enormous daily rations of food-stuffs (some reckoned at 2,100 *debenu* in metal value), supplied by the Prophets of Amon, the King, and the temples of fifteen cities.[2]

This " reign " of the Worshipper of the God [3] did not lead

[1] **XVII**, vol. iv, §§ 935–41. On the Worshippers of the God, see Maspero, " Les Momies royales de Deir el-Bahari," in **III**, i, p. 748, and **I**, v, p. 84 ; also Blackman, " On the Position of Women in the Egyptian Hierarchy," in **XIII**, vii (1912).

[2] Stele of the Adoption, published by Legrain, and translated by Erman, in **XII**, xxxv, pp. 16–29. Cf. **XVII**, vol. iv, §§ 935–58.

[3] There were five Worshippers in succession (by adoption), from Osorkon III to Psammetichus III. A sixth, Amenardis II, was designated, but did not reign.

to the abolition of the First Prophet of Amon, but the latter had lost all his old glory. In the time of Nitocris, Horkheb, the First Prophet, ranked below a prophet of the fourth class named Mentuemhet (Pl. XXIV), who was the confidential adviser of the Worshipper, and probably ruled her, since he managed the Thebaïd in practice.[1] In those troubled times, the moral authority of a woman required to be backed by the strength of a man of action. Nevertheless, in quieter times, at the end of the Saïte period, the last Worshipper of Amon took, not only an essentially royal name, " Female Horus " (*Hort*), not to mention the traditional cartouches, but the title of First Prophet of Amon.[2] It was the logical conclusion

FIG. 64.—Libyan Chief.

of the situation. The foreign Kings kept the substance of power for themselves, but they willingly allowed a woman of their family to hold the traditional authority attaching to sacred names.

This last Worshipper of Amon was Ankhnesneferibra, the daughter of Psammetichus III, adopted by Nitocris. She remained in office until the Persian invasion, and saw the end of Pharaonic Egypt. The story of her presentation to her husband Amon has come down to us as follows :—

---

[1] **XVII**, vol. iv, § 901 ; cf. **XX**, vol. iii, p. 386. Mentuemhet was a " Prince " of Thebes.

[2] **I**, v, p. 85. *Hort* is one of the titles of Queen Hatshepsut.

She came to the Temple of Amon-Ra, King of the Gods. The Prophets, the Divine Fathers, the Priests (*uâb*), the Officiants, and the Lay Priests of the Temple of Amon were in her train, and the Great Ones went before. They did all the rites of the going-up of the Worshipper of the God into the temple, with the Scribe of the God and nine *uâbu* of his house. She put on all the amulets and adornments of the Wife of the God and of the Worshipper of the God Amon ; they crowned her with the Two Feathers and the diadem to make her a Majesty (*hemt*) for the whole circuit of the Sun. And her titles were established : " Princess, Very Lovable, Greatly Favoured, Mistress of Charm, Sweet in Love, Majesty of All Women, Wife of the God, Worshipper of the God (fore-name), Hand of the God (name), Endowed with Life, Royal Daughter of the Lord of the Two Lands, Psammetichus II."

And this is how her position in the temple is described :—

After all the rites and ceremonies had been done to her, as they were done to (the Goddess) Tefnet, the first time, there came to her the Prophets, the Divine Fathers, and the Hour-priests of the Temple, every time that she went to the House of Amon, in his beautiful feast of his Rising. She, the Princess, Greatly Praised, Very Lovable, the Regent of all the Circuit of Aten, the Wife of the God, whose pure hands hold the sistra, when she contents Amon with her voice.

The Persian invasion put an end in 525 to the last independent dynasty, and also to the authority of the Wife of Amon. The ancient kingdom of the Pharaohs, descended from totems and gods, turned into a theocracy, and dismembered by priests and foreigners, now, at the point of death, gives us a last faithful image of itself, in the sacred gesture made before Amon by the two pure hands of the Worshipper of the God.

PART THREE

INTELLECTUAL LIFE

RELIGION—ART—SCIENCE

THIS third part will not give a complete account of religion, art, literature, and science, for good monographs already exist on these subjects. Aiming at instruction, the authors of these works have preferred to study the manifestations of the religion, art, and literature of the ancient Egyptians by themselves, and to separate them from social life. Our point of view is different, for we are considering the whole of Egyptian civilization in its general aspect.

The reader of the previous chapters will have seen that the dividing-line which modern people strive to maintain between religious and social facts was unknown in ancient times, and more so in Egypt than anywhere else. There were no water-tight compartments separating the State from religion, the civil services from the priesthood, profane art from sacred art, science from dogma. In Egypt (and elsewhere, at the beginning of civilizations) what we call religious feeling was at the bottom of institutions of all kinds, art, and literary and scientific inquiry, inspiring thought and stimulating argument. The history of institutions which we have reviewed has constantly illustrated this close connexion between religious and political ideas. So, too, the arts of every sort have expressed, in written, plastic, and pictorial monuments, the religious and political condition of the Egyptians in the Thinite, Memphite, Theban, and late periods. We have, indeed, on our way, met the principal gods, summarized essential doctrines, described characteristic monuments, and quoted illuminating works of literature. If we still have to reconsider, in more detail, certain features of religion, art, and literature, it is because in these domains human thought exercises a fertile activity, and quickly takes flight, going further and further from the limited conception which is the starting-point of dogma, plastic art, and literary work. By curiosity, by continuous reflection, by a noble care for technical perfection, the thinker and artist go on for ever improving their creations. There may be halts and retrogressions, due to factors of decay or social troubles, but they seek, and they find, one in his thought and the other in his work, an end in itself. So, after prescribed ritual, there appear, in various degrees of perfection, metaphysical discovery, the exposition and criticism of dogmas, personal piety, and moral scruple. So, by a parallel evolution, architects, sculptors, and painters escape from canons which are only a kind of ritual, and conceive art for its own sake. Writers produce literature, craftsmen create personal methods, and learned men aspire to scientific inquiry.

For the object which I have in view, it is necessary and sufficient, in the following chapters, to point out the relation of religious, artistic, and literary facts to political and social institutions, and then to define, if possible, the historical meaning of the evolution revealed by rituals, dogmas, temples, tombs, statues, paintings, and books.

CHAPTER I

RELIGION

I

THE GOD. LOCAL CULTS

IN Egypt, at all times, the gods lived in intimate relations with men.[1] The society of the divine beings was superimposed on human society, being modelled on the same organization and living by the same means. In reality, men imagined the gods in their own image, and projected idealized beings and leaders on to a higher plane. In theory, however, the gods were on the earth before men, and revealed to their creatures the means of livelihood and the benefits of social organization. In Egyptian tradition, the divine dynasties reigned before the Pharaohs, and the gods were the first inhabitants of the Black Land.

In Part One I have briefly stated the historical interpretation of these legendary data. After the clans had settled in cities and nomes, their ensigns sometimes became the gods of capitals and of provinces. Indeed, the most ancient religious element which we can reach is these deified ensigns of the nomes.[2] Then came the struggles between various populations for supremacy over the Valley ; for us they are summed up in the conquest of Upper Egypt by the Servants of Horus from Lower Egypt. By the side of the ensigns new gods appeared, Osiris, Horus, Upuat, Anubis, and Thoth, who led the kings and warriors of the North, and then the victors installed their gods in the temples. The patron deities of the Servants of Horus did not drive out the old gods. The latter, when their human subjects made alliance with the Horus-worshippers, kept their cities ; those who resisted and were

---

[1] For Egyptian religion, see Maspero, **XX**, vol. i, chap. 2 ; **XXXVIII**, vols. i–ii ; Erman, **XLV** ; Roeder, **XLIX** ; Naville, *La Religion des anciens Égyptiens,* Paris, 1905 ; P. Virey, *La Religion de l'ancienne Égypte,* Paris, 1910. For the deities and doctrines, see Hastings' *Encyclopaedia* and Roscher's *Lexikon.*
[2] See the Table, pp. 54 ff.

conquered surrendered their capitals to the victors ; even then they survived here and there, as the ensigns of nomes or in secondary temples. The result was a most heterogeneous divine community, in which gods from North, South, East, and West lived amicably together, though as varied in name and appearance as the different peoples which went to make the Egyptian people.

By the beginning of the Old Kingdom, the fusion of these divine elements was complete, as was the unification of the human elements of society. The religious map of Egypt can now be drawn from the map of the nomes ; the ensigns of provinces and the temples of capitals enable us to draw up a table of " the gods of the cities and the gods of the nomes ".

This society of the gods was a reflection of human society. In it the family existed, as far back as we can go, but it was, as it were, conventionalized, being reduced to the typical triad of father, mother, and son. At Edfu, for example, Horus had Hathor for his wife and a little Horus-who-unites-the-Two-Lands for his son. At Thebes, Amon reigned with Mut, and their son was Khonsu. Where a goddess was mistress of the temple, she was the head of the family. At Denderah, Hathor relegated her husband Horus to second place ; her son was a little Horus the Sistrum-player. The rights of a goddess in her city were equal to those of a god in his city. The influence of the gods grew in proportion to the wealth of their city and priests, and was subject to the chances of politics, faith, and fashion. Horus, Hathor, Khnum, Thoth, Min, etc., had several capitals, and where they did not reign they were still admitted as " guests " (*herj-ib*, literally " inside ") of the sanctuaries of other deities. The history of institutions has taken us through the stages of the penetration of Osiris [1] and Ra into most cities, and shown us the supremacy passing in turn to the gods of the successive capitals—Horus, Ra, Amon, Phtah.[2] But every god, great

[1] See the enumeration of the sanctuaries of this god in the *Hymn to Osiris* (above, p. 97).

[2] I have related the conquests of Horus, Ra, and Amon. Phtah of Memphis is less known before the XIXth Dynasty, although he always had a prominent rôle, as god of the city of the King's coronation. He had much influence at the

or small, was " Lord " (*neb*) of his own temple, or city, or nome, and treated his neighbour on equal terms. There were differences in rank due to conquest, the favour of a King, popularity, and other circumstances, but theologically there was no substantial difference between one deity and another.

What, then, was the characteristic quality of a god ? The Egyptians have left no dogmatic treatise containing a definition of what they meant by the word " god ". We have to infer it from the characteristics which they attributed to a divine being.

Let us look through the earliest records, the Pyramid Texts, where they describe the transformation of the dead King into a god. When I explained, in dealing with the Memphites, what became of the resuscitated King, I described a god. He comprises a body (*zet*) and a *Ka*. The body serves as a support for the forms of the god on earth ; we shall discuss it later. The " divine and celestial " element is the Ka.

The Ka is a being whose name, expressed in writing by two arms raised in a gesture of protection [1] and worship [2] (Fig. 48, p. 175), is set up on the stand which supports the clan-ensign. We have been able to place the Ka among the most ancient totems or ensigns (Fig. 9, p. 45). In the course of the ages, it developed to the condition of a god, and then the ancient determinative of a god, the falcon on a stand, accompanies his name (Fig. 13, p. 66).

Who will tell us the etymology of this name ? The root *ka* certainly expresses generative force. [3] With a suitable determinative, the phallus, *ka* writes the name of the bull, which symbolizes generation ; the feminine *ka-t* designates

Courts of Seti I and Rameses II, where he was made the father of Pharaoh (decrees given by Phtah for Rameses II and III, in **XLIX**, p. 158) and associated with Ra and Amon in the government of the universe (above, p. 331). After the Ramessids, the political importance of the Delta gave Memphis, " the Mansion of the Ka of Phtah " (*Het Ka Phtah*), preponderance once more ; Phtah is the universal Demiurge in the text of Shabaka. Cf. M. Stolk, *Phtah*, 1911.

[1] To make a being or thing (e.g. a royal pyramid) live, the god Atum " places his two arms behind them, in the form of a Ka, that his Ka may be in them " (*Pyr.*, §§ 1652 ff.). Cf. above, p. 174.

[2] The usual gesture in all religions.

[3] Hence the translation of Ka by " genius ", in the sense of " author of *generation* ".

the female sexual organ [1] and also the cow; the plural *kau* means the foodstuffs which maintain life; and lastly, *ka*, with the sign of the speaking man, means "thought", intellectual power, while with the cartouche it personifies the royal name (*ren*), or the visible and audible image of a mental concept. The texts of the late period tell us that the gods and the King have fourteen Kas,[2] in which are embodied magical power, (physical) strength, glory, wealth, greenness (health), nourishment, nobility, funerary gear (?), wise intelligence, stability, sight, hearing, knowledge, and taste. These "personifications" belong to the old foundation of beliefs, and are found (e.g. in the royal names) as early as the Old Kingdom. We have no one word which conveys the complex and indefinite attributes of the Ka, which is at once primordial substance and universal substance, the source of life and nourishment, the bestower of physical and intellectual powers, a genius (*genitor*), and protector and creator of the race. There is nothing more like the Ka than the *mana* of uncivilized man, which likewise is a concentration of life, strength, nourishment, intelligence, and magic (cf. *From Tribe to Empire*, p. 47).

Like *mana*, the Ka is both collective and individual. In heaven there is a Ka of all the gods, an essential Ka. " Thou art the Ka of all the Gods. Thou leadest them, thou rulest them, thou makest them live. Thou art *God* (*par excellence*) thou art mighty among all the Gods." [3] " Thou dost not perish, and thy Ka does not perish, for thou art the Ka (*par excellence*)." [4] In the Ka dwell all life, all magical force, all power and authority. [5]

Just as *mana* at first exists in every individual member of the tribe, and afterwards more especially in the gods of the clan, so the essential Ka splits up into individual Kas.[6] In respect of every divine being, the individual Ka acts as a father [7]; " they invoke him to protect them from all fear of death " [8]; he ensures health, strength, and nourishment.

---

[1] *Pyr.*, § 2065.   [2] On this subject, see **XXIX**, p. 209.
[3] *Pyr.*, § 1609.   [4] *Pyr.*, § 149.
[5] Cf. above, pp. 159, 197, on the royal command, personified by Hu and the Ka.
[6] Cf. the text quoted above, pp. 181–3.   *Pyr.*, § 372.
[7] *Ka* and *Kau* are placed parallel with the word *father*.   *Pyr.*, § 136 ; *Mastabas*, p. 195.
[8] *Pyr.*, § 63.

When the body (*zet*) of a being joins his individual Ka, this being " perfects perfection and excels excellence " [1]; he is in the condition of the gods. If they are separated, the body remains incomplete, imperfect, subject to destruction, to death. Such will be the condition of men [2] on earth (until, by the power of rites, their body is united to their Ka).

Joined to its individual Ka, the body (*zet*) becomes indestructible ; it is constantly replenished with vital force, magic, and food (*Kau*). It is said of the god that " he lives fair and healthy with his Ka ",[3] that he possesses it as a Lord (*neb ka*),[4] that " he subjugates the Kas, or the victuals ", an expression used for putting under the yoke, ownership, marriage (*neheb kau*).[5] On the other hand, to destroy the power of a god, it is enough " to remove his Ka from him ".[6]

The perfect being thus made up of Zet and Ka manifests himself as Soul (*ba*), Spirit (*akh*), and Power (*sekhem*). He " takes his form of a god " (*iru neter*),[7] and is henceforth called a god (*neter*).

Has this word *neter* any connexion with the collective *mana* of which the Ka reminds us ? There is no doubt of it, if one accepts the results of a delicate analysis due to M. Victor Loret. The hieroglyph *neter* does not represent an axe (as has often been stated), but is a conventional picture of the scaffold or stand on which the clansman carried the emblem of the clan, the totem.[8] The support of the totem became, in writing, the characteristic sign of the god. According to the same theory, the word *neter* is derived from a root *ter* (written as a date-frond), which expresses the annual growth of the date-palm, and, by extension, the regular rebirth of all plants.[9] " For the primitive Egyptian, a god would be one who, instead of growing up and dying like a man or a beast, always remains in the same state." *Neter* is, therefore, the *Eternal One*, or, rather, *he who is eternally the same*, he who

[1] *Pyr.*, § 375, and above, p. 181.
[2] Except for the King, who, as a god, possesses his Ka on earth, and is the " Ka among men " (above, p. 288).
[3] *Pyr.*, §§ 338, 908.   [4] §§ 598, 906, 1215.
[5] § 315.   [6] § 653.   [7] §§ 372–5 (and above, p. 181), § 762.
[8] Loret, " Les Enseignes militaires des tribus," in **VIII**, x (1902), p. 101.
[9] Loret, " Quelques Idées sur la forme primitive de certaines religions égyptiennes," in **VIII**, xi, p. 69. That a god does not die is another result obtained from worship ; hence the Egyptian explanation of the sign *neter*, for which see p. 390 below.

does not die, a definition which in part fits the Ka, as it does the god. I have quoted (above, p. 358) a text in which the identity of " the Ka of all the gods " with " God *par excellence* " is asserted. We must remember, too, that in the earliest script the word " god " is written in another way, by the falcon on a stand (above, Fig. 13, p. 66), a sign which also accompanies the word " Ka ". All these facts, taken together, suggest that the terms Ka and *neter* are derived from a common stock of beliefs. So the analysis of the idea of god in Egypt in the very early period would take us back to a sort of *mana*.

This hypothesis quite fits in with the historical process described in Part II. It allows us to have a better under-standing of the essential character of the Egyptian god at the dawn of known times. Every god of a city has a potentiality, a vital force, which makes even the *neter* of a small town a being of the same nature as his neighbours of the great capitals. In him resides a portion of that " nameless and impersonal force which recurs in each of these (divine) beings without, however, fusing with any of them ".[1] Every divine being has his portion of the Ka, which does not die. Between the different gods distinctions of rank were based on quantity, not on quality, of Ka, or sacred power. The conseqence was that polytheism always existed in Egypt, whatever might be the political authority of Ra, Osiris, Amon, or Phtah.

II

MATERIAL AND SPIRITUAL FORMS OF THE GODS. BEASTS. STATUES. NAMES

The gods did not assume a " real " appearance until they came down from heaven to earth among men, to rule them and to reveal the arts and all useful truths to them—in brief, to civilize them. " In exchange," as the Egyptians said, they received temples, statues, and offerings—that is, worship.

To live among men the god makes himself visible. In what form ? According to the theologians of Heliopolis, he has, in

---

[1] *From Tribe to Empire*, p. 46.

heaven, an indestructible body (*zet*) [1] of iron, the metal of which the firmament is made. Sometimes this Zet is conceived in the shape of a bird, which, living in the sky, seems suited to representing a god. Indeed, the divine Zet has wings and claws like the falcon [2] (which is the written sign for *neter*). But texts and pictorial monuments tell us that in order to appear to men the god can choose between several " manifestations " (*kheperu*). Let us first see the material forms which a god can assume.

Every Egyptian deity can be represented :—

(i) Under the initial form—beast, plant, object, or being of any kind—in which the spirit dwells which will afterwards develop into a god. Such are, the Lopped Trunk (*zed*) of Osiris, the Knot of Isis, the Falcon of Horus, the Dog of Anubis, the Ram of Amon and of Khnum, the Goat of Herishef, the Ibis of Thoth, the Greyhound of Seth, the Crocodile of Sebek, the Cow of Hathor, the Arrows of Neith, the Thunderbolt of Min, etc.

(ii) By a hybrid figure in which the beast or object is combined with a human body. Usually the man's or woman's body is complete from the shoulders down, but the head is an animal's or, in some cases, represents an object, a fetish. Thus we see the bodies of Horus, Thoth, Anubis, Khnum, Seth, and Hathor, with the heads of a falcon, an ibis or monkey, a dog, a ram, a greyhound, and a cow respectively. [3] Less often [4] the human head is on an animal body or a fetish object ; for example, the Serpent Goddess Mertseger and the Zed of Osiris are represented in this way.

(iii) By a purely human figure, from which the beast or fetish has disappeared altogether ; but these recall their old rôle by a detail of costume or adornment, or by some feature of the divine individual. Thus, Osiris leans his back against the Zed pillar, Isis holds her knot in her hand, Amon has small curved horns about his ears, Isis and Hathor have cow's horns on their heads, and the frame of the sistrum which Hathor bears in her hands or on her head is a bucranium. It is generally the great universal gods or those of the capitals—

---

[1] *Pyr.*, § 749.
[2] §§ 250, 463, 1484, 2043.
[3] Good pictures of hybrid and other forms of gods will be found in Maspero, **XX**, vol. i, chap. ii, and, very fully, in Lanzone, *Dizionario di Mitologia Egizia*.
[4] **XX**, vol. i, p. 130.

Osiris, Isis, Amon, Phtah, Geb, Min—who take an entirely human form.[1]

These three presentations mark the stages of the development from spirit to god, and we can date them fairly exactly.[2] In the protohistoric period, the monuments show only totems on stands, in the form of animals, plants, or objects. About the beginning of the Ist Dynasty, human arms grow from falcons, fish, and even from the staffs of ensigns.[3] At the end of the IInd Dynasty the first hybrids appear, human bodies with the heads of the old totems, which have become anthropomorphic gods. From the IIIrd Dynasty onwards, the development towards human form becomes general and gains in speed. The society of true gods living in heaven is created, and in the sanctuaries beasts and fetishes surrender the first place to the new divine beings, born of more highly developed religious ideas.

The hybrid or human figures of the gods were the product of man's imagination. Nature furnished no living specimens of them. The totem-animals and fetishes of earlier times, on the other hand, did really exist among men. So, to give the hybrid figures a real existence, the sculptor, engraver, draughtsman, and painter step in, and represent the gods as they are imagined. The manufacture of an image is a *creation* in which there is as much magic as art. The sculptor is called " he who makes live " (*sânkh*), for he gives a shape life, or " he who begets " (*mes*). In reality, the statue is a " living image " (*tut ânkh*); at least, magical rites make it so, for its mouth, eyes, ears, etc., are opened (*up ra*, etc.), and its arms and legs are loosened, that it may be able to breathe, speak, eat, drink, see, hear, act, and walk.[4] In this form of a statue, a living image, the god consents to dwell among men. The texts tell us that the statues are the gods' bodies (*zet*), and that they " enter their bodies " (*âk neteru m zet sen*).[5] The

---

[1] In the temple of Sahura (Vth Dynasty) there are very curious anthropomorphic figures of the Ocean, the corn-god Nepri, etc., in which the human body is marked with wavy lines or dotted with seeds.

[2] For details, see Loret, **VIII**, xi, p. 88.

[3] Cf. *From Tribe to Empire*, figs. 7, 9.

[4] Below, pp. 395–6. On this subject, see Moret, *Les Statues d'Égypte, images vivantes* (*Bibliothèque de vulgarisation du Musée Guimet*, vol. 41, 1916, pp. 49–87.

[5] See the text quoted below, p. 386. The ritual making of statues, which caused the gods to be born (*mes*), is mentioned among the notable events of reigns on the Palermo Stone ; cf. above, p. 135, n. 1.

rituals, of which I shall speak later, say that it is the soul, Ba, a bird with a human head, which descends from heaven to " animate " the statue. The learning of the priests and the art of the sculptor combine to produce images which should " satisfy the heart of the gods ". It is, above all, important to give each his characteristic attributes and then his names, which are the personal property of each deity. Crowns, sceptres, ornaments, which vary as much as heads, must be

FIG. 65.—Worship of Sebek-Ra as a Crocodile.
Musée Guimet. XIXth Dynasty.

assigned with pious zeal and reproduced with the most scrupulous accuracy, for otherwise the god, unable to recognize his image, would not enter it, and would refuse to live among men.

Neither the beasts nor the various totems, however, disappear from iconography. Down to the end of Egyptian civilization, the nome-ensigns keep the ancient patrons of the clans alive, in their revered traditional form, in the great public ceremonies. Moreover, a great many of the gods like to show themselves to men in the really living form of a sacred animal. The fifth King of the Ist Dynasty, Usaphaïs, built a shrine for the Goat consecrated to Herishef, the Arsaphes of the Greeks, the god of Heracleopolis.[1] According to Manetho, the second King of the IInd Dynasty, Kakau, founded the cult of the Bull Apis, the living image of Phtah,[2] at Memphis, of the Bull Mnevis, the living image of Ra, at Heliopolis, and of the Goat, the living soul of Osiris, at Mendes. Other god-animals are known to us—the Bull Bakha, which represented Mentu, and afterwards Ra, at Hermonthis ; the Goose and Cat of Amon of Thebes ; the Phœnix (heron), the soul of Ra at Heliopolis ; the Ram of Khnum at Elephantine ; the Crocodile of Sebek at Crocodilopolis, etc. Men also worshipped trees, which concealed under their foliage the goddesses Nut and Hathor or personified Osiris (sycamore, fir, olive, cypress).

In all these cases,[3] the whole species to which the beast or plant belonged was regarded as sacred ; but one individual bull, ram, crocodile, or whatever it was, was " chosen and recognized " by certain signs, and then " brought in as the god ", fed, and worshipped in the temples.[4] After its death, natural or deliberately brought about at a certain age,[5] its body was mummified and laid in a magnificent tomb. Then another bull or falcon was " sought ", and when it had been " recognized " it was consecrated in the place of the deceased and made to " go up into the sanctuary ". From the example of the Bull Apis, whose splendid mausoleum (the Serapeum at Memphis) has been excavated at Mariette, we know that these divine animals formed a kind of dynasty. At least twenty-four Apis-Bulls reigned in succession in the Temple of Phtah, between Rameses II and the Ptolemaic period. Whatever importance these sacred beasts may have enjoyed, we must not forget that they were by no means independent deities. Apis was worshipped as the " repeater " (uhem) and " living image " of Phtah [6] ; he was only the reflection on earth of another, who was the true god of the city.

[1] *Palermo Stone* (Schaefer, p. 20), and Petrie, *Royal Tombs*, ii, pl. 7.

[2] The cult of Apis is mentioned on the Palermo Stone.

[3] On the sacred beasts, cf. Erman, **XLV**, pp. 247 ff. ; Virey, *Religion*, pp. 17 ff. Strabo (xvii, 31 ; 38–40) gives curious details.

[4] For Apis, see Hdt., iii, 28 and ii, 153.

[5] On these subjects, cf. Chassinat, " La Mise à mort rituelle d'Apis," in **IV**, xxxviii (1917), p. 33, and Spiegelberg, **XII**, lvi (1920), p. 1.

[6] Epithets of Apis at Memphis.

The other members of the species which had supplied an Apis, Mnevis, or the like, also enjoyed, if not worship, peculiar veneration.[1] According to Strabo (xvii, 40), they were " sacred ", ἱεροί (whereas their chiefs, established in the temples, were gods θεοί). On this matter we have the evidence of Herodotus, Juvenal, Plutarch, and Clement, who express their surprise, and sometimes indignation, at the devotion inspired by these animals. In certain nomes oxen, cows, cats, dogs, ichneumons, snakes, falcons, wolves, crocodiles, hippopotamuses, and rams were venerated. "While alive they are treated as well as can be, and when they die they are mummified and buried in consecrated sepulchres.[2] If anyone kills one of these beasts willingly, the penalty is death ; if unwillingly, he pays a fine fixed by the priests. But if a man kills an ibis or a falcon, willingly or unwillingly, he must die.[3] Yet the people of the next nome have no scruple about eating these animals, and do not regard them as in any way sacred."

This evidence is based on correct observation. Extensive necropoles have been discovered in which the mummified bodies of cats (at Bubastis and Beni-Hasan), crocodiles (at Manfalut and Kom-Ombo), ibises (at Hermopolis and Abydos), dogs, ichneumons, falcons, etc., had been ritually buried, in immense quantities. The mummies of a given species certainly seem to be localized in the nome where a beast of that kind was worshipped in the temple of the capital. Moreover, Herodotus says that mummified falcons were taken to Buto and ibises to Hermopolis from all parts, to be buried beside Horus the Falcon and Thoth the Ibis.[4] We should note that most of the necropoles discovered are late. It is possible that in the Saïte period, which saw a kind of Renaissance, the worship of animals came back into favour in the general return to the traditions of the past. But I do not think that it is right to regard these practices as a late aberration of religious sentiment, as there is a tendency to do. There was, much rather, a reawakening of traditions thousands of years old, forgotten and perhaps misunderstood,

---

[1] On this subject cf. Wiedemann, *Museon*, vi, 2, p. 117.
[2] Hdt., ii, 67, 69.
[3] ii, 65. Cf. Diodorus, i, 83, who relates the murder of a Roman citizen who, on a visit to Egypt, had accidentally killed a cat at Alexandria.
[4] ii. 67.

which prescribed, among other things, that the animal protector of the nome should be maintained in life and after death, and forbade that it should be slain or eaten.[1]

" Who does not know," writes Juvenal, " what monsters are adored by demented Egypt ? One part worships the crocodile, another goes in awe of the ibis, gorged with snakes . . . Cats here, there fish of the river, and elsewhere dogs are venerated by whole cities, but Diana by none. It is sacrilege to violate the leek and the onion, and to chew them in your jaws—how sainted are they whose gardens grow these divinities ! " [2]

Juvenal's indignation makes us smile. He did not know the meaning and historical rôle of those living images, Thoth's ibis. Wazet's serpent, the plant of Upper or Lower Egypt which in other days had meant a clan.

Was not this " degradation " of religious feeling rather a simple-minded, sentimental aspiration to the heroic past, and a return to the oldest gods of the common people and of the nation, whom public piety set up against the rationalist gods imported from Greece and Rome by the Foreigner ? Moreover, the revival of the worship of beasts coincided in time with the practical application of the life which was in the statues of the gods to the government of men, by oracles, intervention in justice, etc.[3] The part played by beasts and living statues is explained by the importance which had been attached from the earliest ages to the " material forms " of the god when he lived in human society.

Among the *spiritual* " manifestations " of the Egyptian god we must include his Name, *his Names.*[4]

The name of a person or a thing, and also of a god, is, for primitive man, an image which is confused with its object. To call a being by his name is to create him, to cause his individual personality to be born (*mes*).[5] To pronounce his name is to fashion his spiritual image by the voice ; to write it, is to draw his material image, and this is especially true in Egypt, where hieroglyphic writing reproduces living beings and objects in line. In a legend which we shall consider later, Ra declares that his name has been spoken by his father and

---

[1] *From Tribe to Empire*, p. 18. [2] *Sat.*, xv, 1 ff. [3] Above, p. 332.
[4] Cf. **XXVII**, pp. 266 ff. [5] See p. 375.

mother, and then hidden in his bosom by him who begot him, in order not to give power (over him to an enchanter).[1] The name is one of the aspects of the Ka (see above, pp. 121, 358) ; it animates the body which it enters. So, to know the name of a being is to have a means of mastering him ; presently we shall see what use the magician could make of the knowledge of a name.

This explains why we have been able to define the character of Pharaonic kingship by analysing the official names of Pharaoh (above, p. 118). It will be concluded that the names of the gods should tell us as much about the inmost nature of their possessors. Unfortunately, their exact meaning is too often uncertain. In the case of local gods which were originally totems, their names had probably once been collective and common to all the clansmen, and did not become individual and personal to the particular god until after the disappearance of the clans. In order to show who and what these gods were, it was considered expedient to add epithets to their name—geographical, indicating their original abode or the temples and cities which they owned, or descriptive, alluding to an attitude of the idol or an attribute, or genealogical, showing their descent from some other deity, or historical, recording some memorable event in their career. An exact knowledge of these facts was required of the initiated worshipper. Every pious man ought to be able to say : " O God N., *in all thy names*, hear me, I speak to thee." [2] As an example, here is a little hymn of the XIIth Dynasty (Louvre Stele C. 20) ; it will be seen that the utterance of the names, local epithets, and attributes of the god seems to have been the chief concern of the worshipper.

To Min-Horus. I worship Min ; I exalt Horus, (the god) who holds his arm high.[3] Hail to thee, Min, in thy apparitions, thou who hast two feathers ! [4] O son of Osiris, born of Isis, Great God in the temple Senut, [5] mighty in Ipu and at Coptos, [6] Horus whose hand is armed (with the spear), [7] Master of terrors, who dost silence the Violent One (Seth), Prince of all the

[1] Below, pp. 371–2.
[2] Addressed to Ra ; Sethe, *Urk ,* iv, p. 943 (XVIIIth Dynasty).
[3] Min, an ithyphallic god, holds a whip with his right arm raised in the air behind his head.
[4] The characteristic headgear of the god.
[5] The sanctuary of Min is mentioned in *Pyr.,* § 1998.
[6] The capitals of the IXth and Vth Nomes, of which Min was the god.
[7] The attitude of Horus spearing the followers of Seth.

Gods, rich in perfumes when thou comest down from the land of the
Mazoï, feared in Nubia,[1] etc."

In spite of its primitive conciseness, this hymn, which was
written about the year 2000, rises far above the conception of
a local god. In it we see Min contaminated by Horus, Son of
Isis, and promoted to a lofty destiny, since he is called King
of all the Gods. How did he rise to the position of a universal
god, without ceasing to be a local god ? That is what we shall
learn from a rapid examination of the metaphysical
conceptions of the Memphite period.

III

THE UNIVERSAL GODS AND THEOLOGICAL CONCEPTIONS

The unrestricted divine power owned by any particular
god led his worshippers to see his influence, not only in the
little happenings of local life, but in the general events of the
world's history. In Egypt every god of a city became, for his
flock, the King of the Gods and the author of the world. But
we seldom hear of the systems imagined by the inhabitants
of one city or another regarding the creation of the universe
by their own deity. The many texts on the subject which
have come down to us bear, with very few exceptions, the
stamp of Heliopolis. The prevalent cosmogonic conceptions
were those elaborated by the priests of the two greatest
cosmic gods, Ra, the Sun, and Osiris, the god of Nature.
Adopted as patrons by the Pharaohs, Ra and Osiris imposed
themselves over all the rest ; they compelled the gods of
Memphis, Thebes, Hermopolis, Coptos, Saïs, etc., to come
into a single theological system and to accept an uniform
ritual. This religious centralization accompanied, and
explains, the political centralization effected by the Memphite
Pharaohs (Pl. XIV, 1).

With the universal gods, general conceptions were imposed
upon the Egyptian mind. These are set forth in great
collections of religious writings. For the Memphite period,
there are the Pyramid Texts ; for the Middle Kingdom,
the Sarcophagus Texts ; for the New Empire and the late
period, the funerary papyri, called the *Book of the Dead.*

---

[1] As god of the city of Caravan-men, Min was worshipped in the desert.

We cannot go into these theological compositions in detail, and I shall simply indicate the great themes which are expounded in them.

We find two subjects of human interest considered : (i) the aspect of the world, its origin, creation, and government, and (ii) the problem of life and death. The Heliopolitan doctrine dealt with the first point ; the Osirian prevailed for the second. In both cases mythical stories, reflecting popular conceptions, preceded, or at least accompanied, the writings of the priests. Mythological literature, which in the case of the local gods is almost non-existent, or at any rate has not been discovered so far, is most abundant on the subject of the universal gods.

A. *The Doctrine of Heliopolis*

In Part II I described the origins of Heliopolis and the development of its political and social influence. We now have to see its prodigious influence on men's minds, through literature, popular and priestly.

Popular fancy surrounded Atum, the local god of Heliopolis, and the Sun King with a number of myths full of realistic features.[1] In them Atum appears as an ancestor, the author of the historical divine family in which the great gods of the universe are collected. As one would expect of a *primordial* creator, Atum alone lived at the beginning of time. Having no female being with him, he produced out of himself a divine pair of children, Shu (Air) and Tefnet (the Void).[2] Of these a second pair was born, Geb (Earth) and Nut (Sky). The last two were represented as closely united, the Sky (the female) stretching over the Earth, but with the Air, Shu, slipping in between them and holding Nut up above Geb (Fig. 45, p. 154). So the elements were separated. It is a cruel division. The Sky covers the Earth all over, but her hands and feet still touch the ground. The Air holds up her star-spangled stomach and bust with his hands in the attitude

[1] The popular or theological episodes of the creation of the world are often depicted on Theban sarcophagi. See Valdemar Schmidt, *Sarkofager* (Atlas), Copenhagen, 1919.
[2] *Pyr.*, § 1248.

later assumed by Atlas bearing the sky. The wild undulations of the earth's surface come from Geb's struggles against Shu, who has taken his wife from him ; he hoists himself up on one elbow and bends a knee, but remains petrified in the attitude, thus forming the mountains, which are called the " Risings of Geb ". From Nut and Geb there were born Osiris (the Nile) and Isis (the fertilized soil), Seth (the desert) and Nephthys. With Atum these four couples formed the first divine family, the Great Ennead,[1] from which other gods issued.

Whereas at Heliopolis popular belief regarded its god Atum as the creator of the world, in this anthropomorphic form, other Egyptians, perhaps the vast majority, imagined the sky, Nut, as a woman, or a cow, from whose belly there issued every day a child, or " a milk calf with pure mouth ", who was the Sun. At a very early date the Heliopolitans appropriated this conception, but transformed it to suit themselves, saying that Atum had made Nut fruitful and was the father of the Sun. " She who is in the sky conceived (the Sun, Ra) ; he who begot him is Father Atum, before the sky was, before the earth was, before men were, before the Gods were born, before death was." [2] For others, the sun Ra was a scarab-beetle (*kheperer*), rolling his ball in the sky. *Kheperer* sounds like the verb *kheper*, " to become " ; the Heliopolitans adopted the scarab as one of the " becomings " of the Sun. *Khepri*, " he who becomes," was the word for the rising sun ; *Ra* was the name of the sun reigning in the zenith ; *Atum* (on account of a root *tm*, " not to be ") meant the sun in the evening twilight, " he who is not " during the night.[3] These popular inventions were developed by sacred art. In the temples the Sun is represented in the form of a child, born at dawn from an opening lotus (Pl. VI, 1), growing from hour to hour as a youth, then, at noon, as a man in the fullness of his strength and crowned with the royal Pskhent, and lastly, as evening approaches, as a figure bending more and more, until he is like a bowed old man, leaning on a staff to hold up his exhausted frame.[4]

---

[1] *Pyr.*, § 1521. Cf. above, p. 154.
[2] *Pyr.*, § 1466, where the child conceived is the deified King, identified with Ra. I have restored the logical meaning to the formula, substituting Ra for Pepi I.
[3] On these three names, see *Pyr.*, § 1695. Cf. below, p. 372.
[4] At Edfu ; cf. **XX.**, vol. i, pp. 89, 161.

Such is the physical appearance of the complex being Khepri-Ra-Atum, who in his Mansion of the Sar at Heliopolis rules his own city and the whole of Egypt. The Heliopolitan texts in the Pyramids describe, in entirely material terms, the business of kingship which the Sun conscientiously performs ; the picture has shown us what were the real occupations of Pharaoh in Memphite times (see Part II, pp. 157 ff.).

The government of the world was no light task, and the popular traditions tell us that the rule of Ra had its troublous times. At every moment, perilous conflicts endangered his existence and his authority. The snake Apophis hid in the clouds and caused " disturbances of the sky " or lay in wait for the barge of the Sun, to swallow it up with all on board, but the glorious might of Ra and the valour of the gods, " the Followers of Ra," dispelled the darkness and drove away the enemy—who, however, was never annihilated.[1] It was the same unceasing war as that waged by other sky-gods, Horus and Seth (see above, p. 69). Their adventures were blended with those of Ra when the Great Ennead ruled over all the temples ; the victories of Horus became episodes in the story of Ra. On the walls of the temple of Edfu there is a very long narrative,[2] which enumerates the campaigns against Seth (Apophis), commenced in the year 363 of the reign of Ra-Harmachis (a composite deity, made up of Ra and Horus of the Eastern Horizon), and the victories won and sanctuaries founded (*mesent*) by the Harpooners, the warriors of Horus (above, pp. 107–11). Other legends tell how one of Ra's eyes fled from Egypt, and was brought back from Nubia by Horus, who is here called Onuris (*Anhert*, " he who brings back her who was far away," namely, the goddess of the Sun's Eye).[3]

This reign, visited at intervals by cosmic catastrophes, ended when Ra perceived that he was growing old and could no longer maintain his authority over gods and men.

Ra still sailed every day in his celestial barge, but his mouth trembled like an old man's, and dribbled on the ground. A goddess full of wiles, Isis, " skilful in words, whose heart was more artful that those of millions of men, and surpassed millions of gods and spirits," had conceived the plan of robbing Ra of his power, by taking from him his Name, which no god knew.

[1] See Lacau, *Textes religieux*, 35 (XIIth Dynasty) ; for the Theban period, cf. *The Book of War against Apophis*, in **XLIX**, p. 98.
[2] **XLIX**, p. 120.   [3] H. Junker, *Die Onurislegende*.

With earth moistened by the fruitful spittle of Ra, Isis made a sacred snake, and set it in the God's path. Ra was bitten, and groaned with pain. He summoned the Council of the Gods.

"When I was going upon the roads, to contemplate what I have created, travelling over the Two Lands which I made, something, I know not what, hurt me. It is not fire, it is not water, and yet my heart burns, my flesh trembles, and my limbs shake." The Gods came in haste, and among them was "Isis with her magical lore, she whose mouth is full of the breath of life, whose spells destroy sickness, and whose words revive those who stifle." Isis said to Ra, "Tell me thy Name, my divine Father, for a man lives if incantation is made with his Name." Ra wished to evade the question, knowing the danger. "I have many names and many shapes. My shape is in every God. Atum and Horus the Younger are named in me. (As for my secret Name), my father and my mother have spoken that Name. It has been hidden in my body, since my birth, that the force of my magical charm may not go over to an enchanter against me." Then he tried to satisfy Isis with other talk, equally vague. "I am he who created heaven and earth, and put the souls in the Gods. I am he who, by opening his eyes, makes the day, and by closing them makes the night, he at whose command the Nile makes its waters flow, and he whose name the Gods do not know. I am Khepri in the morning, Ra at noon, and Atum in the evening."

But this answer did not give the "true Name" of the God; so the poison continued to burn. Isis pressed for the real Name. Conquered by pain, Ra at last uttered it, "I let Isis persuade me. My Name shall go from my body into her body." Then he hid himself from the other Gods, for the Barge of Millions of Years was great. When the time came that "the heart came out", Isis told her son Horus to take note of the God's gift, and the poison was charmed away. So Ra yielded up his heart and his true Name, the secret of his power.[1]

After the gods, men perceived that Ra was growing weak, and rebelled against him. Hearing their hostile talk, Ra called together his council of the gods, namely, his divine Eye,[2] Shu, Tefnet, Geb, and Nut, the fathers and mothers who had been with him when he was still in the primordial Chaos, and had been the first called to life by him, and with them came the god of Chaos himself, Nun. On their advice, Ra sent against men his divine Eye, which took the form of the goddess Hathor; afterwards she was called Sekhmet, the Mighty One, when she had sown terror abroad by massacring men. Drunk with blood, Hathor-Sekhmet did not cease from killing. Ra had to make a magical drink, composed of pomegranate-juice (?) and beer; seven thousand jars of this mixture, poured on the earth, gave the goddess the illusion that she was drinking the blood of men; she got drunk, and forgot her butchery. So the remnant of the human race survived.

[1] **XLIX**, p. 138.
[2] Here the goddess Hathor, the living form of the will of Ra.

All the horrors of revolt and chastisement made Ra weary of power. He told the gods how he was disheartened, and acknowledged his decrepitude to himself. Nun then decided to place Shu, the son of Ra, on his father's throne, to govern men. Ra mounted on the back of Nut, the Cow of Heaven, and henceforth remained alone in the sky, far from the earth and men. But, at the moment of parting, men and Ra made an end of their strife and concluded an alliance.

" Your sins are forgiven," said the Creator to his creatures. Killing (of the guilty) does away with killing (of the rest); thence come sacrifices.[1]

The reign of Shu, Ra's son and successor, was not free from troubles. The sons of Apophis, the Snake of the Clouds, plotted against him and attacked him in his residence Atnub (el-Arish). He triumphed over his enemies, but sickness assailed his body, in consequence of which there was a palace-revolution and Shu fled to the sky. The earth, deprived of its King, was plunged in darkness. Then Geb, the son of Shu and Tefnet, mounted his father's throne. He, in his turn, knew the bitterness of power. He was badly bitten by the very Uræus which adorns the brows of gods and kings, then attacked by a crocodile, and finally rescued by the victories of Ra-Harakhti over the enemies of the light. Re-established on his throne, Geb devoted himself to the practical government of his realm, and caused his scribes to make a list giving the names of the nomes and cities founded or conquered by his ancestors and himself all over Egypt.[2]

Geb was succeeded by Osiris, whose beneficent reign and tragic death have been described. Then Horus, son of Isis, succeeded his father, and founded the line of sovereigns which, through the Servants of Horus, takes us to the human Pharaohs.

So, in spite of gaps, popular tales and magical literature have preserved traditions about the successive reigns of the great gods of the universe. They created gods and men, and organized their empire by establishing the authority of Ra and his family over the gods of the nomes and cities.

---

[1] **XLIX**, p. 142. The end, according to the interpretation of Naville and Maspero.

[2] This account is taken from a divine chronicle engraved on a late shrine found at el-Arish. Cf. **XLIX**, p. 150.

By the side of the popular tradition, we have a priestly tradition, which presents the creation of the universe and of government by the Heliopolitan gods in a wholly spiritual form. The dogmas, the metaphysics of Heliopolis had a decisive influence on the social and intellectual life of Egypt. The numerous texts in which they are preserved belong to the Theban period, or even later times, but the foundation is certainly as old as the Pyramid Texts, in which, moreover, there are very clear allusions to all these conceptions.

The theologians of Heliopolis had made out a complete, logical picture of the creation of the world. First, they described the condition of the universe before the Creation.

At the beginning there was a water, in which floated the inert germs (*nenu*) of every living being and every thing. This primordial ἄβυσσος was called the *Waters born of the Nun*, the *Secret Place of the Nun*. Later it was personified in the form of the god Nun, who was called the father of the gods; but he was a purely intellectual creation. In essence, the Nun is unorganized chaos, nothingness.[1]

In the Nun lived a spirit which was still undefined, but carried in itself the totality of future existences; this was called Tum, Atum. Feeling the lack of a personality, " finding no place in which to abide " (that is, having no definite character), Atum wished " to found in his heart (spirit) all that exists ". By an effort of his will, he stood up out of the Nun, and rose above the water; thereupon the Sun came into being, Light was, and Atum, duplicated and made external to the primordial Water, took the name of Ra.[2]

After Ra, the other gods, the universe, and all living beings were created by the Demiurge Atum-Ra. According to the theologians of Heliopolis, the first divine family was composed of nine members, who constituted the political and religious Great Ennead whose history I have already related (p. 152 ff.).

What process of creation did Atum employ? According to a " physical " explanation, the gods of the Ennead (or all of them) were a *corporeal* development of Atum. The gods are the " members " of the Demiurge, " the totality of existence and living beings is his body "[3]; sometimes the statement is

[1] For references, see my article, " Le Verbe créateur," in **XXIX**, p. 108.
[2] In the Pyramids we find the composite Ra-Atum; §§ 145, 152, etc.
[3] E. Naville, *Todtenbuch*, var., p. 40.

more precise : " The Ennead is the teeth, the lips, the veins, the hands of Atum." [1] This reminds one of the purely material procreation of the gods in popular tradition (see p. 153) ; but we must not be deceived. The gods are also immaterial beings. In the *Book of the Dead*, chapter xvii, we read : " Ra made, from all his names, the cycle of the Gods. *Gloss* : What is that ? Ra created his members, which became the gods of his following . . . He is the god with the great Name, who spoke his members." The text of Shabaka says in confirmation, " The Ennead is also the teeth and lips of that Mouth, which utters the names of all things."

The creation, therefore, was effected when the mouth of the Demiurge had uttered the names of all that exists.[2] I have described the extreme importance of the name, which gives external being to what was before a purely mental concept, and creates it materially, giving it a visible existence, by writing, and an audible existence, by speech. Before the Creation, " no God yet existed ; the name of nothing was known." [3] If the Demiurge was at this initial moment still unknown, undefined, it was because " there was yet no mother for him, who could have made his name, and no father for him, who could have uttered it ". Nothing, therefore, exists until it is *named*.[4] In the Papyrus of Nesmin, the Demiurge proclaims : " I created all shapes, with what came out of my mouth, in the time when there was neither heaven nor earth "—a creation by the *Word* of which we find echoes in the Hermetic writings, Genesis, the Gospel according to St. John, etc.

It was not only at the beginning of the universe that the divine Word was creative. It has never ceased to act on gods, men, and things ; universal life is constantly being supplied with provisions [5] by a continual creation, of which the Word is the agent. This theory is to be read on a block of stone, now weathered, on which the Ethiopian King Shabaka, seized,

---

[1] Text of Shabaka, quoted below.
[2] Cf. " the divine forms issued from the mouth of Ra," *Pyr.*, §§ 800, 1015, 1720 ; " the gods issued from the mouth of Ra himself," Louvre, Stele C.3.
[3] **XLVIII**, p. 129.
[4] Inversely, a man can be killed by the annihilation of his Name, a method employed by magicians. See also what has been said above regarding the mutilation of names in the time of Hatshepsut and Akhenaten.
[5] *Pyr.*, § 162. The bread of the gods is " spoken by Geb, issued from the mouth of the Ennead ".

like all his family, with pious enthusiasm for ancient theology, made the engraver " copy a book written by the Ancestors, eaten by worms and illegible from beginning to end ". The venerable document was " adapted " by the priests of Memphis, who substituted Phtah, the local god of the White Wall, for Atum as the creator of the gods and the world ; but, apart from this honour done to Phtah, which is explained by the position of the monument at Memphis, the text follows the Heliopolitan tradition.[1]

It sets out to explain the working of the creative thought which incessantly animates the world. The vocabulary used is concrete, as is usual among the Egyptians, whose writing, being, like their minds, essentially realistic, is never good at rendering abstractions. The word " Thought " is written as " Heart ", and the word " Word " by " Tongue " ; and, what is more, the rôle of the Heart is personified by a god of the intelligence, Thoth, while that of the Word is played by the god of active realization, Horus. Now that these points have been explained, the theories of the Memphite priests will be better understood.

The Demiurge who created all the gods and their Kas is in this heart and in this Tongue. Thoth has manifested himself in the Heart, Horus in the Tongue, on the part of Phtah. . . . He (Phtah) presides over everybody, and over every mouth, of all gods, men, beasts, reptiles, who live upon what he thinks and what he commands regarding everything, at his will. . .

When the eyes see, when the ears hear, when the nose breathes, these organs make that rise up to the Heart. It is the Heart which makes all that results (the concept, the result of sensation) to come out, and it is the Tongue which repeats (expresses) the thought of the Heart. . . . That is what causes all the Gods to be born (mes), Atum with his Ennead ; and every divine utterance manifests itself in thought of the Heart and speech of the Tongue.

That is what creates the vital forces (kau) and pacifies (?) the harmful forces (?) creating all foods and all offerings by this speech ; creating what is loved and what is hated (by the God, i.e. good and evil),[2] that is what gives life to the just and death to the unjust. That is what creates every work (ka-t) and every art (iaut) which the hands execute. The legs walk, all the limbs move, when the Tongue utters speech regarding what the Heart has thought and regarding what comes forth from the Tongue.

This theory is curious, first of all, because it analyses the working of sensation which (i) provokes thought, (ii) calls the will into action, the will manifesting itself by the

---

[1] I quote the latest edition, Erman's " Ein Denkmal memphitischer Theologie," in *Sitzber. Preuss. Akad.*, xciii (1911). Cf. **XXIX**, p. 121.

[2] See the application of this definition to the King, above, pp. 123, n. 1, 160.

utterance of speech, command, reflection, etc. It is interesting also because it explains at the same time the working of the authority of gods and kings, and its means of expression, which is the verbal command. We understand why an oral or written order of Pharaoh is called an " utterance of words " (*uzu medu*). We see that, in the mind of the earliest Egyptians, an order of the King is equivalent to an act of creation, of the same kind as that of the Demiurge. That is why the royal command is personified by the Ka, the spirit of the race (p. 197).

Other applications of this thesis will be found later on ; the Tongue operates in all domains. We shall see that it creates the offerings of funeral worship (*pert kheru*) and that it makes gods and the dead " come out at the voice " when it calls them.

This manifold activity of the creative Word among the Egyptians shows, moreover, the extent to which magic permeates metaphysics, entering into the creation and organization of the universe and the existence of beings of every degree, and reaching through the whole of social life, wherever the voice of the chief commands and creates. Let us turn back to the text of the Theban period (above, p. 331), when the Trinity-Unity of Amon-Ra-Phtah ruled the world ; its authority is exerted by a message, which simply transcribes the order uttered by the voice of the Demiurge at Heliopolis.

The divine Word rules the universe in another of its aspects. The great universal gods not only created the world ; they organized it and subjected it to a discipline and order which they themselves obey. They are the responsible authors of natural and moral laws. In the Hermetic books, $\Lambda \delta \gamma o s$ means Reason as well as Word. In the Egyptian texts, Ra, the Demiurge, has a beloved daughter and counsellor in Maat, the goddess of Right or Law and Truth, in other words, of Reason. The texts lay stress upon the interdependence of Ra and Maat. Maat, the substance of the Demiurge and merged in him, is at once his life, his daughter, and himself.[1] She is so like him that she constitutes the essential nourishment of the divine beings ; in the ritual of worship, she represents in herself all the spiritual or material offerings which the King, in the name of men, must present to the god.

[1] **XLVIII**, p. 140.

In the pictures in the temples, the god lives perpetually with Maat (Pl. XVI). The hymns which serve as a commentary to the pictures are an anticipation of the lofty speculations of Plato : " The thought of the gods, contemplating Truth, is nourished, and enjoys bliss. And it sees Justice, and Knowledge of that which really is. Such is the life of the gods." [1]

In Part II we saw the consequences of this association of Ra and Maat on the moral development of the kingship. From the VIth Dynasty onwards, Pharaoh felt himself responsible to the Sun after his death. The " Great God " of the sky, who dispenses justice to every being in Egypt, as among most Eastern peoples, presides over the tribunal which judges the dead Kings (p. 186). The *Teachings for Merikara* (IXth Dynasty) have shown us to what an extent Pharaoh was inspired by the Justice of the Sun and took his duties towards mankind to heart (p. 256). After the social revolution, it is Maat whom the law-loving Kings invoke. In all times the Vizier, Pharaoh's right hand, is the " Prophet of Maat ", and the moral force of the title is recalled in admirable language when the King gives his instructions to the Vizier (p. 288).

To sum up, in the Heliopolitan doctrine a god was conceived as an Intelligence which has thought the world and expresses itself by the Word, *the instrument of continuous creation, the organ of government, and the herald of law and justice.* This theory triumphed in the intellectual domain from the Vth Dynasty at the latest, and it placed its mark upon institutions.

Thanks to its close alliance with the Kings, the doctrine of Heliopolis, strong in the nobility of its spiritual and moral tenets, was accepted by every priesthood and in every temple in Egypt. Heliopolis had most certainly not been the one and only centre of intellectual and metaphysical culture. Every god in every city stored in himself sufficient vital potency to become a Demiurge, at least in the opinion of his worshippers. We see a glimpse of some of the rival systems

[1] *Phaedrus.* 247 *D-E.*

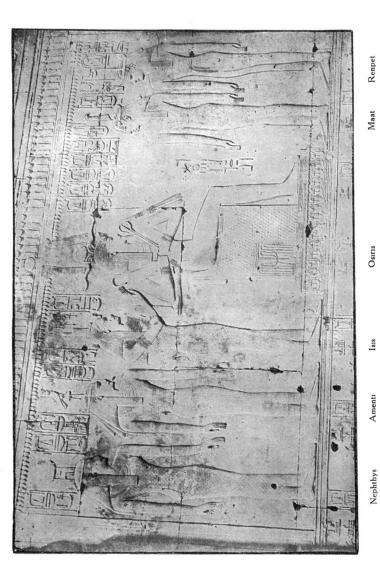

Nephthys   Amenti   Isis   Osiris   Maat   Renpet

OSIRIS WORSHIPPED BY THE GODDESSES

Limestone (Temple of Seti I, Abydos)

[face p 378

in the interpolations in the Heliopolitan texts. Phtah of Memphis and Khnum of Elephantine created all living beings, modelling them on a potter's wheel. Neith of Saïs and Nut, the Cow of Heaven, were also mothers of the Sun before anything existed. The Ibis Thoth hatched the egg of the world at Hermopolis Magna.[1] All these deities, and many others, played the part of Demiurge in systems which explained the Creation, but we hardly hear of these various stories except through the doctrine of Heliopolis. In every sanctuary the priests adapted the " sayings of Heliopolis "[2] to their particular god. This was the origin of the complex types in which Ra was associated with the god of the city— Amon-Ra at Thebes, Horus-Ra at Edfu, Sebek-Ra at Crocodilopolis, etc. So, too, Hathor, who was made the wife of Ra, became the inevitable associate of the goddesses of cities.[3] Finally, most of these gods also became chiefs of Enneads. What we chiefly know is the unifying effect of the doctrine and worship of Heliopolis on the other sanctuaries.[4] In the society of the gods the same levelling process, political as much as religious, was carried out as the Pharaonic kingship had effected in the society of men.

But the centralization of the gods was the result of a political idea rather than of any religious need of the Egyptians. The proof of this is the failure of Akhenaten's attempt at monotheism. Monotheism was never suited to the Egyptian mind. Against the predominance of Atum-Ra, contrary influences made themselves felt. We have seen the encroachment of Amon on Ra in the Theban monarchy and of Phtah on all the gods from the XIXth Dynasty onwards. The text of Shabaka has shown us how, in the late period, they managed, without suppressing Amon, to recognize Phtah of Memphis in him. The most important and earliest opposition came from the god of Hermopolis, Thoth. In himself he represented Intelligence, and also the divine Word, which was expressed, for the general public, by his

---

[1] **XXIX**, p. 114.   [2] Above, p. 186.
[3] Blackman, " Women in the Egyptian Hierarchy," in **XIII**, vii, pp. 12 ff.
[4] See H. Brugsch, *Religion*. The unification of doctrines (syncretism) gives the religion of the Ptolemaic period an air of monotheism, which beguiled the Egyptologists of the generation of Brugsch, Pierret, and Grébaut. Maspero rebelled, and maintained the thesis of the fundamental polytheism which everything confirms in the classical periods of Egypt.

title of " Lord of the Divine Words ", being the inventor
of speech and writing, and, consequently, of magic writings,
and of the magic in general which commands all the forces
of nature and even masters the gods.[1]   The Heliopolitan
theory, as we have seen, gives Thoth an individual rôle in
creation by the Word, describing him as the tongue of Atum,
and therefore the Word incarnate. Other texts declare that
the place where Atum, on emerging from Chaos, manifested
himself as the Sun Ra was a hill at Hermopolis Magna, and
there, too, Shu separated the Sky from the Earth.[2] Finally,
the system of the Ennead (the Demiurge and eight other gods)
was opposed by the school of the City of Eight Gods, Khmunu,
or Hermopolis Magna.   There reigned the Ogdoad, eight
gods whose total was fused in Thoth, without any ninth
god presiding over them all.[3]   Was the Ogdoad an earlier
theological conception than the Nine of Heliopolis ?   Was it
the model copied and developed by the priests of Atum-Ra ?
The question has not been settled.   However it may have
been, we see the theologians striving to reconcile the Eight
and the Nine. On a coffin of the XXIInd Dynasty, a priest
of Amon, identifying himself with the Demiurge, proclaims :
" I am One which becomes Two. I am Two which becomes
Four. I am Four which becomes Eight. I am One which
protects it (the Eight)." [4] Thus formulated, the Ennead is
a compromise between the Ogdoad of Hermopolis and the
Demiurge of Heliopolis. These attempts at fusion, and the
prominent rôle which popular tradition gives to Thoth,
" the Vizier of Horus ", in the divine chronicle, show the
ingenuity with which the priests of Ra managed to extend
their dominion over all sanctuaries.

B.   *The Doctrine of Osiris*

The doctrine of Osiris is at the opposite pole of Egyptian
religious theory. It, too, is the source of a popular and a
priestly literature.

Thanks to the Greeks, and especially to Plutarch, the legend
of Osiris has been preserved better than any other. I have

---

[1] See Boylan, *Thot*, chap. iii.
[2] *Book of the Dead*, chap. xvii.
[3] See **XX**, vol. i, p. 148.
[4] **IV**, xxiii, p. 196.

related (pp. 84 ff.) how in this legend the god of the Nile and of vegetation became the Good Being, slain for the salvation of men; he is also the ancestral king, a model for his son Horus, and the prototype of Pharaoh alive and dead.

The priestly tradition shows that Osiris came into the Heliopolitan Ennead at the beginning of the Memphite period. The process which led to the admission of the earth-god among the gods of heaven and its historical significance have been set forth in their place (Part II, Chap. II, p. 154). Being given the especial funerary character suited to a god who had known death and resurrection, Osiris installed himself in the necropoles, just as Ra had established himself over the gods of the cities among the living. At Memphis he annexed the domain of Sokar; at Abydos, that of Khent-Amenti; and he was given a temple in most cities. The democratic revolution made his triumph secure, for he was a god of the people. We have seen how, under the XIIth

Fig. 66.—Mummy being swathed in wrappings, with a Mask on its Face.
New Empire.

Dynasty, the Service of Osiris, at first strictly confined to the King (the Sed-feast), became a national festival (p. 248). Under the Theban monarchy, Osiris gained in authority with every century. At the end of Egyptian civilization, the Foreigners would honour, in Serapis, a blend of Osiris with Apis; of him, with Isis, Horus, and Thoth, they would make the divine family above all others; and they would seek in the Osirian doctrine for the revelation of the " Egyptian mysteries ".

The prestige of Ra came from his position as Demiurge; that of Osiris from the fact that, as an agricultural god, he had faced death and conquered it. The story of Osiris dealt with the problem of death and the possibility of survival and resurrection. Gods and men were personally interested, and one can understand that Osiris was worshipped universally.

I have described how Seth had brought about the death
of Osiris, and by what means, technical and magical, Isis
and her allies had saved his body from corruption. The body
of Osiris, having been disinfected with natron, was preserved
from contact with the air by a mass of wrappings. Anubis,
according to the legend, was the inventor of these wrappings,
and was called *Ut*, " the Swaddler." [1] To him Ra entrusted
the task of burying Osiris. Isis completed the work by her
magical art ; the spells (*hekau*) and charms (*akhu*) uttered
by her mouth (creative like that of every god) transformed
the corpse into an eternal body. Osiris was the first mummy.
The imitation of movements restored to this incorruptible
body the apparent life which it lacked. In every human family
the son used to perform the funerary cult for his father.[2]
Horus, therefore, behaved to his father Osiris as a " darling
son " (*sa mer-f*). " Thy mouth is opened by Horus, with his
little finger. As the son opens therewith the mouth of
his father, so Horus has opened therewith the mouth of
Osiris." [3] The eyes of Osiris were also opened, that he might
see,[4] and his ears and nose, that he might hear and breathe.[5]
Instruments of (celestial) iron, bits of natron, and food forced
or persuaded his mouth.[6] The mummy would be able to
eat, drink, breathe, speak, and " utter commands " as the
Demiurge.

To the son, too,[7] fell the duty of " creating " an image
(*tut*), representing the deceased, not as a desiccated, invisibly
wrapped-up mummy, but in the physical beauty and mental
vigour of the prime of life. So Horus " caused to be born "
(*mes*) one or more statues, in stone, wood, or metal, of the
god standing with his eyes open and his face full of expression.
This image was " living ", and the life which it contained
would be strengthened by a magical consecration. Horus
and his " allies " (that is, the sons, relations, and friends of
the deceased) opened the mouth and eyes of the statue in
the actual workshop of the sculptors and metal-founders,
the Golden Building (*het-nub*).[8]

The mummy and statue thus became the visible images of

[1] *Pyr.*, § 574.   [2] Cf. p. 144.   [3] *Pyr.*, § 1330.
[4] § 643.   [5] §§ 1673, 1809, 1983.   [6] §§ 11 ff.
[7] *Ritual of the Opening of the Mouth* (Seti I).
[8] *Pyr.*, § 1329 ; *Ritual of the Opening of the Mouth*, l. 1.

the eternal body. Osiris, the first earthly being removed to the sky after death, the first who passed " from the Gods of the earth to the Gods of heaven " (above, p. 155), underwent, on his arrival up above, a " spiritualization " which united his Zet to his Ka, and made of him the complete being who manifests himself as a Soul, a Spirit, a God. In conclusion, we should remember that by a solemn verdict of the tribunal of Ra the accusations of Seth were dismissed and Osiris, " justified " (*maâu*), became the Just One who rose to heaven.

This funerary cult, these rites first applied to Osiris, are what Diodorus calls (i, 25) " the remedy which confers immortality ", the invention of the whole of which was ascribed to Isis, the magician. It was the most precious revelation which any Egyptian god had ever made to the world. Plutarch is a faithful interpreter of Egyptian thought when he says :—

> Isis did not wish that the battles and hardships which she had faced and all her acts of wisdom and courage should be buried in forgetfulness and silence. She therefore instituted very holy mysteries (τελεταί), which were to be images, representations and acted scenes of the sufferings of that time, to be a lesson of piety and consolation to the men and women who should undergo the same trials.[1]

Herodotus tells us that at Saïs he saw the Egyptians " at night doing the play of the Passion of Him (τὰ δείκηλα τῶν παθέων αὐτοῦ),[2] which they call Mysteries (μυστήρια)." [3]

Now, these mysteries were not, as has been maintained,[4] imported by the Greeks into Egypt. From the XIIth Dynasty, at the latest, the episodes of the death, burial, and resurrection of the god were enacted in great festivals, partly out of doors, and partly in special buildings, the " chapels of Osiris ", attached to the temples of the gods of the cities. I have translated (p. 249) the account of the chief officiant who, in the name of Senusert III, directed this funeral feast, the Great Outgoing (*pert âat*) of Osiris. In the feast of the erection of the Zed pillar we were present at the resurrection of Osiris (p. 130). Besides these especial occasions, a daily " service " was held in the chapels of Osiris, to recall, at every hour of the night and day, the incidents of the god's

---

[1] *De Iside*, 27.
[2] " He " is Osiris, whom Herodotus, out of superstitious respect for the sacred Name, abstains from naming.
[3] ii, 171
[4] Sourdille, *Hérodote et la religion de l'Égypte*, p. 334.

death and resurrection.[1] In the month of Choiak, in autumn, the priests used to make " Gardens of Osiris " in which they buried clay statuettes sprinkled with seeds ; the germination of the seeds bore witness to the resurrection of the god.[2]

That the mysteries might be repeated in exact detail, the tradition had to be fixed in written books of rites. We have the texts of these, with illustrations—the book of the Swaddling of the Mummy,[3] that of the Opening of the Mouth and Eyes for the statue in the Golden Building,[4] the description of the rites for making the Gardens of Osiris,[5] receipts for sacred oils and perfumes,[6] etc. These documents are of the Theban and Ptolemaic periods, but in the Pyramids of the VIth Dynasty we have, in many prolix versions, prior to their condensation into rituals, accounts of " the remaking of the body ", " the ascension into heaven ", " the presentation of offerings ", etc.

In most of the rituals we are told who are the people fit to know, recite, and perform them. These are the Officiant (kheri-heb), who holds the actual book in his hands, the Swaddler (ut), the Pure One (uâb), clean in body and purified in spirit, who " enters " into communication with the god, the Server (sam), the Prophet (hem-neter), etc. There has, therefore, since the earliest times, been a professional clergy. In certain cases these priests take the names and masks of the divine kinsfolk of Osiris—Geb, Horus, Isis, Nephthys, Thoth, and Anubis—calling themselves the " son ", " sister ", " wife ", etc., of the god whom they serve. Thus the family worship of the earliest days survives in the Osirian cult which spread over it when the funeral customs of the primitive Egyptians were taken under the protection of the Good Being.

So Osiris shares the supremacy in religion with Ra, as Egypt is subject to the two-fold influence of Nile and sun. He thereby gains material advantages, political and social privileges. All that appertains to creative power and the organization of the world and of society remains the portion of Ra ; everything connected with the maintenance of life,

---

[1] Cf. my Mystères égyptiens, **XXIX**, pp. 20–36.
[2] Cf. "La Passion d'Osiris," in **XXVIII**, p. 89.
[3] Maspero, Mémoires sur quelques papyrus du Louvre.
[4] In tombs, especially that of Seti I.
[5] At Denderah.
[6] At Edfu and Philae.

nourishment, the war with death, and resurrection after death is under Osiris. The union of the two great nature-gods became very close. In the official doctrines of the XIIth Dynasty, Osiris is " the Soul of Ra, his great hidden Name which resides in him " (above, p. 372) ; the two gods have composed " one single Soul in two twins " ever since the day at Mendes, long ago, when Osiris met Ra and the two gods embraced. In the universe, death and life, night and day, are complementary. One is the past, the other the future. " Osiris is called Yesterday, Ra is called To-morrow." [1]

IV

THE RITUALS OF HELIOPOLIS AND OSIRIS APPLIED TO GODS AND MEN

The dogmas and rituals of Ra and Osiris did not affect religious life only. They had a profound influence on social life, in laying down, once for all, the main principles on which the relations of the Egyptian with the sacred beings were to develop. Those who were *sacred* in his eyes were, in the same degree, the gods, the Kings, alive and dead, and dead men who had been buried with the proper rites.

We may conclude from the religious texts that neither the creative power of Ra nor the resurrection of Osiris remained the exclusive property of these great universal gods. As Plutarch says, the Creation of Ra and the Passion of Osiris served as models for other gods, and for men. In reality these were *revelations* regarding the riddle of the universe and the riddle of death. In them the local gods must find an example to imitate in order to obtain complete and eternal security, while men will seek in them for the hope of compensation for their earthly sufferings, in the felicities of a divine life after death.

The local gods, as I have said (p. 246), were compelled to share their power with Ra in the sanctuaries and with Osiris in the necropoles. This subordination in fact was recorded by the theologians and introduced, after it had taken place,

---

[1] *Book of the Dead*, chap. xvii. See Grapow's critical edition, in *Religiose Urkunden.* i.

into the general scheme of the creations ascribed to the
Demiurge when he organized the world. The theorists of
Heliopolis and Busiris end by denying the independent
existence of any god of the nomes or cities, although the
historical monuments show us them, each in his place, even
before there is any mention of Ra and Osiris. For the priests,
the Demiurge has created everything and existed before
everything, and here, with its political consequences, we have
the theory of the Demiurge creating his members by the
Word and giving the gods their names :—

> Atum is he from whom everything has come, with offerings, provisions,
> divine offerings, and all goods. He caused the Gods to be born, he made
> the cities, he founded the nomes. He set the Gods in their sanctuaries, and
> he modelled (made) statues of their bodies (zet), so that their hearts should
> be content. . . . So, the Gods enter their bodies (be they made) of what-
> soever wood, stone, or metal. . . . So he has joined all the Gods to their
> Kas.[1]

Statues need temples, and Atum has made these, too ;
therefore the temples will be built according to rules
elaborated by the priests of Heliopolis (below, pp. 419 ff.).
The statues, being living images, need clothing, ornaments,
attention to their toilet, material and magical nourishment,
security, and adoration—in a word, a cult. Atum created all
this, and his priests have condensed the revelation of it in
the rituals of divine worship.

We have these rituals, written on papyri or on temple-
walls, from the Theban period and onwards. They are the
same everywhere, whatever the god and the city. If we
exclude the great feasts commemorating a personal exploit
of a deity (such as the campaigns of Harmachis against Seth
at Edfu, and the great gatherings of Hathor, the Goddess of
Love, of Min, the God of Fruitfulness, and of the funerary
gods Phtah and Osiris), for every god the ordinary daily
service is celebrated in an uniform manner in every temple,
in accordance with a common ritual, for which we have
evidence at least as early as the Theban Middle Kingdom.

Now, this ritual contains elements which are older than
the supremacy of Heliopolis. It is certain that, in every town,
those who celebrated the cult had, from the earliest times, the

---

[1] Text of Shabaka (Erman, op. cit., pp. 941–2). At the beginning of the text,
Atum surrenders to Phtah of Memphis his own rôle as creator of the gods.
As we have seen (p. 376), this is explained by the Memphite origin of the
document, so I have restored Atum to his place.

cares about which we are told by a prince of Hermonthis, the Director of the Prophets of Mentu, under the XIth Dynasty. The priest, he says, must be one

> who knows the offerings of the temples, with experience regarding the right moment to bring them ; keeping their taboos (*but*) away, and knowing what their heart desires (for) each god, in regard to what comes to him ; knowing (each god's) bread from the (other) offerings ; knowing the sacred images of the district-ensigns, and likewise all their statues ; what touches the sanctuary opens for him ; knowing the House of the Morning (cf. p. 393) ; entering their doors [1] . . . Of what he has laid in his heart, nothing comes out on his lips.[2]

Another great personage, the Vizier User (XVIIIth Dynasty), who was an *uâb*, or Pure One, in the Temple of Amon at Karnak, describes his duties as officiating priest as follows :—

> I held (the office of) the *uâb* who goes into the sanctuary of Amon. I laid the rouge on the divine flesh ; I adorned Amon-Min, and I also shouldered [3] Amon at his feast. I carried Min on his platform. But I do not lift my shoulder in the house of the Master of the Bowed (?), I do not hold my arm high in the house of Him who holds his Arm High (Min), I do not raise my voice in the house of the Master of Silence, I do not tell lies in the house of the Master of Maat, I do not in anything diminish the value of (?) the things purified for the God, I do not place my mouth on his divine offerings. I have, then, performed the office of a Reporting Priest, [4] hearing what is heard in secret (in the sanctuary), and I reveal nothing of the words of the King's House. [5]

Without a doubt, these attentions and precautions, all of a material kind, represent the most ancient part of the ritual. In the very first temples raised by the Thinite Kings to the deified ensign of Neith and to the Ram, and later in those which their successors built to all deities, the gods must have received such attentions and honours from chiefs and Pure Ones.

On the " mystery " part of the rites, which took place inside the sanctuary, we can throw some light with the aid of the formulas in the Theban rituals.[6]

The object of worship in the sanctuary is the statue of the god, of stone, gilded wood, or metal (gold or bronze), enclosed in a shrine of wood or stone, with doors sealed with a clay seal. The sanctuary or a neighbouring room contains a barge, mounted on a pedestal, the cabin of which also contains a

---

[1] **XII,** xxxiv (1896), p. 33.　　　　[2] Ibid., p. 26.
[3] That is, he carried the pole bearing the barge of the god.
[4] Who reports the oracles of the god ? Cf. p. 332.
[5] In **VIII,** N.S., i (1919), pp. 10–13.　　[6] **XLVIII.**

divine statue. This barge is carried on poles on the shoulders of the Pure Ones when the statue leaves the sanctuary for processions and all " Outgoings " or " Risings " (*khâ*) of the god (cf. Fig. 62, p. 305).

The ceremonial of the cult represented in the pictures comprises in the main the following acts.

(i) The King, or the priest who takes his place, purifies the sanctuary and his own person by fumigations and ablutions (Pl. XVII).

(ii) He breaks the seal of the doors of the shrine ; prostrates himself before the statue ; wakes it with the hymn of Morning Worship (above, p. 158) ; purifies it with water

Fig. 67.—Amenophis III sacrificing a Victim to Min. Luxor.

and incense ; takes it in his arms ; and feeds it, presenting it with chosen material offerings and with the symbolical offering of the goddess Maat.

(iii) The King proceeds to make the toilet of the statue— purifications, fumigations, clothing, adornment, crowns, sceptres, rouging, anointing, and scenting.

(iv) After placing the seal on the doors the King leaves the sanctuary, walking backwards, keeping his face to the shrine, and wiping away the trace of his footsteps.[1]

All these actions are accompanied by formulas, which, through allusions of varying transparency, reflect the

---

[1] On this rite of Outgoing, cf. Gardiner, *Tomb of Amenemhet*, p. 93.

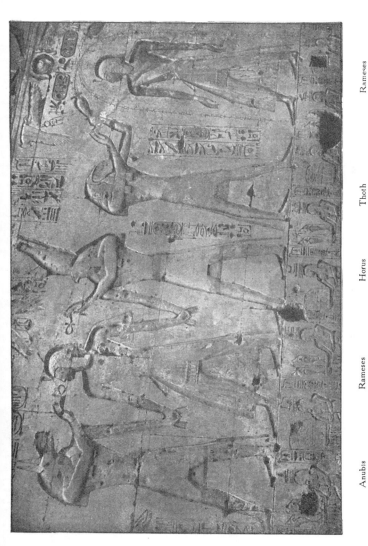

Anubis   Rameses   Horus   Thoth   Rameses

RAMESES II LED BEFORE OSIRIS AND PURIFIED BY THOTH AND HORUS

Limestone (Abydos)

[face p. 388

doctrine of Heliopolis mingled with that of Osiris. Let us remember, once more, that the first " great temples ", which were the expression, not of a local cult, but of a State religion, were those of the Sun built by the Pharaohs of the Vth Dynasty. But it was about this time that Osiris ascended to heaven to reign with Ra. In consequence, in all temples built after this union, the rites are addressed to a divine being conceived on the model of Ra and Osiris, and the life of every god appears as a replica of the divine existence of Ra and Osiris. The essential characteristics of that life, in very brief form, are as follows.

The sanctuary, in which the god dwells, is called the " sky ". When the King or priest breaks the seal of the shrine, he is said to open the two doors of the sky. There, every morning, the god rises (*khâ*) like the sun at daybreak. Hour by hour, till midday, he grows in strength and glory, and when the divine barge comes out of the shrine, crossing the temple to the great entrance, it is really Ra visiting his terrestrial domain, going along the " East " side to the zenith, like the sun. After midday, the god returns by the " West " side of the temple to the sanctuary, where he arrives in the evening, to " rest in his Western horizon " (cf. below, p. 420). During the night, the god, like Ra, disappears from view. He dies, takes the form of a mummy, and visits that nocturnal, unseen side of the universe, the *Duat* (described by the royal hypogea), where the dead of the provincial capitals lie.[1] At the break of the next day he abandons his mummy-form [2] and is reborn in his sanctuary, as in the Eastern sky, in the form of a young sun—a child emerging from a lotus. (Pl. VII, 1)—or of " a milk calf with pure mouth ",[3] proceeding from the body of the celestial Cow Nut. Such is the daily round of the god of every temple.

Every god is just as much Osiris as he is Ra. On opening the shrine, what the King finds before him, in the appearance of a statue, is a body whose limbs, mutilated and scattered

---

[1] The three stages of the sun in its daily course are described by the names Khepri, Ra, and Atum (above, p. 372) ; see the chapters of the Ritual, **XLVIII** pp. 139, 145.

[2] Cf. J. Capart, *Thèbes*, p. 321. In the picture of the twelfth hour of the night, in the *Book of the Duat*, there is a mummy lying full length under a scarab. This is the nocturnal body of the dead Sun, from which the *kheperer*, the scarab, detaches itself, as the Khepri of the new day.

[3] *Pyr.*, § 27.

by Seth, have been piously put together and transformed into a mummy by Isis, Horus, Anubis, and Thoth, like that of Osiris. The King (or officiant) will give his life back to him. To the inert corpse he restores active organs by the rites of the Opening of the Mouth and Eyes, and, to give it back its heart and its Ka, the Horus King takes the statue in his arms and breathes his Soul (*animus*, breath) into the mouth by a kiss (Pl. X, 2). Thus the god again becomes a " perfect Spirit ", through the " spiritualization " conferred by these Osirian rites (p. 181).

The Osirian doctrine, therefore, gives a special colour to the appearance of the god. I have previously (p. 359) attempted to define the ancient notion of a god, as a being who renewed himself at intervals, without loss of substance, *neter*. Since the triumph of Osiris, men have known how they can facilitate the renewal of the *neter*—by applying the Osirian rites. In the Theban temples, the god is a being who has victoriously undergone the trial of death, like Osiris. His body, treated like that of Osiris, is an eternal Zet. It is in this same period that a papyrus [1] defines the hieroglyphic of " god " by these words : " he is *buried* (or *swaddled*) " [2]; and, indeed, the sign *neter* is often represented as the staff of an ensign, wrapped in a bandage. Thus, every god of Theban times is, as it were, impregnated with that death which is the condition of the resurrection of the agricultural god.

FIG. 68.—
Swaddled *Neter*.

The Solar conception and the Osirian conception are intermingled in all the formulas of the ritual. The purifications and fumigations to which the statue is subjected are those with which the Heliopolitans greet the Sun at daybreak [3] and also Osiris at his rebirth. The stuffs in which the statue is dressed are bandages, green, red, and white (" sympathetic " colours) ; in these the Osirian mummy is

---

[1] Griffith and Petrie, *Two Hieroglyphic Papyri from Tanis*, pl. xv, 2.

[2] *Iu-f qeris*. Mr. Griffith translates " embalmed ", that is, properly buried, and then *deified*, being assimilated to Osiris. Loret, commenting on the passage (**VIII**, xi, 1904, p. 83), lays stress on the fact that the determinative of *qeris* is a wrapping ; *qeris* first had the sense " swaddle ", " wrap ", and later that of " bury ".

[3] On this subject, see Blackman, in **XIII**, v, p. 162 ; **IV**, xxxix, p. 44.

wrapped, and so are the statues of the Solar gods. The sceptres, maces, magical whips, talismans, necklaces, and bangles are those which adorn the Kings of the living and the dead. The food is " the Offering which the King gives " (*hetep rdu nsut*) to Ra, as to Osiris, namely, a list of all, or nearly all, the beasts and plants produced by the soil of Egypt and presented to the Creator by the King, in the name of mortal men.

In general, this ritual is essentially practical and formal ; we shall see its moral side. The culminating point in the written accounts of the rites and the principal scene in the pictorial representation of them is the presentation to the god by the King of a statuette of the goddess Maat, a symbolical offering of Right, of Truth and Justice, which, more than all the oxen,[1] cakes, wines, and fruits, is the gift most pleasing to the god.[2] At this moment, the King sings a hymn in praise of the moral qualities of the god in whom Ra, " the father of Maat," and Osiris *maâu*, " justified," are merged. Here are some extracts of the " Chapter of the Giving of Maat ". The King presents himself thus :—

I am come to thee, I, with my two hands joined to carry Maat. Maat is come that she may be with thee. . . . Thou livest on Maat ; thou dost join thy members to Maat ; thou dost allow Maat to alight on thy head. At the sight of thy daughter Maat, thou growest young ; Maat lies like an amulet on thy neck ; she lies on thy breast. . . . Thy right eye (the sun) and thy left eye (the moon), thy flesh and thy members, the breath of thy chest and heart are Maat ; thy bandages, thy garments are Maat. What thou eatest, what thou drinkest, thy bread and thy beer, the incense which thou dost breathe, the air in thy nose are Maat. Thou hast thy Ka, when Maat worships thee and thy members are joined to Maat. Thy daughter Maat is at the prow of thy barge, she alone is in the cabin. Thou art because Maat is, and she is because thou art. When thou comest in the East of the sky. . . . Maat is before thy face in the sky and on earth, whether thou turn to the sky or walk on earth. Maat is still with thee every day, when thou liest in the Duat. Maat is with thee when thou givest light to the bodies in the underworld, and when thou goest up into the hidden region (the necropolis) ; there thou art in peace and strength because of her.[3] (Therefore) the assembled Ennead says to thee, " Thou art *maâ-kheru* (justified and triumphant) for millions of years.[4] . . . Maat is the

---

[1] Above, p. 242 (*Merikara*).

[2] This sentiment appears in the Middle Kingdom in the *Teachings for Meri-kara* (above, p. 242). The daily offering of Maat to Ra was also ritual by that time.

[3] The daily and nightly stages of the life of the Sun and of every god are well described here.

[4] A judgment similar to that undergone by Osiris.

Unique One, Thou hast created her. No other God has shared her with thee. Thou alone (dost possess her) for ever, eternally.[1]

This wordy address, which I have cut down by two-thirds, clearly shows the rôle of the god, as being responsible for order in nature and the creator and guardian of right or law. At the same time, the social interest of the cult is revealed. In the innumerable pictures of the offering of Maat, the King and the god hold short conversations. The King presents Maat as the tribute of men of good will and the product of his own efforts in his royal office ; the god replies that he will make justice and law flourish in heaven and on earth, as a heavenly and earthly recompense for men. If we look back to the *Teachings for Merikara* and the *Instructions to the Vizier*, we shall see how the Solar and Osirian doctrine was applied in the political and social domain.

After the gods, the first to benefit by the " revelation " is the King. He has a right to it on several grounds, which I have stated in Part II. I may recall briefly that Pharaoh is, among men, the incarnation of the Falcon, of Horus-Seth, of Ra, of Ra-Harakhti, of Osiris, of Horus, Son of Isis, and of Amon-Ra, that is, of the king-gods who in turn ruled in Egypt. The Stele of Kuban describes Rameses II as follows :—

Horus of the motley feathers ; beautiful Falcon of electrum. . . . Horus and Seth exulted in heaven on the day that he was born, and the Gods said, " Our seed is in him ! " The Goddesses said, " He is issued from us to exercise the kingship of Ra ! " Amon said " When I created him, I set Maat in his place ! ". . . . Thou art Ra incarnate, Khepri in his very shape, and thou art the living image on earth of thy father Atum of Heliopolis.[2] Hu (Command) is in thy mouth, and Sia (Intelligence) is in thy heart ; the seat of thy tongue is the sanctuary of Maat. God sits on thy lips, and thy words are made real every day, for thy heart has been made like that of Phtah,[3] who invented the Arts.[4]

In consequence, the King is worshipped like Ra and Osiris. In life he is adored with the god of every temple, as an associate god, and in death he has funerary temples of his own. There the ritual of his cult is like that of the gods.[5]

[1] **XLVIII**, pp. 138–48.
[2] The King embodies the Sun in his daily avatars ; cf. above, p. 372.
[3] See Phtah as the Demiurge, p. 376.
[4] *Stele of Kuban*, ll. 2–4, 13–19, in **VIII**, N.S., i (1919), pp. 19 ff.
[5] Cf. **XXX**, pt. iii.

Moreover, the divine nature of the King is renewed daily by the worship paid to the gods. The ritual allows no other officiant than the King himself. It is the King who purifies, dresses, feeds, and protects the god; he plays the part of Horus the Darling Son; he is the son of the family, paying worship to his fathers the gods. But the King cannot officiate every day, in every temple at once. The ritual provides for an acting prophet, entrusted with the material performance of the rites, but he is merely a proxy of the King, and he says to the god, " I am the prophet; I am sent by the King, to see the God." [1] Also, the whole matter of religious offerings is in Pharaoh's own hands, for he alone can speak the releasing formula, " The King gives the offering," which creates the nourishment of the gods on earth.

Now, to enter into effective communication with the gods, Pharaoh must himself be " consecrated ". Several formulas of the divine ritual end with the refrain, " Here is the offering given by the King, for I have purified myself." [2] Only an *uâb*, pure in body and spirit, can approach the god and enter the secret parts of the temple.[3] In consequence, before every royal or divine ceremony in which the King will come into the presence of the gods, he receives purifications by water, incense, natron, etc., which renew his quality as a god. If he is to perform the cult, he first goes into a sacristy, the House of the Morning (*per-duat*), where two priests, wearing the masks of Horus and Thoth, wash and fumigate him, with the same vases and materials as are used for purifying Ra at daybreak, and give him clothing, crowns, sceptres, and talismans of Ra. At the same time, the King is subjected to the Opening of the Mouth and Eyes which makes him a god by the Osirian rite, warding off all danger of death and reuniting him with his Ka.[4] Alone among men, Pharaoh, by his divine birth and the rites of the *per-duat*, possesses his Ka on earth, and so is a " perfect " Spirit, a god. In scenes

---

[1] **XLVIII**, pp. 42, 55, 68, 78, 121, 128, 133, 211.
[2] **XLVIII**, pp. 66, 96, 109, 115, 169, 170.
[3] On the doors giving access to the sanctuaries in the temples one reads, " Every being who enters here must be *uâb*."
[4] We have an intact *per-duat* in the temple of Edfu. It is described by me in **XXX**, chap. vii, p. 212, and published in full by Kees in **IV**, xxxvi (1914), p. 1. He shows that the translation " House of Worship " should be corrected to " House of the Morning ". Blackman brings out the Solar nature of this name and of the purifications received by the King, in **XIII**, v, pp. 118, 148.

of worship the King's Ka is frequently represented in the form of a youth bearing on his head the sign of the Ka, whose raised arms surround the royal name, and holding in his hand an ensign, a staff surmounted by the bust of a god ; this is called the " royal Ka " (Fig. 47, p. 166). This Ka " dwells in the shrine and in the House of the Morning ", and is the genius who protects the life, health, and strength of Pharaoh (Pl. X, 1).

Having become a god, Pharaoh can appear before the gods. Two priests, Horus and Thoth, take his hands and " make the King go up " (nsut bes) into the sanctuary (Pl. XVII), where the god embraces him, or the goddesses suckle him.[1] The professional priests who accompany the King or act as his substitute can only perform this office if they are " pure " [2] ; they therefore undergo the necessary ceremonies of purification.[3]

The King is a god in yet another quality. After his death, he is deified ; but he then belongs to another category of gods, which we have to examine.

The third category of divine beings comprises all the dead who have undergone the Osirian rites. Here we reach the solid ground of facts. What was pure theory in the case of the gods, being mere concepts of the imagination, and even of the living King, is a material reality in the case of the dead. A real body, exposed to corruption, has to be snatched from death, not the statue of a god or the living body of a King. Fictions become practical processes ; the rites of the Osirian-Solar worship and of that of the gods are applied in their entirety to the bodies of dead men who are to be transformed into gods.

The rituals describe how the body of Osiris was dismembered by Seth, put together by Isis, protected from decay

---

[1] **XLVIII**, p. 23, pl. i ; **XXX**, p. 292.
[2] **XLVIII**, p. 17.
[3] For the Director of Prophets and the *uâb*, see p. 387. There were four classes of prophets. Bakenkhonsu gives a good example of the career of a priestly official under the XIXth Dynasty (p. 335).

by Anubis and Thoth, swaddled by Anubis, restored to life
in every organ by the *up-ra*, and
finally presented with sceptres, ornaments, and crowns, the insignia of
gods and kings. In the necropoles we
see with our own eyes skeletons which
really have been dismembered and then
put together, every bone in its place,
and bodies which have been desiccated,
disembowelled, disinfected with natron,
resin, and bitumen,[1] stuffed with
scented, antiseptic substances, wrapped
in bandages to keep out the air, made
incorruptible, in fact, and adorned with
talismans, sceptres, and divine crowns.
These are the mummies, the oldest discovered specimens of which date from
the beginning of the Old Kingdom;
these, in their millions, have revealed
the Egyptian people to us in the actual
bodies of its peasants, townsmen,
princes, and Kings.[2]

FIG. 69.—Ushebti, or
Answerer. Shaped
like a mummy hold-
ing its tools for work
in the next world.

The mummy (*sâhu*) which receives
the rites of the *up-ra* in the sacristy
(*uâbt*) of the embalmers or at the door of the tomb becomes
an eternal body ; but once this body has gone down
to the bottom of a grave it can no longer be reached by
officiants. As in the case of Osiris and the gods, other images
are made as substitutes for the Zet, representing it under the
living aspect which the body once had ; these are the statues
of wood, stone, and metal and the reliefs, which are turned
into living images by the Opening of the Mouth in the House
of Gold.[3] The union of the dead man's personal Zet and Ka,[4]

---

[1] On mummification, see Hdt., ii, 86–8 ; Diod., i, 91–2. A short history
of the processes used (from the IInd Dynasty) is given by G. Elliot Smith,
" Egyptian Mummies," in **XIII,** i (1914), p. 189, and in the *Journal of the
Oriental Society*, Manchester, i (1915), with reference to the entrails kept in
the Canopus jars.

[2] On this subject, see G. Elliot Smith, *The Royal Mummies*, Cairo catalogue,
1912.

[3] *Het-nub*, *Pyr.*, § 1329, and tomb of Seti I.

[4] To die in accordance with the rites was to " go to one's Ka ", that is, to
join one's Ka for a new, divine life. For the Old Kingdom, cf. *Urk.*, i, 50, 71, 73.

which is obtained by " spiritualization ", causes the Zet to pass from the world of mortals to that of the gods. The Soul (*Ba*), now attached to the Zet, comes and " animates " the statues and the mummy, and divides its time between heaven and earth. The Spirit (*Akh*) remains in heaven, while the Name (*ren*) will live in the memory of men, provided that it is written on the walls of the tomb and in the chapel, and repeated by the family and officiants on the days of the funeral feasts. The feeding of the dead man is ensured for eternity :—

(i) By the " Offering given by the King " (*hetep rdu nsut*) to his Imakhu ; this is the abundant meal given to dead men, as to gods and kings ;

(ii) By a magic formula, the *pert kheru*, or " Issuing at the Voice ". When the voice of the King [1] or the officiant representing him proclaims that offerings are given to a deceased man, that voice, creative like the Word of the Demiurge,[2] causes real offerings to " issue ", to appear on the table of the deceased, not only on the day of a funeral, but whenever the *pert kheru* is ritually pronounced. At the magical summons the beasts, viands, loaves, fruit, etc., drawn or enumerated on the walls come to life and " issue " as real dishes on the offering-table. Furthermore, at the bidding of the formula, the deified dead man himself " issues at the voice " (*pert kheru* or *r kheru*) [3] to take his meal in the chapel.[4] So we find in the tombs the statue of the dead man, represented as " issuing " from the inner chambers, descending from the other world to the table of offerings, to sit down to the provisions eternally furnished by the gifts of the King (Pl. V, 1).

[1] *Pyr.*, §§ 58–9. The theory of the *pert kheru* has been elucidated by Maspero, " La Table d'offrandes des tombeaux égyptiens," in **XXXVIII**, vol. vi, p. 357, and amended by Gardiner, *Amenemhet*, pp. 85 ff.

[2] *Inscription of Paheri* (*Urk.*, iv, p. 121). The two great sources of offerings for the dead are mentioned—" an Offering given by the King " (*hetep rdu nsut*), according to what is written in the books, and an " Issuing at the Voice " (*pert r kheru*), according to the oral tradition of the Ancestors, as that which habitually issues from the mouth of the god. Moreover, the " Offering given by the King " is more especially given to the gods, and " the offering which issues at the voice " to the deified Spirits of the dead (*Urk.*, iv, p. 545). On the development of these formulas, see Gardiner, *Amenemhet*, pp. 79 ff.

[3] *Pyr.*, §§ 1713, 796 ; the dead man " issues at the voice of Anubis ".

[4] " The voice issues for the deceased, when he is called (by the officiant) to take incense, water, or air, or to see Ra " (Constantinople Stele, published by V. Scheil in **IV**, xv, p. 197), or " to take his offerings on the altar of Unnefer " *Urk.*, iv, p. 112).

In Part Two I showed that the royal privilege of the Osirian and Solar rites was only extended gradually by the Kings to their subjects. First the royal family, then the oligarchy of princes and priests, and finally the masses obtained these religious rights, which brought political rights as a corollary. By these successive extensions we have been able to follow the development of the social system between 2500 and 2000 B.C. Under the Theban Middle Kingdom, the unification of society from a religious and political point of view was an accomplished fact. All Egyptians were promoted to immortality, and entitled to mummy, Zet, Ka, Ba, and Akh; after death they would be god-kings, equal to Osiris, Ra, and Pharaoh. To instruct the people in its divine rights and duties after death, the speculations of the theologians, the priests of Ra and Osiris, had to be spread abroad. This was the cause of the enormous development of religious literature from this period. We find it written on the sides of sarcophagi and coffins [1] and on the papyri which we call the *Book of the Dead*.[2]

This is not the place for a detailed examination of that literature, which is, besides, obscure and often unintelligible.[3] I shall merely give a short analysis of two essential chapters of the *Book of the Dead*.

Chapter xvii tells the dead man his *rights*, which are important. Since he becomes like Ra, he will be called the Demiurge, Atum-Ra, and will speak in his name. This chapter is, therefore, a monologue by the Demiurge, relating the creation of the universe, defining his divine powers, and explaining the dogmas of the rôle of the gods and the destiny of men, the earthly images of Ra (cf. p. 242), who, when they have died a good death, will be as the gods. Such subjects are never easy to understand. We therefore have this text in a very short version of the Middle Kingdom, with fairly short glosses, or explanatory comments; a version of the

---

[1] Published (without a translation) by Lacau, " Textes religieux," in **IV**, vols. xxvi ff. See Breasted's résumé in **XLI**, pp. 273 ff. There is an English edition and translation by Budge, *The Book of the Dead*, 3 vols., London, 1901 (*Books on Egypt and Chaldæa*). See also Lepage-Renouf's translation.

[2] Those of the XVIIIth Dynasty have been published by Naville, *Das aegyptische Totenbuch der VIII. bis XX. Dyn.*, 1886. A MS. of Saïte period has been published by Lepsius, *Das Totenbuch der Aegypter*, 1842.

[3] An analysis of the *Book of the Dead* will be found in **XXVII**, chap. v. P. Pierret's *Le Livre des Morts*, translated into French from the text of Lepsius, is now out of date.

New Empire, with more extensive glosses ; and a version of
the Saïte period, also with glosses, which is still more prolix.[1]
" He who says this chapter will be on earth by the side of
Ra ; he will arrive happily by the side of Osiris. But he who
does not know this chapter will not enter (into the other
world) ; he will not emerge from ignorance."

Chapter cxxv warns the deceased of his *duties*. The most
urgent is " to separate himself from his sins, to deserve to see
the face of the gods ". Then he will appear before the divine
tribunal, which will ask him for an account of his life on earth.
We should remember that, as early as the VIth Dynasty,
the deceased King is summoned before the Solar gods, who
examine whether he is " justified by his deeds " on earth,
and that a King of the IXth Dynasty assures his son
Merikara and his subjects that nothing escapes the justice
of the gods (above, p. 256). Since the admission of the people
to the Osirian rites, every Egyptian will pass before the
tribunal, the president of which is now Osiris the Justified.

In the Hall of Double Justice, a great balance is set
up before Osiris, sitting on his throne. By the balance stand
Anubis, Thoth, and Maat, and near them is a female monster
with a crocodile's head, a hippopotamus's body, and the mane
and claws of a lion, the " Devourer ",[2] who turns her snout
towards Osiris, as if asking leave to devour " him who comes
from the earth ". All round the hall, the forty-two deities
of the forty-two nomes form a jury to try the deceased, and,
if necessary, to put him to death. But he, being instructed in
chapter cxxv, " knows the names of Osiris and the forty-
two judges " and boasts that he " brings Maat " and can
clear himself. Then follows a list of the sins which the
deceased denies having committed—it is a negative confession.
Here it is, in résumé :—

> I have not done evil. I have committed no violence, I have not stolen,
> I have not caused any man to be killed treacherously, I have not diminished
> the offerings (of the Gods), I have not lied, I have made no one weep, I
> have not been impure, I have not killed the sacred beasts, I have not
> damaged cultivated land, I have not spoken calumniously, I have not shown
> anger, I have not committed adultery, I have not refused to hear the words
> of truth, I have not done witchcraft against the King or my father, I have
> not polluted water, I have not caused a slave to be ill-treated by his master,
> I have not sworn (falsely), I have not tampered with the plumb-line of the

---

[1] There is a critical edition in Grapow, *Religiose Urkunden*, 1916.
[2] In the Pyramids it was a hyena (see p. 187).

Fig. 70.—The Judgment of the Dead by Osiris.

From E. Naville, *Totenbuch.*

balance, I have not taken the milk from the mouth of sucklings, I have not netted the birds of the Gods, I have not turned back the water in its season, I have not cut a water-channel (or dike ?) in its course, I have not quenched fire in its hour, I have not despised God in my heart. I am pure, I am pure, I am pure !

This negative confession sums up the official morality of the Egyptians. It enumerates, without any apparent order, sins which do not seem equally serious to us. We must regard it as a social rather than a religious document, and one composed of successive additions. Many of the sins named are attacks on the persons or property of the gods, such as lack of ritual attentions, theft of offerings, and murder of sacred beasts ; these were probably the crimes which the priests specified earliest. Equally ancient is the condemnation of assaults on the authority of the King or the father. Crimes against one's neighbour were perhaps penalized later— diverting or polluting his water, cutting a water-channel, putting out fire, violence, perjury, adultery. The personal crimes, those which chiefly damage the moral worth of the offender, were probably the last of which the conscience took notice—lying, pride, luxury, anger, cruelty, selfishness.[1] On the whole, the divine tribunal is like a Supreme Court of the State,[2] in which, like an official, every Egyptian must render his account before he leaves the service of the gods, the King, and society.

The complete justification of the deceased, which was hard to admit, from the moral point of view, was a concession which had to be made from the social and administrative point of view. Thoth and Anubis refer to the balance, placing the dead man's heart in one scale and a feather, or a statuette of Maat, in the other. If the scales balance, the deceased is justified. That is the only check. To make more certain, the deceased has taken the precaution of conjuring his heart— that is, his conscience—by reciting chapter xxx :

Heart of my mother, heart of my birth, heart which I had on earth, do not rise in evidence against me ; do not be my adversary before the divine powers ; do not weigh against me . . . do not say, " That is what he has done ; of a truth, he has done it " ; . . . do not make complaints arise against me before the great God of the West.

The accuser most to be dreaded is his own heart ! Here, the Egyptian of the people, panic-stricken, does not attempt

---

[1] On this subject, see **XXVII**, p. 219, and **XXVIII**, p. 128.
[2] Note that each of the forty-two nomes is represented by a judge.

to follow the ideal, too lofty for him, which is preached by the King and priests (cf. the *Teachings for Merikara*, above, p. 256), namely, that divine justice is deaf to prayers and threats. The average Egyptian, in peril before the tribunal of Ra and Osiris, calls in the magician to his aid ; the evidence of his conscience, if he has sinned, will not prevail against a spell which he recites. He will escape from the Devourer, and the trial (ordeal ?) of the Basin of Flames. Thoth, perhaps cheated, pronounces the sentence of the tribunal : " The deceased has been weighed in the balance. There is no fault in him ; his heart is as Maat."

It is, therefore, admitted that the tribunal of Osiris recognizes the complete innocence of anyone who knows the proper formula. Justification is automatic, and is obtained by magical means. It also ensues from the fact that, by the Osirian rites, the deceased becomes an " Osiris justified ", *maâ-kheru*. After that, this Osiris can " go wherever he pleases, among the Spirits and the gods ".

The destinies in store for the new Osiris are as varied as the " transformations " (*kheperu*) permitted to the gods. If he likes, he may rule the world with Ra, in the sky ; or row or tow the barge of the Sun ; or live in the fields of Ialu as a tiller of the soil of heaven [1] ; or visit the Duat by night, in the train of the nocturnal Ra [2] ; or dwell with Osiris in the Lower Region ; or " renew his life " (*uhem ânkh*) in his tomb, and even on earth, in his " house of the living ". The *Book of the Dead* teaches him the names of all the gods, the pass-words which will open the gates of heaven and the Duat, and all the mysteries of the divine forms—falcon, swallow, Phœnix Benu, etc.—which he might wish to assume.[3] Everywhere the gods accept him as one of themselves.[4]

---

[1] The King himself ploughs the fields of Ialu and reaps his harvest, from which his offering-bread will come. But, for the impressed labour of the next world, the man dead in Osiris—King or peasant—can call upon statuettes, usually of enamelled clay, which *answer* his summons and do all the heavy work of the afterlife for him. These Answerers (*Ushebtiu*) are found in every Egyptian tomb, sometimes in hundreds. They are a working class, endowed with a magical life, in the service of the " Lords of Eternity " (see Fig. 69).

[2] In the Theban royal tombs, special books describe the voyage of Ra, himself regarded as dead, in the twelve night-hours of the Duat.

[3] What he calls " making his transformations into a falcon, swallow, etc." There is no analogy here with the metempsychoses of other religions, in which, according to his moral excellence, the dead man goes through a whole series of new existences, until at last he is merged in God.

[4] Chap. cxlviii.

The highest ideal, which consisted in " living on Maat among the Gods ", was that which the theologians conceived for the Kings. There is no doubt that the vast majority of Egyptians imagined a less exalted afterlife for the dead. The essential texts of the *Book of the Dead* are certainly formulas of " spiritualization ", but they have another, less ambitious title—" The Chapter of Coming Out during the Day (*pert m haru*) from the Divine Lower Region ".[1]

Some would translate this expression by " go out of the day ", " die to the world ". But the texts describe the aspirations of the deceased as follows : " You come out every morning, and return (to the tomb) every evening. Torches are lit for you at night, until the sun rises on your body. They say to you, ' Welcome ! Welcome ! ' in your House of the Living. You see Ra on the horizon of the sky, you behold Amon when he rises. (So) you awake happy every day." [2] Therefore, *pert m haru* means " to come out into the day " or " by day ", to live, a happy ghost, among the living. And in some tombs this earthly happiness is described with emotion : " You hurriedly pass the doors of the Lower Region. You will see your House of the Living, and hear the voice of the singers and musicians . . . You protect your children, always and for ever." [3]

Death does not break up family life for those who die piously. One chapter of the texts on the sarcophagi is entitled " The Reunion of a Man's Kinsfolk with him,[4] in the Divine Lower Region ". Ra, Geb, and Nut are summoned to allow the dead man, whether he go to heaven, on to the earth, or on to the water, to meet his people, that is, his father, mother, ancestors and ancestresses, children, brothers, workers, friends, allies, and servants, who perform the funeral rites for him on earth, and also his wife, whom he loves ; and to do this, whatever may be his abode in the next

---

[1] Chap. xvii.

[2] Inscription of Paheri (XVIIIth Dynasty) ; *Urk.*, iv, p. 117.

[3] Gardiner, *Tomb of Amenemhet*, pl. xxvii. Cf. Louvre Stele 55 : " May Osiris and Anubis grant that I may be a Spirit in heaven, Mighty on earth, Justified in the divine Lower Region ; that I may go out of my tomb and stay in it, cool myself in its shade, drink the water of my basin every day. . . . May I walk on the bank of my basin every day. May my soul rest on the branches of the plantations which I have made, may I cool my head beneath the sycamores, may I eat the bread which they give me."

[4] The word *abt*, which is rarely found, means the reunion of relations, clients, and servants, and corresponds to *gens*, or *familia*.

life, the sky, the earth, the Lower Region, or the necropolis of Abydos, Busiris, or Mendes. " If the gods do not grant this favour, men will cease to worship ; they will supply no more bread or meat ; and the barge of Ra will cease to sail." [1] Here, again, practical interest in the family cult brings us down from the heavenly paradise to earth ; by the side of the dogmas of the theologians, we catch a glimpse of the utilitarian sentiments of the people, who, to reach their ends, prefer to employ magic.

V

MAGIC, MORALITY, PERSONAL PIETY

In Egypt magic is hardly distinguished from religion. No doubt the methods which the magician employs in ordinary life are not those of the priest. The latter addresses prayers and offerings to the gods ; the former tries to circumvent them by force or trickery. In Egypt, as elsewhere, the priest supplicates while the magician commands. The latter, by sympathetic magic and imitative magic, makes use of the natural affinities of living beings and things. He thinks that he perceives the law of cause and effect, and claims to apply it everywhere. Where does the magician obtain his knowledge ? From the gods themselves. Thoth is the inventor of magic spells, as the " Lord of the creative Voice, Master of words and books ".[2] Isis is the great magician, who robbed Ra of his Name and possesses the secrets of the gods. Khonsu is the operator who, in the service of the gods, executes—sometimes even in foreign lands [3]— the magnetic passes and charms which subject every being to his will.

The interdependence of religion and magic is explained by the fact that the notion of the *sacred* extends to both alike. The divine potency, the *mana*, of primitive man [4] exists in every being and in every object, but in different degrees. The gods have it in the highest degree of all, though one has it less than another. In them it is expressed, not only

---

[1] Lacau, " Textes religieux," in **IV**, vols. xxvi ff. ; Texts ii and lxxii. For the social importance of these texts, see above, pp. 258–9, 273.
[2] **XXVII**, p. 259.   [3] **XLVI**, p. 188.   [4] Cf. From *Tribe to Empire*, pp. 46–9.

by a Ka, a Spirit, a Soul, a Power, a Name, but by the possession of charms, talismans, "magics" (*hekau*; cf. p. 122). Other beings [1] have it less ; these are the spirits which live among the gods and on earth, like inferior geniuses, and dwell (without always revealing themselves) in some object, animal, or living or dead man. Men as a rule have this power least of all, since on earth they live apart from their Kas. Most live close to gods and spirits without knowing it. Some of them, however, have received, through the sacred Books, the revelation of the magic of Thoth, Isis, Khonsu, etc. These are " wise men " (*rekh ikhet*) ; they " know the names " of gods, spirits, geniuses, and every being, and therefore they have power over them (cf. p. 372), and can tell those beings or objects which are inhabited by spirits and may be used as talismans or vessels for magic.[2] They know the power of the divine formulas, pronounced with the correct intonation ; they have the " right voice " (one of the meanings of *maâ-kheru*), and they claim, if need be, " to create by the voice."

The magician has formulas at his disposal for defence and for attack, for immediate and for deferred action. He protects his own life and that of his clients by talismans and spells. The talismans are amulets of wood, metal, or enamelled clay, whose shape recalls hieroglyphic signs, such as life, health, strength, stability, greenness, beauty, vigilance, protection, etc. Figurines of gods and kings are worn for the same objects. They are made into necklaces, bangles, anklets, belts, and head-ornaments, and all articles of clothing are adorned with them, making an armour which, by its sympathetic force, protects gods, living men, and mummies. Every talisman recalls a story and takes the form of some powerful god ; or else a god has used it in memorable circumstances, and tried its efficacity. From this come the formulas accompanying the talismans. They add the power of the " Voice " to the sacred content stored in them, for they are recited aloud over the talisman. He who says the formula will conquer evil, as the god who used it triumphed in the past—imitative

---

[1] Ibid., pp. 100–1.
[2] In the tomb of Amenophis II there is a list of gods and spirits, containing 540 names. The name " Spirit " (*Akh*) may be used in the magical texts for the *Afrit* which animates beings or objects.

Fig. 71.—Horus the Saviour mastering the Typhonian Beasts.

The child-god is surrounded by Ra, Isis, and Thoth. Above his head is the mask of Bes, which can be placed over the face of Horus, to frighten his adversaries.

In the upper compartment are scenes of the worship of Ra and various gods fighting for the magician who conjures them.

Magical stele known as the Metternich Stele. I have translated and commented on it in *Revue de l'Histoire des religions*, Nov., 1915.

magic. The magical papyri composed on this theme have preserved for us, as test-cases for the efficacity of formulas, the myths of the reign of Ra, the life of Osiris, the youth of Horus, the wars of Horus and Seth, etc.

When he passes to the offensive, the magician uses the same spells, either to quell snakes, lions, scorpions, and wild beasts in general, or to conjure " adversaries ", an evil genius or maleficent god like Seth or Apophis, or to impose his will on Ra or another god. Illness is one such case ; the being who causes it is an " adversary " (kheft), whom the magician alone can track down and master, just as he drives away ghosts, the wandering dead who send bad dreams, etc. These enemies the magician can exorcize for certain, *if he knows their name and conjures them by that name*. He obtains useful indications from the observation of the stars, on account of their influence on the fate of every being. He studies the fortune belonging to every position of the stars, the events which have previously happened in a given conjunction and will inevitably recur if the conjunction does. To be a healer, the magician must also be an astrologer. More, if he knows the names of the gods who have influence over a certain person or country, he can make them serve him and obey his voice ; if they do not, he throws the universe into confusion and terrorizes the gods. By these means he throws spells a long way, bewitches people, makes philtres of love or hate, kills people by destroying wax figures of them, and so on. Kings were no more secure from the perverse science of the enchanter than gods. Rameses III had to protect himself against a magician " who had stolen the secret books of the King, to bewitch and destroy the people of the Court ".[1]

So both black magic and white magic are practised, and are distinguished less by their methods than by their object, according as it is more or less occult, and criminal or lawful. In the cult of the gods and of the dead, magic plays an essential part. The priest worships and protects the god by means which are in no way different from the prescriptions used by the magicians. The embraces, the passes which shed

---

[1] Useful references will be found in my notes : " La Magie," in **XXVII**, pp. 243 ff., and " Horus Sauveur," in *Revue de l'Histoire des religions*, Nov., 1915, where I have made comparisons between the Egyptian texts and the general theory of magic. See also Lacau, *Les Statues guérisseuses* (*Mon. Piot.*, xxv), 1922.

the fluid of life (protection, *setep sa*), the creation of offerings by the *pert kheru*, the perpetual imitation of what was done for Ra or Osiris for the benefit of the King or dead man—all these rites are impregnated with magic.

From this point of view, magic is an official science, and the practice of it is a sure protection for man against the thousand dangers to which he is exposed. One can understand the confidence which Merikara's father places in it. "Ra created magic as an arm to defend men against evil fortunes, and he sends them dreams by night and by day" (above, p. 242).[1] At Court the "wise men", the magical experts, are included among the King's advisers, and the King himself boasts of being "initiated by Thoth into the knowledge of things, and of being, like Thoth, the Great Magician".[2]

But, on the other hand, the *Book of the Dead* tells us that formulas are sufficient to ensure to the dead man automatic triumph in the next world. Thus the high morality of the dogmas comes to nothing in practice. The judgment before Osiris and even the testimony of conscience are nullified by the use of the all-powerful formulas. He who is instructed in the chapters and possesses the ritual talismans will enter the gates of paradise, however well they are guarded; he will be told, "Enter! Thou art pure!" Magic makes up for lack of goodness and deceives men and gods alike.

Since the cult is tainted with magic, are we to deny the morality of religious sentiment among the Egyptians? This would be to say more than is justified by our inquiry, and to ignore the lesson which we have learned from the history of institutions from the time of the Kings who stood for the just laws. Worship retained forms which it had had for centuries, and tradition imposed the use of formulas which were magical rather than religious, but religious sentiment grew continually purer, from the XIIth Dynasty to the end

---

[1] Gardiner, **XIII**, i, p. 35, commenting on the *Teachings for Merikara*, lays stress upon the existence in Egypt of a magic which was the official handmaiden of the State religion. Magical practices also represent a method of individual worship, emancipated from official rites. This conception is derived from the communistic origins of society, in days when sacred gifts were not yet concentrated in the great gods, or in the power of the chiefs alone, but every individual in the clan had a share in the collective *mana*; cf. *From Tribe to Empire*, pp. 44–9.

[2] *Urk.*, iv, p. 20 (King Ahmes I).

of Egyptian civilization, at least among the educated governing classes.

As early as the XIIth Dynasty, a man says : " I have never done ill to anyone, that I may be a Spirit in the divine Lower Region." [1]

Paheri, of the princely family of el-Kab, bases his hope of an afterlife, not on magic, but on the testimony of his good deeds. " If I am placed in the balance I shall be weighed, whole and without deduction. . . . I have told no lie against another, *for I have known the God who is in men* (conscience) ; I have known him, and I have distinguished this from that (good from evil)." So Paheri is promised " the favour of the God who is in him ", [2] to ensure his life beyond the grave.

About the end of the XVIIIth Dynasty, Beki speaks his last words to his contemporaries : " Take pleasure in Justice (Maat) every day, as in a grain (?) of which one does not make a dish, and yet God, the Lord of Abydos, lives on it every day. If you do this, it will profit you. You will go through life in sweetness of heart, till you reach the beautiful West, and your soul will be able to go in, and go out, and walk about, like the Eternal Lords, who will abide as long as the Primordial Lords." [3]

Towards the end of Egyptian civilization, a noble personage declares : " The heart of a man is his own God. Now, my heart is satisfied with what I did when it was in my body. Then, may I be as a God ! " [4]

Such are the sentiments of good men who, like Beki, " just and free of faults, have set God in their heart and are wise by his grace." In these scrupulous spirits a personal religion begins to take shape. Conscience rises above imperative rituals, full of magic, and obscure and incoherent dogmas, to the notion of a justice which seeks and finds an end in itself. It is not only to uphold the social order, to obey the King's law, that Beki does good ; he obeys above all his internal god, his conscience. It is as a believer, not as an official of the King, that he stands for Justice. [5]

In spite of the political convulsions of the last centuries of national life, the germs of personal piety, planted in the human conscience, took root and bore fruit. In the necropoles of Thebes and Memphis of this period we find hundreds of humble stelæ in which worshippers of all classes of society address themselves to the gods directly (not through Pharaoh), to express love, reverence, and trust in their justice. [6] About the same time we see private individuals making donations

[1] Cairo : Piehl, *Inscriptions hiéroglyphiques*, iii, pl. xcii.
[2] *Urk.*, iv, pp. 119 and 117. Same sentiment in Louvre Stele C.26, l. 24.
[3] E. Drioton, *Les Confessions négatives*, in *Bibl. École des Htes. Études*, sec. iv, No. 234 (1922), pp. 551 ff.
[4] Piehl, op. cit., iii, pl. lxii.   [5] Drioton, op. cit., pp. 547–64.
[6] Erman, " Denksteine aus der thebanischen Graberstadt," in *Sitzber. Berlin. Akad.*, xlix (1911), pp. 1086 ff.

of real and movable property to the gods of temples, sometimes without the King intervening.[1] A devotion which shows its fervour by substantial gifts offers some guarantee of sincerity.

Finally, in the last days of Egyptian civilization, belief in the Last Judgment is expressed in the most human and elevated form.

A demotic papyrus, dating from the first years of our era, tells of an infant prodigy, a magician born, who goes down to the underworld with his father and visits the great abode of Osiris, King of the Dead. Before entering, they have passed the funeral procession of a rich man, buried in magnificent state, and the body of a poor wretch, rolled up in a dirty mat and followed by no one. When they come to the hall where Osiris judges the dead, they see a distinguished personage, clad in fine linen, sitting quite close to Osiris. "Father," says the child, "do you not see that high personage ? The poor wretch (whom we saw just now) . . . it is he. He was brought here, his misdeeds were weighed against his merits, and his merits were found more numerous than his misdeeds. Since he was not given a large enough sum of happiness while he was on earth, it was ordered, before Osiris, that the funeral gear of that rich man (whom you saw carried out of Memphis in great honour) should be given over to this poor man here, and that he should then be placed near Osiris. The rich man whom you saw, his misdeeds were found more numerous than the merits which he had on earth. He was bidden to pay here, and you have seen him, lying at the door. The pivot of the door is set in his right eye, and turns in his eye when it is opened or shut, while his mouth gives great cries. . . . He who does good on earth, good is done to him here ; but he who does evil, evil is done to him. These things which you see here have been established for ever, and they will not change ; and they happen in the forty-two nomes where are the gods of the tribunal of Osiris." [2]

Of course, this is only a story ; but, at least, it illustrates the spread among the mass of the people of the religious feeling which had been growing among the few ever since the Middle Kingdom. The gods no longer bow before magical formulas. The house of Osiris is no longer an office of weights and measures, where the total of offences against the social order is weighed against the total of services rendered, with

---

[1] In the classical period, no one can give a piece of land, offering, or object to a god except through the King, as eminent owner of the land, and as sole priest of the cult. It is the King who " gives the offering " in the name of the pious donor. From the XXIInd Dynasty onwards we find the stelæ recording donations on which the King no longer appears (cf. Spiegelberg, "Neue Schenkungsstelen," in **XII**, lvi (1920), pp. 57–9).

[2] Adapted from **XLVI**, pp. 160 ff. Compare the Parable of Dives and Lazarus (Luke xvi, 19). After death, Dives burns in hell while Lazarus lies in Abraham's bosom. "Remember," Abraham says to the rich man, "that thou in thy lifetime receivedst thy good things, and Lazarus in like manner evil things : but now here he is comforted, and thou art in anguish."

a balance and weights which magic falsifies. The Wide Hall of the Double Maat [1] is now a moral tribunal. Divine Justice is inexorably scrupulous, discerning, and, above all, reparative. She corrects the inequalities of fortune ; in the next world she divides men according to their merits.

In the course of centuries, priests and men broke away from the dominion of rituals and shattered the system of formulas. As their thought became emancipated, they became aware of their individual responsibility. A new world was opening. The religion of Egypt, an instrument of government, a State institution, which ignored the individual, a social edifice reinforced by a framework of dogma and ritual, collapsed or was transformed when, in the awakened conscience, personal piety was established.

[1] This same name means, on earth, the Vizier's tribunal (p. 286), and, in the next world, that of Osiris.

CHAPTER II

ART, SCIENCE, AND LITERATURE

OF the modes by which the life of a community expresses itself, the arts are the most subjective. Nevertheless, the physical nature of the country imposes certain methods on the artist, by the materials which it furnishes, and the political system influences his imagination, by the intellectual discipline which it preaches. The Egyptians, like every other people, were subject to these laws. In Egypt, the artist, like the priest, soldier, peasant, and official, worked to increase the chances of society lasting in this world and the next. This explains why the erection of buildings to shelter and magnify the life of gods, Kings, and deified dead is one of the essential manifestations of Pharaonic rule. Every King, " in exchange for the favours which he received " for himself and his people, owed it to his gods, his ancestors, and himself to build monuments in which their names and his own should live for ever. Indeed, most of the evidence with which we reconstruct the history of Egypt comes from the temples and tombs, which have earned their name of " eternal monuments ".

Temples and tombs demanded the collective effort of every art and craft. So architecture was the great " work ", in which the architect directed " all the work " of artists and craftsmen, with whom learned and literary men collaborated. Not until fairly late did the arts come to be differentiated and develop according to the genius of individual artists.

The first characteristic of the arts in Egypt, then, in the broadest sense, is their mutual interdependence. If the historian would ascertain the social effort represented by the artistic achievement, he will for choice point to this unity. We shall find in the production of works of art the centralization, discipline, and faith which governed political life. For in Egypt religious obligation is at the source of art, as of institutions.

411

I

We shall describe Egyptian art by studying the temples and tombs in their materials, plan, and decoration.[1]

A. *Materials*

In very ancient times stone was not used for building. The wood of the country, which only furnishes small beams and round logs, supplied the skeleton of light constructions, the walls of which were made of a wattle of reeds, lotus, and papyrus. Palm-leaves and papyrus-flowers, nailed on the top of walls and pillars, were the earliest decoration, which was copied in the later buildings of stone. The Royal Carpenter (*medeh*) was one of the great personages of the Thinite and Memphite Courts.

A second structural element was supplied by mud, mixed with straw, being used in the form of *pisé* (rammed between boards which were removed when it hardened), or of bricks, baked in the sun (never in the oven). The former method made it possible to " mould " (*qed*) solid walls, straight or circular, provided that they were thick and sloped inwards to the top. The moulder-masons (*iqedu*) enriched their art with new forms—walls with rounded tops, granaries with low round vaults (Fig. 59 and Pl. IX, 3), and domed chapels, which we know chiefly from pictorial representations. Brick gave a uniform, rectangular, light material adapted to all kinds of work. Brick walls, being thinner than those of mud, were adorned with projections and niches (Fig. 41), of which the Thinite tombs give well-preserved examples.[2] From very early times the Egyptian could build false vaults with his bricks, making each course overlap that below, and later he made semi-circular barrel vaults, and even domes on pendentives.[3] The mud buildings, which were weak at the

---

[1] All useful references will be found in G. Jéquier, *Manuel d'archéologie égyptienne*, vol. i : *Les Éléments de l'architecture*, 1924. See also J. Capart, *Leçons sur l'art égyptien*, 1920, and *L'Art égyptien : études et histoire*, vol. i, 1924. There the photographic material is indicated, and the great archæological publications. Cf. G. Bénédite's short but solid résumé, *L'Art égyptien dans ses lignes générales*, 1923.

[2] The Sumerian brick buildings have the same decoration.

[3] Jéquier, op. cit., pp. 304–8 ; for stone vaults, see pp. 309–14.

PLATE XVIII

1 TEMPLE AT DAKKEH PYLON, COURT, HYPOSTYLE, SANCTUARY
Sandstone Ptolemaic period

2 FUNERARY TEMPLE OF RAMESES II, THE RAMESSEUM AT THEBES
Converging lines of roof and ground Sandstone

angles, were protected by bundles of reeds placed at the points of least resistance.

The stone of the country, hewn and dressed, brought new materials. Limestone, sandstone, and granite were used by the time of Usaphaïs (Ist Dynasty) and Khasekhemui (IInd Dynasty); divine and royal edifices could now be " moulded in stone " (*qed iner*). Whereas brick triumphed in the Thinite period, stone made immense progress from the IVth Dynasty onwards—a granite temple, pyramids, Sun-temples. Architects and workmen, in the achievement of those gigantic works, reached a degree of perfection not surpassed by any people since. Under the IVth Dynasty, the desire for solid buildings of colossal size led to the use of huge blocks, even for interiors. Later, monoliths were confined to obelisks, statues of Kings, shrines, and sarcophagi. For building, after the Old Kingdom, medium-sized rectangular blocks were used, in regular layers like bricks.

Architecture in stone preserved some of the features proper to buildings of wood and mud, either from routine or from respect for tradition. The surrounding walls, which were vertical inside, had a pronounced batter outside, which was necessary with *pisé* but useless with stone. At sharp angles in the façade the torus, a round stone moulding, bound round with sculptured ligatures, recalled the bundle of reeds which had protected the corners of the *pisé* wall, and was merely ornamental in purpose. On the tops of walls, palm-leaves were no longer nailed, but the Egyptian hollow cornice was carved in stone, reproducing curving palm-leaves (Fig. 41; Pls. IV, 3; XVIII, 1; and XIX, 2). On the fronts of chapels and in tombs the projections and niches of the brick buildings were imitated. Lastly, the stone pillars, originally square, or cylindrical and quite plain, like wooden posts, became flower-columns, the glory of Pharaonic architecture.

By the side of the plain pillar, standing on the ground without a base and bearing the architrave without abacus or capital, as in the Temple of the Sphinx, there appears in 2900, under Zeser, the cylindrical, fluted column, surmounted by a " Doric " capital, which is enclosed in two long leaves, undulating and fluted, which hang downwards along the shaft.[1] This unexpected, and so far unique type, which seems to combine the elements of the future Doric and Corinthian orders, gives a very high idea of the inventive faculty of the pre-Memphite sculptors.

In the following centuries, the mature taste of the architects decided in favour of other types. First there was the cylindrical column, plain, or fluted, with from eight to twenty-four faces, on a base wider than the shaft and surmounted by a Doric abacus, without other decoration.[2] Then came the various orders of flower-columns (Pl. XX): (1) the palm-column—a conventionalized palm-tree, with a smooth round shaft, surmounted by a capital of nine palm-leaves [3]; (ii) the lotus-column, consisting of from four to six round lotus-stalks rising vertically together in a fasciculated shaft, tied round the neck with a five-fold band, and the flowers at the top just opening, and often surrounded by buds [4]; this order was used in the Old Kingdom, dropped in the time of the Theban temples, and revived in Ptolemaic times ; (iii) the papyrus-column, the chief Egyptian order, which was most often used. The column is of from six to eight fascicles, surrounded by reed-leaves at the base, where it tapers downwards. These fascicles have the triangular section characteristic of the papyrus. In the capital, the flowers are open or closed.[5] In the New Empire the column is often simplified ; a single stalk forms the shaft, without fluting, and a single flower, open like an inverted bell [6] or closed, constitutes the capital.

In the temples of the Græco-Roman period, the architects, initiated by the Greeks into new combinations, such as the acanthus capital, created a composite style, in which lotus, papyrus, and lily, open or closed, rise from palms, palmettes, vine-leaves, and buds of various flowers.[7] The capitals are then enormous bouquets, enlivened by the most brilliant

---

[1] These are pilasters, half engaged in the wall, excavated by the Service of Antiquities near the Step Pyramid of Saqqarah. Cf. I, xxv (1925), p. 149, pl. v (Mr. Firth's report).

[2] Jéquier, pp. 175–83.

[3] The earliest found are in the temple of Sahura (Vth Dynasty) ; Jéquier, p. 196.

[4] Except in the wooden specimens, in which the flower is often open ; Jéquier, p. 202. For the closed capital in the Old Kingdom, see Jéquier, p. 203.

[5] Old Kingdom, Jéquier, p. 211.

[6] Ibid., p. 223.

[7] Jéquier distinguishes twenty-seven types of composite capital.

colours, as, indeed, they were in all the previous periods (Pl. XX, 2).

Thus the wood, the earth, the stone, and the flora of the country furnished the materials and decorative elements of Egyptian buildings.   But it was religious thought which determined their plan, conventionalized their decoration, and revealed their inner significance.

B.   *The Plan of Temples and Tombs*

When Pharaoh decided to build a sanctuary, he consulted the *Book of the Foundation of Temples*, which was believed to have been written by the god Imhetep.   On the appointed day, the King, aided by officiants acting the parts of gods, stretched the line along the four sides, dug the earth along the mark, moulded a brick, pushed a block of stone into the foundations, and deposited underneath it tools, talismans, and tablets in his name, to recall the work done by men in honour of the god.[1]

The architect and stonemasons were under the direction of the high-priest of Phtah (the god of the arts), who bore the title of Great Chief of Works (*ur kherp hemut*).[2]   This shows the religious control to which the builder was subjected.[3] The plan of the temple was inspired by dogma, and varied as dogma varied.

The Thinite temple was a mere hut of wattle, with a fence in front and two ensigns in the form of the sign *neter* (god) at the entrance.   Under the Vth Dynasty, the Sun-temples (Fig. 46, p. 162) were still but little developed architecturally. An obelisk in an open court, an offering-table, libation-vases, and a small sacristy for the priests were the features of a cult which had hardly any earthly *décor*, as was fitting with a sun-god who lived chiefly in the sky.

After the democratic revolution Osiris was associated with Ra, and accordingly the Theban temple was conceived on quite a different plan, which was to prevail from then to the end of Egyptian civilization.   The being whose house had to be built had become a man-god (Osiris) as well as a heavenly

---

[1] **XXX**, p. 130. The Palermo Stone bears witness to these rites in the Ist Dynasty, and they last till Roman times.

[2] Cf. the title *Pontifex*, Bridge-builder, of the priest-architects in Rome.

[3] See above, pp. 251–2.

god (Ra). The temple was therefore suited to an existence which was spent both on earth and in heaven.

The earthly appearance of the temple.—Like the palaces of Kings and the houses of rich men, the plan of the temple comprises three divisions, leading from social to family life, from the outside world to privacy (see Pls. XVIII and XIX).[1]

(i) A door in the outer wall leads into a court, open to the sky, where the people of the house, friends, clients, and visitors go about. In the temple the door, which is of monumental size and flanked by two very high rectangular towers, forms what we, following the Greeks, call the pylon (Egyptian *bekhent*). Inside is the great rectangular court, a kind of enclosed public square, on to which the full light of the sun pours without other shade than a narrow pillared portico along the sides. This wide space (*uskhet*), stretching the whole breadth of the building, is open to visitors, devout or curious, and is the public part of the temple.

(ii) Then comes a second *uskhet*, differing from the first in that it has a roof, borne by columns.[2] This is used by the master of the house as a dining-room and reception-hall. Air and light enter only through the door and through openings at the top of the side-walls, under the roof. We are in the semi-private part of the house, to which only intimates are admitted. In the temple this pillared hall, cool and dim, is the hypostyle. Here the god makes his " rising " (*khâ*), that is, shows himself, in the form of his statue, to his worshippers; and here he takes his meals, that is, the offerings (*hetep*) served to him. In most temples there are two, or even three, hypostyles, in succession ; the " wide hall of the rising " (*uskhet khâ*) is distinguished from the " wide hall of offerings " (*uskhet hetep*), and sometimes both are preceded by a " forehall " (*khent*). Into this semi-private part of the temple only the priests and certain worshippers, the Pure (*uâbu*), are admitted. At the entrance-doors stand the words, " Those who enter here must be pure."

(iii) Last, there is a small hall, closed on all sides, with no opening but the door. In the house this is the most private part, the harem, the bedroom, where only the owner and his

---

[1] Strabo (xvii, 1, 28) gives an accurate general description of the temples which he saw in Egypt.

[2] Hence the Greek name *hypostyle*.

PLATE XIX

1. KARNAK. GREAT HYPOSTYLE HALL OF SETI I AND RAMESES II.
OBELISKS OF THOTHMES I AND HATSHEPSUT

2. EDFU. COURT, HYPOSTYLE, SANCTUARY, CIRCUIT WALL
Ptolemaic period. The lighting is reduced, from the court to the shrine
(the openings in the roof are modern)

family can enter. In the temple it is the "secret part" of the building. In the centre, on the main axis, is a kind of fortified keep, with thick walls, entered only by a door. This is the private chamber of the god, the sanctuary, "the place which one should not know" (*khem, skhem*), the *adyton*. Here the "living image" of the god dwells, in the form of an emblem or a statue, in a granite shrine or in the cabin of a sacred barge, "that which bears the beauties

FIG. 72.—Plan of a Palace at el-Amarna.

Reading upwards, (i) outer wall with great central door; (ii) open court, surrounded by a portico; (iii) pillared hall, for meals and receptions; (iv) private apartments, provisions, bedroom (right).

of the God" (*utest neferu*), mounted on a pedestal. As a rule, the barge is in a first sanctuary, in front of that of the statue, which is, in this case, the true Holy of Holies, the "Great House" (*per-ur*). All round the sanctuaries runs a passage, on to which cells open—sacristies, store-rooms for offerings and sacred apparatus, and chambers for certain secret rites. No one can enter "the mysterious places" save the King and the priests on duty.

Such is the plan of the house in which the man-god lived among his creatures (cf. Pl. XVIII, 1). From the Theban period to Roman times, this edifice was reproduced in thousands of examples, some small and some colossal.[1] With its immense walls, the straight surface of which is broken by no opening or moulding, the Egyptian temple harmonizes

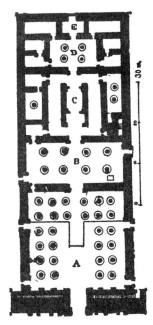

Fig. 73.—Temple of Khonsu at Karnak.

Rameses III. A. Pylon and open court with portico; B. Hypostyle hall of the "rising" and "offerings"; C. Sanctuary of the barge; D. Vestibule; E. Holy of holies (statue).

wonderfully with the undefined, flat lines of the cliffs over-looking the valley. Here, once more, the artist has under-stood the teaching of nature,[2] and has developed from it a sober, powerful style, suitable for "eternal monuments".

[1] e.g., the Ramesseum is 220 feet wide at the pylon and 490 feet long. Karnak and Luxor are aggregates of temples of various periods, in which every part is repeated. The temples hewn in the cliffs (e.g. at Abu-Simbel) have the same general plan, but lack the pylon.

[2] Compare the lines of the temple at Der el-Bahari with those of the Libyan cliff (Plate II, 1); see also those of the Ramesseum (Plate XVIII, 2).

The dogmatic division of the temple.—In addition, the architect had to arrange his temple as a dwelling for a sun-god, the creator of the universe.

The temple, the house of the Demiurge, becomes a reduced image of the universe. Its floor is the land of Egypt, with its plains, high ground, waters, plants, and living inhabitants.[1] Flowers and trees rise from the real or supposed ground, either in the open air, in the court, or supporting the sky, in the hypostyle, in the form of columns shaped like palm-tree, papyrus, and lotus. The roof of the hypostyle and of the sanctuary is the sky. It is painted blue, dotted with golden stars, and on it one sees the star-gods in their boats, the *decani* who preside over the thirty-six parts of heaven, and the deities of the Zodiac. Great vultures, with outspread wings, fly there, to ensure the protection which they symbolize. In the median axis, the winged disk of the Sun hovers everywhere.[2]

This Demiurge is a Sun-god—Atum, Ra, Harakhti, under various local names. The temple is, therefore, a " Solar " building. Its ritual orientation places its face towards the East, and makes the building run from East to West, following the course of the sun. In practice, this orientation is only found in a few places, for example, at Abu-Simbel, but in theory the god, from the depths of his shrine, is supposed to face the East. On the left side [3] of the court there is sometimes an altar, at which, at daybreak, a priest comes to worship the rising sun ; in the evening he turns round towards the sunset.[4] In theory, even if it does not happen in practice, the sun rises between the towers of the pylon on the East. The priests teach that the two towers are Isis and Nephthys, " the two great Goddesses in the Eastern side of the sky." [5] On the walls of the Ptolemaic temples one reads : " The pylons are like the two Sisters lifting up the disk of the Sun. One side is Isis, the other Nephthys. They hold the winged disk Behedeti up in the air

---

[1] See the painted pavement of a palace at el-Amarna, which is an excellent illustration to the *Hymn to Aten* (Plate XIII, 1, and p. 325).

[2] Cf. *From Tribe to Empire*, fig. 31.

[3] Left from the point of view of the god, looking down the temple towards the entrance.

[4] Cf. Maspero, " La Chapelle d'Ibsamboul," in **XII**, xlviii (1910), p. 91.

[5] *Pyr.*, § 2200.

(*tua*) when he shines on the horizon." "The Sun rises in the sky, flying, every morning, and alights every day on the two arms of Isis and Nephthys. He mounts in the sky in the form of Khepri and goes across the firmament." [1] In front of the pylon two or four obelisks, "which give light to the Two Lands like the Sun," [2] announce that the temple is under the protection of the erected stone, the ancient dwelling of the Sun.

In addition the plan of the temple is adapted to a theoretical course of the Sun, as represented by the god residing in the shrine. As in the real sky, there are the horizon of the morning, the zenith, and the horizon of the evening.[3] The small, dark *adyton* is the gorge in the Arabian cliff, dark before dawn, from which the Sun rises. The text say, " Ra is born every morning ; this place of his birth is like the horizon of the sky." The hypostyle, where the light is still very dim, offers a somewhat larger field to the Sun's first rays. One is no longer on the horizon ; one can see " the celestial vault . . . with its columns of papyrus, lotus, and palm, which bear the structure as the four deities of the four cardinal points bear the sky ". Then comes the open court " like Nut (the Goddess of the Sky) who gives birth to light " ; this is the immense plain of heaven, opening before the Sun's course, in the splendid hours of morning. At noon the Sun is above the pylons, which hold him in the air, in the apogee of his might. After midday, the same stages are passed in the opposite direction. Court, hypostyle, and *adyton* receive the declining orb in their respective domains, each smaller and dimmer than the last. The Sun is back in the *adyton*, now called his Western horizon, and alights on the out-stretched hands of the priest-king. " He lies, during the night, in the shrine, until the dawn of the next day." [4]

In this daily journey, the god divides his temple

---

[1] Dumichen, *Tempelinschriften*, i, pl. 2, l. 9.

[2] Mariette, *Abydos*, i, pl. 18*b*.

[3] Cf. Rochemonteix, in works which are old, but deserve to be better known, " Le Temple égyptien," " La Grande Salle hypostyle de Karnak," and " Le Temple d'Apet," collected in **XXXVIII**, vol. iii. The texts which I quote are from the temple at Edfu (Dumichen, in **XII**, 1870, pp. 2 ff.). Cf. Spiegelberg, **XII**, liii (1917), p. 98, and Grapow, *Die bildlichen Ausdrücke des Ægyptischen*, 1924, pp. 24–8, 33.

[4] Rochemonteix and Chassinat, *Edfou*, i, p. 34, pl. xiii*a*.

into two regions, as the real sun divides the sky.[1] What lies to his left as he leaves the shrine forms the Eastern side (attached to the South) of the temple and the sky, the domain of the rising sun, of Ra, the god of life. What lies to his right forms the Western side (attached to the North), the realm of the sinking sun, of Osiris, the god of death, and the region of the necropoles.[2] A central zone between the two sides may be compared to the zenith.

The architect observes these rules of the theologians with scrupulous respect. He endeavours to translate them by the dispositions of the temple, especially in the " secret part ". In some temples, the sanctuary is flanked on the left by the apartments in which the god manifests himself in his solar glory. The Chamber of Fire (?) (*per-nesert*), the Hall of the Throne of Ra, the hall in which the New Year is celebrated, and the altar of the Sun in the court are the places which mark the daily, or annual, triumph of Ra. On the right of the sanctuary, the Chamber of Water (?) (*per-nu*) and the halls in which they celebrate the mysteries of Osiris dead and resurrected remind one that the temple is the scene, not only of the daily decline of the evening Sun, but of the Passion of Osiris, who has there his tomb (*sheta*) and the cradle of his rebirth (*meskhent*).

In the other parts of the temple the architectural decoration displays the same contrasts before the eyes of the people. On the left, the Eastern and Southern side, the attributes of gods and kings, the rites, and the offerings belong to the Southern half of the world over which the sun is here supposed to pass ; on the right, the Western and Northern side, they belong to the Northern half.[3]

---

[1] Rochemonteix, loc. cit., pp. 47, 187. Cf. Grébaut, **IV**, i, p. 74.

[2] The Egyptian takes his bearings with his face to the South. His right is the West, his left the East.

[3] These general dispositions are confirmed in the Ptolemaic temples. For the division into North and South the actual orientation of the monument is sometimes taken into account (Mariette, *Denderah*, text, p. 39). At Denderah the ancient names of the royal palaces of Buto (above, p. 112) designate the two chambers which enclose the sanctuary (*per-ur*) ; but the meaning of these names was widened. *Per-nu*, by a pun on *nuj* (water), here means a libation-chamber (*Dend.*, ii, 56) for Hathor-Wazet, in harmony with the Osirian side of the temple ; *per-neser* (pun on *nesert*, flame) means a chamber where the burnt-offering is made (ii, 72a), where Hathor is Sekhmet, the mistress of fire, in harmony with the Solar side of the temple. It remains to be proved that these denominations were general before the Ptolemaic period. On *per-nu*, cf. Brit.

The same symbolism is expressed by the systematic distribution of the columns, of which some have open capitals and others closed ones. In the great temples the hypostyle has three aisles, the central one being higher than the other two. The capitals of the central nave are always bell-shaped, with open flowers, but those of the side-aisles are bundles of closed flowers.[1] The architect found this contrast in nature ; when flowers are closed they droop, and when they are open they stand up triumphantly. When he reproduces these attitudes in his stone flora, he will think it more artistic to put the tall columns with open flowers in the centre of the building, and to surround them with shorter columns with closed capitals. But it is at night, and also at dawn, that the lotus and papyrus are closed, whereas they open their petals under the influence of light and warmth. Here the religious interpretation comes in, taking us from nature to symbols. First, the papyrus column suggests, by its form, living vegetation, the vegetable *greenness* of which the papyrus (*uaz*) is the symbol in writing ; a hypostyle hall is named *uazit*, the " (green) hall of papyrus ". On the other hand, from the lotus the gods are born.[2] The pictures in the temples, illustrations of the " books ", show us the gods issuing from these flowers as they open ; Osiris, Nefertum, Ra, and the deified dead rise every morning from the unfolded lotus. In the hymns, " the divine lotus which lays its head in the primordial Ocean is the refuge of the Sun " [3] during the night ; at dawn, " in the shape of Nefertum, the Sun rises from the lotus " and mounts on the horizon.[4] Let us return to the temple. In the central nave, on the road followed, in the temple, by the sun in the zenith, the open capitals bear witness to the full expansion of light and vegetation at noon. In the lateral aisles, the papyrus and lotus are closed because, as flowers of the East and of the West, they enclose the unborn god at dawn and the dead god at nightfall.[5]

In the median axis of the temple, over the monumental

Museum, *Stelæ*, ii, 8–9 (XIIth Dynasty) ; on *per-neser*, cf. *Urk.*, iv, 107 (XVIIIth Dynasty).

[1] Jéquier, op. cit., p. 224.
[2] Moret, " Le Lotus et la naissance des dieux en Égypte," in *Journ. Asiat.*, May, 1917, pp. 499 ff.
[3] **IV**, xxvii, p. 190.
[4] *Pyr.*, § 266 ; Plut., *Dei Iside*, 11.
[5] Rochemonteix, op. cit., pp. 57, 178 ; cf. our Plates VIII, 1, and XX, 1.

1. LUXOR. CENTRAL COLONNADE OF TUTANKHAMEN,
WITH OPEN CAPITALS
Closed capitals at the sides. XVIIIth Dynasty

2. PHILÆ. PALM, LOTUS, PAPYRUS, AND COMPOSITE CAPITALS
Ptolemaic period

doors, that is, in the zenith, the sun is represented in the form of a winged disk, which was universally understood as the symbol of the sun before it became that of the Solar Horus localized at Edfu (Horus Behedeti).   At Abu-Simbel the entrance door, in the middle of the façade, is surmounted by a falcon-headed Harakhti, crowned with the disk.

The Solar intention appears in another feature, common to all temples. From the pylon to the hypostyle and sanctuary the ground rises in a series of ramps, while the roofs become lower. The pylon is highest, the hypostyle is not so high, and the sanctuary is lowest of all. The elevation is like a musical *crescendo* sign. The architect seems to have wished to indicate by the lines of the roof and ground, converging

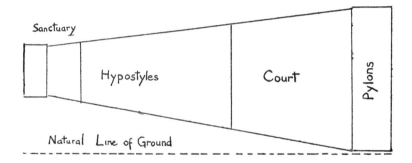

Fig. 74.—Ground and Roof-lines of the Temple.

towards the shrine, the sun's daily rising above the Eastern horizon and daily return to the Mountain of the West, his evening horizon (Pl. XVIII).

Having seen the plan of the temples, let us look at that of the *tombs*.   Here again the architectural plan is laid down by the Osirian doctrine.   Having studied the essentials of that doctrine in previous chapters, let us here briefly recall that the survival of the dead is ensured (i) by the preservation of the body, (ii) by the making of statues, " living images," and (iii) by the celebration of the funeral cult and the regular supply of offerings.   Every tomb will have to answer to these three conditions and will be built on a ritual plan.[1]

[1] See the text quoted above, p. 197.   When the King makes a tomb for a favourite, he entrusts the building to the priest of Phtah, the Great Chief of Works, and himself supervises operations.

In the Memphite period, the mastabas comprise three distinct parts : (i) a vertical pit ending in the funeral chamber where the mummy is to lie ; (ii) a walled chamber (*serdab*), where the statues will live which are visited by the Soul (*Ba*), when it is united to them by the Osirian rites ; and (iii) a chapel open to kinsfolk, friends, and the priests who pay worship and offerings (Pls. IV and V).

The first two chambers, which are closed after the burial, are small and little decorated. The third, which is public, allows the architect to enrich the pomp of the funeral worship by his art. On a wall in this chapel, facing east, is a false door (Pl. IV, 3), adorned in early times like the grooved façades of the Thinite tombs. This is the entrance of Amenti, with its doors and bolts and the grill above, through which the dead man can be seen sitting before his meal, in

FIG. 75.—A Visit to the Necropolis.

In the Libyan cliff are three doors of chapels. A woman mourns, after putting down the offerings under two date-palms and a sycamore. Painting on a wooden stele (XXIIIrd Dynasty). Cairo, LI, p. 342.

the other world (in the form of a bas-relief).[1] Sometimes the door opens, and the dead man appears standing in it (Pl. V, 1), as if about to descend the steps to meet his relations ; or else he puts his head over the top and looks into the chapel.[2] In all these details, as in the decoration of the walls, the architect has adhered strictly to dogma. However, he has some freedom in the arrangement of the chapel. According to the wealth of the owner, the reception-hall to which the family are admitted consists of one or more chambers.

There are mastabas for large families [3] in which the three elements are multiplied. For the Kings, the plan is modified, but the units prescribed by dogma are maintained. The tombs of the Memphite Pharaohs, as we have seen (p. 173), comprise

---

[1] Cf. Moret, *Fragments du Mastaba de Shery* (*Mon. Piot*, vol. xxv), 1922.
[2] **XXVII**, pl. xiii, 1.
[3] See the tombs of Ti, Phtahhetep, and Mera in the Memphite necropolis.

PLATE XXI

1. THE VALLEY OF THE KINGS
On the horizon the Nile and the Plain of Thebes

2. SARCOPHAGI, COFFINS, BOXES FOR CANOPI
Bubastite period (Cairo)

[face p. 424

(i) a portico and road of approach, (ii) a temple for the statues, and (iii) a pyramid. These three elements correspond to the chapel, *serdab*, and funeral chamber of the mastabas of lesser men. The three divisions required by dogma are preserved in all periods. The Theban Kings are buried in rock-hewn hypogea, not in pyramids, but here again we find a temple in the valley (e.g. the Ramesseum, Pl. XVIII, 2), a tomb cut in the Western Mountain (Pl. XXII), to hold the statues and furniture, and a chamber for the mummy. Private individuals, doing things more cheaply, reduce these elements to a chapel outside (Fig. 75), which has usually disappeared to-day, and a hypogeum with a pit.[1]

C. *The Decoration of Buildings*

Draughtsmen, sculptors, painters, and decorators.—In the temple or tomb, when the architect's task is finished, that of the artists and craftsmen under his direction begins, and it is an infinitely complex one. Hieroglyphic inscriptions have to be engraved on stone, every sign being treated as an artistic figure ; images of gods and exact likenesses of dead men must be drawn and carved ; statues intended for the rites and all the furniture and utensils of the funerary or divine cult must be made ; walls must be adorned with complete and faithful pictures of private, social, and religious life ; the statues and furniture have to be gilded and the mural reliefs painted ; the great doors must be made, provided with bronze hinges, staples, and bolts, and covered with chased plates of gold ; and a thousand other details must be carried out by the most expert artists. At Edfu the work of building and decoration took ninety-five years, from the laying of the foundation-line to the installation of the god in his abode.[2]

Let us consider the elements of the technique of drawing and relief-carving.[3]

The Egyptian shows himself a born draughtsman. His pictorial script gives him constant practice. Incised, carved

[1] For the Theban tomb, see A. H. Gardiner, *Tomb of Amenemhet*, the conclusions of which I have summarized in **VIII**, N.S., i, p. 267.

[2] **XII**, viii (1870), p. 3.

[3] For a detailed study, see H. Schaefer, *Von aegyptischer Kunst* (1920), and numerous articles in **XII**, especially about the art of el-Amarna (vol. lii, 1914, p. 1). See also L. Klebs, "Die Tiefendimension in der Zeichnung des alten Reiches," in vol. lii (1914), p. 19 (perspective, foreshortening, etc.).

in relief, drawn, or painted, on walls, bone, wood, or metal, it is a continuous succession of small masterpieces. In the perfect execution of it, the artist learns every refinement of drawing, and his eye is as gifted for observing forms as his hand, when free, is for rendering them. In Egypt, writing is the first of the pictorial arts, and, conversely, every figure is a definition, as if written, of a living being or object. The " name " of beings, a spiritual concept, takes life and shape by the magic of the hieroglyphics, the " divine words ". Among primitive men, and especially in Egypt, to portray a being or object is to call it to life ; the image brings up the reality. We have had evidence of this principle in the case of the statues, the " living images " of gods and men (p. 382). The same principle holds good for every kind of representation, written or artistic. So the object of sculptor, painter, and draughtsman is to make a complete and accurate copy of persons and things, for in this way the souls of the persons or things will be able to " enter " the images which resemble them and to animate them with a divine life.[1]

These are the ideas governing the technical conventions of the pictures drawn, carved, and painted on the walls of tombs and temples ; but there are material difficulties which impose traditional methods on the artist.

Pliny the Elder states that the Egyptians invented the art of painting, six thousand years before the Greeks, beginning by drawing lines round men's shadows.[2] Silhouettes of living beings and objects, copied from their shadows on walls, are often the starting-point of drawing, on the walls of the mastabas as on the sides of Greek vases.[3] Such drawing gives the outside line perfectly but it is only good for *profiles*. The shadow of an object taken from in front shows a featureless mass ; if internal details are to be seen the artist must draw them inside his outline. The Egyptians could draw

---

[1] This belief in the life of images sometimes leads to unexpected consequences. In the Pyramids and in certain tombs the written signs representing men are always mutilated and incomplete, and those of animals, especially dangerous ones, such as snakes and wild beasts, are cut in half or decapitated. The reason is that it was feared that these figures, made alive by rites and recreated by the voice of the man reading the text, might become hostile to the dead man. On this subject, see H. Brugsch and P. Lacau, in **XII**, xix, p. 8, and li, p. 1.

[2] *N.H.*, xxxv, 15–16 : *umbra hominis lineis circumducta*.

[3] E. Pottier, in *Revue des Études grecques*, xi (1898), p. 355.

PLATE XXII

THE GOLDEN HALL OF THE TOMB OF SETI I

Rock-cut architecture.   On the walls, books describing the next world (*Duat*); on the ceiling, the star-gods in the sky. (Photograph of the Metropolitan Museum, New York)

heads and bodies in full face, as we see in their hieroglyphics [1] and reliefs, but they seldom attempted it, and then only for the figures of foreigners, gods or men.[2] Their almost exclusive preference for side views led them into mistakes which cause one a disagreeable surprise in such gifted and conscientious artists. Feet and hands are treated carelessly ; many human figures, in monuments of all periods, even among those best executed (Pls. VII, 3, and XVI), seem to have two left feet or two right hands. Now, in a silhouette the foot or the hand with extended fingers has the same shape, whether it is the right or the left. So the artist has to draw internal lines, separating the big toe or thumb, in order to show which

FIG. 76.—Harem at el-Amarna.
Superimposed scenes.

it is. But the Egyptian draughtsman too often puts the thumb in the same position on the hand, irrespective of which hand it is, and the same with the big toe. This deformation, which jars on us, was accepted by the Egyptians, as a pure convention, and we also find it on Greek vases and many other objects, where the artist has followed the silhouette method.

The reliefs on the temples and tombs contain another curious feature, which is not to be explained on technical

---

[1] e.g., the sign of the human face (*her*), and the owl (*m*).
[2] See Horus Bes (Fig. 71), the goddess Kadesh (*From Tribe to Empire*, fig. 40), and some figures of the Peoples of the Sea (ibid., figs. 44–5).

grounds ; namely, the flattening back of certain parts of the
body, and the absence of foreshortening and perspective. In
a head drawn in profile, the eye, if properly drawn in profile
too, does not show the whole pupil, and does not seem to look
at you. Now, what the Egyptian artist wants, above everything else, is to make a real, living eye, and so he flattens it
back, drawing it in full, as if facing you (Fig. 64). The same
thing appears in the shoulders, which are shown as seen from
in front, in one plane. But the chest, one breast of which is
indicated in the outline, is supposed to be seen in three-
quarters, and so is the stomach, on which the navel is marked ;
both are fitted in somehow with the arms and legs, which are
drawn strictly in profile. The same divergencies appear in the
costume ; a collar drawn full-face lies on the chest which
is drawn in three-quarters, and the waist-cloth spreads out
sideways, in front of the loins.[1] Crowns and headdresses are
sometimes done from in front, with the details flattened
out, so as to be quite visible.

The same conventions appear in the rendering of objects,
buildings, landscapes containing figures, etc. A loaf on a
mat will be drawn above the mat, so as to be seen (Fig. 51).
An arm-chair is drawn in profile, but the seat is in plan, on
the top of the legs. In a drawing of a temple or palace, gate,
court, hypostyle, and inner room are all completely visible,
one above the other. If the artist has to represent a scene
with many figures, supposed to be on the same level, he will
draw them one above the other, and all of the same size.
His eye, concentrating on volume, does not see perspective
or receding lines or foreshortening. So every figure or object
remains complete, real in itself, independent of all its
surroundings. In the total scheme of the picture it retains its
full significance, and is read like a distinct sign of writing
(Fig. 76).

Why these conventions ? Do we explain them when we
put them down to inexperience, the clumsiness of a primitive
art ? Certainly it is in part due, if not to technical inability,
at least to a tradition of simplicity derived from the silhouette
method. This tradition was sternly maintained, for ritual
reasons, in representations which, we must remember, were

---

[1] See Plates VI. 2 : X. 2 : XIII. XVI. and XVII.

intended for religious buildings. But there is another intention, which we shall find in the technique of the statues in the round.

For statues, stone, plastic clay, enamelled or otherwise, wood, ivory, bone, and metal are used, the last being in early times chased over a wooden pattern and later cast in a mould. Gilding, gold and silver overlay, enamel, rare stones, and coloured glass are used to adorn figures or to give animation to their features; sometimes they have enamel eyes in a setting of copper.[1] These works in the round present a complete form, from whatever side they are seen, and the artist has no need of ingenious flattenings of a limb or an ornament, to render the reality correctly. Nevertheless, the statuary, too, has to observe conventions.

First, he has to solve problems of technique. How is he to cut out, from his block of stone or wood, limbs which are difficult to carve and fragile when they are done? We can follow the advance made from century to century. In the Thinite period, all the expression of life is concentrated in the face; the arms remain fixed to the sides, and the legs are not separated (Fig. 40). At the beginning of Memphite times, limbs are disengaged, arms are stretched out, legs are divided, and the left foot advances slightly (Pl. V, 4). In statues of wood, where the material is less inclined to break, the limbs move in the air; a right hand projects in front of the trunk, holding a stick, and legs are separated in quite a stride (Pls. X, 1, and XI, 2). Statues of copper, bronze, or gold, in plates hammered over a wooden pattern, have an even freer action. At the end of the Theban Empire, the use of moulds for the casting of statues, generally small, makes it possible to produce statues with free limbs in large quantities, and they come into general use.

Yet the Egyptians never reached the technical skill of the Greeks. Besides, why should one ask them for qualities at which they usually did not aim? The statuary art was for a long time mainly religious. Most of the statues which we

---

[1] For the technique of the arts, see Maspero's excellent manual of applied archæology, **LI**, and Flinders Petrie, **L.**

possess come from temples or tombs, and consequently represent beings in a " state of grace "—Kings, gods, and deified dead—or, at least, taking part in some sacred task, as officiants in temples or as servants of a dead man in his tomb. Is it surprising that these persons, engaged on a solemn duty, should have a serious, formal air, a ritual, fixed character ? Their attitudes are hardly allowed to vary. Gods and great personages are represented standing with their legs together, or with the left foot forward, or, sometimes, sitting on a throne or arm-chair. Subordinates and servants squat in the Oriental manner, with their legs together, and their arms crossed over their knees, or else with their legs crossed, tailor-fashion (Pl. VI, 1), or, again, on their knees, with their arms extended or raised in adoration. Whatever the attitude may be, every figure, in the round or in relief, is subject to technical and ritual canons.

We have no Egyptian treatise on æsthetics. But Diodorus (i, 98) has formulated the rules observed by draughtsmen and statuaries. The human body was treated as if it were divided into two by an imaginary line running through the middle of the forehead, the nose, the breast-bone, the navel, and the crutch ; the sections on either side of this line being equal and symmetrical. This explanation of Diodorus is confirmed by most of the reliefs and statues ; Julius Lange has based on it his " law of frontality " (a bad name, since there is no necessity, for the application of the rule, that the figure should be shown full-face). The Egyptian work of art is based on the balance of the parts about the central line. The head is not inclined to right or left, and the bust, even in stooping figures, remains a block without any deviation. We may add that the limbs, in the few movements which they perform, are attached to the trunk as rigid pieces, sometimes at a right angle.[1] When two figures are associated, the methods are the same. Look at a god or king holding his divine wife on his knees (Pl. XXIII, 1). The two bodies are independent, the trunks are rigid, and the arms and legs stick out angularly from the bodies.[2]

Here we see the same convention as in the reliefs. The

[1] Plates VI, 1 ; V, 4 ; XI, 2.
[2] Cf. H. Schaefer, " Grundlagen der aegyptischen Rundbildnerei und ihre Verwandtschaft mit denen der Flachbildnerei ", in *Alte Orient*, xxxiii (1923).

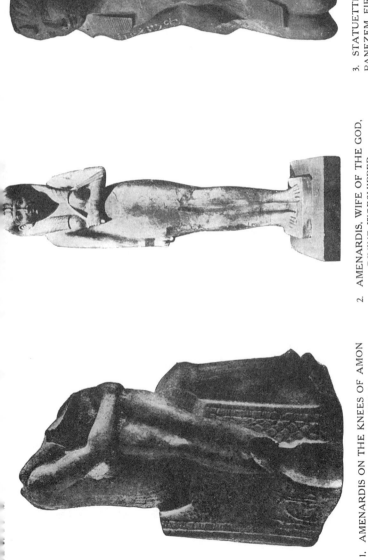

1. AMENARDIS ON THE KNEES OF AMON
Statuette of enamelled clay (Cairo)

2. AMENARDIS, WIFE OF THE GOD,
DIVINE WORSHIPPER
Alabaster (Cairo)

3. STATUETTE WITH THE NAME OF
PANEZEM, FIRST PROPHET OF AMON
Basalt (Cairo)

face p. 430

Egyptian does not render bodies as his eye sees them, at a certain distance and in a certain scale, with bendings, fore-shortenings, and shadows which apparently modify their real lines. He corrects the evidence of his eye by his knowledge, by all that his memory and tactile experience tell him about the total shape of a person or object. So he tries to represent bodies as they are, and not as he sees them—complete and independent, even if they form part of a group. This is the cause of the figures shown one above the other and of the bodies rendered, as it were, limb by limb. This objective conception of art is not peculiar to the Egyptian. It is found in the work of all Orientals, before the Greek, in the fifth century, imposed his subjective conception, which renders bodies as the eye sees them, with foreshortening, shadows, and perspective, and not as experience has shown them to be. We also find the objective vision and rendering in drawings of children [1] and primitive peoples, and even in the work of highly refined artists who, on principle or out of affectation, have come back to trying to render real volume, by cubism and other methods.

We should note that buildings, statues, and reliefs were always painted, and sometimes covered with a thin coat of stucco, which bore the colour. The colour, being laid on in flat washes, added nothing to the rendering of volume or modelling. It is the same with the paintings in the Theban tombs, which are not on reliefs, but laid flat on the walls (Pls. IX and XXII). The painter uses only flat washes, often of conventional colour, to render flesh, flowers, leaves, and decorations. With few exceptions,[2] there is in his painting no shading, modelling, tone, or illusion ; he renders things as he conceives them individually, in repose, in a crude, equal light, and not as his eye might see them, moving and affected by their surroundings in the changing play of light and shade.

These conventions, which govern all pictorial repre-sentation among the Egyptians, may be finally explained by Lionardo da Vinci's profound definition of painting : " It is

---

[1] Cf. Schaefer, op. cit., pl. ii, and " Scheinbild oder Wirklichkeitsbild," in **XII**, xlviii (1911), p. 134.

[2] There is an attempt at diminishing tone in Plate IX, 2 ; this striving after real modelling is characteristic of the art of the el-Amarna period (cf. Plate XIII, 1).

a mental thing." The "deformations" of Egyptian art
proceed from a mentality which is not ours, but is that of the
conscientious primitive man.

Once these rules are laid down, it will be understood that
there might be something mechanical in their application by
the artist.

Diodorus observes (i, 98) that the Egyptian sculptors
followed a canon of proportions. "They divide the whole
body into twenty-one and a quarter parts, and base man's
whole structure on these." This leads to the strange consequence that the different parts of a statue are treated
separately by specialists. "When they have agreed on the
height of the statue, they do each his own work, quite
separately, but in such harmony that one is absolutely
astounded." When the work is done, all the parts fit
perfectly.[1] In reality, such feats were exceptional. The stone
statues are almost all monoliths, and so could not be treated
in the manner described by Diodorus; but there is a statue
of sandstone, found by Legrain at Karnak, which has separate
limbs, carved independently and affixed with tenons.[2] The
wooden statues often have limbs attached, which are sometimes jointed and movable. We need not remember Diodorus's
details, which are exaggerated, but the general idea which
he gives is suggestive.

On the blocks intended for statues or walls to be covered
with reliefs the draughtsman prepared for the sculptor by
squaring the surface with guiding-lines for the important
details. The foreheads, eyes, shoulders, waist-lines, and feet
of the different figures go on the same lines, and arms are
placed at the same level according to the gesture.[3]

For the proportions of the figure, statistics taken from the
monuments show that a canon exists, but it varies with the
period and the school. "The first, which was in use from
the Old Kingdom onwards, divides the upright human figure

---

[1] Diodorus broaches the subject in connexion with the Apollo of Samos,
which had arms extended and legs walking in the Egyptian style. He declares
that the sculptors Telecles and Theodoros each made a half of it, and each part
then fitted the other exactly. From this he deduces the principle of the median
division (from which we have taken the law of frontality) and the canon of
proportions. On this subject, cf. de Ridder and Deonna, *Art in Greece*, in *The
History of Civilization*, p. 243.

[2] Cairo catalogue : *Statues et statuettes*, vol. ii, pl. 1.

[3] Cf. Plates VI, 2 ; X, 2 ; XIV, 1 ; XVI ; XVII.

into eighteen squares. The knee comes in the sixth square, the shoulders in the sixteenth, and the nose in the seventeenth ; the head comprises two squares, and so goes into the rest of the body eight times. The seated figure comprises fifteen squares. The second canon, which is chiefly employed from the Saïte period, gives a slenderer figure with the forehead at twenty-one, the mouth at twenty, the shoulders at nineteen, and the knees at seven." [1]

The composition of the pictures shows us the various trades collaborating in the service of the gods and the deified dead, and taking part in their cult.

In the temples, the huge, windowless walls lend themselves admirably to the sculptor's chisel. I have said, when speaking of the hieroglyphics, that the writing of the Egyptians is drawing ; and the converse is equally true. The drawing on the walls of monuments is also writing ; the whole temple can be read from end to end like an illuminated missal. The pictures suit the special character of the three parts of the temple, and describe what goes on inside.

In the part open to the public, the pylon and court, historical scenes are preferred—the victories and trains of booty which have made it possible to build the temple, the ritual of the foundation, the decrees granting the priests the privileges and land needed for the cult. The decoration here is like a series of notices to the public. It is often cut in deep relief *en creux* (that is, *below* the surface of the stone), a method which gives the maximum effectiveness and legibility.

In the hypostyle, the Hall of the Rising shows us the god in his manifestations, seated on a throne and receiving the worship of the Pure Ones (Pl. XIV), or else borne in his barge on the shoulders of priests in the processions of the great festivals, at which he declares his will by gestures or oracles (Fig. 62). In the Hall of Offerings, the forty-two Niles of the forty-two nomes bring flowers, fruit, and solid and liquid nourishment (Fig. 53). On the walls the King lassos or shoots oxen, antelopes, and goats, the flesh of which will appear on the table of the gods ; he slaughters victims (Fig. 67) ; he

[1] Jean Capart, *Leçons sur l'art égyptien*, p. 130.

causes meat to be roasted ; he presents water, incense, and flowers to the god who rejoices in the smoke of sacrifice and feeds on immaterial Maat.

Now we come to the secret part, the sanctuary. Here the walls reproduce, in pictures one over the other, the daily rites which reanimate the statue in the shrine. In the chambers of the East, the triumphal feasts of the Sun are depicted ; in those of the West, the nocturnal mysteries of the death and rebirth of Osiris. Everywhere, the priest-king converses with the god, and exchanges with him the sacred fluid which, in this holy place, passes from heaven to earth (Pl. X, 2). The King, who is as necessary to the celebration of the cult as the god, appears everywhere in the ritual decoration. Care is taken not to omit scenes of his divine birth, his coronation, his Sed-feasts, his purifications, and his confidential conversations with the gods (Pl. XVII), who consecrate him every day as a god, united to his Ka, among men.

The images of the gods are everywhere, in relief and in the round,[1] on the walls, inside the shrine, and in crypts concealed in the walls. A chief sculptor of the King, the son of a sculptor, under the New Empire, paying homage to Thoth, the god of decorative artists, tells us that the King greeted him in his youth, as chief of works in the temples. Having been introduced solemnly into the Golden Building, to " give birth to " the statues and sacred images of the gods, nothing was hidden from him.

" I am the Chief of the Secrets. I see Ra in his manifestations, Atum in his births (forms), Osiris, Thoth, Min, Horus, Hathor, Sekhmet, Phtah, Khnum, Amon-Ra," etc. (over thirty deities). " It is I who make them rest in their eternal shrines."

In adorning the tombs, whether mastabas or hypogea, the artists also use books of copies,[2] which they reproduce indefinitely when carving and painting the various scenes of the cult (in the burial chambers) or of the new life promised to the deceased (in the chapels).

As for the representations of ordinary life, space lacks to

---

[1] Cf. Plates III, 3, and XIV, 2–3.

[2] Luise Klebs has made a list of the motives treated in *Die Reliefs des alten Reichs* and *Die Reliefs und Malereien des mit leren Reichs* (XIIth to XVIIth Dynasties). Cf. P. Montet, *La Vie privée des Égyptiens*, 1925, based on the reliefs in the mastabas.

discuss in any detail a subject which M. Georges Bénédite sums up in these terms : " The plastic art of ancient Egypt is divided into two contiguous domains, which are very clearly distinct, although the border-line is sometimes badly defined— the domain of free, popular art, and that of canonical, hieratic art." [1]

In scenes of nature and animal life, the artist observes truly, and renders what he has seen easily and happily. So, too, if he has to portray ploughmen in the fields, herdsmen guarding their beasts, craftsmen at their trades, merchants in the market, street scenes, games, or vulgar brawls, his drawing shows hardly any technical constraint or academic methods ; he is realistic, bold, and humorous. Are we to conclude that there was in Egypt a hieratic art distinct from popular art ? Stated thus, the question leads to a mis- understanding. In my opinion, we should distinguish between subjects, not between artistic doctrines or artists. According as the subject is sacred or profane, the artist respects ritual attitudes and canonical traditions in greater or less degree. In every period, the same artists were able to render the aspects of hide-bound dogma and those of free nature equally well. Egyptian art is one; the artists interpret their themes strictly, where they must, and with a certain fancy, where it is allowed.

Besides, it cannot be denied that even in subjects taken from popular life, in which there is a chance for sly observation and a certain liberty of style, the " book of the artist " imposes its forms, for these amusing sallies of pen and chisel are found repeated on several monuments. Even the sprightliness of the people is turned into formulas taught in the art-schools.

A " Director of Artists, painter and draughtsman ", under the XIIth Dynasty, prides himself on his capacity for doing ritual subjects and free subjects, in varied attitudes, equally well. He seems to have specialized in making statuettes of enamelled clay, and he describes, in technical terms, the meaning of which is too often uncertain, his professional skill in the preparation of the plastic paste and in the modelling. Now, on the one hand, he " knows the secret of the divine words (hieroglyphics), the ceremonial of feasts, and every magic, and makes use of them without omitting anything ".

[1] " Signa Verba," in *Recueil Champollion*, p. 23.

On the other hand, he describes the free attitudes which he has
learned to render.

> I know the attitude of a man's statue, the gait of a woman, the carriage
> of . . . the bent (attitude) of one being beaten . . . I can make an eye
> look at another [1] ; I know the frightened look of men on being awakened,
> the swing of the (spear-) thrower's arm, and the stoop of the runner. I know
> how to make clay (?) and materials for overlay (?), so that they will not
> burn in fire or wash off in water. This has been revealed to no one, except
> to myself alone and my eldest son, when the God (the King) ordered that
> there should be someone (?) to whom it should be revealed. I have seen
> things produced by his hand in the post of Director of Works, in every
> precious stone, from silver and gold to ivory and ebony.[2]

We need not smile at his vanity. We see in it an element
which we have not noticed before, and which we must observe
before we end this analysis of artistic production in Egypt—
the professional pride of the artist, " initiated in the secrets
of art and the crafts," and the revelation of his personality.

The personal character of artists and periods.—Technical
mastery brings its own reward. It develops in the artist a
joy in creating and a care for perfection which lead him to
regard his art as an end in itself, and not a means of performing
a religious act. It opens the door to independence of rules and
canons. Some Egyptian artists go through. It is true that the
works of art are almost always anonymous ; only rarely
can the name of a sculptor be attached to a statue. But
professional pride exists. On the tomb of Phtahhetep (Vth
Dynasty), the Director of Sculptors, Phtah-Ankhni, has represented himself.[3] Under Rameses III, a painter seems to have
left his portrait, taken from life ; he is sitting in the Oriental
manner, dipping his brushes into the cups of his palette, and
his long hair, hanging over his shoulders, gives him a
surprisingly " artistic " air.[4] Another painter of the same
period denies that "he is a mere draughtsman-scribe. His
thought is its own guide. He has no superior to set him rules,

---

[1] i.e. give a figure life by its glance.

[2] Louvre, Stele C.14. Cf. the commentary of Sottas, in **IV**, xxxvi, (1914),
and Gardiner, in **XII**, xlvii (1910), p. 96. The stele of this artist is indeed a
masterpiece of engraving on stone.

[3] **XL**, p. 504 ; **XII**, vol. xlii (1905), p. 128, and vol. 1, p. 76 (signature of
relief).

[4] **XII**, liv, p. 77.

for he is intelligent, skilful with his hands, and acute-minded in all things ".[1]

Certain forms give scope to individual mastery more than others, and soon lead the artist to aim at the purely artistic satisfaction which we call art for art's sake. This is the case with the work of goldsmiths, jewellers, furniture-makers, and makers of articles of luxury or the toilet. For centuries, religion inspired the decorative motives of these craftsmen.

FIG. 77.—Cutting Vases in Hard Stone.
Old Kingdom.   The drill (hemt) became the hieroglyphic sign designating " artist ", " craftsman ", " art ".

A chain, a bracelet, a necklace, a crown, before becoming a personal ornament, was a talisman protecting the wrist, ankle, neck, waist, or head. That is why they are adorned with hieroglyphic signs meaning greenness, stability, life-health-strength, and magical protection. Open flowers of lotus and papyrus recall that the sun rises in their cups. Sometimes, as in pectorals, the shape is strictly architectural, the ornament taking the form of a shrine containing one or more divine

FIG. 78.—Talisman Bracelet.
Formed of *sa* (guard) signs. Gold and amethyst. Found on a woman's arm at Negadah (Ist Dynasty).

figures (Fig. 79). For all this, the execution of these phylacteries involves so much training and skill ; the cutting of gold, silver, and bronze, the setting of stones and glass-pastes, and the making of *cloisonné* enamel are such delicate work ; and the richness of the material and the beauty of

<hr />

[1] **IV**, xxiv, p. 185.

forms and colours are so attractive to the eye,[1] that the object takes on an æsthetic value far surpassing its magical utility. Then the golden flies fastening chains, the snakes which coil round arms and ankles, the finger-rings and toe-rings, the bronze mirrors with handles adorned with figures and flowers, the jewel-cases, the gorgeous boxes strewn with the signs of Isis or Osiris, all these articles of luxury, executed in precious materials, are appreciated for the finish of their workmanship, their beauty, and their intrinsic value. Is not this also true of the chairs, arm-chairs, beds, sacred chests, gable-fronted

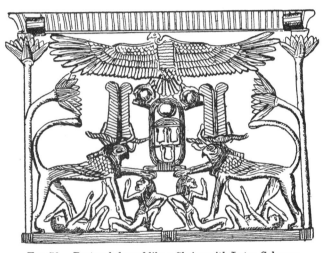

Fig. 79.—Pectoral shaped like a Shrine with Lotus Columns.

Open-work gold plaque, set behind with cornelian, turquoise, and lapis-lazuli. Nekhebt protects the name of Senusert III, who, in the form of griffins, tramples on captives. Cairo, from Dahshur (**L,** p. 103).

shrines (the XIIth Dynasty precursors of the Greek pediment), and, in short, of all the furniture of which such perfect specimens have been found in the tomb of Tutankhamen (Pl. XII, 3) and other tombs of the XVIIIth Dynasty ? Certainly, they still have the ritual decoration and the protecting sacred beasts. Uræi and heads and feet of lions guard their sides ; lotuses, talismans of life and health, and the cheerful, grotesque figures of Bes and Thueris the Hippopotamus keep off evil spirits ; but they are valued for

[1] On the workmanship of the jewels, cf. E. Vernier, "La Bijouterie et la joaillerie égyptiennes," in **II,** *Mémoires*, ii.

their facing of gold and precious stones and their graceful solidity, and have become objects of beauty and luxury. Pottery, which in protohistoric times furnished the essential part of furniture and bore the emblems of the clans, soon lost its racial and local ornament, and is now reduced to a less ambitious but universal office in the form of household articles, vases, and subsidiary ornaments. By the Middle Kingdom the sculptor and metal-founder have to supply not only the King and the privileged classes, but the general public as well. Every man can now worship the gods in person, and accordingly the faithful buy the divine effigies in gold, bronze, enamelled pottery, painted and stuccoed wood, bone, and ivory. Art becomes industrialized. Articles are manufactured in batches, and in the Saïte period statuettes and talismans of metal and enamelled clay are turned out of moulds in millions.

Not only the development of technique and the education of the public taste helped art to break loose gradually from religion. Social evolution and political disturbances also had an influence on the style and expression of works of art, especially in those branches which touch man most closely, sculpture and drawing.[1]

The surviving statues of the Thinite period reveal a realistic art, very close to nature ; but when the monarchy imposes itself on the unified country, the conventional representation of gods and kings appears. The statue of Khasekhem (Fig. 40) announces the canon which will dominate for three thousand years. Under the Memphite Old Kingdom, the august character of the god-king is expressed in all its majesty in the royal statues of Chephren and the reliefs on the Solar and royal temples. Then we see the advance of the aristocracy, in the very characteristic portraits found in the *serdabs* of the Vth and VIth Dynasties. Yet the middle classes of the day inspire sincere and realistic work, like the seated Scribe and the Shekh el-Beled, and the sculptor is aroused to equal enthusiasm by the scenes of popular life which he records in reliefs on the walls of tombs. The decline of the Memphite Kings blights artistic production for a long time ; from the VIIth to the XIth Dynasty the most appalling barbarism

---

[1] Cf. **XLVII.** Our plates have been selected to show this development of art.

prevails, lasting as long as the revolutionary turmoil. With
the XIIth Dynasty, the restored royal workshops bring the
traditions back to honour, but art is more studied and has
lost its vigour and naturalness. The figures of Kings, like the
literature of the day, reveal a scholarly, conscious style, which
no longer aims at might and majesty, but at psychological
analysis. Certain royal heads (Pl. X, 3) betray the anxieties
of power and the bitter cares of the Kings who maintained
the just laws.[1] At the same time art is popularized.
Statuettes are made by the thousand for the use of the people,
to serve as company in the next world. With the XVIIIth
Dynasty a new period opens, characterized in art by technical
perfection, aiming at finish and properly conventionalized
expression. The royal figures observe a conventional
idealization. Meanwhile, Asiatic luxury, introduced by the
conquests in the Near East, enriches the Egyptian style,
invading dress and surroundings. The age of Amenophis III
witnesses the full expansion, in all its delicacy and subtlety,
of an art made fruitful by contributions from Syria,
Mesopotamia, and Crete.[2]

At this moment the reformation of Amenophis IV, by
changing religious tradition, influences the art and intellectual
culture of Egypt profoundly, although not for long. In every
domain a sudden and radical revolution breaks out,
battering a breach in dogmas, canons, and rituals.

In architecture, the temple of the Osirian type is, for the
time, abandoned. There are no more pylons, hypostyle halls,
or fortress-sanctuaries. The reformer King returns to wide-
open buildings like the Sun-temples of the Vth Dynasty.[3]
The temples of Aten consist solely of a court on which the sun
sheds floods of light ; in the centre is an altar, laden with

---

[1] Between the XIIth and XVIIIth Dynasties, archæologists used to place
a group of statues (Niles (?) bringing offerings, human-headed sphinxes) of
granite or diorite, found at Tanis, whose type, energetic to the point of brutality,
seems to indicate foreign origin (cf. **LI**, pp. 150–3). One of the sphinxes had been
appropriated by the Hyksôs King Apophis, and several statues were reutilized
by a King of the XXIst Dynasty (Tanite). Mariette attributed these statues
to the Hyksôs ; Golenischeff saw the features of Amenemhat III in the sphinx
of our Plate XI, 1 ; Capart (**XLIII**, p. 211) ascribes them to the beginning of the
Old Kingdom.
[2] On this period, see G. Steindorff, *Die Blutezeit des Pharaonenreichs*, 1926,
with fine illustrations.
[3] Cf. Blackman, " A Study of Liturgy in the Temple of Aton at el-Amarna,"
in *Recueil Champollion*, p. 505.

offerings on which the hand-tipped rays of Aten descend. The court is surrounded by a portico of flower-columns, with statues at the sides representing, not the god, but the King adoring Aten. In a corner stands the erected stone (*benben*) of the Sun. The walls of the porticoes show the King and his family worshipping the Solar disk, whose rays reach to him.

This new conception of the temple does away with the divine statues and traditional scenes of the Osirian cult. Aten has no anthropomorphic body, and consequently he cannot receive the rites of mummification, or of the Opening of the Mouth, or of resurrection. All the ritual decoration disappears. Only the natural setting of the flower-columns is kept. But there are also painted pavements, representing the gladness of beasts and birds in the awakening of nature, and of flowers and plants opening at the hour when the sun rises on the Eastern horizon (Pl. XIII, 1). These pictures are a direct commentary on the *Hymns to Aten* from which I have quoted passages (pp. 36, 325), a veritable *Magnificat* to the glory of the Sun.

In sculpture, since no more statues or reliefs of the old gods are made, man becomes the chief theme of the artist, and above all the Man *par excellence*, the King, and the royal family. The sculptors reproduce the figure of Amenophis IV Akhenaten to satiety. The King preaches the return to nature, makes the artist work from the living model, and allows a plaster cast of his face to be taken (specimens have been found), to make sure that his features are correctly reproduced (Pl. XII, 1). Now, the King is prognathous, and afflicted with an abnormally large occiput to boot. The sculptors faithfully reproduce the prominent lower jaw and the long, bulging skull, even when these deformities have been further aggravated by disease (Fig. 62). There are reliefs of the King, studio studies, which border on caricature.[1]

This out-and-out realism brings with it profound observation of the nude. For the first time in Egyptian art, we find studies from the living nude model. The Queen and the King's daughters are not afraid of posing. Masterpieces of realistic grace are the result (Pl. XII, 2 and 4).

It can be said that, during this short period, art becomes secular. One logical consequence is the abandonment, at

[1] On the art of el-Amarna, see Schaefer's well-illustrated articles in **XII**. lv.

least in part, of the laws of frontality which used to govern all human figures. The scenes engraved at el-Amarna and on the furniture of Tutankhamen (in that King's youth) show us the King, the Queen, and their daughters in familiar attitudes, in which there is no trace of formality or convention. The artist, having noted picturesque gestures as they occurred, reproduces them, taking an exquisite delight in them (Pl. XII, 3). With freedom, the artist also gains personality. We know the names of three sculptors of the Court—Men, Bek, and Iuti, who work for the King and his mother Tii.[1] Their studios have recently been excavated, and marvellous busts of Akhenaten and his Queen, Nefertiti, have been found in them.

Fig. 80.—A Property of the Theban Period.
The different planes are drawn side by side, not one over the other.

The painting which we find on the pavements of el-Amarna and on the furniture of Tutankhamen also reveals great technical progress. The painter is no longer content with flat, unbroken colour without modelling ; he tries toning off his colour, renders relief by shadows, and begins to understand the effect of lighting (Pl. XIII, 1). Visual truth is sought, instead of mental representation. Care is also taken over the modelling of flesh and the correct drawing of hands and feet ; the careless habits of the old technique are corrected. Lastly, a consideration of perspective, in the grouping of persons and objects, appears for the first time in the frescoes of this period.

[1] **XL**, pp. 503–6.

MENTUEMHET, PRINCE OF THEBES
XXVth Dynasty (Cairo)

[face p. 442

The realistic works of el-Amarna breathe, on the whole, a frank, healthy joy; but in the funeral scenes in the tombs this serenity gives place to uncontrolled grief. The artist is not afraid of giving the King pathetic gestures of woe and despair before the dead body of his daughter. Human distress, like joy, is a source of true inspiration.

In the study of the Egyptian mind, it is very remarkable that, even when art was emancipated, a new tradition was formed. The appearance of the unhealthy King was peculiar, with the enormous backward bulge of the skull, the emaciated face, the sagging belly, and the rounded pelvis and thighs, all visible through his costume of pleated transparent material. The people of the Court affected the outward appearance of the King; all his peculiarities were slavishly imitated, and were copied by the artists. This manifestation of the " herd-spirit " somewhat spoils the style of el-Amarna.

The swing of the pendulum had an equal effect on art, but not all at once. As soon as the sovereignty of Amon was restored, the studios of el-Amarna were abandoned, and the artists of the Court went back to Thebes. There, everything suggested to them the old decorative themes, in which the image of the god, in statues and reliefs, and the rites of worship condemned the artist to an everlasting monotony of treatment. They did not surrender at once, and for several generations they maintained a certain independence of taste, a fidelity to nature, and a striving after correct and delicate drawing. Down to the time of Rameses II, the Renaissance of el-Amarna kept inspiration alive, and this period has given us the last masterpieces of Egyptian official art. A statue of the great Pharaoh shows him, with his head bent, as if listening to the prayers of his subjects,[1] in an attitude very unlike the impassive sovereignty of the Memphite Kings,[2] and expressing, on the contrary, the monarchical socialism in which the King was the fellow-worker of his people. After the XXIst Dynasty there were numbers of statues of high-priests of Amon, cold and correct,[3] and realistic, vigorous portraits of Ethiopian Kings and warrior-chiefs.[4] The Saïte Renaissance tried to galvanize art into life by going for inspiration to the Memphite masterpieces, but slavish

---

[1] Plate XV, 1.
[2] Plate III, 1.
[3] Plate XXIII. 3.
[4] Plate XXIV.

devotion to the past prevented the development of an original style. Great sculpture declined, like the authority of the Pharaohs. It is the day of industrial art. Small objects appear in masses. Artists amuse themselves with technical difficulties, loading bronze with overlay, and make up for lack of genius by talent. Inspiration deserts a decaying religion, and can no longer resist influences from outside, Asiatic and Greek. At the same time as the sap of national life is exhausted, Egyptian art loses its style and personality.

II

SCIENCE

For the Egyptians, what we call science formed part of the revelations, or " divine words ", which the gods, and Thoth (Hermes) in particular, let fall from their lips for the instruction of men. The Greeks held that medicine, chemistry, geometry, and the " exact sciences " in general, had first been cultivated in Egypt. We need not accept these illusory monopolies and pretentious primogenitures. Without a doubt, the Egyptian priests, full of their great antiquity, themselves spread abroad a story which redounded to the glory of their gods. Certainly the immense dikes and irrigation works, the pyramids and obelisks, the monolithic statues, and the plan of the temples prove that in very early times the Egyptians had gone deep into the practical problems of mathematics and geometry involved by the transport and placing of these colossal masses. Work in metal and the manufacture of pottery, coloured glass, and enamels revealed to them the physical and chemical properties of their material. The mummification and dissection of bodies gave them some knowledge of anatomy and pathology. But it seems fairly certain that, expert as they were in applied science and skilful in solving technical difficulties,[1] they were not so gifted for speculation and pure inquiry.

---

[1] The hoisting-machines used for artificial irrigation were those still used by the fellah of to-day : (i) the shadoof, or pole with a counterpoise, which is represented in tombs of the XVIIIth Dynasty (see Plate IX, 1) ; (ii) the *saqiyeh*, or horizontal wheel with scoops, driven by a man or beast, which is never depicted but may be mentioned in a formula regarding the field-work expected from the Ushebtiu in the next world (**XII**, liii, p. 113 ; liv, p. 140).
We do not find the wheel used for vehicles before the Middle Kingdom

Geometry and Mathematics.—According to Herodotus (ii, 109), geometry was born of the need for dividing the soil of Egypt into regular portions. In any case, the social organization of the Valley made it necessary at an early date to have a fixed, universal system of measures.[1] For length the standard measures were taken from the human body. The foot was used by painters and sculptors to establish their canon. The unit of long measure was the cubit, which was divided into two spans, six hands, or twenty-four fingers. The ordinary cubit of about $18\frac{1}{2}$ inches was distinguished from the royal cubit of about $20\frac{1}{2}$ inches, which was more convenient for the purposes of the administration ; this unit was commonly used for the plans of buildings and

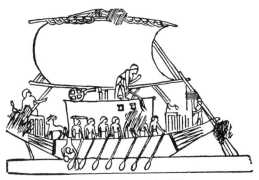

FIG. 81.—Transport by River.
New Empire. Tomb of Paheri.

the usual operations. For longer distances the *itru* was used, the *schoinos* of the Greeks, equal to about 5,000 cubits, and so, at times, was a multiple of 10,000 cubits. The King's surveyors measured land in *arourai* (*sta*), a square with a side of 100 royal cubits, or about 3,300 square yards.

(L. Klebs, *Reliefs M. R.*, p. 65). Did it come from Asia with the horse and chariot ? Yet the Egyptian had the potter's wheel very early. Before wheeled traction, goods were hauled on sledges, which suited the tracks of beaten earth which were the only roads. The very great development of river traffic also took the place of land-transport.

For the machines used by the builders in the transportation and erection of the enormous monoliths, and in building, cf. A. Choisy, *L'Art de bâtir chez les Égyptiens*, 1904. For the machinery which, according to Arabian tradition, existed in certain temples, cf. Berthelot in *Journal des Savants*, May, 1896, and April, 1899.

[1] On this subject see Griffith in **XIV**, 1892, p. 403, and Brugsch, *Die Aegyptologie*, p. 370.

The unit of capacity was the *henu* of about ¾ pint. The standard weight, the *deben*, was on an average 3·21 oz., which is not far off the Babylonian weight. A beam-balance was used for ordinary and for more accurate weighing. Money, properly so called, did not exist in Egypt before the Persian invasion, but the market value of goods was reckoned in weights of gold, silver, and copper, according to a standard-value, the *shât*,[1] even for payments, or exchanges in kind.

The division of the year was based on a duodecimal system, which has survived in the reckoning of the months (12),

FIG. 82.—Gold Chains weighed in the Balance.

Deben weights and ingots shaped like animals (*pecunia*). Temple of Der el-Bahari.

the decads (36), and the hours of the day and of the night (12 each).[2] Arithmetic, however, was on the decimal system. Writing had signs for the units from 1 to 9, and for 100, 1,000, 10,000, 100,000, and 1,000,000 ; there was no 0.

Mathematical treatises have come down to us. The most important is the Rhind Papyrus,[3] which is a copy, made in the time of the Hyksôs, of an older work. It sets forth a series of arithmetical and geometrical problems which arose, in practice, in the assessing of the " incomings and outgoings "

---

[1] On the *shât*, cf. R. Weill, in **XXXVII**, i, p. 83.
[2] Thirty-six decads in the normal year of 360 days.
[3] In the British Museum ; translated by Eisenlohr, 1877.

of the offices of the Treasury, in exchanges, in the measurement of fields, and in estimating the capacity of granaries. Arithmetical calculations are confined to addition and subtraction. Multiplication and division are done by the method of addition. To find the product of 8 × 8, the scribe writes down one column of figures, beginning with 1 and multiplying by 2, until he comes to 8, which he marks with a stroke ; beside this he writes a second column, beginning with 8 and multiplying by 2, until he gets the result, thus :—

$$
\begin{array}{rr}
1 & 8 \\
2 & 16 \\
4 & 32 \\
-\ 8 & 64
\end{array}
$$

To find how many times 7 goes into 77, he makes the same arrangement. The small strokes at the side mark the figures which are used in the sum $1 + 2 + 8 = 11$ times.

$$
\begin{array}{rr}
-\ 1 & 7 \\
-\ 2 & 14 \\
4 & `28 \\
-\ 8 & 56
\end{array}
$$

The calculation of fractions is clumsy. As a rule, the only numerator used is 1, so that $\frac{5}{8}$ is written $\frac{1}{8}\frac{1}{8}\frac{1}{8}\frac{1}{8}\frac{1}{8}$. However, the signs for $\frac{2}{3}$ and $\frac{3}{4}$ are used. Sometimes the scribes get some fun out of this infantile method, and, to write the 24th day of the month, set it out thus, $\frac{2}{3}\frac{1}{10}\frac{1}{30}$; that is, $20 + 3 + 1 = 24$.

In geometry their theory is elementary. Calculations of surface are based on the properties of the triangle, rectangle, trapezium, and truncated pyramid, the definitions of which are not free from errors.[1] In one literary papyrus a scribe propounds such problems to a colleague as : How many bricks are required to build a ramp of given dimensions ? How many men will be needed to drag an obelisk of 110 cubits (187 ft. 9 in.) from the quarry to the capital ? How many, to set up a colossus 30 cubits high (51 ft. 2 in.) and 20 cubits wide (34 ft. 2 in.) ?[2] The monuments which stand prove to us that the Egyptians did solve such problems, on the ground, with a skill which takes us by surprise.

---

[1] **LI**, p. 427.
[2] A. H. Gardiner, *Papyrus Anastasi I*, p. 31.

Medicine.—In the natural sciences the Egyptian's faculty of observation triumphs. He is not much of a mathematician, but he is a first-rate observer ; we have proof of it in his drawings of animals, which are observed with an accuracy and rendered with an animation which make up for the ritual sterotypes of the temples and tombs. The study of the human body was familiar to the Egyptians at an early date. Mummification, which was practised at least by the IInd Dynasty, was preceded by the ritual dismemberment of corpses, and the two processes had revealed the external and internal anatomy of the body. They obtained very clear ideas of pathology from the inspection of bodies which had succumbed to one disease or another. But we must not forget that it was not physicians, but specialists in mummification, who opened the corpse, cleared out the brain and entrails, and raised up the skin above the muscles to stuff the members. That is why, for all the great name the Greeks gave the Egyptian doctors, their books of medicine, several specimens of which have been preserved, have appeared but indifferently scientific to modern physicians.

The name " physician ", *sunu* (perhaps " corrector ", " healer "), was borne by priests ; this implies the religious and magical character of the calling.

In the earliest times we find royal physicians whose chiefs are at the same time officials of very high rank and priests, usually of the goddesses Serqet and Neith of Saïs. Like so many other features of Egyptian civilization, medicine seems to have come from Lower Egypt. Its principal centres were the temples of Atum-Ra at Heliopolis, of Neith at Saïs, of Anubis at Letopolis, and that at Bubastis. The medical books which we possess [1] date from the Middle Kingdom, or from the Hyksôs period, but pious tradition attributes them to a divine revelation. " The Beginning of the Book of Healing Illnesses, found in ancient writing in a chest at the feet of Anubis at Letopolis, in the time of King Usaphaïs " [2]—such

---

[1] These are the Berlin (or Ebers) Papyrus, those of Leipzig, London, the University of California (Hearst), and New York (Edwin Smith), and the medical and veterinary fragments of the Kahun papyri. A new edition of these papyri has been undertaken by W. Wreszinski, *Die Medizin der alten Aegypter*, 4 vols., 1909, etc.

[2] Manetho confirms that anatomy-books were written in the time of Usaphaïs.

are the titles of the Leipzig and Berlin Papyri. By the side of the highly-placed physicians, we find plain " servants of Ka ", who effect the ritual circumcision of young men " painlessly ".[1] The physician was a "Chief of the Secrets"[2] ; a priest tells us that "he has come from Heliopolis with the Princes of the Great House, the Lords of the Safeguard, the Masters of Eternity, and has come from Saïs with the Mothers of the Gods, who have taken him under their protection, that he may destroy every malady ".[3] At Saïs, in the Temple of Neith, there was, by the side of the school of the " Wise Magicians " (the House of Life), a school of medicine. Cambyses destroyed it, but Darius I had it restored, and the man who rebuilt it tells us [4] :—

> On the order of Darius, I founded (this school) with all its students, men of good birth and not of humble condition. Over them I set wise men of every order, for their work. His Majesty caused them to be given all kinds of things suitable for doing this work. I supplied them with everything that was useful, with every instrument according to the books, just as they were before. His Majesty did this because he knew what was useful for this art, to make every sick man live, and to establish the name of every god in every temple.

Medicine, then, was intimately bound up with religious beliefs and magical arts ; we shall see that remedies were very often charms. The great Ebers Papyrus, a sort of manual for the use of students, reveals " the secrets of medicine ". The internal life of the body depends on the " vessels " (*met*) in which blood, water, air, urine, semen, mucus, and fæces circulate ; here arteries, veins, and viscera are confused. These vessels start from the heart. " In the heart there are vessels for all the members. If the physician lays his finger on the head, nape, hands, place of the heart, arms, or legs, everywhere he presses on the heart, since its vessels lead to every member." [5]   Some say that there are twenty-two vessels ; others, forty-six. Most internal maladies are due to their being obstructed, heated, or stiffened ; they are treated with plasters and liniments. Complaints of the intestines, affections of the eyes, tumours, and the diseases

[1] J. Capart, *Une Rue de tombeaux*, pl. 35 ; cf. **XXXVIII**, vol. x, p. 115.
[2] *Urk.*, i, 42. The high-priest of Bubastis bore the title of " Great Physician ". On ranks in the medical profession, cf. **XII**, lv, p. 65.
[3] *Ebers Papyrus*.
[4] H. Schaefer, **XII**, xxxvii (1899), p. 72.
[5] *Ebers Pap.*, 99, 1 ; cf. Schaefer, **XII**, xxx, p. 108.

of women are frequently observed. The following is an account of a case and its cure.

> Remedy (*shesau*, literally, skilfulnesses, trick) for the woman affected in the eyes, so that she can hardly see, and has pains in the neck. *Say of it* : " It is discharges (?) of the vulva that affect the eyes." *Do for it* : A fumigation of incense and fresh oil ; fumigate the vulva with it. Fumigate her eyes with bee-eater's feet, and then make her eat the raw liver of an ass.[1]

Prescriptions are adapted to the patient's age and the season ; a drug which cures in the first month of winter will be inoperative in the third month. The prescriptions would give us a whole pharmacopœia, if we were not so often held up by the uncertain meaning of a technical term, or the impossibility of identifying a plant or substance. The Egyptian physician was great on castor-oil and simples. Certain ointments are compounded of thirty-seven ingredients, and the oddest products are employed—lizard's blood, the humours of a pig's ear, mother's milk, and the fæces of children, asses, dogs, gazelles, etc., combined with oils and fats of similar origin. A good many of these drugs passed, through Hippocrates and Dioscorides,[2] into the stock-in-trade of the mediaeval apothecary, and survive in the panaceas of the strolling quack. There are Egyptian veterinary treatises which apply the same methods to the diseases of animals.[3]

Remedies are often accompanied by incantations, allusions to some deity—Isis, Thoth, Horus, Ra, Anubis, Imhetep, Amon-Ra—who was cured by the same prescription, and will come to the aid of the physician. To speak these spells " in the right voice " made cure fairly certain.

Luckily for the reputation of the Egyptian physician, a papyrus has recently been analysed which reveals a more scientific spirit. The Edwin Smith Papyrus discusses surgical cases, classifying them in order, from the head downwards, in a methodical manner very different from the fanciful exposition of the medical papyri. In the portion preserved, there are ten observations for the head, four for the nose, three for the jaws, five for the temporal region, five for the ear, lips, and chin, six for the throat and cervical vertebræ,

---

[1] *Kahun Pap.* ; cf. Maspero, in **XXXVIII**, vol. viii, p. 414.
[2] Cf. E. Chassinat, in *Bibl. École Htes. Études*, No. 234, p. 447 ; **XL**, p. 460.
[3] *Kahun Pap.*

five for the clavicular and scapular region, nine for the thorax and breasts, and one for the backbone ; the rest is missing. Each case is set forth methodically. The complete exposition of a case comprises : (i) statement—Remedies for a given case ; (ii) observation—If you examine a case presenting so-and-so ; (iii) diagnosis—Say of it, " It is such-and-such a malady " ; (iv) prognosis—If it is mild, say, " It is a malady which I can treat " ; if it is doubtful, " It is a malady which I can combat " ; if it is incurable, " It is a malady for which I can do nothing " ; (v) treatment—For a wound in the temple, " Apply fresh meat the first day ; then treat with an ointment and honey until healed." [1]

In only one case, out of forty-eight, is a magical charm added to the treatment. This papyrus, therefore, affords serious evidence in favour of the Egyptian surgeon in the XVIIIth century before our era. On the back of the papyrus, however, there are incantations, written by another hand. They have the impressive title of " Book for turning an old man into a youth of twenty ". There were Fausts in Egypt.

We need not be surprised that Herodotus proclaims the triumph of medicine in the country.[2] In Egypt, he says, medicine is specialized, like oracles. " Each physician deals with one malady, not more. And the whole place is full of physicians. Some are established as healers of the eyes, others of the head, others of the teeth,[3] others of the region of the belly, and others of internal complaints." Now, this specialization, which, after all, proves a scientific method, was very ancient ; in the Old Kingdom, Pharaoh had physicians " for his two eyes ". As in modern Egypt, the eyes and intestines were subject to frequent maladies. " The Egyptians look after their health with emetics and purgatives, and clear themselves out for three days running, once a month, considering that all the ailments of men come from the food they eat. Thanks to these precautions, and to their climate, I think that the Egyptians are the healthiest of men, next to the Libyans." [4]

---

[1] J. H. Breasted, *The Edwin Smith Papyrus* (*Bibl. École Htes. Études*, No. 234), p. 385.
[2] ii, 84.
[3] Mummies with false teeth have been found.
[4] Hdt.. ii. 77 : cf. Diod.. i. 82.

Chemistry.—Pharmacopœia takes us to the preparations of the laboratory, and here we are in an especially Egyptian domain, since chemistry derives its very name from *Kemt*, the Black Land, or Egypt. Among the products which come under the head of chemistry, we first may mention the Materia Medica, which, in the prescriptions of physicians and sorcerers, is rich in substances from all sources. Drugs, perfumes, and ointments were also manufactured in the laboratories of the temples for the needs of the cult, such as the fumigation, purification, and anointing of statues. The rituals enumerate the plants, rare stones, mineral and vegetable oils, animal fats, resins, herbs, and natron-baths which preserve mummified bodies. In the workshops of the metal-casters, goldsmiths, gilders, and enamellers, a hundred ingenious processes bear witness to thorough-going research into the properties, affinities, and transformations of ores and metals.[1] Thanks to Dioscorides, Hippocrates, Pliny the Elder, and the Alexandrian and Arabian alchemists, this science has not been lost. It feeds the secret laboratories of the seekers of the Philosopher's Stone, and provokes the interest of great chemists like Berthelot and Gabriel Bertrand. Unfortunately the difficulty of translation, here as in other technical matters, prevents our utilizing a great number of the documents.[2]

Astronomy.—Here   observation   is   combined   with mathematics. The Egyptians excelled in the practical part, but their theoretical research was not so profound as has been supposed. Like medicine, astronomy was in the hands of the priests, at least in the case of the higher posts. At Heliopolis, the priest who observed the sun was the " Great Seer ". The temples had night-shifts to study the stars. In the library of the temple of Edfu, the catalogue of which is engraved on the walls,[3] one notices books on the " knowledge of the periodical movement of the sun and moon, or of the stars ", or on " the conjunction of the sun ". The gods lived in the sky ; there

---

[1] See the works of Vernier and Petrie quoted on pp. 429, 438, footnotes. For alchemy, cf. the researches of Berthelot.

[2] M. Victor Loret is a great authority on the interpretation of these technical texts. See his studies in Egyptian botany and drugs, in **IV**, esp. vols. vii, xv, xvii, and his *Flore pharaonique*.

[3] **XII**, 1871, p. 43. Cf. Mariette, *Denderah*, text, p. 247 ; Diod., i, 47 ; Clement of Alex., *Stromateis*, vi.

their birthdays were determined, observed, and celebrated, and nothing of what happened in the firmament, which they crossed in their barges, escaped the priests " who know the ordering of the heavens ".[1]

In 4241 the establishment of the calendar, as I have said, was already based on accurate observation of the annual course of the sun and of the position of Sothis (Sirius) with relation to it. The division of the year into lunar months of thirty days is explained by an exact knowledge of the moon. The stars were divided into two classes, the Indestructible (*ikhemu-sek*), which never disappear from the visible sky, and the Unwearied (*ikhemu-urz*), which wander, the planets. Among these latter, five, corresponding to Jupiter, Saturn, Mars, Mercury, and Venus, are attested at least as early as the New Empire. Of the fixed stars thirty-six were catalogued. Each of them presided over one of the thirty-six decads of the normal year of 360 days, and so these deities were called *decani*. The most ancient list is inscribed inside a coffin-lid of the XIIth Dynasty,[2] and other lists are found in royal tombs (Seti I, Rameses IV), and under the roof of the Ramesseum and Ptolemaic temples. The twelve signs of the Zodiac—Ram, Bull, Twins, Crab, Lion, Virgin, Scales, Scorpion, Archer, Capricorn, Water-bearer, and Fish—only appear in documents of the late period, and derive their names from the Greek Zodiac, which was itself derived from Babylonian astronomy.[3] To the late period, too, the Græco-Coptic names of the months belong. They are taken from ancient names of festivals which were held in honour of the eponymous gods who protected the months.

	1st Season. INUNDATION (*Akhet*)	IInd Season. GERMINATION (*Pert*)	IIIrd Season HEAT (*Shemu*)
	1. Thoth	1. Tybi	1. Pachons
Five intercalary days	2. Paophi	2. Mechir	2. Payni
(the Coptic short month)	3. Athyr	3. Phamenoth	3. Epiphi
	4. Choiak	4. Pharmuthi	4. Mesore

The day (*haru*) was divided into twelve hours of light and twelve of darkness, whatever the real hours of sunlight might

---

[1] The title of the high-priest at Hermonthis, the Heliopolis of Upper Egypt.
[2] Daressy, in **I**, i, p. 79. The dead live in the sky, with the *decani*.
[3] Spiegelberg, in **XII**, xlviii (1910), p. 146. Small sundials (votive offerings ?) have been found. The oldest is of Merneptah's time. Cf. **XII**, lvi (1920), p. 202 ; xlix, p. 67.

be. The time was told by clocks of various types. There
were sundials, on which the sun's course was marked by a
shadow,[1] and vessels which filled with water, or emptied, at
a regular rate, hour-levels being marked on the inside.[2]
At night the hours were also determined by observation of
the stars. In royal tombs of the XXth Dynasty, star-tables
have been found, which indicate, from the 1st to the 15th and
from the 16th to the 30th of each month, hour by hour, the
position of the stars relative to two observers facing each
other, on the roof of the temple, in the north-and-south axis.[3]
When sighting Orion or Sothis, the " Giant's Leg " or the
" Bird's Head ", with the aid of a viewing-instrument,[4]
the observer had to find the star above the head, or about the
eye, or at the level of the elbow of a colleague who was keeping
watch with him. So the star-tables give the position of the
stars in relation to a figure of a seated astronomer, that is,
over his head, near his right or left elbow, etc. The names,
Giant, Bird, Water-star, Lion, etc., indicate constellations
describing these figures in the sky.

Astronomy as applied to the events of human life, that is,
astrology, was held in great esteem by the Egyptians. Every
month, every day, and every hour of the day and night were
in the keeping of a deity who could intervene in the fate of
men on the hour or day or in the month when " the heavens
joined the earth ". The episodes of the life of the gods fell
on certain days, which were accordingly lawful or unlawful
(*fastus, nefastus*). It was most important for men to know
them, and the priests and magicians compiled books for the
purpose. The oldest, which dates from the Middle Kingdom,
merely enumerates the thirty days of the month, with the
remark " good " or " bad ", or even both " good and bad ",
according to the hour. Nine days are bad, three mixed, and
the rest good. Three papyri of the New Empire give, save for
lacunæ, all the days of the year, with the mythological reason
in each case of the prognostic, " good " or " hostile ", the
latter being written in red, the colour of Seth. Chabas has
published one of these under the title, *Calendrier des jours
fastes et néfastes.*[5]

---

[1] See *From Tribe to Empire*, p. 271, " at the hour when the shadow turneth."
[2] **XL**, p. 400, pl. xxvii.   [3] **XL**, p. 401, fig. 174.
[4] **XII**, liii (1917), p. 113.   [5] **XLVIII**, vol. xii, p. 221.

The 26th Thoth is a day on which one should do nothing, absolutely nothing, for it was the day of the battles between Horus and Seth, thrice unpropitious. On the other hand, the 27th Athyr, the day of the apportioning and peace between Horus and Seth, is thrice propitious. The 6th Paophi is the feast of Ra in heaven ; he who is born on this day dies of drunkenness—thrice propitious ! Other days make one liable to be killed by the crocodile and snake. But he who is born on the 10th Choiak will die at table—thrice propitious ! The 16th Paophi is the feast of Osiris at Abydos ; " what you see on that day will be fortunate."

There were pious people who wore these papyri, carefully rolled up, at their necks, as amulets, for " the man who possesses this talisman will prosper in life ". The Greeks had similar beliefs ; what is Hesiod's *Works and Days* but a guide for the effective direction of one's activities at every moment in the year ? Here the fifth day of the month is unpropitious because the Eumenides are going about the world punishing perjury, while the seventh is holy because Leto bore Apollo on that day. The twentieth day is very good at dawn, but dangerous after noon. The science of prognostics is not a brilliant chapter in the history of the human imagination.

What was provided for the advice of the ordinary man was necessarily even more important for the guidance of kings. In Mesopotamia there were collections of omens, which gave the historical events, good or bad, which had occurred when the stars were in certain positions ; according to magical theory, exactly similar things would happen again in the same conjunctions. Collections of this kind probably existed in Egypt,[1] but none has come down to us. Manetho,[2] however, who worked from authentic sources, frequently mentions portents occurring in the sky and on earth with disastrous consequences, which should be a lesson to the Pharaohs.

III

LITERATURE

The Egyptians were a most talkative people, as busy with their pens as with their tongues. What is preserved of Egyptian literature is certainly only a minute part of the production of a nation who talked about themselves for four thousand years. Every great historical period is accompanied

---

[1] Cf. Hdt., ii, 81, and Diod., i, 81, 50, 28.
[2] *F.H.G.*, ii, pp. 539, 543–4.

by works which have their special social character and
literary nature ; so true is it that in Egypt, as everywhere
else, literature is a reflection of social life.

The first period, the Old Kingdom, is marked by an
essentially religious literature, the expression of the priesthood of Heliopolis. This consists of the imposing records
known as the Pyramid Texts, which are our sources for the
history, the religion, and every intellectual activity of the age.
I have used them so much in Part II that we need not return
to them here. These texts are inscribed on stone, and their
adaptation to religious buildings explains why they are
enclosed in frames shaped like the sign for a building, *het*,
and why their commencements are called " door " (*ra*), which
we improperly translate " chapter ". Like sculpture, painting,
and the other arts, literature is, at the beginning, only a
decoration of temples and tombs, and has to conform with the
architectural scheme, even in its outward form.

In the Memphite tombs, the scenes of popular life contrast
vividly, by their free, spontaneous style, with the ritual
decoration.[1] So, too, the inscriptions written above these
rustic scenes give us the common speech, in short fragments,
and sometimes little works of popular inspiration, which are
probably songs. Here is the song of the shepherd, driving his
flock through the swamps.

> The shepherd is in the water with the fish.
> He talks to the silurus and exchanges greetings with the oxyrrhynchus.
> O West ! Whence comes the shepherd ? He is a shepherd of the West.

By this the shepherd means that his hard life will bring him
to the cemetery.

Men carrying big landowners on their shoulders lighten
their labours by singing :—

> The litter-bearers are happy !
> We like it full better than empty.

In the midst of the overwhelming masses of religious
writing, this secular vein is a mere thread, of which one almost
loses sight.

A second period begins with the social revolution, between
the Old and Middle Kingdoms. At no other time is there such
a flow of Egyptian eloquence. First of all, religious literature

---

[1] Cf. Erman, *Reden, Rufe, Lieder* ; P. Montet, *La Vie privée des Égyptiens
sous l'Ancien Empire.*

makes way for a social literature. Writing is done on papyrus for choice, and thought gains lightness by escaping from the heavy medium of stone.[1] All the circumstances arouse interest, observation, reflection. The cultivated class knew anxiety, doubt, despair; the people was excited by curiosity, expectation, and greed, and intoxicated with the success of its audacity. A in all revolutions, intellectual excellence came into conflict with brute force. There was no more leisure for thought; and yet a few spirits taking refuge in themselves, a few isolated observers, managed to scatter some fruitful seeds in the social turmoil. It was to the time of the Kings of Heracleopolis (IXth and Xth Dynasties) that the Egyptians assigned the *Teachings for King Merikara*, the *Satire of the Trades*, and the *Tale of the Peasant*, which are like mirrors of the political circumstances which we have studied in their place. Of the same period (although preserved in later manuscripts) are the various accounts of the time of anarchy which are put into the mouth of an old sage or priest, the lamentations of the Misanthrope conversing with his spirit. It is to be observed that in this disillusioned literature religious sentiment is practically absent; where the social order collapses, it is because its dogmatic substructure has been undermined. We have already made what use we could of these documents, in which the soul of the people is seen pulsating, in the course of our historical narrative (Part II, Chaps. III and IV).

Many years after order was restored, the memory of the disturbances haunted the Egyptian mind. Our copy of the principal text, the *Admonitions*, belongs to the XVIIIth Dynasty. So, too, for a long time the tombs were engraved with the songs of the house of King Antef, which the harpists accompanied on their strings; there the bitter scepticism of the troubled age veils itself in geniality and peaceful resignation (pp. 223–4).

---

[1] The papyri are made of papyrus-fibre, beaten, pressed, amalgamated, and reduced to a flexible state. They were cut into strips of various size, sometimes 40 yards long. Writing was done with a reed pen (calamus). The scribe's palette had two cups, for black and red ink, and a water-pot (Fig. 39). The scribe wrote in hieratic character from right to left, arranging his text in vertical columns or horizontal lines of equal size, which formed pages. He kept the rest of the papyrus rolled up with his left hand. For the scribe's materials, see **LI**, p. 491. For the sake of economy, writing was also done on potsherds and flakes of stone (ostraca).

With the XIIth Dynasty, the disenchantment which followed the turmoil of revolution gives place to confidence and security. Society is reorganized under just laws, and the Osirian rites are no longer a privilege of the few. A new religious literature, written on coffins and sarcophagi, and later on papyri, spreads abroad the releasing formulas which enable all virtuous men to enjoy divine bliss in the next world. At the Court there is now a refined literary school which cultivates fine language and aims at a chaste style. To these anonymous writers we owe delightful stories, such as *Sinuhet* and *The Shipwrecked Sailor*, about the adventures of a traveller who has risked his life in Syria and of one who has sailed on unknown seas.[1] Anxiety to train up well-educated, right-thinking, honourable officials inspires the *Teachings* ascribed to Viziers of the Old Kingdom, Kagemni and Phtahhetep. The King's doctrine is set forth in the *Teachings of Amenemhat I* and in those of Sehetepibra. These documents, and the hymns of gratitude preserved in the Kahun Papyri, have been used above ; they reveal the restored prosperity of Egypt and the wise intentions of the Kings, now become the fellow-workers of their subjects. The narrative, lyrical, and didactic texts of the Middle Kingdom form a rich and varied literature ; if there is an age in which one can speak of a classical literature in Egypt, it is certainly this.

With the New Empire, literature evolves, like society, towards freer and less strictly national forms. The Egyptian Empire beyond the frontiers and the religious reform of Akhenaten have opened new sources of inspiration. Art, in the age of el-Amarna, is secularized. Literature breaks away from the forms of a school of writers, and introduces the simplicity and freshness of popular speech into the official or chastened language of educated circles. It is no mere chance that we should find in the decrees of Akhenaten, for the first time, the grammatical forms of the Late Egyptian invading the legal and administrative style. The speech of the people, with its trivial locutions and its analytical construction (which adds the definite article and the auxiliary verb to the stock of grammatical forms), brings with it a vivacity, a freshness of impressions, the best specimens of which are furnished by the *Tales*, which might have been written for children.[1] Religious literature, too, is refreshed at the popular source ; the famous *Hymns to Aten* are the unaffected expression of the love of humble creatures (p. 326).

The subsequent return to the doctrine of Amon-Ra brings a revival of sacerdotal literature. Hymns to Amon, metaphysical expositions on the creative Word and the government of the universe by a Trinity-Unity,[2] and moral treatises by various scribes [3] are products of this traditional spirit.

Morality is expressed in remarkably refined language in the *Maxims of the Scribe Ani*, in which one finds touching counsel on the duties of a son :

> Double the bread which you give your mother. Support her as she has supported you. . . . When you were born, after months, she still carried you on her neck, and for three years her breast was in your mouth. She was never disgusted by your filth ; she never said, " Why do that ? " She took you to school when you learned to write, and every day she waited there, with bread and beer from the house. When you are grown and take a wife, and have a household of your own, turn your eyes back (to the time) when your mother bore you. . . . May she never have to reproach you, nor to lift her hands to the God, and may he never hear complaint from her ! [4]

Relations with women concern the moralist :—

> Beware of the woman from outside, who is not known in her city. She is a water deep and boundless, and there is no knowing her limits. A woman who, when her husband is away, says to you daily, " I am pretty," when there is no one by . . . it is a sin deserving death to listen to her.[5]

A document which may be based on the author's own experience, or may be purely literary, gives us a suggestive glimpse of married life. A husband complains of his dead wife, who haunts and dogs him, without motive ; so he addresses a letter to her spirit (*Akh*), to rid himself of her obstinate pursuit :—

> Why have you done me evil, so that I am in this sad condition ? What have I done to you, that you lift your hand against me, without my having done you any evil ? I shall summon you before the tribunal of the Nine Gods of the West, and they will decide between you and me, on this letter. . . . What have I done to you ? You were my wife when I was young, and I was by you. When I took employment elsewhere, I did not leave you, and I caused no grief to your heart. Why, when I was an officer in Pharaoh's army, among his chariot-fighters, I let them come near you,

---

XLVI. *The Two Brothers, Predestined Prince, Princess of Bakhtane*, etc.
[2] See above, pp. 331, 376.
[3] The fullest are the *Maxims of Ani* and two papyri recently published by H. Lange, *Das Weisheitsbuch des Amenemope* and the *Papyrus Lansing*, Copenhagen, 1925.
[4] Erman, *Literatur*, p. 299. [5] *Ibid.*, p. 296.

they brought you good things, and I hid nothing from you, as long as you lived. No one ever found that I acted ill towards you. . . . nor that I " went into another house " [1] (on divorce). And when they put me in the place where I am now, and I could not return . . . I sent you my oil, my bread, and my clothes. I never sent anything (of the kind) to another place. . . . When you fell ill, of the malady which you made, I made a physician go to you, and he made remedies, and did all that you said. . . . And when I had to accompany Pharaoh to the South, I was near you in thought, and I spent the eight months without eating or drinking like a man. (After your death) when I returned to Memphis, I entreated Pharaoh, he sent me to you, and I wept much for you with my people before my house. I gave garments and cloths to swaddle you. . . . Why, I have now spent three years living alone, and have not " gone into a house ". . . . And as for the sisters in the house, I have not gone in to any of them ! [2]

But the popular vein does not run dry. Among the characteristic writings of the New Empire and the last period there appear, written in demotic, more *Wonderful Tales* about the adventures of mercenaries [3] who end up as princes and kings, and charming *Love-songs*, the restrained, sincere lyricism of which shows us an interesting side of the Egyptian mind.

These love-poems are *Songs to gladden the heart,* and are therefore accompanied by the harp and flutes.[4] The music is lost, and we cannot follow the metre,[5] but the words remain. Most of these trifles are dialogues in which the man and woman sing in turn, calling each other " my brother " and " my sister ", with an imagery and a sensuality which will blaze out with more fire in the Songs of the Shulamite. Some of the habits mentioned in these poems confirm the entertaining disclosures of Herodotus. He tells us that the women of Egypt are very free in their manner in ordinary life and in the hubbub of religious feasts [6]; it is they who go out for the business of the household, while the men stay at home and do the housework. The Theban tombs also show us the gay humour of the ladies, and many popular stories enlighten us as to their temperament and go-ahead behaviour.[7] This last trait is especially striking in the *Love-songs*.

---

[1] On this expression, see above, p. 274.
[2] *Leyden Pap.*, 371. Cf. **XL,** p. 176.
[3] **XLVI,** p. 231.
[4] We know nothing of Egyptian music, save that certain instruments existed— harp, lyre, lute, flute, oboe, trumpet, castanets, cymbals (*menit*), sistrum, tambourine, and military drum.
[5] The writing does not give the vowels, so we do not know their quantities.
[6] Hdt., ii, 35, 48, 60.
[7] The story of the *Two Brothers* contains the prototype of the episode of Potiphar's wife ; **XLVI,** p. 6.

To begin with, the man plays rather a minor part; it is the woman who always does the talking.

The *man* tells us, not without a certain sentiment of fatalism which tempers his rapture, that he is going down the Nile to Memphis. He will find his " sister " in a garden of perfumes, under an arbour, " and if he kisses her open lips, he will be happy without beer." He knows beforehand that by her side he is like the "bird" which will let itself be caught in the " trap of love ", but . . . the joy of loving is great, and he surrenders to it; it draws more strongly than wine and fermented liquors.

> *The man speaks* :
> I go down the river . . . with a bunch of reeds on my shoulder. I shall come to Memphis, and I shall say to Phtah, Lord of Justice, " Give me my sister to-night ! " The river (is) wine, Phtah (is) its reeds, Sekhmet its lotuses, Earit its buds, Nefertum its flowers [1] . . . Behold the dawn ! Memphis is a bowl of fruits set before the God of the Fair Face (Phtah).
> I shall lie down in my house. I shall be ill (as) if I had been beaten ; my neighbours will come to see me. Then, my sister will come with them. She will be better than the doctors, for she knows what ails me. . . .
> I see my sister coming and my heart rejoices. My arms open to clasp her, my heart shakes in its seat . . . when my mistress comes to me . . .
> If I clasp her and her arms open, it is as if I were in Punt.[2] If I kiss (her mouth) and her lips open, I am happy without beer !

The woman has none of this simplicity, so easily caught and so easily satisfied. Her love is more subtle, more elegiac when waiting, more passionate when fulfilled. She practises all the arts of coquetry, she makes advances ; she sets the trap for the " bird ". Is this mere caprice ? No. Her senses are on fire, but her mind is practical ; what she wants, is a permanent union, marriage. She will watch over the goods of her beloved as the " mistress of his house ", and in lyrical transports she invites him to that felicity.[3]

> *The woman speaks* :
> Beloved brother, my heart follows your love . . . and I say to you, See what I do. I have come and set my trap with my hand. . . . All the birds of Punt alight in Egypt, with myrrh on them ; but he who comes first takes my bait. He brings his perfume from Punt, and his claws are full of frankincense.
> My desire for you, is that we loose him (from the trap) together, I alone with you, that you may hear the plaintive voice of my (bird) scented with myrrh.

[1] For the love-sick one the landscape becomes an enchanted scene, where every detail is animated by a deity of the region.
[2] The country of perfumes.
[3] W. Max Muller, *Die Liebespoesie der alten Aegypter*, 1899 ; **XLIV**, pp. 303 ff.

How good that would be for me, if you were with me when I set the trap ! . . .

The voice of the goose [1] complains, when it is caught by the bait. Your love takes me (to you), and I cannot loose it. I must abandon my nets. What shall I say to my mother, to whom I go back every day, laden with my birds ? " You have set no trap to-day ? " I am the captive of your love.

Your kiss only is what makes my heart live. When I have found it, may Amon give it to me, eternally, for ever !

O fair one, what my heart conceives, is to possess your goods as the mistress of your house (*nebt per*), with your arm laid on my arm. . . . If your love turns away (?), I say in my heart . . . " My great (brother) is far from me to-night," and I am like one in the grave ; for are you not health and life ?

Sometimes we find miniatures, epigrams, which will one day serve as a model for the amorous trifles of the Alexandrian poets. This is how the girl addresses the turtle-dove which wakes her at dawn with his crooning and compels her to rise.

The voice of the turtle-dove speaks to me. . . . He says, " It is dawn. Are you not going out ? " " No, turtle-dove ! You insult me ! I have found my brother in his bed. My heart rejoices. He says to me, ' I shall never leave you ; my hand stays in your hand. I walk about and am with you, wherever it is pleasant.' He has made me the first of girls, and he does not grieve my heart."

After love requited, we have the other side of the passion—suspicions, and complaints uttered when the faithless man has taken another sweetheart. The woman's love is richer in expression and more varied in shades of sentiment than the man's.

The poet also makes the surroundings the accomplices of love. The lady walks in the garden, in flowery groves and among vegetables. A plant or fruit evokes a comparison with some perfection of her form, or an allusion to her full-blown happiness. Trees speak ; it is they who shelter the lovers under their branches and conceal their caresses. In return for their discretion, they expect consideration. A pomegranate-tree complains of neglect, and utters threats. A fig, planted by the woman, declares itself overwhelmed by fate. A little sycamore, which favours amorous trysts, observes the couples slyly, but will keep their secrets.

Other verses sing women " sweet in love ", and describe feminine beauty. These are the features of the Egyptian ideal : " Hair blacker than darkness, teeth more dazzling than chips of flint, a slim waist, and a firm, well-set bosom."

[1] The lover, caught in the trap.

To judge, too, from the statues and pictures, the Egyptians did not admire opulent forms. Unlike the Oriental of to-day, they prized the slenderness of adolescent beauty, which promised them, in the next world, a wife eternally young.[1]

In the literary and artistic production of the Egyptians, as chance has restored it to us, the work of pure imagination remains the exception. Art, science, and literature were made to serve religion and the State ; such is the utilitarian, social character which stamps Egyptian civilization. Old Egypt was but rarely a land of non-utilitarian culture, art for its own sake, pure scientific inquiry, abstract reasoning, or intimate literature. Its great works are anonymous and collective ; they are sternly subordinated to artistic canons, and are directed towards social and religious ends. Therein the Egyptian idea of art too often restricts the field of invention of its mighty creators ; but it expresses what the people set above everything—authority and honesty. And herein its masterpieces possess in high degree the rare quality of exactly symbolizing the race and of being at once recognizable by their noble, disciplined ideal and their unsurpassed, inimitable style.

[1] See Plates XI–XIII.

CONCLUSION

THE known past of Egypt is the longest recorded by history. No doubt Mesopotamia goes back as far ; but there the prehistoric period is still unexplored. Egypt alone offers a field of observation extending from the Palæolithic age to the Christian era. If one counts only from the institution of the calendar, that gives four thousand years of civilization, attested by written monuments. But who will reckon the thousands of years which the Egyptian had taken to pass from the age of knapped stone to the social and political organization of the Thinite monarchy ?

Let us briefly survey the ground covered in the present volume and in *From Tribe to Empire*, and note, too, the lacunæ in our knowledge.

(i) A first period takes us from the most distant origins to the earliest historical monuments. Here all computation of time is approximate, and we can only call it the period prior to the fifth millennium. Palæolithic man has left his tools of flint, but of man's progress in the Mesolithic age we know nothing. We do not know whence the decisive innovations of the Chalcolithic age came—polished stone, pottery, the use of metals (copper and gold), textiles, domestication of animals, agriculture. But we observe that the Egyptians of this age were unrivalled workmen in stone and metal, and they already lived socially, grouped in clans under the protection of fetishes or totems.

(ii) With the settlement of the clans on the soil, a second period begins. The nomes appear, with their local gods and their chiefs, the heirs of the totems. From where, subsequently, did the warriors come who founded the first centralized kingdoms of Upper and Lower Egypt, and the Servants of Horus, with their universal gods, their kings, their pictorial writing, and their already conventional art ?

In the traditions of the next period, this organization, taught to men by the great nature-gods, Horus, Seth, and Osiris, originated in the Delta. Unfortunately, while Upper

465

Egypt has a fair number of monuments, in Lower Egypt the climate of the Delta is responsible for irreparable destruction, which deprives us of direct evidence about the region which sent forth the ideas and doctrines which expanded in later ages. Thanks to the Pyramid Texts, we have been able to work backwards to a tentative account of these doctrines. Much remains to be done in this matter. The reader has been warned that this period of elaboration was of exceptional importance and very long; it includes the date of the inauguration of the calendar (4241) and ends on the accession of Menes (about 3315).

(iii) From the Thinite Monarchy to the end of the Old Kingdom (3315–2360), numerous monuments enable us to define the character of institutions and society. Egypt was united and subjected to the authority, ever growing more centralized, of a despotic kingship by right divine. All social interest was concentrated on the King, alive and dead. Egypt was the personal property of the royal family. The power of the Pyramid-builders collapsed with the VIth Dynasty. Until recent years, the historian noted, without being able to explain it, that about 2360 the Old Empire sank into the unknown. Royal monuments disappear, art becomes barbaric, and there is every sign of civil war and social distress—but how and why did it happen ? The recent discovery of decrees extorted from the last Memphite Kings has enabled us to follow the attacks which priests, officials, and plebeians in succession delivered against the royal despotism ; the dismantling of the monarchical fort was progressive and complete. With the aid of texts which have long been published but have not hitherto been comprehended in their historical significance, I have tried to throw some light on a great democratic revolution, full of bloody or picturesque incidents, which occurred under the Heracleopolite Dynasties, between 2350 and 2150. We have seen its consequences—the access of the mass of the people to religious and political rights. Many obscure points have still to be cleared up ; but it now seems certain that with the Old Kingdom uncontrolled autocracy disappeared.

(iv) A new Egyptian society is revealed by the Theban monarchy (2160–1100), and, through varying political fortunes. it retains its essential characteristics down to the end of national independence (525). In this immense space of time, it is not surprising that there should still be very great lacunæ. The break between the Middle Kingdom and New Empire of Thebes, due to the Hyksôs invasion, the rapid collapse of the Egyptian Empire in Asia after Merneptah, the decline of the Ramessids, the splitting up of the power under the Bubastites, and the Ethiopian and Saïte restorations are all critical periods, of which we know little. Certainly, these are big gaps. But these sudden plunges into chaos are due to accidents of foreign politics. They affect the reigning house rather than society, which survives invasions, goes on with its civilization without a break, and evolves along the lines of its undecaying doctrine.

The reforms of the law-maintaining Kings, who succeeded the absolute monarchs, humanized the conception of power. In the Old Kingdom the royal authority was a dogma, revealed to men by the gods, strictly applied by the Pharaohs, and unreservedly accepted by their subjects. Under the XIIth Dynasty, this dogma assumed a less rigid form in a doctrine, *Teachings*, which strove to be human and reasonable. The Court became the centre of Law—not only of contractual law, applied to political and commercial dealings (in this Babylon innovated more than Egypt), but of social law, which based the relations of men with the King on the divine justice of the other world. The King did not consider that he weakened his authority by associating his whole people with the management of his domains. The constitution was then akin to State socialism ; Pharaoh remained the master of the soil and of his subjects' lives, but on condition that he made everything serve the public good. In the State, the King *served* ; following his example, every man, from the richest to the poorest, worked for the community, on the land and in the workshops and offices of the State ; even the divine and natural powers were enlisted in the public service.

The proof of it is in the enumeration which we find in papyri of the last Theban period : " Teachings to inform the ignorant, as well as the wise, of all that Phtah has created and Thoth has recorded, of all that is under the roof of the sky, of all that is disposed on the back of the earth." First come the elements—sky, sun's disk, sun, star . . . storm, thunder, dawn, darkness, fire, water, inundation, sea, lake, earth, sand, vegetation. Then we have living beings—god, goddess, Akh (Spirit, deified dead), reigning King, Royal Wife, King's mother, royal children, Princes, Vizier, Sole Friend, etc. There follow the officials of the Government, central, provincial, and local (finance, justice, army, temples), and, at the end, the King's scribes, craftsmen, cooks, carpenters, engravers, metal-casters, and cobblers.[1]

Such is the Egyptian society as we find it, all " On His Majesty's Service ". That service embraces the entire universe. Men and the elements alike have their posts, as parts of one whole, fellow-workers in a common task. Heaven, earth, sea, winds, and clouds appear as witnesses to the treaty of peace between Rameses II and Khattusil.[2]

Communistic society in the time of the clans, autocracy by right divine in the Old Kingdom, and monarchic socialism after the revolution—these are the great stages in the history of institutions.

Notwithstanding its limitations, the system to which the Egyptians remained faithful—which was based on a mystical conception of power—has shown, by its vitality, duration, and prosperity, what could be done by intelligent authority and the collaboration of disciplined subjects, to govern men.

In these three successive aspects, Egyptian civilization leaves us the vision of a dense population, homogeneous in race and spirit, which, without being numerically large,[3] gives an impression of strength by its creative and organizing genius, its robust, deliberate art, its intellectual discipline, its belief in another life, and its ideal of justice.

On the one hand, the Egyptian owes his doctrine to the conditions of life imposed on him by the governing powers of the country—the Nile and the Sun. On the other, he is the

---

[1] The end is missing. See Maspero, " Un Manuel de hiérarchie égyptienne," in *Journal Asiatique*, 1888 ; cf. Brugsch, *Die Aegyptologie*, p. 221, and **XLIV**, p. 240.

[2] *From Tribe to Empire*, p. 328.

[3] On the numbers of the population in Pharaonic times the monuments tell us nothing definite. By analogy with modern times, one may reckon that Egypt, properly so called, was able to feed 8,000,000 inhabitants under the Theban monarchy. Diodorus (i, 31) says, " Egypt was formerly more populous than any other country in the world. . . . In a census of the whole population taken in ancient times, seven million inhabitants were counted ; and even at the present day (about 60 B.C.) they are not less than three million."

very close heir of primitive societies. In Egypt, as among primitive men, the individual is subordinated to the community, lives in constant touch with Spirits, and is imbued with filial reverence for tradition.

In its government, as in its manners, Egyptian society, an anachronism compared with Greece and Rome, remained to the end in the stage where the " sacred " dominates. In the temples maintained by the Cæsars, the priests crown their foreign sovereigns, " renew " their life and power by worship, and protect gods and men from death by repeating the rites invented four thousand years ago for the Servants of Horus. Not without reason do we read, in a work of the time of Theodosius : " Egypt is the image of heaven, the temple of the world, the seat of religions." [1]

As Egypt developed, it was still governed by the old mentality in spite of the attempts at adaptation which we have noted. Save at rare times of social crisis, the Egyptian aspired neither to liberty nor to individualism ; he was not made for reflection or critical analysis. It was chiefly in art and the crafts that he was driven to innovation by his love of technical perfection. But the emancipation which sets up the rights of the individual against the demands of the community, which delivers man from the " sacred ", the artist from canons, the worshipper from rituals, and the thinker from tradition, never became general in Egypt. From these bonds the individual would be freed by the lawgivers and philosophers of Greece.

When the Saïte Kings opened Egypt to foreigners, the Greeks were among the first to arrive. Having been brought up in small democratic cities, these sceptical rationalists and creators of a wholly human style in art stood utterly amazed before the colossal hieratic monuments, the strange beast-gods, the god-kings, who ruled a great state as absolute masters, the omnipresent administration, and the people,

---

[1] Pseudo-Apuleius, *Asclepius*, 24 (T. Hoppner, *Fontes Religionis Aegyptiacae*, p. 620). This dialogue between Hermes Trismegistos and Asclepios, one of the last productions of Alexandrian philosophy, is only known by a Latin translation, wrongly attributed to Apuleius. The hero is none other than the architect of King Zeser (IIIrd Dynasty), the Imhetep to whom books of medicine and religious hymns were ascribed (see p. 224) ; the Egyptians had made a demi-god of him, and the Greeks identified him with their Asclepios-Æsculapius (cf. L. Ménard, *Hermès Trismégiste*, 2nd edition, pp. iv, xcvi, 147 ; K. Sethe, " Imhotep, der Asklepios der Aegypter," in **XL**, vol. ii, 4, 1902).

wholly devoted to the service of its gods, its Kings, and its dead. They felt the stupefaction with which we are filled before the gigantic fossils of another age. Neither Herodotus nor the others understood the inmost mind of the Egyptians ; but they felt that they had before their eyes a spectacle of immense interest, unique in the world then known, which they must absorb before they saw it disappear under the tide of " progress ". Egypt offered herself to them as a storehouse of human civilization from its beginnings ; she was the mother of art, science, religion, and institutions, who, in the decline of a life which had miraculously lasted since time immemorial, still stood at their doors for the instruction of " modern " communities. Going back to the past of the human intelligence, the sceptical Greeks came to question the priests of Heliopolis, to learn from the most ancient tradition.

So there begins for Egypt the unexpected rôle of teacher of the Foreigners who invade her. Lawgivers and philosophers took inspiration from her social experiments and metaphysical theories, and those in search of a consoling faith were initiated into her mysteries. To her conquerors she gave a doctrine of authority and of administrative methods.[1] What an example for the empire-builder was afforded by a country where the royal power was defined as " a beneficent office " and was based on a revelation of the gods, accepted by men ! So Alexander the Great crossed the sands of Libya to ask Amon of the Oasis for his paternal investiture. The Macedonian caused himself to be worshipped as the image and son of Amon ; the Ptolemies followed his example ; the Cæsars profited by the lesson and became gods of the Empire.

As for the Egyptian administration, that highly perfected instrument, the fabric in which the whole people worked for the State, its practical usefulness was immediately appreciated by the Ptolemies. Egypt, by the intensive exploitation of its agricultural wealth and industries, became a factory with an enormous output, whose market was the Mediterranean world. When, later, the Cæsars transformed the Roman Republic into an Empire, Egypt was, not only the corn-granary of the Roman world, but the model province for its

[1] Strabo says (xvii, 1, 2) : " The Institutions of Egypt are universally cited and set up as a pattern."

Imperial institutions and the personal property of the Emperor.

But material prosperity, disciplined work, and excellent administration are not enough to make a nation endure. A people needs a doctrine, a faith. For thousands of years the Pharaohs had made and the priests had fed the divine theory of royal authority and social co-operation which had sustained the strength and morale of the people. Bit by bit, mercenaries and Foreigners robbed Egypt of her social ideal, her faith in authority, her customs, her writing, and her religion. Moreover, the Pharaonic conception of society was now worn out and condemned to extinction. Egypt became, to use words taken from her own language, " a body without a soul, a chapel without a god." [1] With her last priests, driven out by the Christians, the secret of the hieroglyphics was lost. The very name of Egypt and her sacred Word sank into oblivion. Let us listen to the poignant lament of one of the last sages educated in the school of Alexandria. For him, to see the dissolution of the last society in which men still believed that they lived in close communion with the gods, was to witness, not only the end of Egypt, but the end of the world. We still feel the melancholy which lies in the farewell which Hermes [2] addresses to what was, in its day, a glorious and beneficent civilization, to all that must vanish and can never be again.

" *A time will come when it will seem in vain that the Egyptians preserved the worship of the gods, with pious minds and scrupulous religion, and all their holy veneration, having availed nothing, will be unrewarded. Godhead will go from the earth to heaven ; Egypt will be abandoned by it, and the land which was the seat of the ancient doctrines will be empty, and deprived of the presence of the gods. For Foreigners fill this region and the land. Not only will the doctrines be neglected, but, still harder fate, it is in the name of the laws, as it were, that religion, piety, and divine worship will be forbidden and punished. Then this very holy land, the seat of sanctuaries and temples, will be filled with dead and tombs. O Egypt, Egypt ! Of thy doctrines only fables will be left, in which thy posterity will no longer believe, and there will survive only words, engraved on stones, to tell of thy piety.*"

[1] *Papyrus Anastasi IV*, pl. 11 ; cf. **XLIV,** p. 244.
[2] Pseudo-Apuleius, *Asclep.*, 24.

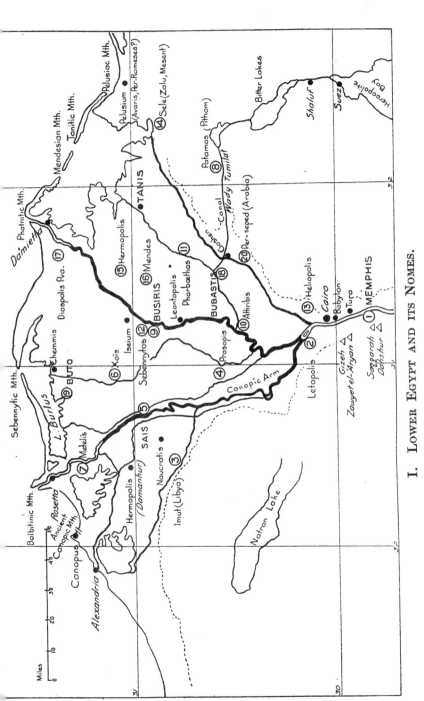

I. LOWER EGYPT AND ITS NOMES.

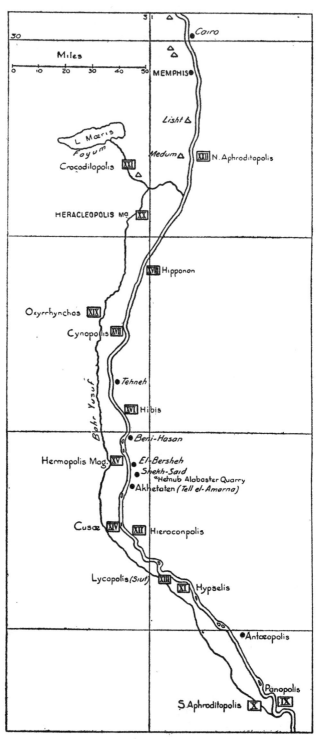

II. UPPER EGYPT AND ITS NOMES.

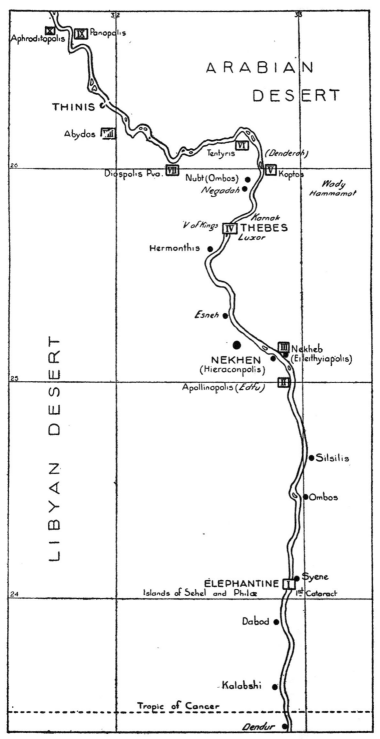

II. UPPER EGYPT AND ITS NOMES.

[*page* 475

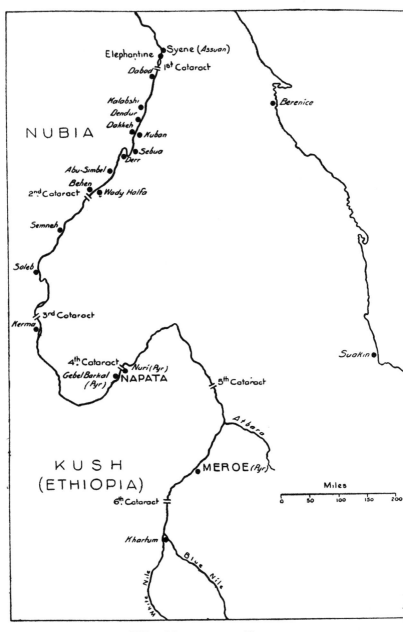

III. Nubia and Ethiopia.

BIBLIOGRAPHY

Note.—For the convenience of English readers, certain English and other editions are quoted in square brackets; but the footnotes do not refer to the pages of these editions.

I. WORKS QUOTED IN THE BIBLIOGRAPHY TO *FROM TRIBE TO EMPIRE*, PARTS II AND III

The reference numbers given in *From Tribe to Empire* are retained.

A. Periodicals

French

Annales du Service des Antiquités de l'Égypte, Cairo . . .	**I**
Mémoires et Bulletin de l'Institut français d'Archéologie orientale, Cairo	**II**
Comptes rendus de l'Académie des Inscriptions et belles-lettres, Paris	**III**
Receuil de travaux relatifs à la Philologie et à l'archéologie égyptiennes et assyriennes, Paris	**IV**
Revue Archéologique, Paris	**V**
Revue Cr.tique, Paris	**VII**
Revue Égyptologique, Paris	**VIII**
Revue de l'Histoire des religions (Annales du Musée Guimet), Paris	**IX**
Sphinx, Upsala and Paris	**X**

German

Zeitschrift für aegyptische Sprache und Altertumskunde, Leipzig .	**XII**

English

The Journal of Egyptian Archæology, London	**XIII**
Proceedings of the Society of Biblical Archæology, London . .	**XIV**

B. General Works

BREASTED (James H.), *A History of Egypt*, London, 1906 . .	**XVI**
—— *Ancient Records of Egypt*, 5 vols., Chicago, 1906–7 . .	**XVII**
MASPERO (Sir Gaston), *Histoire ancienne des peuples de l'Orient classique*, 3 vols., Paris, 1895–7 [8th ed. 1909; *The Dawn of Civilization*, 5th ed., London, 1910; *The Struggle of the Nations*, 2nd ed., 1910; *The Passing of the Empires*, 1900] . .	**XX**
MEYER (Eduard), *Histoire de l'antiquité*, translated from the 3rd ed. by A. MORET, vol. ii, Paris, 1913 [*Geschichte des Altertums*, Stuttgart und Berlin, 1901–13]	**XXII**
—— *Chronologie égyptienne*, translated by A. MORET, Paris, 1912 (*Annales du Musée Guimet, Bibliothèque d'études*, vol. xxiv, No. 2) [*Aegyptische Chronologie*, Berlin, 1904]	**XXIII**

C. Special Works [1]

MORET (A.), *Au Temps des Pharaons*, 3rd ed., Paris, 1922 [*In the Time of the Pharaohs*, translated by Mme MORET, New York and London, 1911]	**XXVII**
—— *Rois et dieux d'Égypte*, 3rd ed., Paris, 1922 [*Kings and Gods of Egypt*, translated by Mme MORET, New York, 1912] . .	**XXVIII**
—— *Mystères égyptiens*, 3rd ed., Paris, 1922 . .	**XXIX**
—— *Du caractère religieux de la royauté pharaonique*, Paris, 1902 (*Annales du Musée Guimet, Bibliothèque d'études*, vol. xv) .	**XXX**

[1] Special monographs are quoted in the footnotes to the passages dealing with the subject in question.

II. WORKS QUOTED IN THIS VOLUME ONLY

A. Periodicals

French

Revue de l'Égypte ancienne, Paris . . . . . . **XXXVII**
Bibliothèque égyptologique, Paris . . . . . . **XXXVIII**

German

Untersuchungen zur Geschichte und Altertumskunde Aegyptens,
Leipzig . . . . **XXXIX**

B. General Works

ERMAN (Adolf) and RANKE, *Aegypten und aegyptisches Leben im
Altertum*, 2nd ed., Tübingen, 1923 [*Life in Ancient Egypt*,
translated by H. M. TIRARD, London, 1894] . . . . **XL**

C. Special Works

BREASTED (J. H.), *Development of Religion and Thought in Ancient
Egypt*, London and New York, 1912 . . . . . **XLI**
CAPART (Jean), *Leçons sur l'art égyptien*, Liège, 1920 [The introductory
chapters translated by W. R. DAWSON, *Egyptian Art*, London,
1923] . . . . **XLII**
—— *L'Art égyptien : études et histoire*, i, 1924 . . . **XLIII**
ERMAN (Adolf), *Die Literatur der Aegypter*, Leipzig, 1923 . . **XLIV**
—— *La Religion égyptienne*, translated, Paris, 1907 [*Die aegyptische
Religion*, Berlin, 1905 (Berlin Kgl. Museum, Handbuch); *A
Handbook of Egyptian Religion*, translated by A. S. GRIFFITH,
London, 1907] . . . . **XLV**
MASPERO (Sir Gaston), *Les Contes populaires de l'ancienne Égypte*,
4th ed., Paris, 1911 [*Popular Stories of Ancient Egypt*, translated
by Mrs. C. H. W. JOHNS, London and New York, 1915] . . **XLVI**
—— *L'Égypte*, Paris, 1908 (*Ars Una*) [*Art in Egypt*, London, 1921] **XLVII**
MORET (A.), *Le Rituel du culte divin journalier en Égypte*, Paris, 1902
(*Annales du Musée Guimet*, Bibl. d'études, vol. xiv) . . **XLVIII**
ROEDER (G.), *Urkunden zur Religion des alten Aegypten*, Jena, 1915 . **XLIX**
PETRIE (Sir W. M. Flinders), *Arts et métiers de l'ancienne Égypte*,
translated by J. CAPART, Brussels, 1912 [*Arts and Crafts of
Ancient Egypt*, Edinburgh and London, 1923] . . . **L**
MASPERO (Sir G.), *Guide du visiteur au Musée du Caire*, 4th French
ed., 1914 . . . . **LI**

The author was unable to use the excellent *Cambridge Ancient History*, which
appeared while his manuscript was in the press.

INDEX

References to notes, plates, and figures are given, but only where there is no reference to the subject in the text of the page.

A figure in brackets after the name of a King indicates his dynasty; after that of a place, the nome.

AAHHETEP I, II, Queens (XVIII), 299, 307–8

Abdu, see Abydos

Abu, see Elephantine

Abu-Simbel, temple, 298, 418 n. 1, 419, 423

Abusir : representations of the Sed, 131 ; tomb of Sahura, q.v.

Abydos, Abdu (VIII), 55 ; battle, 219, 221 ; Greeks at, 347 ; inscription, 142 n. ; mummy ibises, 365 ; Osiris Khent-Amenti, worship of, 97, 110, 246–52, 254–5 ; relief and reliquary of Osiris, q.v. ; other gods, 110, 246 ; princes, 209, 211 ; Tablets, 18–19, 189, 216 ; temples, foundations, immunities, 206–7, 252, 297, 304–5, 378 pl. ; tombs, 141, 146, and see under Osiris

Abyssinia, 28–9

ACHTHOES, KHETI (IX), 151, 218, 233–4

Acquaintances, 159, 190, 192 ; in funerals, 258

Administration, officials : early, 41–2 ; Thinite, 134–40 ; Memphite, 158–64, 188–98 ; officials become independent princes, 208–20, 235–7 ; under Thebans, 237–41, 260–88 ; tombs of Theban officials, 297

Admonitions of an Old Sage, 221, 224–31, 457

ADONIS, 82, 84, 319

AFRICANUS (Sextus Julius), chronology, 4–5, 19

Afterlife, 397, 401–3 ; judgment of the dead, 186–7, 255–8, 398–401 ; Thinite, 141–3 ; Memphite, 168–9 ; 171–3, 175–85, 197 ; for nobles, 197, 199–201, 214–15 ; for people, 203, 226, 229, 248, 253, 255–7, 259–60

Agriculture, 38–9, 43–4, 268 pl. ; in Old Kingdom, 138, 261–2 ; decline in revolution, 225 ; under Thebans, 266, 273, 279 ; House of, 193, 263 ; see also Irrigation

AHA, Horus-name of Menes, q.v.

AHMASI, Q. (XVIII) 308–11

AHMES I (XVIII), 291, 299, 304, 308, 336

AHMES, Chief of the Sailors, 299

AHMES PEN-NEKHEBT, 299

Aï (XVIII), 315, 325 n., 329, 336

Air, see Shu

AKERBLAD, 11

Akh, Spirit, 143, 171–3, 181, 183–6, 396, 404 n. 2 ; see also Horus, Servants of

AKHENATEN, IKHUNATEN, AMENOPHIS IV (XVIII), 315–16, 319–25, 329, 336 ; hymns to Aten, q.v. ; tomb, mummy, 295 n. 1, 329–30 ; influence on art, 440–3 ; portraits, 322 fig., 420 pl., 441–3

Akhetaten, see Tell el-Amarna

Alabastronpolis, see Hetnub

ALEXANDER, K. of Macedon, 3, 24, 336, 470

Amada, temple, 298

Amarna, el, see Tell el-Amarna

AMASIS (XXVI), 336, 346, 348

AMÉLINEAU (E.), 141, 247–8

AMENARDIS I and II, Worshippers of Amon, 344, 350, 430 pl.

AMENEMHAT I, AMENI (XII), 232, 234, 237–8, 241, 244, 294 ; in literature, 221, 222 n. 1, 232 ; Teachings, 237

AMENEMHAT II, 232, 240 ; AMENEMHAT III, NEMAATRA, MENMAAT-RA, 176, 241, 288, 440 n. 1 ; AMENEMHAT IV, 232

AMENEMHAT, Vizier, 234, 241

AMENHETEP, Pharaohs (XVIII), see Amenophis

AMENHETEP, Prophet of Anon, 335

AMENHETEP, scribe, 304

AMENI, Nomarch, 238–9

AMENI, Pharaoh, see Amenemhat I

AMENMESES (XIX), 336

AMENOPE, maxims of, 459 n. 3

AMENOPHIS I (XVIII), 21, 308, 336 ; AMENOPHIS II, 295 nn., 315, 336, 404 n. 2

AMENOPHIS III, 336 ; buildings, founda-
tions, relations with gods, 294–8,
304, 317–19 ; foreign affairs,
315–16 ; Sed, 128 fig., 132–4, 298
AMENOPHIS IV, see Akhenaten
AMENOPHIS, others, see Amenhetep
Amenti, see Iment
AMON, AMMON, AMON-RA : beginnings
of Amon and fusion with Ra, 51,
54, 244–5 ; influence in New
Empire, 306 ff. ; superseded by
Aten, 315–27 ; revival 327 ff. ; in
Ethiopia and under Ethiopian
Dyn., 341–4 ; under Bubastites
and Saïtes, 349 ; in legend, 61–2 ;
= Zeus, 50, 61 ; ram, 261–2 ;
goose, cat, 364 ; hymns to, 66,
330–1 ; temples and foundations at
Thebes, 26 pl., 293–5, 302, 304,
316, 333, 340, 416 pl., 418 nn.,
422 pl. ; other temples, 297–8 ;
1st Prophet of, 305, 313, 320, 324,
328, 334–5, 337–8, 340–2, 349,
351, 443 ; women of, 129, 132,
335 ; Worshipper of, 129, 334,
349–52, 430 pl. ; as father of
Pharaoh, 310–12, 316–17, 323,
337 ; direct intervention in affairs,
309, 332, 338, 343 ; Amon-Ra at
Xoïs, 57 ; oracle at Siwa, 25
n. 1, 470 ; at Kadesh, 161 ; army
division, 300
AMTSI, Q. (VI), 193
Anastasi Papyrus, on Nile, 31 n. 1
ANHERT, ANHOR, ONURIS (falcon), 58,
61–2, 334 ; = Ares, 61 ; = Horus,
371
ANI, maxims of, 459
ANKHNESNEFERIBRA, Worshipper of
Amon, 351
ANKHU, Collection of Sayings, 222–3
Answerers, see Ushebtiu
Ant-eater, see Seth (Beast)
ANTEF, Pharaohs (IX), 219, 234 ;
decree, 218 n. ; stele, 284 n. 4,
286 n. 5 ; Songs of Harpist, 221,
224, 457
ANUBIS (dog, jackal) : early god and
ensign, 47, 56, 86, 93 n. 1, 361 ;
goes South and becomes Khent-
Amenti, 110–11, 171 n. 2 ; in
Heliopolitan legend, 61, 158 ; in
Osiris legend, 87–9, 92, 97, 155,
382 ; feast, 135 ; in Mysteries,
250 ; in funerals, 169–70, 246 ;
in judgment of the dead, 398–400,
402 n. 3 ; House of, 145 ; Offering
of, 200 ; Basin of the Jackal,
181–2, 185 ; temple at Letopolis
and medicine, 448
ANUQET, 54

ANZTI (two feathers), 58, 78–80, 85–7,
97, 103, 105, 110, 126, 171
APHRODITE = Hathor, 50
Aphroditopolis (VI), see Denderah
Aphroditopolis, Northern, Per-hemt
(XXII), 56, 110
Aphroditopolis, Southern, Zebti, Per-
Wazet (X), 49, 55,
APION, 3–4
APIS : Bull (Phtah), 57, 131, 135,
364–5 ; nome, see Libyan Nome
Apollinopolis Magna, see Edfu
APOLLO = Horus Behedeti, 61
APOPHIS (Seth, serpent), 153, 371 ;
sons of, 373
APOPHIS, Hyksôs K., 440 n. 1
APRIES (XXVI), 336, 346
Apu, see Panopolis
APULEIUS, pseudo-, Asclepius, on
Egypt, 469, 471,
Arabian desert, 25, 420
Arabian Nome (20), 59
Arabic writing and language, 8
Archers, Bows (people), 114, 225
Architecture, 412 ff. ; as " great
work ", 411 ; water-channels on
buildings, 35 n. 3 ; see also Palace,
Pyramid, Temple, Tomb
ARES = Anhert and Shu, 61
Arish, el, see Atnub
Army : Thinite, 137 ; Memphite, 161,
194, 210 ; Heracleopolite, 236 ;
Middle Kingdom, 239 ; Theban
organization, 279, 300–1 ; Director
of Soldiers, 238–9 ; mercenaries,
194, 219, 262, 301, 333, 337, 339–40,
345–6 ; soldiers under New Empire,
298–302, 304, 339–40 ; see also
War
Arrows, as ensign, 39, 46–8, 57, and see
Neith
ARSAPHES = Herishef, 364
ARTATAMA, K. of Mitanni, 316
Asasif, stele of Nomarch, 244
ASCLEPIODOTUS, graffito, 297
ASCLEPIOS = Imhetep, 469 n. 1
ASH, name of Beast of Seth, 48
Ash, tree, 81
ASHURBANIPAL, K. of Assyria, 336, 345
Asia, Easterners : Semitic type in
Egypt, 38 ; Semitic (?) origin of
Horians, 107 n. 2 ; early wars,
114–15, 135–6 ; Old Kingdom
wars in Asia, 161, 193–4 ; Asiatics
in Delta at end of Old Kingdom,
219, 221, 225, 234 ; Middle
Kingdom wars, 232, 234 ; Hyksôs
invasion, q.v. ; New Theban
Empire in Asia, 233, 290–2, 314–15 ;
later wars, 333, 340, and see
Assyria ; Asiatic prisoners, 291 ;

mercenaries, 301; Syrian connexion of Osiris, 81–2, 84, 88–9; of Aten, 317–18; Asiatic influence on art, 440

ASPALUT, K. of Ethiopia, 342 n. 2, 343 n. 4, 345 n. 2

Assuan, princes, 209, 211, 214

Assyria, Assur: sources for chronology, 22; alliances, 292, 315; wars and conquest of Egypt, 24, 342, 344–6

Astrology, 406, 454–5

Astronomy, 452–4, and see Calendar

Atbara R., 28

ATEN, 99, 318–27; disk as cartouche, 150; disk in temples, 422–3; hymns to, 36–7, 325–7, 459; temples, 36, 440–1

ATHOTES, see Atoti II

ATHOTHIS, see Khent

Athribis (10), 58, 78

Atnub, el-Arish, 373

ATOTI I (I), see Khent; ATOTI II, ATHOTES, 117; ATOTI III, CENCENES, 117

ATUM, TUM, ATUM-RA: Atum god of Heliopolis, 58; fusion with Ra, 64 n. 3, 153–4; Khepri-Ra-Atum, see Khepri; in legend, as Demiurge, 61, 152, 369–70, 374–5, 386; replaced by Phtah, q.v.; protector of pyramid and dead King, 174–5, 178; dead identified with, 257; books at Heliopolis, 251–2; temple and medicine, 448–9

Avaris, Hyksôs capital, 23

Ba, Ram, see under Khnum

Ba, Soul, 171–2, 183–4, 396

Babylon in Asia: alliances, 292, 315; law, 467

Babylon near Heliopolis, 317

Bahr Yusuf, 28

BAILLET (J.), on slavery, 292 n. 1

BAKENKHONSU, Prophets of Amon, 335

BAKET-ATEN, princess, 322

BAKHA Bull: Mentu, 54, 364; Ra, 364

BARTHÉLEMY, Abbé, 11

BAST (cat), 59, 288

BAZAU (Hetepsekhemui), BOÈTHUS (II) 117

Bee of Buto, in royal title, 121, 151

Beetle (scarab), see Khepri

Behedet (II), see Edfu

Behedet, Diospolis Pva. (17), 59, 108 n. 2, 109

Behedet-meht (14), see Sele

BEK, sculptor, 442

BEKI, on justice, 408

BÉNÉDITE (Georges), on art, 435

Beni-Hasan: family of, 237; inscription, on foundation of cities, 43 n. 1; mummy cats, 365; tomb of Neheri, 254 n. 4

BEQET, Nomarch's daughter, 238

BERENICE, Ptolemaic Q., 250 n. 7

Berlin Papyrus, see Ebers Medical Papyrus

Bersheh, el, 240

BES, 405, 438

Bet el-Wali, temple, 298

Bet-Khallaf, temple, 147

BICHERIS (IV), 148

BINETEREN (Neteren), BINOTHRIS (II), 117

BIUNETER, UBIENTHES (I), 117, 171

BLACKMAN, on House of Morning, 393 n. 4

BOCCHORIS (XXIV), 124 n. 1, 336, 344, 347–8

BOETHUS, see Bazau

Bolbinitic Mouth, 27

Book of the Dead, 257–8, 260, 397–403, 407; on Osiris as corn, 83; on Ra as creator, 375

BORCHARDT (L.), on chronology, 23 n. 1

Bows (people), see Archers

BREASTED (J. H.), on XVIIIth Dyn., 314 n. 4

BROUSSARD, Capt., and Rosetta Stone, 10

BRUGSCH, on monotheism, 379 n. 4

Bubastis (18), 50, 59, 129, 254, 340, 346 n. 2, 365; medicine at, 448, 449 n. 2; Dynasties, 24, 336, 339–41, 343, 347,

Bucranium, as ensign and attribute, 46–7, 55, 361

Bull: bull-calf as emblem, 58; Great Black Bull as emblem, 58, 78 fig.; desert (Ra), 57; in royal title, 121–2, 151; King Bull, 114 n. 4, 121–2; sacred bulls, 364–5; see also Apis, Bakha, Heseb, Khonsu, Mnevis

Burlus, L., 91

Busiris, Zedu (9), 50, 58, 79–80, 85, 97, 103, 105, 254–5

Buto, Per-Wazet (19), 59, 86, 88, 365; early capital, 103, 111–14, 116; emblems in royal title, 120–1; Sed, 132–3; Warden of Pe, 138

BUYUWAWA, Libyan mercenary leader, 339

Byblos, Osiris and, 81 n. 3, 82, 88–9

CÆSAR (C. Julius), 336

CÆSARS, see Rome

Calasiries, 302

Calendar, 20–3, 104–5, 446, 453–4

CAMBYSES, K. of Persia, 336, 49

Canals, 33, 44, 195, 346 n. 2, *and see* Irrigation

Canopus, Decree of, on Mysteries, 250 n. 7

CAPART (Jean): on statues, 432–3; on Tanis sphinxes, 440 n. 1

Carians, in Egypt, 345–6

CARTER (Howard), excavations, 330

Cartouche, 150–1

Cat, 365, *and see* Amon, Bast

Cataract, First, 25, 82

CENCENES, *see* Atoti III

Census, 135, 139–40, 188

Centralization, early, 78, 95, 104, 113, 116, 120, 122, 140

CHABAS, on astrology, 454

CHAÎRES (II), 117

CHAMPOLLION (Jean François), Frontispiece, 11, 18; on Hypostyle Hall, 294

Chancellor, 138, 190, 194, 210, 239, 258

Chapels, *see under* Tombs

Charters of immunity, 204–8, 210, 215, 263–5

Chemistry, 452

Chemmis, 86, 91–2, 99 fig., 111

CHENERES (II), 117

Chenoboscion, princes, 209

CHEOPS, KHUFU (Mazedu), SUPHIS (IV), 148; pyramid, 146 pl., 147, 173, 177; statuette, 246

CHEPHREN, KHAFRA (Userib), SUPHIS, 148, 150; pyramid, 147, 173, 177; statue, 68 pl., 439

CHERES, *see* Khaneferra

Child, Royal, nome-emblem, 59

Children, Royal, 192, 197, 236; in coronation and Sed, 129–30, 132; in funerals and Mysteries (Darling Son), *see under* Horus Yr.

Chronology, 3–5, 17–24; sequence dates from pottery, 106

Circumcision, 449

Cities: hieroglyphic, 41 fig., 42; early, and gods, 41–3, 46–53; Directors of, 211; Protectors, 191; " new cities " with immunities, 204–5, 210; Regents of, 238

Clans, 39–41, 46, 51–2, 95, *and see under* Ensigns

CLEMENT, Bp. of Alexandria: on divine animals, 365; on hieroglyphics, 9

Climate, 34–5

Clocks, 454

Columns, 413–15, 419, 422

Confession, negative, 398–400

Coptic writing and language, 1, 7–9, 14

Coptos, Gebtiu (V), 55, 68, 119, 367; decree of Demzibtaui, q.v.; of

Neferkauhor, 217; statue of Horus, 70 : Temple of Min, q.v.

Coronation rites, 123–6, 312; repeated in Sed, q.v.

Cow, 365, *and see* Nephthys, *and under* Hathor, Isis, Nut

Crete, relations with Egypt, 22, 228, 292, 315, 440

Crocodile, 49, 52, 55–6, 68, 119, 364–5, *and see* Sebek

Crocodilopolis, Fayum, Moeris (XXI), 56, 245, 364

Cronos, 61

Crowns, Red, White, *Pskhent,* 76–7, 111–14, 123–5; in royal title, 120–1, 151

Cusæ, Gesa, Meir (XIV), 56, 110; princes, 209, 211, 235–6

Cynopolis, Dog (XVII), 47, 56, 110, 238–9

Cyprus, alliances, 292

Dahshur, 147, 176

Dakkeh, temple, 412 pl.

DANGA, dwarf, 178

DARIUS, I, K. of Persia, 346 n. 2, 449

DAVY (G.), on conflicts of totems, 52; universal god and political centralization, 65 n.; primitive institutions, 95–6; *nourris,* 167; authority by individual contract, 167 n. 3; *mana,* 172 n. 3

Dead, beliefs and practices regarding the, *see* Afterlife, Funeral rites, Pyramids, Tombs

Debt, laws of Bocchoris, 347–8

Delta: character, 26–7, 35, 73–4; early history, 73 ff., 85–6, 102–16; in civil war and revolution, 219, 221, 225, 233–4; under Thebans, 317; later revival, 337 ff.

DEMZIBTAUI, Pharaoh, decree, 215 n. 2, 217–18

Denderah, Tentyris (VI), 55, 68, 110, 209, 421 n. 3; called Aphroditopolis, 50

Dendur, temple, 298

DENNUT, Uraeus, devourer, 187

Der el-Bahari: burial-pit, 295 n. 2, 314, 338; temple of Hatshepsut, 26 pl., 296, 308, 310–14, 418 n. 2; pyramid and temple of Mentuheteps, 234, 296

Der el-Gebraui, princes, 209, 212, 214

Derr, temple, 298

Description de l' Égypte, 11, 13

Deshasheh, princes, 209

Devourer, 398, 401; *and see* Dennut

Dialogue of an Egyptian with his Spirit, 221, 223, 457

Dikes, *see* Irrigation

DIODORUS SICULUS, 3, 5–6 ; on Amon and direct intervention, 343 n. 4 ; Anubis and Upuat, 87 ; Bocchoris and laws, 347–8 ; cats, 365 n. 3 ; country of Egypt, 25 ; early dyns., 101–2 ; funeral rites, 383 ; hieroglyphics, 9 ; Horus Yr., 91 ; land and soldiers, 302–3, 340 ; Memphis, 124 n. 1 ; Nile, inundation, 28–9, 31 n. 2, 35 nn.; Osiris, 83–5, 87 n. 1 ; Pharaoh's life, 343–4 ; population, 468 n. 3 ; Ramesseum, 296 ; statues, 430, 432 ; written petitions, 279 n. 3

DIONYSOS, resurrection, 84

DIOSCORIDES, debt to Egypt, 450–1

Diospolis Ma. (IV), see Thebes

Diospolis Pva., Het (VII), 47, 55

Diospolis Pva. (17), see Behedet

Director, of Upper Egypt, 194, 213–14, 217, 238

DIVES and LAZARUS, Egyptian parallel, 409

Dog : ensign, 45 fig., 46–7 ; nome, see Cynopolis ; sacred, 365 ; greyhound, see Seth (Beast) ; see also Anubis

Domain, Royal : reduced by immunities, 204–8, 217, 220 ; Theban Kings restore, 237–9, 265 ; Directors of Classes, 239–40 ; Regents, 191 ; Superintendent of Declarations, 191 ; see also Land, Pharaoh's Fields

Drawing, painting, reliefs, 406, 422, 425–9, 431–6, 441–3, 448

DUAMUTEF, s. of Horus, 172

Duat, Morning, 181–2, 185, 389, 391 ; worship, 158, 388

DUDUN, Nubian god, 298

DUMMUZI, Sumerian god, 84

DUSHRATTA, K. of Mitanni, 316

Dynasties, division into, 5

EARIT, 461

Earth, see Geb

East, Iabt, Ingot, Point of East, Khent-iabti, 46, 58, 76–7

Easterners, see Asia

EBERS (Berlin) Medical Papyrus, 21, 448 n. 1, 449

Edfu, Apollinopolis Ma., Behedet (II) : nome, 54 ; takes names Behedet, mesent, from Delta, 107–9 ; Horus at, 47, 107–10, 356 ; Temple of Horus, 107, 416 pl., 420 n. 3, 425, 452 ; Hathor at, 356 ; House of the Morning, 393 n. 4 ; princes, 209, 211, 214 ; inundation at, 32

EILEITHYIA = Nekhebt, 112 n. 2.

Eileithyiapolis, see Nekheb

Elephant, ensign, 39, 51, 54

Elephantine, Abu (I) : calendar from, 21 ; Dynasties, 23, 148, 156 ; as frontier, 25 n. 1 ; gods, 51, 54, 245, 364 ; Nile, source of, 84 n. 1, 145 n. 1 ; Nilometer, 31 n. 2, 32 ; princes, 212.

Enneads, of Heliopolis, 58, 60–3, 93–4, 97–9, 154–7, 174–5, 181, 245 ; poor equalized with, 226, 229, 253

Enneads, other, 379

Ensigns : of clans, 39–40, 45 fig., 46, 54–9 ; of nomes, 39, 45–59 ; development into human form, 362

ERATOSTHENES of Cyrene : visits Egypt, 6 ; on Athothes, 117

ERMAN (A.), on temple property, 333

ESARHADDON. K. of Assyria, conquers Egypt, 336, 345

Esneh, see Latopolis

Ethiopians, Southern Libyans, Temhu : in Ethiopia, 341–3, 345 n. 2 ; in Egypt, 24, 336, 343–6, 348, 443

EUSEBIUS, Bp. of Caesareia, 4–5 ; on protohistoric dyns., 101

Face, ensign, 46

Falcon : ensign, 39, 45 fig., 46–8, 54–6, 58–9, 115 ; falcon and bull, 54 ; and feather, 57 ; on Nubti, 55, 149 ; on oryx, 51 fig., 52, 56 ; flying falcon, 56 ; mummy falcon, 54, 57, 59, 112 ; two falcons, 55, 110, 118–19 ; as sign of " god ", 55, 66 ; in royal title, 110, 118–20, 122–3 ; worshipped and mummified, 365 ; see also Anhert, Horus, Mentu

Family : origins, 96 ; Old Kingdom, 168 pl., 262 ; Theban, 263, 265, 273–5, 326 pl.; in after life, 259, 265 n. 1, 275, 402 ; family worship, 96–7, 143–4

Fayum : pyramids, 296 ; nome, see Crocodilopolis

Feather, ensign, 45 fig., 54, 57–8, 110 ; ostrich, see Iment ; two feathers, see Anzti

Fishing, 38–9, 269

Flesh, ensign, see Meat

Food : food-supply, granaries, 139, 158, 167, 191, 268 pl., 280, 281 fig., 412 ; food of Memphite King, 165–6 ; in afterlife, 172, 184–5, and see Offerings

Foundations, see Offerings

Free men, nemhu, 265–8, 272–3, 302, 347

Friends, Sole Friend, 159, 190, 192, 194 ; in funerals, 258

Funeral rites, 168 pl., 395–6, 407 ; predynastic, 106 ; Thinite, 142–4 ;
Memphite, 168–71 ; extended to
nobles, 198–200, 212 ; neglected in
revolution, 223, 228 ; extended
to people, 226, 232 fig., 253, 257–60 ;
see also Afterlife, Pyramids, Tombs
Furniture, 135, 437–8, 442

GARDINER, on magic and religion,
407 n. 1
GEB (Earth), 30 ; in legend, 61–2, 64,
71, 82, 87, 92–4, 98–100, 154,
175, 369–70, 373, 380 ; in funerals,
170 ; as herald, 160 ; representa-
tions, 154 fig., 262
Gebel Barkal, see Napata
Gebelein, temple, 234
Gebel el-Araq, knife handle from, 107
Gebtiu (City of Caravan-men), see
Coptos
Genesis, Bk. of : on land and taxation,
267 n. 2, 303 ; creative Word, 375
GEORGE the Syncellus : on chronology,
etc., 5–6, divine dyn., 61
Gerf Hussen, temple, 298
Gesa, see Cusæ
Gizeh, pyramids, 147, 173, 177
Goat, see Herishef ; Osiris at Mendes,
364
Gods : idea of god, neter, 66, 355–60,
390 ; Heliopolitan idea of, 378 ;
of nomes, and clan-ensigns, 43–4,
46–53 ; nome-gods in judgment of
the dead, 398, 409 ; universal
gods, 61–5, 368 ff. ; local gods subordinated to Ra and Horus,
385–6 ; centralization and
polytheism, 378–80 ; composite,
379 ; identified with Greek gods,
50 ; magic, 404 ; representations,
360 ff. ; and beasts, 363–6 ;
statues, 362–3 ; Names, 366–7
GOLENISCHEFF, on Tanis sphinx, 440
n. 1
Goose, see under Amon
Goshen, Regent's Wall, 289
Granaries, see under Food
GRÉBAUT, on monotheism, 379 n. 4
Greeks : travellers, traders, and mercenaries in Egypt, 1–3, 6, 345–7 ;
names of nomes, 50 ; resurrection-
god, 84 ; prognostics, 455 ; re-
marks on Egypt, 1–3, 5–7, 444,
448, 470 ; see also Ptolemies
Greyhound, see Seth (Beast)
GRIFFITH, on iu-f qeris, 390 n. 2
Guard : of Palace, 137, 158 ; Pharaoh's
in New Empire, 301–2
Guide of the Country, 191, 209
Gurnah, temple, 296

Gurob, papyri, 264–5
GYGES, K. of Lydia, 345–6

HA, mountain-god, 57
HAMMURABI, K. of Babylon, 22
HANKU, Nomarch, 210
HAPI, see under Nile
HAPUSENB, Prophet of Amon, 313–14
HARAKHTI : Horus, 66, 108 n. 3, 155,
423 ; Ra, 107–8, 120, 176, 243,
297–8, 318, 373 ; fused with Shu
as Aten, 320 ; Harmachis, see under
Khepri ; Temple at Abu-Simbel,
423
HARDEDEF, 224
Hare, Nome, see Hermopolis Ma
HARMACHIS, see under Khepri
HARPOCRATES = Horus Yr., 90 n. 1
Harpoon : ensign, nomes, 46, 47 fig.,
57–8, 106 ; mesent, 108–9
Harvest rites, 89 n. 1
HATHOR : nomes, 47, 49, 53–6, 110,
356 ; as form of Isis, 49, 56, 110 ;
Hathor-Isis of Byblos, 81 n. 3,
82 ; as cow, 47, 49, 54–6, 64 n. 3,
361 ; wife of Horus, 53–5, 110,
356 ; tree, 364 ; Great Mother,
110 ; Aphrodite, 50 ; fused with
Nut, 64 n. 3 ; with Sekhmet, q.v. ;
with Wazet, q.v. ; priests, temple,
208 n. 3, 211, 334 ; under
Akhenaten, 323
Hatiu, Libyan chiefs, 77
HATSHEPSUT, Q. (XVIII), 296, 308–14,
336, 337 n. 1, 351 n. 2
Hau-nebu, People of the North, 99
n. 7
HEARST Papyrus, 448 n. 1
HECATÆOS of Abdera, 3, 6
HECATÆOS of Miletos, 2
Heliopolis (13) : nome, 58 ; early
history and importance, 78 n. 3,
104–6 ; influence in Old Kingdom,
120, 147, 156 ff., 203 ; decline, 218,
222 ; under Middle Kingdom, 243 ;
under New Empire, 306, 331 ;
doctrine, 60–5, 152–6, 369 ff., and
see Pyramid Texts, Ra ; Atum at,
152–4 ; books of Atum, 251–2 ;
adoption of Ra, 153 ff. ; adoption
of Osiris, 97, 106, 251–2 ; judgment of Seth at, 94 ; unification,
" words of Heliopolis," 378–9 ;
Mansion of Sar, 94, 157 n. 3, 371 ;
Temple of Ra (Aten), 36 n. 3,
174 ; temple property, 333 ;
medicine, 448–9 ; astronomy, 105,
452 ; Greeks and priests, 470
HELIOS = Ra, 61
HEMUR, Director of Prophets, 206
HEPHÆSTOS = Atum-Ra or Phtah, 61

Heracleopolis Ma. (XX), 56, 97, 109 ;
Dynasties, 22–3, 218–19, 233–4 ;
later rulers, 339, 341 ; Ram, *see*
Herishef
HERACLES = Khonsu, 61
Heredity, masculine : in Osiris legend,
96 ; in Thinite rites, 144 ; of
office, 213, 217 ; of goods, office,
trade, 265–7, 273 ; of 1st Prophets,
334–5
Heredity, uterine, *see* Woman
HERIHOR (XXI), 336–8, 342
HERISHEF (Ram, Goat), 56, 135, 245,
361, 364
HERMES, *see under* Thoth ; Trisme-
gistus, 469 n. 1, 471
Hermetic writings, on creative Word,
375, 377
Hermonthis, Uast (IV), 51, 54, 209,
244, 320, 364, 453 n. 1
Hermopolis Ma., Khmunu, Hare (XV) :
nome, emblems, 49–50, 56 ; Osiris
at, 97 ; Thoth at, 71, 110, 379–80 ;
princes (tombs at Shekh-Said),
209, 214, 240–1 ; mummy ibises,
365
Hermopolis Pva. (15), 47, 59, 110
Hermopolis, Damanhur (in 3rd Nome),
110
Hermotybies, 302
HERODOTUS, 2–3, 6 ; on Egypt, 6,
470 ; Amon and Egypt, 25 n. 1 ;
divine animals, 364 n. 4, 365 ;
army, 302 ; climate, 35 ; early
dyns., 101–2 ; feasts and Mysteries,
132, 254, 383 ; floods, damage by,
279 n. 2 ; geometry, 445 ; hieroglyphics, 9 ; land system, 266–7,
302 ; medicine, 451 ; Memphis,
124 ; mosquitoes, 269 n. 1 ; Nile,
28–9, 32–3 ; priests, 302 ;
Psammetichus I, 345–6 ; Saite
prosperity, 348 ; Solon's debt to
Egypt, 348 ; swamps of Delta,
109 ; women, 460
Heroonpolis, Patamos, Pithom (8),
58, 78, 346 n. 2.
HESEB Bull, nome, 58
HESEPTI (Den), USAPHAÏS (I), 117,
135–6, 364, 413, 448
HESIOD : on Nile, 28 ; on prognostics,
455
Hetnub, Alabastronpolis, 195, 240
Hetnub, House of Gold, sacred workshop, 250 n. 1, 252, 313, 382, 434
Hibis, White Oryx (XVI), 56, 68,
236, 238–9
Hieraconpolis (III), *see* Nekhen
Hieraconpolis, Serpent Mountain (XII),
55, 110, 210, 213
Hieroglyphics, *see* Writing

HIPPOCRATES, debt to Egypt, 450–1
Hipponon, House of Phœnix (XVIII),
56
Hippopotamus : a beast of Seth, q.v. ;
worshipped, 365 ; goddess Thueris,
438 ; hunting, 109, 135, 161
Hittites, Khatti, alliances with, 292,
315, 468
HOMER, on Thebes, 293
HOR (XIII), 230 fig., 286 pl.
HOREMHEB (XVIII), 295, 329–30, 336
HORKHEB, Prophet of Amon, 351
HORSIATEF, K. of Ethiopia, 345 n. 2
HORUS (falcon), gods of various nomes,
47, 51 fig., 52–6, 58–9, 86, *and see*
various Horuses below
HORUS BEHEDETI OF EDFU (falcon) :
god of nome, 47–8, 54 ; in divine
dyn., 61–2 ; wars with Seth,
originally waged by other Horuses,
107–10 ; gets name Behedeti, 110 ;
as dynastic god, 108, 133–4 ;
fusion with Ra, 108, 245, 423 ;
= Apollo, 61 ; Hathor his wife,
356 ; called Anhert, 371 ; temple
at Edfu, q.v.
HORUS BEHEDETI, other than at Edfu,
55, 57–9, 109–10, 356
HORUS THE ELDER, *see* Horus Presiding over the Two Eyes
HORUS OF THE GODS, 66
HORUS HARAKHTI, *see under* Harakhti
HORUS KHENTI-IRTI, *see* Horus
Presiding over the Two Eyes
HORUS KHENTI-KHET of Athribis, 58,
62
HORUS, LIBYAN, 75–6, 86
HORUS OF THE MORNING, 66
HORUS NUBTI, 55 ; in royal title,
149–51
HORUS PRESIDING OVER THE TWO
EYES, sky-god of Letopolis, afterwards called THE ELDER (falcon),
57, 67, 112 ; in divine dyns., not
Ennead, 61–3, 155 ; distinct from
and later combined with Horus Yr.,
q.v. ; wars with Seth, Geb's
arbitration, 67–72 ; his wars repre-
sented as those of Horus of Edfu,
108–10 ; wars blended with Ra's,
371 ; absorbed by Osirian
conquest, 86 ; Hathor his wife,
110 ; in royal title, 118–19, *and
see* Horus (combined) ; four sons
of, 67
HORUS THE SAVIOUR, 405
HORUS SEPDU, 161
HORUS SEPED, 59
HORUS SHESEMTI, 66 n. 2
HORUS THE SISTRUM-PLAYER, 356

HORUS WHO UNITES THE TWO LANDS, 356

HORUS THE YOUNGER, of Buto : nomes, 57, 59 ; in divine dyns., Ennead, 61, 155–6 ; distinct from and later combined with Horus Er., 66–7, 73, 92, 93 n. 3 ; absorbed by Osirians, 86 ; in legend (Osiris, wars with Seth, judgment of Seth), 83, 90–100, 109, 111, 382 ; exploits and title Behedeti taken by Horus of Edfu, 109–10 ; as K. of Egypt, 94, 99, 101, 103 ; prototype of Kings and sons, 96–7, 161, 251, *and see below* (in funerals); in royal title, 119–20, *and see* Horus (combined) ; and dead King in heaven, 181–2 ; in funerals (darling son), 169–72, 258, 382 ; in Mysteries (darling son), 249, 251 ; in Sed, 76 ; = Harpocrates, 90 n. 1 ; in calendar 105 ; as son of Wazet, 113 ; at Nekhen, 112 ; sons of, 62, 169, 172, 248

HORUS, combined of the above (falcon), 68 pl., 361 ; in royal title, 118–20, 123 ; assumed by princes, 234 ; King embodies, 123–6, 127 fig., 128, 392 ; falcon takes dead King to heaven, 179 ; aids King in war, 161 ; in ritual, 393–4 ; as Word, 376 ; several capitals, 356 ; fusion with Ra, 120, 150, *and see* Harakhti

HORUS, Servants of, Iakhu, Akhu, Shemsu-Hor, 23, 63, 91 n. 2, 93–5, 101–16, 126, 133, 135, 284

HORUS, Service of, 120, 134 n. 2, 135–6, 252–3

HORUS, Director of Works of Amon, 318

House, *per.* : of Flame (?), *see* Palace (of North) ; of Gold, *see* Hetnub ; of King of South, White, Red, 138 ; of Life (school), 159 ; *per-âa*, 137 ; *per-nu*, 112–13, 421 n. 3 ; *per-ur*, *per-neser*, *see* Palaces (of South and North)

HU, god of command, 159, 243

HUI, tomb of, 287 fig.

Hunemmtu, 99 n. 5

HUNI, *see* Neferka Huni

Hunting, 38–9, 109, 135, 161

HUZEFA (II), 117

Hyena, monster of underworld, 187 ; *and see* Devourer

Hyksôs, Shepherds : invasion, 4, 22–3, 232, 290–1 ; art, 440 n. 1

Hypselis, *see* Shashetep

Iabt, *see* East

Iakhu, dead demigods, 62–3, *and see* Horus (Servants of)

Ibhat, quarries, 194

IBI, Nomarch, 212, 214

Ibis : ensign, 45 fig., 46–8, 59 ; worshipped, 365 ; *see also* Thoth

Ichneumon, worshipped, 365

IDI, Vizier, 217–18

Iertet, timber from, 195

IGERNEFERT, prince, 249–51

IHI, son of Horus, 54–5

IKHUNATEN, *see* Akhenaten

Ikhutaten, *see* Tell el-Amarna

Imakhu : Memphite, 190, 192, 196–202 ; in heaven, 179, 258

Imam, timber from, 195

Iment, Amenti, West (ostrich-feather) : ensign, goddess, 57, 75–7 ; abode of dead, *khert neter*, Divine Lower Region, 110, 171, 178, 199–200, 247, 389, 401, 408, 420–3, 456, *and see* Khent-Amenti ; Western Nome, *see* Libyan Nome ; cf. Metelis, 57

IMHETEP, 224, 415 ; = Asclepios, 469 n. 1

IMSET, s. of Horus, 172

INAROS, rebellion against Persians, 2

Industry, trade : Thinite, 138 ; Memphite, 215–16, 261–3 ; decline in revolution, 225 ; Theban, 268–9, 272, 275, 292–3 ; Saite, 348–9, 444

INENI, biography, 313 n. 3

Ingot of East, *see* East

INMUTEF, officiant, 312

Ionians, in Egypt, 345–6

IPOUR, in *Admonitions of an Old Sage*, q.v.

IPU, *see* Panopolis

Irrigation, dikes, 31–4, 39, 44, 136, 236, 279 ; shadoofs, wells, 268 pl., 444 n. ; *see also* Canals

Iseium, 58, 85

ISIS : centres of worship, 57, 85–6 ; in Ennead and divine dyn., 61–2, 64, 154, 175 ; in Osiris legend, 81, 87–92, 98–9, 155, 382 ; steals Ra's Name, 371–2 ; represents soil, 64 ; as magician, 87, 89, 96, 98, 372, 382, 403–5 ; as law-giver, 87, 96 ; and matriarchy, 88, 96 ; and consanguine marriage, 95 ; in calendar, 105 ; in funerals, 169–70 ; and dead King, 171, 181–2 ; Mysteries, 254 ; representations (Knot, cow, woman), 80 n. 2, 361–2 ; pylon, 419–20 ; *see also under* Hathor

ISSI, *see* Zedkara Issi

Itet-taui, royal residence, 242, 296

Iuti, sculptor, 442
Iuya, 316

Jackal, see Anubis
Jerusalem, taken, 340
John, St., Gospel, on creative Word, 375
Joseph in Egypt, 303
Josephus, 3–4
Judges, 190; judge-scribe, 191; Judge of the Door, 193; Judge and Warden, 193; Judge Protectors, 240; see also Justice (administration of)
Justice: administration, 159–60, 279, 282–6, and see Judges; right, truth, 160, 186–7, 408, and see Afterlife (judgment of the dead), Maat, Osiris (justified), Ra (and justice); Theban " just laws ", 237, 284–7
Juvenal, on divine animals, 365–6

Ka, 286 pl., 357–60, 404; arms as clan-ensign, 45 fig., 357; as protective genius, 120, 121 fig., 166 fig., 171, 174, 175 fig., 183, 230 fig., 358; collective, divine substance, 120, 143, 167, 185, 358; reunion with in afterlife, 143, 171, 174, 181–5, 259, 359, 395; King has and is in this life, 120, 288, 311 n. 2, 393–4
Ka (I), see Khent
Ka (IV), Horus-name of Mycerinus, q.v.
Kab, el, princes, 291 n. 1, and see Paheri
Kadesh, battle, 161, 301
Kagemni, Vizier, Teachings, 458
Kagera R., 27 n. 4
Kahun papyri: on army, 300; chronology, 21; life of the people, 264–6; medicine, 448 n. 1, 450, 458; royal revenues, 276–7
Kakaï (Neferirkara), Nephercheres (V), 148, 150, 156, 163, 192, 206–7, 246
Kakau (Nebra), Sechous (II), 117, 364
Kalabshi, temple, 298
Kares, inscr. of, 307 n. 1
Karnak, see Thebes
Kashta, Ethiopian King, 336, 342–4
Kassite invasions, 22
Kati (Sky), 66 n. 3
Kerrt, Osiris at, 97
Khaba, Horus-name of Zeser II, q.v.
Khafra, see Chephren
Khammaat, barge, 250
Khamsin, 35, 69

Khaneferra (Neferkhau), Cheres (V), 148
Khasekhem (II), see Neferkara
Khasekhemui, Zazaï (II), 80–1, 108 n. 3, 117, 119, 136, 141, 413
Khatti, see Hittites
Khattusil, K. of Hittites, 468
Khent, Ka, Atoti I, Athothis (I), 117, 124; tomb, 247–8
Khent-Amenti, Khent-Imenti, Khenti-iment: at Abydos, 55; rules lower world, 171; Offering of, 200; see also under Anubis, Osiris, Upuat
Khepri, manifestation of Ra (scarab), 153, 370, 389 n. 2, 392; Atum as, 174; scarab takes King to heaven, 179; Khepri-Ra-Atum, 371–2; = Harmachis, Great Sphinx, 146 pl., 173, 317–18, 413; Ra-Harmachis = Ra + Harakhti, 371
Khert neter, Divine Lower Region, see under Iment
Kheti (IX), see Achthoës
Kheti, Nomarchs, 236–7
Kheti, Vizier, 285
Khetutet, goddess, 145
Khmunu, see Hermopolis Ma
Khnum: god of nomes, Ba Ram, 47, 49, 51, 54–5, 59, 68, 361, 364; as creator, begetter, 31, 288, 379; as manifestation of Ra, 245; ends famine, 32 n. 3
Khnumhetep, various, 238–9
Khonsu, 61–2, 127 fig., 256, 295, 312, 403–4, 418 fig.; bull as his image, 157–8
Khufu, see Cheops
Kingship, see Pharaoh
Kircher, researches, 8–9
Knife, nome-emblem, 56
Knot of Isis, see under Isis
Kom-Ombo, mummy crocodiles, 365
Kuban Stele, on Rameses II, 392
Kuruw, el, pyramids, 341 n. 4, 343
Kush, see Nubia

Labour, impressed, see under Taxation
Land: Old Kingdom, 136, 138–9, 144, 188–90; under Thebans, 265–7; late period, 347–8; of princes, 210; priests, 303–6, 324; soldiers, 299–302, 339–40; Director of Fields, 279; see also Domain, Pharaoh's Fields
Lange (Julius), law of frontality, 430
Lansing Papyrus, 459 n. 3
Latopolis, Esneh (III), 54
Lebanon, timber from, 135
Lefébure, on maâ-kheru, 186

LEGRAIN (Georges): excavations at Karnak, 323, 335 n. 2, 350, 432; on persecution of Amon, 323

Leipzig Papyrus, 448 n. 1, 449

Leontopolis, 152

Letopolis, Sekhem (2), 50, 57, 67, 75, 86, 97, 107, 448; city of Horus Presiding over Two Eyes, q.v.

Libyan desert, 25, 74–5; oases, 28

Libyan Nome, Apis, West (3), 57, 75–6, 86

Libyans, Tehenu: Libyan type in Egypt, 38; Libyans in Delta, 74–7, 111, 114–15, 219, 233; wars with, 136, 234; mercenaries, 219, 333, 337, 339; costume, 351 fig.; health, 451; Northern Libyans in Egypt (late), 336–7, 344, 346; Southern Libyans (Temhu), see Ethiopians

Life Health Strength, 108 n. 3

Lion, lioness: King Lion, 114 fig., 115, 121; in royal title, 121; hunting, 161; see also Sekhmet, Shu, Sun

Literature: in Old Kingdom, 456; Middle Kingdom, 220–31, 235, 456–7; New Empire, 458–62; folk-tales, 341, 458–60; love-songs, 460–3; see also Teachings

LORET (V.): burial-pits, 295 n. 2; on âsh, 81 n. 4; botany and drugs, 452 n. 2; Horians, 107 n. 2; neter, 359

Lotanu, prisoners, 304

Lotus: emblem of South, 124 fig., 125, 201 fig.; column, 414, 422; sun and gods born from, 202 pl., 370, and see Nefertum

Luxor, see Thebes

Lycopolis, see Siut

MAAT (Truth and Justice), 62–3, 187, 377–8, 388, 391–2, 398–402, and see Justice

MAATKHA, princess, 192

MACEDON, name for Upuat, 87 n. 6

Machinery, 444 n.

MAFEDET, feast of, 135

Magic, 403–7; in Sed, 134; gives life to mummy and statue, 171, 186–7, and see Opening of the Mouth, etc.; in judgment of the dead, 400–1; in medicine, 450–1; use of Name, 371–2, 375 n. 4, 426; talismans, 404, 407, 437–8, 455; Ba, 183; secrets held by King, 188; invented by Isis, q.v.; see also Voice

MANETHO, 3–5, 14–15, 19, 24 n. 1; on Apis, 364; Bocchoris, 344; dynasties (divine), 60–3, (proto-

historic) 101–2, (Thinite) 117, (Memphite) 146, 148, 156, 189, 203, 216; medicine, 448 n. 2; Memphis, 123–4; portents, 455

Manfalut, mummy crocodiles, 365

Mansions, Regents of, 194, 209, 279–80

MARIETTE (Aug. Éd.): Serapeum, 364; on Hyksôs art, 440 n. 1; Old Kingdom tombs, 201

Marriage: 274–5, 459–60; in Osiris legend, 95; consanguine, 95, 307–8; of Queen-mother with god, 310–11, 316–17, 337; Mitannian marriages, 316; see also Woman (position of)

Mashausha, mercenaries, 339

MASPERO (Sir Gaston), 202 pl.; burial-pits, 295 n. 2, 338; on canal, 346 n. 2; Ka, 182; mesent, 107–8; nome, 43 n. 2; polytheism, 379 n. 4; Queens, 307; Thothmes III, 314 n. 4

Mastabas, see under Tombs

Mathematics, 445–8

MAY, courtier, 322

Mazoï: timber from, 195; Nubian mercenaries, q.v.

Meat, flesh, ensign, 46, 47 fig., 57, 110

Medicine, 448–52

Medinet-Habu, temple, 296

Meditations of a Priest of Heliopolis, 221

Mediterranean type in Egypt, 38

Medum, pyramid, 147

MEHTIMSAF (Neterkhau), MERENRA I, METHESUPHIS (VI), 177, 189, 194–5, 211

Meir, see Cusæ

MEKHU, 212

MEMNON, colossus, 296–7

Memphis (1), 57, 124, 147; foundation, White Wall, 50, 124, 125 fig., 126, 138 n. 2; predynastic Kings, 102; under Thinites, 137, 146; Memphite Dynasties, 23, 146 ff.; under Memphites, 147; under Thebans, and later, 278, 317, 331, 356 n. 2; taken by Assyrians, 345; Greek settlers, 346; in legend, 71–2, 94, 97; Phtah at, 50–1; Apis, 364; procession round wall, 123, 125–7; dikes, inundation, 32; palaces, 124; necropolis, 146–7; temples and property, 162–3, 333; Serapeum, 364

MEN, sculptor, 442

Menat-Khufu, 238–9

MENCHERES (IV), see Mycerinus

MENCHERES (V), see Menkauhor

Mendes, Zedet (16), 32, 59, 78, 80, 85, 337, 364, 385

MENES (Aha) (I), 3, 32, 50, 101–2, 117, 124, 126, 136, 141 n. 2; later Pharaohs as Menes, 134
MENKAUHOR (Menkhau), MENCHERES (V), 148, 163
MENKAURA, see Mycerinus
MENMAAT-RA, see Amenemhat III
MENTHESUPHIS, see Zesamsaf
MENTU (falcon, Bakha Bull), 51, 54, 244–5, 364
MENTUEMHET, Prophet of Amon, 351, 442 pl.
MENTUHETEP, Pharaohs (XI), 219, 234, 241; MENTUHETEP III, 246, 296; MENTUHETEP IV, 234, 251, 296
MENTUHETEP, Vizier, 241, 249, 250 n. 1
MERA, tomb of, 168 pl., 424 n. 3
MERBAPEN (Anzib), MIEBIS (I), 117–18
Mercenaries, see under Army
MERENRA I, see Mehtimsaf
MERENRA II, see Zesamsaf
MERIKARA (IX), 218, 234, 236; Teachings for, 219, 221, 237, 256, 261, 286, 407, 457
MERIT-ATEN, princess, 322
MERNEPTAH (XIX), 252, 336
Meroe, 345 n. 2
MERT-NEIT, Q. (I), 136
MERTSEGER (serpent), 361
MES, inscription of: on land, 299; on reaction against Aten, 329 nn.
Mesent, 107–9; nome, see Sele
MESKHENT, goddess of birth, 270
MESMEN, 300
Mesolithic remains, 38–9
Metal-work, jewellery, 39, 104, 135, 404, 437–9; and see Statues
Metelis, Per Ha neb Imenti (7), 57, 76, 78, 106
METHESUPHIS, see Mehtimsaf
MEYER (Eduard): on chronology, 4 n. 4, 17, 22; Thinites, 140
MIEBIS, see Merbapen
Milesians, in Egypt, 347
MIN (thunderbolt), 47–8, 55, 135, 361–2, 367 n. 3, 388 fig.; at Coptos (temple), 205–8, 217; in Wady Hammamat, 251 n. 3; Solarized 245; Hymn to, 267–8
Mitanni, relations with Egypt, 292, 313, 315–16.
MNEVIS Bull (Ra), 58, 321, 364–5
MOELLER (G.), on Hermotybies, 302 n. 3
Moeris, L., nome of, 56 n., and see Crocodilopolis
Money, 446
Morality: right to heaven, 185–7, 398–402, 408–10; see also Justice, Teachings
MORGAN (J. de), Thinite tombs, 141

Mountain: ensign, 39, 46, 55, 57; of Serpent, see Hieraconopolis (XII)
MTEN, tomb and career, 191–3, 215 n. 3
Mummies, 89–90, 170–1, 295–6, 381 fig., 382, 390, 394–6, 448; of animals, 365
Music, 460 n. 4
MUT, 251, 295, 313
MUTEMUIA, Q. (XVIII), 316
MYCERINUS, MENKAURA (Ka), MENCHERES (IV), 142 fig., 147–8, 177, 192, 208 n. 3

Name, importance of, 366–7, 371–2, 375 n. 4, 396, 426
Napata, Gebel Barkal, 297–8, 341–3, 345 n. 2
NAPOLEON: in Egypt, 9, 11; on administration of Egypt, 34
NARAM-SIN, K. of Akkad, 22
NARMER, K., 114–15; palette of, 110 n. 3, 114, 138 n. 1
NASTESEN, K. of Ethiopia, 345 n. 2
Naucratis, 346
NAVILLE (E.), excavations, 314 n. 4
NEBKA (II), 117
NEBKA (Sanekht), NEBKARA (III), 148
NEBKAU, Horus-name of Sahura, q.v.
NEBKAURA, Heracleopolite Pharaoh, in Peasant story, 283 n. 1
NEBT-HET, see Nephthys
NEBUNNEF, Prophet of Amon, 334
NECHO I, K. of Sais, 345 n. 3
NECHO II (XXVI), 336, 346
Nedit, Osiris at, 93, 251
NEFERFRA (V), 163, 193
NEFERHETEP (IX), 221
NEFERHETEP (XIII), 251–2
NEFERIRKARA, Horus-name of Kakai, q.v.
NEFERKA HUNI, NEFERKARA HUNI (III), 147–8
NEFERKARA (Khasekhem), NEPHER-CHERES (II), 117, 125 n. 2, 139 fig., 147, 154, 439
NEFERKARA (VI), see Pepi II
NEFERKARA HUNI (III), see Neferka Huni
NEFERKASOKAR, SESOCHRIS (II), 117, 147
NEFERKAUHOR, Pharaoh, 217
NEFERKHAU, Horus-name of Khanferra, q.v.
NEFERREHU, Sentences, 221, 231
NEFERTARI, Q. (XVIII), 308
NEFERTITI, TADUKHIPA, NEFER-NEFRU-ATEN, Q. (XVIII), 316, 320 pl., 322, 442
NEFERTUM (lotus), 57, 422, 461, and see Lotus

Negroes in army, 194, 262
NEHERI, various, 238, 240, 254 n. 4
NEHSI, official, 313–14
NEITH (two arrows): emblems and worship, 47–8, 57, 75–7, 361; in legend, 86, 109, 379; crowns, 76, 111–12; and Queen, 136, 310; school of medicine, 448–9
NEIT-HETEP, Q. (I), 136
NEKANKH, prince, 211
NEKHEB, Eileithyiapolis (III), 54, 103, 111–13, 138
NEKHEBT (vulture), 54, 112–13, 120–3, 125 n. 2; = Eileithyia, 112 n. 2
Nekhen, Hieraconpolis (III): early royal city, 112, 114, 116; Warden, 138, 193; objects from, 68 pl., 80–1, 106, 135 n. 3, 139 fig.
NEKHT, of Hibis, 238
NEMAAT-HAPI, Q. (II), 136
NEMAATRA, see Amenemhat III
Neolithic remains, 39, 104
NEPHERCHERES (II), see Neferkara
NEPHERCHERES (V), see Kakaï
NEPHTHYS, NEBT-HET (cow): nome, 55; in Ennead and divine dyn., 61–2, 154, 175; as desert, 64; in Osiris-legend, 81, 89; in calendar, 105; in funerals, 169, 171; and dead King, 181–2; pylon, 419–20
NEPRI, corn-god, 31, 83, 99, 362 n. 1
Nertu, 99 n. 5
NESAMON, Prophet of Amon, 335
NESHA, sailor, 299–300
Neshemt, barge, 250–1
NESMIN, papyrus of, on creation, 375
NESSUMENTU, General, 244 n. 3
Neter, 66, 359–60, 390
Neter, see Sebennytos
NETERAQERT, NITOCRIS, Q. (VI), 189
NETERKHET, Horus-name of Zeser I, q.v.
NEUSERRA (Isitibtaui), RHATHURES (V), 17–18, 148, 163, 192
NEWBERRY: on Osirian trees, 81 n. 4; Sed, 129; Zed, 81
Nile: valley, 25–7; river, 27–34; Blue Nile, 28–9; White Nile, 29; raises ground-level, 38–9; inundation, 28–32, 35 n. 4, 135, 140, 145; 280; Nilometers, 31 n. 2; as Hapi, 28, 30, 82–4, 172; as Osiris, 64, 82–4, 145; Hymns to, 30–1, 145; made by Aten, 37, 326; Niles in representations, 125 n. 4, 201 fig., 433; statue in Vatican, 32; see also Irrigation
NITOCRIS, Q. (VI), see Neteraqert
NITOCRIS, Worshipper of Amon, 350–1
Nobles. see Princes

Nomarchs, 44, 79 n. 2, 190, 194, 208–14, 235–41, 279–80; children at Court, 211–13
Nomes: hieroglyphic, 33, 41; development, 40–53; gods of, see under Gods; table of, 54–9; Niles of, 433; Protectors of, 191; Regents, 191, 239, 341; Chiefs, 209, 241
Nubia, Kush: wars with Old Kingdom, 136, 161; with Middle Kingdom, 234, 239; with New Empire, 313, 315; prisoners, 291, 304; mercenaries (Mazoï), 194, 219, 301, 333; Royal Son of Kush, 278, 287 fig.; gold from, 136; Min in, 368; in Egyptian kingdom, 337; see also Ethiopians
Nubt, see Ombos
NUBTI, see Horus Nubti, and under Seth
NUN, primordial Ocean, 98, 178, 362 n. 1, 372–4
Nuri: pyramid, 342 n. 2; inscr., 343 n. 3
NUT (Sky): in Ennead, 61, 64, 154, 369–70; mother of Seth and Osiris, 68, 82, 98, 171, 370; cow, mother of Sun, 153–4, 370, 373, 389, 420; fused with cow Hathor, 64 n. 3; separated from Geb by Shu, 154 fig., 369–70, 380; as tree, 364; as Sarcophagus, 171; court of temple, 420
Nyavarongo, R., 27 n. 4

Oasis, Great, Greeks in, 347
Obelisk, symbolism of, 175–6
Ocean, primordial, see Nun
Offerings: King's Offering, to secure food in next world, 165–7, 172–3; extended to others, 200, 258–9, 391, 396; domains founded for offerings, 205–6, 304–5; offerings and foundations of officials, 212, 217; private donations to temples, 408–9; "King gives Offering," formula, 393, 396; Field of Offerings, 184–5; Regents of, 185; Offerings of Anubis, Osiris, Khent-Amenti, 200
Officials, see Administration
Ogdoad, see under Thoth
Ombos, Nubt, 68, 103, 119; Seth of, see Seth (Nubti)
ONNUS, see Unas
ONURIS, see Anhert
Opening of Mouth, Eyes, etc., 168 pl., 170, 199, 362, 382, 390, 393, 395
Oryx, white, see under Seth; Nome of, see Hibis

OSIRIS : nomes, 47, 55, 57–9, 80, 85, 110 ; temples, domains, 97, 206–7, 246, 249, 252, 304–5, 381 ; tombs and relics, 43 n. 4, 89, 91 n. 4, 202 pl., 247–8 ; reliquary at Abydos, 55, 246–7, 250 n. 9 ; god of vegetation, 64, 82–5, 88, 90, 92, 105–6 ; of Nile, Hapi, 64, 82–4 ; of water, 82 ; Water of Renewal, Renpu, 83, 143 ; connexion with Syria, 81–2, 88–9 ; legend, 6, 81, 86–95, 97–100, 155, 250 n. 8, 251 n. 1, 382, 394–5 ; historical foundation of legend, 95–7, 103–4 ; absorbs, Anzti, 79–80, 85, 87 ; conquers Delta, 85–8, 103 ; spread to Upper Egypt, 106, 110–11 ; raised to Ennead and heaven by Heliopolis, 61–2, 64, 97 n. 2, 98 n. 5, 154–5, 168, 175, 245, 255, 381 ; Osirian reaction against Ra, 218, 245–60 ; revival after Akhenaten, 329 ; doctrine and supremacy, 380–5 ; influence on ritual and temples, 385–6, 389–93, 421 ; representations, attributes (corpse, goat, shepherd, tree, Zed), 85, 127, 328 pl., 361–2, 364 ; Osirian nature of coronation and Sed, 124–34, 142 ; Sed of Osiris, 131 ; as god of dead, mummy, 247, 381–5, 394–5, and see below (Osirian afterlife) ; as Khent-Amenti, 57, 80 n. 1, 171, 246–50, 254, 381 ; Osirification of pre-Osirian funeral rites, 143–4 ; Osirian afterlife and funeral rites, 142, 168–75, 178, 182, 188, 253–60, 394–403, 423 ; Osiris justified, 94, 203, 383, 391, and see Afterlife (judgment of dead) ; Mysteries, 254, 383–4, (Zed) 132–4, (funeral) 169–70, 255, (Abydos) 248–55 ; Offering of, 200 ; Hymn to, 87 n. 2, 97–100 ; in calendar, 105–6 ; as Sokar, 381 ; Serapis, 381 ; see also Zed
OSORKON I, II (XXII), 336, 339–41
OSORKON III (XXIII), 32, 336, 344
OSYMANDYAS, tomb of, see Ramesseum
OTHOËS, see Teti
Oxyrrhynchos (XIX), 56, 68
Oxyrrhynchus fish, ally of Seth, 68, 89

PAHERI, inscr. of, 396 n. 2, 402 n. 2, 408
Painting, see Drawing
Palaces : early, 142 fig. ; Thinite, 137 ; architecture, 416–17 ; of South and North (per-ur, per-neser), 112–13, 157–8, 312, 421 n. 3
Palæolithic remains. 38

Palermo Stone : on Apis, 364 ; buildings and statues, 162, 362 n. 5 ; census, 140 ; chronology, 17–18 ; coronation rites, 123 ; inundation, 31 n. 2, 136 n. 1 ; predynastic Kings, 103 n. 2 ; Sed, 127 n. 1 ; Queens, 136 ; rites of founding temples 415 n. 1 ; Thinites, 134–5
Palettes, 39, 104, 107, 121, 135–6, and see Ensigns (of clans), Narmer
Palm : Nome-emblem, 46, 49, 56, 97 ; column, 414
PANEZEM I (XXI), 338
PANEZEM, Prophet of Amon, 430 pl.
Panopolis, Apu, Ipu (IX), 47, 55, 209, 367
Papyrus : emblem of North, 124 fig., 125, 201 fig. ; column, 414, 422 ; manufacture of papyri, 457 n. 1 ; evidence of papyri, 16 ; literary papyri, 220 ff., 457 ff., and see Teachings ; see also Anastasi, Ebers (Berlin), Gurob, Hearst, Kahun, Lansing, Leipzig, Nesmin, Rhind, Sallier, Smith, Turin
Pa-Rameses, 278, 330
PASAR, priest, 332
PASHEDENBAST, 343 n. 3
Patamos, see Heroönpolis
Pâtu, people, 99 n. 5
Peasant, story of, 256, 266 n. 1, 272, 273 n. 1, 283–4, 457
Pelusiac Mouth, 26 n. 2
PENTAUR, poem, 301
People, common : under Old Kingdom, 138, 143, 201–2, 215–16, 261–4 ; advantages by revolution, 226–9 ; under Theban, 260–1, 263–76 ; later, 347–8 ; tombs, afterlife, 143, and see under Afterlife
Peoples of the North, see Hau-nebu
Peoples of the Sea, 291, 332–3
PEPI I (Meritaui), MERIRA, PHIUS (VI), 124, 147, 177, 193–4, 197, 205, 207, 211 ; PEPI II, NEFERKARA, PHIOPS, 177, 189, 203, 205–8, 213, 217
PEPI, Black, prince, 211
PEPI-ANKH, princes, 211, 235
PEPINEFER, Nomarch, 211–12
Peqer, Ra-Peqer, Umm el-Gaab, 248–51, 254
Per (various), see House
PERENMAAT (Sekhemib), UZNAS, TLAS (II), 117
PERIBSEN (Seth) (I), 117–18, 146–7
Persians, in Egypt, 2, 24, 32–3, 352, and see Cambyses, Darius
Pert-kheru, see Voice (issuing)
Per-Wazet (X), see Aphroditopolis, Southern

Per-Wazet (19), *see* Buto
PETRIE (Sir W. M. Flinders): Kahun and Gurob papyri, 264; Thinite tombs, 141, 246; on predynastic boats, 107 n. 1; pottery and dating, 106; Sed, 132
PETUBASTIS (XXIII), 336, 341
Pharaoh, kingship: natural conditions (Nile, sun), 33–4, 36, 145; based on that of Osiris, Horus, and Seth, 72, 95–7, 100–1, 103–4, 118–19; early, 40, 42–4, 103, 111 ff., Thinite, 116 ff.; Memphite kingship by right divine (Ra), 146–52, 157 ff.; occupations of Memphite King, 160–7; Memphite justice, 185–7; Memphite decline, 203 ff.; Thebans restore monarchy, 237–41; in new form, 260–1; doctrine, just laws, 284–7, *and see under* Justice, *Teachings*; concessions to soldiers and priests, 298 ff.; struggle with priests, 306 ff.; priests triumph, 327 ff.; King as priest, alone having relations with gods, 135, 162, 201, 208, 388–90; worshipped in life, 392–4; afterlife, 141–4, 168–87, 200; and Ka, q.v.; architecture as "King's work", 411; meaning of "Pharaoh", 137; *see also* Administration, Centralization
Pharaoh's Fields, 266, 291
Pharbæthos, Hesebt (11), 58, 78
Philæ, temple, 422 pl.
PHIOPS, *see* Pepi II
PHIUS, *see* Pepi I
Phœnicians circumnavigate Africa, 346
Phœnix: House of, *see* Hipponon; *see also under* Ra
PHTAH: at Memphis, 50–1, 57, 356 n. 2; = Hephæstos, 61; as craftsman, 30, 318 n. 2, 392; high-priest as Great Chief of Works, 139, 192 n. 3, 197, 415; in Ennead, 61–2; substituted for Atum as Demiurge, 61 n. 1, 356 n. 2, 376, 379, 386 n. 1; as dynastic god, 286 pl., 297–8, 356 n. 2; in Theban Triad, 331, 377; under Akhenaten, 323; in Rosetta Stone, 128 n. 3; army division, 300; *see also* Apis Bull, *and under* Sokar
PHTAH-ANKHNI, Director of Sculptors, 436
PHTAHHETEP, tomb, 146 pl., 424 n. 3, 436
PHTAHHETEP, Vizier, *Teachings*, 221, 273, 284, 458

PHTAHMES, Viziers, 278, 320
PHTAHSHEPSES, career, 192–3
PIANKHI (XXIV), 336, 342–4
PIERRET, on monotheism, 379 n. 4
PITHOM, *see* Heroönpolis
PLINY the Elder: on drugs, 452; obelisks, 176; painting, 426; swamps of Delta, 109
PLUTARCH: on Egypt, 6; Horus Er., 67; Horus and Seth, wars, 70; Mysteries, 383; Osiris legend, 6, 83–5, 87 n. 1, 88, 90 n. 2, 380; sacred animals, 365
Population, 468
Pottery: predynastic, 39, 104, 106; later, 439; wheel, 444 n.
Priests: various special priests, 137, 170, 258, 385; belong to royal family, 190; feudal priesthood, 203 ff.; later influence, 241–2, 302 ff.; under Akhenaten, 324; influence, *see under* Amon, Heliopolis, Ra; *see also* Prophets
Princes, nobles, 137, 194, 208–16, 235–7, 291, *and see under* Administration
Prognostics, 454–5
Property: movable, 139–40, 144, 347–8, *and see under* Heredity (masculine); landed, *see* Land
Prophets: Directors of, 194, 209–10, 235, 241, 313, 334; 1st Prophet of Amon, *see under* Amon; *see also* Priests
Prosopis (4), 47, 57, 75
Protector of Country, 79 n. 2, 138
PSAMMETICHUS I (XXVI), 336, 345–6, 349–50; PSAMMETICHUS II, 336; PSAMMETICHUS III, 336, 351
Pskhent, see Crowns
PTOLEMIES: rule, 24, 34, 470; kingship, coronation, 116, 126, 470; canal, 346 n. 2; and scholars, 3, 6; decree of Ptolemy V Epiphanes, *see* Rosetta Stone
Punt: expedition of Hatshepsut, 314; perfumes from, 461 n. 2
Pyramids: Old Kingdom, 146 pl., 147, 173–7, 425; Middle Kingdom, 234, 296; Ethiopia, 342–3; priests of royal, 204–6, 208, 215; tenants of, 213
Pyramid Texts, 73–4, 177, 202 pl., 348, 456; no mention of Amon, 244; on Anzti, 79–80; Buto, 116; conquests, early, 122–3; Delta, early, 74 n., 78; Enneads, divine and protohistoric dynasties, 64–5, 102, 154–6; funeral rites, 143–4, 384; gods of nomes and towns, 49: Horuses. Seth. 66–72. 90

n. 2 ; justice, 186 ; Ka, 357–60 ; Kings, kingship, 121, 125–6, 157–60, 163–4, 166, 169 ff., 179 ff., 199 ; *neter*, 359 ; Nile, inundation, 30, 82–4, 145 ; Osirian afterlife, 169 ff. ; Osiris legend, 86, 89, 91, 93–4 ; Saru of clans, 40 ; *sez* tree, 81 ; Solar afterlife, 179 ff. ; sun, 153 ; Zed, 81

QEBEHSENUF, s. of Horus, 172
QEBEHU (I), *see* Sen
QEBEHUT, goddess of coolness, 158
Qenbet, Qenbetiu, 270–1, 278–80, 284–5
Queen : power, importance, 96, 136, 306–8 ; title, 119, 136 ; in rites, 129–32, 133 fig., 169–70 ; wife of Amon, 310–11, 316–17, 337

RA : nomes, 57–8 ; origin, fusion with Atum, and progress, 64 n. 3, 65, 106, 152–7, 368, 374–5, 384–5 ; introduced into Osiris legend, 100, 155 ; Solarization of all gods and rites, 245, 379–80, 385–6, 389–92 ; influence on kingship, 120, 147, 149–51, 156–7, 161–2, 176, 392 ; Sun-temples, 162–3, 177 ; influence on pyramids, 175–7 ; Solar afterlife for King, 178–87 ; for all dead, 257, 394, 397, 401–2 ; Osirian reaction, 218, 233 ; revival under Thebans, 242–6 ; fusion with Amon, 244–5 ; Amon-Ra in nomes, 54, 59 ; Amon-Ra in divine dyn. = Zeus, 61 ; relations with Osiris, 97, 368, 384–5 ; special devotion to Ra under New Empire, 317–19, *and see* Aten ; in Theban Triad, 331, 377 ; course in temples, 419–23 ; in Ennead and divine dyns., 61–2, 64, 154, 370 ; = Helios, 61 ; reign, 371–3 ; wars with Apophis, 153, 371 ; Isis steals Name, 371–2 ; revolt of mankind, 230, 372 ; occupations, 157–60 ; and justice (Maat), 186–7, 230, 256, 377–8, 391 ; and magic, 134, 405, 407 ; army division, 300 ; as Harakhti, q.v. ; as Harmachis, *see under* Khepri ; as Horus, 120, 176, *and see* Harakhti ; as Bakha Bull 364 ; as Mnevis Bull, q.v. ; as Phœnix, 58, 364 ; as scarab, *see* Khepri ; in other manifestations, *see under* Sun
Race of Egyptians, 38, 106
Ram, 365, *and see* Amon, Herishef, Khnum

RAMES, Vizier, inscr., 321 n. 2
RAMESES, meaning of name, 14
RAMESES I (XIX), 294, 336
RAMESES II, 18–19, 151, 334 pl., 336 ; and Amon, 161, 334 ; buildings, foundations, 294–5, 297–8, 305, *and see* Ramesseum ; canal, 346 n. 2 ; and Hittites, 468 ; inscriptions, 142 n., 392 ; and Phtah, 356 n. 2 ; representations, 334 pl., 388 pl., 443 ; soldiers' land, 301–2
RAMESES III (XX), 295–7, 333, 336, 406 ; RAMESES IV, 252, 336 ; RAMESES V–XII, 336
RAMESESNEKHT, Prophet of Amon, 335
Ramesseum, 296, 412 pl., 418 nn., 425
Ra-Peqer, *see* Peqer
RATOESES (IV), 148
Regents : of Foreign Countries, 195 ; Nomes, q.v. ; Royal Domain, 191 ; Regent's Wall, *see* Goshen
REISNER, excavations at Napata, 342–3
Rekhetu, 99 n. 5, 114
REKHMARA, Vizier, 278, 280–2, 285–6
Reliefs, *see* Drawing
Renpu, Water of Renewal, *see under* Osiris
REVILLOUT, on laws of Bocchoris and Amasis, 348
RHATHURES, *see* Neuserra
RHIND Papyrus, 446
Risings of King, 123–4, 128 fig., 129, 312 ; Servants of, 137
Rome : rule in Egypt, 24, 34, 116, 123, 126, 469–71 ; idea of Emperor's divinity, 470
ROME, Prophet of Amon, 335
Rosetta Stone (Decree of Ptolemy V Epiphanes), Frontispiece, 10–13 ; on King's title, 128 n. 3
ROY, Prophet of Amon, 335
RUSCH (Adolf), on pre-Osirian funeral rites, 144
Rushes, Fields of, 181, 184, 401 n. 1

SA, *see* Sia
SAAKARA (XVIII), 315, 327, 336
SABU, career, 192–3
SAHURA (Nebkau), SEPHRES (V), 148, 156, 197 ; buildings, 163, 177, 414 n. 3 ; representations from temple, 83 n. 5, 108 n. 2, 161, 362 n. 1
Saïs : early history, 47, 57, 75–7, 86, 103, 105, 111 ; later, 341, 344 ; feast, 254 ; Neith, q.v. ; school of medicine, 448–9 ; Saïte dynasties, 24, 336, 345–52 ; Saïte art, 348–9, 443–4
Sakhebu, 156
SALLIER Papyrus, on Nile, 31 n. 1

Samians, in Egypt, 347
SAMSU (Smerkhet), SEMEMPSES (I), 117
SANEKHT (III), Horus-name of Nebka, q.v.
SANEKHT (XX), 336
Saqqarah: early column, 413–14; pyramids, 147, 149, 177; Tablet, 18–19, 147, 189, 219; tomb of Horemheb, 329; tomb of Mten, q.v.
Sar: = Elder, see Saru; Mansion of, see under Heliopolis
SARCOPHAGUS, name of Nut, 171
SARGON, K. of Akkad, 22
Saru: of clan, 40; Old Kingdom, 140, 193, 270; under Thebans, 263, 269–71, 278–9, 283, and see Qenbet
SATIS, see Setet
Saut, see Siut
Scarab, see Khepri
Sceptre, as emblem, 54, 56, and see Uast
SCHAEFER, on Mysteries, 250 n. 6
Scorpion: clan-ensign, 46; King, 114–15
Scribe, 137, 138 fig., 158, 191, 269–71, 276, 286; of Fields, 217; of Foreign Lands, 138; Seated (statue), 198 pl., 439
Sculpture, see Drawing, Stone-work, Statues
Seals: from Thinite tombs, 134 n. 2, 136, 137 n. 2, 138, 140; Director of Seal, 276–7, 280, 282; Sealer of King's Goods, 139
SEBEK (crocodile), 56, 245, 361, 363 fig., 364
SEBEK-AA, sarcophagus, 155
SEBEKMSAF, Q., 299
SEBEKNEFERURA, Q. (IV), 233
Sebennytos, Neter (12), 58, 78, 85 Sebennytic Mouth, 26 n. 2
SEBERCHERES, see Shepseskaf
SEBNI, of Elephantine, 212–13
Sebua, temple, 298
SECHOUS, see Kakau
Secrets: stolen, 225–6, 253; Chiefs of, 159, 190, 192, 249, 434, 449; Chiefs in funerals, 258
SED, god of Old Kingdom, 135
Sed feast, 76–7, 126–36, 139 fig., 163, 234, 237, 252–3, 298, 312, 320, 340 n. 7
Sehel I., 32, 51
SEHETEPIBRA, Teachings, 241, 249, 286 n. 5, 287–8, 458
SEKHMET (lioness), 57, 288, 328 pl., 461; Hathor-Sekhmet, 372, 421 n. 3
Sele, Zalu, Mesent, Behedet-meht (14), 58. 78. 109

SEMEMPSES, see Samsu
Semites, see under Asia
SEN (Qa), QEBEHU (I), 117
SENBI, princes, 235
SEND, SENTI, SETHENES (II), 117, 147
SENMUT, architect, 313–14
SENTI, see Send
SENUSERT I, SESOSTRIS (XII), 232, 241, 243, 244 n. 2, 246, 286 pl., 294, 346 n. 2; SENUSERT II, 232, 238, 240; SENUSERT III, 21, 232, 241, 249, 286 pl., 288
SEPHRES, see Sahura
SEQENINRA TIUAQENA (XVII), 307
Serapeum, 364
SERAPIS, 381
Serpent: 43, 365, and see Apophis, Mertseger, Wazet
Serpent Mountain, see Hieraconpolis (XII)
SERQET, 310, 448
SESHEPENUPET I, Worshipper of Amon, 344, 350; SESHEPENUPET II, 350
SESOCHRIS, see Neferkasokar
SESONCHOSIS, see Sheshonq I
SESOSTRIS (of Diodorus), see Sheshonq I
SESOSTRIS (of Herodotus), New Empire King, division of land, 266–7
SESOSTRIS (of Strabo), see Senusert I
SETET, SATIS, 51, 54, 156 n. 3
SETH: nomes, 46, 47 fig., 51 fig., 52–3, 55–6, 68, 119; in Ennead and divine dyn., 61–2, 64, 154; god of sky, desert, storm, drought, 64, 69, 88, 181 n. 2; god of evil, 69; = Typhon, 70, 88; in calendar, 105; wars with Horus Er., 69–72, 94; murder of Osiris and wars with Horus Yr., 88, 91–4, 100, 155; wars with Horus of Edfu, 107–9; wars with Ra, see Apophis; K. of Upper Egypt, 68–9, 71–2, 126; as dynastic god, and in royal title (Nubti), 103, 118–20, 123, 125, 127 fig., 149–51, 161, 180–1; Nubti of Ombos, 68, 119; Nubti at Hieraconpolis, 55; Beast (greyhound or ant-eater), 45 fig., 46, 48, 55, 64 n. 3, 68, 119, 361; called Ash, 48; white oryx, 47 fig., 51 fig., 52, 56, 68, 161; hippopotamus, 108–9, 161; oxyrhynchus, 68; crocodile, 68, 119; hunting of wild beasts, 161; Followers of Seth, 103, 107–8; Companions, in Mysteries, 254
SETH, Director of Works of Amon, 318
SETHE (Kurt): on early history, 74 n.; on XVIIIth Dyn., 314 n. 4
SETHENES, see Send
SETH-NUBTI. Pharaoh. 17 n. 2

SETI I (XIX), 166 fig., 336; buildings, tomb, 18, 252, 294, 296–7, 305, 384 n. 4, 426 pl.; and Phtah, 356 n. 2; Sed, 129
SETI II, 336
Sez tree, 81
SEZES (III), 148
SHABAKA (XXV), 336, 342–3; monument, on arbitration of Geb, 71 n. 9; on creation, Phtah, 356 n. 2, 375–6, 386
SHABATAQA (XXV), 336, 342–4
Shaluf, stele of, 346 n. 2
Shardana, 333
Shashetep, Hypselis (XI), 54–5, 68, 97
Shekh el-Beled, statue, 439
Shekh-Said, *see under* Hermopolis Ma.
SHEMAJ, Vizier, 217
Shemsu-Hor, *see* Horus, Servants of
Shepherd Kings, *see* Hyksôs
SHEPSESKAF, SEBERCHERES (IV), 148
SHEPSESKARA, SIOPHES, SISIRES (V), 148
SHESHONQ, Pharaohs (XXII), 336; SHESHONQ I, SESONCHOSIS, SESOSTRIS, 339–40; SHESHONQ II, 339
Shinar, 22
SHU (Air), 61–2, 64, 152, 154, 172, 175, 186, 320, 369–70, 373, 380
SIA, SA, god of knowledge, 243, 288
Silurus fish, nome emblem, 59
Sinai, copper from, 136
SINUHET, story of, 197–8
SIOPHES, *see* Shepseskara
SIPHTAH (XIX), 336
SISIRES, *see* Shepseskara
Sistrum, 460 n. 4; emblem, attribute, 55, 356, 361
Siut, Lycopolis, Saut (XIII), 49, 55, 110, 218–19, 234, 236
Siwa, oracle of Amon, q.v.
Sky, *see* Kati, Horus Presiding over Two Eyes, Nut, *and under* Seth
Slaves, 291–2
Sma, 124 fig., 125, 127
SMENDES (XXI), 336–7
SMITH (Edwin), Papyrus, 448 n. 1, 450–1
SMITH (Elliot), Dr.: on Akhenaten, 319 n. 2; on Iuya, 316 n. 3
SNEFRU (Nebmaat), SORIS (IV), 147–8, 150, 151 fig., 191, 204–5; in literature, 222 n. 1
SOKAR, 57, 135, 145, 147, 172, 381; Phtah-Sokar, 125, 244
Soleb, 129, 298
SOLON, debt to Egypt, 348
Songs of the Harpist, see under Antef
SORIS, *see* Snefru
SOSIS, SOSOS = Shu, 61
Sothis, 20–2, 105, 175, 280

Spedu, gods over offerings, 167
Sphinx: Great, *see under* Khepri; from Tanis, q.v.
SPIEGELBERG, on army, 302 n. 3
Spiritualization rites, 99 n. 3, 181, 199, 383, *and see* Opening of Mouth, etc.
Statues, 104, 135, 235, 287, 429–33, 439–44; in funeral rites, 170–1, 382, 395–6; of the gods, in worship, 362–3, 386–91, 417, 434; jointed, intervention by, 309, 332, 338, 343, 432
Stock-breeding, 38–9, 138, 269 pl.
Stone-work, 38–9, 104, 135, 437 fig., *and see* Drawing, Statues
STRABO: on Egypt, 6; canal, 346 n. 2; divine animals, 365; Nilometer, 31 n. 2; temples, 416 n. 1
Su, 71
Sudan, Egyptian expedition, 212
Sumerians, resurrection-myth, 84
Sun: influence in Egypt, 34; worship, 152–3, *and see* Harakhti, Harmachis, Horus, Ra; as calf, child, 153, 170; falcon, 153; lion, 152; scarab, *see* Khepri; Asiatic Sun-god, 317; represents justice in East, 186, 378; disk as clan-design, 39, 46, 58, 153; disk on monuments, 36–7, 419, 423; disk worshipped, *see* Aten
Sundials, 453
SUPHIS, *see* Cheops, Chephren
SUTEKH, army division, 300
SYLVESTRE DE SACY (Isaac), 10–11
Syria, *see under* Asia

TADUKHIPA, *see* Nefertiti
TAHARQA (XXV), 336, 342, 345, 350
TAKELOT, Pharaohs (XXII), 336; Takelot I, 339
TANCHERES, *see* Zedkara Issi
Tanis, 24, 336–8; statues and sphinxes, 290 pl., 440 n. 1
TANUTAMON (XXV), 336, 342 n. 2, 345
Taxation and impressed labour, 139–40, 262–3, 239–40, 267–8, 276–7, 280–2; tax-collectors, 191; soldiers relieved of, 302; *see also* Charters of immunity
Teachings, King's doctrine, 235–7, 269, 285, 458, 467, *and see* Amenemhat I, Merikara, Phtahhetep, Sehetepibra
TEFEN, 186
TEFNEKHT, K. of Saïs, 336, 341, 344
TEFNET (lioness), 61, 64, 152, 154, 172, 175, 186, 352, 369
Tehenu, *see* Libyans
Tehneh. 208 n. 3. 211

Tell el-Amarna, Akhetaten, Ikhutaten, 315, 321, 330; art, 320 pl., 323, 325, 366 pl., 427 fig., 431 n. 2, 442–3; letters, 22; palace, 417 fig., 419 n. 1; Temple of Aten, 36; tombs, 329

Temhu, see Ethiopians

Temples: building of, 135, 415; architecture, decoration, 386–9, 415–23, 433–4, and see Columns; Thinite, 135, 415; Solar, 162–3, 177, 413, 415, 439; of Aten, 440; donations, see Charters of immunity, and under Offerings; see also Thebes (buildings), and under various gods

Tenants, Pharaoh's: Inspector of, 193; Director, 193–4; of Pyramids, 213

Teni, see Thinis

Tentyris, see Denderah

Tepehet, source of Nile, 85

Terebinth, nome-emblem, 46, 49, 55–6

TETA-SHERA, Q. (XVIII), 304

TETI (Seheteptaui), OTHOËS (VI),171–2, 177, 189, 192–3, 207, 211, 246

THAMPHTHIS (IV), 148

Thebes, Uast, Diospolis Ma., Karnak, Luxor (IV): beginnings, 50–1, 54, 244; as capital, 292–8; decline under Akhenaten, 323–4; revival, 328, 330–1; later, 336–41; sacked by Assyrians, 345; Theban dyns., 23–4, 219, 234 ff.; necropolis, see Tombs, Valleys of Kings, etc.; buildings, 26 pl., 244, 292–7, 304, 335, 340, 412 pl., 416 pl., 418 fig. and nn., 422 pl., and see Ramesseum; other monuments, 308, 313, 320; temple property, 333; king-list from, 18; Vizier as Director of, 234; Stele of Adoption, 350; foundations, influence of priests, see under Amon

THEODOSIUS, Emp. of Rome, 1

Thinis, Teni, 49, 137, 141–2, 246; dyns., 23, 46, 48, 102, 110, 116 ff.

THOTH, TITHOËS (ibis): nomes, 47, 49, 56, 59, 110–11; in Ennead and divine dyn., 61–3; Ogdoad, 56, 379–80; = Hermes, 50, 444; in legend, 70–1, 86–7, 89, 91–4, 97, 155; Solarized, 245; in various rites, 124 fig., 125 n. 3, 169, 250, 393–4; and dead King, 179; in judgment of dead, 256, 398–401; scribe, arts, 87–8; heart, intelligence, 376; magic, 403–5; science, 444; representations, 361

THOTHETEP, Nomarch, 240–1

THOTHMES, meaning of name, 14

THOTHMES I (XVIII), 252, 294, 304, 308–14, 336; THOTHMES II, 308–9, 312–14, 336; THOTHMES III, 18, 21, 127 fig., 294–5, 297, 308–9, 311–15, 336; THOTHMES IV, 315–18, 336

THUERIS (hippopotamus), 438

Thunderbolt, 45 fig., 46–8, 55, and see Min

THUTI, official, 313–14

TI, tomb, 168 pl., 424 n. 3

TII, Q. (XVIII), 316, 319, 330

TITHOËS, see Thoth

TLAS, see Perenmaat

Tombs, burials, 168 pl., 423–5, 426 pl.; chapels, 412, 424; Thinite, 141–3, 146–7, 169, 412; Memphite (mastabas), 146 pl., 201–2, 424–5; tombs of nobles, 197–8, 209, 235; violation in revolution, 228, 233; Middle Kingdom, 202–3, 258–60, 275; Theban hypogea, 295–7; see also Pyramids

TOSORTHRUS, see Zeser I

Totems, 39–40, 45 fig., 48–9, 120–1, 362, 367

Trade, see Industry; Satire of Trades, 268–70, 457

Transport, 39, 106, 193–5, 444, 445 fig., 447

Trees: as ensigns of nomes and clans, 39, 46, 47 fig., 49, 55–6, 97; as gods, 364; Osirian trees, 81–2, 364, and see Zed; palm-column, 414

Troglodytes, wars with, 135, 289

TUM, see Atum

Tura: arbitration at, 71; quarries, 71 n. 8, 193, 197

Turin Royal Papyrus, 18–19; on divine dyns., etc., 62–3, 101–2, 107; Thinites, 147; Memphites, 156, 189, 216; Pepi II, 203; end of Old Kingdom, 218

Turks, decay of Egypt under, 34

TUT, courtier, 323

TUTANKHAMEN (XVIII), 295, 315, 322, 327–9, 336; inscr., 323–4, 327–8; tomb, mummy, 295 n. 1, 320 pl., 331, 438, 442

TYPHON, see under Seth

Uag feast, 98

Uast, sceptre, see Hermonthis, Thebes

Uauat, timber from, 195

UBIENTHES, see Biuneter

UCHOREUS, mythical Pharaoh, 124 n. 1

UENEPHES, see Zet

UKHETEP, princes, 235

Umm el-Gaab, see Peqer

UNAS (Uzataui), ONNUS, UNUS (V), 148, 173, 192 ; funeral texts, 177, 179–84, 186–7
UNEG, god, 158
UNI, career, 193–5, 197, 205
UNNEFER, name of Osiris and royal name, 100, 251
UNUS, see Unas
UPUAT (wolf) : Khenti-iment, Khent-Amenti, 76–8, 171 n. 2, 246 ; in Delta, 76, 86 ; conquered by Osiris, 86–7 ; in legend, 87–8, 93, 110–11 ; goes South to Siut and Abydos, 49, 55, 110–11, 246 ; feast, 135 ; in Sed, 127 ; in Mysteries, 250, 254
Uraeus : of Wazet, on crown, 111, 113, 120, 122, 373 ; on Aten-disk, 320 ; Dennut, devourer, 187
USAPHAÏS, see Hesepti
USER, Vizier, 278, 282 n. 3, 387
USERKAF (Irmaat), USERCHERES (V), 148, 156, 163, 192
Ushebtiu, Answerers, 259–60, 395 fig., 401 n. 1
UTO, see Wazet
UZNAS, see Perenaat

Valleys, of Kings and Queens, 295–6, 338, 424 pl.
Vizier, early, 138 n. 1 ; Memphite, 190, 193 ; under Thebans, 234, 241, 276–86, 291, 297, 300, 313, 320 ; Teachings of, see Phtahhetep
Voice, issuing, pert-kheru, 168 pl., 198 pl., 199–200, 258, 396 ; power in spells, 404 ; gives life to images, 426 n. 1 ; Pharaoh's voice makes realities, 197, 199 ; see also Name, Words
Vulture, 112 n. 2, and see Nekhebt

Wady Hammamat, inscr., 251 n. 3
Wady Maghara, relief, 151
War : records of wars, 135–6 ; early, 107, 121, 136, 161 ; civil, 218–19, 234 ; IXth Dyn., 234 ; XIIth Dyn., 232, 289 ; New Empire wars and conquests, 233, 290–1, 308 ; wars with Asiatics, see under Asia ; prisoners, 136, 291–2, 304 ; see also Army
Warden : of King's Goods, 139 ; of Nekhen and of Pe, 138, 193
WAZET, UTÓ (serpent), 48 ; at Buto, 59, 76, 111–13 ; conquered by

Osirians, 86, 111 ; at Nekheb, 113 ; at S. Aphroditopolis, 55 ; at Denderah (Hathor-Wazet). 421 n. 3 ; Red Crown, 76, 111, 120–1, 123 ; see also Uraeus
WEILL (Raymond), on charters of immunity, 205 n. 1, 207, 217
West, see Iment ; Nome, see Libyan Nome
White Wall, see under Memphis
Wolf, 45 fig., 46, 55, 110, 365, and see Khent-Amenti, Upuat
Woman, matriarchy, uterine heredity : in Osiris legend, 96 ; in King's title, 113 ; position of women, 273–5, 306, 461, and see Literature (love-songs) ; see also Queen
Words : King utters, 159 ; creative Word, 375–8 ; see also Voice
Writing, 1, 7–15, 40, 104, 347, 366, 425–6, 460 n. 5 ; official, 269 ; in Ethiopia, 345 n. 2 ; written petitions, 279

Xoïs, 32, 57 ; Dyn., 23

YOUNG (Thomas), Dr., 11

ZAU, Vizier, Nomarch, 206, 211, 213
ZAUTI, Nomarch, 214
Zawyet el-'Aryan, pyramid, 147
Zawyet el-Meitin, prince, 209
ZAZAÏ, see Khasekhemui
Zazat, 270, 279–80
Zebti, see Aphroditopolis, S. (X)
Zed, 58, 80–2, 85, 89, 130–4, 247 fig., 361
ZEDEFRA (Kheper) (IV), 148
Zedet, see Mendes
ZEDKARA ISSI (Zedkhau), TANCHERES (V), 148
Zedu, see Busiris
Zefau, gods over offerings, 167
ZESAMSAF, MERENRA II, MENTHESUPHIS (VI), 189
ZESER I (Neterkhet), TOSORTHRUS (III), 108 n. 3, 147–50 ; ZESER II (Khaba), 148–9 ; ZESER (one of the above), Famine Stele ascribed to, 32
Zet, eternal body, 89–90, 171, 179, 181–4, 361, and see Mummies, Statues
ZET, UENEPHES (I), 117
ZEUS, see under Amon
Zodiac, 419, 453 ; zodiacal light, 175

A CATALOG OF SELECTED
DOVER BOOKS
IN ALL FIELDS OF INTEREST

A CATALOG OF SELECTED DOVER
BOOKS IN ALL FIELDS OF INTEREST

CONCERNING THE SPIRITUAL IN ART, Wassily Kandinsky. Pioneering work by father of abstract art. Thoughts on color theory, nature of art. Analysis of earlier masters. 12 illustrations. 80pp. of text. 5⅜ x 8½.   23411-8

ANIMALS: 1,419 Copyright-Free Illustrations of Mammals, Birds, Fish, Insects, etc., Jim Harter (ed.). Clear wood engravings present, in extremely lifelike poses, over 1,000 species of animals. One of the most extensive pictorial sourcebooks of its kind. Captions. Index. 284pp. 9 x 12.   23766-4

CELTIC ART: The Methods of Construction, George Bain. Simple geometric techniques for making Celtic interlacements, spirals, Kells-type initials, animals, humans, etc. Over 500 illustrations. 160pp. 9 x 12. (Available in U.S. only.)   22923-8

AN ATLAS OF ANATOMY FOR ARTISTS, Fritz Schider. Most thorough reference work on art anatomy in the world. Hundreds of illustrations, including selections from works by Vesalius, Leonardo, Goya, Ingres, Michelangelo, others. 593 illustrations. 192pp. 7⅛ x 10¼.   20241-0

CELTIC HAND STROKE-BY-STROKE (Irish Half-Uncial from "The Book of Kells"): An Arthur Baker Calligraphy Manual, Arthur Baker. Complete guide to creating each letter of the alphabet in distinctive Celtic manner. Covers hand position, strokes, pens, inks, paper, more. Illustrated. 48pp. 8¼ x 11.   24336-2

EASY ORIGAMI, John Montroll. Charming collection of 32 projects (hat, cup, pelican, piano, swan, many more) specially designed for the novice origami hobbyist. Clearly illustrated easy-to-follow instructions insure that even beginning papercrafters will achieve successful results. 48pp. 8¼ x 11.   27298-2

THE COMPLETE BOOK OF BIRDHOUSE CONSTRUCTION FOR WOODWORKERS, Scott D. Campbell. Detailed instructions, illustrations, tables. Also data on bird habitat and instinct patterns. Bibliography. 3 tables. 63 illustrations in 15 figures. 48pp. 5¼ x 8½.   24407-5

BLOOMINGDALE'S ILLUSTRATED 1886 CATALOG: Fashions, Dry Goods and Housewares, Bloomingdale Brothers. Famed merchants' extremely rare catalog depicting about 1,700 products: clothing, housewares, firearms, dry goods, jewelry, more. Invaluable for dating, identifying vintage items. Also, copyright-free graphics for artists, designers. Co-published with Henry Ford Museum & Greenfield Village. 160pp. 8¼ x 11.   25780-0

HISTORIC COSTUME IN PICTURES, Braun & Schneider. Over 1,450 costumed figures in clearly detailed engravings–from dawn of civilization to end of 19th century. Captions. Many folk costumes. 256pp. 8⅜ x 11¾.   23150-X

STICKLEY CRAFTSMAN FURNITURE CATALOGS, Gustav Stickley and L. & J. G. Stickley. Beautiful, functional furniture in two authentic catalogs from 1910. 594 illustrations, including 277 photos, show settles, rockers, armchairs, reclining chairs, bookcases, desks, tables. 183pp. 6½ x 9¼. 23838-5

AMERICAN LOCOMOTIVES IN HISTORIC PHOTOGRAPHS: 1858 to 1949, Ron Ziel (ed.). A rare collection of 126 meticulously detailed official photographs, called "builder portraits," of American locomotives that majestically chronicle the rise of steam locomotive power in America. Introduction. Detailed captions. xi+129pp. 9 x 12. 27393-8

AMERICA'S LIGHTHOUSES: An Illustrated History, Francis Ross Holland, Jr. Delightfully written, profusely illustrated fact-filled survey of over 200 American lighthouses since 1716. History, anecdotes, technological advances, more. 240pp. 8 x 10¾. 25576-X

TOWARDS A NEW ARCHITECTURE, Le Corbusier. Pioneering manifesto by founder of "International School." Technical and aesthetic theories, views of industry, economics, relation of form to function, "mass-production split" and much more. Profusely illustrated. 320pp. 6⅛ x 9¼. (Available in U.S. only.) 25023-7

HOW THE OTHER HALF LIVES, Jacob Riis. Famous journalistic record, exposing poverty and degradation of New York slums around 1900, by major social reformer. 100 striking and influential photographs. 233pp. 10 x 7⅞. 22012-5

FRUIT KEY AND TWIG KEY TO TREES AND SHRUBS, William M. Harlow. One of the handiest and most widely used identification aids. Fruit key covers 120 deciduous and evergreen species; twig key 160 deciduous species. Easily used. Over 300 photographs. 126pp. 5⅜ x 8½. 20511-8

COMMON BIRD SONGS, Dr. Donald J. Borror. Songs of 60 most common U.S. birds: robins, sparrows, cardinals, bluejays, finches, more—arranged in order of increasing complexity. Up to 9 variations of songs of each species.
Cassette and manual 99911-4

ORCHIDS AS HOUSE PLANTS, Rebecca Tyson Northen. Grow cattleyas and many other kinds of orchids—in a window, in a case, or under artificial light. 63 illustrations. 148pp. 5⅜ x 8½. 23261-1

MONSTER MAZES, Dave Phillips. Masterful mazes at four levels of difficulty. Avoid deadly perils and evil creatures to find magical treasures. Solutions for all 32 exciting illustrated puzzles. 48pp. 8¼ x 11. 26005-4

MOZART'S DON GIOVANNI (DOVER OPERA LIBRETTO SERIES), Wolfgang Amadeus Mozart. Introduced and translated by Ellen H. Bleiler. Standard Italian libretto, with complete English translation. Convenient and thoroughly portable—an ideal companion for reading along with a recording or the performance itself. Introduction. List of characters. Plot summary. 121pp. 5¼ x 8½. 24944-1

TECHNICAL MANUAL AND DICTIONARY OF CLASSICAL BALLET, Gail Grant. Defines, explains, comments on steps, movements, poses and concepts. 15-page pictorial section. Basic book for student, viewer. 127pp. 5⅜ x 8½. 21843-0

THE CLARINET AND CLARINET PLAYING, David Pino. Lively, comprehensive work features suggestions about technique, musicianship, and musical interpretation, as well as guidelines for teaching, making your own reeds, and preparing for public performance. Includes an intriguing look at clarinet history. "A godsend," *The Clarinet*, Journal of the International Clarinet Society. Appendixes. 7 illus. 320pp. 5⅜ x 8½. 40270-3

HOLLYWOOD GLAMOR PORTRAITS, John Kobal (ed.). 145 photos from 1926-49. Harlow, Gable, Bogart, Bacall; 94 stars in all. Full background on photographers, technical aspects. 160pp. 8⅜ x 11¼. 23352-9

THE ANNOTATED CASEY AT THE BAT: A Collection of Ballads about the Mighty Casey/Third, Revised Edition, Martin Gardner (ed.). Amusing sequels and parodies of one of America's best-loved poems: Casey's Revenge, Why Casey Whiffed, Casey's Sister at the Bat, others. 256pp. 5⅜ x 8½. 28598-7

THE RAVEN AND OTHER FAVORITE POEMS, Edgar Allan Poe. Over 40 of the author's most memorable poems: "The Bells," "Ulalume," "Israfel," "To Helen," "The Conqueror Worm," "Eldorado," "Annabel Lee," many more. Alphabetic lists of titles and first lines. 64pp. 5³⁄₁₆ x 8¼. 26685-0

PERSONAL MEMOIRS OF U. S. GRANT, Ulysses Simpson Grant. Intelligent, deeply moving firsthand account of Civil War campaigns, considered by many the finest military memoirs ever written. Includes letters, historic photographs, maps and more. 528pp. 6⅛ x 9¼. 28587-1

ANCIENT EGYPTIAN MATERIALS AND INDUSTRIES, A. Lucas and J. Harris. Fascinating, comprehensive, thoroughly documented text describes this ancient civilization's vast resources and the processes that incorporated them in daily life, including the use of animal products, building materials, cosmetics, perfumes and incense, fibers, glazed ware, glass and its manufacture, materials used in the mummification process, and much more. 544pp. 6⅛ x 9¼. (Available in U.S. only.) 40446-3

RUSSIAN STORIES/RUSSKIE RASSKAZY: A Dual-Language Book, edited by Gleb Struve. Twelve tales by such masters as Chekhov, Tolstoy, Dostoevsky, Pushkin, others. Excellent word-for-word English translations on facing pages, plus teaching and study aids, Russian/English vocabulary, biographical/critical introductions, more. 416pp. 5⅜ x 8½. 26244-8

PHILADELPHIA THEN AND NOW: 60 Sites Photographed in the Past and Present, Kenneth Finkel and Susan Oyama. Rare photographs of City Hall, Logan Square, Independence Hall, Betsy Ross House, other landmarks juxtaposed with contemporary views. Captures changing face of historic city. Introduction. Captions. 128pp. 8¼ x 11. 25790-8

AIA ARCHITECTURAL GUIDE TO NASSAU AND SUFFOLK COUNTIES, LONG ISLAND, The American Institute of Architects, Long Island Chapter, and the Society for the Preservation of Long Island Antiquities. Comprehensive, well-researched and generously illustrated volume brings to life over three centuries of Long Island's great architectural heritage. More than 240 photographs with authoritative, extensively detailed captions. 176pp. 8¼ x 11. 26946-9

NORTH AMERICAN INDIAN LIFE: Customs and Traditions of 23 Tribes, Elsie Clews Parsons (ed.). 27 fictionalized essays by noted anthropologists examine religion, customs, government, additional facets of life among the Winnebago, Crow, Zuni, Eskimo, other tribes. 480pp. 6⅛ x 9¼. 27377-6

FRANK LLOYD WRIGHT'S DANA HOUSE, Donald Hoffmann. Pictorial essay of residential masterpiece with over 160 interior and exterior photos, plans, elevations, sketches and studies. 128pp. 9¼ x 10¾. 29120-0

THE MALE AND FEMALE FIGURE IN MOTION: 60 Classic Photographic Sequences, Eadweard Muybridge. 60 true-action photographs of men and women walking, running, climbing, bending, turning, etc., reproduced from rare 19th-century masterpiece. vi + 121pp. 9 x 12. 24745-7

1001 QUESTIONS ANSWERED ABOUT THE SEASHORE, N. J. Berrill and Jacquelyn Berrill. Queries answered about dolphins, sea snails, sponges, starfish, fishes, shore birds, many others. Covers appearance, breeding, growth, feeding, much more. 305pp. 5¼ x 8¼. 23366-9

ATTRACTING BIRDS TO YOUR YARD, William J. Weber. Easy-to-follow guide offers advice on how to attract the greatest diversity of birds: birdhouses, feeders, water and waterers, much more. 96pp. 5³⁄₁₆ x 8¼. 28927-3

MEDICINAL AND OTHER USES OF NORTH AMERICAN PLANTS: A Historical Survey with Special Reference to the Eastern Indian Tribes, Charlotte Erichsen-Brown. Chronological historical citations document 500 years of usage of plants, trees, shrubs native to eastern Canada, northeastern U.S. Also complete identifying information. 343 illustrations. 544pp. 6½ x 9¼. 25951-X

STORYBOOK MAZES, Dave Phillips. 23 stories and mazes on two-page spreads: Wizard of Oz, Treasure Island, Robin Hood, etc. Solutions. 64pp. 8¼ x 11. 23628-5

AMERICAN NEGRO SONGS: 230 Folk Songs and Spirituals, Religious and Secular, John W. Work. This authoritative study traces the African influences of songs sung and played by black Americans at work, in church, and as entertainment. The author discusses the lyric significance of such songs as "Swing Low, Sweet Chariot," "John Henry," and others and offers the words and music for 230 songs. Bibliography. Index of Song Titles. 272pp. 6½ x 9¼. 40271-1

MOVIE-STAR PORTRAITS OF THE FORTIES, John Kobal (ed.). 163 glamor, studio photos of 106 stars of the 1940s: Rita Hayworth, Ava Gardner, Marlon Brando, Clark Gable, many more. 176pp. 8⅜ x 11¼. 23546-7

BENCHLEY LOST AND FOUND, Robert Benchley. Finest humor from early 30s, about pet peeves, child psychologists, post office and others. Mostly unavailable elsewhere. 73 illustrations by Peter Arno and others. 183pp. 5⅜ x 8½. 22410-4

YEKL and THE IMPORTED BRIDEGROOM AND OTHER STORIES OF YIDDISH NEW YORK, Abraham Cahan. Film Hester Street based on *Yekl* (1896). Novel, other stories among first about Jewish immigrants on N.Y.'s East Side. 240pp. 5⅜ x 8½. 22427-9

SELECTED POEMS, Walt Whitman. Generous sampling from *Leaves of Grass.* Twenty-four poems include "I Hear America Singing," "Song of the Open Road," "I Sing the Body Electric," "When Lilacs Last in the Dooryard Bloom'd," "O Captain! My Captain!"–all reprinted from an authoritative edition. Lists of titles and first lines. 128pp. 5³⁄₁₆ x 8¼. 26878-0

THE BEST TALES OF HOFFMANN, E. T. A. Hoffmann. 10 of Hoffmann's most important stories: "Nutcracker and the King of Mice," "The Golden Flowerpot," etc. 458pp. 5⅜ x 8½.
21793-0

FROM FETISH TO GOD IN ANCIENT EGYPT, E. A. Wallis Budge. Rich detailed survey of Egyptian conception of "God" and gods, magic, cult of animals, Osiris, more. Also, superb English translations of hymns and legends. 240 illustrations. 545pp. 5⅜ x 8½.
25803-3

FRENCH STORIES/CONTES FRANÇAIS: A Dual-Language Book, Wallace Fowlie. Ten stories by French masters, Voltaire to Camus: "Micromegas" by Voltaire; "The Atheist's Mass" by Balzac; "Minuet" by de Maupassant; "The Guest" by Camus, six more. Excellent English translations on facing pages. Also French-English vocabulary list, exercises, more. 352pp. 5⅜ x 8½.
26443-2

CHICAGO AT THE TURN OF THE CENTURY IN PHOTOGRAPHS: 122 Historic Views from the Collections of the Chicago Historical Society, Larry A. Viskochil. Rare large-format prints offer detailed views of City Hall, State Street, the Loop, Hull House, Union Station, many other landmarks, circa 1904-1913. Introduction. Captions. Maps. 144pp. 9⅜ x 12¼.
24656-6

OLD BROOKLYN IN EARLY PHOTOGRAPHS, 1865-1929, William Lee Younger. Luna Park, Gravesend race track, construction of Grand Army Plaza, moving of Hotel Brighton, etc. 157 previously unpublished photographs. 165pp. 8⅞ x 11¾.
23587-4

THE MYTHS OF THE NORTH AMERICAN INDIANS, Lewis Spence. Rich anthology of the myths and legends of the Algonquins, Iroquois, Pawnees and Sioux, prefaced by an extensive historical and ethnological commentary. 36 illustrations. 480pp. 5⅜ x 8½.
25967-6

AN ENCYCLOPEDIA OF BATTLES: Accounts of Over 1,560 Battles from 1479 B.C. to the Present, David Eggenberger. Essential details of every major battle in recorded history from the first battle of Megiddo in 1479 B.C. to Grenada in 1984. List of Battle Maps. New Appendix covering the years 1967-1984. Index. 99 illustrations. 544pp. 6½ x 9¼.
24913-1

SAILING ALONE AROUND THE WORLD, Captain Joshua Slocum. First man to sail around the world, alone, in small boat. One of great feats of seamanship told in delightful manner. 67 illustrations. 294pp. 5⅜ x 8½.
20326-3

ANARCHISM AND OTHER ESSAYS, Emma Goldman. Powerful, penetrating, prophetic essays on direct action, role of minorities, prison reform, puritan hypocrisy, violence, etc. 271pp. 5⅜ x 8½.
22484-8

MYTHS OF THE HINDUS AND BUDDHISTS, Ananda K. Coomaraswamy and Sister Nivedita. Great stories of the epics; deeds of Krishna, Shiva, taken from puranas, Vedas, folk tales; etc. 32 illustrations. 400pp. 5⅜ x 8½.
21759-0

THE TRAUMA OF BIRTH, Otto Rank. Rank's controversial thesis that anxiety neurosis is caused by profound psychological trauma which occurs at birth. 256pp. 5⅜ x 8½.
27974-X

A THEOLOGICO-POLITICAL TREATISE, Benedict Spinoza. Also contains unfinished Political Treatise. Great classic on religious liberty, theory of government on common consent. R. Elwes translation. Total of 421pp. 5⅜ x 8½.
20249-6

MY BONDAGE AND MY FREEDOM, Frederick Douglass. Born a slave, Douglass became outspoken force in antislavery movement. The best of Douglass' autobiographies. Graphic description of slave life. 464pp. 5⅜ x 8½. 22457-0

FOLLOWING THE EQUATOR: A Journey Around the World, Mark Twain. Fascinating humorous account of 1897 voyage to Hawaii, Australia, India, New Zealand, etc. Ironic, bemused reports on peoples, customs, climate, flora and fauna, politics, much more. 197 illustrations. 720pp. 5⅜ x 8½. 26113-1

THE PEOPLE CALLED SHAKERS, Edward D. Andrews. Definitive study of Shakers: origins, beliefs, practices, dances, social organization, furniture and crafts, etc. 33 illustrations. 351pp. 5⅜ x 8½. 21081-2

THE MYTHS OF GREECE AND ROME, H. A. Guerber. A classic of mythology, generously illustrated, long prized for its simple, graphic, accurate retelling of the principal myths of Greece and Rome, and for its commentary on their origins and significance. With 64 illustrations by Michelangelo, Raphael, Titian, Rubens, Canova, Bernini and others. 480pp. 5⅜ x 8½. 27584-1

PSYCHOLOGY OF MUSIC, Carl E. Seashore. Classic work discusses music as a medium from psychological viewpoint. Clear treatment of physical acoustics, auditory apparatus, sound perception, development of musical skills, nature of musical feeling, host of other topics. 88 figures. 408pp. 5⅜ x 8½. 21851-1

THE PHILOSOPHY OF HISTORY, Georg W. Hegel. Great classic of Western thought develops concept that history is not chance but rational process, the evolution of freedom. 457pp. 5⅜ x 8½. 20112-0

THE BOOK OF TEA, Kakuzo Okakura. Minor classic of the Orient: entertaining, charming explanation, interpretation of traditional Japanese culture in terms of tea ceremony. 94pp. 5⅜ x 8½. 20070-1

LIFE IN ANCIENT EGYPT, Adolf Erman. Fullest, most thorough, detailed older account with much not in more recent books, domestic life, religion, magic, medicine, commerce, much more. Many illustrations reproduce tomb paintings, carvings, hieroglyphs, etc. 597pp. 5⅜ x 8½. 22632-8

SUNDIALS, Their Theory and Construction, Albert Waugh. Far and away the best, most thorough coverage of ideas, mathematics concerned, types, construction, adjusting anywhere. Simple, nontechnical treatment allows even children to build several of these dials. Over 100 illustrations. 230pp. 5⅜ x 8½. 22947-5

THEORETICAL HYDRODYNAMICS, L. M. Milne-Thomson. Classic exposition of the mathematical theory of fluid motion, applicable to both hydrodynamics and aerodynamics. Over 600 exercises. 768pp. 6⅛ x 9¼. 68970-0

SONGS OF EXPERIENCE: Facsimile Reproduction with 26 Plates in Full Color, William Blake. 26 full-color plates from a rare 1826 edition. Includes "The Tyger," "London," "Holy Thursday," and other poems. Printed text of poems. 48pp. 5¼ x 7. 24636-1

OLD-TIME VIGNETTES IN FULL COLOR, Carol Belanger Grafton (ed.). Over 390 charming, often sentimental illustrations, selected from archives of Victorian graphics–pretty women posing, children playing, food, flowers, kittens and puppies, smiling cherubs, birds and butterflies, much more. All copyright-free. 48pp. 9¼ x 12¼. 27269-9

PERSPECTIVE FOR ARTISTS, Rex Vicat Cole. Depth, perspective of sky and sea, shadows, much more, not usually covered. 391 diagrams, 81 reproductions of drawings and paintings. 279pp. 5⅜ x 8½. 22487-2

DRAWING THE LIVING FIGURE, Joseph Sheppard. Innovative approach to artistic anatomy focuses on specifics of surface anatomy, rather than muscles and bones. Over 170 drawings of live models in front, back and side views, and in widely varying poses. Accompanying diagrams. 177 illustrations. Introduction. Index. 144pp. 8⅜ x11¼. 26723-7

GOTHIC AND OLD ENGLISH ALPHABETS: 100 Complete Fonts, Dan X. Solo. Add power, elegance to posters, signs, other graphics with 100 stunning copyright-free alphabets: Blackstone, Dolbey, Germania, 97 more–including many lower-case, numerals, punctuation marks. 104pp. 8⅛ x 11. 24695-7

HOW TO DO BEADWORK, Mary White. Fundamental book on craft from simple projects to five-bead chains and woven works. 106 illustrations. 142pp. 5⅜ x 8. 20697-1

THE BOOK OF WOOD CARVING, Charles Marshall Sayers. Finest book for beginners discusses fundamentals and offers 34 designs. "Absolutely first rate . . . well thought out and well executed."–E. J. Tangerman. 118pp. 7¾ x 10⅝. 23654-4

ILLUSTRATED CATALOG OF CIVIL WAR MILITARY GOODS: Union Army Weapons, Insignia, Uniform Accessories, and Other Equipment, Schuyler, Hartley, and Graham. Rare, profusely illustrated 1846 catalog includes Union Army uniform and dress regulations, arms and ammunition, coats, insignia, flags, swords, rifles, etc. 226 illustrations. 160pp. 9 x 12. 24939-5

WOMEN'S FASHIONS OF THE EARLY 1900s: An Unabridged Republication of "New York Fashions, 1909," National Cloak & Suit Co. Rare catalog of mail-order fashions documents women's and children's clothing styles shortly after the turn of the century. Captions offer full descriptions, prices. Invaluable resource for fashion, costume historians. Approximately 725 illustrations. 128pp. 8⅜ x 11¼. 27276-1

THE 1912 AND 1915 GUSTAV STICKLEY FURNITURE CATALOGS, Gustav Stickley. With over 200 detailed illustrations and descriptions, these two catalogs are essential reading and reference materials and identification guides for Stickley furniture. Captions cite materials, dimensions and prices. 112pp. 6½ x 9¼. 26676-1

EARLY AMERICAN LOCOMOTIVES, John H. White, Jr. Finest locomotive engravings from early 19th century: historical (1804–74), main-line (after 1870), special, foreign, etc. 147 plates. 142pp. 11⅜ x 8¼. 22772-3

THE TALL SHIPS OF TODAY IN PHOTOGRAPHS, Frank O. Braynard. Lavishly illustrated tribute to nearly 100 majestic contemporary sailing vessels: Amerigo Vespucci, Clearwater, Constitution, Eagle, Mayflower, Sea Cloud, Victory, many more. Authoritative captions provide statistics, background on each ship. 190 black-and-white photographs and illustrations. Introduction. 128pp. 8⅞ x 11¾. 27163-3

LITTLE BOOK OF EARLY AMERICAN CRAFTS AND TRADES, Peter Stockham (ed.). 1807 children's book explains crafts and trades: baker, hatter, cooper, potter, and many others. 23 copperplate illustrations. 140pp. 4⅝ x 6.   23336-7

VICTORIAN FASHIONS AND COSTUMES FROM HARPER'S BAZAR, 1867–1898, Stella Blum (ed.). Day costumes, evening wear, sports clothes, shoes, hats, other accessories in over 1,000 detailed engravings. 320pp. 9⅜ x 12¼. 22990-4

GUSTAV STICKLEY, THE CRAFTSMAN, Mary Ann Smith. Superb study surveys broad scope of Stickley's achievement, especially in architecture. Design philosophy, rise and fall of the Craftsman empire, descriptions and floor plans for many Craftsman houses, more. 86 black-and-white halftones. 31 line illustrations. Introduction 208pp. 6½ x 9¼.   27210-9

THE LONG ISLAND RAIL ROAD IN EARLY PHOTOGRAPHS, Ron Ziel. Over 220 rare photos, informative text document origin (1844) and development of rail service on Long Island. Vintage views of early trains, locomotives, stations, passengers, crews, much more. Captions. 8⅞ x 11¾.   26301-0

VOYAGE OF THE LIBERDADE, Joshua Slocum. Great 19th-century mariner's thrilling, first-hand account of the wreck of his ship off South America, the 35-foot boat he built from the wreckage, and its remarkable voyage home. 128pp. 5⅜ x 8½.
40022-0

TEN BOOKS ON ARCHITECTURE, Vitruvius. The most important book ever written on architecture. Early Roman aesthetics, technology, classical orders, site selection, all other aspects. Morgan translation. 331pp. 5⅜ x 8½.   20645-9

THE HUMAN FIGURE IN MOTION, Eadweard Muybridge. More than 4,500 stopped-action photos, in action series, showing undraped men, women, children jumping, lying down, throwing, sitting, wrestling, carrying, etc. 390pp. 7⅞ x 10⅝.
20204-6 Clothbd.

TREES OF THE EASTERN AND CENTRAL UNITED STATES AND CANADA, William M. Harlow. Best one-volume guide to 140 trees. Full descriptions, woodlore, range, etc. Over 600 illustrations. Handy size. 288pp. 4½ x 6⅜.   20395-6

SONGS OF WESTERN BIRDS, Dr. Donald J. Borror. Complete song and call repertoire of 60 western species, including flycatchers, juncoes, cactus wrens, many more–includes fully illustrated booklet.   Cassette and manual 99913-0

GROWING AND USING HERBS AND SPICES, Milo Miloradovich. Versatile handbook provides all the information needed for cultivation and use of all the herbs and spices available in North America. 4 illustrations. Index. Glossary. 236pp. 5⅜ x 8½.
25058-X

BIG BOOK OF MAZES AND LABYRINTHS, Walter Shepherd. 50 mazes and labyrinths in all–classical, solid, ripple, and more–in one great volume. Perfect inexpensive puzzler for clever youngsters. Full solutions. 112pp. 8⅛ x 11.   22951-3

PIANO TUNING, J. Cree Fischer. Clearest, best book for beginner, amateur. Simple repairs, raising dropped notes, tuning by easy method of flattened fifths. No previous skills needed. 4 illustrations. 201pp. 5⅜ x 8½. 23267-0

HINTS TO SINGERS, Lillian Nordica. Selecting the right teacher, developing confidence, overcoming stage fright, and many other important skills receive thoughtful discussion in this indispensible guide, written by a world-famous diva of four decades' experience. 96pp. 5⅜ x 8½. 40094-8

THE COMPLETE NONSENSE OF EDWARD LEAR, Edward Lear. All nonsense limericks, zany alphabets, Owl and Pussycat, songs, nonsense botany, etc., illustrated by Lear. Total of 320pp. 5⅜ x 8½. (Available in U.S. only.) 20167-8

VICTORIAN PARLOUR POETRY: An Annotated Anthology, Michael R. Turner. 117 gems by Longfellow, Tennyson, Browning, many lesser-known poets. "The Village Blacksmith," "Curfew Must Not Ring Tonight," "Only a Baby Small," dozens more, often difficult to find elsewhere. Index of poets, titles, first lines. xxiii + 325pp. 5⅝ x 8¼. 27044-0

DUBLINERS, James Joyce. Fifteen stories offer vivid, tightly focused observations of the lives of Dublin's poorer classes. At least one, "The Dead," is considered a masterpiece. Reprinted complete and unabridged from standard edition. 160pp. 5$\frac{3}{16}$ x 8¼. 26870-5

GREAT WEIRD TALES: 14 Stories by Lovecraft, Blackwood, Machen and Others, S. T. Joshi (ed.). 14 spellbinding tales, including "The Sin Eater," by Fiona McLeod, "The Eye Above the Mantel," by Frank Belknap Long, as well as renowned works by R. H. Barlow, Lord Dunsany, Arthur Machen, W. C. Morrow and eight other masters of the genre. 256pp. 5⅜ x 8½. (Available in U.S. only.) 40436-6

THE BOOK OF THE SACRED MAGIC OF ABRAMELIN THE MAGE, translated by S. MacGregor Mathers. Medieval manuscript of ceremonial magic. Basic document in Aleister Crowley, Golden Dawn groups. 268pp. 5⅜ x 8½. 23211-5

NEW RUSSIAN-ENGLISH AND ENGLISH-RUSSIAN DICTIONARY, M. A. O'Brien. This is a remarkably handy Russian dictionary, containing a surprising amount of information, including over 70,000 entries. 366pp. 4½ x 6⅛. 20208-9

HISTORIC HOMES OF THE AMERICAN PRESIDENTS, Second, Revised Edition, Irvin Haas. A traveler's guide to American Presidential homes, most open to the public, depicting and describing homes occupied by every American President from George Washington to George Bush. With visiting hours, admission charges, travel routes. 175 photographs. Index. 160pp. 8¼ x 11. 26751-2

NEW YORK IN THE FORTIES, Andreas Feininger. 162 brilliant photographs by the well-known photographer, formerly with *Life* magazine. Commuters, shoppers, Times Square at night, much else from city at its peak. Captions by John von Hartz. 181pp. 9¼ x 10¾. 23585-8

INDIAN SIGN LANGUAGE, William Tomkins. Over 525 signs developed by Sioux and other tribes. Written instructions and diagrams. Also 290 pictographs. 111pp. 6⅛ x 9¼. 22029-X

ANATOMY: A Complete Guide for Artists, Joseph Sheppard. A master of figure drawing shows artists how to render human anatomy convincingly. Over 460 illustrations. 224pp. 8⅜ x 11¼. 27279-6

MEDIEVAL CALLIGRAPHY: Its History and Technique, Marc Drogin. Spirited history, comprehensive instruction manual covers 13 styles (ca. 4th century through 15th). Excellent photographs; directions for duplicating medieval techniques with modern tools. 224pp. 8⅜ x 11¼. 26142-5

DRIED FLOWERS: How to Prepare Them, Sarah Whitlock and Martha Rankin. Complete instructions on how to use silica gel, meal and borax, perlite aggregate, sand and borax, glycerine and water to create attractive permanent flower arrangements. 12 illustrations. 32pp. 5⅜ x 8½. 21802-3

EASY-TO-MAKE BIRD FEEDERS FOR WOODWORKERS, Scott D. Campbell. Detailed, simple-to-use guide for designing, constructing, caring for and using feeders. Text, illustrations for 12 classic and contemporary designs. 96pp. 5⅜ x 8½. 25847-5

SCOTTISH WONDER TALES FROM MYTH AND LEGEND, Donald A. Mackenzie. 16 lively tales tell of giants rumbling down mountainsides, of a magic wand that turns stone pillars into warriors, of gods and goddesses, evil hags, powerful forces and more. 240pp. 5⅜ x 8½. 29677-6

THE HISTORY OF UNDERCLOTHES, C. Willett Cunnington and Phyllis Cunnington. Fascinating, well-documented survey covering six centuries of English undergarments, enhanced with over 100 illustrations: 12th-century laced-up bodice, footed long drawers (1795), 19th-century bustles, 19th-century corsets for men, Victorian "bust improvers," much more. 272pp. 5⅝ x 8¼. 27124-2

ARTS AND CRAFTS FURNITURE: The Complete Brooks Catalog of 1912, Brooks Manufacturing Co. Photos and detailed descriptions of more than 150 now very collectible furniture designs from the Arts and Crafts movement depict davenports, settees, buffets, desks, tables, chairs, bedsteads, dressers and more, all built of solid, quarter-sawed oak. Invaluable for students and enthusiasts of antiques, Americana and the decorative arts. 80pp. 6½ x 9¼. 27471-3

WILBUR AND ORVILLE: A Biography of the Wright Brothers, Fred Howard. Definitive, crisply written study tells the full story of the brothers' lives and work. A vividly written biography, unparalleled in scope and color, that also captures the spirit of an extraordinary era. 560pp. 6⅛ x 9¼. 40297-5

THE ARTS OF THE SAILOR: Knotting, Splicing and Ropework, Hervey Garrett Smith. Indispensable shipboard reference covers tools, basic knots and useful hitches; handsewing and canvas work, more. Over 100 illustrations. Delightful reading for sea lovers. 256pp. 5⅜ x 8½. 26440-8

FRANK LLOYD WRIGHT'S FALLINGWATER: The House and Its History, Second, Revised Edition, Donald Hoffmann. A total revision–both in text and illustrations–of the standard document on Fallingwater, the boldest, most personal architectural statement of Wright's mature years, updated with valuable new material from the recently opened Frank Lloyd Wright Archives. "Fascinating"–*The New York Times*. 116 illustrations. 128pp. 9¼ x 10¾. 27430-6

PHOTOGRAPHIC SKETCHBOOK OF THE CIVIL WAR, Alexander Gardner. 100 photos taken on field during the Civil War. Famous shots of Manassas Harper's Ferry, Lincoln, Richmond, slave pens, etc. 244pp. 10⅝ x 8¼. 22731-6

FIVE ACRES AND INDEPENDENCE, Maurice G. Kains. Great back-to-the-land classic explains basics of self-sufficient farming. The one book to get. 95 illustrations. 397pp. 5⅜ x 8½. 20974-1

SONGS OF EASTERN BIRDS, Dr. Donald J. Borror. Songs and calls of 60 species most common to eastern U.S.: warblers, woodpeckers, flycatchers, thrushes, larks, many more in high-quality recording. Cassette and manual 99912-2

A MODERN HERBAL, Margaret Grieve. Much the fullest, most exact, most useful compilation of herbal material. Gigantic alphabetical encyclopedia, from aconite to zedoary, gives botanical information, medical properties, folklore, economic uses, much else. Indispensable to serious reader. 161 illustrations. 888pp. 6½ x 9¼. 2-vol. set. (Available in U.S. only.) Vol. I: 22798-7
Vol. II: 22799-5

HIDDEN TREASURE MAZE BOOK, Dave Phillips. Solve 34 challenging mazes accompanied by heroic tales of adventure. Evil dragons, people-eating plants, bloodthirsty giants, many more dangerous adversaries lurk at every twist and turn. 34 mazes, stories, solutions. 48pp. 8¼ x 11. 24566-7

LETTERS OF W. A. MOZART, Wolfgang A. Mozart. Remarkable letters show bawdy wit, humor, imagination, musical insights, contemporary musical world; includes some letters from Leopold Mozart. 276pp. 5⅜ x 8½. 22859-2

BASIC PRINCIPLES OF CLASSICAL BALLET, Agrippina Vaganova. Great Russian theoretician, teacher explains methods for teaching classical ballet. 118 illustrations. 175pp. 5⅜ x 8½. 22036-2

THE JUMPING FROG, Mark Twain. Revenge edition. The original story of The Celebrated Jumping Frog of Calaveras County, a hapless French translation, and Twain's hilarious "retranslation" from the French. 12 illustrations. 66pp. 5⅜ x 8½. 22686-7

BEST REMEMBERED POEMS, Martin Gardner (ed.). The 126 poems in this superb collection of 19th- and 20th-century British and American verse range from Shelley's "To a Skylark" to the impassioned "Renascence" of Edna St. Vincent Millay and to Edward Lear's whimsical "The Owl and the Pussycat." 224pp. 5⅜ x 8½. 27165-X

COMPLETE SONNETS, William Shakespeare. Over 150 exquisite poems deal with love, friendship, the tyranny of time, beauty's evanescence, death and other themes in language of remarkable power, precision and beauty. Glossary of archaic terms. 80pp. 5³⁄₁₆ x 8¼. 26686-9

THE BATTLES THAT CHANGED HISTORY, Fletcher Pratt. Eminent historian profiles 16 crucial conflicts, ancient to modern, that changed the course of civilization. 352pp. 5⅜ x 8½. 41129-X

THE WIT AND HUMOR OF OSCAR WILDE, Alvin Redman (ed.). More than 1,000 ripostes, paradoxes, wisecracks: Work is the curse of the drinking classes; I can resist everything except temptation; etc. 258pp. 5⅜ x 8½. 20602-5

SHAKESPEARE LEXICON AND QUOTATION DICTIONARY, Alexander Schmidt. Full definitions, locations, shades of meaning in every word in plays and poems. More than 50,000 exact quotations. 1,485pp. 6½ x 9¼. 2-vol. set.
Vol. 1: 22726-X
Vol. 2: 22727-8

SELECTED POEMS, Emily Dickinson. Over 100 best-known, best-loved poems by one of America's foremost poets, reprinted from authoritative early editions. No comparable edition at this price. Index of first lines. 64pp. 5³⁄₁₆ x 8¼. 26466-1

THE INSIDIOUS DR. FU-MANCHU, Sax Rohmer. The first of the popular mystery series introduces a pair of English detectives to their archnemesis, the diabolical Dr. Fu-Manchu. Flavorful atmosphere, fast-paced action, and colorful characters enliven this classic of the genre. 208pp. 5³⁄₁₆ x 8¼. 29898-1

THE MALLEUS MALEFICARUM OF KRAMER AND SPRENGER, translated by Montague Summers. Full text of most important witchhunter's "bible," used by both Catholics and Protestants. 278pp. 6⅝ x 10. 22802-9

SPANISH STORIES/CUENTOS ESPAÑOLES: A Dual-Language Book, Angel Flores (ed.). Unique format offers 13 great stories in Spanish by Cervantes, Borges, others. Faithful English translations on facing pages. 352pp. 5⅜ x 8½. 25399-6

GARDEN CITY, LONG ISLAND, IN EARLY PHOTOGRAPHS, 1869–1919, Mildred H. Smith. Handsome treasury of 118 vintage pictures, accompanied by carefully researched captions, document the Garden City Hotel fire (1899), the Vanderbilt Cup Race (1908), the first airmail flight departing from the Nassau Boulevard Aerodrome (1911), and much more. 96pp. 8⅞ x 11¾. 40669-5

OLD QUEENS, N.Y., IN EARLY PHOTOGRAPHS, Vincent F. Seyfried and William Asadorian. Over 160 rare photographs of Maspeth, Jamaica, Jackson Heights, and other areas. Vintage views of DeWitt Clinton mansion, 1939 World's Fair and more. Captions. 192pp. 8⅞ x 11. 26358-4

CAPTURED BY THE INDIANS: 15 Firsthand Accounts, 1750-1870, Frederick Drimmer. Astounding true historical accounts of grisly torture, bloody conflicts, relentless pursuits, miraculous escapes and more, by people who lived to tell the tale. 384pp. 5⅜ x 8½. 24901-8

THE WORLD'S GREAT SPEECHES (Fourth Enlarged Edition), Lewis Copeland, Lawrence W. Lamm, and Stephen J. McKenna. Nearly 300 speeches provide public speakers with a wealth of updated quotes and inspiration–from Pericles' funeral oration and William Jennings Bryan's "Cross of Gold Speech" to Malcolm X's powerful words on the Black Revolution and Earl of Spenser's tribute to his sister, Diana, Princess of Wales. 944pp. 5⅜ x 8⅜. 40903-1

THE BOOK OF THE SWORD, Sir Richard F. Burton. Great Victorian scholar/adventurer's eloquent, erudite history of the "queen of weapons"–from prehistory to early Roman Empire. Evolution and development of early swords, variations (sabre, broadsword, cutlass, scimitar, etc.), much more. 336pp. 6⅛ x 9¼. 25434-8

AUTOBIOGRAPHY: The Story of My Experiments with Truth, Mohandas K. Gandhi. Boyhood, legal studies, purification, the growth of the Satyagraha (nonviolent protest) movement. Critical, inspiring work of the man responsible for the freedom of India. 480pp. 5⅜ x 8½. (Available in U.S. only.) 24593-4

CELTIC MYTHS AND LEGENDS, T. W. Rolleston. Masterful retelling of Irish and Welsh stories and tales. Cuchulain, King Arthur, Deirdre, the Grail, many more. First paperback edition. 58 full-page illustrations. 512pp. 5⅜ x 8½. 26507-2

THE PRINCIPLES OF PSYCHOLOGY, William James. Famous long course complete, unabridged. Stream of thought, time perception, memory, experimental methods; great work decades ahead of its time. 94 figures. 1,391pp. 5⅜ x 8½. 2-vol. set.
Vol. I: 20381-6   Vol. II: 20382-4

THE WORLD AS WILL AND REPRESENTATION, Arthur Schopenhauer. Definitive English translation of Schopenhauer's life work, correcting more than 1,000 errors, omissions in earlier translations. Translated by E. F. J. Payne. Total of 1,269pp. 5⅜ x 8½. 2-vol. set.
Vol. 1: 21761-2   Vol. 2: 21762-0

MAGIC AND MYSTERY IN TIBET, Madame Alexandra David-Neel. Experiences among lamas, magicians, sages, sorcerers, Bonpa wizards. A true psychic discovery. 32 illustrations. 321pp. 5⅜ x 8½. (Available in U.S. only.) 22682-4

THE EGYPTIAN BOOK OF THE DEAD, E. A. Wallis Budge. Complete reproduction of Ani's papyrus, finest ever found. Full hieroglyphic text, interlinear transliteration, word-for-word translation, smooth translation. 533pp. 6½ x 9¼. 21866-X

MATHEMATICS FOR THE NONMATHEMATICIAN, Morris Kline. Detailed, college-level treatment of mathematics in cultural and historical context, with numerous exercises. Recommended Reading Lists. Tables. Numerous figures. 641pp. 5⅜ x 8½. 24823-2

PROBABILISTIC METHODS IN THE THEORY OF STRUCTURES, Isaac Elishakoff. Well-written introduction covers the elements of the theory of probability from two or more random variables, the reliability of such multivariable structures, the theory of random function, Monte Carlo methods of treating problems incapable of exact solution, and more. Examples. 502pp. 5⅜ x 8½. 40691-1

THE RIME OF THE ANCIENT MARINER, Gustave Doré, S. T. Coleridge. Doré's finest work; 34 plates capture moods, subtleties of poem. Flawless full-size reproductions printed on facing pages with authoritative text of poem. "Beautiful. Simply beautiful."–Publisher's Weekly. 77pp. 9¼ x 12. 22305-1

NORTH AMERICAN INDIAN DESIGNS FOR ARTISTS AND CRAFTSPEOPLE, Eva Wilson. Over 360 authentic copyright-free designs adapted from Navajo blankets, Hopi pottery, Sioux buffalo hides, more. Geometrics, symbolic figures, plant and animal motifs, etc. 128pp. 8⅜ x 11. (Not for sale in the United Kingdom.) 25341-4

SCULPTURE: Principles and Practice, Louis Slobodkin. Step-by-step approach to clay, plaster, metals, stone; classical and modern. 253 drawings, photos. 255pp. 8⅛ x 11. 22960-2

THE INFLUENCE OF SEA POWER UPON HISTORY, 1660–1783, A. T. Mahan. Influential classic of naval history and tactics still used as text in war colleges. First paperback edition. 4 maps. 24 battle plans. 640pp. 5⅜ x 8½. 25509-3

THE STORY OF THE TITANIC AS TOLD BY ITS SURVIVORS, Jack Winocour (ed.). What it was really like. Panic, despair, shocking inefficiency, and a little heroism. More thrilling than any fictional account. 26 illustrations. 320pp. 5⅜ x 8½. 20610-6

FAIRY AND FOLK TALES OF THE IRISH PEASANTRY, William Butler Yeats (ed.). Treasury of 64 tales from the twilight world of Celtic myth and legend: "The Soul Cages," "The Kildare Pooka," "King O'Toole and his Goose," many more. Introduction and Notes by W. B. Yeats. 352pp. 5⅜ x 8½. 26941-8

BUDDHIST MAHAYANA TEXTS, E. B. Cowell and others (eds.). Superb, accurate translations of basic documents in Mahayana Buddhism, highly important in history of religions. The Buddha-karita of Asvaghosha, Larger Sukhavativyuha, more. 448pp. 5⅜ x 8½. 25552-2

ONE TWO THREE . . . INFINITY: Facts and Speculations of Science, George Gamow. Great physicist's fascinating, readable overview of contemporary science: number theory, relativity, fourth dimension, entropy, genes, atomic structure, much more. 128 illustrations. Index. 352pp. 5⅜ x 8½. 25664-2

EXPERIMENTATION AND MEASUREMENT, W. J. Youden. Introductory manual explains laws of measurement in simple terms and offers tips for achieving accuracy and minimizing errors. Mathematics of measurement, use of instruments, experimenting with machines. 1994 edition. Foreword. Preface. Introduction. Epilogue. Selected Readings. Glossary. Index. Tables and figures. 128pp. 5⅜ x 8½. 40451-X

DALÍ ON MODERN ART: The Cuckolds of Antiquated Modern Art, Salvador Dalí. Influential painter skewers modern art and its practitioners. Outrageous evaluations of Picasso, Cézanne, Turner, more. 15 renderings of paintings discussed. 44 calligraphic decorations by Dalí. 96pp. 5⅜ x 8½. (Available in U.S. only.) 29220-7

ANTIQUE PLAYING CARDS: A Pictorial History, Henry René D'Allemagne. Over 900 elaborate, decorative images from rare playing cards (14th–20th centuries): Bacchus, death, dancing dogs, hunting scenes, royal coats of arms, players cheating, much more. 96pp. 9¼ x 12¼. 29265-7

MAKING FURNITURE MASTERPIECES: 30 Projects with Measured Drawings, Franklin H. Gottshall. Step-by-step instructions, illustrations for constructing handsome, useful pieces, among them a Sheraton desk, Chippendale chair, Spanish desk, Queen Anne table and a William and Mary dressing mirror. 224pp. 8⅛ x 11¼. 29338-6

THE FOSSIL BOOK: A Record of Prehistoric Life, Patricia V. Rich et al. Profusely illustrated definitive guide covers everything from single-celled organisms and dinosaurs to birds and mammals and the interplay between climate and man. Over 1,500 illustrations. 760pp. 7½ x 10⅛. 29371-8

Paperbound unless otherwise indicated. Available at your book dealer, online at **www.doverpublications.com**, or by writing to Dept. GI, Dover Publications, Inc., 31 East 2nd Street, Mineola, NY 11501. For current price information or for free catalogues (please indicate field of interest), write to Dover Publications or log on to **www.doverpublications.com** and see every Dover book in print. Dover publishes more than 500 books each year on science, elementary and advanced mathematics, biology, music, art, literary history, social sciences, and other areas.